AUSCHWITZ & THE ALLIES

Martin Gilbert

ARROW

Arrow Books Limited
17–21 Conway Street, London W1P 6JD

A division of the Hutchinson Publishing Group

London Melbourne Sydney Auckland
Johannesburg and agencies throughout
the world

First published in Great Britain by
Michael Joseph Ltd and George Rainbird Ltd 1981
Hamlyn Paperbacks edition 1983
Arrow edition 1984

Printed and bound in Great Britain by
Cox & Wyman Ltd, Reading

ISBN 0 09 939140 6

Contents

Leningrad
besieged

River Volga

Moscow

(Shavli)

Vitebsk

*Rudniki
forests*
Ilna

SOVIET   UNION

Minsk

WHITE RUSSIA

Pinsk

t-Litovsk

VOLHYNIA   Kiev

Rovno

UKRAINE   Poltava

Kamenets Podolsk   Dnepropetrovsk

Czernowitz   TRANSNISTRIA   Verkhovka

B   BESSARABIA

Jassy   Odessa   CRIMEA

Focsani   Sebastopol   Kerch

RUMANIA

Bucharest

Ruschuk

BULGARIA

Sofia

T   *Bosphorus*

Istanbul

Dardanelles

Athens   Cesme

KOS

RHODES

CRETE   **CYPRUS**

Kharkov

Taganrog

Mariupol   Rostov-on-Don

Sea of Azov

Krasnodar

Maikop

German front line at the end of 1942

Stalingrad
River Volga

*Caspian
Sea*

Baku

Caucasus mountains

Black   Sea

Constanta

Ankara

T U R K E Y
neutral

Mersin

S Y R I A

Aleppo

PERSIA

Haifa   **PALESTINE**

	Greater Germany of 1942
	Wartime international borders
	Internal frontiers

M Macedonia
T Thrace
AL Alsace-Lorraine
S German-occupied Slovenia
NS Nice and Savoy, occupied by Italy
EG Eastern Galicia
IZ Italian Zone of Croatia
B Bukovina
SW Switzerland

*Aegean
Sea*

0   miles   300
0   kilometres   400

© Martin and Natalie Gilbert 1981

Introduction

In this book I have told the story of how and when the Allies learned of the Nazi extermination of the Jews, and of how they responded. To this end, I have given particular prominence to those atrocity reports which were received in the west during the war itself, and I have traced the Allied reaction to them. This book is not, therefore, a history of the suffering of European Jewry, but an account of the facts of the exterminations as they filtered out of Nazi-dominated Europe, and of the Allied reaction to these facts, beginning when a series of explicit but incomplete reports reached London and Washington during the summer and autumn of 1942.

In order to show the gap between what was known at any given time, and what was really taking place, I have also set out the barest facts of the principal deportations, murders and gassings as they happened, making it clear whenever these facts were unknown to the Allies at the time.

By July 1944 the Allies knew both the location and purpose of Auschwitz, including the way in which Jews, deported to the camp from all over Europe, were killed by gassing. These facts had been smuggled out of Auschwitz itself by two young Jewish escapees. That same month the Allies also received a long and detailed account of daily life inside Auschwitz, explaining all the horrors which that entailed. This account had been brought to the west by a Polish Major, a non-Jew, who had likewise escaped from the camp.

The aim of this book is to show how the Allies responded to each new piece of information as it reached them. As the story unfolds, it becomes possible to see how the most terrible crimes could be committed with scarcely any effort being made to halt them.

There were many reasons for this lack of effort. At the beginning, the Allies themselves knew almost nothing about the crimes. Often, they only learned of specific killings long after they had taken place. In addition, the period during which the facts first became known in any detail, and during which the most Jews were being killed, coincided with the period of maximum German military superiority, and corresponding Allied military weakness. At the same time, the Germans themselves pursued a policy of deliberate, and frequently effective deception. In 1944, as that deception began to fail, and while a series of detailed reports of continuing Nazi atrocities were reaching the west, it was not German policy, but Allied scepticism and disbelief, as well as political considerations and even prejudice, that served to inhibit action.

Martin Gilbert
Merton College, Oxford
9 January 1981

Acknowledgments

In the course of writing this book, I have received valuable help from those individuals who participated in the events which I have described, and who gave me both their personal recollections and access to their private papers. In this regard I should like to thank Benjamin Akzin, Sarah Altusky, Chaim Barlas, Arieh Ben-Tov (formerly Hassenberg), Reuven Dafni, Mrs Eve Gibson, Dr Nahum Goldmann, Rosine de Jong, Dr M. Kahany, Lilli Kopecky (General Secretary, Public Committee of Auschwitz survivors in Israel), Dr M. Krausz, Erich Kulka, Professor Shalom Lindenbaum, Joseph Linton, the late Arthur Lourie, Jona Malleyron, Oskar Krasnansky, Count Edward Raczyński, and Ya'acov Yannay.

I also received considerable help from three other eye-witnesses of the events which I describe: from Chaim Pazner (formerly Pozner), Vice-Chairman of the Directorate of Yad Vashem, Jerusalem, who provided me with documents and recollections of his wartime work in Geneva, and who gave me great encouragement at every stage of the writing of this book; from Gerhart Riegner, who put at my disposal the Geneva archives of the World Jewish Congress, scrutinized the book in typescript, and gave me his own personal account of the events and atmosphere of those years; and from Professor Rudolf Vrba, who was extremely patient in answering my many questions about his escape from Auschwitz in the spring of 1944, and in putting material about his escape at my disposal. A second escapee, Czeslaw Mordowicz, also gave me details of the journey during which he and a colleague brought to the west the first eye-witness account of the murder of Hungarian Jews at Auschwitz in May 1944.

Because this book arose out of two lectures which I was asked to give at Yad Vashem, Jerusalem, I should like to thank in particular both the organizer of those lectures, Dr Yisrael Gutman, for his personal encouragement, and his colleague Dr Shmuel Krakowski, Director of Archives at Yad Vashem, for having shown throughout the period of my researches the greatest patience in answering my many queries, and in providing me with documentary material. No one who has worked in the Yad Vashem archive can fail to be impressed by the courtesy and consideration of all its staff, headed by the Chairman of its Directorate, Dr Yitzhak Arad.

I also received important help from the Director of the Central Zionist Archives, Jerusalem, Dr Michael Heymann, and from his staff; I am indebted in particular to Israel Philipp, Deputy Director of the Central Zionist Archives, for guiding me through their comprehensive collection of wartime documents.

I am also grateful to those librarians, custodians of archives, and directors of different institutions who made available previously unpublished material:

the BBC Written Archives Centre, Caversham; the Jewish Chronicle Library; the Institute of Jewish Affairs; the Kressel Collection, Oxford Centre for Postgraduate Hebrew Studies; the Library and Archives of the Polish Institute and Sikorski Museum, London; the Public Record Office, London (for the records of the Air Ministry, the Colonial Office, the Foreign Office, the Ministry of Information, the Prime Minister's Office, the War Cabinet and the War Office); the Franklin D. Roosevelt Library, Hyde Park (for the records of the President, and of the War Refugee Board); the United States National Archives (for the records of the Defense Intelligence Agency, of the State Department, and of the United States Strategic Bombing Survey); the Weizmann Institute, Rehovot (for the Weizmann papers); the World Jewish Congress archives, New York; and the World Jewish Congress archives, General Secretariat, Geneva.

Each new book on any aspect of Jewish history in the Second World War must derive both inspiration and guidance from books and articles already published, and from material in preparation. This book is no exception, and I should like to thank those historians and writers whose work has been of importance to me in directing the course of my own researches. I am particularly grateful to the pioneering efforts of Yehuda Bauer, John Conway, Józef Garliński, Serge Klarsfeld, Walter Laqueur, Miriam Novitch, Bernard Wasserstein, and Ronald W. Zweig, each of whom has also been most generous in discussing various points with me, and providing me with material. I am also grateful to Danuta Czech, Raul Hilberg and the late Arthur D. Morse whose published work is indispensable for all students of the war years.

I am also indebted to David S. Wyman, whose own work in this field has marked him out as a pioneer, and who sent me copies of many essential documents from the archives of the War Refugee Board, including much previously unpublished material.

For the full texts both of Henry Morgenthau's 'Personal Report to the President' of 16 January 1944, and of the combined Vrba-Wetzler and Mordowicz-Rosin reports as published by the War Refugee Board on 26 November 1944, I am grateful to William R. Emerson, Director, Franklin D. Roosevelt Library, Hyde Park, New York, and to Louise Sieminski.

Many other individuals have answered specific questions, or put me in contact with those who were able to help me. I should like above all to thank: Martin J. Callow, Library and Records Department, Foreign and Commonwealth Office; George C. Chalou, Assistant Chief, Reference Branch, General Archives Division, General Services Administration, National Archives and Records Service, Washington D.C.; Rudolf A. Clemen, Jr., Information Research Specialist, Library, American Red Cross, Washington D.C.; Dan Clemmer, Acting Librarian, Department of State, Washington D.C.; James N. Eastman Jr., Chief, Research Division, Albert F. Simpson Historical Research Centre, Maxwell Air Force Base, Alabama; Barbro Edwards, Cultural Department, Swedish Embassy, London; Dr Elizabeth E. Eppler, Assistant Director, Institute of Jewish Affairs; Oded Eran; Emanuel Frieder, Chairman, Hitachduth Oley Czechoslovakia, Israel; Mark Friedman, World Jewish Congress, New York; Roland Gant; Lloyd Heaslip, Director, Information and Reference Branch, Library of Parliament, Ottawa; G. Ronald Howe, National Council of YMCAs; Gwyniver Jones, BBC Written Archives Centre; Dr L. de Jong, Netherlands State Institute for War Documentation, Amsterdam; Richard Judd, Librarian, Oxford Centre for Postgraduate Hebrew Studies; Jacqueline Kavanagh, BBC Written Archives Centre; Warren Kimball; Arthur Koestler; Roland de Lagerie, Chief, Personnel Administration Section, United Nations Office at Geneva; A. J. van der Leeuw, Research Associate, Netherlands State Institute for War Documentation, Amsterdam; Elana Markowitz; Rev W. R. G. Marshall, Overseas Council, Church of Scotland; E. Martinez, Secretariat of State, Vatican; David Massel, Clerk to the Board, The Board of Deputies of British Jews; Yoram Mayorek, Central Zionist Archives; Captain Waclaw Milewski, Keeper of Archives, the Polish Institute and Sikorski Museum Ltd; Eric Moonman; Timothy P. Mulligan, Modern Military Branch, Military Archives Division, General Services Administration, National Archives and Records Service, Washington D.C.; Rt Rev Mgr David Norris; Avi Pazner, Embassy of Israel, Washington D.C.; Françoise Perret, Dissemination and Documentation, Comité International de la Croix-Rouge, Geneva; Gordon Phillips, Archivist and Researcher, Times Newspapers Ltd; General Porret, Service Historique, Etat-Major de L'Armée de Terre, Ministère de la Defense, Vincennes; M. V. Roberts, Keeper of Enquiry Service, Guildhall Library; Jakob Samek, Vice-Chairman, Hitachduth Oley Czechoslovakia, Israel; Dr Anton Schlögel, Secretary General, German Red Cross, Bonn; Elizabeth Scott, Reader's Digest; Mary L. Shaffer, Director, the Army Library, Department of the Army, United States Army Service Center for the Armed Forces, Washington D.C.; Michael Wallach; Mrs M. Wojakowska, Librarian, The Polish Institute and Sikorski Museum; and Caroline Zelka.

I should like to thank all those who gave me access to their photographic archives, and whose photographs are reproduced in this book: the Central Zionist Archives, Jerusalem, for photographs 10 (L 17/2266) and 11 (L 17/931/2); Martin Gilbert collection, for photographs 22, 24, 26, 33 and 34; Hasifria Hazionit, Tel Aviv, for photograph 3; International Publishing Corporation, for photographs 13 and 14; Keren Hayesod, Jerusalem, for photographs 1, 2, 17 and 18; Erich Kulka, for photographs 19, 20 and 23; National Archives and Records Service, Washington, for photographs 27, 28 and 32; Nowoczesny Zaklad Fotograficzny, 'Polonia', Zakopane, for photograph 12; Dr Chaim Pazner, for photographs 5, 6, 7, 8, 9 and 15; Dr Gerhart Riegner, for photograph 4; United States Signal Corps, Still Section, Studio Division, for photograph 25; Professor Rudolf Vrba, for photograph 21; World Jewish Congress, General Secretariat archive, Geneva, for photograph 16; Yad Vashem, Jerusalem, for photographs 29, 30 and 31.

I have also been helped considerably in the course of my researches by Dr Christopher Dowling, Keeper of the Department of Education and Publications at the Imperial War Museum London, who provided important material in connection with the Allied bombing missions which flew from southern Italy across Europe, and into the Auschwitz region; by Carl Foreman O.B.E., who gave me access to his film, made in 1944, of the Operation Frantic air shuttle mission between Italy and the Ukraine; by Rabbi Hugo Gryn, who read the book in typescript; by Taffy Sassoon, for her help in sorting a vast mass of material; by Richard Grunberger and Anita Mittwoch for their help with translations; by T. A. Bicknell for his work on the maps; by Gerry Moeran of Studio Edmark, Oxford, for his photographic help, together with that of his assistant, Jean Hunt; and by those who undertook the typing of the manuscript in its different stages: Judy Holdsworth, Phyllis Jenkinson, Esther Gerber and Sue Rampton.

In assembling the documentary material, I received valuable assistance at every stage from Larry P. Arnn, of Claremont, California, who worked in various newspaper libraries and archives on my behalf. I should also like to thank Michael O'Mara, Erica Hunningher and Elizabeth Blair, of George Rainbird Ltd, for the impressive combination of encouragement and hard work which each of them exerted in order to bring this book before the public.

Above all, I am indebted to my wife Susie, whose judgment and guidance have been beyond compare.

List of maps

Specially drawn for this volume

Prelude

Hitler's pledge:
'The complete annihilation of the Jews'

Adolf Hitler had written and spoken against the Jews without respite, from the end of the First World War until the beginning of the Second. In his book *Mein Kampf* and in his speeches, he had portrayed the Jew as a parasite, a bacillus and a vampire, bleeding all nations to death and corrupting all that was noble and healthy in 'Aryan' and German life.

In *Mein Kampf* Hitler blamed the defeat of Germany in the First World War on the 'marxist leaders', and he argued that if, at the beginning of the war, or even during it, 'twelve or fifteen thousand of these Jews who were corrupting the nation had been forced to submit to poison gas', then the millions of deaths at the front 'would not have been in vain'. Indeed, Hitler added, 'If twelve thousand of these malefactors had been eliminated in proper time probably the lives of a million decent men, who would be of value to Germany in the future, might have been saved'.[1]

Immediately on coming to power in 1933, Hitler's laws began to deprive German Jews systematically of all their rights of citizenship. These rights were finally taken away in 1935 by the Nuremberg Laws. At the same time a brutal, crude, daily anti-semitism drove more than 250,000 Jews, half of German Jewry, into exile. In every town and village, public slogans declared: 'The Jew is our misfortune', 'Jews not wanted here', and 'Let Judah Perish!'

Threats against the Jews were the stock-in-trade of Nazism. So too was open violence, culminating in November 1938 in the destruction of hundreds of synagogues. And on 30 January 1939, six years after the Nazis had come to power, Hitler declared publicly that in the event of war, 'the result will not be the bolshevisation of the earth, and thus the victory of Jewry, but the annihilation of the Jewish race in Europe.'[2]

Within a few weeks of the German invasion of Poland on 1 September 1939, many hundreds of Jews had been murdered in the streets of a dozen towns, and thousands more had been savagely beaten up throughout German-occupied Poland. Jewish shops were looted, homes ransacked, and synagogues destroyed by the SS. Yet an even worse fate it seemed, was planned for the two million Polish Jews who were now under German rule, for on 16 December 1939 *The Times* published an article which included the headline:

A STONY ROAD TO
EXTERMINATION

[1] Adolf Hitler, *Mein Kampf*, London 1939 (two volumes in one), translated by James Murphy, page 553.
[2] Norman H. Baynes (editor), *The Speeches of Adolf Hitler, April 1922–August 1939*, London 1942, volume 1, page 741, text taken from the authorized English translation published in pamphlet form, Berlin, in February 1939.

This article told of the establishment inside German-occupied Poland of a special 'remainder State', which was to be set aside 'as a Jewish reserve'.

According to *The Times*, the Germans intended to deport more than a million Jews into this 'concentration area'. These Jews would be brought from every country then under German rule: all 180,000 Jews who were still living in Germany itself, all 65,000 from Austria, all 75,000 from the Czech Protectorate, and all 450,000 from the western provinces of Poland, now annexed to Germany. In addition, nearly one and a half million Jews from Poland itself would be uprooted from their homes, and sent to this special area. It was 'clear', *The Times* added, that the aim of the scheme was to set up 'a place for gradual extermination, and not what the Germans would describe as a *Lebensraum* or living space'.

The article in *The Times* pinpointed the area concerned as 'the barren district around Lublin', and included a map. The whole programme, it stated, 'amounts to a mass massacre such as Nazi imagination can conceive but even Nazi practice can hardly carry through in full.'

The deportations to this 'Lublinland' had already begun. As many as ten thousand Jews had already been taken there by train from the former Czech town of Moravska Ostrava. An escapee, who had reached the west through Russia, had told the story of this early deportation, and *The Times* reported it fully. Even those who were seriously ill had not been exempted from deportation.[1]

At the same time, hundreds of thousands of Jews remained in the newly created ghettoes of Poland, or were sent to labour camps on the Soviet border, to build fortifications, while hundreds of thousands more Jews came under Nazi rule as the German armies conquered Denmark and Norway in April 1940, France, Belgium, Holland and Luxembourg in June 1940, and Greece and Yugoslavia in April 1941.

Meanwhile, the 'Lublinland' scheme had been abandoned, and nearly three million Jews throughout Poland, central Europe, and western Europe, lived in their homes and ghettoes. Gradually, throughout 1940, they had been isolated from the communities around them, of which they had for so long been a part. In country after country they were forced to wear the yellow badge, were turned out of the schools, were forbidden to practise as doctors, teachers or lawyers, and were made to suffer the daily indignities of prejudice and scorn.

Another feature of Nazi rule was the concentration camp; by the summer of 1941 there were more than a dozen of these camps, and hundreds of smaller labour camps and prison centres, scattered throughout the Reich. These camps were filled with German opponents of Nazism, with homosexuals and others judged to be enemies of the new social order, with Polish intellectuals and political prisoners, and, but to a lesser extent, with Jews. Brutality ruled supreme in these camps, where death from savage beatings was a daily event.

On 3 May 1941 the Polish Government-in-Exile sent a formal Note to the Governments of all the Allied and neutral powers, describing how 'tens of thousands' of Polish citizens had been 'incarcerated in concentration or intern-

---

[1] *The Times*, 16 December 1939.

ment camps', and it went on to refer specifically to four such camps, 'Oswiecim (Auschwitz), Oranienburg,[1] Mauthausen and Dachau' as camps whose names 'will mark the most horrible pages in the annals of German bestiality'.

In a series of appendices the Polish Note contained nearly two hundred eye-witness reports of ill-treatment and torture in several dozen concentration camps and detention centres. Appendix 168A was a three-page summary of 'testimonials and reports' about Auschwitz. This summary referred to events at Auschwitz up to November 1940, at a time when Poles, not Jews, constituted the majority of the prisoners there. It described, for example, how, as a reprisal for the killing of two guards, 'a large group of prisoners were taken out into a field, ordered to run about, and machine-gunned by the Germans'. The dead were then 'burned in the local crematorium'.

On another occasion a man who had been shot in the stomach for the 'crime' of obtaining a double ration was thrown into the crematorium while still alive. At one prolonged roll-call, eighty-six prisoners had died 'from exposure and beatings'.

The report on Auschwitz ended with a summary which contained its only reference to the Jews. The summary read:

At the end of November, 1940, 8,000 Poles were at the Oswiecim camps. Theoretically, the prisoners were divided into three groups: (1) political prisoners; (2) criminals; (3) priests and Jews. This last group was persecuted most of all. Scarcely any of them came out alive.

In the first days of December, Warsaw post offices despatched several hundred death notices relating to Oswiecim prisoners. In the Warsaw district of Zoliborz alone, 84 such notifications were received. About December 20, 260 more of them were sent. Some 200 bodies of prisoners are being burned in the crematorium each week.[2]

Although by 1941 Hitler had been fulminating against the Jews for eight years, the persecution of Jews was still not thought of as a specially important propaganda theme in Allied broadcasts and articles. Indeed, on 25 July 1941, a Ministry of Information document had warned British policymakers that to make the Nazi danger 'credible' to the British people, it should not be 'too extreme', as concentration camp stories 'repel the normal mind'. A certain amount of horror was needed, the document conceded, 'but it must be used very sparingly and must deal always with treatment of indisputably innocent people. Not with violent political opponents. And not with Jews'.[3]

But Hitler's threat to 'annihilate' the Jews of Europe had not been mere rhetoric. All Hitler lacked was opportunity, and that opportunity came in June 1941, as the German armies, already masters of western Europe, invaded the Soviet Union. From the very first days of the German invasion of Russia, special Nazi killing squads, or Einsatzgruppen, had moved eastwards behind the German army, using the terror and confusion of war as a cover under which to round up hundreds of thousands of Jews in town after town and

[1] The camp just north of Oranienburg is more usually called Sachsenhausen, the nearby village in which it was located.

[2] Ministry of Foreign Affairs, Republic of Poland. The German Occupation of Poland. London. 3 May 1941. Appendix 168A was reprinted as 'Oswiecim Concentration Camp', in the Polish Fortnightly Review, London 15 November 1941, with the additional information that 'during the winter months three crematorium furnaces were insufficient to cope with the bodies to be cremated'.

[3] 'Plan to Combat the Apathetic Outlook of "What Have I Got To Lose Even if Germany Wins"'. Ministry of Information papers, 1/251.

village after village, and to shoot them down on the spot. The systematic mass murder of the Jews had begun.

The slaughter of as many as half a million Jews in the newly conquered territories of western Russia and the Baltic States did not satisfy the Nazi desire to eliminate Jewish life from Europe. Instead, it stimulated the search for a 'final solution'. In the autumn of 1941 experiments had been made in seizing Jews in German-occupied Yugoslavia, and in killing them in specially sealed vans, where the exhaust pipe had been turned back into the interior of the van.

In September 1941 a further experiment had been made on non-Jews, when seven hundred Soviet prisoners-of-war and three hundred Poles at Auschwitz were forced at gunpoint into a hermetically sealed cellar into which poison gas was then pumped. Throughout the night their screams had sounded throughout the camp. But by morning, all had been killed and other prisoners made to carry the bodies from the cellar to the camp crematorium.

News of this particular experiment did not become known in the west for more than six months.

Continuing with the experiments, in November 1941 the Gestapo selected some 1,200 Jewish slave labourers who were then in Buchenwald concentration camp, inside Germany itself, certified them as 'insane', took them by train to the Euthanasia Institute at Bernburg, near Berlin, and gassed them in rooms specially prepared for the experiment.

The 'success' of these various experiments suggested to the Nazi leaders a possible means of murdering hundreds of thousands, and indeed millions of people.

In the late autumn of 1941, as the war entered its third year, there were still as many as two million Jews living in German-occupied Poland alone. Smaller but once flourishing Jewish communities were to be found throughout the confines of German-dominated Europe, bringing to more than four million the number of Jews living in areas ruled or dominated by Germany.

In Poland, the Jews had been confined to crowded ghettoes since the beginning of the war. They had already suffered terribly from forced labour, hunger and disease. At the same time, tens of thousands of Jews had been deported from Germany and Austria to these eastern ghettoes. During 1941, more than 15,000 Jews died of starvation in the Lodz ghetto, and more than 40,000 in the Warsaw ghetto, as a result of deliberate German policy.

These facts were not entirely unknown to the western Allies. On 16 November 1941 the British Minister to Sweden, Victor Mallet, spoke at length to a Swedish economic negotiator who had just returned from Germany. The Swede told the Englishman, who at once reported it back to London, that many Germans were 'disgusted at the way in which Jews are being deported from German cities to Ghettoes in Poland'. The fate of those deported, the Swede had been told, was 'a lingering death'.[1]

On November 19, only three days after this meeting in Sweden, a member of the British Legation in Switzerland, David Kelly, reported from Berne on a conversation with a Polish diplomat, responsible now to the Polish Government-in-Exile in London, who told him 'that about 1½ million Jews who were

[1] Foreign Office papers, 371/26515, C 13440.

living in Eastern (recently Russian) Poland have simply disappeared altogether; nobody knows how or where'. At the same time, the Dutch Minister
in Berne had told Kelly, 'that 50 per cent of the Dutch Jews sent to camps are
now dead'.[1]

On November 22 a junior Brazilian diplomat, Carlos Buarque de Macedo,
who was then Second Secretary at the Brazilian Embassy in Berlin, arrived in
Lisbon for an eight-day visit to Portugal. During his visit, he and his wife
spoke to a member of the British Embassy in Lisbon, who noted down their
remarks and sent them to the Foreign Office in London. 'The treatment of
Jews,' the Brazilian reported, 'is getting more appalling every day. Thousands
are being packed into open lorries and sent off to Poland without food or
water or stops at night.' The Brazilian added: 'So bad is the treatment of
Jews now that even pro-German Portuguese diplomats are so horrified that
they have helped to organize the marriage of six Jews with money to Portuguese, to enable them to be got out of Germany'.[2]

The Jews living outside Nazi-dominated Europe had no access to these
diplomatic reports. But the Zionist movement, once so strong in central and
eastern Europe, did have its own listening-posts, in both Switzerland and
Turkey, to which information was continually being smuggled. In Geneva,
the World Jewish Congress, a body set up shortly before the war to keep a
special watch on anti-Jewish activities, was likewise the recipient of news and
reports. In Jerusalem, the Jewish Agency for Palestine, the Zionist body which
had been set up twenty years earlier by the British Government as its liaison
with the Jews of Palestine, likewise received reports on an almost weekly
basis, from Switzerland, and from Istanbul.

One such report was sent from Gerhart Riegner, the World Jewish Congress
representative in Geneva, to his superiors in New York, in a letter dated 27
October 1941. It told of renewed deportations from Germany and Czechoslovakia to Poland, of the 'horror of deportation', and of the terrible conditions inside Poland itself. 'An eye-witness told me recently', Riegner reported, 'that there are currently 2,000 cases of typhus in the Warsaw ghetto ...'

Riegner urged the dispatch from neutral governments of a 'humanitarian
mission' of Protestant leaders to the deportation regions, as well as Protestant
intervention with the Red Cross, and a 'solemn declaration' by the many
Governments in exile in London, declaring all anti-Jewish laws passed by the
occupying powers and their collaborators as 'null and void'.[3]

A month later, on November 27, a second report from Geneva was sent to
Istanbul by the Jewish Agency representatives, and then forwarded from
Istanbul to Jerusalem. The subject of this further report was Hitler's 'new
order' in Europe. The message was brief but succinct. 'With regard to the
Jews,' Jerusalem was informed, 'it seems that no place whatever has been
allotted to them in Hitler's Europe, and the remnants who escaped the
massacres, starvation and oppression of the ghettoes are no doubt intended to
be sent somewhere overseas.'[4]

[1] Foreign Office papers, 371/26515, C 13826.
[2] Foreign Office papers, 371/26515, C 13706.
[3] Letter to Nahum Goldmann, World Jewish Congress Archives, General Secretariat.
[4] Central Zionist Archives, Z 4/14779.

But according to the evolving Nazi intentions not even the 'remnants' were to be spared. The massive death tolls of the ghettoes were no longer sufficient for the now triumphant Nazis, as they pondered the twin success of their eastern killing squads, and Germany's military dominance in Europe.

At the existing death rate, high though it was, Warsaw Jewry, for example, would not be destroyed completely for another ten years. But with the German army at the gates of Moscow, and most of the capitals of Europe at Germany's beck and call, the Nazis were attracted by the idea of a more rapid and systematic plan, by which the murder of millions of Jews could be carried out according to a clear and competent schedule. By using the most efficient and modern methods, it was clear that there need not be even 'remnants' once the plan was completed.

The first step in carrying out this new plan was taken on 8 December 1941, when several hundred Jews from three small Polish towns were taken to a wood outside the village of Chelmno, and gassed in a specially designed building. The experiment was judged a 'success' by the Nazi planners. It was also a closely guarded secret.

The Chelmno gassing had begun as an experiment. The decision to destroy all the Jews of Nazi-controlled Europe was still to be discussed, and finalized, at a meeting summoned for December 9, in the Wannsee suburb of Berlin. Those invited to Wannsee were senior officials from all the German Ministries, including the Ministry of Justice and the Foreign Office. The details of the Conference were prepared by Adolf Eichmann, head of the special 'Jewish Section' of the SS. Two days before the Conference was due to meet, however, the Japanese attacked Pearl Harbor, and on December 11 Germany declared war on the United States. The Conference was therefore postponed until January 20.

Meanwhile, as the German officials waited to assemble on the new date, the Soviet Government published details of hundreds of atrocities that had been committed against Russian civilians as the German armies had advanced across Russia during the six previous months, between June and December 1941. These details were set out on 6 January 1942, in a note signed by the Soviet Foreign Minister, Vyacheslav Molotov, one of the signatories, scarcely two years earlier, of the notorious Nazi-Soviet pact.

The Molotov note of January 6 gave a stark town-by-town account of what it described as 'abominable violence, outrage and massacre'. Although in no way concerned with separating the fate of Soviet Jews from other Soviet citizens, the note made clear in several of its paragraphs the extent to which the Jews had been singled out as victims. Indeed, one paragraph of the Molotov note dealt explicitly with the fate of the Jews of Kiev, as reported by 'Soviet citizens' who had escaped. The paragraph read:

A large number of Jews, including women and children of all ages, was gathered in the Jewish cemetery of Kiev. Before they were shot, all were stripped naked and beaten. The first persons selected for shooting were forced to lie face down at the bottom of a ditch and were shot with automatic rifles. Then the Germans threw a little earth over them. The next group of people awaiting execution was forced to lie on top of them, and shot, and so on.

A further paragraph of the Molotov note of January 6 gave details of the work of the 'mass murders' of the killing squads in the Ukraine. 'These bloody executions,' the note pointed out, 'were especially directed against unarmed and defenceless Jewish working people,' and it went on to give the numbers killed, according to what were called 'incomplete figures'. These figures were: 'no less than 6,000' in Lvov, 8,000 in Odessa, 'over 8,500 killed or hanged' in Kamenets-Podolsk, 'over 10,500 persons shot down with machine guns' in Dnepropetrovsk, 'about 7,000 persons' in Kerch, and 'over 3,000' shot in Mariupol, 'including many old men, women and children, all of whom were robbed and stripped naked before execution'.

The Molotov note was made public in the Soviet city of Kuibyshev on 7 January 1942, when it was handed to all foreign diplomats in the city, to which the diplomatic corps had been withdrawn in the face of the German advance.[1]

In London, on January 13, representatives of nine occupied countries, Poland, Belgium, Czechoslovakia, France, Greece, Yugoslavia, Luxembourg, Holland, and Norway, having constituted themselves an Inter-Allied Conference on War Crimes, issued a joint declaration condemning German atrocities against civilians in occupied Europe. One of the groups pressing for just such a declaration had been the World Jewish Congress.

While not mentioning the Jews by name, the joint declaration spoke of 'a regime of terror characterized in particular by imprisonments, mass expulsions, execution of hostages and massacres', and agreed to place, among its 'principal war aims', the punishment of those 'guilty and responsible for these crimes, whether they have ordered them, perpetrated them, or in any way participated in them'.[2] But it was not until four months later that the Board of Deputies of British Jews was to receive an assurance from the Inter-Allied Conference on War Crimes that the 'crimes and excesses committed against Jews' were covered by the Conference declaration.[3]

Among the signatories of this declaration of January 13 were the Prime Minister of the Polish Government-in-Exile, General Sikorski, who also served as President of the Conference, and General de Gaulle, the President of the Free French National Committee. All, however, were powerless: in the Far East, the Japanese forces were advancing steadily against the Americans, British and Dutch; over much of Europe, Nazi control was complete; in Russia, the German armies had reached the outskirts of Leningrad and Moscow. It was a bleak picture. And yet, in a speech in the House of Commons on January 27, Winston Churchill spoke of how, although the weight of the war pressed on him even more than in 1940, he still felt confidence in what he called the 'broadening swell of victory and liberation', a swell which was, he added, 'bearing us and all the tortured peoples onwards safely to the final goal.'[4]

When the Nazi and German Government leaders met in the Berlin suburb of Wannsee on January 20 they studied the figures, prepared by Adolf Eich-

---

[1] Subsequently published as a special *Information Bulletin* by the Soviet Embassies in Washington and London, January 1942.

[2] The Inter-Allied Information Committee, London, *Punishment for War Crimes*, His Majesty's Stationery Office, January 1942.

[3] Foreign Office papers, 371/30917; letter of 16 May 1942 from General Sikorski to the Board of Deputies of British Jews.

[4] Hansard, 27 January 1942.

mann, of the number of Jews to be destroyed.[1] Ten days later Hitler addressed an enormous crowd at the Sports Palace in Berlin. He spoke that day of his own confidence in victory, and also of the Jews, telling his listeners, as the Allied monitoring service reported on the following day, 'they are our old enemy as it is, they have experienced at our hands an upsetting of their ideas, and they rightfully hate us, just as much as we hate them'. The Germans, Hitler added, were 'well aware' that the war could eventually only end when the Jews had been 'uprooted from Europe', or when 'they disappear'. Hitler then went on, as far as the Allied monitoring service could record it, to declare that the Jews:

. . . have already spoken of the breaking up of the German Reich by next September, and with the help of this advance prophesy, and we say that the war will not end as the Jews imagine it will, namely with the uprooting of the Aryans, but the result of this war will be the complete annihilation of the Jews.

Now for the first time they will not bleed other people to death, but for the first time the old Jewish law of An eye for an eye, a tooth for a tooth, will be applied.

And the further this war spreads, the further will spread this fight against the world of the [Jew], and they will be used as food for every prison camp, and [   ] in every family, which will have it explained to it why [   ], and the hour will come when the enemy of all times, or at least of the last thousand years, will have played his part to the end.

Such was Hitler's message, as received in London and Washington: the war would end with 'the complete annihilation of the Jews'.[2]

Hitler's subordinates already understood what was required of them. In the six weeks before Hitler's speech the gassings at Chelmno had continued to draw in victims from a wider and wider radius: Jewish communities in Poland which had already been forced into ghettoes, and cut off from contact with the outside world. To enforce this isolation, and to ensure secrecy, the German, Austrian and Czech Jews in the Theresienstadt ghetto were informed on December 10 that the penalty for 'illegal' correspondence was, henceforth, death. Only postcards passed by the Gestapo censor could be sent to the outside world. Six days later Hans Frank, the Governor of the General Government region of Poland, boasted to his senior officials in secret conclave: 'As far as the Jews are concerned – and this I shall tell you quite openly – they must be done away with in one way or another'.[3]

[1] The Wannsee conference discussion is in Nuremberg Trials document NG-2586, published in full in Raul Hilberg (editor), *Documents of Destruction: Germany and Jewry 1933–1945*, London, 1972, pages 89–99.

[2] Franklin Watts (editor), *Voices of History 1942–43* New York, 1943, page 121; text as monitored by the Foreign Broadcast Monitoring Service, Federal Communications Commission. The gaps in the monitored text are shown with square brackets.

[3] Stanislaw Piotrowski (editor), *Dziennik Hansa Franka*, Warsaw 1956, pages 303–4.

Chapter 1

Humanity versus high policy

The Jews who lived in safety, beyond the limits of Nazi rule, made repeated efforts to seek help, and to find avenues of rescue, for those whose lives were now in danger. Since 1917 the Zionists had, with British support, been building up in Palestine a Jewish National Home, and between the wars, more than 300,000 Jews had reached Palestine from Europe, the majority of them from Poland. The rise of Hitler in Germany in 1933 had intensified the pressure of immigration, so much so that in 1936 the Arabs of Palestine, supported by several nearby Arab States, had risen in revolt against Britain, demanding a halt to Jewish immigration. The British Government had sought, first, to suppress the revolt. But, in the early months of 1939, as Britain's own military weakness exposed her to increasing danger from Nazi Germany, the British Government had agreed to the demands of four independent Arab States, Egypt, Saudi Arabia, Iraq and the Yemen, and of the Palestinian Arab leaders, to restrict future Jewish immigration to an upper limit of 75,000, at a rate of no more than ten thousand a year.

This restriction became law, despite a strong Parliamentary protest by Winston Churchill, in May 1939. The Jewish leaders felt betrayed. In their hour of greatest need, as they saw it, the door of safety had been slammed in their faces. Henceforth, in the four months leading up to the German invasion of Poland, and in the successive war years, one dominant aim of their political efforts was to persuade the British Government to abandon this restriction, and to allow any Jew who could escape from Europe to be given a place in Palestine. These efforts, however, were in vain, leading to much bitterness on the Jewish side, and no little vexation on the part of the British officials concerned. This vexation was increased by the flow of 'illegal' refugees. Jews without permission to enter Palestine, who had escaped from Europe and came by boat across the Black Sea and the Aegean, sought to evade the British naval blockade, landed secretly on the coast of Palestine, and 'disappeared' over the sand dunes into friendly homes and settlements. When one such 'illegal' ship, the *Salvador*, sank in the Sea of Marmara on 12 December 1940, and more than two hundred refugees were drowned, T. M. Snow, the head of the Refugee Section of the British Foreign Office, noted: 'There could have been no more opportune disaster from the point of view of stopping this traffic'.[1]

A year later, in December 1941 the refusal of the British authorities in Palestine to allow one of these 'illegal' refugee ships, the *Struma*, to proceed through the Dardanelles to Palestine, had created a storm of Jewish protest in

[1] Foreign Office papers, 371/25242, W 2451, folio 229.

both London and Jerusalem.[1] There were more than 750 Jewish refugees on board the *Struma*, most of them from Rumania, a country which had been pursuing a violently anti-Jewish policy which had already resulted in the murder of tens of thousands of Jews. None of the *Struma* refugees had been able to acquire visas for Palestine, or immigration certificates, as the British Government considered Rumania to be an enemy country. At the same time, under the terms of the 1939 White Paper itself, more than 40,000 Palestine immigration certificates were still unused, including more than 6,000 of a total of 15,000 which had been specially reserved for emergency situations.

When the *Struma* reached Istanbul from the Rumanian port of Constanta, the Turkish authorities would only allow a single passenger, a pregnant woman, to leave the ship. The Turkish Government then asked the British Ambassador if the refugees could proceed to Palestine. Otherwise the boat must be sent back into the Black Sea. There was to be no haven in Turkey.

On learning of the Turkish attitude, the British Ambassador to Turkey, Sir Hughe Knatchbull-Hugessen, pointed out to the Turks that the British, also, were not willing to help. His Majesty's Government, he said, 'did not want those people in Palestine'; they had 'no permission to go there'. But the Ambassador added, as he explained to the Foreign Office by telegram on December 20, that from a humanitarian point of view he did not like the Turkish proposal to send the ship back into the Black Sea. 'If the Turkish Government must interfere with the ship,' he said, 'on the ground that they could not keep the distressed Jews in Turkey, let her rather go towards the Dardanelles. It might be that if they reached Palestine, they might despite their illegality receive humane treatment'.

As soon as the Ambassador's report of his conversation reached London, the Colonial Office protested at his suggestion that the refugees on board the *Struma* might 'receive humane treatment' if they arrived in Palestine without certificates. On 23 December 1941 a Colonial Office official, S. E. V. Luke, noted: 'This is the first occasion on which, in spite of numerous efforts, the Turkish Government has shown any signs of being ready to help in frustrating these illegal immigrant ships, and then the Ambassador goes and spoils the whole effect on absurdly misjudged humanitarian grounds'. Another official, E. B. Boyd, added: 'Sir H. Knatchbull-Hugessen had a heaven-sent opportunity of getting these people stopped at Istanbul and sent back to Constanta and has failed to avail himself of it'.[2]

On 24 December, Christmas Eve, the Colonial Secretary, Lord Moyne, informed Eden's Parliamentary Under-Secretary at the Foreign Office of what he saw as the Palestine aspect of the problem:

The landing of seven hundred more immigrants will not only be a formidable addition to the difficulties of the High Commissioner . . . but it will have a deplorable effect throughout the Balkans in encouraging further Jews to embark on a traffic which has now been condoned by

[1] The *Struma* had been built in 1867 in Newcastle, and first sailed as the *Xantha*. In 1888 she had been lengthened, and substantially altered, and was still British-owned until 1902, when bought by a Greek shipowner. In 1934, as the *Esperos*, she was sailing under the Bulgarian flag. As the *Struma*, in 1942, she was registered in Panama, 226 tons gross, 140 net, with a Bulgarian captain and crew.

[2] The Ambassador's telegram and the minutes of Luke and Boyd, are in Colonial Office papers, 733/449/P3/4/30.

His Majesty's Ambassador. We have good reason to believe that this traffic is favoured by the Gestapo, and the Security Services attach the very greatest importance to preventing the influx of Nazi agents under the cloak of refugees.[1]

As to Knatchbull-Hugessen's humanitarian feelings about sending the refugees back to the Black Sea countries, it seems to me that these might apply with equal force to the tens of thousands of Jews who remain behind and who are most eager to join them.

Lord Moyne's letter ended:

I find it difficult to write with moderation about this occurrence which is in flat contradiction of established Government policy, and I should be very glad if you could perhaps even now do something to retrieve the position, and to urge that Turkish authorities should be asked to send the ship back to the Black Sea, as they originally proposed.[2]

The Jewish leaders in Britain and Palestine knew nothing of this particular discussion. But they did know that the fate of the refugees on board the *Struma* was to be decided upon in London and Jerusalem. They also knew that the British Cabinet had decided, shortly after the outbreak of war, to refuse refugee status to anyone reaching British territory from enemy territory. Clearly, almost all refugees came from enemy territory: they had only become refugees in order to escape from a life of persecution in Nazi-dominated Europe. But it was this very fact which made them unacceptable to the British authorities.

On 18 February 1942 a distinguished British Jew, Professor Lewis Namier, one of the leading Zionist officials then in London, wrote direct to Lord Moyne in the hope of influencing his decision. Namier urged Moyne to give the *Struma* refugees 'a chance of regular and legal admission to Palestine'. Namier gave Moyne information which had been received both from the Jewish Agency in Jerusalem, and from the Zionist Emergency Committee in New York. The *Struma* was 'no longer seaworthy'. Being without visas, the refugees could proceed no further on their journey. Sanitary and food conditions on the ship were reported to be 'desperate'.

Professor Namier pointed out to Lord Moyne that an American Jewish organization, the Joint Distribution Committee, a non-Zionist body, was prepared to pay the cost of transportation from Turkey to Palestine, and to contribute £6,000 towards the absorption of the refugees in Palestine. Namier's letter continued:

The difficulty seems to lie in the general ban against people coming from enemy territory. But this ban is not, and never has been, absolute.

A few months before the outbreak of war, nearly 3,000 Jewish immigrants from Germany and Austria were admitted to Palestine, and no ill results appear to have followed.

Norwegians, Dutch, French, Poles, etc., who have been under the enemy, are constantly being admitted to this country, and other parts of the Empire, including Palestine. . . .

Namier ended his letter of February 18 with a plea that refugee applications

---

[1] No Nazi agents were ever found among these refugees, despite strict surveillance. The use of the 'Nazi agent' argument is carefully examined, and the claim itself shown to have been a false one used for political ends, in Ronald W. Zweig's doctoral dissertation, 'British Policy To Palestine, May 1939 to 1943', Cambridge, June 1978.

[2] Lord Moyne's letter is in Colonial Office papers, 733/449.

be undertaken 'in a humane and friendly spirit'.[1] Namier knew nothing, of course, of the Colonial Office argument about 'absurdly misjudged humanitarian grounds', or of Lord Moyne's own argument to Eden of the 'deplorable effect' which the arrival of the *Struma* refugees would have 'in encouraging further Jews to embark'.

Many of the *Struma* refugees, Namier pointed out in his letter to Lord Moyne, had close relatives in Palestine itself, relatives who were already taking a share in the British war effort, and he ended: 'We beg that this fact may be taken into consideration'.

But neither humanitarian nor military considerations were able to change British policy in time to save the refugees on board the *Struma*. Faced with British hesitations, the Turkish authorities took independent action, boarding the ship, overpowering those passengers who resisted, and towing the *Struma* back into the Black Sea. On the following morning it blew up, possibly struck by a German mine. All but one passenger was drowned. On 1 March 1942 the British High Commissioner in Palestine, Sir Harold MacMichael, telegraphed to the Colonial Office: 'The fate of these people was tragic, but the fact remains that they were nationals of a country at war with Britain, proceeding direct from enemy territory. Palestine was under no obligation towards them'.[2]

Sir Harold MacMichael continued to uphold this principle of non-obligation when, a few weeks later, the question arose of admitting to Palestine a further group of twenty refugees stranded in Turkey, among them the one survivor of the *Struma* explosion, and the pregnant woman who had been allowed to leave the *Struma* in Istanbul – her husband had died when the *Struma* sank, and her newborn child had died in an Istanbul hospital. On 19 March 1942 MacMichael ruled against their admission to Palestine, insisting that the 'basic principle that enemy nationals from enemy or enemy-controlled territory should not be admitted to this country during the war applies to all immigrants'.[3]

Even while the fate of the *Struma* had been in the balance, the 793 'illegal' Jewish refugees on another boat, the *Darien*, which had been intercepted by the Royal Navy, were awaiting deportation to the Indian Ocean island of Mauritius. From both Jerusalem and London, the Jewish Agency fought this decision, and on 4 February 1942, the Prime Minister's own son, Randolph Churchill, had written to his father about it. Churchill reacted at once, writing to Lord Moyne on the following day to urge that the refugees be released from internment and allowed to remain in Palestine. In urging this course Churchill pointed out to Moyne that until the original decision to deport the *Darien* refugees had been taken: 'It looked as if we should be subjected to a wave of illegal immigration, but now that the whole of south-eastern Europe is in German hands, there is no further danger of this. . . .'[4]

Lord Moyne, however, remained in favour of deportation, writing to Churchill on February 7: 'Any relaxation of our deterrent measures is likely

[1] Central Zionist Archives, Z 4/14908 II.
[2] Colonial Office papers, 733/446/76021/42, telegram No. 257, distributed as Most Secret.
[3] Colonial Office papers, 733/446/76021/42, telegram No. 359, distributed as Most Secret.
[4] Prime Minister's Personal Minute, M 27/2, Premier papers, 4/51/1.

to encourage further shipments of the same kind.' The fate of the *Darien* passengers, Moyne wrote, would be a test case of the Government's determination to adhere to their proclaimed policy, and any concessions would cause great damage to the British Government's 'reputation in the Middle East for trustworthiness and firmness'.[1]

Eventually, as Churchill had urged, the *Darien* passengers were allowed to remain in Palestine. But at a further meeting on 5 March 1942, the War Cabinet laid down, as a basic principle of British policy, that: 'All practicable steps should be taken to discourage illegal immigration into Palestine.'

This decision was actually taken against the advice of Lord Moyne's successor, Lord Cranborne, who had advocated that Jewish refugees from central Europe should be allowed not only the six thousand outstanding refugee certificates, but also the 36,000 regular certificates, still not issued.

Lord Cranborne had set out this view in a letter to Churchill on March 3. But the Cabinet decided, nevertheless, that there was 'a grave risk that, if we agreed to admit to Palestine illegal immigrants fleeing from enemy oppression, even if subject to the conditions suggested by the Colonial Secretary, the influx would soon reach large proportions'.[2]

The Jewish Agency leaders were not informed of the Cabinet decision of March 5. Nor did they, or the Cabinet, know that plans were now nearing completion for the deportation of Jews from all over Europe to camps in German-occupied Poland. They did not even know that throughout January and February, tens of thousands of Jews had been deported from Germany itself, and from the Protectorate of Bohemia and Moravia, to the distant cities of Riga and Kovno, where, immediately on arrival, most of them had been taken to nearby forests and shot.

All this was as yet unknown. But the Jewish leaders who lived in safety knew that some terrible fate was in store for those who were trapped under Nazi rule. On March 6, when Dr Weizmann himself wrote to Lord Cranborne to appeal for Government approval for the establishment of a specifically Jewish fighting force to go into battle alongside the other Allied armies, a request first made in September 1939, he added that the 'survival of the Jews nationally' depended upon the victory of the Allies because, as Weizmann went on to explain, 'in the matter of exterminating the Jews, Hitler is as good as his word'.[3]

Despite his understanding of Nazi aims and methods, even Weizmann could not know just how those aims were to be carried out. For within three months of the opening of Chelmno death camp in December 1941, three similar camps were set up in different parts of German-occupied Poland, the sole purpose of which was to murder those who entered them, and to do so with a few hours at the most of their arrival. These camps, at Belzec, Treblinka, Sobibor and Chelmno itself, began to receive trainloads of Jews from all over Europe during the spring of 1942, and in less than a year, more than two million Jews had been murdered, in conditions of the utmost brutality, secrecy and deception.

---

1 Colonial Office papers, 733/446/76021/40, folio 63.
2 War Cabinet 29 of 1942, Cabinet papers, 65/25.
3 Central Zionist Archives, Z 4/14908 II.

1. Europe, Greater Germany, and the first four death camps (in white lettering, with swastikas).

Those Jews who were forced into the cattle trucks, and those who watched them go were told that the trains were going to work camps 'in the east'. The Jews of Poland were to be 'resettled' in a more distant land. Greater Germany, and the General Government of Poland, were to be made 'Jew free'. But, the Nazis added, there was room enough for the Jews elsewhere. If they went quietly, no harm would come to them. If they resisted, they would be shot.

The Nazi promises seemed plausible enough. All over Europe, labour camps had indeed been built to serve the needs of Germany; camps and ghettoes in which clothes factories, armament factories, and machine tool factories made use of Jewish slave labour to help the German war machine. Conditions were harsh, and rations meagre; many died of starvation, or of deliberate brutality by the German guards; but it was still possible to survive. And it was to some such camps, so the Nazis promised, that these deportations of 1942 were bound. The deportation trains had, however, only one destination, a death camp 'somewhere in the east'.

The fact that the Germans had been murdering Jews in Europe was well known to the Allies. Since the outbreak of the war, German brutality had received wide publicity. But none of the Allies yet knew that these killings were part of a deliberate plan to murder every Jew in Europe. The Wannsee Conference, and the setting up of the eastern death camps, had been closely guarded secrets. The deliberate attempt to destroy systematically all of Europe's Jews was unsuspected in the spring and early summer of 1942: the very period during which it was at its most intense, and during which hundreds of thousands of Jews were being gassed every day at Belzec, Chelmno, Sobibor and Treblinka.

The murder of Jews during the first two years of the war had aroused much public sympathy in the west. The war was being fought, after all, against the evils of the Nazi system. But with the United States remaining neutral throughout those first two years, with France defeated, and Britain alone, there was nothing that could be done to loosen the Nazi grip on Europe. Even after the German invasion of the Soviet Union in June 1941, Russia, far from being an effective ally, seemed more likely to succumb to the German attack. The United States did not enter the war until December 1941; she too, in the early months of 1942, was in a weak position, losing vast territories to Japan in the Pacific, and having little immediate involvement in Europe, beyond Hitler's own ill-timed declaration of war. At the same time, the British were facing the prospect of defeat in North Africa, at the hands of Rommel's Africa Corps.

Thus it was that the beginning of the 'final solution' in March 1942 coincided with the moment at which the Allies were at their weakest. In several ways, it was intended to do so; it was the Nazi aim to murder the Jews of Europe without provoking a world reaction, to do so secretly and silently, and to complete the task while Britain, Russia and the United States could do nothing about it. Even the Jews of neutral Switzerland, Sweden, Turkey, Spain, Portugal and southern Ireland had been on the list submitted by Eichmann to the Wannsee Conference. So too were the three-quarters of a million Jews living within Hungary's wartime borders, and the 330,000 Jews of Britain. All were to be destroyed. Only the Jews of Estonia were not listed: they had already been murdered by the killing squads in September and October 1941.

Chapter 2

Warnings and forebodings

That some terrible fate was in store for the Jews had been clear from all the information which had reached the Jewish leaders for more than a year; information which had been smuggled out of Germany, often with incredible difficulty and at great risk. As early as the end of 1940 the senior Jewish Agency representative in Geneva, Richard Lichtheim, a leading German Zionist who had remained in neutral Switzerland on the outbreak of war, warned that for hundreds of thousands of Jews the war 'has become unbearable in the literal sense of the word: they have perished'.

By the end of 1940, Lichtheim, assisted by several other Jewish leaders who had remained in Switzerland after September 1939, had made contact with more than thirty cities in Nazi-dominated Europe. By means of couriers, including Germans willing to risk their lives, and smugglers concerned only with money, the Geneva listening-post was in constant receipt of messages. Some were very brief and cryptic. Others were detailed and precise. And the picture which they built up was unmistakable. At the centre of the tragedy, as Lichtheim reported it, were the million and a quarter 'humiliated and destitute human beings' in the ghettoes of Poland: 'there are the forced-labour battalions of unpaid, unclothed, undernourished Jews, the children dying from hunger and cold, the walls and barbed-wire fences which Jews must not pass, the yellow badges, and the concentration camps.'

Much of Lichtheim's information came from Gerhart Riegner, the World Jewish Congress representative in Switzerland, whose task since the outbreak of war had been to maintain contact with as many Jewish communities in Europe as possible. 'I felt I had to report the facts, and try to make suggestions,' Riegner later recalled. 'But the responsibility lay outside. Our freedom of information was limited. We were in the trap, albeit on a little island. We didn't know sufficiently what was going on altogether. But we had to do what we could do. . . .'[1]

Lichtheim urged his Zionist colleagues in London, New York and Jerusalem to take the reports of Nazi actions seriously. 'Life in Europe is indeed not very pleasant today,' he wrote, 'but it cannot be bettered by those who do not wish to be disturbed by the aspect of ugly things, and turn away from it.'[2]

Throughout 1941, Lichtheim, Riegner and their colleagues in Geneva had sent regular messages to the Jewish leaders in Britain, Palestine and the United States. It was clear from these messages just how harsh were conditions in the ghettoes, and how cruel the restrictions on German Jews who had been deported in October 1940 to camps in Vichy France, including one at Gurs,

---

[1] Gerhart Riegner, conversation with the author, Geneva, 1 October 1980.
[2] Central Zionist Archives, L 22/45.

near the Pyrenees. It was also clear from these messages how drastically the situation had worsened with the German invasion of Yugoslavia in April, and of Russia in June. Jews were rarely seen on the streets of Belgrade, a Zionist representative, Dr Kahany, stated on June 25 in a letter from Geneva, 'because they are practically all taken by the Germans for hard labour'.[1] And on July 16 Dr Kahany sent a message to Jerusalem, based on the report of a Swiss journalist in Berlin, who had been shown a film giving 'some idea of the fate' of the Jews in Russia as the German armies advanced eastwards. In the film, the journalist reported, less than three weeks after the German invasion of Russia one could see 'how the Jews are carrying in one place the bodies of executed or massacred men from the cellars of private houses, from prisons and from offices'.[2]

The messages from Geneva made it clear that there was to be no relaxation of terror. On September 4 Lichtheim reported to Jerusalem, his letter being sent through Istanbul, that there were now as many as nine thousand Croat Jews in labour camps, and that their situation was becoming 'more desperate from day to day'.[3] In a further letter of October 20, he gave details of the expulsion of thousands more German Jews, not this time to France, but east-wards to the ghettoes of Poland. These Jews 'were given between 10 minutes and three hours to leave their flats, with a hand bag and not more than 100 marks'. Similar expulsions had also taken place from Vienna and Prague. All deportees were to be used for 'hard labour', and Lichtheim was afraid that with all the degradations of yellow badges, expulsion from their homes, and deportation, 'added to actual starvation and brutal treatment', the Jewish communities of Germany, Austria and western Czechoslovakia – the new Greater Germany – 'will probably be destroyed before the war ends and not too many will survive'.[4]

What could be done to counter such brutality? In a letter to his superiors in New York on October 27, Riegner urged that the maximum publicity should be given by the Allies to the desperate situation of the Jews of Europe.[5] And twelve days later Richard Lichtheim, in a telegram to Dr Weizmann, asked his own Zionist leaders 'to consider worldwide publicity'. Declarations by statesmen, Lichtheim added, and 'representations by neutrals' might possi-bly have 'some effect'.[6] And in a letter to London two days later Lichtheim elaborated on what he believed would be the fate of the central European deportees, whose total number, he now felt, was nearer 25,000. 'It may be,' he wrote to Joseph Linton, the Secretary of the Jewish Agency in London, 'that in the end their position will be the same as that of the majority of the Polish Jews under German domination: starvation by cold, hunger, filth, ill-treatment and epidemics, with a minority of the younger and stronger sur-viving.' As for the deportations as far east as Minsk, 'which of course lies in ruins, without money, food-reserves, or bedding', this, for the deportees,

[1] Central Zionist Archives, L 22/27.
[2] Central Zionist Archives, Z 4/14901.
[3] Central Zionist Archives, L 22/338, Letter No. 469.
[4] Central Zionist Archives, L 22/149, Letter No. 506.
[5] Archives of the World Jewish Congress, General Secretariat.
[6] Central Zionist Archives, L 22/134, telegram of 8 November 1941.

with the Russian winter setting in, was, in Lichtheim's words, 'murder combined with torture'.

Lichtheim believed that the Jews of Nazi Europe would be encouraged by 'a word of sympathy and consolation'. But he saw no means of direct mitigation of their fate. 'We are witnessing the most terrible persecution of the Jews which has ever happened in Europe', he wrote, and the purpose of protests from Britain and America, as he saw it, was to give the Jews who were thus condemned 'at least some moral satisfaction', and to remind 'certain smaller States', as well as millions of other people, 'that moral values still exist, and that they include and make imperative the condemning of this persecution of the Jews'.

In the practical sphere, Lichtheim wanted the United States to warn the various German 'satellites', Vichy France, Rumania, Hungary, Slovakia and Croatia, not to collaborate in the deportation of Jews from their territories, and not to participate in the slaughter of Jews. Non-Germans taking part in such slaughter, he believed, should be warned by Britain and America 'that they will be held responsible' for such action. As far as the 'satellites' were concerned, such warnings, Lichtheim wrote, 'might have had and *may still have*, a deterrent effect'.[1] The emphasis was his own.

In a letter of 11 February 1942, sent to Arthur Lourie, Secretary to the Emergency Committee for Zionist Affairs in New York, Lichtheim described the ever worsening situation of Jews throughout Europe. Only in Hungary, he reported, was the Government 'still resisting the repeated demands of the Nazis for harsher treatment of the Jews on the German model'. From Holland, where the majority of Jews were 'at least still alive and sleeping in their beds', some Jews had nevertheless been sent to the camp of Mauthausen, in Austria, 'where they have been set to work in the usual Nazi manner with the result that most of them died within the first 3 or 4 weeks after their arrival'.

There were 'many hundreds' of Dutch Jews, Lichtheim reported, who had died in similar circumstances; one man, whom both Lichtheim and Lourie knew personally, had been sent from Amsterdam 'to the concentration camp of Buchenwald, where he died'. In Poland the Jews were being forced to do 'the well-known slave work' for the German armies, in workshops and on the roads. But the worst news came from German-occupied Yugoslavia, where, Lichtheim wrote, '8,000 Serbian Jews are dead or have fled or are now in labour-camps', while 30,000 Croatian Jews were being 'worked to death under the supervision of the "Ustaschi", the gangster organisation of the Croat Chief of State', while in Rumania, as Rumanian troops advanced eastwards into Russia, tens of thousands of Jews had been 'butchered'. The number 'of these murdered Jews', Lichtheim noted, 'is said to be 90,000'.

Lichtheim's letter of February 11 continued on a note of deepest pessimism. It was 'obvious', he said, that as the war continued, 'the number of Jewish victims will increase', and he ended: 'The number of our dead after this war will have to be counted not in thousands or hundred-thousands, but in several millions. . . .'[2]

---

[1] Central Zionist Archives, L 22/134.
[2] Central Zionist Archives, L 22/10.

In London, the Foreign Office was also receiving messages from Switzerland about the persecution of the Jews. On February 9 the British Legation in Berne had sent to London a report which had reached Switzerland that young Jews were being taken to Germany from Nazi Europe 'for Gas experiments'.

The Foreign Office at once asked its representatives in Berne if this report could be confirmed. On February 18 the answer came that the Legation had consulted 'a prominent local private banker', one of the leading members of the Jewish community at Basle. He too had heard of such a report from a 'visitor' who had come to Basle from Vienna, but the visitor 'could furnish no confirmation'.[1]

Confirmation of some gas killings, but not necessarily of Jews being the victims, did reach London on February 19, from the British Legation in Stockholm, in the form of a report direct from Germany. Its author was a Swedish citizen, Dr Höjer, who had just returned from a visit to Germany, and who reported 'that the lunatic asylums are being cleared to make room for the wounded from the Eastern front'. While not mentioning the Jews in his report, Dr Höjer had spoken 'of one asylum where 1,200 people had been removed by poison'.

This Swedish report seemed a definite indication that murder by gas was indeed current practice in Germany. The British official who forwarded the report from Stockholm, Cecil Parrott, noted that what Dr Höjer reported 'should be fairly reliable as he is a man in a responsible government position'.[2]

In London, the Postal and Telegraph Censorship prepared, at the beginning of March, a report on conditions in Germany, based on its censorship work, and on a careful reading of the European Press during the previous three months. The report was dated March 5. One section, headed 'The Jews', gave details of a ruthless new drive to clear the Reich of Jews' at the end of 1941 and the beginning of 1942, based on a scrutiny of Red Cross postal messages from Germany that had reached England during January, the majority of which were from 'unfortunates on the eve of their departure to Poland or unknown destinations'.

The Censorship report of March 5 included the information that rumours 'leaking into Germany' about the fate of the deportees 'have caused a number of Jews to prefer suicide to deportation'. The report also mentioned what it called a 'horror story' of thousands of inmates of a ghetto probably somewhere near the Russian front 'being put to death in an attempt by the authorities to stamp out typhoid'.

One section of the Censorship report of March 5 dealt with conditions in the Warsaw ghetto. 'There are quite a number of people,' it noted, 'who really die in the streets and they are simply covered up with old newspapers where they lie for days until a cart comes round to pick them up. Then they are taken outside the town and dumped into a common grave. . . .' All over German-occupied Poland, Jews of all ages were taken away to forced labour, where 'thousands die while they toil under whips'. In the ghettoes of Cracow, Warsaw and Katowice, any medical supplies found by the Germans had

1 Foreign Office papers, 371/30898, C 2345.
2 Foreign Office papers, 371/30898, C 1898.

been confiscated, 'including bandages'. In Cracow, in the third week of January 1942, Governor Hans Frank had opened a 'special school' to train Germans in 'a more rigid policy' with regard to both Jews and Poles.

After describing the harsh conditions for those Jews who had not yet been deported from Germany itself, the Censorship report of March 5 contained a section which suggested that for some Jews at least, life was believed to be better in the east than in Germany. 'I have even heard,' an intercepted message of 30 December 1941 stated, 'that people are actually very glad to be sent to Poland, as they have left their troubles behind them, including the possibility of being put in a concentration camp.' There was certainly 'no comfort' in Poland, the message added, 'but the Jews are better off there because the Poles are good to them now, for they are under the same yoke. . . .'

The Censorship authorities realized that this latter type of message may have been written in order 'to re-assure' those who received it. But no one who read the report inside the Foreign Office proposed publicizing its more horrific aspects, or taking any further action on it.[1]

In Geneva, Richard Lichtheim was not so reticent about the reports which continued to reach him from Nazi Europe. Indeed, on March 4 news of a disturbing new development had reached the Geneva listening-post. For on that day Lichtheim reported to the Jewish Agency leaders in Jerusalem that some 70,000 Jews, living in the Protectorate of Bohemia and Moravia, formerly the western part of Czechoslovakia, were being driven from their homes and sent to a specially designated ghetto in the small garrison town of Theresienstadt, formerly Terezin. Once there, Lichtheim warned the Jewish Agency leaders, the deportees 'will be slowly starved as in the ghettoes of Warsaw and Lodz', and he added: 'This scheme is probably part of the Nazi plan to destroy the Jews in Greater Germany before the war is finished'.[2]

On the day after Richard Lichtheim sent news of the Theresienstadt ghetto to his colleagues in Jerusalem, a very small chink of light was shone on Jewish rescue efforts by the British Government. Aware of the need to prevent any more disasters like the *Struma*, on March 4, less than two weeks after the *Struma* had sunk, the Passport Control Officer at the British Embassy in Istanbul, A. W. Whittall, informed the Director of the Emigration Department of the Jewish Agency, Chaim Barlas, who was based in Istanbul, that the Immigration Department of the Government of Palestine 'has decided in principle to permit the immigration into Palestine of identified Jewish children resident in Rumania and Hungary aged 11–16 years'. Visas to enter Palestine would be granted to these children on their arrival in Istanbul.[3]

In Geneva, Lichtheim was pessimistic about this concession. 'I feel,' he wrote to a colleague in Istanbul on March 10, 'that this is zero hour and I am very much afraid that for reasons quite outside our control, there may be another case of "too late".'[4] The ghetto system, Lichtheim informed his colleagues in London on March 13, had now been extended to Slovakia, and it was said that it would apply 'to the whole Jewish population'. Once this were

[1] Foreign Office papers, 371/30898, C 2642.
[2] Central Zionist Archives, L 22/134, Letter No. 633.
[3] Barlas papers.
[4] Central Zionist Archives, L 22/10.

done, 'no further emigration will be possible'. In Hungary, labour camps were 'in preparation' for all Jews over the age of sixteen. In Rumania, a thousand 'hostages' had been taken, 'and new persecutions and pogroms are to be foreseen'.[1]

Lichtheim was convinced that something could be done to halt this new wave of persecutions. In the case of Slovakia, he wrote to London and New York on March 16, 'one word from the Pope would be enough. The country is deeply devoted to the Catholic Church', and the Prime Minister, Tiso, 'himself being a priest would perhaps try to stop the brutal excesses and abstain from the wholesale expulsions.[2]

In a telegram to the Jewish Agency in London that same day, March 16, Lichtheim warned that some 70,000 Slovak Jews were about to be deported to a 'ghetto near Polish border'. Each Jew deported would be allowed only 'one suit, one shirt, one pair boots'.[3] It was essential, he added, to approach the Vatican to persuade the Slovak Government to halt the deportations; and on March 18 both Lichtheim and Riegner appealed directly to the Apostolic Nuncio in Berne, Monsignor Philippe Bernadini, speaking to him for three-quarters of an hour, and then submitting a detailed aide-mémoire about the desperate situation of the Jews of Europe, including those of Slovakia, and urging an immediate intervention by the Vatican. The Nuncio, Lichtheim noted on the following day, had been 'most sympathetic and friendly', and promised not only to report to the Vatican, but 'to recommend certain steps in favour of the persecuted Jews.'[4]

What more could be done to halt the impending deportation from Slovakia to the 'ghetto near Polish border'? On March 19 Lichtheim again appealed to his colleagues in London, Jerusalem and New York for 'formal protests and warnings against the ruthless persecution of the Jews in Continental Europe'. These protests and warnings, he wrote, should be made 'over the radio and by speeches of the Statesmen of the democracies'. The Catholic Church, too, should use its 'great influence' in some of the countries concerned.[5]

On March 23 a success was registered for the first small rescue efforts in which the Jewish Agency and the British Government had cooperated. But because of the German mastery of Europe, these efforts were on a minute scale, their initial success marked by the arrival in Istanbul, from across the Black Sea, of two small cutters carrying Rumanian refugees: the *Mihai*, with fifteen refugees on board, and the *Mircea*, with thirteen.

The Jewish Agency had already asked the British Government to issue Palestine certificates still available under the White Paper for 870 Jewish children from Hungary and Rumania. But Sir Harold MacMichael, the High Commissioner in Palestine, was opposed to 'so high a total', being afraid, as he explained to the Colonial Secretary on March 20, that the Germans'

[1] Central Zionist Archives, L 22/134.
[2] Central Zionist Archives, L 22/149.
[3] Central Zionist Archives, L 22/149.
[4] Central Zionist Archives, L 22/149.
[5] Central Zionist Archives, L 22/134.

thoroughness would then make 'more and more ships available', with the result that 'a stream of refugees from South-East Europe will assume most serious proportions and become almost continuous.'[1]

MacMichael would authorize only a hundred Rumanian children in the first instance, to be followed 'probably' by a hundred Hungarian children. All other Jews who tried to reach Palestine, whether overland or by boat, would still be regarded as 'illegals', their boats intercepted, and the refugees themselves taken to internment camps elsewhere. When the war was over they would be sent back to the European countries from which they had fled.

For most of the Jews of Slovakia, however, it was, as Lichtheim had feared, 'too late'. Even as the *Mihai* and the *Mircea* dropped anchor off Istanbul with their twenty-eight refugees, the first trains were being assembled in the railway sidings of Slovakia to deport tens of thousands of Slovak Jews northwards. The railway schedule had been prepared on March 12, allowing for seven trains within the first month, each with specially sealed goods wagons, enabling more than a thousand Jews to be transported in each train.

Lichtheim's telegram of March 16 had spoken of a 'ghetto near Polish border' as the destination for these Slovak deportees. Their actual destination was indeed near the Polish border. It was not, however, a 'ghetto', but a concentration camp scarcely fifty kilometres beyond the Slovak frontier, at the town of Auschwitz.

The first two trains to reach Auschwitz arrived on 26 March 1942. In the sealed and stifling cattle trucks of the first train were 999 women from Ravensbrück concentration camp,[2] north of Berlin, who were tattooed on the forearm with the numbers 1 to 999. Two hours later the second train arrived, bringing a further 999 Jewesses from Slovakia. They also were tattooed, with the numbers 1,000 to 1,998, and like the women from Ravensbrück, sent to the camp barracks. Two days later, on March 28, a further 798 Jewesses from Slovakia reached the camp, their tattoo numbers being likewise meticulously recorded by the camp's clerks as 1,999 to 2,796. On March 30 a third train, with 1,112 Jewish men sealed into its trucks, reached Auschwitz from Paris. They too were tattooed and then sent to the barracks.[3]

Very few of these first arrivals were to survive until the end of the year, and only nineteen of the Frenchmen were to survive the war.[4] But for more than two months their task was to work: they were beaten, starved, shot at the slightest pretext, and forced to extend the camp itself, so that it could eventually receive hundreds of thousands of deportees.

Although the gas chamber at Auschwitz had already been used in the

[1] Colonial Office papers, 733/445/76021/42.

[2] These women from Ravensbrück were non-Jews. Many of them were convicted prostitutes, and other German women condemned by the Nazis as 'asocials'. On reaching Auschwitz, they became the reserve from which the first kapos and block-leaders in the women's camp were drawn. Some were to be among the cruellest, and most feared, of all the 'staff' in Birkenau.

[3] These details, and all subsequent facts concerning the arrival of trains at Auschwitz and the fate of the deportees, are taken from Danuta Czech, 'Kalendarium der Ereignisse im Konzentrationslager Auschwitz-Birkenau', published in *Hefte von Auschwitz*, volume 3, Auschwitz, 1960, and subsequent issues.

[4] The names, ages, birthplaces and fate of all the French deportees between 1942 and 1944 can be found in Serge Klarsfeld, *Le Memorial de la Deportation des Juifs de France*, Paris 1978.

experiment on Soviet prisoners-of-war and Polish political prisoners six months before, the Jews who arrived at Auschwitz during March were not gassed, but kept in the camp barracks, a reserve of slave labour, to which were added before the end of April more than five thousand Slovak Jews and two thousand Jewesses brought to Auschwitz in nine further trains. But few of these early deportees were to live long. Of the 973 men who reached the camp from Slovakia on April 17, only eighty-eight were still alive four months later; and of the 423 Slovak Jews who received their tattoo marks on April 29, only twenty were to survive until mid-August. The reason for so high a death rate was the SS decision that anyone who was considered to be too weak or sick to work, was sent to the gas chamber.

The first gassings at Auschwitz took place on May 4, when 1,200 of those who had arrived in March and April were specially 'selected' by a member of the SS medical service, and their names and numbers meticulously recorded. Then, all 1,200 were sent to the gas chamber, gassed, and their bodies cremated.

Henceforth, it was not only those who had served as slave labourers who were 'selected' to die. Eight days after this first selection, on May 12, a train with some 1,500 Jews reached the camp from the nearby Silesian town of Sosnowiec. All 1,500, including the children, were taken straight from the train to the gas chamber, gassed, and their bodies then cremated.

The news of these first gassings at Auschwitz was not to reach the west for more than two years. But from Geneva, Richard Lichtheim continued to send out what information he could assemble on the general pattern of murder and deportation. 'Such reports ought to be published from time to time,' Leo Lauterbach, head of the Organization department of the Jewish Agency wrote to him from Jerusalem on April 12, 'in order to keep alive public conscience and to awaken the sense of responsibility towards the innocent victims of this modern savagery.'[1]

---

[1] Central Zionist Archives, L 22/10, Letter No. 725.

Chapter 3

Britain's dilemma

Following the German military victories in North Africa, the friendship of the Arab States of the Middle East had become a matter of grave concern for Britain, especially with regard to the maintenance of British power at Suez. For this reason, Arab attitudes towards Jewish immigration to Palestine, and towards Zionist aspirations, were continually cited by British Ministers during the spring and summer months of 1942. Nevertheless, in the aftermath of the sinking of the *Struma* at the end of February, Lord Cranborne, the Colonial Secretary, had continued to advocate a relaxation of the Cabinet rules which had been enforced at the time of the sinking; rules which had led to diplomatic pressure being put on Turkey to ensure that Jewish refugees reaching Turkey from enemy countries would not be allowed to continue towards Palestine.

Cranborne's desire to moderate the Government's policy towards Jewish refugees did not, however, go unchallenged. On 19 March 1942 the High Commissioner in Palestine informed the Colonial Office that: 'If we abandon the principle on which we have hitherto gone we are likely to open the flood-gate and completely undermine our whole policy regarding illegal immigration',[1] and in the first week of April Lord Cranborne's Colonial Office advisers pointed out to him that under the existing British regulations, any Jewish refugees who did manage to reach Palestine from Europe would in any case have to be deported. The former Italian province of Eritrea had been suggested as a possible site for these deportees, and Cranborne put this suggestion forward to the British military authorities in Eritrea. But on April 5 General Auchinleck telegraphed his opposition to the plan, and when Anthony Eden's Private Secretary, Oliver Harvey, asked Eden if he would endorse it, Eden minuted:

No! I think that Lord Cranborne is going to land us with a big problem and that it would be more merciful in the end to turn these ships back.[2]

Lord Cranborne was determined, however, to prevent a repetition of the *Struma* disaster, and at the beginning of May he suggested that any Jews managing to reach Palestine should be allowed to land, their numbers being deducted from the 42,000 remaining immigration certificates. Yet even this concession was severely limited for on May 13 the Colonial Office laid down that 'all practicable steps should be taken to avoid publicity for the new arrangements'.[3] The Department explained that if news of the concession were

---

[1] Telegram No. 359, Secret, Colonial Office papers, 733/445, 76021/42; distributed as Most Secret.
[2] Foreign Office papers, 371/32663, W 5318.
[3] 'Illegal Immigration into Palestine', War Cabinet paper 209 of 1942, presented to the War Cabinet by the Colonial Office, Cabinet papers, 66/24.

made public, many more refugees would be tempted to risk the journey, and the Germans themselves might provide the shipping, in an attempt to drive a wedge between Britain and the Arabs.

Even this concession seemed too much for the Foreign Office, and at the War Cabinet on May 18 Eden himself insisted that if the concession did lead to a 'serious increase' in Jewish immigration, it must be reviewed once the existing White Paper certificates had been used up.[1]

On May 9, while Lord Cranborne's concession was still being discussed in London, the leading Zionists, including Dr Weizmann, were holding a special conference at the Biltmore Hotel in New York. The theme of their meeting was made clear by the Chairman of the Jewish Agency Executive, David Ben Gurion, who declared that, as a result of the 1939 White Paper, the Jews could no longer depend upon Britain to establish a Jewish national home in Palestine. It was therefore necessary, he said, for the Jewish Agency itself to replace the British Mandate as the government of Palestine. At the close of the Biltmore conference on May 11, a majority of the delegates present pledged themselves to work for the establishment of a 'Jewish Commonwealth' in Palestine, and for an end to all immigration restrictions.

Despite the Biltmore programme, Lord Cranborne continued his search for a more flexible policy for refugees. Indeed, on May 22, only eleven days after Biltmore, he set out this new policy in an official letter to the London representatives of the Jewish Agency, whom he had seen that same morning in his room at the Colonial Office.

In his letter of May 22, the Colonial Secretary reiterated the Cabinet's decision that 'all practicable steps' would be taken 'to discourage illegal immigration'. To this end, he wrote, 'nothing whatever' would be done to 'facilitate' the number of Jewish refugees in Palestine. Nevertheless, Cranborne went on, 'shiploads of illegal immigrants' who did succeed in reaching the coast of Palestine would be allowed to go ashore. Once ashore, they would be placed in 'detainment' camps, and those who passed the double test of security and 'the overriding principle of economic absorptive capacity' would be released 'gradually', against the existing half-yearly immigration quotas under the White Paper.

Cranborne's letter of May 22, despite this concession, went on to set out certain continuing restrictions on an 'open' policy. From the Cabinet's decision to discourage illegal immigration, he pointed out, 'it necessarily follows that no facilities can be granted to Jewish refugees who may become stranded in Turkey or in other neutral countries while attempting to enter Palestine from enemy-occupied territory'. And he went on to explain that it would therefore 'not be possible' for the British to 'facilitate the journey to Palestine', either of a group of twenty Rumanian Jews who had earlier escaped from an intercepted illegal ship, the *Dor de Val*, and who were then at Istanbul, or of a second group of refugees on board the *Euxine*, then at the Turkish port of Cesme. Cranborne's letter continued:

While His Majesty's Government do not admit responsibility for the safety of the passengers

[1] War Cabinet 64 of 1942, Cabinet papers, 65/26.

of these two vessels, they are prepared, as an act of grace, to allow them to proceed to Cyprus, if the Jewish Agency can make the necessary arrangements for their transportation from Turkey to the Island.

If however, the *Euxine* succeeds in reaching Palestine, her passengers will be landed and like those from the *Mihai* and the *Mircea* they will be transferred to a detainment camp.

But the offer of refuge in Cyprus for the passengers of the *Dor de Val* and the *Euxine* must not be taken as extending to any refugees who may in future make their way into Turkey. Towards these His Majesty's Government cannot admit that they have any responsibility or obligation.

The Cranborne concession, for all its qualifications and caveats, did mean that those very few who managed to escape, under their own initiative, from the well-guarded prison of Nazi Europe, and who reached Palestine, were now allowed to stay there. But the potentially positive effects of the new policy were sharply curtailed by the Government's insistence that it remain a closely guarded secret. As Lord Cranborne expressed it, bluntly, at the end of his letter:

. . . in view of the extremely delicate position in the Middle East, His Majesty's Government are anxious that the new arrangements should have the minimum of publicity. It is not intended therefore that there should be anything in the nature of a public declaration or announcement concerning them either in this country or in Palestine.

I shall be glad if you will observe similar reticence though I realise that you will no doubt find it necessary to communicate in confidence with Dr Weizmann and the Executive of the Jewish Agency in Jerusalem, and others whom it may seem to you essential to inform.

'In your communication to Dr Weizmann,' Lord Cranborne added, 'you will no doubt stress the importance of avoiding publicity in the American Press.'[1]

Lord Cranborne's letter of May 22 served as a small, somewhat qualified, but nevertheless welcome gesture to the Jews of Europe. As a result of it, several hundred Jews were spared the uncertainties and dangers of being cast adrift into the Black Sea, or of being refused permission by the Turks to cross into Turkey from Bulgaria.

[1] Central Zionist Archives, Z 4/14908.

Chapter 4

'Unbelievable crimes': May 1942

The fate of the Jews under Nazi rule had been one of the topics of discussion at the Special Zionist Conference at the Biltmore Hotel. In his opening address on May 9, Dr Chaim Weizmann had told the delegates that according to a 'calm, statistical estimate', it was believed that '25 per cent of Central European Jewry will be, to use the modern term, "liquidated" – 25 per cent!'[1]

Another speaker, Dr Nahum Goldmann, warned his colleagues that by the time the war was won it might well be found that even Dr Weizmann's figures were too optimistic, and that no more than 'two or three million' Jews would have survived in Europe, out of a pre-war total of eight million.[2] According to Goldmann's calculations, it appeared that up to six million Jews might be murdered before the end of the war.

This was a grim warning. But already events in Europe, as yet hidden from Allied eyes, were proving Goldmann's forecast correct: for this warning came just six days after the first gassings at Auschwitz.

Although these gassings were a closely guarded secret, even as Goldmann spoke, two reports, detailed, horrific, and authentic, were being smuggled out of Nazi Europe. The first came from 'a gentleman from Budapest' who was on his way through Switzerland to South America. He brought to Geneva, and gave to Richard Lichtheim, a message from the Jewish community in Hungary. Lichtheim sent it on, through Istanbul on May 13, to Jerusalem.

Of the 90,000 Jews living in Slovakia, it was reported, 20,000 had already been 'sent to Poland'. In many cases the men had been separated from the women and children. What had happened to the deportees on their arrival in Poland 'is not yet known'. But it was stated 'on good authority' that a large number of girls between the ages of sixteen and twenty-six 'have been sent to the military brothels created at the Polish frontier'.

One story which had come with the traveller from Budapest was of fifty-two Slovak Jews, including women and children, who had managed to reach the Hungarian frontier after the payment 'of enormous sums', and with a promise that they would be allowed to cross into Hungary. But at the last moment, as Lichtheim reported, 'somebody gave the alarm and they were turned back and handed over to the Slovakian frontier-guards who murdered the 52 persons on the spot'.[3]

The second report reaching the Allies in May had been smuggled out of German-occupied Poland, reaching London at the end of the third week in May. It had been sent to London by the underground Jewish Socialist Party

[1] Quoted in the *New York Times*, 10 May 1942.
[2] Central Zionist Archives, Z 5, Minutes of the Emergency Committee, 9 May 1942.
[3] Central Zionist Archives, L 22/10, Letter No. 710 via Istanbul.

in Poland, the Bund, and was addressed to the Polish Government-in-Exile. The Bund Report began with the statement that from the beginning of the Russo-German war in June 1941 'the Germans embarked on the physical extermination of the Jewish population on Polish soil'.

According to the Bund Report, the Germans had used Lithuanian and Ukrainian 'fascists' for the killings, which had begun in Eastern Galicia in the summer months of 1941. The 'following system', it stated, was 'applied everywhere':

. . . men, fourteen to sixty years old, were driven to a single place, a square or a cemetery, where they were slaughtered or shot by machine guns or killed by hand grenades. They had to dig their own graves. Children in orphanages, inmates in old-age homes, the sick in hospitals were shot, women were killed in the streets. In many towns the Jews were carried off to 'an unknown destination' and killed in adjacent woods.

The Bund Report then listed the numbers who had been killed in these 'murder actions', including 30,000 Jews in Lvov, 15,000 in Stanislavov, and 5,000 in Tarnopol. The same killings took place in every town in Eastern Galicia, and in some, as in Lvov, 'they are still in progress'. In the pre-war Polish city of Vilna, the Report stated, 50,000 Jews had been murdered by special SS killing squads, leaving only 12,000 still alive. In all, in Vilna and the region around it, 300,000 Jews had been butchered, and figures for specific towns were given as examples of the scale of this slaughter. In Rovno, for example, in the first three days of November 1941, 'over 15,000 people, men women and children were killed'.

The Bund Report then told of the methods of killing in the Polish territories which, renamed the Wartheland, had been incorporated into the German Reich. Here, the Report stated, thousands of Jews had been murdered 'by gassing' in the hamlet of Chelmno:

A special automobile (a gas chamber) was used. Ninety persons were loaded each time. The victims were buried in special graves, in an opening in the Lubard Woods. The victims themselves had to dig their own graves before being killed.

This was the first time the name of Chelmno, or details of the gassing of Jews, had reached the west. Once again, the details given in the Bund Report were precise, and, as we now know, accurate.[1] According to the report, 'on average' a thousand people a day had been gassed at Chelmno between the winter of 1941 and March 1942, including some 5,000 from the nearby towns and villages, and as many as 35,000 from the Lodz ghetto, as well as 'a number of Gypsies'.

In addition to the Eastern Galician, the Vilna region, and the Wartheland killings, the Bund Report also described the 'extermination of Jews' in the German-occupied region known as the Government General of Poland. According to the Report, the killings there had begun in February 1942, when Gestapo and SS men had gone each day to the Jewish quarters of two large

[1] See *Obozy hitlerowskie na ziemiach polskich 1939–1945: Informator encyklopedyczny*, Warsaw 1979, pages 129–30.

2. The eastern regions of Greater Germany, the 'General Government of Poland' and 'Lublinland'.

towns, Tarnow and Radom, 'killing the Jews in the streets, in the courtyards and in the homes'. In March 1942 the mass expulsion of Jews from Lublin had begun, but first, children in orphanages and people in old-age homes had been murdered 'in a beastly fashion along with patients in the hospital for general and epidemic diseases. . . .' In all, two thousand Jews had been murdered in this way, and a further 25,000 'carried off to "an unknown destination" out of Lublin, in sealed railway cars. They disappeared without a trace'. A further 3,000 Jews had been 'interned in barracks' at Majdanek, a suburb of Lublin.

Two more towns were mentioned at the end of the Bund Report. The first was Cracow, where, during the last days of March 1942, 'fifty Jews were picked out from a list and shot in front of the gates'. The second was Warsaw, where, on the night of April 17, 'the Gestapo arranged a blood-bath. . . .' This 'bloodbath' was then described, by those who had written from Warsaw:

They dragged fifty Jews, men and women, from their homes, picking them from a prepared list, and killed them in a beastly fashion in front of their gates. Some they could not locate in their homes. Every day since April 18, they kill a couple of Jews in their homes or in the streets during the day time. This action proceeds according to a prepared list and embraces Jews of all levels in the Warsaw Ghetto. There is talk about more bloody nights.

In all, according to the Bund Report, an estimated 700,000 Polish Jews had been killed between June 1941 and April 1942 in German-occupied Poland, a fact which showed, the Report said, 'without a shadow of doubt, that the criminal German Government has begun to carry out Hitler's prophecy that in the last five minutes of the war – whatever its outcome, he will kill all the Jews in Europe'.

At the end of its Report, the Bund asked for an immediate Allied response. Although the Germans would, the authors of the Report believed, 'be held fully accountable for their fearful bestialities at the proper time', this, for the Jewish population 'which is going through an unheard of hell', was not a sufficient 'consolation'. Something had to be done 'to prevent the destruction of Polish Jewry'.

The authors of the Bund Report wanted the Polish Government-in-Exile, and through it the United States and the other Allied Powers, to 'apply the policy of retaliation' on German nationals living in Allied countries. It was essential that these Germans should, 'already *now*, be held responsible for the bestial extermination of the Jewish people'. A policy of reprisals, the Report declared, was 'the only possibility of saving millions of Jews from inevitable destruction'.[1]

The Polish Government-in-Exile, by whom the Bund Report was received at the end of May, contained in its National Council two Jewish members, Szmul Zygielbojm and Dr Ignacy Schwarzbart. Zygielbojm was a member of the Bund, and Schwarzbart was a Zionist. Both men at once made details of the Report known to the British authorities, to the BBC, and to the head of the Polish Government-in-Exile, General Sikorski, who broadcast over the BBC setting out details of the Bund Report, and telling his listeners: 'The Jewish population of Poland has been doomed to destruction in accordance with the Nazi pronouncements on destroying all the Jews regardless of the outcome of the war'.

Sikorski added: 'Massacres of tens of thousands of Jews have been carried out this year. People are being starved to death in the ghettos. Mass executions are held; even those suffering from typhus are shot.'[2]

The Bund Report stimulated substantial interest. On June 24 it was summarized by the BBC, in its daily internal directive of news which it believed to be worthy of special attention. The BBC had always put stress on that aspect of German policy which it called 'The Terror'. And in its directive of June 24 it noted that 'The most ghastly aspect of this at the moment is the news, now confirmed, of the mass shooting of Jews in Vilna and Poland'. The directive continued:

In Vilna 60,000 Jews have been executed during the last few months. Other information is of the concentrating of Jews in the Lublin district. Brought from all over Europe, they have been

[1] The full text of the Bund Report was published in its original Polish and in English translation, by Yehuda Bauer, in 'When Did They Know?', *Midstream*, April 1968.
[2] Reported in *The Times*, 10 June 1942.

massed in one great camp, shot in great numbers, starved, and allowed to perish of diseases, so that the number of victims amounts to scores of thousands.

Brutal German excesses against Jews in Lvov, Jaslo and other towns of the Lublin and Lodz departments have also been reported.

The BBC directive ended: 'Please give full prominence to this. This also will have to be paid for. There will be retribution for Jewish victims.'[1]

Meanwhile, a further document issued on June 24 by the Polish Ministry of Foreign Affairs in London, stated that rumours were current in Warsaw 'that Jews are used in testing of poisonous gasses', that the number of Jews killed in eastern Poland and the 'occupied provinces of Russia' was estimated at 700,000, and that at a census taken by the Germans in the Ukrainian city of Dnepropetrovsk 'only 128 Jews were registered, whereas before the war their number must have been at least 500 times as many'.[2]

In an effort to publicize the fate of his fellow Polish Jews, Zygielbojm had written an article based on the Bund report, and had published it in the *Daily Telegraph*. The BBC's internal directive for June 25 referred directly to this article. 'The ghastly story of the massacre of the Jews in Poland . . .' it advised, 'should be given the fullest possible publicity in all languages.' And the directive continued: 'It should be made the subject of commentaries, not least to Catholic countries. This is one of the great crimes of history. If the Germans can treat the Jews in this way, what security from extermination have other "inferior" races, the Poles, the Serbs, the French?'[3]

The Bund Report story was printed in the *Daily Telegraph* on June 25, as the main news item on page five, the principal inside news page, under a bold headline:

GERMANS MURDER 700,000
JEWS IN POLAND

and a third line which read:

TRAVELLING GAS CHAMBERS

The facts of the Bund Report were, the paper added, 'wholly in keeping with Hitler's many times avowed policy'.[4]

On June 29 the World Jewish Congress held a press conference in London, at which Dr Schwarzbart presided. Once more the Bund Report of May 22 was read, and this time more newspapers responded. Three headlines of June 30 were unambiguous:

MASSACRE OF JEWS—OVER 1,000,000 DEAD SINCE THE WAR BEGAN
The Times
GREATEST POGROM—ONE MILLION JEWS DIE
Daily Mail
JEWISH WAR VICTIMS MORE THAN A MILLION DEAD
Manchester Guardian

[1] General Directive, 24 June 1942, BBC Written Archives Centre.
[2] Polish Ministry of Foreign Affairs, 'German Administration of Occupied Countries', copy in Foreign Office papers, 371/30900, folio 96.
[3] General Directive, 25 June 1942, BBC Written Archives Centre.
[4] *Daily Telegraph*, 25 June 1942.

On July 2 the *New York Times* gave a summary of the Report on page six of the paper. On page one, greater coverage was given to Governor Lehman's tennis shoe, which the Governor had donated to the scrap rubber drive, to encourage the civilian war effort. To the dismay of the Polish National Council, no other leading newspapers yet seemed interested at all, even to the extent of an inside page story, and on July 8 the Council repeated its earlier resolution of June 10, pointing out that it had in its possession 'newly revealed facts of the systematic destruction of the vital strength of the Polish nation, and the planned slaughter of practically the whole Jewish population'.[1]

On June 26, in a further effort to publicize the details of the Nazi policy against the Jews, Zygielbojm broadcast the main facts of the Bund Report over the BBC. He could not, he said, promise effective retaliation, but Germany was certain to be defeated, and the Allies, when victorious, would find, as Zygielbojm expressed it, the 'proper means of compelling the German barbarians to pay for all their unbelievable crimes'.

In his broadcast, which was in Yiddish, Zygielbojm gave an assurance to Hitler's victims 'that Jews in free lands will strain every nerve to put an end to systematic slaughter', and he read out a letter from a Jewish woman in one ghetto to her sister in another. The letter read:

My hands are shaking. I cannot write. Our minutes are numbered. The Lord knows whether we shall see one another again. I write and weep. My children are whimpering. They want to live. We bless you. If you get no more letters from me you will know that we are no longer alive.

'This letter,' Zygielbojm told his listeners 'is in reality a cry to the whole world.'[2]

A further digest of information from Poland had been published on July 1 by the Polish Ministry of Information in London, in its Press Bulletin, the *Polish Fortnightly Review*. The theme of the issue was the 'German attempts to murder a nation', in this case, the Polish nation. But one section was also devoted to the 'destruction of the Jewish population' of Poland: to mass shootings in four towns, and to the transfer of Jews from the Lublin ghetto to the village of Majdan Tatarski, where, the report stated, 'almost the entire population was exterminated'.

A number of Lublin Jews, according to the *Polish Fortnightly Review*, had been locked into railway wagons, shunted beyond the town, 'and left on a siding for two weeks, until all inside had perished of starvation'. But the majority of Lublin's Jews:

. . . were carried off over a period of several days to the locality of Sobibor, near Wlodawa, where they were all murdered with gas, machine-guns and even by being bayoneted.

It is an authenticated fact that Lithuanian detachments of *szaulis*, who have recently been brought into Poland, were used for these mass executions.

The fetor of the decomposing bodies in Sobibor is said to be so great that the people of the district, and even cattle, avoid the place. One Pole working in Sobibor wrote a letter pleading to be granted a transfer elsewhere, as he could not remain in such conditions.

[1] The Archives of the Polish Institute.
[2] *Jewish Chronicle*, 10 July 1942.

As well as the killings at Sobibor, the *Polish Fortnightly Review* confirmed other mass murders in the former eastern provinces of Poland, including 'several thousand Jewish children' massacred at Pinsk in the autumn of 1941, and some 12,000 German Jews deported from the Reich 'only to be massacred when they reached Poland'.

The locality of Sobibor, and the Majdan Tatarski village near Lublin, were the only two death camp sites mentioned in the Jewish section of this Polish Ministry of Information report. But in another section, concerned with the non-Jewish 'victims of German arrests', the report described how Polish prisoners, after being held, and tortured, in the Pawiak prison in Warsaw, were then 'transported to work in Germany, or to the concentration camp at Oswiecim'.

There followed a detailed, and harrowing account of conditions at Oswiecim–Auschwitz. The account made no reference whatsoever to any Jewish victims at Auschwitz. Indeed, the word 'Jew' was not mentioned. But the account made it clear that Auschwitz was a camp of particular barbarity. As well as describing the experimental gassings of September 1941, in which seven hundred Soviet prisoners-of-war and three hundred Poles had been murdered, the account told of how:

In addition to the main camp, built near Oswiecim, there is an additional camp near by, in which the brutalities are so terrible that people die there quicker than they would have done in the main camp. The prisoners call this supplementary camp 'Paradisal' (presumably because from it there is only one road, leading to Paradise). The crematorium here is five times as large as the one in the main camp. The prisoners of both camps are finished off in three main ways: by excessive labour, by torture, and by medical means.

The prisoners of the 'Paradisal' camp especially have very heavy work to perform, chiefly in building a factory for artificial rubber production near by. The tortures, which are in accordance with the well-known German methods, have the effect of driving a number of prisoners every day to despair, and flinging themselves against the wire surrounding the camp. The wire is guarded by guards with machine-guns, and the prisoners are shot down.

One of the favourite tortures in Oswiecim is to seize the victim by the arms and legs and swing him against a post until his back is broken. But the 'scientific' method of killing off prisoners is by injections which work slowly on the internal organs, especially on the heart. It is universally believed that the prisoners are used for large-scale experiments in testing out new drugs which the Germans are preparing for unknown ends. . . .

According to this report of July 1, among the other experiments being tried on the prisoners 'is the use of poison gas'. The report continued:

Recently the situation in Oswiecim has worsened, in consequence of the formation of a women's section. The women are put on those few lighter jobs (scrubbing potatoes, cleaning, etc.) which previously were performed by a number of the men, who thus escaped heavier labour. Now the men are used exclusively for heavy physical labour, and are divided into categories according to their strength. It is estimated that the Oswiecim camp can accommodate fifteen thousand prisoners, but as they die on a mass scale there is always room for new arrivals.[1]

There had been no mention in the Bund report of Auschwitz. As a result, the name of the camp had not been mentioned either by the BBC, or by any

---

of the Allied newspapers which had given the report publicity. Yet it was at Auschwitz that the scale of killing, already substantial, was at that very moment being deliberately and methodically extended.

During a visit to Auschwitz earlier that summer, Heinrich Himmler had ordered an extension of the camp. For even by the time of his visit, the single gas chamber and crematorium had become inadequate for the killing process which the Nazi leaders had in mind. Yet the location of Auschwitz on the main Vienna to Cracow railway line, and so easily linked to the Berlin, Breslau, and Warsaw lines, was clearly ideal, if the camp were to continue to receive Jewish deportees from all over Europe.

Following Himmler's visit, land had been set aside near the Polish hamlet of Birkenau, alongside the railway. There, new barracks were built, a women's camp was opened on 16 August 1942, electric fences erected, and a deep ditch dug around the whole site. At the same time, a German construction firm was asked by the SS to design and to install a new type of gas chamber at Birkenau, with crematorium attached, and with a far greater capacity than that in Auschwitz Main Camp.[1]

On July 3 a meeting was held at the BBC to discuss the broadcasting of news of anti-Jewish atrocities in Poland. During the discussion, the Assistant Director of European Broadcasting, D. E. Ritchie, told the meeting, which included a Polish Government and a Foreign Office representative, 'that it was felt that the best news value of the Massacre story had been lost owing to its having been given to the *Daily Telegraph* first'.

Rebuked, the Polish representative agreed that in future the BBC would have 'priority' for any such stories.[2]

The British Government now took a direct part in publicizing the Bund Report, for on July 9 the Minister of Information, Churchill's friend Brendan Bracken, was present at a specially summoned press conference together with the Minister of Home Affairs of the Polish Government-in-Exile, Stanislaw Mikolajczyk, and the two Jewish members of the Polish National Council, Zygielbojm and Schwarzbart. Once again, the facts in the Bund Report were repeated, together with information about German plans to terrorize the Polish non-Jews.

The Press conference of July 9 was again publicized in the *Daily Telegraph*, although once more the front page was devoted to a new German advance of some seventy miles on the eastern front, and to the manoeuvring of the British and German armies in the western desert in anticipation of 'the next phase of the battle'. There was, however, a smaller front page report on the massacres in Poland, 'in which Roman Catholics have been heavy sufferers', and in which the 'Polish intellectual classes' were being threatened with 'annihilation'. The Jewish aspect of the atrocities formed a part of the main story on page five, based on the Press conference, and giving prominence to Brendan Bracken's assurance that the German 'gangsters' would be punished 'with the utmost rigidity of the law'.

[1] See map on page 193, and plan on page 195.
[2] Minutes of 21st Meeting to Discuss BBC-Polish Broadcasts, 3 July 1942, BBC Written Archives Centre.

The report of July 10 in the *Daily Telegraph* drew two Jewish items from the Press conference; Zygielbojm's personal account of life in the Warsaw ghetto, and the details of anti-Jewish massacres given by Mikolajczyk. Among the remarks of Zygielbojm which were reported was one that the Germans 'were deliberately carrying out their monstrous plan to exterminate Jews'. In some Polish towns, Zygielbojm added, 'not a Jew had been left alive'.

The details published from Mikolajczyk's remarks included an account of how, on the night of March 23, the Jews of Lublin had been driven out of their homes, the sick and the infirm 'killed on the spot', and 108 Jewish orphans aged between two and nine taken from their orphanage to outside the town, where, 'together with their nurses', they were murdered. Altogether, in that one night, Mikolajczyk added, '2,500 people were massacred'.[1]

The Polish National Council's press conference of July 9 was also mentioned in *The Times*. But the headlines in *The Times* put first the fate of the non-Jewish Poles, as the people whom it stated to be in danger of 'extermination'. The secondary heading referred simply to the Jewish 'plight'.[2] Nevertheless, both these reports were explicit, as was a radio broadcast by Cardinal Hinsley, who spoke of his 'horror' at the massacres, and stressed the reliability of the reports on which he based his condemnation.[3]

The question of what could be done was the hardest of all to answer. The war was going badly for the Allies. Leningrad was still besieged. The German armies were less than a hundred miles from Moscow. In North Africa, the frontiers of Egypt stood exposed to German attack.

A sense of helplessness pervaded those who learned, and believed the increasingly ominous news. On May 27, Weizmann's private secretary, Doris May, had written to Arthur Lourie of the Emergency Committee for Zionist Affairs in New York: 'One wonders, vaguely and guiltily, what one is doing, sitting warm and dry, and well-fed, and comfortable, in the midst of all this? Or indeed, what it is physically possible for the ordinary person to do to redress the balance of injustice?' And on June 15 Richard Lichtheim wrote from Geneva, also to Lourie: 'The destruction of the Jewish communities is continuing. The whole of Europe is anxiously awaiting the day when the Allied nations will liberate this tortured continent'.[4]

Lichtheim himself was certain that this day of victory was not too far off. On May 30 the first thousand bomber raid had taken place over Germany, when the Royal Air Force dropped a total of 1,455 tons of bombs on Cologne. Thirty-nine of the thousand bombers had been lost during the raid. But in the first week of June two further such raids were carried out, on Essen and Bremen. Reflecting on these raids, Lichtheim wrote to Nahum Goldmann on June 15 of his 'personal belief' that the war could be 'finished this year by heavy bombardments from the air'.[5]

Lichtheim's confidence in the speedy effect of Allied bombing on German

[1] *Daily Telegraph*, 10 July 1942.
[2] *The Times*, 10 July 1942.
[3] BBC Written Archives Centre.
[4] Lourie papers.
[5] Central Zionist Archives, L 22/149.

morale was misplaced. But his realization that only an Allied victory could save those Jews who were still alive was widely shared. 'Our consciences often feel troubled,' a member of the Jewish Agency Executive, Leo Lauterbach, wrote to Lichtheim on June 16, 'when, after reading your heart-rending reports on the situation, we can do no more than express our sorrow and indignation.'[1]

Twelve days later Lauterbach wrote again, having been sent by Lichtheim a further report, published in the *Tribune de Genève*, describing the confiscation by the Gestapo of all Jewish property in Holland. This report, Lauterbach wrote, revealed 'one more step in the catastrophic developments' of which Lichtheim had already written in his earlier letters. Lauterbach added: 'It is like an avalanche which cannot be stopped and at best can be observed by those who have escaped being buried by it'.[2]

Throughout June 1942 there was another reason for the sense of helplessness among Jews outside Europe, and in particular among those in Palestine. Not only had the German army launched a new offensive against the Russians on the Kharkov front on June 10, and Japanese forces landed on the Aleutian islands of Alaska three days later, but on June 17 the British forces in North Africa, having been steadily pushed back by Rommel, were forced to withdraw to the Egyptian frontier. A garrison had been left in the Libyan town of Tobruk to bar the German advance, but on June 21 Tobruk fell to Rommel's forces, and three days later, on June 24, the Germans had advanced fifty miles inside Egypt.

Suddenly Britain's ability to defend even Egypt was cast in doubt. And beyond Egypt lay Palestine, relatively defenceless. The Jews of Palestine now realized that the war might come to them at any moment. It was no longer a question of believing or disbelieving news of Nazi atrocities committed two thousand miles away: it was a question of the possible arrival of these same Nazis, as conquerors, in Tel Aviv and Jerusalem. On June 25 Doris May wrote from London to Arthur Lourie in New York: 'It may yet fall to our handful of half-trained, half-equipped people to put up the only effective resistance to the advance – to crack the jaws that seek to devour them'. She had hoped, she said, that Palestine, the Land of Israel, might be spared, 'but it does not look very like it'.[3]

In London, Churchill continued to support the Zionist request for the formation of a specifically Jewish military force to fight as an integral part of the Allied armies. But both the War Office and the Colonial Office were opposed to this scheme, which had first been put forward by the Zionist leaders within a few weeks of the outbreak of war. In a personal minute on July 5 to the Colonial Secretary, Lord Cranborne, Churchill wrote:

The strength of opinion in the United States is very great, and we shall suffer in many ways there by indulging the British military authorities' and Colonial Office officials' bias in favour of the Arabs and against the Jews.

---

[1] Central Zionist Archives, L 22/10, Letter No. 779.
[2] Central Zionist Archives, L 22/10, Letter No. 785.
[3] Lourie papers.

Now that these people are in direct danger, we should certainly give them a chance to defend themselves.

Churchill ended his letter:

It may be necessary to make an example of these anti-Semite officers and others in high places. If three or four of them were recalled and dismissed, and the reasons given, it would have a salutory effect.[1]

No such action was taken. Nor would the Cabinet Ministers concerned withdraw their opposition to a Jewish army. Meanwhile, Polish, Czech and Free French forces continued to reinforce the Allied strength on land, at sea, and in the air, and although hundreds of thousands of Jews were serving, as individuals, in the different Allied forces, the Zionists felt aggrieved that there could not be a specific Jewish force, to challenge Hitler's armies with its own sacrifice, its own zeal, and its own flag.

[1] Premier papers, 4/51/9.

Chapter 5

Evidence and omissions

In German-occupied Europe, a new wave of terror had begun, following the shooting in Prague on May 27, by Czech patriots, of Richard Heydrich, ruler of the German Protectorate of Bohemia and Moravia. Heydrich died of his wounds on June 4, and six days later all 250 male inhabitants of the Czech village of Lidice were killed as a reprisal. As well as the Christians of Lidice, several hundred Jews were also murdered inside Greater Germany as a reprisal for Heydrich's death, and the pace of the deportations to the death camps was intensified.

The Lidice killings were widely publicized in Britain, and on June 17 the Prime Ministers of the Allied Governments-in-Exile urged the British Foreign Secretary, Anthony Eden, to propose direct Allied reprisals against Germany. One proposal, suggested by a Conservative Member of Parliament, Sir Thomas Moore, was an 'immediate warning to the German Government that, in future, a German undefended town or village will be obliterated by the Royal Air Force in retaliation for every innocent person murdered by the Nazis in any occupied country'. Churchill's immediate reaction was: 'There would not be enough German villages to go round', but instead the Allied bombing effort would continue to be directed 'to the most effective points'.[1] This view was supported inside the Foreign Office, where Frank Roberts, of the Central Department, noted on June 18 that it seemed to him 'preferable to continue our present policy and to leave the European populations to draw their own conclusions from the heavy bombing of German cities'.[2]

Collective reprisals were therefore ruled out. Individual reprisals, as asked for in the Bund Report at the end of May, had also been ruled out by the Allies. One Allied concern was that reprisals against individual Germans in Allied custody could so easily be followed by counter-reprisals against Allied prisoners-of-war in German hands. Rather than taking reprisals on German nationals who had been caught in Allied hands on the outbreak of war, it had always been hoped, and especially by the Jewish leaders, to organize exchanges of such German nationals for Jews caught in Nazi Europe on the outbreak of war who held British, Palestinian, or other Allied passports. One such exchange involving forty-six Palestinian Jews had already taken place in December 1941, and negotiations for a second exchange were still in progress.

These negotiations were prolonged and difficult, carried out through the good offices of neutral Switzerland. But having been successful once, it was hoped that they would work again. Any reprisal action could only endanger such plans for rescue, as well as the lives of thousands of Allied prisoners-of-

---

[1] Prime Minister's Draft reply, Foreign Office papers, 371/30916, C 6108.
[2] Foreign Office papers, 371/30916, C 6108.

war, including 40,000 British soldiers captured at Dunkirk in June 1940, and hundreds of bomber pilots and crew who had been shot down over Germany during 1941, and were being held in camps and castles throughout Germany.

Only two avenues of action seemed open in the spring of 1942: massive protests which might stimulate neutral, satellite, and even German public opinion, and the threat of retaliation once the war was over.

The first suggestion, publicity, was taken up by A. G. Brotman, the Secretary of the Board of Deputies of British Jews, in a discussion on July 11 with P. Stanczyk, the Minister of Social Welfare in the Polish Government-in-Exile. Three days later Brotman wrote to Stanczyk, setting out his ideas in some detail. The Jewish aim, he explained, was to make 'an organised endeavour to keep the conscience of the civilized world alive to the crimes and atrocities committed by the Nazis and their associates against all the rules of warfare'.[1]

More details concerning the atrocities themselves were published in London on July 15, in the *Polish Fortnightly Review*. But they concerned atrocities against Poles in general, not specifically against Jews. This issue of July 15 contained a map, showing twenty-two concentration camps in which, the caption explained, 'Poles were held'.

The Polish report of July 15 made no reference to Jews in its section on these concentration camps. Nor did it mention Jews in the two paragraphs devoted to Auschwitz itself. These paragraphs read:

Further batches of prisoners are continually being sent to Oswiecim concentration camp from all the prisons in Poland. In the second half of March a couple of hundred persons were sent from Warsaw to the camp; among them were several Polish warders of the Warsaw prison. In April several hundred more prisoners, women as well as men, were sent from Warsaw. News is continually being received of deaths in Oswiecim of prisoners who are unable to stand up to the rigours of the camp.

Large parties of Oswiecim prisoners go to work every day on the building of a synthetic petrol works which is being erected in the vicinity. The mortality among prisoners is indicated by the following details. Of a party of prisoners transferred to the camp from Milano-wek[2] in July, 1940, three have returned home, two are still in the camp, and 35 have died—of a group of 12 workers in the former Warsaw Committee for Social Self-help, taken to Oswiecim in July, 1941, only one remains; the others have all died in Oswiecim. . . .[3]

Although this report on Auschwitz, like the previous Polish report of July 1, made no reference to any Jewish victims, or Jewish deportations, other reports, in which Auschwitz itself was not mentioned, did refer to Jews. On July 16 the weekly magazine *News Review* told of 'large gas stations' which had been set up in Poland 'to kill off Jews who had been expelled from Germany to the Lublin district as well as the Polish Jews who lived there. No sleeping-drugs were wasted on them. They were just trussed up and finished off'.[4]

Another report on Nazi atrocities was published five days later, on July 21, by the Polish Government-in-Exile. Like previous Polish reports, it dealt primarily with the killing of non-Jewish Poles, of whom it was estimated that a total of 70,000 had been killed by April 1941. But the report of July 21 also

[1] Foreign Office papers, 371/30917.
[2] Thirty-five kilometres southwest of Warsaw, on the Warsaw-Lodz railway.
[3] *Polish Fortnightly Review*, 15 July 1942.
[4] *News Review*, 16 July 1942.

referred to the mass murder of 'Polish citizens of Jewish faith' at Lublin, Lvov. Stanislavov, Vilna and Chelmno, some of the places which had been listed in the Bund Report two months before, and noted that at Chelmno 'tens of thousands were killed in gas chambers'.

The Polish Report of July 21 also mentioned Auschwitz by name, but as in the two earlier reports of July 1 and July 15, no reference was made to Jews, or to any deportation of Jews to Auschwitz. At Auschwitz, the report stated, more than eight hundred people had been gassed on 5 September 1941: about two hundred Polish lawyers, engineers and students, and six hundred Soviet prisoners-of-war, mostly officers, while 274 women had been sent from Ravensbrück on 28 September 1941 followed by 243 more women on 30 May 1942.[1]

Yet the day-by-day gassing of Jews at Auschwitz had been carried out, unknown in the west, since the previous May. During June, more than seven thousand Jews had been brought to Auschwitz from Silesia, France and Slovakia. During July more than eight thousand had arrived. Some were 'selected' to be sent to the barracks at Birkenau for slave labour. But most were taken by truck from the railway siding, along the Birkenau perimeter road, to the gas chambers. Thus on July 11, out of more than a thousand deportees from Slovakia, only 182 men and 148 women were sent to the barracks, and the rest, including all the old people and children, were gassed. Six days later, on July 17, a total of two thousand Jews reached the camp from Holland. That same day 449 of them, the old, the infirm, and all women with children, were gassed. The rest were sent to the barracks.

All this was unknown to the Allies, or to the Jewish organizations in the west. Equally unknown was the decision of the SS, on July 10, to hand over a thousand Jewish women then in the barracks at Birkenau to the authority of a German medical professor, Dr Clauberg, who wished to carry out experiments in forcible sterilization in special laboratories set up at Auschwitz itself.

Although these facts, recorded at the time by the Gestapo, were unknown in the west, further evidence that Jews were still being deported from western Europe came immediately after the Gestapo had seized some 18,000 Jews in Paris on July 16. All these Jews, Berlin radio announced boldly on July 17, 'will be deported to the East, as previously announced'.

The Allied monitoring stations heard and recorded this broadcast as it was being made, and it was quoted in the New York Times on July 18. Four days later in London, a report in The Times gave details of painful scenes at the deportation camps as the men, described as 'Jews and Communists', were seen by their wives being marched handcuffed to the deportation trains 'between files of German soldiers with fixed bayonets'. Some of the men, according to The Times, 'incensed by the distress of their women', had instinctively sprung forward to take a last farewell, only to be driven back by the German soldiers 'with their rifle butts'.

The Times' report on July 22 also noted that the Germans had 'casually notified' the French that those deported eastward 'would not return to France'.[2]

[1] 'Pologne: communiqué par le Gouvernement polonais', copy in Foreign Office papers, 371/30917.
[2] The Times, 22 July 1942.

Meanwhile, the second suggestion which Zygielbojm had made in his broadcast, post-war retribution, was being seriously considered by the Allied leaders, and was mentioned explicitly by President Roosevelt himself in a message to a mass protest meeting held in New York on July 21. 'Those who carry out the crimes,' Roosevelt declared, 'will be called to account on the day of revenge.'[1]

Six days later, in London, Anthony Eden was the senior Minister present at a special Committee of the War Cabinet to discuss the question of the 'Treatment of War Criminals'. Following this meeting, the legal experts at the Foreign Office began to examine the question of a possible British Government statement on the subject, to be made in conjunction with the United States. One proposal, which the American Ambassador in London, John G. Winant, was asked to pass back to Washington, was that the actual terms of any armistice with Germany should contain a clause demanding that the Germans surrender their war criminals to the Allies.[2]

In the summer of 1942 the Foreign Office in London received a report from an American citizen, Edwin Van D'Elden, who had just been repatriated from Germany. In his report, which was sent on July 24 from the British Embassy in Washington to the Foreign Office, Van D'Elden described the deportation of Jews from Frankfurt-on-Main to the east. He himself had only left Frankfurt on May 15, having been released from internment on account of illness, and he reported the fate of several thousand of the deportees, who, he said, had been forced to leave the train in 'open territory' in German-occupied Poland, been stripped of their clothes, and then 'summarily executed by Nazi firing squads who mowed the victims down by machine-gun fire'.[3]

Inside the Foreign Office, it was decided not to publicize Van D'Elden's report. The official concerned explained his reasons thus: 'I cannot understand why it should be necessary to send broadcasts to the Germans about persecution of the Jews, on the ground that they know very little of what is happening. The movement is surely tolerated and even encouraged by many, and is certainly known to all Germans – since they are forced to participate.'[4]

With such an argument, the Van D'Elden report was consigned to the files, and disappeared within them. But by now too much was known for the facts to be overlooked. On August 7 Richard Lichtheim wrote gloomily from Geneva to Jerusalem: 'the position in Europe is quite desperate and I am suffering from a permanent feeling of frustration because there is so little we can do about it.' Lichtheim added:

Considering the conditions under which millions of Jews are now living in Poland and the other occupied territories I am afraid that the number of Jewish victims will be much higher than hitherto anticipated. If the war goes on for another year or longer there will probably be three million dead and three million broken in health and spirit.[1]

[1] Quoted in the *New York Times*, 22 July 1942.
[2] Foreign Office papers, 371/30917.
[3] 'Persecution of Jews'. Copy in Foreign Office papers, 371/30900, folios 178–80.
[4] Foreign Office papers, 371/30900, C 7610, minute signed by A. David.
[5] Central Zionist Archives, L 22/177.

On August 3, in a leading article headed 'Uprooted Peoples', *The Times* had written of the deportation of non-Jews from Slovenia, and of Jews from France and Holland. These latter 'seemed to suggest', *The Times* commented, 'Nazi determination to purge western Europe of all its Jews'. From Holland, it added, six hundred Jews 'are said to be deported every day'. And the leading article continued: 'These exiles are herded together in Poland in conditions of degradation and misery. Their eventual fate is either extermination or wretched survival in the vast eastern ghetto around Lublin, beyond the pale of the German Reich.'[1]

Five days later, on August 8, *The Times* reported widespread French indignation at the deportation of Jews from France 'to an unknown destination', while a second article in the same column told of a report which had just reached London of Nazi brutality towards Dutch Jews. Girls 'of school age', it reported, 'were placed in trains and sent to a camp – it is not known what kind of camp'. In addition, whole families were awakened in the early morning, ordered to take food for three days with them, marched to the station, and sent huddled together in trains 'which leave for an unknown destination'.

The actual destination was in fact Auschwitz–Birkenau. It was still an 'unknown destination' as far as the Jewish deportations were concerned. Ironically, however, the very next item in the same column named the true destination: 'the Ocwiecim concentration camp'.[2] But it named the camp, not in connection with the Jewish deportations, but as the place to which non-Jewish Poles were being sent as a result of a wave of sabotage 'spreading all through Poland'. Twenty such 'saboteurs' had been arrested near Radom, and executed on the spot; the rest, according to the report, some 540 in all, were sent to Auschwitz.[3]

The 'unknown destination' had still not been connected with Auschwitz, and the secret of its work and purpose remained intact.

[1] *The Times*, 3 August 1942. Lublin and the 'Lublinland' reservation were, in fact, both inside the boundary of Greater Germany, as created in October 1939, following the German conquest of Poland.
[2] The correct Polish spelling is: Oswiecim.
[3] *The Times*, 8 August 1942.

Chapter 6

'Camps are being prepared'

At the end of July 1942 news reached the west which seemed to confirm the details of the Bund Report, and to suggest that Poland's largest surviving Jewish community, that of Warsaw, was about to suffer the same fate as the Jewish communities of Eastern Galicia, the Vilna region, and the Wartheland.

This new information was published in the *New York Times* on July 29. Its source was the Polish Government-in-Exile. In publicizing it, however, the *New York Times* mixed it with other news, and gave the items a combined headline:

YUGOSLAVS DRIVING
AXIS FROM BOSNIA

It was only the fourth headline which referred to a Nazi plan for 'wiping out' 600,000 people in the Warsaw ghetto. The word 'Jews' did not appear at all in these headlines, but the ninth paragraph of the report itself stated starkly: 'Nazi authorities in Poland are planning to "exterminate" the entire Warsaw ghetto whose population is estimated at 600,000 Jews. . . .'

The report of July 29 made clear, as had not been stated in the Bund Report of two months before, that nearly 100,000 Jews had already died in Warsaw as a result of deliberate starvation, privation and disease, between the time when the Germans had sealed off the ghetto in November 1941, and the summer of 1942. But now it appeared that the Nazis were seeking a new and more rapid means of destroying Warsaw Jewry, deportation to the east, and there seemed equally little doubt, according to the Polish Government-in-Exile, that this deportation meant death for as many as 400,000 Jews.[1]

In fact, these Warsaw deportations had already begun on July 22, when nearly ten thousand Jews had been sent in sealed cattle trucks to Treblinka, and gassed immediately they reached the camp, less than three hours away from Warsaw by train. But the Polish Government-in-Exile's message of July 29 mentioned neither Treblinka itself, nor the fact that the deportations had actually begun.

News of the continuing deportations from France was published in London on July 29 in *The Times*, in a report of opposition inside Vichy France to a number of German measures, among them 'the brutality of the Germans towards French Jews'. Under a headline:

BRUTALITY TO JEWS

The Times correspondent at the French frontier reported on the 'indignation'

[1] *New York Times*, 29 July 1942.

which had 'flared up' following the Gestapo 'drives' throughout the previous week in which 20,000 Jews had been rounded up. The report continued:

The Jews were arrested in the streets, in shops, or in their homes, and then, without distinction of age, sex, or origin, were taken, as they were, and herded into camps. Vichy was then officially notified, in curt language by the German authorities that they would all be deported to Poland.

There were indescribable scenes of despair, and whole families are reported to have committed suicide. All through the week along the whole demarcation line, especially along the banks of the rivers Cher and Saone, Jews were shot attempting to escape into unoccupied France.

In addition to that, however, Berlin peremptorily demanded the surrender to the Gestapo of the inmates of the Jewish and Polish refugee camps in unoccupied France, in particular those from a camp in the Pyrenees. . . .[1]

What did these sudden round-ups mean? Could they be, in fact, part of a plan for total extermination? As yet there was no evidence that such a plan existed. But the first news of such a plan was about to reach the west; not further statistics of the spread of mass murder or of deportations 'to the east', but news of a definite and comprehensive extermination plan aimed at the destruction of all European Jewry.

Not only did the news reaching Switzerland at the end of July tell of a specific extermination plan. It also came from German sources. All earlier reports of mass murder had come from Polish or Jewish sources. Now it was from highly placed Germans that the shattering message came.

One such source was Dr Arthur Sommer, an economist attached to the Army High Command in Berlin, and belonging to a group opposed to the Nazi regime. Since the outbreak of war, Sommer's contact in Switzerland had been a University Professor and fellow economist, Edgar Salin, who had passed on a series of messages about the German war effort to one of the Geneva Zionists, Chaim Pozner, a former pupil of Salin's. Now an ominous message came:

In the East camps are being prepared where all the Jews of Europe and a great part of the Russian prisoners-of-war will be exterminated by gas.

Please relay this information immediately to Churchill and Roosevelt personally.

If the BBC comes out every day with a warning against lighting the gas ovens, then perhaps they may not be put into operation, for the criminals are doing everything to prevent the German people from finding out what they are planning to do and will certainly carry out.[2]

Although the 'gas ovens', that is to say the gas chambers and the crematoria, had already been in operation, at Auschwitz for nearly three months and at Belzec for more than four months, this was an unmistakable reference to a specific plan whereby 'all the Jews of Europe' were to be killed. It was also a plea for action to stop a process from being 'put into operation'. But in fact that process was already far advanced.

---

[1] *The Times*, 29 July 1942.

[2] I am grateful to Dr Chaim Pazner (formerly Pozner), for the text of this message, which he recalls having handed to V. C. Farrell, the British Passport Control Officer in Berne, for transmission to London, as well as to the leaders of the Swiss Jewish Community, and to a leading American citizen in Switzerland, the head of the Bank for International Settlements, for transmission to Washington.

An equally ominous message which reached Gerhart Riegner, of the World Jewish Congress, had also come to Switzerland from Germany. It too had come from a German who hated Nazism, and who had likewise passed such messages to Switzerland before. This German, said to be an industrialist, also had access to high policy. His message had apparently been brought by the man himself, who gave it to a Jewish businessman living in the German-speaking part of Switzerland.

Before passing the message on, Riegner cross-questioned the contact. The German industrialist, he was told, 'is the head of a big factory, employing 30,000 people for the war effort, with access to the military and to Hitler'.

Could the report of an actual extermination plan be believed? 'We had first to convince ourselves that the message was true', Riegner later recalled, and he added: 'When you get such a bombshell it is also not easy. It took me two days fully to take it in, to grasp it. But I was of German origin. I knew the real character of the Nazi movement. I knew they were capable of doing such things'.

Before passing on the message to the Allies, Riegner looked for further facts which might confirm the alleged extermination plan. He found them in two details which, as he later recalled, 'gave a sense to the whole thing'. The first was Hitler's own constant reiteration that the war would end with the annihilation of the Jews, 'he had announced it all the time'. The second was the pattern of recent deportations.[1]

Riegner now prepared a note of all that was known in Geneva of the current deportations. It was a formidable list. As many as 28,000 Jews 'to be arrested and deported' from Paris on July 16, the arrest of 'several thousand' French Jews in the provinces, especially Tours and Poitiers, the recent daily seizure of Jews in Lyons, Marseilles and Toulouse, the 'daily big deportation' of Jews from Holland, the announcement by the Germans themselves of 'increased deportations' from Berlin and Vienna, the much reduced number of Jews in Prague, and the recent deportation of 56,000 Jews from Slovakia.[2]

Suddenly, in the light of the new message, all these diverse deportations made sense: they were part of a pattern and a plan. On August 8, convinced that the message was as accurate as it was terrible, Riegner handed an identical telegram both to Howard Elting, the American Vice-Consul in Geneva, and to H. B. Livingston, the British Consul, for transmission to the World Jewish Congress leaders in London and New York. The telegram read:

Received alarming report stating that, in the Fuehrer's Headquarters, a plan has been discussed, and is under consideration, according to which all Jews in countries occupied or controlled by Germany numbering $3\frac{1}{2}$ to 4 millions, should, after deportation and concentration in the East, be at one blow exterminated, in order to resolve, once and for all the Jewish question in Europe.

'Action is reported,' the message added, 'to be planned for the autumn.'

Once again, nothing was said, or even known, about the plan having already been in operation for nearly four-and-a-half months. Indeed, in Riegner's version, it was only 'under consideration'. There was, however, an added

---

[1] Recollection of Gerhart Riegner, in conversation with the author, Geneva, 1 October 1980.
[2] Draft telegram from Riegner to Stephen Wise, dated 8 August 1942, Archives of the World Jewish Congress, General Secretariat.

detail. 'Ways of execution are still being discussed,' Riegner reported, 'including the use of prussic acid.'

In his message Riegner went on to discuss the reliability of the message. 'We transmit this information,' he wrote, 'with all the necessary reservation, as exactitude cannot be confirmed by us.' But he did add, in a final sentence: 'Our informant is reported to have close connections with the highest German authorities, and his reports are generally reliable.'[1]

The British and American diplomats at once passed back Riegner's message to London and Washington. At Riegner's request, it was to be forwarded in the United States to Rabbi Stephen Wise, head of the American Jewish Congress, and in Britain to Sydney Silverman, a Labour Member of Parliament, and Chairman of the British Section of the World Jewish Congress. Neither message, however, had a simple path. The one to Stephen Wise had a life of only nine days. At first, it seemed that it might be taken seriously, for it reached the State Department in Washington with a covering note from the Vice-Consul, reporting that when he had mentioned to Riegner 'that this report seemed fantastic to me', Riegner had replied that 'it had struck him in the same way', but that if one took into account that mass deportations were known to have taken place from Paris, Holland, Berlin, Vienna and Prague since July 16, 'it was always conceivable that such a diabolical plan was actually being considered by Hitler'.

The Vice-Consul himself was not entirely sceptical. Riegner, he said, was 'a serious and balanced individual' who would not have come to see him had he not had 'confidence in his informant's reliability', and if he did not seriously consider 'that the report might well contain an element of truth'.

Inside the State Department, it was, however, scepticism that prevailed. In the Division of European Affairs, the Assistant Chief, Paul Culbertson, commented on August 13: 'I don't like the idea of sending this on to Wise, but if the Rabbi hears later that we had the message and didn't let him in on it he might put up a kick.' Another official, Elbridge Durbrow, went even further. It did not appear 'advisable', he wrote that same day, in view of what he called 'the fantastic nature of the allegations and the impossibility of our being of any assistance if such action were taken', to pass the message on to Wise 'as suggested'. The message was therefore held back, and on August 17 the United States Minister in Berne, Leland Harrison, was informed that Riegner's message had not been delivered to Wise 'in view of the apparently unsubstantiated nature of the information'.[2]

---

[1] Foreign Office papers, 371/30917, C 7853. Telegram No. 2831, Berne to Foreign Office. Dr Pazner has suggested that the message which he was sent by Sommer was also the direct and sole source of the telegram sent by Riegner to London and Washington. But the Riegner telegram contains no mention of the principal feature of the Sommer message, that it might perhaps be possible to prevent the 'gas ovens' from being put into operation by daily warnings over the BBC. In addition, the Sommer message referred to Russian prisoners-of-war, of whom no mention was made in the Riegner telegram. The Sommer message also told of extermination by 'gas', while the Riegner telegram told of 'prussic acid', of which no mention was made in the Sommer message. The Riegner telegram also reported that different 'ways of execution' were being discussed. The Sommer message told *only* of gas. It is these various differences which lead me to believe that although both the 'Pozner' and 'Riegner' messages refer to an extermination plan, it is unlikely that the one was merely a telegraphic version of the other.

[2] The State Department reaction to the Riegner telegram is in United States National Archives, 862-4016, Race Problems, Germany, 2234.

A week later Riegner himself was informed bluntly, by Paul C. Squire, the American Consul in Geneva, that the American Embassy in Berne had received telegraphic instructions from the State Department 'which indicate that it is disinclined to deliver the message in question in view of the apparently unsubstantiated character of the information which forms its main theme'. Squire told Riegner, however, that if he received 'corroboratory information', he should at once advise the Consul, whereupon 'further consideration will immediately be accorded the matter'.[1]

Meanwhile, the British Consul in Geneva, acting as his American counterpart had done in answer to Riegner's request, had forwarded the message to London. He made no comment of his own, but gave the message to the British Legation in Berne for transmission to London by the fastest possible route. At 4.48 on the afternoon of August 10, it was coded in the British Legation in Berne, and telegraphed to London, where it reached the Foreign Office at 6.25 that same evening.

In the message as sent to London, Riegner asked Silverman to 'inform and consult New York'. But when the coded telegram reached the Foreign Office in London, it was not immediately passed on. Instead, several officials within the Foreign Office studied the decoded version, and made their own critical comments on it. The first to do so was David Allen, of the Central Department. 'We have no confirmation of this report from other sources,' he wrote, 'although we have of course received numerous reports of large scale massacres of Jews, particularly in Poland.'

The only recorded comment of the Under-Secretary of State for Foreign Affairs, Richard Law, was to ask 'what we know of Mr Riegner', and after a search of the files in the Refugee and Eastern Departments, it appeared that nothing was known. 'We have never heard of Dr Riegner,' the Refugee Department noted. It was then agreed to consult 'the Zionists', and in particular Professor Namier, in London. But here too the Foreign Office drew a blank, noting on August 15: 'the Jewish Agency have no information'.

Five days had now passed since the Riegner telegram had reached the Foreign Office. But still it had not been passed on to the Member of Parliament to whom it was addressed. 'I do not see how we can hold up this message much longer,' noted Frank Roberts on August 15, 'although I fear it may provoke embarrassing repercussions,' and he added: 'Naturally we have no information bearing on this story.'

Silverman was finally given Riegner's message on August 17. He at once telegraphed a copy to Stephen Wise, in New York, and at the same time asked for an interview with the Foreign Office, in order to discover what could be done. This interview took place on the morning of September 9, a month after Riegner's message had been telegraphed to London. At the interview, Silverman began by describing Riegner as 'entirely trustworthy', and went on to say that he himself 'had received reports of transportation of Jews from occupied territories and Germany towards the east, which might be a confirmation of this alleged plan'.

Silverman had already repeated the text of Riegner's telegram to Stephen

Wise. He now asked the Foreign Office if he could have 'permission' to talk to Wise on the telephone, 'in order to find out the reactions of the American Jewish Congress to this story', and to find out 'whether there was any action which could be taken'. This request, he was told, would be considered.

Silverman's final point was to ask the Foreign Office whether they thought 'that any good would be done by giving publicity to this rumour by getting it into Germany', or whether the British Government could by any means 'bring some pressure to bear on the Germans, e.g. through the Vatican'. Once again, Silverman was told that his question would be considered.

The report of an 'extermination plan' was now known in both London and Washington. But following Silverman's visit to the Foreign Office on September 9, certain reservations were expressed by those who studied his requests. The Vatican, it was noted by David Allen on September 10, had already been asked 'to take a more positive line in condemnation of German atrocities', and Allen felt that Britain 'should *not* help matters by taking any further action on the basis of this wild story', As regards the publicity for which Silverman asked, it was agreed in the Foreign Office 'that the most we could say to Mr Silverman was that, if Jewish organisations themselves wished to give publicity to the story, the F.O. could see no objection, although we could take no responsibility for the story'.

Silverman's request to telephone to the United States was likewise not accepted. 'We think it would tend to give away sources of information in Germany,' one official noted, 'and, as the Germans always listen to such conversations, it would not be of much use for Mr Silverman to plan any joint action with Dr Weizmann.'[1]

In his note of September 10, Allen expressed the general scepticism of the Foreign Office at Riegner's report of an actual extermination plan, informing his colleagues:

We have also received plenty of evidence that Jews deported from other parts of Europe have been concentrated in the Government-General and also that Jews once there are being so badly treated that very large numbers have perished: either as a result of lack of food or of evil conditions, i.e. in the Warsaw ghetto, or as a consequence of mass deportations and executions.

Such stories do provide a basis for Mr Riegner's report but they do not of course amount to 'exterminations at one blow'.

The German policy seems rather to eliminate 'useless mouths' but to use able bodied Jews as slave labour.

Allen added that he saw 'no particular reason' why Silverman 'should be given special telephone facilities to speak to Dr Weizmann about this', and he was reluctant to make use of what he called 'this story' in British propaganda to Germany 'without further confirmation'.

A second barrier to any official British reaction to the report of the extermination plan came from Colonel Ponsonby, who also spoke to Silverman, in the second week of September, telling him that he 'should consider whether any action taken by the Jewish Associations might not annoy the Germans and make any action they were proposing to take even more unpleasant than it might otherwise have been.'

[1] The Foreign Office had mistaken Chaim Weizmann for Stephen Wise.

It was clear that the impact of Riegner's telegram had been lost. Colonel Ponsonby told Silverman that the argument that it might be dangerous to 'annoy' the Germans applied not only to any action the Jewish 'Associations' might take, but also to any publicity that might be given to the report by the British Government.[1]

No one in the Foreign Office saw any link between the Bund Report of May 22, and Riegner's telegram eleven weeks later. Yet the Bund Report had specifically mentioned gassing, at Chelmno, as well as giving a clear indication of the scale of the slaughter.

Riegner's telegram was sent from Geneva to London on August 10. On that same day, Richard Lichtheim sent yet another of his detailed reports to Jerusalem. It was an account of the situation in France, which had reached him four days before, and which described the Paris round-ups of July 15 and 16.

The report from Paris told of three to four hundred suicides, including a woman who had killed not only herself, but her six children. It gave details of the seizure of men and women who, 'dispossessed of their money', were then separated, and taken either to the Vélôdrome d'Hiver or the Parc des Princes. The report continued:

Neither sick nor patients just operated on were spared. Thus the Rothschild Hospital's surgery, reserved for operated patients from the camp of Drancy, was suddenly emptied and the patients brought to the camp, however recently they had undergone operation, however serious was their state of health.

The children from 3 years of age upwards were taken away by force from their mothers, and were loaded on lorries. They were crying, weeping, calling for 'mother' across deserted and dark streets. . . .

As many as five thousand children had been taken from their parents within forty-eight hours. The children were then placed in three special schools, and their parents deported. On August 13 Lichtheim wrote to the Emergency Committee for Zionist affairs in New York: 'I am surrounded by so much misery and despair, and there is so little hope left. The fact is that five million European Jews are going down the drain.'[2]

Neither the Bund Report, nor Riegner's telegram, nor Lichtheim's messages, had made any mention of Auschwitz itself. And yet, in the last week of July alone, eight trains had reached Auschwitz; five from Paris, one from Slovakia and two from Holland. Nor did the rate of deportation slacken in August, when eight trains arrived from Holland, one from Slovakia, five from Belgium, six from Yugoslavia, and fifteen from France. The conditions inside the trucks were so terrible that many people died during the two, three and four day journeys.

In August 1942, the month during which, according to Riegner's message, a plan of extermination was 'under consideration', these deportations had brought more than 30,000 Jews to Auschwitz, of whom at least half had been gassed within a few hours of reaching their destination. Among those gassed were 344 children under the age of ten, sent from Paris on August 17. Most of them had been deported without their parents.

[1] The British Foreign Office reaction to the Riegner telegram is in Foreign Office papers, 371/30917. C 7853.
[2] Central Zionist Archives, L 22/177.

These 'children's' transports now became a feature of Gestapo policy. Before the end of August, four more trains reached Auschwitz from Paris, carrying a total of more than 1,500 children. So large was the scale of the slaughter that new gas chambers were being designed, and new crematoria constructed.

Equally unknown in the west, at regular intervals during August more than seven hundred sick Jews had been taken from the camp hospital at Auschwitz, and killed by Phenol injections in the heart. On August 21 a further 746 Jewish men and women, some suffering and others convalescing from typhus, were taken from their sick beds and gassed.

Throughout August the gassing of deported Jews was also taking place further east, at Treblinka, Belzec and Sobibor; and a fourth set of gas chambers was at that very moment in preparation in the Majdanek suburb of Lublin, where the already brutal concentration camp was also about to become a death camp. With their armies victorious in Europe and North Africa, the Germans were able to carry out a war of total destruction against millions of captive civilians, in conditions of secrecy and deception, knowing that even if the secret became known, the Allies were in no position to take any effective military action, either to liberate the captives, or to reverse the tide of war.

Chapter 7

Towards 'an unknown destination'

Almost every day, following the arrival of Riegner's telegram, news of the killing of Jews on a massive scale began to reach the Allies. Among the main features of such news, were the tens of thousands of deaths in the Warsaw ghetto, as a result of the Nazi policy of deliberate starvation.

On August 17, *The Times* published a short news item, sent from Zurich two days earlier by Reuter, that the mayor of the Warsaw ghetto, Adam Czerniakow, had committed suicide. He had indeed killed himself on July 23. The reason for Czerniakow's suicide was likewise correctly reported. He had refused to submit lists to the Gestapo of some 100,000 Jews whom the Gestapo wished to deport to what Reuter called 'an unknown destination in the east'.[1] The report added that Czerniakow had realized 'that the 100,000 would most probably be massacred'.[2]

On August 19, two days after this report was published, the Belgian Embassy in London gave the Foreign Office what purported to be an eye-witness account of just such a massacre. The events it referred to related to the massacre of Jews in Riga the previous April. Among more than 14,000 Jews killed, the account stated, had been several hundred deportees from Holland, and between fifty and a hundred Belgians, likewise deported 'to the east' a month or two before: 'As the executions took place in the day, they were filmed.'

The account of August 19 was explicit. The Jews had been taken to a field outside Riga, where a large trench had been dug. Then, under the direction of the chief of the Gestapo, and in the presence of several Estonian officers:

... the order was given for the Jews to undress completely. There followed a scene impossible to describe, men and women weeping, falling on their knees, beseeching the German executioners to desist. But all in vain.

These unfortunate people, among them young children, were lined up at the edge of the trench, and machine-gunned. The execution over, the trench was searched to ensure that there was no one alive among the victims.

One of the Estonian officers present was unable to stand it, and went suddenly mad.

In sending on this account to the Political Warfare Executive, for possible use as anti-German propaganda, an official of the Foreign Office noted: 'I think they will be interested in the décor, e.g. the stripping and filming of these unfortunate people.'[3]

Not only the nature of these eastern massacres, but the full extent of the

---

[1] In fact, Treblinka. The SS had originally intended to kill the Jews of Warsaw at Sobibor, but because the killing process there had become chaotic by July 1942, following five months of ceaseless mass murder, the SS leaders decided to send Warsaw Jewry to Treblinka instead.
[2] *The Times*, 17 August 1942.
[3] Foreign Office papers, 371/30918, C 8108.

sufferings in the ghettoes, was becoming more clear with each report that reached the Allies. One such report reached Washington from London in the last week of August. Its author was Ernest Frischer, a member of the Czecho-slovak Government-in-Exile in London.

In his report, Frischer made no mention of Treblinka, Sobibor, Belzec or Auschwitz. His information was centred, instead, around the German policy of sealed and starving ghettoes. Among the facts which he reported were the comparative weekly food rations in German-occupied Poland. The Germans in Poland received 80 ounces of bread a week, the Poles 62 ounces, the Jews 14 ounces. A similar ratio was in force for meat, sugar and fats. 'There is no precedent,' he stressed, 'for such *organised wholesale dying* in all Jewish history, nor indeed in the whole history of mankind.' The emphasis was his own.

Believing that it was this policy of starvation which constituted the Nazis' method of destruction, Frischer urged a relaxation of the Allied blockade of Germany, so that the International Red Cross could send food parcels to the ghettoes as it already did to the prisoner-of-war camps in Nazi Europe. Such a scheme, he wrote, was essential in 'putting a stop to boundless, unscrupulous destruction'.[1]

Frischer handed his report to the United States Ambassador to the Czech Government-in-Exile, who forwarded it on August 26 both to the State Department in Washington, and to the White House. On the following day, from Geneva, the United States Consul sent the State Department details of the continuing deportations of Jews from France. The source of this informa-tion was Dr Donald A. Lowrie, an American citizen, and a member of the World Alliance of the YMCA. Lowrie had just returned from Vichy France. In mid-August, he said, 3,500 Jews had been deported eastwards from camps in Vichy France, and he added that 'new orders announce that between August 23 and mid-September, 15,000 others will meet the same fate.' What was that fate? According to Lowrie, deportation 'meant either forced labour or slow extermination in the Jewish "reservation in Poland"', and he concluded that 'the critical task is to secure immigration permission from America.'[2]

Neither Frischer nor Lowrie had mentioned the death camps. Both still believed that the murder of the Jews was taking place primarily by slow starvation in the eastern ghettoes. But other information reaching Geneva in the second week of August seemed to confirm Riegner's telegram of the previous month, that the total destruction of European Jewry was planned, for on August 15 Richard Lichtheim, noted down in a memorandum information brought by two eye-witnesses, one a Jew and one a non-Jew, who had just reached Switzerland from Poland, one having arrived only the previous day.

The facts which the two Polish escapees reported were horrific. They were also specific, unlike the general warning of extermination passed on by the German industrialist at the end of July. The memorandum which Lichtheim prepared was in six parts. The first part began curtly: 'The liquidation of the Warsaw Ghetto is taking place', and it went on to report that Jews were being 'removed from the Ghetto in groups and shot', irrespective of age and sex.

---

[1] United States National Archives, 740-00116 European War 1939/536.
[2] Quoted in Arthur D. Morse, *While Six Million Died: A Chronicle of American Apathy*, New York, 1967, pages 11–12.

According to the second paragraph of the report, these 'mass executions' were not taking place in Warsaw itself, 'but in especially prepared camps for the purpose'. No mention was made of gassing, the main method of killing, or of Treblinka, where these gassings were taking place. But the report did give the name of one of the camps, Belzec. Certain statistics were also listed: 'About 50,000' Jews had been killed in Lvov (Lemberg); this was 20,000 more than the number reported nearly three months before, in the Bund Report of May 22. A further 100,000 'have been massacred in Warsaw'. There was not one Jew left in the 'entire district' east of Poland, 'including occupied Russia'. In addition, the report claimed 'the entire non-Jewish population of Sebastopol was murdered'. And the second paragraph ended, ominously: 'So as not to attract the attention of foreign countries, the butchering of the Jewish population in Poland was not done at one single time.'

The third paragraph of Lichtheim's memorandum reported, tersely and accurately: 'Jews deported from Germany, Belgium, Holland, France, and Slovakia are sent to be butchered, while Aryans deported to the east from Holland and France are genuinely used for work.'

Paragraph four reiterated that the aim of the deportations to the east was to enable the 'butcherings' to be carried out where 'less opportunity is afforded to outsiders of knowing what is going on'. Even the Theresienstadt ghetto, which the Nazis spoke of as a 'model' ghetto, was 'only an interim station', as the Jews deported there from Germany, Austria, Bohemia and Moravia, 'await the same fate'.

The final paragraphs of the Lichtheim memorandum were likewise true:

(5) Arrangements are made for new deportations as soon as space is made by executions. Caravans of such deportees being transported in cattle cars are often seen. There are about forty people in each cattle car. It is especially significant to note that Lithuanian non-Jews are entrusted with fetching the candidates from the death Ghetto in Warsaw.

(6) It is a tragedy that the Polish population is being incited by the Germans against the Jews and the relationship between the Poles and the Jews has been aggravated to the last degree. In Lemberg this is particularly true.[1]

Lichtheim held back the Polish eye-witness report for two weeks, explaining, when he did eventually send it on to the Zionist leaders in London, Jerusalem and New York on August 26 that the details it contained were 'so terrible that I had some doubts whether I should forward it or not'. But Lichtheim concluded in his covering letter: 'In fact, I believe the report to be true and quite in line with Hitler's announcement that at the end of this war there will be no Jews in Continental Europe.'[2]

Even while Lichtheim had been holding back his report of August 15, new evidence had reached him which seemed to confirm it. On August 27 he sent on to Jerusalem the text of a postcard which had been posted to Geneva only three weeks before from the Polish town of Czestochowa. The postcard gave the impression, for the German censor, of being a purely personal one. It declared that 'Eliezer', by which it in fact meant 'Warsaw', was 'in very bad health and that he sees no way out. He is being treated by Dr Kilajon' –

[1] Central Zionist Archives, L 22/149.
[2] Central Zionist Archives, L 22/149.

the Hebrew word for 'Extermination' – 'who gives him no hope. He is becoming more and more ill and his lungs are bleeding constantly.'

All the reports he had received from Warsaw, Lichtheim stressed, 'are to the effect that a considerable number of people from the ghetto have been transported elsewhere, and there are reports that they have been murdered'. He had already, he explained, sent on to Jerusalem the previous day, 'the most dreadful details'.[1]

One distressing piece of news which Lichtheim sent to Jerusalem, London and New York that same week concerned the attempt by many French Jews to escape deportation by crossing over the frontier into Switzerland. On August 13 the Swiss Police authorities had closed the frontier altogether, and now it appeared that several would-be refugees who had managed to get inside Switzerland had then been taken to the border by the Swiss Police, and forced back into France. 'You can easily imagine what it meant for these unfortunate people,' Lichtheim wrote on August 28, 'led to the frontier and forced to cross it.' He added: 'Nobody knows what then happened to them.'[2]

Lichtheim had been particularly upset by the report of a debate in the House of Commons, held on August 6, in which several speakers, sympathetic to the Jewish plight, had spoken of the need to provide homes after the war for '9½ million Jews', and of the problem which would be created by the existence of '7 million dispossessed Jews in Eastern Europe'. Writing to his Jewish Agency colleagues in London on August 27, Lichtheim commented that these figures 'show that people in England do not know what is now going on in Europe'. Even 'the Jewish leaders', he noted, still believed that after the war there would be some 'five or six million homeless Jews' in Europe. 'In fact,' Lichtheim wrote, 'no more than two million would have survived, most of them, about 800,000, in Hungary'.

In his letter of August 27 Lichtheim stated emphatically: 'We now know that deportation means death – sooner or later', and he added: 'This process of annihilation is going on relentlessly and there is no hope left to save any considerable number.'

It was 'no exaggeration', Lichtheim concluded, 'to say that Hitler has killed or is killing 4 million Jews in Continental Europe', and that no more than two million had any chance of survival; those only because German rule had not been extended to the countries in which they lived.[3]

The daily budget of news reaching Switzerland held out no hope of a change. On August 31, in his 807th letter of the war to Jerusalem, Lichtheim reported on new expulsions from the Rumanian-ruled cities of Czernowitz and Timisoara, and of the arrest of Jews in Vichy France, Jews who were then handed over by the Vichy authorities to the Gestapo for deportation. 'All these happenings . . . ,' Lichtheim reflected, 'confirm the impression conveyed in my previous reports that there is a general plan behind these measures, to deport and destroy the Jews all over Europe.'

How was it possible to believe that the Jews of Europe were not only to be destroyed, according to a deliberate plan, but that the process had actually

---

[1] Central Zionist Archives, L 22/177.
[2] Central Zionist Archives, L 22/177.
[3] Central Zionist Archives, L 22/149.

begun, and was indeed far advanced? Many of the Jewish leaders who received these reports had themselves been born in Poland or had Polish parents. It was their own families, colleagues and friends, who were being thus murdered. Bewildered and uncomprehending, on September 28, the head of the Organization Department of the Jewish Agency, Leo Lauterbach, wrote privately to Lichtheim to express what he called his 'grave doubts' at the accuracy of many of the facts of the report. Lauterbach added:

One must also learn from experience to distinguish between reality, grim as it is, and figments of an imagination strained by justified fear and which grows to believe what is whispered without being able, in the circumstances, to check its veracity.[1]

Yet Lauterbach went on to accept the main burden of Lichtheim's letter, and Lichtheim himself went on sending information to Jerusalem, London and Washington, all of which seemed to confirm the extermination plan.

The Allies had no military means of preventing the deportations. Nor did there seem to be any other possible reaction except publicity. Those who learned of the deportations could do nothing more than report them. From the most recent reports reaching him, Lichtheim wrote from Geneva on September 3 to London, New York and Jerusalem, 'the intention cannot be to get labour supply but simply to kill off the deportees'. Lichtheim added:

All the relief organizations in Europe, Jewish and non-Jewish, constantly dealing with these horrors are in a state of despair because no force on earth can stop them. Announcements lately made that the perpetrators would be punished after the war have of course no effect. Also there is no adequate punishment for those crimes.[2]

On September 4 Dr Weizmann's secretary, Doris May, wrote to Arthur Lourie in New York of how the news from Geneva about the deportations from France was 'curiously shattering', and she went on to explain:

. . . barbarism in Germany, however deplorable, is not really surprising, or even shocking— the Hun is always the Hun, and must be expected to behave accordingly. But the same things should happen in *France*, and that Frenchmen, even though they do not co-operate, should stand by and see them done, somehow strikes at the roots of confidence! Yet what active resistance can be expected of anyone after two years of starvation and suppression? (And how inadequate are words!)[3]

The deportations from France continued throughout September 1942. On September 3 the World Jewish Congress in Geneva had learned of eleven deportations in August from the main internment camps in southern France and the Pyrenees, including Gurs and Les Milles, and five days later, in a letter to Jerusalem, Lichtheim reported that 'at least 10,000 have already been deported'[4], despite a strong protest by two leading clergymen in southern France, the Archbishop of Toulouse and the Bishop of Montauban.

In London, *The Times* published full reports of the deportations of Jews from France, throughout the first two weeks of September. It had received

[1] Quoted in Walter Laqueur, *The Terrible Secret*, London 1980, pages 179–80.
[2] Central Zionist Archives, L 22/134.
[3] Lourie papers.
[4] Central Zionist Archives, L 22/136.

these reports from its own correspondent at the frontier between Vichy France and neutral Spain in the Pyrenees. With the advantage of Spanish neutrality, each report was published on the day after it was sent to London.

On September 7 the main article on the Imperial and Foreign page of *The Times* was headed:

VICHY'S JEWISH VICTIMS
CHILDREN DEPORTED TO GERMANY

and it told of the 'unabated ruthlessness' of the deportation campaign. Women and children, it stated, 'suddenly notified' that they could visit their relatives in various internment camps, were then 'forced to accompany the deportees without being given any opportunity to make preparations'. At Les Milles there had been eighty-six attempted suicides: 'some men had cut their veins with broken glass.' Recently, 'a train containing 4,000 Jewish children, unaccompanied, without identification papers or even distinguishing marks, left Lyons for Germany.'[1] But where in 'Germany' was not known. It was in fact Auschwitz.

The impact of the news from France was considerable: on September 8, in his first speech in the House of Commons for nine weeks, Churchill referred to the deportations during the course of a comprehensive survey of the war situation. The 'brutal persecutions' in which the Germans had indulged, he said, 'in every land into which their armies have broken', had recently been augmented by what he described as:

. . . the most bestial, the most squalid and the most senseless of all their offences, namely, the mass deportation of Jews from France, with the pitiful horrors attendant upon the calculated and final scattering of families.

This tragedy fills me with astonishment as well as with indignation, and it illustrates as nothing else can the utter degradation of the Nazi nature and theme, and the degradation of all who lend themselves to its unnatural and perverted passions.

Pausing for a moment, Churchill declared: 'When the hour of liberation strikes in Europe, as strike it will, it will also be the hour of retribution.'[2]

In the days following Churchill's speech, *The Times* continued to report the deportation of Jews from France, and to stress the opposition of the French people to the collaboration of the Vichy Government in these measures. On September 9 it published news of the dismissal by the Vichy authorities of General de St-Vincent, the Military Governor of Lyons, who had 'refused to obey Vichy's order', on August 28, 'to cooperate in the mass arrests of Jews in the unoccupied Zone'. General de St-Vincent had, it appeared, refused to place his troops at the disposal of the authorities in order to round up Jews.

The news item of September 9 also told of a Vichy order for the arrest of all Roman Catholic priests who were sheltering Jews in the unoccupied zone. 'Some arrests,' it added, had already been made. But in reply to these arrests, Cardinal Gerlier, the Archbishop of Lyons, had already issued a 'defiant

[1] *The Times*, 7 September 1942.
[2] Hansard, 8 September 1942.

refusal' to surrender those Jewish children whose parents had already been deported, and who were being 'fed and sheltered' in Roman Catholic homes.[1]

A main news item in *The Times* on September 11 reported 'popular indignation' in Lyons following the arrest and imprisonment of eight Jesuit priests who had refused to surrender 'several hundred' children for deportation; children whom they had kept hidden 'in buildings belonging to the religious order'. *The Times* also reported that the Papal Secretary of State, Cardinal Maglione, had informed the French Ambassador to the Vatican 'that the conduct of the Vichy Government towards Jews and foreign refugees was a gross infraction' of the Vichy Government's own principles, and was 'irreconcilable with the religious feelings which Marshal Pétain had so often invoked in his speeches'.[2]

Watching these events from Geneva, Richard Lichtheim was convinced that nothing could be done to save the Jews of western Europe and Poland. But he was equally convinced that it was not too late to save those Jews living in lands not yet under direct German control. On September 15 he set out his thoughts on rescue to Linton, in London: 'far too little,' he wrote, 'has been said and done to warn the Nazis and their associates against the consequences of these crimes.' Lichtheim added: 'I am still under the impression that the Jewish organizations in England and the USA should have done much more on previous occasions to inform the public, the press and the leading statesmen of what is happening to the Jews.'

Lichtheim then wrote of the potential danger to those Jewish communities not yet under direct Nazi control, in particular the 750,000 Jews in Hungary, and the 300,000 Jews who had not been deported from Rumania in the mass expulsion of the summer and autumn of 1941. 'In these countries,' Lichtheim wrote, 'and also in Italy, there is still a chance left that the Jews might be spared, if the Governments of these three countries are warned in time that they will be held responsible if they allow the Gestapo to do what it has done in the other countries of Europe.'

Lichtheim was aware that Churchill, Roosevelt, and the Governments-in-Exile had already issued statements warning that those who committed crimes against humanity would be searched out at the end of the war, brought to trial, and punished. But what he believed should be done was for the Allies to issue 'some special warning', directed not to the public in general in Hungary, Rumania and Italy, but to the leaders, Horthy, Antonescu and Mussolini.

Lichtheim argued that were these three rulers made aware that 'their specific attitude in this specific matter' was being '*closely watched*', and if the special warning he had suggested were directed 'to *them*', then in his view 'they may abstain from these extreme measures against the rest of the Jews *for which Hitler will certainly ask in due course*'. The emphasis was again his own.

Lichtheim suggested that the warnings might come from the Vatican, or some neutral power, and he added:

I do not know what action the Jewish organisations in England and America have taken so far to save the remnants of European Jewry. But I feel that the present moment is a favorable one.

[1] *The Times*, 9 September 1942.
[2] *The Times*, 11 September 1942.

The tide is turning. The prospects of the Allied Nations to win the war are better than they have ever been before and this is felt all over Europe. In Italy, Hungary and Roumania, there are many influential people who are dissatisfied with the pro-Nazi policy of their governments.

It is certainly the right moment to warn these governments against a renewal of the persecution of the Jews – especially so because public opinion has now been roused as never before by the latest events in France and the many protests coming from all sides.[1]

From his listening-post in Geneva, Lichtheim had become convinced that the German policy towards the Jews was one of complete destruction. On September 18, angered by a request from the United States to 'review the position of the Jews of Europe', he replied that he could not give such a review 'because the Jews of Europe are today no more in a "position" than the waters of a rapid rushing down into some canyon, or the dust of the desert lifted by a tornado and blown in all directions'.

In his letter of September 18, Lichtheim stated that of the six million Jews in Nazi-controlled or dominated countries, not counting Hungary and Italy, 'one or two millions are already dead, and the other four or five millions are somewhere between life and death – I do not know if nearer to life or to death'. If one or two million were already dead, he added, 'one or two million more will be dead next year. Those who did not die from hunger and disease may be killed by other methods. Hitler has sworn that in his Europe there will be no Jews at the end of this war'.

Lichtheim wrote pessimistically of the 'second front' which the Allies were then discussing; the plan for a military landing on the western coast of Europe. 'Maybe there will be one day such a second front,' he wrote, 'which will free the Dutch, the Belgians, the French, from the invader. But the Jews in these countries will not be among the freed people. Hitler is seeing to that. The deportations have now started for the Jews in Belgium, Holland, and occupied France, and even for the 10,000 Jewish refugees in non-occupied France.'

Lichtheim was right; and although he made no mention of gassing, which had first been described in the Bund report four months before, or of the extermination plan of the Riegner telegram of August 10, or indeed of Auschwitz, which had not yet been mentioned in any document to reach the west as a place to which Jews were being deported and killed, the statistics and tone of his letter were remarkably acute and accurate. His letter ended:

You wanted a survey of the position of the Jews in Europe. You wanted facts and figures. Have I stated the facts? Some of them, but very few. Think of the facts behind the facts, of the rivers of tears and the streams of blood, the broken limbs and the naked bodies, the bleeding feet and the crying children, the stench and the filth, the biting cold and the gnawing hunger, the black despair in millions of hearts.

Try to think of the last thoughts of the three Jews who were paraded through a Polish town and hanged for having tried to obtain some food from non-Jews. Feel the feelings of the Jewish mother in Paris who threw her six children, and then herself out of the window when the police came to take her away to a camp and then to Poland.

Have I stated the facts?

I have written 4,000 words and I have said nothing.

Use your imagination, friend.[2]

[1] Central Zionist Archives, L 22/136.
[2] Central Zionist Archives, Z 4/14901.

Details of the mass murder of Jews were now circulating widely among the Allies. So strong an impact did Lichtheim's Geneva memorandum of August 30 make in Washington, where it had been sent to the White House, that on September 26 President Roosevelt's Personal Representative to Pope Pius XII, Myron Taylor, sent a copy of it to Cardinal Maglione, the Vatican Secretary of State. In his covering note, Taylor asked Maglione whether the Vatican had any information 'that would tend to confirm the reports contained in this memorandum', and if so, 'whether the Holy Father has any suggestion as to any practical manner in which the forces of civilized public opinion could be utilized in order to prevent a continuation of these barbarities'.[1]

Unfortunately, as the State Department learned three weeks later in a dispatch from Harrison, the Minister in Switzerland, 'reports of severe measures taken against non-Aryans have also reached the Holy See from other sources, but that up to the present time it has not been possible to verify the accuracy thereof'. The Holy See, Harrison added, 'has no practical suggestions to make'.[2]

It was not only the Vatican which had no suggestions to make. 'Unhappily,' Arthur Lourie wrote to Richard Lichtheim on September 25, from New York, 'there has been no real awakening of the public conscience here on the whole issue.' Among Jews, Lourie added, 'certainly there is some knowledge and a sense of horror and ineffectiveness in the face of calamity, but as far as the general American public is concerned – while from time to time there are news stories dealing with the deportations and massacres – the whole thing remains remote, and interest centres, perhaps inevitably, on affairs nearer home.'

The picture emerging from Europe, Lourie wrote, 'is such as defies belief', and he added that Lichtheim's most recent letter had left him 'with a sense of almost hopelessness'.[3]

But Lichtheim did not despair altogether, and in a telegram to the Jewish Agency in London on September 26, he proposed that 'strong pressure' and the 'sternest warnings' were necessary, to save what he called the 'remnants' of European Jewry in Bulgaria, Rumania and Hungary. All the information reaching Geneva, he declared, 'confirmed previous reports about extermination Jews following deportation from various countries to Germany or Poland, also following deportation within Poland.' Apart from a 'small minority' of Jews working as artisans for the German army, both the Warsaw and Lodz ghettoes were, as he phrased it, 'nearly emptied'.[4] And in a letter which he sent three days later to London, Jerusalem and New York, he stated: 'The total destruction of the Jewish communities in Belgium and Holland is nearly complete.'[5]

Lichtheim's letters from Geneva were read by most of the Zionist leaders in London, Jerusalem and New York. 'I know of no other source,' the Executive Director of the United Palestine Appeal, Henry Montor, wrote to him from New York on September 29, 'from which one can obtain so startling and de-

[1] United States National Archives, 121-866A/302.
[2] United States National Archives, 740-00116 European War 1939/605.
[3] Central Zionist Archives, L 22/149.
[4] Central Zionist Archives, L 22/134
[5] Central Zionist Archives, L 22/136.

pressing a picture of the rapidity with which hundreds of thousands of Jews are perishing without a murmur on the part of the civilised world.'[1]

For the 'civilised world', however, it was the possibility of an imminent German victory which now dominated the news, and confronted both decision makers and the public. Throughout September, German forces were battling within a few hundred yards of the river Volga, and appeared likely to capture Stalingrad. Faced with this prospect, the Russians were forced to salvage what they could of their largest tank factory by transporting it up the Volga on barges. All month, German artillery pounded the city centre. On September 21 all the remaining women and children were evacuated, and five days later some German troops reached the bank of the Volga itself, south of the city.

In the Caucasus, German troops advanced towards the Baku oilfields. Once at the Caspian Sea, Persia, and even India, lay within their reach.

Hitler was elated. Even the British success in Egypt on August 31, at the battle of Alam Halfa, in halting Rommel's advance to Alexandria and holding the line just inside the Egyptian–Libyan border, did not seem a serious setback. Hitler's armies were still masters of Europe. The North African coast was under German control from the Atlantic coast of Morocco to the Egyptian border. And in the Far East, Japanese forces continued to advance across the Pacific, landing in September on several islands in the Solomons, and severely bombing United States naval and artillery installations on Guadalcanal.

Speaking in Berlin on September 30, Hitler surveyed the course of the war. As usual, his speech was monitored by the Allies, and widely reported. The Germans were marching from victory to victory. The Russian was 'a kind of swamp man'. The British leaders were 'nonentities' and 'swashbucklers'. Roosevelt was 'this demented man in the White House'. Under the lead of Germany, the Rumanians, Hungarians, Croats, Slovaks, Finns and Spaniards were taking part in a 'European crusade', a fight for 'honour and decency', against Britain, the United States and the Soviet Union, 'the vilest coalition that the world has ever seen'. But Churchill, Roosevelt, 'and their Jewish backers' would, Hitler warned, 'begin to squirm and whine if the end for England is more horrible than the beginning'.

Hitler then spoke specifically about the Jews, reminding his audience that on 1 September 1939 he had declared that 'if Jewry is starting an international world war to eliminate the Aryan nations of Europe, then it won't be the Aryan nations which will be wiped out, but Jewry'.

Hitler now had a further prophecy to make. Just as the Jews had, as he put it, 'managed actually to draw one nation after the other into this war', so, to just the same degree, 'a wave of anti-Semitism has swept over nation after nation'. And, he prophesied, 'it will move on further. State after State that enters this war will one day become anti-Semitic'. Hitler then declared:

In Germany too the Jews once laughed at my prophesies. I don't know whether they are still laughing, or whether they have already lost the inclination to laugh, but I can assure you that everywhere they will stop laughing.

[1] Central Zionist Archives, L 22/218/1.

'With these prophesies,' Hitler added, 'I shall prove to be right'.[1]

The name 'Auschwitz' had still not appeared in the growing list of camps in which Jews were being killed, nor had it yet been mentioned as a destination of any of the Jewish deportations. But many of the September deportations had in fact gone straight to Auschwitz. Of 957 Jewish men, women and children reaching Auschwitz from Paris in the early hours of the morning of September 2, a total of 918 were gassed by the late afternoon. The gassing was witnessed by an SS doctor, Johann Kremer, who noted in his diary: 'Compared with what I saw, Dante's inferno seems to me like a comedy. Not without reason do they call Auschwitz an "annihilation" camp'.[2]

Throughout September, trains reached Auschwitz from Belgium, France and Holland. Most of the deportees were gassed on arrival, a few sent to the barracks, but even here there was no safety. On September 5 some eight hundred sick Jewish women were taken from their barracks and gassed, while later that same day a total of 714 Dutch Jews reached Auschwitz, of whom 661 were gassed by the following morning.

Although Birkenau and its gas chambers remained a secret, the deportations themselves continued to be reported to the west through Switzerland. 'I understand,' Lichtheim had written to Joseph Linton in London on September 17, 'from information received from Croatia that there are practically no children left because the whole Jewish population has been evacuated. . . .' But where had the deportees been sent? Lichtheim wrote to Linton of two destinations: 'to labour camps or to Poland (Ost-Oberschlesien)'.[3] This latter area had not been mentioned before: it was, in fact, the exact region, Eastern Upper Silesia, of Auschwitz itself.

But 'Auschwitz', the death camp, remained a secret, even after September 17. Indeed, twelve days later, on September 29, when Lichtheim sent London, New York and Jerusalem a report of the continuing deportations from Holland, and of the systematic destruction of 'the once flourishing community of 180,000 souls', he added:

The arrests and deportations are made with the usual brutality. Everything the Jews possess is taken away from them. 40 or 50 persons are herded together in one carriage otherwise used for cattle, and then they are sent to their 'unknown destination'.

Lichtheim himself put the phrase 'unknown destination' in quotation marks. There was 'more and more evidence', he added, that many of the deportees were dying 'on their way' in the cattle trucks, and that others, especially the older men and women, 'are shot after reaching the German frontier'. Where the rest of the deportees were, he wrote, 'and if they are still alive, I cannot tell. There are most gruesome reports. . . .'[4]

[1] Foreign Broadcast Monitoring Service, Federal Communications Commission, quoted in Franklin Watts (editor), *Voices of History 1942–43*, New York 1943, pages 507–25.
[2] Quoted in Danuta Czech, 'Kalendarium der Ereignisse in Konzentrationslager Auschwitz-Birkenau', published in *Hefte von Auschwitz*, volume 3, Auschwitz 1960, entry for 2 September 1942.
[3] Central Zionist Archives, L 22/136.
[4] Central Zionist Archives, L 22/136.

Chapter 8

Rescue and refuge

Roosevelt's pledge of July 21, that those who had carried out the crimes would be 'called to account', had given satisfaction in Jewish circles, where it seemed this was one of the only avenues of action open to the Allies. At the same time, the Jewish leaders were anxious to be represented on any inter-Allied body dealing with war crimes. It was clear, as the Board of Deputies of British Jews had pointed out in July, that the Jews had already been 'specially marked out for brutal attack'. But the Foreign Office was opposed to any specifically Jewish representation. As Frank Roberts wrote on August 21 to a colleague in the Ministry of Information: 'His Majesty's Government of course do not recognize a distinct Jewish nationality'.[1] And Roberts' colleague, Roger Allen, expressed his support for the view that 'Jews must be treated as nationals of existing States and not as having any separate Jewish nationality apart from the nationality shown on their passports'.

In a further internal note written on August 21, A. W. G. Randall set out the reasoning behind Foreign Office opposition to any Jewish participation, as Jews, on a war crimes tribunal. Firstly, he wrote, 'HMG do not recognise a distinct Jewish nationality.' In addition there was, in his view, 'plenty of evidence' of what he described as 'the extreme Zionist campaign for recognition of a distinct Jewish nationality'; a campaign which the Foreign Office considered to be 'part of the propaganda for a Jewish sovereign state in Palestine, and it also no doubt aims at securing separate Jewish representation at any Peace Settlement'. The 'campaign' for a Jewish army, Randall added, 'has this in view'. So too did the attempts 'by various British Jewish bodies to obtain specific recognition of the sufferings of Jews in the Allied declaration of 13th January on war crimes', a declaration which had in fact not mentioned Jews by name.

In his note of August 21 Randall pointed out that this Zionist 'campaign' which, he added in brackets, 'is a dangerous one even for the Jews themselves, as many of them privately recognize', did not appear to have had any 'notable success'. But he went on to warn that 'several of our allies are susceptible to such pressure', among them the Poles and the Czechs. When the former Czech Foreign Minister, Jan Masaryk, announced his support for Jewish representation at any war crimes trial, Frank Roberts described him as a man 'whose humanity is better than his judgement'.

The Foreign Office had been particularly angered on August 17, when General Sikorski had sent a message to a conference being held by the New

[1] This, and the subsequent comments during August 1942 about war crimes and Jewish nationality, are in Foreign Office papers, 371/30917.

Zionist Organization. In his message, Sikorski expressed Polish sympathies with the Jewish longing for a National Home. The actual phrase which Sikorski used, and which annoyed the Foreign Office, was: 'a state of their own in Palestine'.

But no message from Sikorski, however sympathetic it might be to Zionism, could advance in any way the request for Jewish representation at the forthcoming war crimes conference. Determined not to recognize any Jewish 'nationality', the Foreign Office resolutely, and successfully opposed any such representation.

Another priority for the Jewish leadership in London and Jerusalem during September 1942 was the question of rescue: how to persuade the Allies to accept those Jews who did escape from Nazi Europe.

On September 9 the Jewish Agency office in London received a telegram from the Agency's representative in Istanbul, Chaim Barlas. A group of Jews who had managed to escape from Rumania were about to be sent back there by the Turkish authorities. This group had already reached Mersin, on the southern coast of Turkey, but would still have to be returned. It was urgent, Barlas insisted, for the British Government to intervene, and to prevent the Turks from returning these refugees.[1]

Such an appeal could not be ignored. The lives of twenty or thirty people were at risk. For them to be allowed to continue to Palestine, or even to an internment camp in Cyprus, meant safety. But if forced back to Rumania, who could tell what their fate might be? In January 1941 more than a hundred Jews had been slaughtered in the streets of Bucharest: men, women and children shot down where they stood, or as they ran from the mob. In June 1941 more than four thousand Jews from Jassy had been forced into two trains, and shunted about the railway lines of eastern Rumania, without food or water, until more than three thousand were dead, their bodies left at the side of the tracks to be stripped and pillaged by local looters.

Whereas the Bund and Riegner messages had told of death and dangers far away, and beyond succour, the Barlas telegram offered the possibility of actual rescue. Hence its importance, and the importance of all such appeals on behalf of small groups of Jews who had actually managed to take the first steps away from torment.

Confronted with the telegram from Istanbul, the Jewish Agency took immediate action, and on the afternoon of September 10, Professor Namier himself was received at the Colonial Office by a member of the Middle East department, E. B. Boyd.

Namier showed Boyd the telegram from Barlas, and asked the Colonial Office to telegraph to the British authorities in Turkey, 'to prevent the Turks from returning these refugees to Rumania'. But Boyd replied that if such a telegram were sent, the British authorities 'would make themselves responsible for these Rumanian refugees', a responsibility, he felt, that Lord Cranborne's letter of May 22 had not envisaged.

Namier was angered by this reply. If the British Government 'refuse to take

---

[1] Central Zionist Archives, Z 4/14908 I.

any notice of these refugees', he warned, or refuse 'to offer them any refuge', then the only alternative was their being delivered into the hands of the Rumanians, 'which would mean death'.

Had not Lord Cranborne said there would be 'no more *Strumas*', Namier asked? But Boyd pointed out that the cases were different. The present refugees had travelled by rail, whereas the *Struma* was, as he put it, 'a ship-wreck'. But Namier interjected to say 'that it did not make much difference whether they were returned across a land frontier or allowed to perish in the Black Sea' and he added that if Boyd considered 'what was now happening to the Jews of France, Poland, etc., he must realize what a returning of these refugees to Rumania would mean'.

On behalf of the Jewish Agency, Namier asked Boyd to give these Ru-manians certificates to Palestine, telling him 'that they were literally refugees from death – not illegal immigrants'. But Boyd replied that he 'did not think' certificates for Palestine could be given, nor was there 'any obligation' on the British Government to provide for a refuge in Cyprus.

At one point in their conversation, Namier noted, Boyd 'came out with the argument that if these people are helped there would be a procession of such boats.' Namier replied that such an outcome 'was not likely', as so few Jews were in fact able to escape, but that the Colonial Office must not expect the Jewish Agency to 'take a tragic view of it if a few hundred Jews escape massacre.' The Colonial Office, Boyd replied, 'had to take a practical view.'

For the Colonial Office, maintenance of the six-monthly Palestine quotas was the cornerstone of their policy. As they saw it, it was essential not to antagonize the Arabs of the Middle East. The German army was victorious in North Africa; the German navy patrolled the Aegean; German aircraft were based in Crete and Rhodes. British control of Egypt, the Suez Canal and Palestine hung on a slender thread. Without Arab goodwill, Britain could find herself defeated in her most vulnerable region.

Namier was not without an answer to this line of argument. There was, he said, a shortage of manpower in Palestine. There were many new immigrants, refugees, 'willing and fit to serve in the army'. They should not be sent to Cyprus. If 'properly vouched for', as Namier phrased it, they should be given their chance 'to participate in the Palestine war effort'.

These arguments were not effective, even though, as Namier noted, it seemed 'obvious' to him that many of Boyd's remarks were 'mere "official reservations" and not expressions of any ill-will or indifference'.[1] But there were others who took a different view of the attitudes which lay behind the evolution and rigidity of Britain's Palestine policy. Indeed, on the very day that Namier was talking with Boyd at the Colonial Office, the Prime Minister, Winston Churchill, was cautioning a friend, 'against drifting into the usual anti-Zionist and anti-Semitic channel which it is customary for British officers to follow.'[2]

In July 1942 the Vichy regime had agreed to hand over to the Germans ten

---

[1] 'Interview with Mr Boyd at the Colonial Office at 3.30 p.m on 10th September 1942', Central Zionist Archives, Z 4/14908 I.

[2] Prime Minister's Personal Minute, D.M. 1/2. Premier papers, 4/52/5. The friend was Sir Edward Spears, the British Government's representative in Syria.

thousand foreign Jews living in the unoccupied zone of France. These Jews were to be deported by the Germans to Poland: Berlin radio, monitored in Britain, had announced the fact of these deportations. Thousands of those affected tried to flee to Switzerland. But on August 13 the Swiss Government had closed its frontiers to all those seeking to cross them 'illegally'. So strict were the Swiss authorities that more than a thousand Jewish refugees who had managed to cross into Switzerland without permission were taken to the border and forced to cross back into France.

The British Government were asked to take at least the children of these Vichy Jews. But it was felt in the Foreign Office that priority in any relaxation of the immigration laws should be given to children of Allied nationality as 'it would be very difficult to justify to our Allies the grant of visas to enemy aliens, however sound our humanitarian reasons. The Permanent Under-Secretary of State, Sir Alexander Cadogan, gave as his considered opinion: 'It seems to me wrong to support bringing children to this country at present.'[1]

In London, the Chairman of the Jewish Refugee Committee, Otto Schiff, asked the Home Secretary, Herbert Morrison, to allow children and old people with close relatives in Britain to be admitted. Schiff estimated, on a narrow interpretation of the concept of 'close relatives', that 'the total number of such children and such persons over 60 would not exceed 300 or 350'. In addition, Schiff told Morrison, the Jewish Refugee Committee would give a financial guarantee to ensure that 'there would be no question of any such children or persons over 60 becoming a charge on public funds'.

Herbert Morrison was regarded by the Jewish organizations in Britain as a friend. But in the secrecy of a Cabinet memorandum on 23 September 1942, he explained to his Cabinet colleagues why he was against accepting the Vichy children. The official minutes of the meeting recorded Morrison's actual words:

The general policy has been not to admit during the war additional refugees to the United Kingdom unless in some quite rare and exceptional cases it can be shown that the admission of the refugee will be directly advantageous to our war effort. Any departure from this rigid policy is liable to fresh claims and additional pressure for the admission to the United Kingdom of persons who are in danger or distress, and I am convinced that it would not be right to make any general departure from the principle that the United Kingdom is unable during the period of the war at any rate, to accept additional refugees.

Morrison went on to state that British public opinion was not all that enthusiastic about the large number of Jewish refugees already in Britain, and that if more Jews were allowed in, it might, as he put it, 'stir up an unpleasant degree of anti-Semitism (of which there is a fair amount just below the surface), and that would be bad for the country and the Jewish community'.[2]

Throughout the autumn and winter of 1942, the Jewish Agency leaders persevered with four main rescue attempts. Although small in scale, these efforts took up a great deal of time, the more so as it was not always easy to obtain the support of the Allies, or of neutrals, or of the protecting power.

Since June 1942, the Jewish Agency had been trying to bring a group of 270

[1] Foreign Office papers, 371/32683. Minutes dated 8 September 1942.
[2] War Cabinet of 23 September 1942, Cabinet papers 66/29/18.

Hungarian Jewish children to Palestine from Hungary, a country which was not yet under direct Nazi rule. The British Government made no objection. Indeed, the British were not only willing in this instance to waive the restrictions on Jews coming from enemy countries, according to the Cranborne letter, but also to facilitate the transfer of the children from Europe to Palestine, help which was specifically barred by the terms of that letter.

Throughout August a British official in the Berne Legation, Douglas Mackillop, had been active in passing on lists of the children from the Swiss Consulate in Istanbul to the Special Division of the Swiss Legation in Budapest. But there had been long delays, and on September 22 Mackillop explained to Dr Kahany of the Jewish Agency that it was the Swiss Government that had, for nearly three months, shown a 'somewhat reserved' attitude. As Mackillop noted, the Swiss had 'observed that the matter goes far beyond the framework of the ordinary business of the protecting Power (as the children are not British) and they apparently feared to have difficulties with the governments of the two countries concerned': Hungary, where the children were living, and Rumania, through which territory they must pass on their way to Palestine.[1]

During September, as a result of British pressure, the Swiss Government agreed that its Legation in Budapest would undertake the necessary identification of the children. But at the very moment when this helpful gesture was made – the first fifty children reached Palestine four months later – another Swiss authority, the Ministry of Police, was insisting that the Swiss border with France remain closed to Jews trying to escape deportation. After a month and a half of protest by all the rescue organizations in Switzerland, Jewish, Protestant, Catholic and Quaker, the Swiss agreed to modify the ban. Parents who were accompanied by children under the age of sixteen would be allowed to cross the border. But on October 2 Richard Lichtheim reported from Geneva to the Zionist Emergency Committee in New York that adults alone would not be allowed across the Swiss border, unless they were over sixty years old. Indeed, Lichtheim wrote, 'the frontier guards are taking them back', and once back in France the likelihood was that they would be deported, which, he added, 'as you know, means they will be sent to their doom in Germany or Poland'.[2]

The Hungarian children and the Swiss border were only two of the problems of rescue with which the Jewish leaders were confronted in the autumn of 1942. From mid-August to the first week of September the Soviet Government had authorized the departure of five thousand Polish Jews, most of whom had fled eastwards into the Soviet Union in September 1939, at the time of the German invasion. Three thousand were Jewish soldiers formerly in the Polish army. Nine hundred were adults, three hundred were accompanied children, and seven hundred were 'orphans or abandoned children'. All had received British permission to proceed to Palestine. But now another obstacle arose: the Government of Iraq, an independent Arab State, refused to allow them to cross Iraqi territory.

---

[1] Conversation reported by Dr Kahany to Joseph Linton on 23 September 1942, Central Zionist Archives, L 22/136.

[2] Central Zionist Archives, L 22/136.

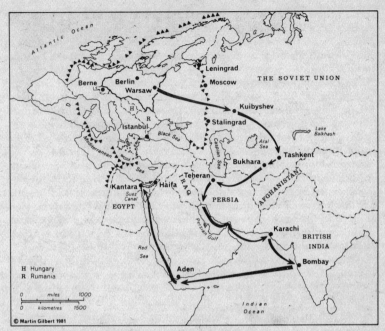

3. The route of the Teheran children from peril to safety.

The Head of the Immigration Department of the Jewish Agency, Eliahu Dobkin, hurried to Teheran to report on the condition of these Polish Jews. 'Most of the refugees,' he wrote on October 12, 'are men and women whose spirit has been broken; who, to a greater or lesser degree, are disillusioned and eaten up by despair.' There were even those, he noted, who had become 'completely demoralized', and who were as a result capable 'of anything: of theft, even of murder'. Dobkin added: 'They are lost souls, not only to Palestine but to human society as a whole. Our only comfort is that they constitute a minority.'[1]

The Jewish Agency could not leave these wretched people in Teheran. They were, after all, Jews, victims of the war, and homeless. Most of them were destitute. To help them therefore became a priority. Both the Foreign Office and the State Department were asked to persuade the Iraqi Government to grant transit visas, in the 'first instance' to the children. Both Governments agreed to do what they could, but on November 1 it was learned that the Iraqi Government had rejected the Allied request. No Jewish children were to be allowed to make the overland journey from Iran to Palestine, 'in spite of State Department intervention'.[2]

On November 11 one of the leading Arab experts in the Jewish Agency, Eliahu Epstein, discussed the Iraqi refusal with the British Ambassador to

[1] Central Zionist Archives, Z 4/15161.
[2] Letter from Nahum Goldmann to Moshe Shertok, Central Zionist Archives, S 25/1681.

Iraq, Sir Kinahan Cornwallis, who was then in Palestine. 'When I pointed out the humane side of the immigration of the children,' Epstein reported to the Agency, 'he observed that to those Iraqis who objected to Jewish immigration into Palestine, age made no difference, since "a little Jew is bound to become an adult".'[1]

The Teheran children eventually reached Palestine, but only after a long sea voyage through the Persian Gulf to Bombay, then on to Aden and the Red Sea, the Suez Canal and Palestine. This act of rescue, which ought to have been so swift and simple, took more than three months, and hundreds of messages, to complete: it absorbed energies which might have been used to good effect in other spheres, more directly linked with Nazi-dominated Europe.

Even before the Teheran children's future had become clear, the Jewish Agency found itself in a lengthy dispute with the British Government, following an appeal by the Agency to the British High Commissioner in Palestine, to allow Jews from Bulgaria to enter Palestine within the White Paper quota. Sir Harold MacMichael passed on this request to the Colonial Office in London, together with his own recommendation that it should be rejected. As MacMichael informed the Colonial Office on 9 November 1942:

I fear that if the Bulgarian Government were to know that we were prepared to accept Jews, they would send out as many as the trains could hold, without regard to numerical or other qualifications. There could be no process of selection in connection with immigrants and we could not send back any who came out of Bulgaria.

It seems to me that the door would then be thrown open to any number and condition of Jews whom any Axis country felt disposed to get rid of, with or without German instigation, nor could we any longer maintain our refusal to facilitate the journey to Palestine of illegal immigrants who arrive in Turkey.[2]

On November 17 an interdepartmental conference met to discuss Mac-Michael's argument. One official minuted: 'This question was taken towards the end of the meeting this morning, in fact nearly at 1 o'clock, and there was not much time to discuss it.' Nevertheless, it was decided to support Mac-Michael's ban on Bulgarian Jewish refugees. As the official minutes of the conference recorded, 'to accede to the Jewish Agency's request would mean that we should be opening the floodgate.'[3]

[1] Central Zionist Archives, Z 4/14797.
[2] Foreign Office papers, 371/32.698, W 15197.
[3] Colonial Office papers, 733/438.

Chapter 9

Slaughter in the east

Throughout October the messages from Geneva poured in to London, New York and Jerusalem in a steady stream. On October 5 Lichtheim sent a seven-page report on the 'brutal assassination' of thousands of Jews in Riga eleven months before, in December 1941. As well as Latvian Jews, the report stated, there were several thousand German Jews 'who were deported last autumn to the Ghetto of Riga and of whom no more was heard'.

Lichtheim emphasized the veracity of this report. It had been brought, he said, by a Jew who had lived in Riga under false papers, outside the ghetto itself, and who had 'the extraordinary luck' of escaping from Latvia to Switzerland. His report consisted of what he had himself seen, and what he had been told by members of the Latvian police. On telling his story in Geneva, he had been cross-questioned for three hours by Gerhart Riegner, who had then written down all he had heard.[1]

'I must repeat what I have said in previous letters,' Lichtheim stressed, 'the Jews in Hitler-Europe are doomed,' and he went on to urge the Jewish Agency leaders to do all they could 'to save at least the still remaining communities in the semi-independent states of Bulgaria, Italy, Roumania, Hungary, and in Vichy France.'[2]

Lichtheim's reports met with a mixed reception. One in particular, that of August 15, had seemed too far-fetched to be believed. This was the report in which Lichtheim had written of 'mass executions' in Poland, in camps 'especially prepared' for the purpose, and had named Belzec as one of these camps. This was also the report that stated that the deportees from France, Germany, Holland, Belgium and Slovakia had not been sent east to labour camps, but 'to be butchered'.

On October 6 a senior member of the Jewish Agency Executive, Yitzhak Gruenbaum, telegraphed to Lichtheim: 'shocked your latest reports regarding Poland, which despite all, difficult to believe.' Gruenbaum added that the Jewish Agency had not yet published these reports, and urged Lichtheim to 'do everything possible' to verify them.[3]

Lichtheim replied by telegram on October 8: 'Report fifteenth August confirmed by two quite different sources. Verification extremely difficult. No eye-witnesses available for obvious reasons. Also, numbers unknown. There-

[1] The escapee's name was Gabriel Ziwian. Born on 8 October 1923, he was at the time of the German invasion of Russia a medical student. Forced into the Riga Ghetto in October 1941, he ran away in December 1941, and hid in 'Aryan' Riga until March 1942, when he worked his way to the Baltic port of Stettin. From June to August 1942 he worked in the hospital at Stettin, and in September he escaped to Switzerland, reaching Geneva on 22 September 1942.
[2] Central Zionist Archives L22/136.
[3] Central Zionist Archives, L 22/136.

fore don't publish.'[1] But in a letter to Gruenbaum later that same day, Lichtheim explained that other evidence continued to reach him along similar lines. 'In fact,' he wrote, 'I have been told that there are somewhere in the East two establishments destined for the purpose indicated in the report.'[2]

As an example of the often cryptic, and yet explicit reports reaching him, Lichtheim quoted from two recent letters which had reached Switzerland from Warsaw. The first, dated September 4, stated that '*Mea Alafim* has had to leave and has been invited by *Herr K* to his country house *Kever*.' This seemed a simple message about a Mr Alafim. But in Hebrew, *Mea Alafim* meant 100,000, *Herr K* indicated the Germans, and *Kever* was the Hebrew for grave.

A second letter from the same man, sent from Warsaw on September 12, stated briefly: 'What a pity that the nice citrus fruits you have sent me are now rotting, but my uncle *Achenu* is now dead and cannot make use of them. I feel very lonely.' *Achenu* was Hebrew for 'our brothers' or 'our brethren', a reference to the Jews of Warsaw.

In forwarding these two messages to Jerusalem, Lichtheim commented: 'Maybe this man is exaggerating, but we have heard the same things from other sources, especially with regard to the large number of Jews from Warsaw who have been killed after being sent to other places', and he added: 'Putting all these pieces of evidence together, there can be little doubt that the deliberate destruction of Jewish communities in Poland is not only contemplated but already on its way'.

Reflecting on the Allied warnings about war criminals being tracked down after the war, and brought to trial, Lichtheim felt that whereas these warnings might have some effect in Rumania, Italy and Bulgaria, and would as a result 'help a number of Jews to survive', it was a fact, as he expressed it, 'that in the case of Hitler, nothing we or others would do or say could stop him'. The Jews outside Nazi Europe must therefore 'face the fact that the large majority of the Jewish communities in Hitler-dominated Europe are doomed'. Lichtheim went on to warn: 'There is no force which could stop Hitler or his SS, who are today the absolute rulers of Germany and the occupied countries.'[3]

Lichtheim sent this letter to Jerusalem on October 8. But a week later, in a private letter to another member of the Jewish Agency Executive, Leo Lauterbach, he expressed his unease at the reception of his information. 'I have the impression', he wrote, 'that my previous reports,' that is, before his report of August 30, 'have not always found the necessary understanding. Some of our friends did not want to believe that something like this can happen, others may have been misled through different (i.e. less alarming) reports.' And Lichtheim added: 'It is pointless to deal now with motives which have caused this,' and he went on to write of his own convictions, and helplessness, telling Lauterbach: 'Events speak an inexorable language and we face these events impotently, or almost so. . . .'[4]

Four days later, on October 20, Lichtheim wrote again to Lauterbach. Once

[1] Central Zionist Archives, L 22/136.
[2] There were in fact five main killing centres in operation by October 1942: Chelmno, Belzec, Treblinka, Sobibor, and Auschwitz-Birkenau.
[3] Central Zionist Archives, L 22/149. Letter No. 845.
[4] Central Zionist Archives, L 22/136.

more, the information was precise, and offered no hope of any effective countermeasures, or opposition. In June or July, it appeared, Hitler had held a discussion with his senior advisers 'regarding new and even more ruthless methods in order to annihilate the Jews more quickly, that is within the next three or four months'. One of those at the meeting, the Governor-General of Poland, Hans Frank, had, according to this report, argued that, on economic grounds, the Jews should not be killed on such a scale, as the able-bodied were needed for slave labour. But another of those present, a member of the Ministry of Economics, Dr Backe, had pointed out, also on economic data, that the food situation in Germany itself 'would be considerably bettered by the death of three or four million Jews who otherwise would have to be fed'.

The actual decision, Lichtheim commented, 'lay of course with Hitler, and he decided as was to be expected. Economic arguments and counter-arguments are not of great importance to him. His decision was dictated by hatred of the Jews.' According to reports of this discussion, and its aftermath, Hitler had signed 'a formal order' at the end of July to the effect that all Jews were to be seized, deported, and killed, 'at some remote places of Poland and occupied Russia'. It was this decision, Lichtheim told the Jewish Agency leaders in Jerusalem, that 'explains the otherwise inexplicable brutal mass deportations from all over Europe of men, women and children, as well as old people "quite unfit for any kind of work",' and he cited a further report which had reached Geneva from Holland, of the deportations from Groningen of all people up to the age of seventy-five.

Lichtheim pointed out in his letter of October 20, that whereas in 1940 or 1941 there had already been mass executions of Jews, these were carried out at a local level, and 'under this "system" there was still a chance left that at least the younger and stronger might survive, and that some of the communities, especially in western Europe, but also in the ghetto-districts of Poland, would not be completely destroyed'. But now, he warned, 'even this outlook was too optimistic'. All chance of survival had disappeared. The 'plan' behind the present deportation measures was 'to exterminate immediately the largest possible number of Jews'.

There was no respite in the terrible news which continued to reach Geneva from Nazi Europe. On October 20 Lichtheim sent to London, New York and Jerusalem a summary based on letters from a number of Slovak Jews who had been deported to Poland. The letters had been sent from Poland to Bratislava, to the eminent Slovak rabbi, Dov Weissmandel, who then sent them on by courier to Switzerland. According to Lichtheim's summary, as many as 70,000 Slovak Jews had been 'sent lately to that "unknown destination" which means death by shooting or poisoning'. Those who had been sent instead to the eastern ghettoes 'will probably share their fate or will perish owing to intolerable conditions of life and lack of food'. As for those used as slave labourers, a Belgian Jew who had been sent east, escaped, and managed to get to Switzerland, confirmed that 'if they became ill or too weak they are shot'. Trains taking Slovak deportees away were called coloquially, Lichtheim added, *Vernichtungstransporte*, or 'annihilation trains'.[1]

---

[1] 'Note regarding the deportees from Slovakia', Geneva, 20 October 1942. Central Zionist Archives, Z 4/14901.

What did all this new information mean? Was it proof that the report of an extermination plan which had been brought to Geneva more than two and a half months before was indeed true. For Gerhart Riegner, the spate of messages in September and October constituted 'the confirming pieces of evidence' that a mass murder plan did indeed exist. Riegner himself had questioned both the Latvian student who had seen the massacres in Riga and the Belgian Jew who had returned from German-occupied Poland, from the town of Rawa-Russka. Nor did Riegner doubt their stories. The Latvian, he later recalled, 'was a very fine young intellectual, a medical student, who told the story of the extermination of tens of thousands of Jews nine months earlier, an extermination of which the world has no knowledge'. As for the Belgian, he had turned out to be 'a simple man, a car mechanic who had worked in a garage. He told his story with many details, I had never heard it before in such clear terms: the people who were able to work were working, those who couldn't work were killed, and those who were no longer able to go on working were killed too. . . . He had heard it from a German officer who was sick of the war'.[1]

With so much information now having reached Geneva, including eye-witnesses from Latvia and Russia, and letters from Poland and Slovakia, as well as the second report of Hitler's intentions brought, apparently, from Berlin itself, the World Jewish Congress leaders in New York telegraphed to Riegner on October 8 instructing him and Lichtheim to contact the American Minister in Berne 'immediately', and to give him a detailed report of the new information, 'including sources'.[2]

That same day, Paul Squire, the American Consul in Geneva, wrote direct to Riegner to state that henceforth the American Legation in Berne would be glad 'to offer you such assistance as may be appropriate' in forwarding any further reports to the Jewish leaders in the United States.[3]

The meeting between Riegner, Lichtheim and Leland Harrison, the American Minister to Switzerland, took place in Berne on October 22. The two Jews had compiled a complete and formidable folio: all the reports and eye-witness accounts which had reached them since the first news of the extermination plan in August. 'We put it all together,' Riegner later recalled. 'He read it for twenty minutes. Lichtheim and I were sitting there like little schoolboys. He then began to put questions, to ask for affidavits.'[4]

Among the documents which Riegner and Lichtheim gave Harrison were copies of the letters from Warsaw and Slovakia, the reports of the Belgian Jew who had escaped from Rawa-Russka and of the medical student who had seen the slaughter in Riga and had likewise managed to escape to Switzerland. All this was introduced by a five-page note of their own, summarizing the Jewish fate under Nazi rule country-by-country.

The facts showed, Riegner and Lichtheim wrote, how the Germans were

---

[1] Recollections of Gerhart Riegner, in conversation with the author, 1 October 1980.

[2] Telegram 8 October 1942, signed Nahum Goldmann and Irving Miller, archives of the World Jewish Congress, General Secretariat.

[3] Letter of 8 October 1942, marked 'Strictly Confidential', archives of the World Jewish Congress, General Secretariat.

[4] Gerhart Riegner, conversation with the author, Geneva, 1 October 1980.

carrying out 'the policy of constant and deliberate annihilation of all European Jewish communities'. The three million Jews of Poland were being expelled, deported and executed 'to the point of complete annihilation'. Of the 100,000 Jews living in Latvia in 1939, 'there are now only 4,000 left'. Of the 150,000 Lithuanian Jews, no reports concerning their fate were available, but there were 'persistent rumours that they have shared the fate of Latvian Jewry'. From Holland at least one-third of the 180,000 Jews 'have already been deported'. All the Jews of Old Serbia had 'disappeared'. Some 50,000 French Jews had 'already been deported'; so had 70,000 of the 90,000 Jews of Slovakia. As to the fate of these deportees, Lichtheim and Riegner were emphatic:

A great number of the deported people are starving in the trains in consequence of the in- describably inhuman conditions in which the transports are carried out. According to a report from a German source, many of the deportees from the Western countries are no longer alive when reaching the German frontier but are killed before by various methods.

Younger deportees are being taken to work either in the industries of Silesia or for the construction of fortifications in the coastal zones of France or at the Eastern front. Those unfit for work are killed, and those engaged in slave labour are nearly worked to death and if unfit for work they also are killed.

Persisting rumours say that young Jewish girls and women after having been sterilised are brought to the military brothels.

In the East-European countries, notably in Poland, pogroms and mass executions on a large scale are constantly taking place. Thus the deliberate policy of extermination of European Jewry is systematically carried out quite in accordance with the announcements made in the last speeches of the Head of the German Government.[1]

The material handed to Harrison contained, as Riegner later recalled, 'all that we knew at that date'. Riegner and Lichtheim also submitted the same dossier, within a few days, to the British Minister, Clifford Norton.[2]

The facts were becoming more and more widely known, and on October 27 the *Manchester Guardian* warned its readers not to take Hitler's claim that he would annihilate European Jewry 'as just another wild and whirling threat'. Hitler, the newspaper wrote, 'aims literally at the "extermination" of the Jews in Europe so far as his hand can reach them. . . .' Between one and two million Jews 'are believed to have already been destroyed'. Perhaps four and a half million remained to be killed, 'if Hitler has his way'.[3]

A further report of Hitler's intentions was compiled by the United States Consul in Geneva, Paul Squire, who took a sworn testimony, on October 29, from a distinguished Swiss lawyer, Professor Paul Guggenheim, who had been told by 'a very important Swiss personality' that there existed 'an order of Hitler demanding the extermination (*Ausrottung*) of all Jews in Germany and in the occupied countries up to December 31, 1942'. Professor Guggen- heim's informant, Squire added, 'is under the impression that the order is in the course of being executed'.[4]

The names 'Auschwitz' and 'Birkenau' had still not appeared in the reports

[1] 'Note regarding the German policy of deliberate annihilation of European Jewry', 22 October 1942, Central Zionist Archives, L 22/56.
[2] Gerhart Riegner, letter to the author, 28 August 1980.
[3] *Manchester Guardian*, 27 October 1942.
[4] Central Zionist Archives, L 22/56.

reaching Geneva, or in the messages from Geneva. But during October many thousand French, Dutch and Belgian Jews were deported there, and murdered. Even the 'model' ghetto at Theresienstadt was no longer spared, bearing out Lichtheim's report of August 30 that it was 'only an interim station' whose deportees would themselves be deported again, to their deaths. This was indeed so; on October 28 a train, its cattle trucks sealed, its 'passengers' denied food or water, and forced together without room even to move, let alone to lie down, reached Auschwitz from Theresienstadt. There were 1,866 Jews on this train, many of them old people. On arrival 215 men and 32 women were tattooed and sent to the barracks. The remaining 1,619 were gassed.

In October, a ship set off from Norway. It too was carrying Jews to their death. Transferred to a sealed train at the German coast, these 250 Norwegian Jews, men and boys, were likewise taken to Auschwitz.

Three other death camps were working at full stretch during October: Treblinka, Sobibor, and Belzec. There, no one was taken to barracks or slave labour, but all were gassed on arrival; more than 25,000 at Treblinka alone in the last ten days of October. In the same ten-day period, at least five thousand Jews had been gassed at Sobibor and more than ten thousand at Belzec.

A fourth camp had also participated in this mass killing in October. Just outside Lublin, the suburb of Majdanek, not originally intended as a death camp, had become the site where many thousands were now being killed, including 1,800 survivors of the Lublin ghetto at the end of October. At the same time, east of German-occupied Poland, those few towns where Jews had not been murdered by the killing squads twelve months before, were the object of renewed Nazi action: in Brest-Litovsk the Nazis began to 'liquidate' the ghetto on October 15, when as many as 25,000 Jews were murdered.

Thousands tried to hide in cellars, or in specially prepared underground bunkers, but were searched out by German forces, and destroyed. On October 28 the killing was repeated in Pinsk, where ten thousand Jews were hunted down and shot. Many tried to break through the ring of German troops, and reach the forests. A few succeeded, but even then the local population caught them and handed them over to the Germans. Only 150 artisans were kept alive to work for the Germans until they too were murdered two months later.

In the second two weeks of October, a minimum of 108,000 Jews had been murdered by the Germans, a daily average of more than seven thousand.

A small percentage of the deportees were not gassed, but sent to labour camps instead. In the Auschwitz region alone, more than thirty industrial centres used Jewish slave labour. Both Krupp and I. G. Farben had set up factories near Auschwitz, specifically to take advantage of this cheap labour. Thousands of Jews died each month in these labour camps, but a fragment survived. As Lichtheim wrote from Geneva to Jerusalem on November 2, to Yitzhak Gruenbaum, who was trying to trace his son: '. . . in spite of all the terrible things which have happened to the deported Jews, a certain number of them are actually working in the coal and iron industry of Upper Silesia and in various other places in Poland. Therefore let us hope as long as there is any hope left'.[1]

The areas of hope were, however, strictly limited. 'I am sure,' Lichtheim wrote on November 9 to another Zionist friend in Jerusalem, 'you will not be deluded – as so many of our friends in Palestine – by wishful thinking.' There was 'a great difference,' he added, 'between being an optimist and living in a fool's paradise, and that is exactly what a considerable number of our friends are now doing.'[1]

There was no longer any reason for anyone in the west to live in a 'fool's paradise'. Publication of the terrible facts had become an almost daily event. In New York City in September the magazine *Jewish Frontier* had published a detailed account of the gassings at Chelmno, and in November it devoted its whole issue to the fate of the Jews. 'In the occupied countries of Europe,' the November issue declared, 'a policy is now being put into effect whose avowed object is the extermination of a whole people.' There followed a series of reports prepared by the American Jewish Congress, the World Jewish Congress and the Institute of Jewish Affairs, describing Nazi barbarism in Poland, Lithuania, Yugoslavia, France, Holland, Rumania, and Germany. 'The tempo of this planned slaughter,' *Jewish Frontier* told its readers, 'is being speeded up with every new Hitler invasion,' and about a million Jewish civilians had perished 'through massacre and deliberate starvation' since 1939.

For three years, *Jewish Frontier* stated, 'the Nazi plan' for the Jews had been in progress. The successive stages did not appear 'simultaneously' in every occupied country because of the exigencies of time and completion, but the trend was plain: 'Nazi savagery climbs inexorably from step to step. . . .' It was in this context, the magazine added, that the recent deportation of Jews from France to Poland to 'unknown destinations' allowed only 'the most sinister explanation'.[2]

Auschwitz had now kept its secret for six months.

[1] Letter to Dr A. Hantke. Central Zionist Archives, L 22/136.
[2] *Jewish Frontier*, volume 9, November 1942. Special Issue, 'Jews Under The Axis, 1939–1942'.

Chapter 10

Eye-witness

On 11 November 1942 the Germans occupied the 'Free Zone' of France. The quasi-independence of Vichy France was no more. There could now be no local protest against the deportation of Jews without that protest coming up against direct Gestapo reaction. The full range of Nazi terror was at once imposed upon southern France. That same day, Lichtheim reported from Geneva that the deportations from Holland were continuing.[1]

The destination of the deportees remained unknown, but was still, in fact, Auschwitz. On one day alone in November, sixty-three of those sent from the train to the gas chamber were children under twelve.

Neither the names, destination or fate of these deportees was known in the west. But two new sources of information were about to send their own shock waves throughout the Allied world. The first source was to have its strongest impact in Palestine, for on the morning of November 16 further Palestinian subjects to be exchanged for German internees had reached the Holy Land. There were 114 of them in all, 69 of them Jews. All had been eye-witnesses of Nazi brutality. Each one had horrific tales to tell of deportation, brutality or mass murder.

Almost all of the information brought by the returning Palestinians had already been forwarded to London, Washington and Jerusalem in the previous three months, from the Jewish Agency representatives in Geneva, or had been publicized in London by the Polish Government-in-Exile. But as the Agency leaders listened, throughout November 16 to 19, to people who had actually lived through and seen these horrors, the facts so often stated in the Geneva letters took on a new dimension.

Hitherto, the reaction to much of the news from Geneva had been shock followed by disbelief. Now shock was followed by belief. There were too many eye-witnesses, and their stories were too detailed, and too vivid, to be disbelieved. On November 20 the first summary of these stories was telegraphed from Jerusalem to London: 'tales of horror', Moshe Shertok informed Linton, 'which outmeasure anything yet reported of progress annihilation Jews Central Europe by Germans'. Among the facts reported were 'Harrowing details recounted by eyewitnesses of people thrown into flames, specially constructed crematorium, locked up poison gas chambers, and other forms of torture'.

At the end of his telegram, Shertok admitted: 'Confess if not reported by persons coming from spot would not have believed', and he went on to urge Linton to make the 'utmost efforts' to ensure the widest publication in what

[1] Central Zionist Archives, L 22/218/1.

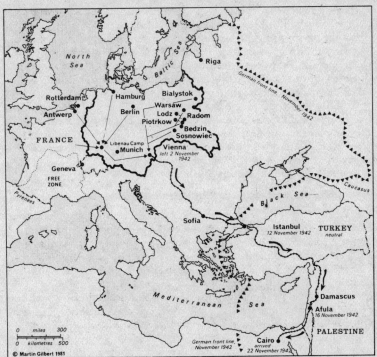

4. The first eye-witnesses of Nazi terror leave Greater Germany, France and Holland for safety, in exchange for German subjects returning to Germany, November 1942.

he called the 'authoritative press'. Shertok then reiterated, almost as if still convincing himself: 'Emphasise these no atrocity tales but accounts eye-witnesses who were carefully cross-examined'.

One serious problem remained with these new and decisive reports: their source could not be divulged as this, Shertok stressed, 'would further damage exchange schemes'.[1]

This telegram did not reach London for another seventeen days. But inside Palestine, the news led to an outburst of anguish. On November 23 the *Palestine Post* announced in its main headline:

SLAUGHTER OF EUROPE'S JEWS

and in a sub-headline:

ANNIHILATION OF ENTIRE COMMUNITIES

But in giving details of the news to the Press, the Jewish Agency insisted that the actual source was not revealed, and the newspapers referred only to 'harrowing accounts received by the Jewish Agency Executive in Jerusalem from reliable sources'. No mention was made of the eye-witnesses. At one point the

[1] Central Zionist Archives, S 25/1681.

Palestine Post referred simply to 'Reports received from the Warsaw and Lodz ghettoes'. But it did not say how these reports had been received.

But the reports were graphic. In addition to the details sent by Shertok to London on November 20, the *Post* on the following day told of Jewish children under the age of twelve who had been 'executed in their thousands', of elderly people 'murdered wholesale', of able-bodied Jews sent in groups 'to unknown destinations', all trace of whom 'has vanished'.

From the Kielce ghetto, the *Post* reported, 1,500 Jews had been massacred 'on the spot' and the rest, some 27,000 people, 'it is said were slaughtered on their journey: in any case nothing has been heard of them'. At Piotrkow only 2,600 were still alive of a pre-war community 20,000 strong, and of these survivors 'only 160 are women and children'.

Ironically, under its main sub-headline:

EXECUTION OF HITLER'S DESIGN

the *Palestine Post* of November 23 gave exactly equal prominence to a report from Geneva about 24,000 Riga Jews who had been 'forced to dig their own graves', and then shot. Indeed, the Geneva report was at the top of column one of the front page, the unidentified eye-witnesses' report only in column two.[1]

Expressing their complete confidence in these 'harrowing accounts', and declaring that Palestine Jewry 'had not given adequate expression to the ghastly tragedy now being unfolded', the Jewish Agency declared four days of official mourning, culminating in a 'general fast' on December 2. Flags were flown at half mast. Newspapers were published with black borders. And at a specially summoned General Assembly of Palestinian Jewry, strong words were spoken about the atrocities, and bitter words about the Allies.

In his opening address, Itzhak Ben-Zvi, the head of the National Council, after referring to the 'unparalleled' catastrophe facing Jewry, pointed out, as reported by the local Jewish News Agency, 'that a heavy burden rested on the civilised nations which refused to open the gates of their lands to the refugees, and did not give a helping hand to the Jews who are rebuilding their ancient home'. This was also the theme of David Ben Gurion, the Chairman of the Jewish Agency Executive, who, at the same meeting, 'blamed the democratic world for depriving the Jews of their rights as a nation, and for refusing them an independent Homeland'.

The General Assembly ended by adopting a manifesto 'declaring their horror and their sorrow, and sending a cry for help to all the Allied Governments and Church leaders throughout the world to stop the slaughter of the Jews'.[2]

In Geneva, Richard Lichtheim was not impressed by these revelations and declarations. 'The facts now published in Palestine are not new to me,' he wrote to a friend in Jerusalem on December 9, and he added: 'You cannot divert a tiger from devouring his prey by adopting resolutions or sending cables. You have to take your gun and shoot him.'[3] For the Jews, and for all other victims of Nazi rule, the tragedy was that in Europe, in December 1942,

---

[1] *Palestine Post*, 23 November 1942.

[2] *Palestine Post*, 1 December 1942.

[3] Letter to Leo Lauterbach, Central Zionist Archives, L 22/218/4, Letter No. 913.

the Allies had no 'guns'. Hitler's forces, although they had failed to capture either Stalingrad or Alexandria, were still the masters of Europe. The main unoccupied countries, Hungary, Rumania, Slovakia, Finland, Bulgaria and Italy, still did Germany's bidding.[1]

The telegrams which Lichtheim now received were the inevitable response of the Jewish Agency leaders, jolted into telegraphic action by the Palestinian exchange. 'Can you move International Red Cross', Bernard Joseph had telegraphed to Lichtheim from Jerusalem on November 25, to 'intervene to stop massacres Jewish children, women, Poland, and obtain permission remove children neutral countries'.[2] And in a letter sent to Lichtheim that same day, Joseph reiterated his suggestion that the International Red Cross might be able to save 'at least part of the children by transferring them to neutral countries'.[3]

Lichtheim received this appeal from Jerusalem on November 30. 'Red Cross fully aware situation,' he replied at once, and he added: 'All possible steps have been taken months ago here, also London, Washington.' In a long letter that same day, Lichtheim set out his reasons for believing that it was now too late for any such initiative to succeed. In Poland, he wrote, the larger ghettoes had been 'nearly emptied, which means that the inhabitants have been sent further east to some "unknown destination".' There had even been a deportation of a thousand Jews, 'men, women and children', from Norway to Poland. 'There could never have been any doubt,' he added, 'as to the meaning behind these deportations which have been carried out with the utmost brutality.' And he went on to ask: 'How can we now expect the Nazis to release from their grip the remnants of the Jewish communities still in their power? There is not the slightest chance that anything like the release of women and children can be achieved by the Red Cross or the Church or any other body.'

In his letter of November 30 Lichtheim reiterated what he had already stressed in his earlier letters of August 30, September 18 and October 10. There were Jews who had still not been deported to the 'unknown destination', and who were still being confined inside ghettoes, but these ghettoes were, he wrote, 'certainly only a formal step to achieve their starvation and annihilation'. Lichtheim added with some bitterness:

I am under the impression that some of our friends in Palestine have been unwilling to believe what I have told them in my numerous reports written during the last six or eight months about the position in Poland and the rest of German-dominated Europe, while these same reports have been read with much attention and have been acted upon in London and New York.[4]

Lichtheim's attitude was not without justification. 'Perhaps we have sinned', one Agency leader, Eliahu Dobkin, had told a meeting at Tel Aviv on Novem-

---

[1] But Finland, although allied to Germany in the war against the Soviet Union, had successfully refused to deport any more of its 2,000 Jews, following the murder of 11 Jewish refugees whom the Finnish Government had returned to Germany, at the request of the German Government. Bulgaria, Italy and Hungary had likewise rejected several German requests to deport Jews to 'resettlement areas' in German occupied Poland.
[2] Central Zionist Archives, S 25/1681, Telegram.
[3] Central Zionist Archives, S 25/1681, Letter.
[4] Central Zionist Archives, L 22/218/1.

ber 25, 'as the first terrible news came to us two months ago via Geneva and Istanbul, and we did not believe it'. Dobkin also reported to his colleagues Ben Gurion's comment, based on his personal experience, 'that in America they thought this was one of the methods of atrocity propaganda'.

'There is no knowledge', the Executive of the Labour Federation were told on November 25, 'of the fate of hundreds of thousands who were sent in an "unknown direction". There hasn't been a letter, or even a message'. What the eye-witnesses did report, however, was 'all sorts of rumours' which told 'of large concrete buildings on the Russian-Polish border where people are killed by gas and are burned'. Both Belzec and Treblinka were on this border. 'A woman from Oswiecim, west Galicia, told of 3 ovens for burning Jews that were set up in that town'. The woman was, in fact, from Sosnowiec, only 20 miles from Auschwitz. She said nothing of deportees reaching Auschwitz from further away.

As for almost 25,000 Dutch Jews and 15,000 Belgian Jews 'already deported', and 2,500 Dutch and 250 Belgian Jews still being deported each week, none of the eye-witnesses knew where these tens of thousands of Jews had been sent; only that they had been deported 'somewhere'.

This report was in Hebrew. It was not translated into English, or published, even in Hebrew.[1]

On November 26 the Jewish Agency's Information Department issued a closely-typed ten-page bulletin, also in Hebrew, giving details of the eye-witness reports. Among these reports was the one from the woman from Sosnowiec, who told of 'three stoves' that had been built near Auschwitz, for the purpose of 'burning Jews'. Two more chimneys, she said, 'were now being built'. From time to time, she added, Jews 'from the neighbourhood' were brought to the camp.[2]

This piece of information, published in Hebrew in a mass of other material, was likewise not translated into English. Nor was it published in the English-language press in Palestine. Nor was it sent on to London or New York. Indeed, no mention was made of Auschwitz, its stoves, chimneys, or deportees from nearby towns, in the telegraphic summary of the eye-witness reports sent to London by Shertok that same day, although his summary did mention by name two concentration camps, 'at Tribilanki and Lesitz'; telegraphic errors for Treblinka and Belzec.

Amid the plethora of horrible news, and the stress on Treblinka and Belzec in many of the eye-witness reports, the name 'Auschwitz' had simply not registered either as a principal killing place of Jews – which no one had reported it to be – nor as the main 'unknown destination' for the deportees from western Europe, a fact likewise not reported by any of the eye-witnesses.

Yet during the sixteen days between the arrival of the eye-witnesses on November 16 and the day of fasting on December 2, the gassings at Auschwitz, which had already been in progress since May 4, continued unabated: during those sixteen days alone at least five thousand were gassed. The 'unknown destination' had become one of the best kept secrets of the war.

[1] Protocols, Executive of the General Federation of Jewish Labour (unpublished).
[2] Central Zionist Archives, quoted in Walter Laquer, *The Terrible Secret*, London 1980, page 23 note 1, and page 192.

Chapter 11

'This bestial policy'

On November 25, at the very moment when the half-million Jews in Palestine were learning of the mass murder of their fellow Jews in Europe, yet another report had reached the Jewish leadership in London. This new report described 'the liquidation' of the Warsaw ghetto, and the gassings at Belzec. It had been brought from Poland to the Polish Government-in-Exile in London by an eye-witness, Jan Karski, a non-Jew.

Jan Karski had entered the Polish Foreign Ministry in 1938, at the age of twenty-four, and having served in the Polish Army in September 1939, then joined the Warsaw underground. Early in 1940 he had made his first clandestine mission out of Poland, to Angers in France, then the place of exile of the Polish National Council. In 1941 he had returned to Warsaw, and in the late autumn of 1942 had been sent back by the Polish underground through France and Spain to Gibraltar, and then to London.

'There is no doubt that his visit prompted us to act' the Polish Ambassador in London, Count Raczynski, later recalled.[1] And indeed, on the evening of November 25, the Polish Government-in-Exile handed Karski's report to A. L. Easterman, the Political Secretary of the British Section of the World Jewish Congress. Easterman at once telephoned the Foreign Office, and asked if he and Sydney Silverman, the Labour Member of Parliament, could show the report to Richard Law, the Under-Secretary of State for Foreign Affairs, and Eden's deputy. The meeting took place on November 26. Easterman handed Law a copy of the report, which told a tragic story.

In March 1942, according to this latest report, Himmler had ordered 'the extermination of 50 per cent of the Jewish population' in German-occupied Poland, 'to be carried out by the end of 1942'. But although the killing had then begun, 'with extraordinary gusto', the results had apparently not satisfied Himmler, who, in July 1942, during a visit to the General Government, had ordered new decrees, 'aiming at the total destruction of Polish Jewry'.

Karski's report went on to describe how the 'persecutions' had begun in Warsaw on 21 July 1942, when German police cars suddenly drove into the ghetto, and German soldiers 'immediately started rushing into the houses, shooting the inhabitants at sight, without any explanation'. On the following day a 're-settlement' decree was issued. All the Jews of Warsaw, 'regardless of sex or age', were to prepare for what had been called 're-settlement' in 'the Eastern part of Poland'. The daily quota of 'people to be re-settled' was fixed at six thousand a day, and the order was to be carried out by the Jewish

---

[1] Count Raczynski, letter to the author, 18 September 1980. See also Raczynski's book, *In Allied London*, London 1963, pages 127–8.

Municipal Council, 'under pain of death'.

The report went on to describe how, on July 23, as had already been reported in *The Times*, the German police had ordered the chairman of the Council, Adam Czerniakow, 'to deliver 10,000 people the next day and 7,000 daily on the following days', despite the original quota of 6,000. A few minutes after the Germans had left him, Czerniakow had committed suicide. Karski then reported, and this was new, how the manhunts had begun immediately after Czerniakow's suicide, and how these manhunts had been carried out by the Gestapo with the help of Ukrainian, Latvian, and Lithuanian 'security battalions'. These battalions, he noted, 'under the command of SS men, are characterized by their utter ruthlessness, cruelty and inhumanity', and he continued:

The Jews, when caught, are driven to a square. Old people and cripples are then singled out, taken to the cemetery and there shot. The remaining people are loaded into goods trucks, at the rate of 150 people to a truck with space for 40. The floor of the truck is covered with thick layer of lime and chlorine sprinkled with water. The doors of the trucks are locked. Sometimes the train starts immediately on being loaded. sometimes it remains on a siding for a day, two days or even longer. The people are packed so tightly that those who die of suffocation remain in the crowd side by side with the still living and with those slowly dying from the fumes of lime and chlorine, from lack of air, water and food. Wherever the trains arrive half the people arrive dead. Those surviving are sent to special camps at Treblinka, Belzec and Sobibor. Once there, the so-called 'settlers' are mass murdered.

Even the need for slave labour was not being met from Warsaw. According to Karski's report, 'out of a total of 250,000 "re-settled", only about 4,000 have been sent to auxiliary work. . . .' and he went on to stress that neither children, nor even babies, had been spared. In addition, the orphans were also evacuated. The director of the largest Jewish orphanage in Warsaw, the well-known writer, Janusz Korczak, whom the Germans had allowed to stay behind in the ghetto, 'preferred to follow his charges to death'.

The Polish report of November 25 reiterated the figure of 250,000 as the number of Warsaw Jews murdered between July and September 1942. Nor had the deportations and killings ended. While 120,000 ration cards had been printed for September, the number issued for October 'was only 40,000'.

It was not only the Jews of Warsaw who were being killed, the report continued. Simultaneously, the ghettoes in the provinces 'are being liquidated'. There followed an account of the different methods of 'mass extermination': execution by firing squads, electrocution, and 'lethal gas-chambers', and the report continued with an account of the 'electrocuting station' at Belzec camp:

Transports of 'settlers' arrive at a siding, on the spot where the execution is to take place. The camp is policed by Ukrainians. The victims are ordered to strip naked—to have a bath, ostensibly—and are then led to a barrack with a metal plate for floor. The door is then locked, electric current passes through the victims and their death is almost instantaneous. The bodies are loaded on to waggons and taken to a mass grave some distance from the camp.

The report then described how, at another death camp, Treblinka, a large digging machine had recently been installed:

It works ceaselessly digging ditches—mass graves for Jews who are to meet their death there. The Ukrainian guards, witnesses of the mass murders, are allowed to keep the money and jewellery robbed from the victims. These bestial murders sometimes take place in the presence of the local non-Jewish Polish population, who are helpless and overcome with horror at the sight of such inhuman violence. . . .

The Polish report of November 25 ended with a reference to a pamphlet circulating inside Poland which contained 'a strongly worded protest against the terrible extermination of Jews', and estimated that the total number of Jews murdered in Poland since the outbreak of war 'exceeds one million'.[1]

Such was the information which two British Jews, A. L. Easterman and Sydney Silverman, put before the Under-Secretary of State for Foreign Affairs, Richard Law, on November 26. Law himself recorded the course of their conversation. Whatever the British view might be, Silverman said, 'it was now clear' that the State Department 'accepted the substantial truth of these stories'. But Law replied that he did not think that the State Department 'had any more evidence than we had', although, he added, on the State Department's knowledge 'of the German character and of Nazi ideology', it probably seemed to them that there was 'nothing intrinsically improbable about the story'.

Law went on to say that the British 'had had no more evidence'. The British Minister in Berne, Clifford Norton, had seen Gerhart Riegner about his August telegram of a German extermination plan, 'but had been unable', Law reported, 'to get from him the facts on which his evidence was based'.

Silverman told Law that the British might take the view 'that there was nothing that could be usefully done at the moment'. But if that was the British Government's view, he added, 'it meant that nothing in fact could ever be done'. Even if the British thought that any steps which they took 'would be ineffective', the Government would be 'in an impossible position' if it did not do something.

Silverman made two suggestions. The first was a Great-Power Declaration to the effect that the United Nations had been informed of the extermination plan, and that 'if it was carried out', those responsible for it 'would receive their due punishment', while at the same time the German people themselves 'could not escape responsibility for the acts of their government'. The second suggestion was 'that some use should be made' of broadcasting, not to threaten the Germans, 'but to encourage the Jews and to encourage those non-Jews who might be willing to give the Jews their protection'.

Richard Law circulated his account of this conversation within the Foreign Office. 'I doubt very much,' he noted, 'whether his proposals, if we were able to carry them out, would do very much good, and I think Mr Silverman agrees.' On the other hand, he added, 'I think that we should be in an appalling position if these stories should prove to be true and we have done nothing whatever about them.'

At the end of his account, Law noted that Silverman 'and his friends' had been 'very forbearing on the whole', but that he was 'afraid' that 'unless we can make them some kind of gesture they will cause a lot of trouble'.

Within the Foreign Office, it was now a Great Power Declaration, such as

---

[1] The report of 25 November 1942, and the Foreign Office comments on it, are in Foreign Office papers, 371/30923, C 11,923, folios 62–7 and 71–3.

Silverman had requested, which was the object of discussion. Yet there were still some hesitations: 'our declaration', David Allen wrote on November 27, 'should, in the absence of clearer evidence, avoid too specific a reference to the *plan* of extermination'. Instead, it should concentrate 'on condemnation of the general German *policy* of getting rid of useless Jews'.

Commenting on these arguments, Frank Roberts wrote that although there was 'no actual proof of these atrocities', he thought that their probability was 'sufficiently great to justify action . . .', particularly if such action was considered necessary 'with a view to satisfying Parliamentary opinion here'.

Further pressure for action came from the Polish Ambassador, Count Raczynski, who, at a meeting with Anthony Eden on the morning of December 1, 'drew attention', as the Foreign Office noted, 'to the wholesale destruction of Jews in Poland'. This destruction, Raczynski told Eden, 'was causing great agitation among Jews all over the world'.

Raczynski had two suggestions: a 'warning to Laval' concerning the deportations from France, and a meeting of representatives of the occupied countries to discuss and publicize the persecution.[1] But the Foreign Office rejected the idea of such a meeting. The Polish Government, Frank Roberts noted that same day, 'are always glad of an opportunity (1) to make a splash as leader of the minor Allies and (2) to show that they are not anti-Semitic'. In any case, he added, although atrocities 'are undoubtedly taking place, we have no reliable evidence. Nor are we sure', he wrote, 'that world Jewry as a whole wishes to draw public attention to what is going on'. Roberts had yet another objection to a protest meeting of the Governments-in-Exile, writing in his minute of December 1:

It also occurs to me that this is not a very suitable moment to breathe fire and fury against the Germans in connexion with their treatment of the Jews, since Hitler now has in his power our former friends in France and in particular M. Reynaud, M. Mandel, M. Daladier and M. Blum.[2] He also has in his power various Spanish and other left-wing refugees in France. In addition Hitler seems to be in a very difficult mood about prisoners of war. It therefore seems to me inadvisable to irritate him more than is necessary, particularly on a Jewish issue.

Also on December 1 the British Section of the World Jewish Congress issued a three-page typed bulletin headed: 'Annihilation of European Jewry. Hitler's policy of total destruction'. The bulletin was based largely on the Polish report of November 25, which itself had been publicized at a meeting of the Polish National Council on November 27. But the bulletin also included details from the various other reports which had reached Britain since the Bund message of the previous May.

Two million Jews at least had already been 'murdered, tortured and deliberately starved to death in Eastern Europe', the bulletin stated. The number was probably 'much greater'. Almost the entire Jewish population of the Baltic States had been 'exterminated'. Hundreds of thousands of Jews of Rumania had been deported to Transnistria, 'and there massacred'. In addi-

---

[1] Raczynski's meeting with Eden, and the Foreign Office comments on it, are in Foreign Office papers, 371/30923. C 11,923, folios 68–70.

[2] Reynaud, Daladier and Blum – each of them a former French Prime Minister – survived the w.r. Mandel, a former Colonial Minister and, like Blum, a Jew, was handed over by the Gestapo to the Vichy militia in 1944, and shot.

tion, 'scores of thousands' of German, French, Belgian, Dutch, Czechoslovak and Yugoslav Jews had been deported to Poland and the occupied areas of the Soviet Union 'for mass slaughter'.

In March 1942, the bulletin stressed, 'The holocaust took on a formal design, under an explicit policy . . .', and it went on to mention, not Auschwitz, but the three death camps already known, Treblinka, Belzec and Sobibor.[1]

On the morning of December 2 both the BBC, and the Foreign Office News Department, telephoned to the Central Department to ask what they should do about the 'story emanating from the World Jewish Congress', about the German Government's order 'for the extermination of the Jews in Eastern Europe'. They were told that the question of an official statement was being considered, 'and that meanwhile it seemed desirable to soft pedal the whole thing'. At the same time, the Central Department pointed out, they would not wish 'the impression to be given' that the Department 'were deliberately trying to kill the story'.[2]

Meanwhile, Sydney Silverman's suggestion of a Great-Power Declaration was followed up, albeit in the slightly modified form of separate, but identical declarations to be issued in London, Moscow and Washington. On the evening of December 2 Eden saw the Soviet Ambassador, Ivan Maisky, who gave his 'purely personal' approval to the idea of such a declaration, which might, he said, 'give the unhappy Jews some comfort'. Eden explained to Maisky that it was also hoped by the declaration 'to encourage the populations of the occupied countries, who were already giving some help to those unhappy people, to continue with this course'.[3]

Eden now put his authority as Foreign Secretary behind the declaration, sending both Maisky and the United States Ambassador, John Winant, a British draft, to be issued, if approved, 'as soon as possible'. Eden explained, in a letter drafted by Frank Roberts, that the idea was for Britain, the Soviet Union and the United States to condemn the German atrocities, and to 'remind their perpetrators that certain retribution awaits them'. There was, the letter added, 'growing public interest in this question, and it is therefore desirable to make our attitude known at the earliest possible moment'.[4]

On December 3 Sydney Silverman let it be known that he would be asking a question in the House of Commons about the Allied response. Indeed it was noted in the Foreign Office on December 4 that an immediate '3 power declaration' would have the effect of 'forestalling Mr Silverman's question in the House, and also satisfying the public interest'.[5] This public interest, David Allen noted that same day, had been aroused 'as a result of the publicity which the Jewish bodies in this country have succeeded in organizing', and made it 'desirable that the reactions of H.M. Government should not be too long delayed'.[6] The declaration itself, drafted by Allen, was forthright in its con-

---

[1] 'Annihilation of European Jewry, Hitler's Policy of Total Destruction', 1 December 1942. Copy in Foreign Office papers, 371/30923. C 11923, folios 122–4.

[2] Foreign Office papers, 371/30923. C 11923, folio 72.

[3] Eden's report on his conversation with Maisky is in Foreign Office papers, 371/30923. C 11923, folios 113–14.

[4] Foreign Office papers, 371/30923. C 12147, folio 149.

[5] Foreign Office papers, 371/30923. C 12201, folio 186.

[6] Foreign Office papers, 371/30923. C 12201, folio 188.

demnation of what it called 'this brutal policy of cold-blooded extermination'.[1]

Before the declaration could be issued, Washington and Moscow had to give their approval. It was also decided to associate all the Governments-in-Exile with it. This took time. Meanwhile, the Jewish Agency continued to press the British Government for help in the rescue of the Jewish children from three States which were not yet entirely within the Nazi grip, Hungary, Rumania and Bulgaria.

On December 4 the Colonial Secretary, Oliver Stanley, agreed to discuss the question of rescuing the children with three Jewish Agency representatives, Professor Namier, Berl Locker, the head of the Jewish Agency's Political Bureau in London, and Blanche Dugdale, the niece of Lord Balfour, and herself a lifelong supporter of Zionism. These three were accompanied by Joseph Linton, the secretary of the Jewish Agency in London.

According to the official British record of the interview, Namier, Locker and Mrs Dugdale had raised the question of finding a refuge for persecuted Jews from Nazi-occupied territories, 'preferably Palestine, but if that was impossible, in some other territories in the British Empire'. The present British policy 'in regard to non-admission to Colonial territories of Jews in enemy countries' should, they urged, be changed, 'in order to save the remnant of the Jewish people in Europe'.

Namier, Locker and Dugdale then stressed 'the need for saving as many children as possible'. Jewish parents, they told the Colonial Secretary, 'would willingly agree to part with their children in order to safeguard the continuance of their race'. They realized, they said, 'that only some portion could be sent to Palestine'. But they went on to urge 'that it was the duty of HMG and corresponding nations to regard Jews as an Allied people suffering more than any others at the hands of the oppressors'. In the margin opposite the phrase 'Jews . . . an Allied people' the Colonial Office official responsible for Jewish immigration, J. S. Bennett, noted: 'This is a major fallacy'.

The three emissaries suggested that 'the most fruitful field' for rescue was Bulgaria. The Jewish Agency, they said, still had an 'organisation' there. The Bulgarian Government 'would allow them to go'. And there was a common land frontier between Bulgaria and Turkey.

The Colonial Secretary did not reject the Jewish Agency's appeal out of hand, and suggested to his advisers that Britain might at least try to help the 'substantial immigration' of Bulgarian Jewish children. This would, however, 'take time', he noted, 'and on present information will probably not be feasible as regards Palestine'.[2]

In reporting on the meeting to the Jewish Agency in Jerusalem, Linton telegraphed two days later that the deputation had urged that Jews coming from enemy or occupied countries should cease to be regarded 'as enemy aliens or contaminated'. He added that the Zionists had 'strongly appealed to help us save the remnant of our people', and had themselves suggested, if Palestine were impossible, temporary asylum in Cyprus, Kenya, and even Mauritius.

In his telegram to Jerusalem, Linton noted that the Jewish Agency repre-

[1] Foreign Office papers, 371/30923. C 12147.
[2] The Colonial Secretary's report of this interview, telegraphed to the High Commissioner in Palestine, is in Foreign Office papers, 921/10.

sentatives had declared that the Agency itself, the Jews of Palestine and the Jewish communities in the free world, would take 'all responsibility' for any children who were brought out. To help bring them out, the help of the Red Cross, and the Protecting Power, Switzerland, could also be utilized. 'We underlined again,' Linton reported, 'absurdity argument political unreliability.' Previous potential adult refugees had been barred for security reasons. But there was no way that the children could be a threat on security grounds.

Linton ended his account by reporting that Stanley himself had said he was 'extremely moved' by the Jewish Agency representations, but that he was unable to give an 'immediate answer' because the present policy was 'shaped' not by himself but by the Government.[1]

Unknown to the Jewish Agency emissaries, even the Colonial Secretary's sympathetic suggestions that something might be done to get the children out of Bulgaria had been too much for some of his advisers. On December 7 J. S. Bennett, noted: 'it is difficult to present a convincing case on *security* grounds against letting in *children* as proposed here; particularly in view of our reception of Greek (non-Jewish) children'. Bennett added:

What is disturbing is the apparent readiness of the new Colonial Secretary to take Jewish Agency 'sob-stuff' at its face value. As a political manoeuvre this will establish a good precedent which the Agency will no doubt exploit.[2]

The Colonial Office decided to advise rejection of the Jewish Agency request, which was to be put before the War Cabinet in seven days time.

Also on December 7, the Colonial Office received a full report of the facts reported by the Palestinian eye-witnesses who had been exchanged for German nationals in November. This was a report which the Jewish National Council had sent from Jerusalem, following the decision of its special General Assembly to 'send a cry of help' to all the Allied Governments. Reading the details as reported by the eye-witnesses, and passed on by the General Assembly, J. S. Bennett noted: 'Familiar stuff. The Jews have spoilt their case by laying it on too thick for years past'.[3]

It was not, however, the Palestinian eye-witnesses, or the reports forwarded from Jerusalem, but the information provided by the Polish Government-in-Exile which had made the headlines in both Britain and the United States, and which was leading, throughout the first and second weeks of December, to the publication of a Three-Power Declaration. On December 4 *The Times* had published a report from its diplomatic correspondent, headed 'Nazi War on Jews', and with the sub-heading 'Deliberate Plan for Extermination'.

The article in *The Times* referred first to a Swedish newspaper correspondent in Berlin, who had reported at the end of November that, 'under a recent German order, the entire Polish General-Government would be "Jew-free" by December 1'. The Warsaw ghetto alone would remain. A total of 1,700,000 Jews would be 'liquidated, which means either transported eastward in cattle trucks to an unknown destination, or killed where they stood'. Accounts of

[1] Central Zionist Archives, Z 4/14758.
[2] Foreign Office papers, 921/10.
[3] Foreign Office papers, 921/7.

punitive conditions inside the ghetto, and reports that the Lublin district, which formerly had 313,000 Jews, was 'to be cleared at the shortest notice', had to be read, *The Times* suggested, 'against the background of Hitler's recent and apparently irrelevant outbursts against the Jews'.

At the end of his article, the diplomatic correspondent referred to the Polish Government-in-Exile's information of November 25, which it described as having 'just reached this country from the underground labour groups in Poland', and which had been compiled there 'little more than a month ago'. From this it was clear, he said, that 'the Poles themselves believe that few of the Jews who are sent east in cattle trucks, crowded together without food, survive the journey'. The diplomatic correspondent then quoted from the final paragraph of the Polish memorandum:

One of the war aims of Hitler's regime, and one which has been publicly proclaimed by its highest authorities, is a complete extermination of Jews wherever the rapacious hand of German Fascism made its way.

All other war aims of Nazism will fail in the end—and the defeat of German Fascism is inevitable—but this particular aim, a complete extermination of Jews, is already being enforced.

At the end of his article, the diplomatic correspondent of *The Times* commented that on the Germans' 'own showing', according to 'their own boasts', what he called 'terrible measures' were now being applied. And he added: 'It appears that the veil across the whole truth is only now being drawn aside.'[1]

This report caused a considerable stir, so much so that on the following day, December 5, *The Times* gave prominence to a letter from William Temple, Archbishop of Canterbury, who praised the paper for publicizing 'the appalling facts now coming to light with regard to Hitler's project for the extermination of the Jews'. This emphasis was in fact maintained by a triple headline over the Archbishop's letter:

NAZI WAR ON JEWS
THE NEW BARBARISM
RESPONSE OF THE CIVILISED WORLD

In his letter, the Archbishop stated: 'It is a horror beyond what imagination can grasp'. But he wished to express, both on behalf of the Church of England and the Free Church, 'our burning indignation at this atrocity, to which the records of barbarous ages scarcely supply a parallel'. It was hard, the Archbishop added, 'to see what can be done'. But he did have two suggestions, one concerning refugees, the other concerning retribution:

At least we might offer to receive here any Jews who are able to escape the clutches of the Nazis and make their way to our shores. In comparison with the monstrous evil confronting us the reasons for hesitation usually advanced by officials have an air of irrelevance.

Further, it could be announced that any person proved to be directly or indirectly concerned in this outrage would be held responsible when the war is over.

The Archbishop ended on a religious note. The matter, he said, seemed in fact to be 'beyond earthly resources'. It should, he reflected, 'be the subject of our constant, united, and most earnest prayer to Almighty God'.[2]

---

[1] *The Times*, 4 December 1942.
[2] *The Times*, 5 December 1942.

On December 7 the Jewish Agency in London received the telegram from Jerusalem, sent seventeen days before, setting out the horrific account brought by the Palestinian eye-witnesses. That same day, while the Jewish Agency leaders were deciding on various extra efforts at publicity in the British Press, the Foreign Office telegraphed to the British Ambassador in Washington, Lord Halifax, with the text of the proposed declaration. Halifax was also told, in an explanatory note, that 'we have little doubt that a policy of gradual extermination of all Jews, except highly skilled workers, is being carried out by the German authorities'. In addition, Halifax was told, the Polish Government had recently received reports 'tending to confirm this view', and the reports themselves 'read convincingly'. The Jewish organizations in London, the telegram noted, 'have recently organised considerable publicity', and had proposed a Three-Power Declaration 'condemning German policy and threatening retribution'. The reaction of the Soviet Ambassador had been favourable. What was required of Halifax was that he should now 'press the United States Government for an early reply, as there is considerable public interest here and early action is advisable'.[1]

All the indications were now favourable for the issue of the Declaration. On December 8 Joseph Linton informed Lord Melchett: 'We understand (very confidentially) that the Prime Minister has been much moved by the reports'.[2] In Washington, President Roosevelt received a delegation of Jewish leaders, and the leading United States newspapers carried long stories, and editorial comment. On December 10, the Polish Ambassador in London, Edward Raczynski, sent Eden an extremely detailed twenty-one point summary of all the most recent information regarding the killing of Jews in Poland; confirmation, he wrote, 'that the German authorities aim with systematic deliberation at the total extermination of the Jewish population of Poland', as well as of the 'many thousands of Jews' whom the Germans had deported to Poland from western and central Europe, and from the German Reich itself.

It was necessary, Raczynski's letter ended, not only to condemn these crimes and to punish the criminals, but also to find means 'of offering hope that Germany might be effectively restrained from continuing to apply her methods of mass execution'.[3]

It was not clear to what extent the mass of information and publicity would have a long-term effect, either of sympathy or of action. On December 8 Weizmann's secretary, Doris May, wrote to Arthur Lourie at the Emergency Council for Zionist Affairs, in New York:

I don't know what one can say about the news that reached us—and no doubt you—from 'behind the veil'.

After a certain stage horrors cease to horrify, because one's imagination cannot cope with more than a limited amount without rebelling.[4]

'The facts do indeed surpass imagination', Blanche Dugdale wrote in the

---

[1] Foreign Office papers, 371/30923. Telegram No. 7686. War Cabinet distribution.

[2] Central Zionist Archives, Z 4/14758.

[3] Foreign Office papers, 371/30924. C 12313. This report was published almost immediately as, Republic of Poland, Ministry of Foreign Affairs, *The Mass Extermination of Jews in German Occupied Poland*, London, December 1942.

[4] Lourie papers.

Spectator on December 11, and she went on to describe how there was 'a spontaneous reaction against "atrocity-stories" and a desire to believe them exaggerated, which is rooted as much in the healthier forms of incredulity as in the instinct to spare oneself pain'. Nevertheless, she argued, 'no room seems to be left' for doubting the new 'facts and figures' recently made public by the Polish Government-in-Exile, about the deportation and murder of Warsaw Jewry at the 'camps of execution' at Belzec, Sobibor, Treblinka, places, she explained 'east of Warsaw'. And she went on to write of how, at these places:

... the Polish peasantry can hardly endure the continual stench of putrefying flesh, for when the trucks are opened they reveal a mass of the dead and dying, standing upright for lack of room to fall down. Those who still breathe are shot, electrocuted or gassed. The Germans do their butchery assisted by Ukrainian, Lithuanian and Latvian Fascists. ...

These things, Mrs Dugdale wrote, had been happening all through 'this November of cheerful memory'. They were still happening 'now'. Scepticism could no longer serve 'as excuse for inaction'.

Mrs Dugdale went on to urge a repetition of earlier pledges 'to exact full retribution for war crimes'. It would, she argued, 'be a shameful thing' if the British Government, the Parliament, and the nation 'were to remain supine, or mere critics of what others try to do on behalf of tortured people'. And she went on to stress that the 'jaws of the trap' were not yet closed everywhere, 'at any rate not yet'. As it was now known what would happen 'if, or when, they shut', that knowledge, she declared:

.... lays a heavy responsibility on the Governments and nations who have it in their power to provide refuge. The Jewish communities in the free countries are willing and able to carry the financial burden of the old, the sick and the children. Palestine has an acute labour-shortage due to its contribution to the war-effort.

But Palestine is not the only place within the British Empire where safety awaits those who succeed in escaping. Men who do not open doors to those who are hunted by murderers participate in the crime.[1]

Both the question of a special declaration on war crimes, and the question of refugees, were on the War Cabinet agenda on December 14, only three days after Mrs Dugdale's article was published. And it was at that very War Cabinet that Anthony Eden presented the arguments in favour of the Declaration to his colleagues. There were, he told them, 'indications' that large-scale massacres of Jews were taking place in German-occupied Poland. 'It was known,' Eden told his colleagues, 'that Jews were being transferred to Poland from enemy-occupied countries, for example Norway; and it might be that these transfers were being made with a view to wholesale extermination of Jews.'

Given such a report by the Foreign Secretary, the Declaration was approved by the War Cabinet. The next item on the agenda was the recent request from the Jewish Agency; that 4,500 Bulgarian Jews, the majority of them children, should be allowed to leave Bulgaria for Palestine. This immigration, it was pointed out, would fall within the existing immigration quotas. But the Colonial Secretary, Oliver Stanley, opposed the request. 'This proposal,' he told the War Cabinet, 'had been rejected on security grounds'; that was to say,

[1] *Spectator*, 11 December 1942.

he explained, in accordance with a much earlier Cabinet decision three years before, which had rejected the 'exodus of nationals from a country with which we were at war'.[1]

No one at the War Cabinet drew any link between the planned policy of extermination in German-occupied Europe, and the request to allow children to leave an 'enemy' country. Nor did Stanley tell his colleagues that Churchill himself had approved the plan for the admission of 4,500 Jewish children and five hundred accompanying adults. 'Bravo!', Churchill had written to Stanley on December 11, adding: 'But why not obtain, as you will, the hearty endorsement of the War Cabinet'.[2]

Meanwhile, the final stages of the Declaration went ahead, coordinated by officials in London, Moscow and Washington, and the impact of the Declaration, when issued on 17 December 1942, was considerable. Its central paragraph associated not only Britain, the Soviet Union and the United States, but also the Governments-in-Exile of Belgium, Czechoslovakia, Greece, Luxembourg, Holland, Norway, Poland and Yugoslavia, as well as General de Gaulle's French National Committee, in a condemnation 'in the strongest possible terms' of what it described as 'this bestial policy of cold-blooded extermination'.

In describing the deportations, the Declaration was graphic: 'None of those taken away are ever heard of again,' it stated. 'The infirm are left to die of exposure and starvation or are deliberately massacred in mass executions.' And the Declaration went on to estimate the number of victims 'of these bloody cruelties' as being 'reckoned in many hundreds of thousands of innocent men, women and children'.[3]

In London, the Declaration was read out by Anthony Eden himself in the House of Commons. 'I regret to have to inform the House,' he said, 'that reliable reports have recently reached His Majesty's Government regarding the barbarous and inhuman treatment to which Jews are being subjected in German-occupied Europe.'

After Eden had read out the Declaration, several Members of Parliament spoke briefly. A Labour MP, Reginald Sorensen, a former Minister of the Free Christian Church, asked about the possibility of 'co-operation with the non-belligerent and neutral Governments' to secure the emigration of Jews from German-occupied Europe to Sweden, 'or to some other neutral country'. A Liberal MP, James de Rothschild, speaking as a British Jew, hoped that the Declaration, broadcast by the BBC, might 'percolate throughout the German-infected countries', and that, in doing so, it would give 'some faint hope and courage to the unfortunate victims of torment and insult and degradation'.

James de Rothschild hoped that when news of the Declaration reached the Jews inside Europe, they would feel 'that they are supported and strengthened by the British Government and by the other United Nations', and that the Allies would 'continue to signify that they still uphold the dignity of man'.

The House of Commons had been shocked and moved by all that the Declaration revealed: so much so that a Labour MP, William Cluse, himself

[1] War Cabinet minutes, Cabinet papers, 65/28.
[2] Premier papers, 4/51/2.
[3] Final text in Premier papers, 4/100/3, Annex No. 4 of the War Cabinet minutes of 14 December 1942.

an orphan since the age of five, asked the Speaker if MPs could 'rise in their places and stand in silence in support of this protest against disgusting barbarism.'

All Members of Parliament then stood, heads bowed, in silent recognition of the terrible facts. In the House of Lords, Lord Samuel, told his fellow peers: 'This is not an occasion on which we are expressing sorrow and sympathy to sufferers from some terrible catastrophe due unavoidably to flood or earthquake, or some other convulsion of nature. These dreadful events are an outcome of quite deliberate, planned, conscious cruelty of human beings.'[1] And on that same day, December 17, at a mass protest meeting held by the Women's International Zionist Organization at the Wigmore Hall in London, a message was read out from Churchill's wife, in which she spoke of Hitler's 'satanic design to exterminate the Jewish people in Europe', and informed the assembled ladies: 'I wish to associate with you in all your grief, and I pray your meeting may help to keep the attention of the British people focussed upon the terrible events which have occurred and are impending in Nazi Europe.'[2]

The Polish Government-in-Exile also participated in the publicity given to the Declaration. Speaking over the BBC on December 17, Count Raczynski, who had been one of the signatories of the nine-Government declaration of the previous January, described the German nation as 'so powerful in its armed might and owning so gigantic a war machine, and at the same time so cowardly, accepting the destruction of an entire race, the representatives of which, such as Heine, Mendelsohn and Einstein, contributed so much to the glory of Germany's civilization. . . .'[3]

Both the British and American Governments tried to persuade Pope Pius XII to associate himself with the Declaration of December 17. On the day after the Declaration was issued, the British Minister to the Vatican, Francis d'Arcy Osborne, was instructed 'to urge the Pope to use his influence either by means of a public statement in connection with Christmas, or through some less obvious action through the German bishops', to encourage German Christians 'to do all in their power to restrain these excesses'.[4] But he was unsuccessful, and on December 26 President Roosevelt's personal representative to the Pope, Myron C. Taylor, reported to Washington that the Cardinal Secretary of State, Maglione, while 'deploring cruelties that have come to his attention', added that the Holy See 'was unable to verify Allied reports as to the number of Jews exterminated etc.'[5]

Three days later, the Pope told Osborne that he felt that his Christmas message had in fact condemned the Nazi crimes. In this message he had spoken of the need for mankind to vow to bring men back to the law of God and to the service of their fellow-men; a vow, the Pope had said, that mankind owed to all the victims of the war, to the widows, to the orphans, to the homeless, to the dispossessed, and also to the 'hundreds of thousands of persons who,

[1] Hansard, 17 December 1942.
[2] Palcor Bulletin, 17 December 1942.
[3] BBC Written Archives Centre.
[4] Foreign Office papers, 371/34361.
[5] Foreign Relations of the United States 1942, volume 1, Washington 1960, pages 70–71.

without any fault on their part, sometimes only because of nationality or race, have been consigned to death or to a slow decline'.[1]

The Pope considered this sentence a clear and sufficient reference to Nazi crimes against the Jews. At the same time, he was reluctant to endorse specific atrocity stories, for, as Myron Taylor's assistant, Harold H. Tittman reported on December 30, after his own audience with the Pope: 'he "feared" that there was a foundation for the atrocity reports of the Allies but led me to believe that he felt that there had been some exaggeration for the purposes of propaganda'.[2]

A week later, Osborne asked the Vatican specifically to associate itself with the Allied Declaration. But on 5 January 1943 he reported back to London that the Pope considered his broadcast to have been 'clear and comprehensive in its condemnation of the heartrending treatment of the Poles, Jews in occupied countries, hostages etc.', and that it had 'satisfied all demands recently made upon him to speak out'.[3]

The name 'Auschwitz' had not been mentioned in the Declaration of 17 December 1942. Yet throughout November and December the pace of deportation and slaughter there had not slackened. The other death camps, whose names were now so widely known, Belzec, Treblinka and Sobibor, had also continued to act as killing centres, as had Majdanek. So too had Chelmno, the first camp in which the Jews had been gassed, in December 1941, and the first one to be mentioned by name in the west.

On December 17, the day of the Allied Declaration, Richard Lichtheim wrote from Geneva to both London and Jerusalem, with news which he had just heard 'from a reliable source' that the deportations from Holland were continuing, and that a train left Holland with deportees 'every week'. Many Dutchmen had helped Jews to escape, or had hidden them, although the death penalty had been proclaimed for such actions. This 'menace', Lichtheim reported, had actually been carried out twice 'in the last weeks', when Dutchmen found guilty of helping Jews 'have been sent to the well-known place Mauthausen, where people are killed. . . .'

It was known that the Dutch non-Jews had been sent to Mauthausen. But where had the Jews been sent? Lichtheim's 'reliable source' could not give him the answer. Nor did the Joodsche Raad, the Jewish Council in Amsterdam, know the answer. As Lichtheim wrote: 'Of the deported people there has been no news, in spite of publications from the Joodsche Raad that people will be allowed to write'. With the exception of a few high SS officials, Lichtheim added, 'nobody knows to what place the transports are being sent'.[4]

After seven and a half months, Auschwitz still kept its secret.

[1] *War and Peace Aims of the United Nations September 1, 1939–December 31, 1942*, Boston 1943, page 626.
[2] *Foreign Relations of the United States 1943*, volume 3, Washington 1963, pages 911–13.
[3] Foreign Office papers, 371/34363, C 216.
[4] Central Zionist Archives, L 22/218/1. In the month before the Allied Declaration and totally unknown to the Allies or to the Jewish leaders in the west, trains had left Holland for Auschwitz on November 20 (726 deportees), November 24 (709 deportees), November 30 (826 deportees), December 4 (812 deportees), December 8 (927 deportees) and December 12 (757 deportees). *Overzicht van de uit Nederland Gedeporteerde Joden*, Netherlands State Institute for War Documentation, Amsterdam, n.d.

Chapter 12

'Everything has to be tried'

Eight days after the Allied Declaration of 17 December 1942, stating that there was a German plan 'to exterminate the Jewish people in Europe', the Polish Ambassador to London, Count Raczynski, went to see Churchill's Private Secretary, John Martin. Raczynski brought with him a memorandum addressed to Churchill from the Polish Government-in-Exile, stating that the Germans were proceeding 'with mass expulsion of the Polish population, slaughter and mass executions', in the neighbourhood of Lublin, and in four other districts in German-occupied Poland. In one district alone, the memorandum noted, 'they have deported the entire population of 54 villages'.[1]

In presenting this evidence of the mass killing of non-Jews, Count Raczynski asked for the British Government to consider taking some action, including, as Martin reported that same day to the Foreign Office, 'air reprisals', assistance 'from the air' to those Poles who were resisting deportation, and 'representation to the Soviet authorities with a view to such assistance from the Russian side'. This request of December 25 was supplemented five days later by a telegram sent direct to Churchill from the head of the Polish Government-in-Exile, General Sikorski, who was then in Mexico City.

On December 31 the Polish appeal was discussed at a meeting of the British Chiefs of Staff Committee. During the meeting Churchill himself asked the Chief of the Air Staff, Sir Charles Portal, to consider 'the bombing of certain targets in Poland' as a reprisal, as the Polish Government-in-Exile had asked. Churchill also suggested that it might be more effective, and technically easier, to attack instead an important city in Germany, such as Berlin, and that if there were to be a routine bombing raid on Berlin in the near future, 'leaflets should be dropped during the raid telling the Germans that air attacks were reprisals for the persecution of the Poles and the Jews'.

Replying to Churchill's suggestions on 2 January 1943, Portal opposed any specific reprisal action, as a matter of principle. 'We have, I think, always insisted,' he wrote, 'that air attacks are ordinary operations of war against military (including of course industrial) targets, and intended to destroy the enemy's war output. We have thus deprecated the carrying out of air attacks as reprisals.' Such reprisal attacks, Portal added, 'would be an explicit admission that we were bombing civilians as such and might well invite brutal vengeance on our air crews'.

Sir Charles Portal had a further reason for rejecting the Polish request. It was, he wrote, 'more strictly a political warfare matter and relates to the

---

[1] This memorandum, and the other documents cited here concerning the Polish request for reprisals and the British response, are in Premier papers, 3/351/4.

Jews'. The point was, as Portal explained it, that Hitler 'has so often stressed that this is a war by the Jews to exterminate Germany that it might well be, therefore, that a raid, avowedly conducted on account of the Jews, would be an asset to enemy propaganda'.[1]

On January 6 Portal set out his reasons for rejecting both the bombing of a target in German-occupied Poland, or for 'devastating a German city', or for labelling any raid a 'reprisal one'. As for a target inside Poland, from a military point of view, Portal wrote, it would be 'very unprofitable to divert our best bombers to Polish targets and to keep them waiting for long periods for the moonlight and good weather without which they could not locate such distant objectives'. In addition, 'the small scale of attack' which Britain could produce at such a distance 'would not be impressive as a reprisal'. It would be more effective, Portal wrote, after a successful air-raid over Germany, to emphasise 'to the world' the part played in such a raid by the Polish Air Force.

The objections to leaflets about reprisals, Portal added, were 'rather formidable', and he went on to argue that once a raid were to be labelled as a reprisal, 'even on Berlin', Britain would automatically abandon its position 'that air attacks on cities are attacks on military objectives (including industry) and therefore "lawful" and justifiable'. In addition, if Britain were to claim that the reprisal raid had been 'an especially violent or effective one', would there not then be two comments to be faced, 'Why not always do the same?' and 'You are competing in brutality with the Germans'?

In opposing reprisals, Portal also warned Churchill that if this particular reprisal were carried out, the Royal Air Force would be 'overwhelmed with requests from all the other Allies that we should also redress their grievances in the same way'. This, he said, would result 'in nothing but a series of "token" reprisals which would not only be completely ineffective as deterrents but would also destroy the last shreds of the cloak of legality which at present covers our operations'.

There was yet another argument against reprisals. They would, Portal warned, 'make it much easier for the Germans to institute reprisals against our captured air crews'.

Portal's arguments were effective, and on January 10 Sikorski was informed by telegram that no reprisal raids over Poland were possible. In addition to the military reasons already set out by Portal, a further reason was added; that the United States Air Force 'is not at present equipped with aircraft which could successfully bomb any place in Poland'.[2]

Following the arrival of the eye-witnesses in Palestine, the Jewish Agency intensified the search for avenues of rescue. On December 18 the Jewish Agency Executive in Jerusalem telegraphed to the senior member of the Executive then in London, Moshe Shertok, instructing him to consult the British authorities on three possible measures. The first was to approach national Governments, 'including Argentine', in the hope that they would make 'direct representations' to the German Government, urging the Germans

---

[1] Air Ministry papers, 8/433.
[2] Foreign Office to Washington, telegram No. 234, in Premier papers, 3/351/4.

to 'discontinue annihilation Jews'.

The second suggestion was to ask the Swiss Government to persuade the International Red Cross 'actively' to help 'get children out'. The third suggestion was radio broadcasts to 'warn' the satellite countries 'by respective names'.[1]

On the following day, December 19, another appeal for help was sent direct to Churchill by Szmul Zygielbojm, one of the two Jewish members of the Polish National Council in exile. In his telegram, Zygielbojm quoted what he called 'a last appeal of despair' from the Warsaw ghetto, an appeal which he had received more than three months before, on August 31. 'No longer thousands, or tens of thousands,' the appeal read, 'but this time hundreds of thousands are perishing. The whole population is being exterminated, children, women and men. Out of three and a half million only one million and a quarter are still alive, while the slaughter goes on.'

Zygielbojm added that the Jewish community of Poland 'begs you to find means to save those few Polish Jews who still may have survived'.[2] But of how they could be saved, he made no mention. Four days later, on December 23, a deputation from the Board of Deputies of British Jews called on Anthony Eden at the Foreign Office. Its request was a specific one, that the British do their 'utmost' to provide for the reception of such Jews as were able to escape from enemy-occupied territory, either through Bulgaria or through Portugal. In reporting this request to the War Cabinet later that same day, Anthony Eden told his colleagues that he had referred in reply 'to the grave practical difficulties' of arranging for the reception of such refugees, and had 'entered into no commitment'.

This reply had been a grave disappointment to the Board of Deputies. But to his War Cabinet colleagues Eden had gone on to say that he thought the British Government 'should consider very carefully whether there was anything we could do to assist these people'.[3]

Following Eden's request, a special committee was set up, composed entirely of members of the War Cabinet, to examine the question of where the refugees could be sent. Known as the Committee on the Reception and Accommodation of Jewish Refugees, its four members were Eden himself, Clement Attlee, Herbert Morrison and Oliver Stanley.

These four Ministers held the first meeting of their Committee on 31 December 1942. At the start of the meeting the head of the Refugee Department at the Foreign Office, A. W. G. Randall, explained that there were more than ten thousand refugees already in Spain, of whom about half were Jews, and that new refugees were arriving in Spain at the rate of about fifty a day. Although it was proving 'extremely costly' for the Allies to maintain these refugees in Spain, the American Government had turned down, on military grounds, a proposal that they should be evacuated to North Africa.

Herbert Morrison wanted to press the Americans to agree to a civilian administered 'reception' camp in North Africa 'in which the refugees could

[1] Central Zionist Archives, S 25/1681.

[2] Premier papers, 4/51/8.

[3] War Cabinet, 172nd Conclusions of 1942. Copy in Premier papers, 4/51/8.

be sorted out'. He added, as the official minutes recorded, 'that he deprecated the tendency to regard the United Kingdom as the sole repository for refugees'.

Various possible destinations were then discussed. As for Dutch Guiana, the Committee were told, the Dutch had already shipped 'a small number of Dutch Jews' there, and 'would definitely refuse Jews of enemy origin'. Oliver Stanley felt that Palestine should be reserved for Jews from eastern Europe, who were 'in much greater danger' than those in Spain; but in any case adult males 'could not be accepted on security grounds'. There could be 'no question', he said, of Palestine accepting Jews from either Spain or North Africa.[1]

Randall told the Committee that the War Office was being consulted about the possibility of sending Jews to Madagascar. Oliver Stanley ruled out Trans-Jordan 'in view of the political and safety problems involved'. As for Britain, Herbert Morrison was again emphatic. The Home Office, he said, 'would not refuse to take a limited number of refugees, say from 1,000 to 2,000, but certainly not more' and only on the condition 'that they were sent to the Isle of Man and stayed there as long as he thought it necessary'. Morrison added:

He could not, however, agree that the door should be opened to the entry of uncategorised Jews. It should be borne in mind that there were already about 100,000 refugees, mainly Jews, in this country, and that the accommodation problem was already most difficult and would become critical in the event of renewed air attacks.

There was, Morrison added, 'considerable anti-Semitism under the surface in this country. If there were any substantial increase in the number of Jewish refugees or if these refugees did not leave this country after the war, we should be in serious trouble'.[2]

The Committee held its second meeting on 7 January 1943, having in the meanwhile dropped the word 'Jewish' from its title. During the meeting, Clement Attlee told his colleagues that Canada had taken in five hundred Jewish refugee children in 1942 'and did not wish to take any more', while Australia and New Zealand were 'too far away to justify the provision of shipping' to convey refugees there. As for the presence of Jewish refugees in Eire, this 'might be undesirable from the security point of view'.

There were problems, the Committee was told, as to how 'the Parliamentary aspect of the problem should be dealt with', particularly as Morrison 'might be pressed' to allow the refugees already in Spain to enter Britain.

The Colonial Secretary, Oliver Stanley, also spoke, telling his colleagues:

There was reason to believe that it was the policy of certain Axis countries, notably Rumania, to extrude Jews from their territories, as an alternative to the policy of extermination. This made it all the more necessary that the policy of His Majesty's Government to accept into Palestine only the limited number of Jewish children with a small number of accompanying women from Eastern Europe should be firmly adhered to.[3]

As a result of the Committee's discussions on January 7, a telegram was sent

---

[1] At this point in time, there were still available more than 30,000 ordinary Palestine certificates under the White Paper, and a further 3,000 emergency certificates. See page 133, note 2.

[2] War Cabinet Committee on the Reception and Accommodation of Jewish Refugees, 1st meeting, 31 December 1942, Cabinet papers, 95/15.

[3] War Cabinet Committee on the Reception and Accommodation of Refugees, 2nd meeting, 7 January 1943, Cabinet papers, 95/15.

on the following day to the British Ambassador in Washington, Lord Halifax, telling him that a joint Anglo-American effort was now needed to deal with the refugee problem. The refugee problem, Halifax was told, 'is not wholly Jewish', and there was so much 'acute suffering' among non-Jews in Allied countries 'that Allied criticism would probably result if any marked preference were shown in removing Jews from territories in or threatened by enemy occupation'. In addition, the telegram stated, there was 'the distinct danger of stimulating anti-Semitism in areas where an excessive number of foreign Jews are introduced'.

It was also explained to Lord Halifax that the possibility of the Germans changing over 'from the policy of extermination to one of extrusion' would be aimed, as it had been 'before the war', at what was described as 'embarrassing other countries by flooding them with alien immigrants'.[1]

On January 9 the *New Statesman and Nation*, in an article headed 'Our Part in Massacre', appealed to the British Government for a change in policy. The article was unsigned.[2] It began by discussing the difficulties which people found, 'even now', in realizing that Hitler 'is engaged in exterminating the Jews of Europe, not metaphorically, not more or less, but with a literal, totalitarian completeness, as farmers try to exterminate Californian beetles'. The article continued:

We were slow to believe it ourselves. We passed over the earlier stories of wholesale massacre in Kiev and Odessa in silence: we feared that something ugly had happened but this butchery in batches of several thousands seemed incredible.[3]

It was clear, the *New Statesman* added, that Hitler was 'clearing the whole Jewish population' from Vienna, and that most of the German towns 'were now "clean" of Jews'. 'We did not doubt,' the article explained, 'that in the process they would be robbed, and that hunger, cold, disease and ill-usage would kill off the infants, the aged and the infirm. But we supposed that some kind of slave-colony was being formed from the survivors, somewhere in Eastern Poland.'

Hitler's own speeches in February and November 1942 were proof, the *New Statesman* noted, that Hitler 'has actually done what his sadism would always have prompted him to do'. The plan was 'systematic', nor was any attempt being made to conceal it. The evidence produced by various Allied governments, all of it 'from non-Jewish sources', was 'irresistible'. Everything that had been done in Warsaw, Vilna, Lublin 'and a dozen other towns'

---

[1] Telegram of 8 January 1943, Cabinet papers, 95/15.

[2] On 7 December 1942, the day on which the eye-witness reports had reached the Jewish Agency in London, Blanche Dugdale had agreed to write an article for the *Spectator* and Professor Namier had suggested 'keeping in touch' with Kingsley Martin, the editor of the *New Statesman*. Central Zionist Archives, Z 4/14758.

[3] Lord Dacre (formerly, as Hugh Trevor-Roper, Regius Professor of History at Oxford, and during the war a member of British Intelligence working in Britain), has written 'I remember well the moment when I first saw the evidence – a fragment of the evidence – about the extermination of the Jews. It was explicit, factual, documented. But could it be believed? Between the reception of evidence and belief in its conclusion there is a great psychological gulf; and in wartime, when so much is uncertain – when hatred breeds passion and passion is exploited by propaganda – it is prudent to suspend judgment. I recall that I suspended my own judgment and only gradually, many months later, drew from that dreadful evidence the conclusion which it entailed' (*The Listener*, 1 January 1981).

pointed to 'a plan imposed from the High Command of the New Order'.

The 'continental massacre', reported the New Statesman, had begun in July 1942; it had 'wiped out' a million Jews by October; and it was 'presumably, still going on'. It would take 'some time yet' to kill all 'six million' of the Jewish population of pre-war Europe. The question now was: 'What is to be done?' And the answer, according to the New Statesman, was an international open door policy for Jewish refugees, and the 'right' of the remaining 40,000 under the 1939 White Paper to enter Palestine.[1]

Any refugees over the 40,000 would, under the New Statesman plan, be given 'temporary refuge' elsewhere. There was no question of any permanent settlement. 'Unless these Jews can, after victory,' the paper argued, 'go back to security in any land of the Continent, we shall have fought this war in vain.' The Dutch, the French, the Czechs would 'welcome the survivors back'. If the Rumanians would not do so, 'they must be taught their lesson'. As for the Germans, 'our belief is that Hitler's propaganda has infected only a minority'. There was, therefore, 'no permanent problem of resettlement', only a problem of keeping alive 'such Jews as we can help to escape, until the war is won'.

The New Statesman proposed, as an immediate step 'to get the doomed Jews out of the grip of the Nazis', that Britain should 'beg' the neutral Governments of Turkey, Sweden and Switzerland 'to speak to Berlin jointly in their own names' and to offer, with the help of the Red Cross, 'to collect the surviving Jews first of all on their own soil.' Britain would undertake to bear, or to share the cost of housing these refugees until the end of the war 'in, say, Cyprus, Palestine, North Africa, the Isle of Man and Canada'. Such a scheme would have a greater chance of success if the Pope 'would publicly associate himself with this intervention of the neutrals'.

The New Statesman article went on to urge that 'as no consular machinery survives in Europe' for Jews wishing for permits to go to Palestine within the remaining 40,000 vacant certificates, all formalities connected with acquiring such permits 'should be waived'. At the same time, what it called 'the scandal' of Britain's own immigration restrictions should be removed. The article ended: 'When historians relate this story of extermination, they will find it from first to last all but incredible. For Hitler there is the excuse of madness. But this nation is sane.'[2]

Ten days later, on January 19, William Cluse, the Labour Member of Parliament who had suggested the two minute silence at the time of the Allied Declaration of December 17, asked in the House of Commons for a relaxation of the Government's policy towards Jewish refugees. His specific request was that the Government 'ease the immigration arrangements' for Palestine, so that what he called 'a large number' of Jews could enter. But in reply Clement Attlee told the House of Commons that there could be no such relaxation of the rules, and he added, by way of explanation, that 'efforts to save the Jews cannot be simply British efforts', and that 'the only real remedy for the consistent Nazi policy of racial and religious persecution lies in an Allied victory',

[1] In fact, 33,000 certificates were still available, see page 133, note 2.
[2] New Statesman, 9 January 1943.

to which every Allied resource 'must be bent'.[1]

Attlee said nothing to the House of Commons about Canada, having taken in five hundred refugees in 1942, being unwilling to take in more. Nor did he refer to Oliver Stanley's argument that the prospect that some Axis countries might 'extrude' their Jews instead of killing them 'made it all the more necessary', as Stanley had phrased it, to accept into Palestine only a 'limited number' of Jewish children.

The War Cabinet Committee on refugees held its third meeting on January 27, and discussed what should be said to an All Party Deputation which was to be received on the following day, and which would press for an 'open door' policy towards refugees. The Committee members were clear as to what their attitude should be. As the official and secret minutes recorded: 'It was essential to kill the idea that mass immigration to this country and the British Colonies was possible'. Nor should any figures be given about the numbers of Jewish children 'whom we might hope to bring into Palestine' from the Balkans. Instead, 'emphasis should be laid on the complicated negotiations involved . . .', particularly in regard to the transport of the children to Palestine, and their 'maintenance in that country'.

As for the possibility of exchanging Jews under Nazi rule for Germans interned in the Isle of Man, this, the Committee felt, should be answered on the lines that such a proposal was 'undesirable on security grounds', and that 'in any case, measures for exchange of British subjects in Germany should come first'.[2]

While the makers of British policy thus seemed to bar any efforts at large scale rescue, the Jewish Agency tried to continue those small and individual attempts at rescue and aid that were open to them. Knowing nothing of the deliberations of the War Cabinet's Committee on refugees, the Agency's representatives in Geneva, Istanbul, London and Jerusalem continued to press for Palestine certificates, travel documents and visas for as many Jews as would still be allowed to leave Europe.

The first success of the Agency's policy was the departure from Hungary of fifty Jewish children on January 5. Their departure had been held up for six weeks, when at the last moment, the German Government had used its growing authority in the Balkans to refuse to allow the children to embark on a boat for Istanbul at the Danube port of Ruschuk, and new arrangements had had to be made with the Bulgarian Government to allow them to reach Turkey by train through Bulgaria. Once they began their journey, only six days separated danger from safety: for on January 11 the Jewish Agency in Istanbul was able to telegraph to the Palestine Office in Geneva: '46 first group 50 children Budapest arrived',[3] and eight days later these forty-six children reached Palestine by train through Turkey and Syria, their Syrian transit having been secured by a British Government guarantee. On arrival in Palestine the forty-six children were admitted within the remaining 32,000 White Paper certificates. 'We must derive what comfort we can from these

[1] Hansard, 19 January 1943.

[2] War Cabinet Committee on the Reception and Accommodation of Refugees, 3rd meeting, 27 January 1943, Cabinet papers, 95/15.

[3] Yad Vashem archive, P 12/29 (Pazner papers).

driblets of child immigration', wrote one Zionist magazine. 'They barely touch the fringe of our appalling problem; but every life saved is so much to the good.'[1]

The 856 'Teheran children' were likewise on their way to Palestine. But the earlier refusal of the Government of Iraq to allow any Jewish children at all to cross Iraq, even in transit, was followed on January 11, after the long sea route to Suez had been agreed upon, by the refusal of the Egyptian Government to grant the children transit visas from the Suez Canal to the borders of Palestine.[2] Once more, the Jewish Agency was obliged to devise new schemes, to seek yet again the help of busy Ministers and officials, and to send telegrams and messages through the long and difficult wartime censorship and telegraphic machinery. On learning of the Egyptian ban, the British authorities decided that the children, who were already at the Persian Gulf, would have to go to India instead of to Palestine, and to remain in India until the end of the war.

The Jewish Agency still hoped, however, to bring the children to Palestine, and suggested that the Government of Transjordan might allow the children to disembark at the Red Sea port of Akaba, thus avoiding Suez altogether. When this proved impossible, a third disembarkation point was suggested, Moses Wells, on the western coast of the Sinai desert, and thence by truck and train across Sinai to Palestine.

All these suggestions and negotiations took up time and energy. The Egyptian refusal to grant the children transit visas, like the earlier Iraqi refusal, led to exacerbation of feeling and a sense of unending struggle against limitless forces, for relatively small and simple goals. For the Jewish Agency, these were desperate times, the desperation of which was accentuated by the contrast in the effort needed to bring a few hundred to Palestine, and the simultaneous distant slaughter of so many hundreds of thousands.

In German–occupied Europe the policy of extermination proceeded without delay or hesitation. No problem of transit visas impeded the regular and relentless dispatch of deportation trains across former frontiers, or within the borders of Greater Germany. In January alone, more than 40,000 Jews had been taken by train from northeast of the General Government to Auschwitz, where almost all of them had been gassed, while at the same time, from the General Government itself, some 13,000 had been deported to Treblinka, where all had been murdered, and eight thousand from Lvov to Belzec, likewise to be killed immediately on reaching the death camp.

On January 25, a total of seventeen letters, forwarded under an International Red Cross scheme, reached Jerusalem. Some were from Poland, others from Holland, Belgium, Hungary and Rumania. All spoke, in the veiled language needed to pass the censor, of hunger, deportations and death. It was clear from these letters, as from the Palestinian eye-witnesses and the Polish reports of the previous November, that those deported had been, for the most part, murdered. Three days later, on January 28, the Foreign Office in London handed the Labour Member of Parliament, Sydney Silverman, a message which had been received for him, from Geneva, with further news of the deportations of

[1] *New Judaea*, January 1943.
[2] Central Zionist Archives, S 25/1,675.

the previous month. The message had been sent from Geneva eight days before, through the British Consul, having been compiled by Lichtheim and Riegner, on the basis of new information reaching them from Nazi Europe.

Not only had more Jews been deported from Berlin, this message read, but reports received in Geneva from both Berlin and Prague had stated 'that by the end of March no Jew will be left in either city'. In addition, according to reports which had been received in Geneva from Berlin, special Gestapo agents from Vienna, where the deportations were 'nearly completed', had been sent both to Berlin and to Holland 'to hasten the deportations' there.[1]

In this letter of January 20 there was also a report of the fate of those Jews whom the Rumanians had deported eastwards in the autumn of 1941, from Russian territory which had been occupied by Rumanian troops at the time of the German invasion of Russia. According to this further report, 'signed Fildermann', a total of 136,000 deportees were confined in ghettoes and labour camps east of the Dniester river. This report was one of the few to reach the west from a Jewish leader who was already a well-known figure in the Jewish world before the war.[2] 'Living conditions are indescribable,' Fildermann reported, 'prisoners being deprived of all their possessions and having no money to buy foodstuffs. Twenty or thirty people are housed in deserted cellars, sleeping in one unheated room on the floor.'

The result of such conditions was disease, 'especially spotted typhus'. Of the 136,000 deportees, Fildermann reported, 'about 60,000 are already dead, while 70,000 are starving'.

It seemed that nothing could be done to save the Jews deported across the Dniester, except perhaps large sums of money. In his report, Fildermann appealed for 'urgent help': funds, which the Jews remaining in Rumania could not raise.[3]

The Jewish Agency, the World Jewish Congress, and the smaller Jewish organizations of Palestine, Britain and the United States, were already in debt. The Teheran children, the Hungarian children, the tens of thousands of Jewish refugees in special refugee camps in Switzerland, the 'illegal' refugees deported by the British to Mauritius at the end of 1940, the destitute refugees who had managed to reach Palestine after the Cranborne concession of May 1942: all were heavy financial burdens, especially in wartime, when funds were hard to raise and almost impossible to transfer. Of course, every effort was made to meet this new financial appeal from Rumania: but the fact that Rumania was now 'enemy' territory meant that no funds could be transferred legally.

To try to help the few remaining Jews of Poland, two methods had been tried, with some small degree of success, throughout the summer and autumn of 1942, and were continued in the early months of 1943. The first was the dispatch of food parcels, from Sweden, Portugal and Switzerland. These parcels, which were delivered to the surviving Jewish communities by the Red Cross, contained small amounts of coffee, chocolate, sugar, sweets, and

---

[1] There is a copy of the Lichtheim-Riegner letter, as handed to the British Consul, in Central Zionist Archives, L 22/56.

[2] For a brief outline of Fildermann's career, see the biographical note on page 344.

[3] There is a copy of the Fildermann report, as received in London, in Central Zionist Archives, Z 4/14901.

tinned sardines, a vital supplement to the starvation rations of the ghetto.

The daily deportation continually reduced the number of addresses to which parcels could be sent. As the Co-Director of the Palestine Office in Geneva, Chaim Pozner, wrote to his colleagues in Istanbul on December 12: 'Unfortunately, it is indescribably difficult to ascertain the new addresses of our relations – the pre-condition for efforts at providing direct assistance'.[1]

The second area of help was also one of potential rescue: the smuggling into German-occupied Poland of passports, issued in Switzerland by diplomats of several Latin-American countries, including those of Salvador, Venezuela, Honduras and Paraguay. These passports were taken eastward by courier. If they reached those for whom they had been made out, they could sometimes act as a protection against deportation, and even as a means of emigration. But the cost of buying these passports was high and the risks formidable: not only for the recipient, but also for those who issued them, and whose Governments could, and often did, annul them.

Food parcels and passports were both small and, as had already become clear, belated efforts at help and rescue. 'It is a terrible pity', Chaim Pozner wrote to a Jewish Agency contact in Istanbul on 9 February 1943, 'that Palestine Jewry's readiness to render help has only assumed concrete form so late – far too late'.

In this same letter, Pozner reported on the return to Switzerland of several Swiss citizens who had recently visited Holland. 'Unfortunately', he wrote, 'what they had to tell us is worse by far than everything we have heard up to now.' 'At all events,' Pozner added, 'what matters now is to save what is still to be saved. So everything has to be tried, even if the real possibilities are very slight.'[2]

The possibilities of rescue by the Jewish Agency were tragically small, compared with the pace of destruction. At Auschwitz, still a secret, expansion continued, and following the establishment of Crematorium No. 2 at Birkenau, the SS had ordered the construction of a third gas chamber and crematorium there, according to the same design, and with the ability to 'dispose' of two thousand bodies every twelve hours.[3]

---

[1] Central Zionist Archives, S 6/4683.

[2] Central Zionist Archives, L 15/191.

[3] On 29 January 1943 the SS construction unit had reported that Crematorium II was completed except for a few 'minor construction details' (Nuremberg documents NO 4473). The final completion date was 20 February 1943.

Chapter 13

Rescue and massacre

On 3 February 1943 the British Government was confronted by a serious challenge to its refugee policy when nine Members of Parliament, of all political parties, pressed Anthony Eden and Oliver Stanley to relax the existing restrictions. A Labour MP, Arthur Greenwood, asked about the possibility of allowing into Palestine 'Jewish refugees from enemy and enemy-occupied countries', and another Labour MP, Reginald Sorenson, asked if arrangements could be made 'for any number of Jews temporarily to reside in Palestine'. But Stanley answered: 'No, Sir,' and he added that it was 'essential, from the point of view of stability in the Middle East at the present time', that the numerical limits laid down in the 1939 White Paper 'should be strictly adhered to'.

A Liberal MP, Sir Richard Acland, asked the Government: 'Do not the claims of humanity come before your quota restrictions?' and he added: 'Why not take all you can get under all conditions?' But Stanley answered bluntly: 'Winning the war is the most important of all.'

During the course of these questions, Oliver Stanley announced that arrangements had provisionally been made to admit 270 Jewish children from Rumania and Hungary, 'and some of them are now in transit to Palestine'. In addition, it had 'now been decided' to admit further children from Rumania and Hungary 'up to a total of 500', while 'some weeks ago' the Government of Palestine had agreed to admit, from Bulgaria, four thousand Jewish children with five hundred adults to accompany them on their journey.[1]

On the day after Stanley's announcement, the British Passport Control Officer in Istanbul, A. W. Whittall, informed the Jewish Agency representative, Chaim Barlas, that Barlas had been appointed 'as delegate of the Jewish Agency for Palestine for the selection and transport of these immigrants', and that all the children and adults whom Barlas selected within this scheme would be issued with the necessary visas for Palestine 'on their arrival in Turkey'.[2]

This decision was welcome to the Jewish Agency, which at once sought means of locating and transporting the children out of Europe, itself a slow and formidable task. Only seventy-two children were able to be brought out in March, twenty in May and forty-nine in June.

One idea which arose after the Palestinian exchange of November 1942 was to extend the exchange lists to include Jews who were not Palestinian subjects. This idea came from Lieutenant-Colonel Stanley Cole, a former

[1] Hansard, 3 February 1943.
[2] Central Zionist Archives, L 22/168.

regular Army officer employed at the Colonial Office in charge of prisoners-of-war and civilian internees. Joseph Linton later recalled lunching with Cole, who said to him:

We are running out of the Germans we've got for exchange. But the Germans don't know how many Germans we've got. Why don't you send me more lists of Jews. The Germans won't be able to exchange them because there will be so many. But they may set them aside. It may just save their lives.

Henceforth, the Jewish Agency representatives in London, Jerusalem, Istanbul and Geneva were to compile larger and larger lists, and to send them into Holland, France, Belgium and even Poland. 'It was Cole's idea', Linton stressed. 'He thought it up, and he encouraged me'.[1]

One problem which troubled the Jewish Agency leaders in Jerusalem was what they regarded as the lack of effort in refugee and protest matters on the part of the leaders of United States Jewry. On February 11 Bernard Joseph telegraphed from Jerusalem to Nahum Goldmann in New York: 'Amazed apparent failure appreciate extreme urgency make every effort save Jews while we can'. Joseph added: 'Apprehend by end March few remaining avenues escape may be closed. Moreover latest reports state have begun expelling, liquidating ghetto communities',[2] that is to say, those few ghettoes that had been kept in existence after the massive deportations of the summer and autumn of 1942.

Unknown in either Jerusalem or New York, on February 11, the day of Bernard Joseph's telegram, yet another sealed train had left Paris for Auschwitz. Among those on board were several hundred children, all of whom were gassed as soon as the train reached its distant destination. What could be done to help those Jews who were not yet under direct Nazi control? On February 12 an independent member of Parliament, Eleanor Rathbone, had circulated a private note about 'many thousands of Jews in Bulgaria, Hungary and Roumania under threat of massacre, whom those Governments would probably be equally ready to let go to any neutral State willing to receive them'. Miss Rathbone then set out five suggestions to make a larger exodus possible: persuading the Turkish Government to arrange 'some large refugee camp, pending evacuation'; evacuating Jews who had escaped from France into Spain and Portugal to some refugee camp 'possibly at Casablanca', or elsewhere in North Africa, or Cyprus; 'inducing' Allied or neutral States to offer at least 'temporary asylum' by promising to give those States 'relief from their burden' in feeding and clothing the refugees; and influencing as many States as possible 'to greater generosity, and not only for children, since few children can escape secretly over frontiers'.

In her note, Miss Rathbone suggested several possible temporary places of refuge: Sweden, Switzerland, Spain, Turkey, the United States, Argentina, Brazil, Eire 'especially for children: de Valera is said to be very humane', and even, as far as Britain was concerned, the Isle of Man.

The key to rescue, Miss Rathbone argued, was to organize it in a far more

---

[1] Conversation with Joseph Linton, London, 1 July 1980.
[2] Central Zionist Archives, S 25/1670.

vigorous way than at present. A problem affecting the lives 'of possibly several millions', she wrote, and 'at least hundreds of thousands', deserved 'something better than the amount and quality of the attention it is now receiving from Governments'. Ministers concerned with the heavy responsibilities of the war effort could only give 'small and spasmodic attention' to refugees and refuge. Her hope was for 'a man of first-class standing' to be put in charge of these rescue efforts, with a world wide authority; a man with 'energy, initiative, foresight, tenacity and sagacity'.

Eleanor Rathbone had one more immediate suggestion, a 'public declaration' over the BBC and other Allied broadcasting networks stating that the United Nations 'will find asylum for those able to leave enemy or enemy-occupied territory'. This could, in her view, obtain 'the same object' as a direct 'offer to Hitler', to which the Allied States were unlikely to agree. The offer of asylum, as she saw it, might influence both Hitler, and the rulers of countries still not directly under German rule. Her reasons were as follows: it was unlikely that Hitler 'has leisure at present for much attention to the Jewish problem', while at the same time power inside Germany 'may be passing into the hands of less sadistic Nazis'. These men, she continued: '. . . may be beginning to fear the consequences of further outraging world opinion'.

Eleanor Rathbone felt that the 'satellite countries especially', realizing the probability of the defeat of the Axis, 'have increasing motives for desiring to placate the United Nations by showing generosity in this relatively minor matter'. Even Pierre Laval, Prime Minister of Vichy France, may have become unwilling, she wrote, 'to outrage further Allied and humane French opinion'. Could not a way be found, Miss Rathbone asked, whereby 'all these motives' could be worked on, either through broadcasts from the BBC and the United States, or 'by negotiations' through the Protecting Powers or the International Red Cross.[1]

Following Miss Rathbone's criticisms, on February 18 the Foreign Office prepared a note on the refugee situation for members of the War Cabinet's refugee Committee. Negotiations were continuing, the note explained, on behalf of the four thousand Jewish children and five hundred adult Jews from Bulgaria, whose admission to Palestine had been announced in the House of Commons two weeks before. But 'in the present condition of the Turkish railways' the transport difficulties were likely to prove formidable, while the Turks themselves 'show no enthusiasm over the passage of Jews through their territory.' Nor had the United States Government yet replied to a Foreign Office request of January 12 about helping in the destination and shipping of refugees in Spain. It may be deduced, the Foreign Office concluded, 'that there is a striking difference between the intensive propaganda campaign regarding Hitler's victims carried out here, and the apparently negligible publicity in the US'.[2]

When the War Cabinet's refugee Committee met on February 19, Eden spoke of how the 'Parliamentary situation' might, as he put it 'become

[1] Eleanor Rathbone, 'The Nazi Massacres of Jews and Poles: What Rescue Measures Are Practically Possible?' Copy in Central Zionist Archives, Z 4/14758.

[2] Note by the Foreign Office, 18 February 1943, Cabinet papers, 95/15.

difficult'. Herbert Morrison agreed: 'we must expect,' he said, that 'the pressure upon the Government to undertake relief measures would increase.' Of course, Morrison added, 'it would not be impossible for him to admit between 1,000 and 2,000 refugees into the UK, but he was not in favour of this course.' Nor were the refugees in Spain 'in any real danger'.

The Committee then discussed one possible Parliamentary demand, that the British Government should approach the German Government with a view 'to obtaining permission' for certain categories of refugees to be allowed into neutral countries. But the Committee was emphatic and, as its secret minutes recorded, 'repudiated any question of trying to do business with Hitler'.

The Norwegian Government, the Committee were told, had suggested to the Foreign Office that five hundred Norwegian Jews, 'who were about to be deported to Germany', should be exchanged for the same number of German prisoners-of-war in Britain who were 'unfit for military duties'. But, as the minutes again recorded, the Committee considered 'that this proposal should not be entertained'.[1]

The Parliamentary questions, of which Eden warned his refugee Committee colleagues on February 19, came six days later. The first questioner was a Conservative, Sir Percy Hurd, who had been a Member of Parliament for more than twenty-five years. Was Eden aware, he asked, 'of the growing public uneasiness caused by the comparative inaction of the United Nations in succouring the tortured Jewish people of Europe?' Hurd wanted Eden to suggest 'the appointment of someone of international experience' to focus his attentions on the difficulties, 'and effect a remedy'.

Another Conservative MP, Dr Little, a Presbyterian minister from Northern Ireland, wanted Eden both to 'explore further resources of help for the Jews', and to seek the assistance of neutral countries 'in a united effort to prevent Hitler from exterminating the Jewish race in Axis and subjugated countries'. A Labour MP, William Brown, wanted Eden to 'initiate representation by the United Nations to the German Government to permit Jews to leave the occupied countries of Europe', as well as to 'offer protection' to Jews who were liberated, or who escaped from occupied territory. Brown also wanted the Government to make available 'the fullest possible facilities' for the immigration of Jewish refugees to Palestine.

Eden's reply disappointed the questioners. 'The only truly effective means of succouring the tortured Jewish, and I may add, the other suffering peoples of Europe,' he said, 'lies in an Allied victory.' In devoting their energies towards this victory, the Government was therefore 'seeking to bring relief to all the oppressed'.

Following Eden's answer, the Labour MP, Sydney Silverman, who was himself a Jew, pointed out that while he realized there was 'no great hope' until an Allied victory had been won, ten weeks had nevertheless passed since the Allied Declaration, 'and that many of us are afraid that by the time the Allied nations have concerted their plans there will be nobody left to save'.[2]

---

[1] War Cabinet Committee on the Reception and Accommodation of Refugees, 4th meeting, 19 February 1943, Cabinet papers, 65/15.

[2] Hansard, 25 February 1943.

In Palestine itself, the arrival of the first group of 'Teheran' children, 858 in all, on February 18, had stimulated feelings both of joy and grief. There was joy at so many young lives saved, after more than three years of suffering and wandering. But there was grief at the realization that the eight hundred children who had arrived, and the four hundred who were still to follow, represented hundreds of thousands who had already perished.

Seeking also to follow up the small but successful exchange scheme of November 1942, the Jewish Agency had persuaded the British to continue negotiations with the Germans through the Swiss Government, and had prepared a much longer list, of 802 Jews, all of whom were holders of Palestinian passports, and were known to have been seized by the Germans on the outbreak of war, or after the German conquest of Poland. On March 8 one of the Jewish Agency representatives in Geneva, Dr Kahany, was able to report to his superior in Istanbul that the Germans 'are ready to let out the 802 – provided that they can all be found – and ask in exchange a certain number of people formerly in the Near East, in whom *they* are interested'.

The Germans even offered, so Kahany was able to report, 'a fair proportion, i.e. 100 of ours against 80 or even 60 of theirs'.[1] That same day, in a second letter sent from Geneva, Richard Lichtheim was able to report to the Jewish Agency Executive in Jerusalem that he had already heard of a few cases in Holland where Jews with Palestinian passports 'had been officially informed that they are on such an exchange list'. It seemed, therefore, that the mere act of sending the lists to Germany 'might help the people concerned, at least', as Lichtheim wrote, 'in this sense, that for the time being they will not be deported'.[2]

On March 16, in a further letter to the Jewish Agency office in Istanbul, Dr Kahany explained that one problem that had just arisen was that some of the people asked for by the Germans in order to carry out the exchange were no longer in the Middle East, but in Australia. And three days later Richard Lichtheim explained to the Jewish Agency leaders in Jerusalem the even greater difficulties involved in fulfilling the Agency's wider hope of including in the exchange lists not only 'women and children of Palestinians or Palestinian residents', but also veteran and distinguished Zionists and their families who were in fact Dutch or German nationals. 'Unfortunately,' Lichtheim wrote, 'the system has been worked out too late. For instance I do not know of anybody of our people in Berlin who could be included, because they are no longer there and their addresses are unknown, provided they still have an address.'[3]

On March 15, in another letter to Jerusalem, Lichtheim passed on details of reports which had just reached Geneva from Berlin, 'showing that the last remnants of the Jewish community have now disappeared'. In a 'sudden round-up', all those Jews who were still working in various industries throughout Germany had been 'arrested and taken away'. Their number was estimated at 15,000, 'the rest of what was once the German–Jewish community'. Between one and two hundred had been 'shot on the spot' during the round-up.

[1] Central Zionist Archives, L 22/146.
[2] Central Zionist Archives, L 22/146, Letter No. 1005.
[3] Central Zionist Archives, L 22/146.

The rest had been deported 'in the usual way', and, Lichtheim added, 'there is not much hope we shall ever hear of them again.'[1]

In his letter of March 15, Lichtheim also passed on information which had reached Geneva from Holland. Between eighty and ninety thousand Dutch Jews, he wrote, 'have now been deported'. Those who had been sent to 'certain labour camps, especially in Upper-Silesia', had been allowed to write to the Jewish community council in Holland, 'and to give their address'. But those who had written, Lichtheim pointed out, 'number only a few hundred, and this shows what has become of the large majority'.[2]

None of the reports of early 1943 mentioned Auschwitz. Yet it was to Auschwitz that the majority of the Dutch deportees, as well as continuing deportees from France and Belgium, had been sent, and it was at Auschwitz that they had been gassed. Unknown to Lichtheim, of the so-called 'labour camps' which he mentioned, the one in 'Upper-Silesia' was in fact Auschwitz itself and several hundred letters and postcards had indeed been received in Amsterdam with 'Auschwitz' as the address of the deportees. By allowing some of the Dutch Jews who were in the labour camp section of Auschwitz to send these formal cards to the Jewish Council, the Gestapo skilfully maintained the deception that Auschwitz was simply another labour camp. In this way, its true function remained hidden. Indeed, on 22 January 1943, the Jewish Council in Amsterdam had discussed the fact that despite the hundreds of cards, 'no message or other news had been received from women with children, or from the aged'. Yet although this was a disturbing fact, the Council's main conclusion was, not that women with children, and old people, were being murdered, but that the Germans had broken their promise, made on the eve of the deportations, that once deported, families would be kept together; and it was the separation of the families, rather than the possibility of their extermination, that seemed to be the only plausible explanation of the lack of letters.[3] It was not the leaders of Dutch Jewry, but the Jewish Agency and World Jewish Congress representatives in Geneva, who drew an accurate conclusion. But there was an unbridgable gulf between the accurate conclusion that the Jewish deportees were being murdered, and the lack of knowledge of where that killing was taking place.

By March 1943 the destruction of Polish Jewry was almost complete. More than 700,000 Jews from the Galician provinces of pre-war Poland had been murdered at Belzec, and the camp itself had been closed. The Jewish communities in the regions around Chelmno and Sobibor had likewise been destroyed. At Treblinka, more than 300,000 Jews from Warsaw had been murdered between July and September 1942, leaving only 70,000 in the ghetto, starving, sick and isolated. At Majdanek, Jews from both Poland and western Europe were being assembled and gassed.

[1] This was the 'factory action' of 27 February 1943, when 7,000 Jews were deported from Berlin, and at least 3,000 more from Hamburg, the Ruhr and Munich to the death camps in the east. It had been preceded by three separate deportations from Berlin to Auschwitz on February 3 (952 deportees), February 19 (1,000 deportees) and February 26 (913 deportees).

[2] Central Zionist Archives, L 22/146. Letter No. 1006, via Istanbul.

[3] From 11 July to 23 February 1943, nine trains were sent from Holland to Auschwitz (with a total of 7,877 deportees). From 2 March to 20 July 1943, all Dutch Jews were sent to Sobibor (19 trains, more than 32,000 deportees), and thereafter, from August 1943 to September 1944 mostly again to Auschwitz (16 trains, more than 12,000 deportees): see also pages 145–6.

But it was still Auschwitz, its activities a secret in the west, where the systematic deportations and gassings continued on the largest scale, with medical experiments and sadism unabated. In the first week of March alone, more than five thousand deportees were gassed on arrival, among them Jews from Paris and Berlin, and before the end of March a further five thousand had been gassed, many of them Greek Jews, who had been brought to Auschwitz from Salonica, a railway journey of nearly a thousand kilometres.[1]

Although all these deportations were secret, rumours of one area of deportation had reached the west on March 16, when Richard Lichtheim telegraphed from Geneva to Joseph Linton in London: 'Understand number Jews probably younger generation Bulgaria now also menaced by deportation Poland'. Lichtheim added: 'Suggest you contact New York, consider appropriate measures, warnings'.[2]

It was not in fact from Bulgaria itself, but from Bulgarian-occupied Macedonia, seized in 1941 from Yugoslavia, and from Thrace, seized in 1941 from Greece, that the deportations had begun, in the first week of March. Nor was it only the 'younger generation' but whole communities; in all 7,122 Macedonian Jews and 4,221 Thracian Jews. Within a week, all had been deported to Treblinka, where they were gassed as soon as they arrived at the death camp. By the time that Lichtheim's telegram had reached London, the fate of these 11,000 was sealed.

The first news of the Macedonian and Thracian deportations was published in Switzerland on March 23, by the Swiss Telegraphic Agency. This stated accurately that 'about 12,000' Jews of Thrace and Macedonia were being deported to the Reich. But it went on, inaccurately, to say that the deportees 'will be employed in agriculture'.[3]

In Bulgaria itself, the King and Parliament opposed the deportation of Bulgarian-born Jews. On learning that pressure for their deportation was mounting, Chaim Barlas, the Jewish Agency representative in Istanbul, decided to appeal to Angelo Roncalli, the Papal Delegate in Turkey, to use his influence. Barlas knew that Roncalli had served in Bulgaria before being posted to Turkey, and that he was godfather to the King's son. 'I came to Roncalli', Barlas later recalled, 'and he immediately wrote a cable to the King, asking him to save Jews'.[4]

In a visit to Berlin in the first week of April the King himself argued that he needed the Jews for 'road construction', and could not therefore spare them for deportation. Ribbentrop, the German Foreign Minister, told the King that Germany would prefer him to agree to a more 'radical solution'. But the King was not to be deflected from his own, and his Government's decision. Bulgaria, although allied to Germany, was not occupied. Nor, despite a year of pressure, were the Germans able to persuade the Bulgarians to change their minds. As a result, more than 48,000 Bulgarian Jews survived the war.[5]

[1] Danuta Czech, 'Kalendarium der Ereignisse im Konzentrationslager Auschwitz-Birkenau', published in *Hefte von Auschwitz*, volume 4, Auschwitz 1961.

[2] Central Zionist Archives, L 22/146.

[3] *Agence Télégraphique Suisse*, 23 March 1943.

[4] Chaim Barlas, conversation with the author, Jerusalem, 15 April 1980.

[5] For an account of the saving of Bulgarian Jewry, see Frederick B. Chary, *The Bulgarian Jews and the Final Solution, 1940–1944*, Pittsburgh, 1972.

Not only the Jews of Bulgaria, but also the 120,000 Jews then in Italy seemed likely to be protected by those allies of Germany unwilling to bow to German demands for deportation. On March 29 Lichtheim informed the Jewish Agency leaders in Jerusalem that the Germans were reported to have asked the Italian Government to hand over all Jewish refugees in Italy for 'general mobilization of manpower'. For the Jews, Lichtheim commented, such mobilization 'means slave-labour for a minority of younger men and women, and death for the others'. But the Italians, he wrote, had apparently 'flatly rejected this demand'.[1]

In Geneva, the Secretariat of the World Jewish Congress and the World Council of Churches had issued a joint appeal to the Allies on March 18, urging them to encourage the neutral states to grant 'temporary asylum' to Jewish refugees. In order to make this arrangement effective, the neutral states should be given 'definite guarantees' by Britain and America that the refugees would be repatriated or re-emigrated 'as soon as possible after the war'. Such rescue action was particularly urgent, the appeal pointed out, as 'reliable reports' had reached Geneva 'that the campaign of deliberate extermination of the Jews organized by the Nazi officials in nearly all countries of Europe under their control, is now at its climax'.[2]

The Jewish Agency representatives in Geneva were likewise seeking means of help and rescue, their principal effort being the compilation of exchange lists, and the sending of certificates to the internment camps at Westerbork in Holland and Drancy in the suburbs of Paris, and to the few remaining Polish ghettoes in southwest Poland. On March 25 Lichtheim wrote from Geneva to Yitzhak Gruenbaum in Jerusalem that, according to information received in Switzerland from the Bedzin ghetto, in southwest Poland, 'photocopies of certificates even if not certified by any authority would help protect people'. Lichtheim added: 'suggest issuing certificates there, sending photocopies here soonest possible . . .',[3] and almost every day names obtained from inside Nazi Europe were telegraphed from Geneva to Jerusalem, and then the serial number of the Palestine certificate was telegraphed back to Geneva, for dispatch into Nazi Europe.

So the search for addresses continued. During 1941, several hundred Jews were able to smuggle out their names and addresses from Poland, for inclusion on such lists. And when, in German-occupied Poland, the Gestapo were presented with the actual South American passport holders, they not only held many of them back from deportation, but transferred them out of Poland altogether, some to an internment camp at Tittmoning, in Bavaria, some to Bergau, near Dresden, some to the concentration camp at Bergen–Belsen, where they were kept in a special 'protected' part of the camp, and some to the French town of Vittel, near Nancy, in preparation for their actual emigration.

But within the German State, two conflicting interests were at work. From Berlin, the Foreign Ministry had suggested to Eichmann that 'approximately

---

[1] Central Zionist Archives, L 22/146. Letter No. 1031 via Istanbul.
[2] 'Summary' sent on 19 March 1943 to the American Minister in Berne, Leland Harrison, and on 22 March 1943 to the British Minister, Clifford Norton; archives of the World Jewish Congress, General Secretariat.
[3] Central Zionist Archives, L 22/146.

30,000 Jews of diverse nationality' should be kept 'in reserve' for exchange purposes. But one of the senior SS officers in Riga, a city to which many such Jews had been deported from Germany and Austria, warned the Foreign Ministry on April 5 that 'Since, as is well known, in the course of time many thousands of local and German Jews have been shot in the Riga area, it seems very doubtful if any Jews could be eligible for exchange purposes without the mass shootings becoming known abroad and used as propaganda against us.'[1]

---

[1] Letter No. 438/43g, Nuremberg Trial Documents, NG-2652/B. The letter writer was Adolf Windecker, SS Obersturmbannführer, and Foreign Ministry Representative with the Reichskommissar Ostland.

Chapter 14

Warsaw and Bermuda

The impact of the Allied Declaration of 17 December 1942 continued to be felt among the Allies throughout the early months of 1943. In Britain, the Government had been embarrassed by a series of Parliamentary questions, culminating in those of 24 February 1943, urging an 'open-door' policy for any Jews who managed to escape from Nazi control.

The State Department in Washington, and the Colonial and Home Offices in London, clung to their quota systems with tenacity, but on February 18 the Foreign Office had asked the State Department if something might not be done 'for the relief of refugees on a United Nations basis', in view of the 'intense public interest' shown in Britain over the fate of the Jews. As the Foreign Office explained, there had been 'intensive representations' by distinguished public men, the Archbishop of Canterbury, Members of Parliament 'of all Parties', and 'innumerable responsible public bodies'; so much so, indeed, that the refugee issue had become the 'main problem' then 'agitating the public conscience'.

In reply, on February 26, the State Department had suggested that both Britain and America undertook 'a preliminary exploration of the problem' at a Conference in Ottawa,[1] and this suggestion was approved by the War Cabinet's refugee Committee on March 5. The Committee's two Cabinet Ministers, Anthony Eden and Oliver Stanley, also invited the Foreign Office and the Home Office 'to consult together as to the line which should be taken' if the British Government were 'pressed to receive additional refugees in the United Kingdom'.[2]

During March, the Jewish Agency continued with its efforts to obtain modifications to the existing quotas. On March 23, when the Swiss Telegraphic Agency reported the deportation of 12,000 Jews from Bulgarian-occupied Thrace and Macedonia to Germany, Dr Weizmann wrote to Lord Halifax, begging him to allow the Jews still in Bulgaria to enter Palestine:

The idea that thousands of these people, who might be saved are being left to their fate is simply unendurable. When we pleaded for rescue—not merely for pity—we were told that the Jews in Poland cannot be reached, that Hitler would not let them out, that their number is too large to be manageable, that other people are killed there besides the Jews etc. etc.

But here in the case of Bulgaria, there is a definite and practicable proposition. Every thousand people admitted is a thousand less murdered, and it may not yet be too late to save a remnant.[3]

[1] Aide-Memoires of 19 and 26 February 1943, Cabinet papers, 95/15.
[2] War Cabinet Committee on the Reception and Accommodation of Refugees, 5th Meeting, Cabinet papers, 95/15.
[3] Weizmann papers. Quoted in Michael J. Cohen (editor), *The Letters and Papers of Chaim Weizmann*, volume 21, series A, Jerusalem, 1979, pages 14–15.

Opposition to the maintenance of these Allied quotas reached a peak on the very day that Weizmann sent this letter, for on March 23, the Archbishop of Canterbury, William Temple, moved a resolution in the House of Lords, urging what he called 'immediate measures on the largest and most generous scale', to give 'temporary asylum' in Britain to all Jews who did manage to escape from Nazi control.

The Archbishop warned the House of Lords that the Jews in Europe were confronted with 'wholesale massacre'. It was essential, he argued, to devise some scheme of rescue. It was not enough to turn down schemes which involved indirect contact with the Germans 'merely on the grounds that we will have nothing to do with these barbarians'. Nor was it right to argue that an influx of Jewish refugees into Britain would create 'danger of an Anti-Semitic feeling' in Britain. It would be easy for the Government 'by skilful use of the wireless', to win British sympathy for any rescue proposals, 'especially if a large number of those who were brought out were children, and were being delivered from almost certain death'.

Speaking in the same debate, Lord Samuel stressed that if Britain's immigration rules could be relaxed, 'some hundreds, and possibly a few thousands, might be enabled to escape from this holocaust'.

The British Government had already tried to deflect criticism by making two points: first, that negotiations were beginning with the United States to evolve a common policy, and to see what could be done to receive the refugees; and second, that in Britain itself food shortages and the problems of unemployment made it difficult to contemplate more refugees being received. In his speech, Lord Samuel tried to answer both points:

The declaration of the United Nations was made on December 17. Today is March 23, and, so far as is publicly known, nothing has happened except discussions, conferences and exchanges of notes. We are glad to learn that measures are afoot for securing close cooperation between this country and the United States. But there seems to be a great danger that action is liable to be lost in the sands of diplomatic negotiations. . . .

While Governments prepare memoranda and exchange notes and hold conferences, week after week, month after month the Nazis go on killing men, women and children.

Lord Samuel continued, with reference to the Home Office arguments about Britain's own limited capacity to receive these refugees:

So small is the number that it seems monstrous to refer to difficulties of food supply, in this country of forty-seven million people, or to difficulties of employment, when we know that here also there is a shortage of labour. . . .

There is still in this country, however, a rigid refusal to grant visas to any persons who are still in enemy-occupied territory.

The British Government was not prepared, however, to change its policy, and the former Colonial Secretary, Lord Cranborne, reiterated official policy that if Britain did open its doors to refugees, it would create problems of housing accommodation and food supply. Indeed, Cranborne added, as far as food was concerned, 'the difficulties are no less in the Colonial territories. There are not unlimited supplies'.[1]

[1] Hansard, 23 March 1943.

Conscious of the lack of satisfaction at this attitude, and of the mounting pressure in non-Jewish circles that some gesture should be made on behalf of the Jews under Nazi rule, the British Government announced that it would organize a Conference, to be held at Bermuda, to discuss the refugee question, and on March 27, only four days after the House of Lords debate, Anthony Eden, who was then in Washington, discussed the forthcoming Bermuda Conference with President Roosevelt, Cordell Hull and Sumner Welles. It was made clear to the Americans, however, that on the issue of Jewish refugees, the British Government intended to maintain its pre-war policies.

During the Washington discussions, the Americans raised the question of the Jews of southeast Europe, who were said to be 'threatened with extermination unless we could get them out'. According to one official's secret record of the discussions, the Americans 'very urgently pressed Eden for an answer to the problem'. For his part, however, Eden stated that it was necessary 'to move very cautiously about offering to take all Jews out of a country', and he told the Americans:

If we do that, then the Jews of the world will be wanting us to make similar efforts in Poland and Germany. Hitler might well take us up on any such offer, and there simply are not enough ships and means of transportation in the world to handle them.[1]

Eden told the Americans that the British were prepared to admit a substantial number of Jews to Palestine, '60,000 more Jews', but he stressed shipping difficulties and security risks, adding that 'the Germans would be sure to put a number of their agents in the group'.[2]

In preparation for the Bermuda Conference, the Jewish Agency asked, among other requests, for a direct approach by Britain to the German Government, and for the rescue of Bulgarian Jewish adults. In Washington, these points had been put direct to Eden by Stephen Wise and Joseph Proskauer, a former Justice of the New York Supreme Court. But as Moshe Shertok telegraphed to the Jewish Agency Executive in Jerusalem on April 10: 'Results discouraging. Eden described proposal approach Germany for release Jews as fantastically impossible'. At the same time, Shertok noted, all other Jewish Agency proposals were to be referred to the Inter-Allied Conference.[3]

On March 25, as part of the British preparations for the Bermuda Conference, a special meeting of all the Departments concerned was held in the Foreign Office. The meeting agreed that if the American delegate at Ottawa were to offer, and 'this was thought improbable', to take into the United States 'several thousand refugees' then in Spain, on condition that the United Kingdom and Colonies took the rest, 'this would be an embarrassing development'. In this event, Britain should remind the Americans 'of the limits we have reached in the African colonies', should warn them 'that the neutral Spanish Government would be embarrassed by such an offer', and should

[1] Between 1942 and the end of the war, shipping was found to transport a total of 371,683 German prisoners-of-war, and 50,273 Italian prisoners-of-war, across the Atlantic to the United States (*History of Prisoner of War Utilization by the U.S. Army, 1776–1946*, Department of the Army, Washington, June 1955).

[2] Note by one of the United States' participants, Harry Hopkins, published in *Foreign Relations of the United States 1943*, volume 3, Washington 1963, pages 38–9.

[3] Telegram to Bernard Joseph, Central Zionist Archives, S 25/1670.

make a 'cautious promise' to look into the United Kingdom and non-African colonial possibilities.

The meeting of March 25 also agreed on certain guidelines for British refugee policy. The first was that the refugee problem was not confined 'to persons of any particular race or faith'. In addition, in view of 'transport limitations', refugees should be housed 'as near as possible to where they are now, or to their homes'. Plans should also be made to maintain them in neutral countries in Europe, with assurances for their support, and also 'for their return to their native countries at the end of the war'.

It was also felt at the meeting of March 25 that the United States could help in persuading the countries of Latin America 'to be more liberal in regard to accommodating refugees'.[1]

The War Cabinet's Committee on refugees met on April 1, with Clement Attlee in the Chair, and with Oliver Stanley and Herbert Morrison the other two Ministers present. The main feeling of the meeting was that, once Tunisia was cleared of German forces, the objections to setting up a refugee camp in North Africa 'will it is hoped, largely disappear', but that it would be 'inadmissable' of the Americans to claim that such a camp constituted 'an American contribution' to the solution of the refugee problem. Instead, the American delegation at Bermuda should be urged to accommodate refugees in the United States itself, 'up to the limit of their quotas', on which, according to the Committee, there was still 'a margin'.

As regards the proposal to evacuate Jewish refugees from Bulgaria and Turkey, the War Cabinet Committee felt that it would be necessary 'to make quite sure that these refugees would stay in Turkey and would not be passed on, e.g. to Palestine'.

Another point made by the Committee in its secret conclusions was that owing to the 'serious food situation' no more refugees could be received at present in Britain's East African colonies. But during the discussion it was stressed that Britain itself had problems in this regard, for Herbert Morrison, the Home Secretary, told his colleagues that the 'maximum number' of Jewish refugees who could be accommodated in the United Kingdom 'would be 2,000'. The only other possible havens were, according to the Committee, a further two thousand in Canada, and five hundred in Jamaica 'provided the Americans supplied the additional food required'.

The Committee also discussed the possibility of allocating 'some suitable area' as a place to settle Jewish refugees after the war. In this connection however, as the minutes recorded, 'it was pointed out that the Jewish element in the population of Poland was proportionately higher than was healthy'.[2]

The refugee debate was also being carried on in public, and a leading article published in *The Times*, on April 3, while sympathetic to the plight of Jewish refugees, went on to describe the 'sterile and unsatisfactory policy' of trying to settle these refugees 'in Palestine or Africa or Brazil'.[3] This comment provoked Professor Namier to reply that far from being 'sterile' of economic or

---

[1] Note by the Foreign Office, 31 March 1943, Cabinet papers, 95/15.
[2] War Cabinet Committee on the Reception and Accommodation of Refugees. 6th Meeting, 1 April 1943, Cabinet papers, 95/15.
[3] *The Times*, 3 April 1943.

cultural achievement, the Jewish National Home had received 'about one-third of the refugees from Greater Germany, with great benefit even to the Arab population'.[1]

Other voices gave a different perspective: four days later *The Times* published a letter from a Conservative MP, Wing Commander Archibald James, arguing that in Britain even second generation Jewish refugees were, 'particularly when Zionist, strongly resistant to assimilation; a respect in which they differ from such earlier arrivals as Huguenots'. If the 'larger problem' of distressed Jewry were to be faced, outside those who came within the existing Palestine quota, then James advised 'the creation under the peace treaties of a Jewish State in south-east Europe'. This area, James added, was 'their age-long majority habitat', and he ended his letter:

Jewish leaders would be well advised to face realities, and not to seek to over-exploit sympathies aroused by Nazi beastliness at a time when Jews are not alone in suffering wrongs as well as in having rights to maintain.[2]

In Geneva, Richard Lichtheim was worried about the future of those Jews who still lived beyond the range of Nazi deportation orders. 'I only hope,' he wrote to the Jewish Agency Executive in Jerusalem on April 13, 'there will be no change for the worse in Italy and Hungary, the only countries on the Axis side where the Jewish communities are still comparatively safe, but nobody can tell what the next morning will bring.'[3]

One small area of goodwill and rescue during April was the decision of the International Red Cross, communicated to the British Government on April 5, 'to provide for the transport by sea of Jewish emigrants travelling to Palestine under the protection of the Red Cross emblem. . . .' As soon as a ship could be chartered for the 270 Rumanian children, the Red Cross would 'apply to the belligerent States' to recognize this protective measure.[4]

Other efforts to enlist Red Cross support had been made by the World Jewish Congress Secretariat in Geneva, which was able to report to New York on April 14 the 'considerable dispatch' of food parcels to Theresienstadt. These parcels had been paid for largely by the Congress, which also reported that the Red Cross 'intend obtain same possibility for labour camps in Upper Silesia, Auschwitz, Sosnowitz, Birkenau, Jawischowitz, other places where many young deportees concentrated'.[5]

It is clear from this telegram that Birkenau was neither specifically associated with Auschwitz, of which it was an integral part, nor regarded as being more than a labour camp for deportees; a camp moreover, to which food parcels might be dispatched.

Unknown to those who were assembling for the Conference at Bermuda, and unknown to the Jewish leaders for whom the Conference seemed so essential an opportunity for rescue, the deportations to Auschwitz continued throughout the first three weeks of April. On April 3 a total of 2,800 Greek

---

[1] *The Times*, 6 April 1943.

[2] *The Times*, 10 April 1943.

[3] Letter to Lauterbach, Central Zionist Archives, L 22/156.

[4] 'Note for the Foreign Office Concerning the Assistance to the Jews', Foreign Office papers, 371/36661, W 7159.

[5] Gerhart Riegner to Stephen S. Wise, telegram of 14 April 1943, archives of the World Jewish Congress, General Secretariat.

Jews reached the camp by train from Salonica, of whom 2,208 were gassed. Indeed, so great were the numbers to be gassed and burnt that on the following day, April 4, orders were given for the construction of a fifth gas chamber and crematorium.[1]

These details were unknown to the Allies. But on April 18, a report was being drafted in London which contained an eye-witness account of Auschwitz. It was never made public.

The report of April 18 was written by a Pole, a non-Jew and a member of the Polish underground, who had just reached Britain after spending eleven consecutive months in Poland, from November 1941 to December 1942. For the largest part of this time he had been in Warsaw, where he had made contact with the Polish underground, which had sent him to the town of Auschwitz, adjacent to the camp, in order to find out what was 'going on' in the camp itself. He had information 'from people who were freed'. According to his account, 'masses of Jews' were brought to Auschwitz from countries beyond Poland, and were 'exterminated en masse'. His report went on to state that when he had left Auschwitz at the end of September 1942, 'at least' 60,000 of the 95,000 registered prisoners had been murdered, and he went on to describe what he had ascertained to be the methods of killing, on the basis 'of information which I collected on the spot'. He described four such methods:

a. Gas Chambers, the victims were undressed and put into those chambers where they suffocated.

b. Electric Chambers, these chambers had metal walls, the victims were brought in and then high tension electric current was introduced.

c. The so-called Hammerluft system. This is a hammer of air. Those were special chambers where the hammer fell from the ceiling and by means of a special installation victims found death under air pressure.

d. Shooting. This was used as a collective form of punishment, in cases of lack of subordination, thus killing every tenth.

According to this report, the first three methods were those 'used most frequently'. During the gassing 'Gestapo men stood in a position which enabled them to watch in gas masks the death of the masses of victims'. After the killing, the corpses were taken outside the camp, and were put into huge pits covered in lime. 'The burning of the victims by means of electric ovens', the report stated, 'was seldom applied'. This was because 'in such ovens only about 250 people could be burnt within 24 hours'.[2]

There were several errors in this report. But its message was correct: Auschwitz was at last shown to be the site of the mass murder of Jews. There is no evidence, however, that its revelations made any impression, or that it was quoted or mentioned again. The events it referred to were those of the previous September, more than six months earlier, and the Auschwitz section had been preceded by a long section on the Warsaw ghetto, the facts of which were already well known. Perhaps, for this reason it was overlooked. The report specifically states that it was 'drafted on the 18th of April in London'.

It was two events which took place on the following day, April 19, that

---

[1] In all, nineteen trains left Salonica for Auschwitz, and within four months a total of 43,850 Jews, amounting to 95 per cent of Salonica Jewry, had been deported.

[2] 'Report Drafted on the 18th of April in London'. Copy in Yad Vashem archive, 0-67.

were to dominate all discussion for the rest of April, and for much of May: the opening of the Bermuda Conference and the start of the Warsaw ghetto uprising.

There were also two other items of news which provoked a substantial reaction in the second and third weeks of April: the report of the discovery of the mass grave of some ten thousand Polish officers, including many Jewish officers, who had been disarmed and then murdered in the Katyn forest, apparently by the Soviets, and the simultaneous announcement by the Soviet authorities themselves that they had executed two leading Polish Jewish socialists, Henryk Ehrlich and Viktor Alter. The shooting of these two well known political figures, announced with 'sorrow and distress' by the Polish National Council in London, was at once made public.[1]

The first news of the Warsaw uprising was published in the western press on April 22. Its source was a United Press dispatch from neutral Sweden, reporting an appeal over 'secret Polish radio' on the night of April 21. The appeal, as heard in Sweden, said:

The last 35,000 Jews in the Warsaw ghetto have been condemned to execution.
   Warsaw again is echoing to musketry volleys.
   The people are murdered.
   Women and children defend themselves with their naked arms.
   Save us—.[2]

At that point, the radio station had gone dead.

Five days later, on receiving several Warsaw addresses for the next exchange list, Dr Kahany wrote from Geneva to his Jewish Agency colleagues in Istanbul: 'the Warsaw ghetto is now entirely evacuated and *none* of the original (or changed) addresses is now valid'.[3]

The Jewish resistance in Warsaw was in fact continuing. But with each day, stronger German forces were sent against it, and those in the western world were forced to remain distant spectators of Polish Jewry's most heroic and desperate act of resistance.

The Bermuda Conference opened on 19 April 1943, just as the Warsaw ghetto uprising began. It was the eve of Passover, the Jewish festival of rejoicing at the escape from pharoah's Egypt, and the invocation of the prayer 'Next year in Jerusalem'. At Bermuda, by mutual Anglo-American agreement, the United States quota system, and the 1939 Palestine restrictions, were subjects to be avoided.

During the Conference the British delegation stressed Great Britain's own limited capacity to absorb refugees. The '60,000' figure, which Eden had spoken of in Washington three weeks earlier, was never mentioned. Indeed, as one of the British delegates, Osbert Peake, told the Conference on April 24:

At one time they had been told that there were 20,000 children in Vichy France, but in the present overcrowded state of the UK, difficulties of transport, food, and accommodation, such a number could not be contemplated. It would be embarrassing to the war effort of both the USA and the UK.

[1] *The Times*, 19 April 1943.
[2] *The Times*, 22 April 1943.
[3] Central Zionist Archives, L 21/168.

There was a vociferous minority of people in the UK who wanted HMG to do this, but the majority there thought that quite as many refugees as they could cope with in war circumstances had been admitted.

The head of the British delegation at Bermuda, Richard Law, asked whether the United States might approach the various Latin American governments to see if some place of refuge could be found. But the United States dismissed this suggestion as 'impracticable'. Senator Lucas, one of the United States representatives, asked whether the British Honduras ought not to take in some Jews. But the British replied that there were already twenty Jewish refugees, and two Jewish internees, in British Honduras; and that there was no room for further 'Europeans unaccustomed to manual labour in a tropical climate'.[1]

On the question of relaxing the regulations for entry into Palestine, the British Government would make no concessions. This was, apparently, the view of Anthony Eden himself. On April 25 Eden's Private Secretary, Oliver Harvey, noted in his diary: 'Unfortunately A.E. is immovable on the subject of Palestine. He loves Arabs and hates Jews'.[2]

This was not an attitude shared by Eden's chief, the Prime Minister. Indeed, on April 27, in a secret War Cabinet memorandum, Churchill informed his colleagues with stark brevity: 'I cannot in any circumstances contemplate an absolute cessation of immigration into Palestine at the discretion of the Arab majority'.

In his memorandum Churchill suggested the possibility not only of a Jewish self-governing regime in Palestine, but also of turning two former Italian colonies, Eritrea and Tripolitania, 'into Jewish colonies, affiliated, if desired, to the National Home in Palestine'.[3] But Churchill's sympathies to Zionist aspirations were not shared by the majority of his Cabinet. Nor did these Ministers seem at all eager to open the doors of Britain itself to those relatively few Jews who might still escape from Europe. In recent years, Eden explained to his colleagues, at the War Cabinet on April 27, 'our policy had been only to admit to this country certain very limited categories of stateless refugees'.

The War Cabinet then accepted Eden's proposal, that the Americans should be told that Britain would only be 'prepared to make an effort' to admit a number of stateless refugees into Britain if the United States 'were prepared to do the same'.[4]

Four Ministers were present at the next meeting of the War Cabinet's refugee Committee on May 3: Attlee, Eden, Morrison and Stanley, and they discussed 'what could be said in the House of Commons' by the Government about Bermuda. It was 'necessary', they agreed, to make 'some kind of statement' as soon as possible, in order, as the minutes of the meeting expressed it, 'to satisfy opinion both in the House and in the country'.[5]

[1] Bermuda Conference, minutes of the discussion of 24 April 1943, Foreign Office papers, 371/36725.

[2] Diaries and Papers of Oliver Harvey (Lord Harvey of Tasburgh), Diary entry for 25 April 1943, quoted in Bernard Wasserstein, *Britain and the Jews of Europe 1939–1945*, London and Oxford 1979, page 34.

[3] War Cabinet paper 178 of 1943, Cabinet papers, 66/36.

[4] War Cabinet No. 59 of 1943, Minute No. 3. As circulated to the War Cabinet Committee on the Reception and Accommodation of Refugees, Cabinet papers, 95/15.

[5] War Cabinet Committee on the Reception and Accommodation of Refugees, 7th Meeting, Cabinet papers, 95/15.

On May 3 the British delegate at Bermuda, Richard Law, sent an account of the course of the discussions to Eden, who circulated it to the War Cabinet. 'We are,' Law wrote, 'subjected to extreme pressure from an alliance of Jewish organisations and Archbishops.' And he went on:

There is no counter-pressure as yet from the people who are afraid of an alien immigration into the country because it will put their livelihood in jeopardy after the war. I have no doubt in my own mind that that feeling is widespread in England, but it is not organised so we do not feel it.

In the United States, on the other hand, there is added to the pressure of the Jewish organisations the pressure of that body of opinion which, without being purely anti-Semitic, is jealous and fearful of an alien immigration *per se*. And in contradistinction to the position at home, that body of opinion is very highly organised indeed. The Americans, therefore, while they must do their utmost to placate Jewish opinion, dare not offend 'American' opinion.[1]

On May 8, as the Bermuda Conference was coming to an end, the High Commissioner in Palestine, Sir Harold MacMichael, reported to the Colonial Office that, as far as Palestine was concerned, there were still more than 33,000 vacant certificates out of the 75,000 total of the 1939 White Paper.[2] At the Conference itself, however, this fact had not been the subject of any of the discussions. Nor had this figure been used, either by the British or by the Americans, to indicate at least one possible avenue of rescue and immigration.

When the War Cabinet met on May 10, Eden gave an account of the three decisions which had been reached at Bermuda: that the refugee problem could not be solved by Britain or the United States alone but concerned 'the whole community of civilised nations' all of whom should be invited to share 'in the relief of these refugees'; that a temporary refugee camp should be set up in North Africa 'to relieve the immediate pressure on Spain'; and that the Inter-Governmental Committee on Refugees which had been set up in 1938 by the Evian Conference should be revived.

During the discussion that followed several points were made. The first was that there were 'signs of increasing Anti-Semitic feeling' in Britain itself, and that it would therefore be 'preferable' in any public statement 'to avoid implying that refugees were necessarily Jewish'. Instead, refugees should be referred to 'by nationality rather than by race'. Another point was that the Allied Governments would do their best to ensure that after the war, conditions were created in former enemy territories 'which would enable refugees to return to them'.

The War Cabinet then discussed the forthcoming debate in the House of Commons. Its conclusion was a forthright one. 'In view of the risk,' it read, 'that a disproportionate number of the speeches might be by Members holding extreme views in favour of the free admission of refugees to this country, the Whips were invited to arrange that some Members would intervene in the debate who would put a more balanced point of view.'[3]

[1] Foreign Office papers, 371/36731, W 6933.

[2] Colonial Office papers, 733/436/SF/308/42, Secret. According to the statistical summary supplied by MacMichael, between 1 April 1939 and 31 March 1943 the total number of Jewish immigrants into Palestine, both legal and illegal, was 41,169. This left 33,831 places to be filled.

[3] War Cabinet 67 of 1943, 10 May 1943; minutes as circulated to the War Cabinet Committee on the Reception and Accommodation of Refugees on 11 May 1943, Cabinet papers, 95/15.

In Warsaw, after more than three weeks of fighting in houses, cellars and sewers, the last of the Jewish resistance was being overcome by three thousand heavily armed German troops, who had moved systematically from street to street, bombarding and burning. The leader of the uprising, Mordechai Anielewicz, had been killed on May 15, and within a week of his death, more than 55,000 Jews, many of them women and children, had surrendered to the advancing forces. More than seven thousand were shot immediately they surrendered. Fifteen thousand were then deported to Majdanek, and seven thousand to Treblinka, where they were murdered. A few hundred escaped to the relative security of 'Aryan' Warsaw.

On May 7 the Archbishop of Canterbury wrote to Anthony Eden about a Swedish proposal to approach the German Government direct, and to offer to receive in Sweden 20,000 Jewish children from Nazi Europe. In his letter the Archbishop urged the British Government to do 'everything possible to bring this about'.

The Archbishop's letter was discussed inside the Foreign Office throughout the second week of May. The Swedes, noted A. W. G. Randall, 'want to get rid of the children when the war ends'. There was some feeling that, coming so soon after the Bermuda Conference, the offer could not easily be rejected out of hand. Anthony Eden, however, was sceptical of the proposal. 'I am still not enamoured of this,' he noted on May 16. 'We want to make Europe a place in which Jews can live and cannot anyway transport them all abroad.'[1]

There was a further blow to Jewish hopes of rescue during the spring of 1943 when the British Government informed the Jewish Agency that an Afghan offer to take in fifty-two Bulgarian Jews was rejected. At the beginning of March the Afghan Ambassador in Istanbul, Faiz Mohammed Khan, offered, on behalf of his Government, to pay the fares and salaries of the fifty-two, twenty of whom were to be physicians, the rest engineers, chemists, nurses, teachers, architects and mechanics.[2] But at the end of April the Jewish Agency was informed that 'difficulties' had arisen with regard to the transit of these Jews through Palestine and Syria.[3]

The real cause of the scheme being rejected was never revealed to the Jewish Agency. In fact, on April 17 the Government of India had expressed to the Foreign Office its 'reluctance' to agree to 'a large number of Jews of enemy nationality' being allowed to enter Afghanistan, and warned that 'Axis sympathisers may be among them'. In the following weeks this objection received support inside the Foreign Office, where an official noted that the Government of India, the British Embassy in Kabul, the India Office 'and ourselves' were all agreed 'that we cannot run the risk of allowing a fresh German colony to be formed in Kabul, even though the people in question are Jews and are said to be anti-Nazi'.[4]

At the India Office, Algernon Rumbold had suggested that one way of making it possible to allow these Jews to go to Kabul, and at the same time to

[1] Foreign Office papers, 371/36661. W 7131.
[2] Central Zionist Archives, L 15/90.
[3] Barlas papers.
[4] The British documents on the Afghan scheme are in Foreign Office papers, 371/34934.

ensure 'a better hold on them' would be to grant them 'some form of British protection'. But this idea found no favour inside the Foreign Office. 'I think it would be best to stamp on this scheme straight away,' wrote J. R. M. Pink, and he added: 'Treaty Department confirm that if we were to give any form of protection to stateless Jews in one part of the world, the news would soon leak out and it would be extremely difficult for us to explain why we are prepared to give such protection in some cases and not in others.' Moreover, Pink commented, 'the Jews could be relied upon to make the utmost use of such a concession, which might well prove extremely inconvenient.'

In any case, Pink noted, the British Ambassador to Turkey, Sir Hughe Knatchbull-Hugessen, had already pointed out that 'we should not be able to grant visas to people coming from enemy-occupied territory', although a single exception might 'possibly' be made in favour of a Bulgarian Jewish gynaecologist.

The Afghan scheme had been undermined, and when the Secretary of the Jewish Agency in London, Joseph Linton, pressed for its acceptance, the Foreign Office refugee expert, Ian Henderson, referred privately to the 'formidable difficulties of transport and administration' and commented that Linton 'is probably seizing at any straw which may enable him to get a few more refugees out of Axis-controlled territory'.

On May 18 the India Office noted that the Afghan Government had now withdrawn support for the scheme, 'no doubt', as Rumbold commented, 'through fear that any further discussion of this question with us may lead us on to raise with them the question of Axis intrigues in Afghanistan generally'.

On what could the Jews rely for their rescue or survival? On May 2 the United States Assistant Secretary of State, A. A. Berle, speaking in Boston at a mass meeting in protest against German atrocities, had told his largely Jewish audience of what he called 'the blunt and cruel conclusion' which was the 'only honest' answer. 'Nothing can be done to save these helpless unfortunates,' he declared, 'except through the invasion of Europe, the defeat of the German arms, and the breaking of the German power. There is no other way.'[1]

But it was the Allied policymakers themselves, in London, Washington, and Bermuda, who had made sure that no other way was even to be tried. Before the Bermuda Conference the Allies had rejected the Jewish Agency's request for direct negotiations with the Germans, in order to see if Hitler was prepared to let the surviving Jews leave Nazi-controlled Europe. At Bermuda itself the much less controversial and widely publicized 'open door' policy for refugees had also been rejected.

On May 12, in London, one of the two Jewish representatives on the Polish National Council, Szmul Zygielbojm, had committed suicide, tormented by the news that the Warsaw ghetto uprising had been crushed. 'My companions of the Warsaw Ghetto,' he wrote in his suicide note, 'fell in a last heroic battle with their weapons in their hands. I did not have the honour to die with them but I belong to them and to their common grave. Let my death be an energetic cry of protest against the indifference of the world which witnesses the

---

[1] Jewish Telegraphic Agency, *Daily News Bulletin*, volume 24, No. 102, 4 May 1943.

extermination of the Jewish people without taking any steps to prevent it.'

The 'responsibility' for the destruction of Polish Jewry, Zygielbojm wrote, rested 'above all on the murderers themselves'. But he added, bitterly, that it also fell 'indirectly' on the whole human race, on the Allies, and on their Governments 'who so far have taken no firm steps to put a stop to these crimes. By their indifference to the killing of hapless men, to the massacre of women and children, these countries have become accomplices of the assassins'.[1]

The decisions of the Bermuda Conference were a grave disappointment to those Jews and non-Jews alike who had advocated an 'open door' policy: for the Conference agreed in its public communique merely that the pre-war Inter-Governmental Committee on refugees was to be revived; that several thousand Jewish refugees already in Spain were to be dispersed 'to temporary residence in North Africa', and that there were to be 'further limited admissions' of refugees to both Britain and the United States. The official, and secret, Conference Report had stressed that 'under war conditions' the numbers of refugees who could be given even temporary refuge 'must necessarily be limited'.[2]

The British War Cabinet met in London on 17 May 1943. During the course of the discussions, Anthony Eden spoke of his concern about the statements 'which were likely to be made' in the House of Commons debate in two days' time. Members would probably ask, he said, 'about the facilities for refugees to escape from Nazi oppression through Spain'.

It was decided that Eden should take the opportunity of the forthcoming Secret Session of the House on May 18 to tell Parliament that because of previous public discussion on the transfer of Jewish refugees through Bulgaria to Palestine, 'the Germans had now taken special steps to prevent refugees from leaving Bulgaria',[3] and to 'warn Members' of the importance in the debate of May 19 to 'avoid any statement' which might lead the Germans to take similar action in respect of Spain.[4]

Despite this caution, many English men and women, including Members of Parliament, were distressed at what they still regarded as the Government's over-cautious attitude, particularly during the Bermuda Conference, on which such hopes had been founded. 'The Bermuda business is sickening,' Weizmann's secretary, Doris May, wrote to a friend in New York: 'a nice Riviera holiday for a bunch of officials engaged in exploring avenues and turning stones – and meanwhile the people perish.'[5] On May 18 George Bell, the Bishop of Chichester, appealed in *The Times* for a more active policy

---

[1] Zygielbojm's letter was published in full in the *New York Times* on 4 June 1943, under the headline: 'Pole's suicide note pleads for Jews'. A further headline declared: 'He denounced apathy'.

[2] 'Bermuda Conference', Report in Colonial Office papers, 733/449/76208/2. Printed for the War Cabinet as W.P.(43)193, designated Secret.

[3] On 12 May 1943 the exiled Haj Amin el-Husseini, former Mufti of Jerusalem, had protested to Hitler about the possibility of 4,500 Bulgarian Jews being allowed to go to Palestine (Nuremberg Trial Documents, NG 2757). The Mufti's protest had been successful. Two years earlier, at a meeting with Hitler on 8 April 1941, Haj Amin had offered Hitler his active help in bringing about the downfall of the 'English-Jewish coalition' (Nuremberg Trial Documents, NG 5720).

[4] War Cabinet minutes, 17 May 1943, circulated to the War Cabinet Committee on the Reception and Accommodation of Refugees on 18 May 1943, Cabinet papers, 95/15.

[5] Lourie papers.

towards refugees. The guilt 'lies with the Nazis,' he wrote. 'But can we escape blame if, having it in our power to do something to save the victims, we fail to take the necessary action, and take it swiftly?' It was quite certain, the Bishop added, 'that if the British and American Governments were determined to achieve a programme of rescue in some way commensurate with the vastness of the need, they could do it.'[1]

[1] *The Times*, 18 May 1943.

Chapter 15

The debate of 19 May 1943

The long-awaited Parliamentary debate of May 19 was opened by the Government spokesman, Osbert Peake, the Under-Secretary of State at the Home Office, who stressed that the total number of Jews who were able to escape, or who had escaped, 'is of course infinitesimal in proportion to the size of the problem as a whole'. Hitler, he added, 'is determined not to let these people go', and the 'rate of extermination' was such that 'no measures of rescue or relief, on however large a scale, could be commensurate with the problem.'

Peake then reiterated the Government's argument that, as far as those living in Nazi Europe were concerned, it was the approach of an Allied victory which would contribute 'more to their salvation than any diversion of our war effort in measures of relief, even if such measures could be put into effect'.

Later in his speech, Peake criticized those like Eleanor Rathbone, who were demanding that the British Government issue visas to individual Jews inside Nazi Europe, whose relatives were in the west and had applied on their behalf for visas, in the hope that this might enable them to leave. Peake rejected this request, telling the House of Commons: 'The suggestion that visas should be promised to such persons is really asking the impossible. We should be pledging ourselves in advance to receive persons about whom we know nothing and whom we could not identify.'

Speaking of those who had expressed the view that not enough was being done to help refugees, or would-be refugees, and mentioning in particular the Bishop of Chichester's letter to *The Times*, Peake quoted from a speech by Macaulay of more than a century before, on 'the effect of distress on the human mind'. Distress, Macaulay had said: 'makes even wise men unstable, unreasonable, credulous, eager for immediate relief, heedless of remote consequences. There is no quackery in medicine, religion or politics, which may not impose even on a powerful mind, when that mind has been disordered by pain or fear.'

This quotation, said Peake, had given him 'some comfort', when he read letters such as the one which the Bishop of Chichester had written to *The Times*.

Peake was followed by Eleanor Rathbone, who argued that the opening speeches at the Bermuda Conference had 'breathed the very spirit of defeatism and despair', a spirit which she felt still animated all official discussion of the refugee issue. There had been, she said, 'no sense of urgency at Bermuda', nor was there a sense of urgency now. What mattered, Eleanor Rathbone insisted, was 'of caring enough and of giving your whole time and thought to doing the thing'. At the Bermuda Conference it had become clear that neutral countries would only take in refugees from Nazi Europe if they had the possibility of passing them on to Allied countries. Would these neutrals not be 'more in a position to pass people on', Miss Rathbone asked:

. . . if Great Britain has in the hands of the Consuls some hundreds of unnamed visas available for Palestine or Great Britain or some camp under their control in North Africa or elsewhere, if the United States has another block of such visas and any other friendly country also has a block of such visas?

Miss Rathbone went on to speak of how United States visa procedure 'has been even more difficult and slow than our own', and she added, bitterly, 'If the blood of those who have perished unnecessarily during this war were to flow down Whitehall, the flood would rise so high that it would drown everyone within those gloomy buildings which house our rulers'. How many more, she asked, 'who might be saved will perish' if the problem were approached in the spirit of the Bermuda Conference, and she ended:

. . . the deaths of which we are thinking to-day, are so utterly useless, squalid and unspeakably cruel. They serve no purpose, except to gratify one man's lust for cruelty, for wreaking vengeance on the weak when he cannot reach the strong.
Only victory will put an end to it all. But meantime let no one say: 'We are not responsible.' We are responsible if a single man, woman or child perishes whom we could and should have saved. Too many lives, too much time has been lost already. Do not lose any more.

The 'more balanced view' which the Cabinet had hoped to see was put forward shortly after Miss Rathbone's appeal, by a Conservative MP, Colonel Sir Lambert Ward, a former Lord Commissioner of the Treasury. Ward told the House of Commons that he felt there was 'something' to be said for the view that 'to admit a large number of refugees of the Jewish religion might easily fan the smouldering fires of anti-Semitism which exist here into a flame'.

Ward was also worried about the certainty, as he expressed it, that if Jewish refugees were admitted to Britain 'in any large numbers', they would 'automatically gravitate' towards the East End of London, where, as a result of the blitz, there was a severe housing shortage. He did, however, propose one solution: Jewish refugees should be settled, particularly after the war, in Libya, Tripoli and Tunisia, where there was already a large local Jewish population, 'so that any Jews who were admitted there would not be breaking fresh ground, for they would have their co-religionists there already to help them'.

The debate continued with further criticism of the Government, and much sympathy for the Jews. A Labour MP, John Mack, pointed out to his fellow MPs that the Jews were unlike others who were suffering, in that 'they have no Government to speak for them, they have no consul and no flag. They have no status in any land and they are not likely to have a place at any future peace conference'. John Mack added: 'Our hearts go out to them because of their hopeless plight.'

A Conservative MP, Victor Cazalet, who was shortly to be killed in the same air crash as General Sikorski, spoke of 'a camp called Treblinka', where the horrors of the massacres 'would put to shame the massacres of Genghis Khan or the sufferings of the Albigenses in the past'. Treblinka was the only death camp mentioned in the debate. Of the Jews of Belgium, Cazalet was able to say only that they had been deported 'to concentration camps in Poland or in Germany'. In fact, they had been deported to Auschwitz.

Speaking of what he called the 'increasing' anti-Semitism in Britain itself, Cazalet declared: 'When Jews are massacred in tens of thousands in Europe, it ceases to become news, but when half a dozen Jews are implicated in a black market transaction, that is almost headline news'.

Cazalet appealed to the Government to let refugees into Britain, even if as a result there were a 'risk' of an increase in anti-Semitism. But a later speaker, the Liberal National MP Herbert Butcher, was emphatic that 'we must not allow anti-Semitism to increase', and he went on to tell his fellow MPs that not only was anti-Semitism increasing in Britain, but that 'it is going to increase if Jews receive special treatment'. The only way to bring relief to Europe, he said, was an Allied victory, at the earliest possible moment, and he went on to ask: 'How much shipping are we willing to divert at the risk of delaying that victory?'[1]

A Conservative MP, Arthur Colegate, who had earlier been President of the Industrial Property Committee of the International Chamber of Commerce, was critical of the behaviour of Jewish refugees already in Britain, and gave the House of Commons an example, from his own rural constituency, where there was a hostel for Jewish refugees who had been sent there to do agricultural work. Colegate declared:

The Jews in that hostel had been received handsomely, they had been fed and housed and clothed, but they refused to milk cows after 4 o'clock on Friday. An Hon. Member: 'That is their Sabbath'. Yes, but let me finish. Agricultural labourers who had been working hard had to go in and do their work.

One Member of Parliament interrupted to say that 'Scottish farmers will not milk on Sunday', but Colegate continued:

This case has caused a great deal of prejudice. I have tried to help to get the matter cleared up, because I do not want anti-Semitism to be created. It is a small point, but it is not merely a question of 2 ozs of food per head of the population.

There is a difference of custom, but it is a very awkward difference, and friends of the Jews should exercise great care to prevent such things happening. The farmer himself is naturally very indignant about it.

Such incidents, Colegate warned, 'create prejudice'. But a Jewish MP, Sydney Silverman, appealed to Colegate to 'forgive' the Jews their attachment to their religion, and to ask if he could not 'himself be their spokesman and interpreter in an area where he has such influence?'

In bringing the debate of May 19 to a close, Eden himself spoke on behalf of the Government. There were, he said, '30,000 vacancies in Palestine', and he added: 'We want to get the children there, and despite the transport difficulty we would like to make special efforts to do so, but we cannot get them out without Sofia and Berlin. That is the blunt fact. I have no control over either Sofia or Berlin.'

'I do not believe,' Eden added, in answer to the criticisms which had been levelled against the Government, 'that until the war is over we can deal with

[1] For another aspect of the shipping argument, see page 127, footnote 1.

more than the fringe', and it was, he added, the fringe 'with which we have to deal'.[1]

Although Eden could not say so in the debate, it was, ironically, United States policy towards refugees which was at that very moment proving so strict as to hinder even those initiatives which the British Government had wanted to take.

At the Bermuda Conference it had been agreed to allow those Jewish refugees who were already in Spain, to cross over the Straits of Gibraltar into Allied-controlled North Africa. But on May 19, the very day of the House of Commons debate, Eden telegraphed direct to Churchill, who was then in Washington:

I am dismayed and depressed by the refusal of the United States Chiefs of Staff to agree to our recommendation that a small camp should be established in North Africa into which to draft refugees from Spain. This suggestion has long been pressed forward by us. . . .

It is our main hope of getting refugees out of Spain and so not only satisfying British and American public opinion, but also keeping open the escape routes from France into Spain which are essential to our military and intelligence services. This is the only remaining way of getting our pilots and other prisoners out of France. . . .

The numbers involved are not large and agreement to open a camp even for one thousand would ease the situation. It is difficult to believe that this would put any particular strain on shipping. . . .

As for the last objection, namely resentment on the part of the Arabs, this could surely be eliminated by putting the camp in a place sufficiently remote from important Arab centres.

Eden added that one of the causes of his concern was the possibility of 'extremely serious Parliamentary criticism' if nothing were done.[2]

Six weeks later Churchill himself telegraphed to Roosevelt, urging implementation of the Bermuda scheme for refugee camps in North Africa. As Churchill informed Roosevelt, the 'need for assistance to refugees, in particular Jewish refugees, has not grown less since we discussed the question'; and he added: 'Our immediate facilities for helping the victims of Hitler's anti-Jewish drive are so limited at present that the opening of the small camp proposed for the purpose of removing some of them to safety seems all the more incumbent on us'.[3]

[1] Hansard, 19 May 1943.
[2] Foreign Relations of the United States, The Conferences at Washington and Quebec 1943, Washington 1970, page 345.
[3] Prime Minister's Personal Telegram T.910/3, Personal and Most Secret, Premier papers, 4/51/4.

Chapter 16

'I have never forgotten the terrible sufferings . . .'

By the beginning of 1943, British and American bombers, based in the United Kingdom, had begun to strike with devastating power against the principal cities and industrial centres of western Germany, the Ruhr, the Hamburg area, and Berlin itself. On 8 February 1943 Heinrich Himmler, concerned that as the Allied air-raids reached the region of the concentration camps they might enable the inmates to organize mass escapes, ordered stricter defence procedures. Each camp was to be divided into blocks of four thousand prisoners each. Each block was to be surrounded by barbed wire. Each camp was to be surrounded by a high wall, on the top of which search lights were to be mounted on poles. Barbed wire was to be laid on both sides of the wall, and the interior wire was to be electrically charged. The outer side of the wall was to be mined. The inner side was to be patrolled by dogs. Outside the camp perimeter, guards were to patrol with dogs, which had been trained 'to tear a man apart'.[1]

The growing effectiveness of the Allied bombing had further direct effect on the concentration camp system. On 5 March 1943, during an Allied attack on Essen, the Krupp fuse plant had been destroyed. Within two weeks it had been decided to move what machinery could be salvaged to Auschwitz, where a growing industrial zone already absorbed tens of thousands of the deportees, in slave-labour conditions which held out little hope of survival, but which did offer those sent to the factories a hope which did not exist at all for those 'selected' for the gas chambers immediately on arrival. Indeed, as Auschwitz was out of the range of the Allied bombers in the spring of 1943, the number of factories in the Auschwitz region grew considerably, and thousands of Jews were deported there especially for work in them. Not only Krupp, but several other leading German industrial companies, found it convenient both from the point of view of cheap labour, and freedom from air-raids, to move to the Auschwitz area.

In May 1943, despite Allied bombing raids, the Germans were still masters of Europe. Militarily, they still seemed unperturbed either by the Anglo-American victories in north Africa, or by the slow, distant advance of the Red Army in the east. Looked at from Berlin, no imminent or insurmountable danger seemed to threaten the German mastery. Nor was there any way in which any of the Allied armies could come to the rescue of those Jewish communities which had not yet been deported.

The Allies were confident, however, that the German grip on Europe could eventually be destroyed, and all the subject peoples liberated from tyranny.

[1] Himmler letter of 8 February 1943, quoted in Raul Hilberg, *The Destruction of the European Jews*, Harper Colophon edition. New York, 1979, page 584.

On May 14 the British and American leaders took an important step in this direction, when their highest military planning group, the Combined Chiefs of Staff, approved Operation Pointblank, a joint Anglo-American bomber offensive against Germany, aimed at the very sources of German military power.

The objectives of Operation Pointblank were set out as 'the progressive destruction and dislocation of the German military system, and the undermining of the morale of the German people to a point where their capacity for armed resistance is fatally weakened', at which point it would be possible 'to permit initiation of final combined operations on the Continent'; that is, the opening of a second front in western Europe, and the military defeat of the German control of Europe by armies advancing simultaneously from east and west into Germany itself.

Operation Pointblank was to constitute the principal Anglo–American war effort in the air for more than twelve months, and was intended to reach its maximum force by March 1944, when the United States Air Force alone would be contributing more than 3,500 bombers. The Operation was intended to destroy six German war making systems: submarine construction yards and bases, the German aircraft industry, ball-bearing production, natural and synthetic oil production and storage, synthetic rubber and tyre production, and the manufacture and assembly of military transport vehicles.[1]

If Pointblank were to succeed, a second front could be opened during the summer of 1944. Once such a front were in being, the liberation of Europe would be assured. But by the time liberation came, who could tell how many Jews, or rather how few Jews, would still be alive to celebrate the Allied victory? And what form would their celebration take when, even by May 1943, so many millions were already dead, the Warsaw ghetto uprising crushed, and Polish Jewry, the largest single Jewish community of pre-war Europe, already almost entirely destroyed.

By May 1943 the attempts at rescue, even in the limited ways hitherto available, had become increasingly difficult. Tracing individuals for exchange was now virtually impossible. So few were now left alive.

There were other fears, also, in the minds of the Jewish leaders: following the destruction of the Möhne and Eder dams during the night of May 16–17, when considerable flooding was caused throughout the Ruhr basin, Dr Weizmann expressed his concern to Churchill's secretariat about an Allied press release reporting the fact that Jewish scientists were among those involved in the Allied scientific war effort. Weizmann's fear was that if this news item were repeated, the Germans would carry out further anti-Jewish reprisals.[2] The news item was dropped. But the reprisals took place.

The British Government also continued to cooperate with the Jewish Agency in transmitting lists of Palestinian Jews to the German authorities, through the good offices of the Swiss Government. The hope of survival lay not necessarily in any actual exchange but, as Lichtheim wrote to Istanbul on May 21, in the fact that the Germans had given the Swiss 'a general assurance

[1] Sir Charles Webster and Noble Frankland, *The Strategic Air Offensive Against Germany 1939–1945*, volume 4, Annexes and Appendices, Appendix 23, pages 273–83.
[2] Weizmann papers.

that these people would be treated differently if they could be found'. Even where there could be no possibility of an actual exchange, Lichtheim noted, 'the British authorities wish to be helpful, in case these people can get out'.[1] The original list of eight hundred names had therefore been followed in March 1943 by a second list, with new names, and addresses prepared by the Jewish Agency.

During May the continuing attempts to bring the four thousand children and five hundred adults from the Balkans were collapsing because, after the Bulgarian refusal to allow transit, only Rumania offered a transit route from Hungary to the Black Sea. But on May 21 the Swiss authorities told Lichtheim that 'according to their information a boat from Rumania cannot sail without permission from Berlin'.[2]

The South American passport scheme was likewise continuing. It too was on a small scale, determined principally by the pace of the German deportation plan. On May 22 some sixty Jews reached the French town of Vittel, from Warsaw. Each was the holder of a South American passport. Each had already been saved, by that passport, from deportation to Treblinka. Each now hoped either to be allowed to survive in Vittel, or to be allowed to leave for South America.

One of those who reached Vittel on May 22 was the poet Yitzhak Katznelson, together with one of his sons. His wife and their two other sons had been deported from Warsaw to Treblinka, and murdered there, the previous September.[3] Other Warsaw Jews were included on the exchange lists, but it had proved impossible to find them.

By May 22 the Warsaw ghetto was known to have been destroyed, and the killing of Jews to have spread to other cities; for on that day the *New York Times* reported a speech by the Polish Minister of Information, Professor Stanislaw Kot, who, at a memorial service in London for Szmul Zygielbojm, had told of underground radio reports from Poland that 'the Nazis had started liquidating the ghettos of Cracow and Stanislawow as reprisals for the British bombing of German dams, shooting Jews wherever they were found, or killing them in gas chambers'.[4]

On May 25 *The Times* published the text of two messages which Zygielbojm's Jewish colleague on the Polish National Council, Dr Schwarzbart, had received from the Warsaw ghetto. These messages, he said, were 'one of the last appeals of a fighting and dying people'. The first message was dated April 28, and told of Jews battling against German artillery, flame throwers, and aeroplanes which 'shower high explosives and incendiary bombs'. It also demanded that 'the powerful retaliation' of the United Nations should fall on the Germans 'immediately, and not in some distant future', and in such a way 'which will make it quite clear what the retaliation is for'.

The second message from Warsaw had been sent on May 11, and said, as Schwarzbart reported, 'that the resistance was nearing its end'.[5]

---

[1] Letter to Chaim Barlas. Central Zionist Archives, L 22/168.

[2] Central Zionist Archives, L 22/168.

[3] For Katznelson's story and experiences, see Yitzhak Katznelson, *Vittel Diary*, Kibbutz Lohamei Hagettaot. (Israel), 1972.

[4] *New York Times*, 22 May 1943. The location of the 'gas chambers' was not mentioned.

[5] *The Times*, 25 May 1943.

On May 26, the day after this report of the destruction of the Warsaw ghetto, a report appeared in *The Times*, from its correspondent in Istanbul, which told of the deportation of 50,000 Jews from Salonica 'to Poland', and gave an eye-witness account of the cattle wagons in which the Jews had been deported. Each wagon had only 'one small opening in the roof' for ventilation. Eighty people had been deported in each wagon 'where they had to stand up all the time, pressed against each other like sardines'. Each person was provided with a single loaf of bread. Each wagon contained a jar with 'a small supply of water for all'. There had been 'no provision whatever' for sanitation. Many had died during the journey. At a place in Yugoslavia they had been taken to a camp where they had been 'disinfected', and their heads, including those of the women, had been shaved. From there, the report ended, 'the survivors were sent to Cracow, where all trace of them has been lost'.[1]

In fact, they had been taken to <u>Auschwitz, less than twenty miles from Cracow</u>, and at Auschwitz most of them had been gassed. Once more, the name Auschwitz did not appear in the report. But on June 1, under the heading 'Nazi Brutality to Jews', *The Times* diplomatic correspondent did give <u>the camp's Polish name, Oswiecim,</u> as having been mentioned in several reports as the destination for Jews from nearby Cracow. The Cracow ghetto, he said, had been 'emptied', a thousand Jews having been murdered in the streets and houses, the others 'taken off to the Oswiecim concentration camp'. But he did not say what had become of them there. Nor did he know the destination of Jews deported from several other Polish towns 'under conditions harder than life can bear for long', and, he added, 'the journeys are often very long'.[2]

On June 18 a telegram from the Palestine Office in Geneva to the Jewish Agency in Jerusalem, warned of Jews, brought earlier from the Dutch provinces to Amsterdam, who had now been rounded up and sent to Westerbork camp, 'where lately thousands deported'. This telegram also brought the bad news that documents sent from Switzerland to Holland giving 'protected' status to the recipient, as part of a future exchange scheme, were 'losing progressively' their efficacy, 'which means immediate danger for tens thousands'. The telegram added: 'Only realisation exchange action can help in last hours. Do everything accelerate action, and urge Government transmit immediately veteran lists Protecting Power. Please cable us second veteran list for action.'[3]

The urgency of this telegram was not misplaced. Throughout April and May, thousands of Dutch Jews had been deported to the death camp at Sobibor, where they had been murdered on arrival; 5,594 in four deportations in April and 14,029 in six deportations between May 4 and June 8. Now, on June 20, a further 5,500 Jews were seized in south Amsterdam and sent that same day to Westerbork, for deportation to Sobibor, with others rounded up at that time. They too were murdered on arrival at the camp.[4] Meanwhile, on June 25 more than a thousand French Jews had reached Auschwitz from Drancy; half were gassed that same day.

[1] *The Times,* 26 May 1943.

[2] *The Times,* 1 June 1943. Cracow is only 36 miles east of Auschwitz.

[3] Central Zionist Archives, S 25/1670.

[4] Details of the numbers of Dutch Jews deported, with the dates of deportation are in *Overzicht van de uit Nederland Gedeporteerde Joden,* Amsterdam, no date, issued by the Netherlands State Institute for War Documentation.

Neither the dates nor the statistics of these deportations were known to the Allies. Nor was the fact that nearly 30,000 Dutch Jews had been deported and murdered since the beginning of April. Once more, the news of the mere fact of the deportations had reached Geneva only after the bulk of those deportations had taken place, and the deportees murdered. But although the deportations of Dutch Jews to Sobibor ended on July 20, they were to resume, on August 24, to Auschwitz, and between August 24 and November 16, more than eight thousand Dutch Jews were deported to Auschwitz, the majority of whom were gassed.

Yet Auschwitz was still unmentioned in the almost daily messages of fear and alarm which were reaching the Jewish and Allied leaders. Thus on July 2 Gerhart Riegner telegraphed to the Czechoslovak Government-in-Exile in London, for transmission to the World Jewish Congress:

We receive alarming reports from camps in Upper Silesia. A French deportee worker reports large concentrations of Frenchmen, English prisoners-of-war, ordinary convicts and Jews in labour camps. Large factories with accommodation for workers are being constructed directly above coal mines for the purpose of producing synthetic rubber. 36,000 men work on one building site; 24,000 on another one. Among them are several thousand Jewish deportees between the ages of 16 and 24 who are treated worst.

Guards carry leather whips with which they constantly beat their victims. The deportees are still dressed in the clothes they wore when arrested, which are completely tattered by now. Their daily food ration consists of two small portions of soup, a hundred grams of bread and some black coffee. They sleep on the bare soil, so crowded together that it is impossible to stretch. The ill and injured receive no medical attention. The rate of mortality is so high that in some camps the Jewish personnel has been entirely replaced many times over. Non-Jewish workers are forbidden any contact with the Jews.[1]

This news was alarming. It was also accurate, as far as the labour camps of Upper Silesia were concerned. But it made no mention of Auschwitz, which lay at the centre of the Upper Silesian camp system, and which was the scene of daily gassings and killings of a never-ending flow of deportees.

Towards the end of June the British Home Secretary, Herbert Morrison, learned for the first time of the policy of sending Palestine certificates through the Swiss Government to individual Jews inside Nazi-occupied Europe. Was not this procedure, he asked the War Cabinet's refugee Committee on June 28, 'contrary to the Committee's recommendation that in no circumstances should there be any negotiation whatever with the German Government'. Both Eden and Stanley hastened to put Morrison's mind at rest, explaining that this system of sending a list to the German Government 'of the names of individual Jews to whom immigration certificates could be granted' had been in operation since the beginning of the war. It was not a question of negotiating with the Germans, 'but merely of notification of names which would not be the subject of discussion, but would either be accepted or rejected by that Government'.[2]

Meanwhile, the question of a home in Britain itself for those refugees who

---

[1] Archives of the World Jewish Congress, General Secretariat.
[2] War Cabinet Committee on the Reception and Accommodation of Refugees, 8th Meeting, 28 June 1943, Cabinet papers, 95/15.

might escape from Nazi Europe remained a controversial one. On June 30 Lord Samuel led a delegation of six members of Parliament, himself, Lord Perth, Eleanor Rathbone, David Grenfell and Quintin Hogg, to the Foreign Office. This all-Party delegation produced evidence of individual refugees who had been refused entry to Britain itself. But the Foreign Office did not wish to pursue the complaints by means of an inter-departmental conference, as suggested by the delegation. As A. W. G. Randall noted, Lord Samuel 'was not encouraged to think that this was possible'.[1]

During the summer of 1943 the British Government returned yet again to the Palestine issue. On June 25 Lord Cherwell, the Paymaster General, pointed out to Churchill that the Middle Eastern War Council had recommended 'a firm reassertion' of the White Paper policy of 1939, 'which as you remember gives the Arabs the right to stop Jewish immigration after the end of March 1944, and thus stereotype the existing Arab majority in Palestine'.

Cherwell also drew Churchill's attention to a memorandum by Anthony Eden, who 'wishes to ask the American Government to try to damp down Zionist propaganda in the United States so as not to hurt Arab susceptibilities'.

Lord Cherwell went on to suggest that the problem 'of establishing a state capable of sheltering the whole of Jewry' might be solved by creating two such States, one, 'a smaller National Home in Palestine', the other, 'a larger area, elsewhere', either in Eritrea or Tripolitania as Churchill himself had already suggested, 'or possibly in Madagascar', to serve as 'a colony of the National Home'.

In part of a partitioned Palestine, Cherwell added, the Jews would have 'their own state, in which they can do what they like and accept as many immigrants as they like'. The Arabs inside it would be compensated and moved out; the Jews outside it, elsewhere in Palestine, would be compensated and moved in. As to any 'stir' this might create in the Muslim world, this could be 'allayed by concessions elsewhere', such as in Syria or Pakistan. Cherwell ended:

On the whole I am inclined to think that too much attention is being paid to the Levantine Semites who have annexed the romantic appellation of 'Arabs', and too little to the influence of Jewry, reinforced as it is by world wide sympathy with them in their afflictions. After the last war Arabia (as big as Western Europe) was conquered by us from the Turks and handed over to the Arabs; it seems strange that one corner of it, the size of Wales is grudged to the Jews.[2]

Lord Cherwell's support for a small Jewish State inside a partitioned Palestine was challenged, in part, by the Minister of Aircraft Production, Sir Stafford Cripps, who wrote, in a Memorandum of July 1, in favour of making one 'definite' Allied war aim, what he called 'the relief and honourable rehabilitation of the Jews in their former homes in Europe', as well as the principle of 'full and equal citizenship rights' for all Jews, in all countries freed from Nazi rule. With such a policy, he argued, Zionism would be seen 'to offer very little attraction for the Jews compared with what post-Nazi Europe

[1] Note of 1 July 1943, Colonial Office papers, 733/446.
[2] Premier papers, 4/52/5, folios 1130–2.

may have to offer for their depleted numbers'. But without such a set of war aims, Cripps saw danger in the existing 'hysterical mood' of Zionism, telling his Cabinet colleagues, of the current situation:

. . . the unbalanced emotional attitude of American (and to a less extent British) Zionists towards the Palestine situation are symptoms of the hysteria which, for reasons which are understandable, has overcome the Jewish community in the free world.

With the tragedy of racial extermination running its course before their eyes in Europe it is not surprising that increasing numbers of Jews elsewhere should have come to feel with passionate intensity that the creation of a Jewish State in Palestine is vital for their survival as a community.

So long as this hysterical mood persists the dangers of grave embarrassment for the United Nations and final calamity for the Jews need no emphasis.[1]

The War Cabinet met to examine these arguments on July 2. But first it discussed the question of Jewish refugees from Nazi Europe. The Colonial Secretary, Oliver Stanley, explained that the scheme to bring four thousand Jewish children, with five hundred adults, from Bulgaria to Palestine, a scheme approved by the War Cabinet the previous December, had been 'frustrated by German pressure on the Bulgarian Government', with the result that the frontier between Bulgaria and Turkey 'had now been closed to all Jews'. He added that a later approach to the Rumanian Government, made through the Swiss, 'showed little sign of bearing fruit'.

As it was unlikely that any immigration whatsoever would now be allowed by the Germans from enemy-occupied countries into Palestine, Stanley recommended a relaxation in the existing War Cabinet policy, as set out in Lord Cranborne's letter of 22 May 1942, that illegal immigration, the only other method of escape, 'should be discouraged by all practical means' and that 'no steps should be taken to facilitate the arrival of Jewish refugees' in Palestine. Instead of this, Stanley suggested, 'any Jews who might in future escape to Turkey or other neutral countries would be regarded as eligible for onward transport to Palestine', where, after being placed in camps, they would be released gradually as legal immigrants under the existing immigration quotas.

This concession, which was approved by the War Cabinet, was a definite advance on Cranborne's letter. But as with the earlier concession, it was accompanied by a War Cabinet decision that there should be 'no public announcement' of the change of policy.[2] The Jewish Agency leaders were to be told of the concession, but not the Jewish, or non-Jewish public.

At the end of June the distinguished socialist thinker, Harold Laski, complained direct to Churchill that in a recent speech Churchill had made no reference to the Jews. 'Although in my speech at the Guildhall,' Churchill replied on July 5, 'I referred only to the wrongs inflicted by Hitler on the Sovereign States of Europe, I have never forgotten the terrible sufferings inflicted on the Jews; and I am constantly thinking by what means it may lie in our power to alleviate them, both during the war and in the permanent settlement which must follow it.'[3]

[1] Premier papers, 4/52/5. Memorandum by Sir Stafford Cripps, 1 July 1943.
[2] War Cabinet 92 of 1943. Minutes 1, 2, and 3. Copy in Premier papers, 4/52/5.
[3] Premier papers, 4/51/8.

Chapter 17

The spread of Nazi power

On 10 July 1943 the British and United States Armies landed on the Italian island of Sicily. For the first time since the war began, it seemed almost certain that one of Hitler's allies would be defeated. As the Allied armies landed, more than 43,000 Italian Jews were among those who awaited liberation, including some 13,000 Jewish refugees from elsewhere in Europe who were being held in a special internment camp at Ferramonti, in the south, or were in hiding elsewhere.

On July 17 further evidence of earlier mass murder was ma :e public at a trial held in the Soviet city of Krasnodar, which had been liberated by the Red Army. The trial was a public one, effectively the first 'war crimes' trial of the war, and Allied journalists were encouraged to attend. The facts again referred to an area outside that of the death camps, and to Soviet civilians, rather than to Jews. But the trial did help to establish the scale and nature of Nazi atrocities, and in particular the use of 'murder vans', inside which the victims were locked, and then gassed. Evidence was produced during the trial to show that some seven thousand civilians had been killed in this way in Krasnodar alone. 'Men, women and children,' the court was told, 'were bundled into the van without discrimination,' including most of the patients in the Municipal Hospital. 'The gravely sick patients,' one witness stated, 'were brought out on stretchers and the Germans flung them in the van too.' The van was then driven to a specially dug anti-tank ditch on the outskirts of the city. By the time it arrived, all those in it had been gassed. Their bodies had then been dumped into the ditch.[1]

The gruesome details of the Krasnodar trial could only be described because the German armies were now in retreat. But the death camps and concentration camps in German-occupied Poland were still a long way from the front line, and inside them the mass killing of Jews continued, uninterrupted by Germany's growing military needs, both on the eastern and Italian fronts. Indeed, on the very day that the Krasnodar trial opened on newly liberated Soviet soil, the Polish Government-in-Exile in London sent the Foreign Office two reports, which had been smuggled out of German-occupied Poland, of atrocities still being committed against the Jews. These reports, both dated July 17, referred specifically to the deportations of Jews to Majdanek concentration camp.

According to the first report, from a resistance leader, the Commander-in-Chief of the underground forces in the Lublin district had told him 'that he had evidence that some of the people are being murdered in gas cells there'.

[1] *The People's Verdict: A Full Report of the Proceedings at the Krasnodar and Kharkov German Atrocity Trials*, London, 1944. The proceedings of the Krasnodar trial are on pages 7–44.

The second report was even more specific: 'It has been ascertained that on July 2nd and 5th two transports made up of women, children and old men, each consisting of thirty wagons, have been liquidated in gas cells.'

These two reports were discussed in the Foreign Office. When one official, Roger Allen, asked a colleague to evaluate them, he also added: 'However, you may not consider this of sufficient importance to warrant action.' His colleague William Cavendish-Bentinck, the Chairman of the Joint Intelligence Committee, whose task it was to evaluate the truth or falsehood of all such reports from Nazi Europe, replied, on August 27: 'In my opinion it is incorrect to describe Polish information regarding German atrocities as trustworthy. The Poles, and to a far greater extent the Jews, tend to exaggerate German atrocities in order to stoke us up.'[1]

The reports were in fact the opposite of exaggerated. Thus on July 20 a thousand Jewish men, women and children had reached Auschwitz from Paris, the fifty-ninth such deportation from France in sixteen months. Within a few hours 440 had been gassed, including 126 children. The rest, 369 men and 191 women, were tattooed, and sent to the barracks. Yet even of these, only twenty-seven of the men and sixteen of the women survived the war.[2]

On July 20, the day this particular train reached Auschwitz from Paris, the Jewish Agency representatives in Istanbul sent on to Jerusalem a digest of the messages which they had recently received from Europe. Some of these messages were cryptic postcards; terse, oblique hints to pass the censor. But added together, they told a terrible story: of deportees from the few remaining ghettoes gassed at Treblinka and Belzec; of life in the ghettoes being 'terribly crowded with death'; and of 'a number of deportations' even from the 'model' ghetto of Theresienstadt. The deportees from Theresienstadt, the messages stated, had started on a journey 'of which none knew the end'.

The Istanbul letter of July 20 also brought bad news about the Jews of Zagreb, the capital of the satellite State of Croatia. A message had reached Istanbul two months earlier that no more than four hundred Jews, including forty-five children, were left of the once flourishing Jewish community of many thousands. These thousands, the message stated, had 'moved to take up residence in the suburb of Kever'. Kever was the Hebrew for 'Grave'. Now there was more news. Of the four hundred survivors of two months earlier, 350 had been deported 'to an unknown destination'. The last letter received in Istanbul from Zagreb was dated June 27. 'It is a terrible cry for help.'

The news from Rumania was also distressing; the 'descriptions of the appearance of orphan children are harrowing', Istanbul reported. As for the Polish ghetto of Bedzin, which earlier had been 'comparatively, a ray of light', even from Bedzin 'of late' the listeners in Istanbul had heard 'of deportations and slaughter there'.[3]

This bad news was quickly substantiated, in a letter sent from Bedzin itself on July 17, by four young Zionists. As soon as their letter, smuggled across Nazi-dominated Europe, reached Istanbul, in mid-August, the scale of

[1] Foreign Office papers, 371/34551.
[2] See Serge Klarsfeld, *Le Memorial de la Deportation des Juifs de France*, Paris 1978
[3] 'Extracts from a letter from Istanbul (translated from the Hebrew original)', Central Zionist Archives, Z 4/14758.

slaughter was confirmed. During the first year and a half of the war, the letter declared, the Polish Zionists had been able to set up an 'immense' network of training farms, and a strong Zionist youth movement, 'much larger and stronger than in normal times'. But then, suddenly, all 'regular work', the preparation for Palestine, had been disrupted, 'the ovens were installed, and the systematic extermination began'.

The letter from Bedzin went on to tell of 80,000 Jews from German-occupied western Poland who had been gassed at Chelmno and of the remaining 40,000 Jews of the Lodz ghetto who were sealed in the ghetto, 'doomed to die of hunger and wasting away'. Only 20,000 Jews were still alive in Lithuania, in three ghettoes, at Vilna, Kovno and Shauliai. The rest of Lithuania had become _Judenrein_, 'purged of all Jews'. As for the cities of Warsaw, Lublin, Czestochowa and Cracow, each of them once with flourishing Jewish communities, 'today there are no longer any Jews'. They had been exterminated in Treblinka, the 'famous extermination camp' not only for Polish Jews, but also for Jews from Holland, Belgium and elsewhere.

The letter of July 17 went on to tell of the Warsaw uprising, 'the finest chapter in our struggle', after which 'all the Jews were destroyed and the ghetto completely destroyed'. Outside Warsaw, there were some 30,000 Jews still alive in labour camps, but 'in two weeks time these will also be gone'. A few thousand Jews were in hiding in the 'aryan' side of Warsaw. In Bialystok some 20,000 were living 'under relatively better conditions'. All the Jews of the Lublin region had been gassed in Belzec and Sobibor.

The letter from Bedzin went on to state that only in East Upper Silesia, where Bedzin itself was located, were Jews still living in 'something resembling human conditions'. But even here, things were changing. Three weeks earlier, seven thousand Jews had been 'transferred' from Bedzin, and had been killed in Auschwitz: 'There they were killed by shooting and burning'.

The letter continued: 'In the next few weeks the district from which we write will now become _Judenrein_. By the time this letter reaches you, none of us will be alive.'

For several months, the Jews of Bedzin had been among those who managed to receive South American passports from Switzerland. But in their letter of July 17, the four young Zionists noted that those who had received these protective documents had 'simply vanished'. At first it had been thought that they were safe, 'but we now know that they were sent to Auschwitz'.[1]

What did the name 'Auschwitz' mean to those in Istanbul who read this letter of July 17? Three days later a further letter was sent from Istanbul to Jerusalem. It had been sent to Turkey from the Slovak city of Bratislava just over three months earlier, and it too mentioned Auschwitz. But not as a centre of mass murder. Instead, the letter referred to 'those main centres' to which men and women had been sent: 'Auschwitz in Upper Silesia', 'Birkenau in Upper Silesia' and 'Lublin'. And the letter went on to explain that 'the life in these camps is that of protective custody'.[2]

What then was the truth?

[1] Yad Vashem archive, o-67.
[2] Letter dated 20 July 1943, Central Zionist Archives, Z 4/14779.

Even while the letter from Bedzin was on its way to Istanbul, the Jews of Bedzin were being destroyed, as the letter said they would be. A second transport of four thousand had already been sent to Auschwitz on June 22. Almost all were gassed on arrival.

In London, for both the Government and the Zionists, it was the post-war future of Palestine that re-emerged as a point of controversy towards the end of July. Churchill himself was stimulated by a telegram from General Smuts to the Secretary of State for the Dominions, sent on July 22, and arguing that it would be 'impossible', as had been proposed by several Ministers, 'to send Jews back to Germany and similar persecuting countries'. Other provision would have to be made, Smuts wrote, 'in spite of Muslim intransigence'.

As Smuts saw it, 'Jewish sufferings and massacres make their reasonable requirements a first charge on Allied statesmanship'. This charge, he believed, 'should take precedence over efforts to placate Arabs or the like'. Smuts added: 'Jewish weakness should not make us forget moral strength of their case which goes to the root of whole issue in this war. If we fail the Jews it means Hitler's triumph in the fundamental item of his satanic creed'.[1]

On reading Smuts' argument, Churchill replied by telegram on July 24 that it 'expresses my personal views exactly', and that he was giving it a 'special circulation' to the Cabinet.[2]

That same day, at Chequers, Churchill discussed the war with two of his guests, the air ace, Wing-Commander Guy Gibson and his wife Eve. Churchill wanted Gibson to go on a goodwill tour of Canada and the United States. Eve Gibson later recalled how: 'We were shown a film, captured from the Germans, depicting the atrocities inflicted on the Jews and inhabitants of the occupied countries. It was quite ghastly and the Prime Minister was very, very moved. He told me that it was shown to every American serviceman arriving in this country.'[3]

On July 25 it was announced that Mussolini had been overthrown. For the Jews who heard this news in Allied lands, it was full of danger. Suddenly the future seemed at risk not only for the 43,000 Jews of Italy whom Mussolini had protected from deportation, but also for many thousand more Jews who lived, or had found refuge, in the Italian-occupied zones of France and Croatia, along the Dalmatian coast, in Albania, in Greece, Corfu, and as far east as the island of Rhodes. On July 27, two days after the Duce's fall, but before either the military or political future of Italy was known, Richard Lichtheim and Gerhart Riegner telegraphed from Geneva to New York: 'Recent events Italy and forthcoming retreat Italian troops from Italian-occupied zone France constitute great danger for large number of Jews concentrated this zone, as in German-occupied zone anti-Jewish terror growing daily.' The Geneva telegram suggested a direct intervention by the World Jewish Congress with the Vatican, with a view to ensuring that the retreating Italian troops 'should protect Jews under their domination'.[4]

[1] Premier papers, 4/52/5, folios 1074-5.
[2] Prime Minister's Personal Telegram T.1102/3. Premier papers, 4/52/5.
[3] Letter to the author from Eve Gibson, 17 May 1980. Gibson himself was killed in action September 1944.
[4] Central Zionist Archives, L 22/92.

While the fate of the Jews of Italy and the Italian territories remained uncertain, the deportations from elsewhere in Europe continued without interruption. On August 2 the clerks at Auschwitz recorded the arrival of three
trains: one, the sixth in two days, from Bedzin, from which all but 385
deportees were gassed; one from Paris, from which 218 men and fifty-five
women were taken to the camp, and the rest, 727 in all, were gassed; and one
from Malines, in Belgium, with 1,556 deportees, of whom 1,090 were gassed.

The Nazi military dominance did not prevent the Jews from striking back,
as they had done in Warsaw. But as in the Warsaw ghetto, they were, in each
instance, crushed by the overwhelming German military superiority. Nevertheless, the revolts continued: in Treblinka itself, on August 2, prisoners
fought with guards, set fire to buildings, and cleared a way through the wire
for escapees. Of the seven hundred prisoners then in the camp, more than 150
escaped. One by one they were hunted down. No more than a dozen survived.[1]
Two weeks later, on August 16, a revolt broke out in the Bialystok ghetto, as
the 40,000 Jews were suddenly assembled, and informed that they were to be
deported to labour camps.

Five hundred young Jews and Jewesses who had been preparing to organize
a revolt, fought for four days with guns, grenades and explosives against
German and Ukrainian units equipped with machine guns, light artillery, and
as much ammunition as they cared to use. On August 20 the revolt was
crushed, and the survivors deported to Treblinka and Auschwitz, as planned.[2]
One train was sent elsewhere: on to the 'model' ghetto at Theresienstadt. In
its sealed cattle trucks were 1,260 children. On August 24 they arrived at
Theresienstadt. Two and a half months later, they too were deported to their
deaths at Auschwitz.

The Treblinka and Bialystok revolts led to no pause in the Nazi policy of
seeking out the remaining Jews for death, and during August Jews were
brought to Auschwitz from Salonica, Holland, western Poland and Pomerania;
almost all were gassed.

At the same time, the Germans let it be known publicly to the Allies that all
Jews who were on 'exchange lists' would not be 'molested'. As a result of this
assurance, the Jewish Agency representatives in Geneva had continued to press
their colleagues in Jerusalem to forward as many names and addresses as
possible. Jews with Palestinian citizenship, the parents or children of such
Jews, and even veteran Zionists with European nationality, were considered
eligible for such exchanges. The British approved of the scheme, made the
necessary Palestinian visas available, authorized the Jewish Agency's Palestine
Offices in Geneva and Istanbul to prepare the lists, and instructed the International Red Cross to pass on the necessary letters to the fortunate few.

By the autumn of 1943, reports of Nazi atrocities had become frequent and
detailed. But at the same time the Nazi efforts at deception continued. It had

---

[1] The revolt at Treblinka is described in Jean-François Steiner, *Treblinka*, London 1967 and in Samuel
Rajzman, 'Uprising in Treblinka', in Yuri Suhl (editor), *They Fought Back: The Story of Jewish Resistance
in Nazi Europe*, London 1968, pages 150–7.
[2] The Bialystok Ghetto revolt is described in Szymon Datner, *Walka i zaglada bialostockiego ghetta*,
Lodz 1946, and in Reuben Ainsztein, 'The Bialystock Ghetto Revolt', in Yuri Suhl (editor), *They
Fought Back: The Story of Jewish Resistance in Nazi Europe*, London 1968, pages 158–66.

become clear in the west that the principal phrase of deception, 'resettlement', meant deportation to a concentration camp. This had been clearly stated in the Allied Declaration of 17 December 1942. But the Nazis still hoped to create the impression that these camps were not death camps.

To this end, on 6 September 1943, two 'eastern transports' were sent from the Theresienstadt ghetto to Auschwitz, arriving on the following day. On arrival, no 'selection' at all was made for the gas chambers. Nor were the men and women sent to different camps. Instead, amid scenes of politeness which were in extraordinary contrast to the usual brutality, the 5,007 deportees were taken to a special area of Auschwitz, thirty stables, and allowed to live together as they had done previously in Theresienstadt.

The thirty stables became 'Work-Camp Birkenau'. No SS doctors appeared, as they did in all the other labour barracks, to mark off the sick and weak for gassing. Instead, the deportees were encouraged to send postcards: to write to their relatives and friends both in Theresienstadt, and in their former homes in Czechoslovakia. The message was clear, and in the case of these five thousand, accurate. They had indeed been deported, and deported to Auschwitz, but they were still alive.

Despite the 'horse-stable deception', as it later became known, the news that filtered out of Nazi Europe in the autumn of 1943 made it clear that at least those Polish Jews who had been deported 'to an unknown destination' the previous autumn had all been shot or gassed. It was also clear that rescue possibilities, where they existed at all, were on a minor scale. On September 1 a report was smuggled from Slovakia to Switzerland by a group of Slovak Zionists who were actively organizing an escape route from Poland, across Slovakia, and into Hungary for those Jews who had not yet been deported. In six months, more than seven hundred had managed to escape southwards across the Polish-Slovak and Slovak-Hungarian border. Now two groups of children were being brought out of Poland. Twenty-three had reached the Slovak capital, Bratislava, and twenty were at the Polish-Slovak border.

'Operation Children', as it was called, was one of urgency and danger. In many cases the children's parents had already been killed, or were in concentration camps. Unless these children were at once moved on into Hungary, the report stated, 'their fate does not bear thinking about'. Money was urgently needed, for the necessary bribing of frontier guards, customs officials, and 'professional Aryan smugglers'. Peasants had to be bribed to give shelter in the woods near the frontiers. The very same officials who had to be bribed, and the smugglers without whose help the border could not be crossed, could become rapacious, robbing the escapees of what little money they had left.

Unlike adult escapees, the children normally had no money or valuables to buy their way forward. Hence the urgency of this appeal to Switzerland. It was surely, the report asked, 'of paramount importance' to rescue children, as 'both from the human and the Jewish aspect there is still a great potential in children. . . .'

The Geneva-based Zionists responded to this appeal, sending money by couriers through Austria to Slovakia. For them, it was a dangerous but necessary task. What they could not do anything about were the three factual reports enclosed in the Bratislava report of September 1: reports which, however, they at once passed on to Istanbul, Jerusalem, London and New York. These three reports provided further confirmation of a deliberate Nazi plan to murder all Jews: to destroy the whole fabric of Jewish life and culture. 'One feels as though paralysed after reading these reports,' the Bratislava Zionists wrote, 'and wonders whether it is possible that such diabolical plans have been hatched in human brains. Now we understand where these innumerable people got to, of whom we informed you that suddenly in the autumn of last year they were transferred across the river Bug in their hundreds of thousands, and we heard no more of them. Their silence is now explained, for we know that their fate led them to annihilation.'

The Bratislava report noted that this news tallied with the testimony of the escapees who had reached Slovakia, and it went on: 'Today we know that Sobibor, Malkinia-Treblinka, Belzec and Auschwitz are liquidation camps', where, in order to produce 'the semblance of a labour camp', small work forces were maintained. That was why, the report added, 'from time to time a few individuals could send us a sign of life'.[1]

Auschwitz had now been mentioned twice in three months as a place of the mass murder of deportees. But the name of the camp made no particular impact, and led to no specific action. Nor was it again referred to as a 'liquidation' camp in any of the many messages from Geneva to Istanbul during the next eight months.

Meanwhile, Auschwitz continued its destructive course. On September 2, while the Bratislava report was on its clandestine way to Switzerland, 1,004 Jews from Holland reached Auschwitz. Within a few hours 498, including all the children and old people, had been gassed. On September 3 a 'selection' was made inside the women's camp, and a hundred women, those judged too weak or too sick to work, were taken away to the gas chambers. On September 4, a thousand Jews reached Auschwitz from Paris. Likewise within a few hours, 662, including more than a hundred children, were taken to their death. By the end of the month, three more trains from Holland, and one from Belgium, had reached the camp.

On September 24 a summary of the Jewish situation throughout Europe was sent by Richard Lichtheim, in Geneva, to the Jewish Agency in Jerusalem. It was a bleak survey: in France, 'the Germans seem to make no longer any difference between French or Foreign Jews'; in Slovakia, 70,000 of the 90,000 had been deported: in Holland, 'there are not more than 20 or 30,000 Jews left', of the former total of 160,000, and the deportations from Westerbork were continuing. Those Dutch Jews who had been deported had been sent partly to 'labour service' in Germany, Lichtheim added, and partly to Poland, 'and you know what that means for most of them'. Of the Jews of Germany and Austria, those not in labour camps 'are dead or deported'. Of the Jews of Poland, even those on the Palestine exchange list could not be contacted. The Germans had promised that women and children on the exchange list 'would be spared', but, Lichtheim commented, 'I am very much afraid that for most of these women and children this action has come too late.'

[1] The original of the Bratislava report of 1 September 1943, in German, is in Central Zionist Archives, S 26/1428.

In a telegram from the Jewish Agency in Jerusalem to the Palestine Office in Geneva, a question had been raised about the Jews of Denmark. In his letter of September 24 Lichtheim commented that no 'direct reports' had yet reached Geneva about Danish Jewry, a community of more than seven thousand. 'So far,' Lichtheim reported, 'I have not heard of deportations as in the other German-occupied countries.'[1]

Unmolested since the German conquest of Denmark in April 1940, Danish Jewry was in fact about to face its moment of trial. On August 29 Hitler himself, frustrated by the degree of autonomy which the Danes had been accorded, ordered the internment of the Danish army and the resignation of the Government. Two days later, the Gestapo seized the Jewish community records in Copenhagen, together with the names and addresses of all Jews throughout Denmark, and on September 8 the German Minister in Denmark, Dr Werner Best, telegraphed to the Foreign Office in Berlin, suggesting that advantage should be taken of the political emergency to deport the Jews. All he would need from Germany were soldiers, policemen and ships. Ten days later, Hitler gave his approval to these new deportations.

Dr Best acted swiftly, and on September 28, only ten days after Hitler's approval, he reported to Berlin that he was ready to carry out the deportations in a single night, on October 1. But that same day a German shipping expert, G. F. Duckwitz, who was in Copenhagen, passed on the secret to the Danes, who passed it on to the Jews. On the evening of September 29, while gathered in synagogue at the beginning of the Jewish New Year, the Jews of Copenhagen were told of the impending deportation, and advised to hide with their non-Jewish neighbours.

The people of Denmark hurried to the aid of their Jewish fellow citizens. In churches throughout Denmark, a pastoral letter was read out, reminding the congregants that Jesus too was a Jew. As the Germans began their raids on Jewish homes, less than five hundred Jews were caught, and deported. Meanwhile, the Swedish Government offered refuge to all Jews who could be smuggled by boat to Sweden, and, by the end of October, helped not only by the Danish people, but even by the Danish police, more than seven thousand men, women and children were ferried the five to fifteen miles across the Oresund and to the safety of the Swedish shore: 5,919 were Jews, 1,301 were part Jews, and 686 were Christians married to Jews.[2]

The Jews of Italy were less fortunate than those of Denmark. At first it had seemed that they too might be saved, not only by Mussolini's refusal to deport Jews to Germany, but, after the fall of Mussolini in July 1943, by the liberation of Italy by the Allied armies. On September 8, only six weeks after the fall of Mussolini, the Italian Army surrendered to the Allies.

The Italian surrender came, however, at a difficult moment for the Allies, whose troops were only in possession of southern Italy. As a result, the Germans were able immediately to occupy not only the whole of northern Italy itself, including Rome, but also all the former territory controlled by

---

[1] Central Zionist Archives, L 22/143. Letter No. 1173 via Istanbul.
[2] There is an account of the saving of Danish Jewry in Raul Hilberg, *The Destruction of the European Jews*, Harper Colophon edition, New York 1979, pages 357–63. See also Leni Yahil, *The Rescue of Danish Jewry*, Philadelphia, 1969.

Italy since 1940: southeastern France, the Adriatic coast of Yugoslavia, southern Croatia, Albania, southern Greece, Crete, Corfu, Rhodes and Kos.

One of the first Italian-controlled areas into which the Gestapo moved was southeastern France. Since 1940 thousands of Jews had found refuge there, from German-occupied France, from Belgium and Holland, and after November 1942 from Vichy France. Now the Gestapo began their search for deportees. Even to those who watched events from outside Nazi Europe, their fate was clear. On September 14 Weizmann's secretary, Doris May, wrote from London to a friend in New York:

. . . one wonders what has happened to the 15,000 or so Jewish refugees who found 'refuge' in Italian-occupied S. France. Or rather, one doesn't wonder very much: too late, again.

'How *can* some of our panjandrums even sleep at nights?' Doris May added. 'Or do they (like me alas!) take refuge in the comfortable thought that "there's nothing *I* can do about it"?'[1]

In northern and central Italy, as in southern France, the Gestapo acted swiftly, sending Captain Theodor Dannecker, the officer who had successfully organized the systematic deportation of French Jewry, to repeat his success in Italy. Even those Jews who were able to escape northwards, and reach the Swiss border, were not necessarily safe: the Swiss border authorities, Richard Lichtheim reported from Geneva to Jerusalem on October 4, 'have become most severe'.[2]

Meanwhile, as the Swiss authorities made it extremely difficult for refugees to cross the border into Switzerland, and even turned back many of those who did manage to cross on to Swiss soil, Captain Dannecker worked efficiently and quickly. On October 9 he was ready to act. That day, the Gestapo seized several hundred Jews in Trieste, and deported them to Auschwitz. On October 18 a total of 1,007 Jews were arrested in Rome itself, despite a protest from the Vatican 'to stop these arrests' at once. Like the Jews of Trieste, those of Rome were also deported to Auschwitz. Only twelve were to survive the war.

In the first two weeks of November Jews were seized by the Gestapo throughout German-occupied Italy, and six weeks after the first deportation from Trieste, nearly ten thousand Italian Jews had been deported to Auschwitz, where more than 7,750 of them were murdered.

The Italian surrender was also the moment of disaster for the Jews of Athens and southern Greece, who, unlike those of Salonica, Thrace and Macedonia, had not been deported earlier in the year. Now the arrival of the German armies was followed, as in Italy itself, by the arrival of the Gestapo, and on October 2 the Jewish Agency representatives in Istanbul telegraphed to Jerusalem, their message arriving three days later: 'Telegrams from Athens acknowledge extreme danger expulsion whole Greece Jewry to Poland.' The message, which was incomplete, continued: 'Conjure to save their lives and demand Greek radio instructions for population aid their . . .'[3]

The Jewish Agency in Jerusalem acted immediately, telegraphing on October 6 to the Greek Legation in Cairo to ask the Greek Government-in-

[1] Lourie papers.
[2] Central Zionist Archives, L 22/338. Letter No. 1178 via Istanbul.
[3] Central Zionist Archives, S 25/1670.

Exile to broadcast 'radio instructions' to the Greek population, to help their Jewish compatriots with a view to 'prevent deportation'.[1] The Greeks agreed to do so, and the broadcast appeal was made on October 14. That same day, unknown in the west, six hundred Jews in Sobibor, one of the worst of the eastern death camps, rose up in revolt. They were led by a Jewish officer of the Red Army who had been taken prisoner by the Germans and brought to the camp only three weeks before, to join the 600 in the small labour section of the camp.[2] At least ten SS men, and several of the Ukrainian guards, were killed, and nearly four hundred of the prisoners succeeded in breaking out. More than half of them, however, were killed on the land mines with which the Germans had surrounded the camp, or caught by the massive hunting party of police, soldiers and SS men which went in search of them. Two days later, Himmler ordered the camp to be levelled to the ground. In a year and a half, it had become the graveyard of 600,000 Jews, deported there from all over Europe, and gassed within hours of their arrival.[3]

At Auschwitz, the killing continued without cease. On October 3 an SS doctor made a 'selection' of those in the camp, and 139 Jews, judged too sick to work, were taken away and gassed. Five days later, during the opening hours of Yom Kippur, the holiest moment in the Jewish year, a further 'special' selection was made, and a thousand men and women, likewise judged too sick to work, were sent to their doom.

On October 23 a total of 1,700 Jews reached Auschwitz from Bergen-Belsen. Of various European nationalities, they had been told that they were being sent to Switzerland, and safety. Their shock at being deceived was intense. Despite the formidable apparatus of guards, dogs, machine guns, electric fences and watch-towers, as the deportees were being 'selected' a Jewess among them seized a revolver from an SS man standing by her, and shot at two SS officers. All at once other women in the group hurled themselves on the guards, attacking them with their bare hands. As the women fought, tore and scratched, many of them were shot, and others killed by grenades. The rest were then seized, and taken to the gas chamber. One of the wounded officers died on the way to a nearby hospital.

News of the revolt of these unarmed women was not to be known in the west for another nine months. Nor did the revolt itself lead to any pause in the deportations or in the gassing. On October 28 several hundred Jews from the Pabianice labour camp near Lodz were brought to Auschwitz and gassed, and at the end of the month 613 Jews from Paris were gassed, the women and children on October 30, the men on October 31.

At the War Cabinet on October 8, Churchill had referred 'to the atrocities which the Germans are now committing in the various countries which they were holding in subjection, or from which they were now being driven'. An eye-witness had reported that on the island of Kos, a hundred Italian officers

---

[1] Central Zionist Archives, S 25/1670.
[2] The officer's name was Alexander Pechersky. He survived the uprising, rejoined the Red Army, and was living (in 1980) in Rostov-on-Don.
[3] For an account of the death camp at Sobibor, and the revolt, see Miriam Novitch, *Sobibor Martyrdom and Revolt: Documents and Testimonies*, New York 1980.

'had been shot by the Germans in cold blood'. This was only the most recent example. 'Other instances of German "frightfulness",' Churchill told his colleagues, 'were continually being received.'

Churchill cast about for some means of halting the German atrocities. It might, he felt, have a 'salutory effect' on the Germans if Britain, the United States and the Soviet Union were to make an immediate declaration 'to the effect that a number of German officers or members of the Nazi Party, equal to those put to death by the Germans in the various countries, would be returned to those countries after the war for judgement'.[1]

The War Cabinet approved Churchill's suggestion that he draft a declaration on these lines, to submit to Roosevelt and Stalin. In the draft, Churchill pointed out that as the Allied armies were advancing, 'the recoiling Hitlerites and Huns are redoubling their ruthless cruelties'. All those responsible for, or having taken a consenting part 'in atrocities, massacres and executions', were to be sent back to the countries 'in which their abominable deeds were done in order that they may be judged and punished according to the laws of those liberated countries. . . .'

Churchill's draft declaration went on to list those countries in which German atrocities had taken place. No mention was made of the Jews, but the draft did speak of 'the slaughters inflicted on the people of Poland' and 'in the territories of the Soviet republic which are now being swept clear of the enemy', and it went on to warn:

Let those who have hitherto not imbrued their hands with innocent blood beware lest they join the ranks of the guilty, for most assuredly the three allied powers will pursue them to the uttermost ends of the earth, and will deliver them to their accusers in order that justice may be done.

Such a declaration, Churchill believed, would make at least 'some of these villains shy of being mixed up in butcheries now that they know they are going to be beat'.[2]

But Anthony Eden was not happy about Churchill's message. 'Broadly,' he informed Churchill on October 9, 'I am most anxious not to get into the position of breathing fire and slaughter against War Criminals and promising condign punishment, and a year or two hence having to find pretexts for doing nothing.'[3]

The Jewish Agency and the World Jewish Congress continued to do what they could to mitigate the ferocity of Nazi persecution. On October 23 Dr Pozner was able to send from Geneva to Istanbul, for transmission to Jerusalem, the names and addresses of twenty-four Jews known to be in Belgium, whom he had placed on his Geneva Exchange List, and for whom he now needed Migration certificates from Palestine. That same week, in the United States, the World Jewish Congress asked the Chairman of the American Red Cross, Norman Davis, to announce that all surviving Jews in the ghettoes of

---

[1] War Cabinet Conclusions 137 of 1943. Minute 2. Copy in Premier papers, 4/100/9.
[2] Prime Minister's Personal Telegram, T.1601/3. Personal and Most Secret. Premier papers, 4/100/9, folios 511–4.
[3] Premier papers, 4/100/9, folio 508.

eastern Europe would henceforth be recognized as prisoners-of-war, and thus obtain the direct protection both of the International Red Cross, and of the relevant Geneva convention.

This proposal was rejected, because, as Davis wrote on October 20, the Germans considered their treatment of the Jews as an internal matter. In addition, Davis went on to explain, the protection of 'civilian internees' had not yet received legal sanction in a separate convention. Thirdly, 'it would seem', Davis wrote, 'an exceedingly doubtful procedure to jeopardise the smooth operation' of existing activities protecting prisoners-of-war in an attempt to broaden the existing Convention. Fourthly, the International Red Cross was not in a position to threaten Germany that if Jews continued to suffer privations and death it would not help German prisoners-of-war or German civilian internees. 'Civilian internees', that is, German civilians interned in Allied hands, were in a quite different category to 'detained civilians', that is Jews who were nationals of conquered lands being detained by the conqueror. And fifthly, for Davis was not short of reasons for declining the proposal: 'Our first duty is to individuals regardless of their nationality, creed or race.'[1]

The Jewish Agency understood the Red Cross dilemma. As Dr Kahany later recalled, of his own appeals to Red Cross officials in Geneva: 'The Nazis told them, "don't touch the concentration camps or we will not keep the prisoners-of-war convention".'The Red Cross also pointed out that it had more than a million Allied prisoners-of-war for whom it was responsible, 'while at that stage, on the other side, there were very few German prisoners-of-war'.

Kahany was also told that the International Red Cross had indeed asked the German authorities if the Red Cross could visit the concentration camps: 'The German reply had been, "never, never, never. The question of Jews is an internal German question".' Nevertheless, hoping to advance further, Kahany had suggested that something might be gained if the International Red Cross were at least to announce publicly that they had made the request, and that it had been refused. This suggestion, however, was turned down.[2]

Despite Eden's hesitations about a new war crimes declaration, Churchill had persisted in his belief that as the Soviet armies advanced westwards, such a declaration, issued by Stalin, might give at least the satellite rulers cause to hesitate in the continuing slaughter. 'I attach great importance,' he wrote to Eden on October 21, 'to the principle that the criminals will be taken back to be judged in the countries or even in the districts where these crimes have been committed.'[3]

Churchill's wish was met, resulting on 1 November 1943 in the Moscow Declaration, of which Churchill himself had been the author. It followed almost exactly the wording of his draft declaration of October 9, as approved by the War Cabinet: lists of the 'abominable deeds' would be compiled 'in all possible detail', from all Nazi Europe. The Allies would pursue those who had

[1] Archives of the World Jewish Congress, R & R/Red Cross 1943. Letter addressed to Dr S. Z. Kantor.
[2] Dr Menahem Kahany, conversation with the author, Geneva, 2 October 1980.
[3] Prime Minister's Personal Telegram, T.1682/3, Personal and Secret, Premier papers, 4/100/9, folio 487.

joined 'the ranks of the guilty . . . to the uttermost ends of the earth', and would deliver them to their accusers 'in order that justice may be done'.[1]

A week later, the Institute of Jewish Affairs published in the United States a statement about the murder of Jews in Europe. According to this statement 'Hitler has murdered or destroyed by planned starvation, pogroms, forced labour, and deportations more than three million of Europe's Jews'. The statement was published in the British press, the headline in the *People* read:

HITLER MURDERED THREE MILLION JEWS IN EUROPE.

By itself this was an impressive headline, but it appeared as one of the smallest items of the day in the very bottom of the corner of the front page.[2] Meanwhile, news of the eastward deportations continued to reach the west. On November 5 Gerhart Riegner telegraphed from Geneva, both to the Czechoslovak Government in London, and to his own World Jewish Congress colleagues there: 'Transports out of Theresienstadt have recently shown a marked increase. Between July 15 and September 30, 6,800 Czech Jews – among others – were deported from Theresienstadt to Birkenau. They were put aboard the deportation trains under cover of mounted machine-guns ready for firing'.[3]

As far as the Geneva listening-post was concerned, the fate of these Czech Jews, once they reached Auschwitz-Birkenau, was unknown.

[1] Premier papers, 4/100/3.
[2] The *People*, 17 October 1943. See photographs 13 and 14.
[3] Archives of the World Jewish Congress, General Secretariat.

Chapter 18

'A quite unmanageable flood'

Despite the presence of Allied forces south of Rome, deportations to Auschwitz from Italy and western Europe continued throughout November 1943. These deportations remained secret, unknown to the Allies. Yet they included two hundred Jews deported from Florence on November 6, several hundred from Rome on November 14, a total of 531 from Holland on November 17, and 1,200 from Paris on November 20, of whom more than nine hundred were gassed on arrival at the camp.

Inside Auschwitz itself, even those sent to the camp continued to be 'selected' for the gas chambers: on November 19 a selection was made in the women's camp, and 384 Jewesses driven away to their deaths. Two of the women, Bina Braun and Rosa Thieberger, managed to jump out of the motor lorry in which they were being driven through the camp to the gas chambers. They tried to hide among the other inmates, but were captured and shot.

Meanwhile, the advance of the Red Army from the east was preceded by Nazi atrocities against those Jews who had survived the earlier deportations and massacres. On November 3 the SS instituted what they called a 'harvest festival' at Majdanek, killing 18,000 prisoners in a single day, and a further 34,000 within the next few weeks. On November 5 several hundred Jews in the concentration camp ghetto at Riga were deported to Auschwitz and gassed.

There was resistance also in the east during November: in the Janowska concentration camp in Lvov, in the Poniatowa labour camp southeast of Warsaw, and at Kovno, where 150 young Jews, men and women, managed to escape to the Rudniki forests and join the Soviet partisans.

But little could be done from outside Nazi Europe to help these efforts, or to prevent the killings. On November 10 the Jewish Agency in Jerusalem suggested to Nahum Goldmann in New York that the British and American Governments should be approached with a view to warning the Rumanian authorities that 'they will be held responsible' if they failed to prevent the Germans from carrying out a 'wholesale slaughter' of Jews as Soviet troops approached the Rumanian border.[1]

Exchange Lists and Palestine certificates continued to be the one area of hope and rescue. During the first three weeks of November, eighty-three Jewish refugees from Hungary, as yet not under direct German rule, succeeded in reaching Palestine through Rumania, Bulgaria and Turkey, as did nineteen refugees from Rumania. All 102 had been given certificates by the British authorities. They were all wives and children of Palestinian Jews, or Zionist veterans, whose names had been given by the Jewish Agency to the British,

[1] Central Zionist Archives, S 25/1670.

and passed on by the British Legation in Switzerland to the Swiss Government, which had then forwarded the documents to the Hungarian and Rumanian Governments.

The attempt to add names and addresses to the Exchange Lists continued without respite, with Geneva as the principal point of dispatch. In all, ten lists were sent into Holland, with a total of 2,748 names; twelve lists to Rumania, with more than 2,909 names; twenty-one lists into Hungary, half from Geneva and half from Istanbul, with more than 7,193 names, and at least one list to Belgium.

On November 28 another rescue action came to a climax: the smuggling out of German-occupied Greece of 127 Greek Jews, who were taken by boat to the Turkish coast, and safety. With the approval of the British authorities in Turkey, the Jewish Agency was then able to send the Jews on to Palestine by rail. In December, a further 83 Greek Jews were rescued in this way.

These various efforts by the Jewish Agency saved several thousand lives. Although this was a small total in the shadow of the murder of millions, there seemed nothing more substantial that could be done. As one of the survivors of the Warsaw ghetto revolt himself wrote in a letter sent on to Palestine on November 26, no armed forces nor the representatives of the Polish Government-in-Exile could have saved their lives; they had only wanted 'such assistance as would enable us to die with honour'.[1]

A similar sense of powerlessness is evident from a note circulated by Richard Law to the War Cabinet's refugee Committee on December 2. The Foreign Office, he said on enquiring through the Swiss Government, 'had been unable to confirm any effective desire on the part of the Bulgarians and Rumanians' to allow any 'substantial' number of Jews to leave. Negotiations were still taking place 'in regard to certain small parties' from southeastern Europe, but it seemed clear that until the satellites' fear of Germany grew less, and fear of the Allies grew greater, 'there is little hope of any large movement'.

Law added that Jewish organizations had warned of the 'precarious' position of 70,000 Rumanian Jews who had been deported to Transnistria, and who were now in the line of advance of the Russian army. The Rumanian Government, it was urged, would be willing to 'facilitate' their removal. But Law warned that not only was this course 'impracticable' for as long as Germany was in control of Transnistria, but that 'there is also no destination for the Jews in question available'. Nor was there sufficient shipping for the evacuation by sea 'even for a small number'.

A more 'practicable proposal', Law suggested, was to supplement the previous 'general warning to our enemies in regard to atrocities' by a specific warning 'in this particular case'.[2]

The Zionist leaders, both in London and Jerusalem, continued to worry about the future of Palestine, and about the danger, as they saw it, of Britain's refusal to agree to any form of Jewish State, however small. At Chequers on

[1] The writer of the letter was Yitzhak Zuckermann, a leader of Jewish resistance in Poland, who survived the war, and subsequently settled in Israel. His letter was published by the Ghetto Fighters' House, Kibbutz Lokamei Haghetaot, Israel, in its journal, Historical Records, number 10, 1958.

[2] War Cabinet Committee on the Reception and Accommodation of Refugees. Note by the Minister of State, 2 December 1942, Cabinet papers, 95/15.

October 25, Churchill promised Dr Weizmann that he would deal with the question of Palestine when the war was over. 'Mr Churchill then said', Weizmann recorded at the time, 'that after they had crushed Hitler they would have to establish the Jews in the position where they belonged.' Churchill also said 'that of every fifty officers who came back from the Middle East, only one spoke favourably of the Jews – but that has merely gone to convince him that he was right. . . .'[1]

In Palestine itself, the relationship between the Jewish leadership and the British administration was indeed becoming more bitter. In the second of two arms smuggling trials, which had begun on August 11 and ended on September 27, accusations had been made by the prosecution which caused offence to the Jewish community in Palestine, particularly when the prosecutor, Major J. L. Baxter, referred to the 'Nazi discipline' of the General Federation of Jewish Labour. The Federation was one of the principal and most respected organizations of Palestine Jewry. It protested at once to the High Commissioner that, as The Times reported on September 30 'the word "Nazi" has a very unpleasant meaning among Jews', and it went on to note 'that Jews have voluntarily and willingly undertaken enlistment in the forces of the United Nations and risked their lives in all phases of the struggle'.

In its report The Times noted that this arms trial had 'released the pent-up resentment' of the Jews of Palestine against what they considered to be 'unjust assertions upon Jewish individuals and organisations';[2] and on November 2 the 'foreign minister' of the Jewish Agency, Moshe Shertok, sent a thousand-word telegram to Joseph Linton in London, to protest against what he called the 'anti-Jewish atmosphere' of the trial, in which the whole conduct of the case had given the impression, Shertok said, of having as its aim, not to establish the guilt of the accused, but to 'calumniate' the Jewish community, the Jewish Agency, and the war effort of Palestinian Jewry.

Shertok went on to describe what he called the 'brutal' and 'cynical' cross-examination during the trial of prominent members of the Jewish community, during which it had been suggested that the Jews were arming for 'anti-British purposes'. The prosecution's case had been marked, Shertok added, by 'anti-Jewish political tirades', and foreign journalists had been 'specially encouraged' to come from Egypt to attend the proceedings.[3]

On November 16, there was further friction between the British authorities in Palestine and the Jews, when police and troops raided the Jewish settlement of Ramat Hakovesh, near Haifa, in search of arms. In a telegram to Weizmann on November 19, Moshe Shertok described the violence of the search, the clash between the British and the settlers, and what he called the 'excessive brutal violence' of some of the police, who were seen 'clubbing with rifle butts men fallen', and who had continued to inflict injuries on 'those already bleeding'. A total of twenty-seven men and twenty women had been injured, two 'gravely', and as the police were leaving, accompanied by booing and some stone throwing, two men were shot in the legs when the police officer in charge 'without warning fired two revolver shots into crowd'.

[1] Weizmann papers.
[2] The Times, 30 September 1943.
[3] Central Zionist Archives, S 25/1670.

The policy revealed by the Ramat Hakovesh raid was, Shertok warned, a disastrous course', and he urged 'prompt action' by Weizmann in London to counter it.[1] But on November 21 Sir Harold MacMichael informed the Colonial Secretary that in his view these protests were 'undoubtedly a deliberate and determined attempt by the Jewish Agency to solidify the Jewish nationalist spirit' by 'playing upon' the contrasts of Jewish suffering in Europe and 'the utter lack of sympathy and the brutality of the present regime in Palestine. . . .' This attempt was being helped, MacMichael added, 'by the masochistic tendency, which is so strongly developed in the Jewish temperament, to excite self-pity.'[2]

On the morning of December 13 the American Secretary of State, Cordell Hull, sent for the British Ambassador in Washington, Lord Halifax, to tell him, as Halifax reported later that same day to Anthony Eden, 'of increasing pressure under which United States Government were from Jews'. Cordell Hull 'feared', as Halifax phrased it, 'that unless he could find means of steadying position, they might run into real trouble over it, and Jewish extremists would get control'.

Cordell Hull wanted to be able to tell the 'four million' Jews of America that the United States Government was following the Palestine problem 'with close and constant attention', but did not want to say anything 'embarrassing' to Eden and the British Government. Halifax promised to let him have Eden's comments on the proposed statement in the next few days, explaining to Eden that Hull was 'anxious to forestall what he expects to be "a Jewish blast"'.[3]

Eden replied by telegram on December 21, asking Halifax to express to Cordell Hull 'our candid view that in the long run it would be advantageous to all parties if, apart from a public statement, he felt able to warn Zionist leaders of the dangers of their present policy'. There was a grave danger, Eden explained, of an outbreak of violence in Palestine 'if the Zionists press their maximum demands'. For this reason it was hoped that Hull, 'using his great prestige', would warn the American Zionists 'of the disaster that they may bring on the Jews in Palestine and the damage they may cause to the common war effort if their attitude continues strident and provocative'.[4]

It was not only in Washington, but also in London, that pressure had begun to mount, particularly with regard to British policy towards Jewish refugees. On December 14 this subject was raised in the House of Commons by that persistent campaigner, Eleanor Rathbone. It was almost exactly a year before, she recalled, that Eden had disclosed 'the horrible truths about the cruelties being perpetrated on innumerable Jewish victims on no other ground than their race'. Ever since then, she said, 'the atrocities have continued, and they are continuing day by day'. The number of victims had risen from hundreds of thousands to millions. In Poland alone 'it is estimated that between 1,500,000 and 2,000,000 Jews have been massacred, starved or worked to death by unspeakably sadistic measures'. Every week brought news in the Press 'of the dreadful truck loads of victims that are going across Europe to the murder

---

[1] Central Zionist Archives, S 25/1670.
[2] Letter No. C.S.408, Most Secret, Colonial Office papers, 733/445, 75998/2.
[3] Viscount Halifax, telegram No. 5630, War Cabinet Distribution, copy in Premier papers, 4/52/5.
[4] Foreign Office telegram No. 8792, War Cabinet Distribution, copy in Premier papers, 4/52/5.

camps of Poland, from one European country after another, from France and from Holland, most recently from Greece'.

The Government had promised 'punishment for the war criminals', Miss Rathbone noted. But that, she said 'will not restore the dead to life'. A year ago the practical British public had asked: 'What can be done for rescue before it is too late?' But the result of the Bermuda conference, she argued, was 'pitiably little'. It was essential, she said, to convince the Germans that the question of refugees was one 'about which we care passionately, so much so that if they continue with their massacres and cruelties it may affect their future position and our treatment, after victory, of their peoples'. As for the satellite States, she argued, they were becoming 'increasingly aware of the danger of further outraging world opinion and may yield to pressure where formerly they hardened their hearts'.

Eleanor Rathbone then spoke bitterly of the British Government's earlier policy towards Jewish immigration:

If it had not been for the restrictions placed on immigration to Palestine in pre-war years, even before the Palestinian White Paper, imposed partly for economic reasons and partly to please the Arabs, tens of thousands of men, women and children who now lie in bloody graves would long ago have been among their kindred in Palestine.

That is something I shall never forget, and I hope the House will never forget it either.

There were 'many others', Eleanor Rathbone declared, 'who like me think of this terrible question day and night. It is on our consciences all the time. We are not satisfied that the utmost has been done for rescue'.

Miss Rathbone went on to appeal to the Government to agree to take responsibility, 'not for unlimited numbers' of refugees, but for a proportion of those accepted by the neutral States, 'and so make it possible for the neutral States to offer further large numbers.' Her speech ended with a direct appeal to Eden, and through him to every member of the Cabinet:

Let them not be content with urging the neutral States to take larger numbers in. Let them say plainly what we are prepared to do ourselves and to ask our Dominions and the United States what they are prepared to do. If the Government do that it will have the support of every section of opinion in the country worth consideration. Do not let them be deterred by the mean jealousies and selfish fears of a mere handful of contemptible people who have been influenced by anti-Semitic or by anti-foreigner propaganda. . . .

Our people and the people of the United States are both generous-hearted and deeply humane peoples. Do not let us forget, too, that both these peoples are, professedly at least, Christian peoples. Then let them remember the example of Chaucer's priest of whom it was said,

'Christ's law and that of his apostles
   twelve he taught,
But first he followed it himself.'

During her speech of December 14, Eleanor Rathbone had strongly critic-ized the existing official attitude towards the refugee question. 'Neither we nor the United States,' she said, 'have shown a shining example to the world in this matter.'[1] Unknown to Miss Rathbone, an example of her complaint was

[1] Hansard, 14 December 1943.

taking place as she spoke. Eight months before, the World Jewish Congress
had begun to seek United States support for a possible rescue scheme, put forward by Gerhart Riegner in Geneva.

Riegner's scheme had its origin in a telegram which he had sent from
Geneva on 14 April 1943, to his superiors in New York. My aim, he later
recalled, was 'the beginning of the breaking of the financial blockade against
the Germans, with regard to the victims'.[1] The telegram itself had reported a
'new, urgent appeal for assistance' on behalf of the Rumanian Jews deported
to Transnistria. Money was needed for clothing, especially for children and
orphans 'who should be transferred Palestine'.

Riegner's plan was to avoid the direct transfer of money to Rumania, a
transfer which would have been in breach of the Allied financial blockade, but
to enable the Rumanian Jews to obtain the money they needed by means of a
'definite guarantee' that an identical amount would be deposited in a Swiss or
American bank, 'and paid after war'. Similar funds were needed urgently for
France, 'especially for rescue children being lodged at non-Jews or hidden'.[2]

Despite the initial hostility of the State Department, Riegner's scheme had
been pressed throughout the summer and autumn of 1943, and as it evolved,
it became clear that once the scheme were accepted, and dollars transferred to
a blocked Swiss account, as many as 70,000 Rumanian Jews would be allowed
to leave Rumania for Palestine. But the State Department still hesitated and
delayed, so much so that on 22 July 1943 Stephen Wise went direct to Roosevelt, to explain the scheme personally to the President. To Wise's astonishment, Roosevelt listened without comment, and turned to him with the
words: 'Stephen, why don't you go ahead and do it?' When Wise replied
that he did not feel he had the authority to deal direct with the Secretary of
the Treasury, Henry Morgenthau Jr., Roosevelt simply lifted up his telephone, got through to Morgenthau, and told him: 'Henry, this is a very fair
proposal which Stephen makes about ransoming Jews out of Poland and
Hungary'.[3]

Even Roosevelt's support, however, could not persuade the State Department to look favourably on the scheme for another five months, to the distress
of the World Jewish Congress. Then, on December 15, just as the United
States Treasury was about to issue Riegner with the necessary authorization,
the British Ministry of Economic Warfare informed the United States
Embassy in London that:

The Foreign Office are concerned with the difficulties of disposing of any considerable number
of Jews should they be rescued from enemy-occupied territory. . . .

They foresee that it is likely to prove almost if not quite impossible to deal with anything
like the number of 70,000 refugees whose rescue is envisaged by the Riegner plan. For this
reason they are reluctant to agree to any approval being expressed even of the preliminary
financial arrangements.[4]

[1] Gerhart Riegner, conversation with the author, Geneva, 1 October 1980.
[2] Riegner to Wise, telegram of 14 April 1943, archives of the World Jewish Congress, General Secretariat.
[3] Stephen Wise, *Challenging Years*, London 1951, pages 193–4.
[4] Quoted in Bernard Wasserstein, *Britain and the Jews of Europe 1939–1945*, London and Oxford 1979, page 247.

In reply, the British Ambassador in Washington, Lord Halifax, warned the Foreign Office that American Jewry, 'Zionist or non-Zionist', would regard such a decision as 'inhumane', and on December 21 the American Legation in Berne authorized Riegner to proceed with the scheme, the blockade regulations 'notwithstanding'.[1]

Opinion within the Foreign Office was unchanged. On December 23, Ian Henderson minuted: 'The question at issue is one of balancing the advisability of helping the State Department and Treasury to meet Jewish electoral pressures and of their avoiding a crescendo of US criticism about our Palestine policy, and, on the other hand, of meeting the requirements of the Colonial Office in relation to practical politics and Arab wishes.' Henderson's colleague, A. W. G. Randall noted, on December 24: 'Once we open the door to adult male Jews to be taken out of enemy territory, a quite unmanageable flood may result. (Hitler may facilitate it!).'[2]

It was not the sudden 'unmanageable flood', however, but the painfully slow, small trickle that continued to absorb the energies of the Jewish Agency from day to day. On December 10 one of their Istanbul representatives, Dr Joseph Goldin, reported to Jerusalem that eight Jews had reached Istanbul: from Hungary, four holders of 'ancient' Palestine visas, and two relatives, a wife and a child, of Palestinian residents; and from Bulgaria, two 'veteran Zionists'.[3]

Two days later Goldin telegraphed to his colleague Chaim Barlas, who was then in Ankara, about the six or seven hundred South American passport holders who had been saved from deportation in Warsaw, and taken to Vittel, in France, pending their emigration. It now appeared that they were in some danger, and that 'immediate measures' would have to be taken through the Swiss Government to avoid deportation back to the east.[4]

Henceforth, for more than six months, the fate of these few hundred Polish Jews was to be of acute daily concern to the Jewish Agency. They were, after all, so nearly rescued, and yet so far from safety. All their relatives had been murdered at Treblinka. They alone had been sent by the Germans towards freedom. But the journey was not yet over, and the dangers seemed to grow as the months progressed. These 'Vittel Jews' became, not merely a test case, but almost the only rescue possibility, after the destruction of so many.

Further evidence of the scale of the slaughter of Warsaw Jewry reached the Allies, and western Jewry, on December 15, with the opening of the second Soviet trial of German war criminals, at Kharkov, one of the largest Soviet cities to be liberated from German rule.

During the Kharkov trial a twenty-four-year-old SS Lieutenant, Hans Ritz, was questioned about the use of gas vans in Kharkov. On first hearing the

---

[1] Daniel J. Reagan, Commercial Attaché, to Gerhart Riegner, 21 December 1943, archives of the World Jewish Congress, General Secretariat. Despite Roosevelt's personal support for the scheme, five months had passed between Riegner's initial proposal, and the State Department's acceptance of it. 'Let history, therefore, record for all time', Stephen Wise wrote in his autobiography, 'that were it not for State Department and Foreign Office bureaucratic bungling and callousness, thousands of lives might have been saved and the Jewish catastrophe partially averted'. (*Challenging Years*, page 174).

[2] Foreign Office papers, 371/36747, W 17687.

[3] Central Zionist Archives, L 15/108.

[4] Central Zionist Archives, L 15/108.

words 'gas van' mentioned in Kharkov, Ritz told the prosecutor, 'I remembered the vehicle from my stay in Warsaw, when I witnessed the evacuation in it of the unreliable sections of the Warsaw population.' While in Warsaw, Ritz added, 'I got to know that part of the Warsaw population were evacuated by railway and another part were loaded into the "gas vans" and exterminated.'

Hans Ritz also gave evidence of the mass shooting, in sandpits and stone quarries, of tens of thousands of people in the Soviet cities of Krasnodar, Vitebsk and Taganrog. During the shooting of some three hundred people at a village near Kharkov, Ritz recalled, a woman, trying to save her child, 'covered it with her body. But this did not help her, because the bullet went through her and the child'.[1]

At Auschwitz, the 'horse-stable deception' was continuing, and on December 16 a further 2,491 Jews were brought from Theresienstadt, not to be gassed, but to be put in the special family camp, men, women and children together. Another 2,473 Theresienstadt deportees were added to the family camp four days later, bringing the total since it was begun in September to ten thousand. Their postcards, sent regularly, told of their safe arrival, and of their being alive. They were allowed to receive food parcels from the International Red Cross, and to acknowledge receipt of them.

But even between the arrival of these last two trainloads from Theresienstadt, taken from the railway platform to the stables, there were other arrivals for whom no such deception was required. On December 17, the day after the first new Theresienstadt train, a trainload of Jews arrived from Stutthof concentration camp, near Danzig. Nearly all of them were gassed immediately. On December 20, the very day of the arrival of the second Theresienstadt train, a trainload of 849 Jews reached Auschwitz from Paris; more than five hundred were taken away to be gassed. And throughout December, sick women were taken out of the women's barracks, and sent to the gas chambers, the monthly total being recorded as 4,247.[2]

The family camp at Auschwitz served its purpose well. The postcards sent out, and the food parcels received, were important and successful features of the Nazi deception policy, aimed at lulling those who thought they had no illusions, and confusing others into a sense of uncertainty.

In vain, the World Jewish Congress had continued to press the American Red Cross to give all 'segregated' European Jews the protected status of civilian internees. On December 17 Dr Leon Kubowitzki had urged his senior colleagues to put such a plan 'in the foreground' of their activities. If such status could be secured, he wrote, 'we would perhaps succeed in saving the remainder of the Jewish population of Axis-occupied Europe'.[3] But the American Red Cross again declined even to consider Jewish concentration camp inmates as the legal equivalent of prisoners-of-war, and thus protected by the Geneva Convention.

---

[1] *The People's Verdict, A Full Report of the Proceedings at the Krasnodar and Kharkov German Atrocity Trials*, London 1944. The Kharkov trial proceedings are on pages 45–124.

[2] Danuta Czech, 'Kalendarium der Ereignisse im Konzentrationslager Auschwitz-Birkenau', published in *Hefte von Auschwitz*, volume 6, Auschwitz 1962.

[3] Archives of the World Jewish Congress, New York, R & R/Red Cross 1943.

As 1943 came to an end, and 1944 began, the stories of German atrocities were still not fully believed. One of those concerned by this fact was a Hungarian Jewish refugee, Arthur Koestler, then working as a journalist and lecturer in Britain. 'At present', he wrote in an article which was published in the *New York Times Magazine* in January 1944, 'we have the mania of trying to tell you about the killing, by hot steam, mass-electrocution and live burial, of the total Jewish population of Europe. So far three million have died. It is the greatest mass-killing in recorded history; and it goes on daily, hourly, as regularly as the ticking of your watch.'

Koestler's own 'emotion and bitterness' arose, he wrote, because he had on his desk in front of him photographs of the killings; photographs which had been smuggled out of Poland. 'People died to smuggle them out', he commented, and added caustically, 'they thought it was worth while'. Koestler's article continued:

I have been lecturing now for three years to the troops, and their attitude is the same. They don't believe in concentration camps, they don't believe in the starved children of Greece, in the shot hostages of France, in the mass-graves of Poland; they have never heard of Lidice, Treblinka or Belzec; you can convince them for an hour, then they shake themselves, their mental self-defence begins to work and in a week the shrug of incredulity has returned like a reflex temporarily weakened by a shock.

Clearly all this is becoming a mania with me and my like. Clearly we must suffer from some morbid obsession, whereas you others are healthy and normal. But the characteristic symptom of maniacs is that they lose contact with reality and live in a phantasy world. So, perhaps, it is the other way round: perhaps it is we, the screamers, who react in a sound and healthy way to the reality which surrounds us, whereas you are the neurotics who totter about in a screened phantasy world because you lack the faculty to face the facts.[1]

---

[1] Reprinted in Arthur Koestler, *The Yogi and the Commissar*, London 1945 (Danube Edition, London 1965, page 90).

Chapter 19

Towards a second front

As 1944 opened, the Allied peoples awaited the landing of American and British forces in western Europe. But although this 'second front' had long been spoken of as the only certain means of destroying Nazi tyranny, the Jews of Palestine were nervous of what it might entail. On 29 December 1943 Eliahu Dobkin, head of the Immigration Department of the Jewish Agency, had appealed for the creation of Jewish 'rescue squads' to be sent to the European countries as they were being liberated,[1] while on 11 January 1944 the British Political Intelligence Centre, Middle East, reported that at the end of a five-day conference, the Jewish Labour Federation had expressed its 'considerable anxiety' lest an invasion of Europe 'should lead to even more severe enemy action against those Jews who still remain in enemy territory'.

The Intelligence Centre also reported that speakers at the Jewish Labour Federation had 'emphasised' that the Allied powers 'have so far done nothing political to save the Jews from complete extinction'.[2] Also on January 11, Sir Harold MacMichael warned London, in connection with Dobkin's appeal, that any Jewish 'commando squads' sent into Nazi-dominated Europe 'would undoubtedly be chiefly Zionist propaganda squads charged with the duty of preparing the ground for the emigration of as many Jews as possible to Palestine, rather than of assisting with the task of relief on the spot'.[3]

In London, the Foreign Office continued, during the early months of 1944, to seek a solution for Palestine which would make either a Jewish majority throughout the country, or a smaller partitioned Jewish State, impossible. Churchill, then convalescing in North Africa, asserted his authority against all such moves. He was particularly angered when he read a telegram from Eden to Halifax in which it was suggested that the State Department might wish to help Britain to maintain its pre-war policy. On 12 January 1944 Churchill telegraphed to both Eden and Attlee:

This raises very serious issues. I have always considered the White Paper a disastrous policy and a breach of an undertaking for which I was prominently responsible. Surely we are not going to make trouble for ourselves in America and hamper the President's chances of re-election for the sake of this low-grade gasp of a defeatist hour. The Arabs have done nothing for us during this war, except for the rebellion in Iraq.

We must bring matters to an issue in the Cabinet when I return. Meanwhile we must not commit ourselves to any new defence of the White Paper.

[1] Extract from the newspaper *Davar*, 30 December 1943, sent from H.Q. Palestine to Lord Moyne, Foreign Office papers, 921/152, 6(5) 144/2.
[2] 'Political Intelligence Centre Middle East, Political and General Intelligence Summary (Non-Operational)', Issue No. 18, War Office papers, 169/15698.
[3] Letter No. C.5.300, Most Secret, Foreign Office papers, 921/152, 6(5) 144/1.

'Some form of partition,' Churchill added, 'is the only solution.'[1]

In the United States itself, pressure was growing, particularly in Jewish circles, for a greater official effort on behalf of European Jewry. On 16 January 1944 one of the leading American Jews, the Secretary of the Treasury, Henry Morgenthau, sent President Roosevelt a 'Personal Report' in which he condemned what he called 'the utter failure of certain officials in the State Department' to take effective action 'to prevent the extermination of the Jews in German-controlled Europe'. Morgenthau alleged that the State Department had deliberately sought to prevent news of the mass murders from reaching the public, and had delayed or obstructed pro-Jewish action. Attacking by name the Assistant Secretary of State, Breckenridge Long, Morgenthau denounced the 'indifferent, callous, and perhaps even hostile' attitude of the State Department towards the Jewish issue.

In his nine-page report, Morgenthau gave copious details of two specific acts: the holding up of Riegner's plan to transfer funds to Switzerland for the rescue of Rumanian Jews, and a State Department telegram of 21 January 1943, to Harrison in Berne, advising him not to accept in future 'reports submitted to you to be transmitted to private persons in the United States'. Morgenthau pointed out that this telegram 'was designed to countermand the Department's specific request for information on Hitler's plan to exterminate the Jews'.

Morgenthau insisted that there was nothing 'innocent and routine' about the telegram to Harrison; it was a deliberate concealment, which he had only learned about by accident a year after the event. How many other such concealments, he wrote, 'of the same character are buried in the State Department files is a matter I would have no way of knowing. Judging from the almost complete failure of the State Department to achieve any results, the strong suspicion must be that they are not few'.[2]

Following Morgenthau's protest, Roosevelt made important changes in the organization of American policy. Long himself was no longer to supervise refugee matters at the State Department. A War Refugee Board was established, made up of the Secretaries of State, Treasury, and War, and forming part of 'the executive office of the President'.

On 22 January 1944 Roosevelt himself announced the establishment of the Board. In doing so, he stressed 'that it was urgent that action be taken at once to forestall the plan of the Nazis to exterminate all Jews and other minorities in Europe'.

The aim of the War Refugee Board, according to the White House statement of January 22, was to 'inaugurate effective measures' for the rescue, transportation, maintenance and relief 'of the victims of enemy oppression', as well as the establishment of 'havens of temporary refuge' for such victims. Special Attachés were to be appointed, with diplomatic status, to represent the Board overseas. They would 'accept the services' of agencies of all foreign governments in pursuing their purpose. And the Board would be 'directly

---

[1] Most Secret, Frozen No. 1256, Premier papers, 4/52/5, folio 1029.
[2] 'Personal Report to the President', Secret, 16 January 1944; War Refugee Board archives, Franklin D. Roosevelt Library, Hyde Park, New York.

responsible to the President' in carrying out its policy, and would report to him 'at frequent intervals' about its progress, making any necessary recommendations to him as it might consider appropriate 'for further action to overcome any difficulties encountered in the rescue and relief of war refugees'.[1]

The British Government was embarrassed by the establishment of the War Refugee Board, particularly after an Independent MP, Daniel Lipson, put down a Parliamentary question asking the Government 'to establish a counterpart to the President's Board'. On February 7 Eden circulated a note to his colleagues on the War Cabinet's refugee Committee, in which he criticized Roosevelt's motives in setting up the Board. In 'addition' to what Eden described as 'the humanitarian aim' of rescuing immediately, by all possible means, the victims of enemy savagery, Roosevelt had also been intent, 'with the particularly active support of Mr Morgenthau', on 'placating the large Jewish vote', and 'spiking the guns' of Congress, whose Foreign Affairs Committee had recently been putting pressure on the State Department for a more active rescue policy for refugees.

Eden also warned his colleagues of signs of 'increasing American pressure' on Britain in respect of visas for Palestine 'as a means of getting Jewish children out of France'; a pressure which contrasted 'strangely', Eden added, with the American Government's 'reticence over admission to their own territory'. This reticence, Eden noted, had recently been the subject 'of sarcastic comment in American Jewish papers'.[2]

Three months later, Eden was to circulate to his Committee colleagues a note by Sir Herbert Emerson, who, while on a visit to Washington, had learned that the War Refugee Board had been created 'as a result of Jewish pressure, especially from the extremist groups', and that apart from the humanitarian motives, there was the political consideration 'that the Jewish vote is large, and this is particularly the case in New York State, which is of first-rate importance in a Presidential election'. The Board's director, John W. Pehle, 'is not a Jew', Emerson added, 'but many of the officers are'.[3]

The establishment of the War Refugee Board gave new hope to all Jewish groups concerned with rescue and emigration. But in reality, the scale of rescue possibilities remained small. During 1943 less than four hundred Jews had managed to reach Istanbul, and through Istanbul, Palestine; 120 from Rumania, 109 from Bulgaria, 107 from Hungary, seventeen from Bohemia and Moravia, eight from Slovakia, and seven from Holland. On December 26 the British Government had authorized nine Jews, then in Rumania, to enter Palestine: four were refugees from Poland, three from Rumania itself, one from East Prussia, and one from France.

On January 22, the day of the establishment of the War Refugee Board in Washington, the slow rescue efforts on behalf of Jewish refugees already outside Nazi clutches won an unexpected success with the departure from Lisbon of 757 Jews on board the *Nyasa*, bound for Palestine. Their departure across the Mediterranean had been the dream of a German Jewish refugee,

---

[1] Department of State, Radio Bulletin No. 19, copy as issued by the American Legation in Berne on 23 January 1944 in Central Zionist Archives L 22/135.

[2] Note by the Secretary of State for Foreign Affairs, 7 February 1944, Cabinet papers, 95/15.

[3] Letter of 16 May 1944, Cabinet papers, 95/15.

Wilfrid Israel, who had been sent to Lisbon by the Jewish Agency in 1943. Israel himself had been killed in an air crash in June 1943, but for six months his successor in Lisbon, Fritz Lichtenstein, had worked to effect the transfer.[1]

At the beginning of January 1944 a new Exchange List had been drawn up by the Palestine Office in Geneva, with the names and addresses of 590 Jews 'resident in the Netherlands'. The British authorities accepted the list at once, and on January 4 Douglas Mackillop of the British Legation in Berne informed Dr Kahany, one of the Jewish Agency representatives in Geneva that 'we have requested the Swiss Government to ask the German Government that any deportation order which may have been made against these prospective immigrants may be rescinded in the light of the knowledge that immigration certificates have been granted to them'.[2]

Three weeks later, on January 24, Dr Chaim Pozner was able to write direct from Geneva to the Jewish Council in Amsterdam that a further list of 118 individuals and families had now been approved by the British for Palestine certificates, and he forwarded with his letter the list of names, together with their potentially life-saving 'M' registration numbers.[3]

At the same time, also in Geneva, Pozner's colleague Richard Lichtheim was seeking to secure the emigration of the Polish deportees in Vittel. On February 25 he was informed from Jerusalem that the poet Yitzhak Katznelson, who already held a Honduras passport with which he had left Warsaw for France, was now included on the list of 'Veteran Zionists' submitted by the Jewish Agency to the Palestine Government on December 30, for a Palestine certificate, 'and approved under number M/438/43'.[4]

These efforts at rescue were small, but real; they concerned individuals and families who could still be saved. Whereas the death camps at Chelmno, Belzec, Treblinka and Sobibor had now completed their evil task, with the murder of more than two million Jews between the beginning of 1942 and the end of 1943, at Auschwitz the gassing of the remnants of European Jewry, those still under Nazi rule, continued without interruption. In January alone, more than five thousand Jews from France, Belgium, Holland and Poland were gassed, including 749 Jews from Paris on January 22, the day of the establishment in Washington of the War Refugee Board.

Allied intelligence still did not know the destination of these deportation trains, and the name 'Auschwitz' did not figure in its reports. On January 2 the British Political Intelligence Centre, Middle East, circulated a Secret note on the situation in Greece. Copies were sent to several other intelligence groups, and to the British and United States diplomatic representatives with the Greek Government-in-Exile. Under the section on the Jews of Greece, it was noted that the 70,000-strong Jewish community of Salonica had been 'entirely dispersed', and the report added: 'After being persecuted by the Germans in

---

[1] Israel was killed in the same aeroplane crash as Leslie Howard. Their aeroplane had possibly been mistaken for Churchill's (the Prime Minister was also flying back to England). For Israel's career, see *Wilfrid Israel July 11th, 1899–June 1st, 1943*, London 1945. At the time of his death, 97 Palestine certificates prepared by him were lost with him in the Bay of Biscay.

[2] Central Zionist Archives, L 22/56.

[3] Central Zionist Archives, L 17/914.

[4] Central Zionist Archives, L 22/135.

Salonica, the majority are believed to have been sent to Poland.'[1]

Where in Poland was not mentioned. As in earlier reports, Auschwitz still guarded its secret. In the camp itself, equally unknown to the Allies, the death toll for February was as high as for the previous month. The trains had come from France, Italy, Berlin and Vienna.

On January 15 the SS began work on a special railway spur to link the Vienna–Cracow railway with Birkenau itself. Instead of the deportees being taken from a siding near Auschwitz station, and driven in trucks for more than a mile along the perimeter of the camp to the gas chambers, the new spur was designed to bring their trains to within a few yards of the gas chambers themselves. Hitherto ten trucks had been needed to bring each trainload of deportees to the gas chamber. Now both petrol and time would be saved, and the deportees, emerging from the darkness, squalor and stench of the cattle trucks, would have hardly any time either to work out what was happening to them, or to react. For although scarcely any Polish Jews were left to be deported, the death trains had not yet finished their work, and many more months were needed to complete the deportations from France, Holland, Italy, Belgium and Greece. In Hungary and Rumania hundreds of thousands of Jews were still alive, some 300,000 in Rumania and 750,000 in Hungary, saved from deportation because their rulers, although allied to Germany, had refused to agree to deportations.

At Auschwitz itself, a new pattern had emerged. More than a million and a half Jews had been killed there, but the regular 'selection' of able-bodied men and women to the barracks had created a substantial reservoir of slave labour. On February 22 the number of Jews in the barracks was noted by the Germans at 73,669, of whom 24,637 were women.

This mass of slave labour was used intensively in the area around Auschwitz. On the day on which there were 73,669 prisoners in the camp, 13,477 of them were working in ten different industrial complexes in the Auschwitz region, and doing so in conditions of extreme hardship. The nearest factory to Auschwitz itself was the I.G. Farben petrochemical plant at Monowitz, only six miles from the gas chambers. At Monowitz, on that same February 22, a total of 6,603 Auschwitz prisoners were at work. Indeed, since November 1943, the slave labour barracks at Monowitz had been known as Auschwitz III.

The existence and extent of the factories at Auschwitz–Monowitz continued to contribute most effectively to the secrecy of Auschwitz–Birkenau. Towards the end of February 1944, two weeks after Ira Hirschmann, the War Refugee Board representative, reached Turkey, a group of 112 Turkish Jews were repatriated from Paris to Istanbul. The news they brought to the Jewish Agency was later described by one of the Agency representatives in Istanbul, Menahem Bader. 'They told us,' Bader recalled, 'that each week a deportation train, loaded with a thousand Jews from France and the Netherlands, left for Poland. We wondered how the Germans could spare oil cars and locomotives to transport Jews at this time, when their own cities were being bombed incessantly, and merciless battles were raging in Italy, and along the eastern front.'

Shortly afterwards, Bader added, a letter which reached Istanbul from Slovakia 'telling about the increased number of Jews at Birkenau near Auschwitz solved the mystery. I.G. Farben had built large factories near Birkenau, and the seventy thousand Jews recently concentrated there were serving both as labour force and raw materials'.[1]

It was late February 1944. Still no mention had been made of the gas chambers and crematoria of Birkenau. Yet these same I.G. Farben factories which continued to give the impression that 'Auschwitz' was primarily a labour camp were soon, with Birkenau itself, to come within the range of Allied reconniassance aircraft, and of Allied bombers. And it was the factories around Auschwitz, but not the camp, that were to become Allied targets in the continuing campaign of Operation Pointblank, with its goal of destroying Germany's capacity to make war.

One concern which the British policymakers continued to discuss during the early months of 1944 was Britain's future relations with the Arab world. On March 1, in a letter from Cairo, the British Minister of State, Lord Moyne, warned Anthony Eden, that any post-war plan for Palestine, other than partition, would involve 'some provision for Jewish immigration' throughout Palestine. But any such immigration, he warned, would result, as far as Britain was concerned, in the prospect 'of permanently embittered relations with the Arab world'.

The question of Jewish immigration would become urgent, Moyne explained to Eden, as soon as the Aegean ports were freed from German occupation, as this might lead to 'a large influx of Jewish immigration illegal and otherwise'; so large, in fact, as to 'absorb any balance of unauthorised immigration under the White Paper'. If these Jews were allowed 'to spread throughout the whole of Palestine', Moyne added, there would be 'a much greater danger of an Arab outbreak' than if they could be 'restricted' to a smaller Jewish State within a partitioned Palestine.[2]

On March 4 the Foreign Office set out its view of the British priority. It did so in a telegram to the British Ambassador in Washington, Lord Halifax, giving him the text of a message to be sent to the American Palestine Committee, a Zionist body. The message began by expressing 'British sympathy with the sufferings of persecuted Jewry', sufferings which the British people and the British Government 'have done their utmost to alleviate'. In the past five years, the message read, 48,000 Jews had entered Palestine. A further 27,000 certificates were still available 'under existing arrangements', that is to say, under the 1939 White Paper. But the message continued with what was described as 'a friendly word of warning'. The controversy in America over Palestine, it pointed out, 'has begun to create serious apprehensions in the Middle East', and it ended:

We stand on the brink of the greatest military struggles of our life time. Anything that distracts our two nations from pursuing the struggle with the utmost vigour, must inescapably raise the cost in human lives. The British and American peoples and Jews throughout the

[1] Menahem Bader, *Sad Missions*, Tel Aviv 1979, page 87.
[2] Lord Moyne to Oliver Stanley, Most Secret, Colonial Office papers, 733/461 Part One.

world have in early victory an overwhelming common interest, and by this alone can the mass of European Jewry be saved.[1]

On March 6 the Foreign Office, in a letter to the Polish Foreign Minister in Exile, Count Raczynski, acknowledged receipt of an address by the Representation of Polish Jews on the subject 'of the latest outrages committed by the Germans against the Jewish population of Poland'.[2] Copies of this address had been sent to Churchill and Eden. Churchill told Eden: 'I ought either to keep out of this thing, or make some vigorous public protest. A mere acknowledgement would be rather unsuitable.'[3] But Eden's attitude was: 'I cannot myself see that a further protest could help',[4] and no protest was made.

Churchill was also sent a copy of a further Foreign Office telegram to Lord Halifax, on the need for 'stopping Zionist agitation in America'. This telegram contained the sentence: 'You could point out that the Zionists are deliberately and unjustifiably using the refugee situation, which naturally appeals to public opinion in America and England, to advance their own sectarian ends regardless of the effect upon the true interests of the United Nations.' In a message to Eden on March 8, Churchill insisted on the deletion of this sentence, which could not, he wrote, 'be squared with a decision not to descend into the arena of controversy'. Churchill added: 'I might as well come out and say that the White Paper was a fraud and a breach of faith.'[5]

On March 9 Eden sent Churchill a message which Roosevelt had sent recently to the American Zionist Emergency Council. The United States had never given its approval to the 1939 White Paper, Roosevelt had said. The American people, he added, had always had 'the deepest sympathy' with those who sought a Jewish National Home, 'today more than ever in view of the tragic plight of hundreds of thousands of homeless Jewish refugees'. Churchill noted on this report, in his own handwriting: 'Prime Minister cordially concurs with the President and like him has never given his approval to the White Paper of 1939. On the contrary, he described it at the time as a fraud and breach of faith, and holds the same opinion still.'[6]

Eden's own concerns were centred on the activities of the recently established War Refugee Board, and on March 10, in a note to the War Cabinet's refugee Committee, he pointed out that the Board's allocation of $100,000 to be spent by the International Red Cross in Hungary and Rumania 'for the relief of Jews in enemy territory' was, as he expressed it, 'an obvious departure from the principles of economic warfare agreed upon by our two governments'. Nor was this payment 'a single exceptional one', but rather 'a deliberate departure of policy'.

British policy was faced with a 'disagreeable' dilemma, Eden noted. If the British Government were to object to the War Refugee Board payment, he warned, then the British Government would risk 'being held up by the War Refugee Board, which is engaged in a publicity campaign, as obstacles to a humanitarian measure which would probably save many Jewish lives'. But

---

[1] Foreign Office telegram No. 1922, copy in Colonial Office papers, 733/461 Part Four.
[2] Foreign Office papers, 371/42790, W 4399.
[3] Prime Minister's Personal Minute, M.252/4, original in Foreign Office papers, 371/42790, W 4399.
[4] Handwritten note by Eden, Foreign Office papers, 371/42790, W 4399.
[5] Prime Minister's Personal Minute, M.245/4, Premier papers, 4/52/5.
[6] Viscount Halifax, telegram No. 1208, and Churchill's handwritten comment, Premier papers 4/52/5.

if the British Government acquiesced in the payment, 'we allow the US Government to get the credit for a piece of rescue work which critics will say should have been attempted long ago'. To relax the financial blockade, however, 'may prove of real advantage to the enemy'.

In his note of March 10, Eden also opposed a new public declaration condemning German atrocities against the Jews. Some people, he said, advocated such a declaration because the Moscow Declaration of 1 November 1943 'failed to mention Jews', and that this omission should therefore be repaired. Eden disagreed, feeling that 'these repeated threatenings debase the currency', and that certain Allied Governments might be reluctant 'to be associated with an exclusively Jewish declaration'. The latest Russian atrocity report from Lvov, he noted, 'did not specify Jews as the victims'.[1]

Three days later, on March 13, Eden revealed in a further note to the Foreign Office another reason for his dislike of the $100,000 being sent by the War Refugee Board for refugee relief in Hungary and Rumania. 'The majority of the adults who would benefit' by these feeding and rescue schemes, he explained to his refugee Committee colleagues, 'are Jews, and the political difficulties involved in this are obvious'. It would be easier to justify abandoning a basic Anglo-American principle of economic warfare if the scheme were put on 'an at least ostensibly general and not preponderately Jewish level'.[2]

These views were echoed by Eden's colleagues when the War Cabinet's refugee Committee held its first meeting of 1944 on March 14. Eden told the meeting that the money now authorized by the War Refugee Board to be spent in Hungary and Rumania 'had now reached 700,000 dollars'. But the Minister of Economic Warfare, Lord Selborne, said he would 'regret the further development of these activities', while the Chancellor of the Exchequer, Sir John Anderson, thought it desirable to aim at imposing 'suitable limits on the scheme', rather than run the risk of 'inciting the Americans to go ahead' by adopting what he called 'too stiff an attitude'.

Later in the discussion, the Committee agreed with Eden that a further declaration about German atrocities 'would do no good, and might do harm'. But it favoured a declaration 'addressed to the satellite powers'.[3]

Late in February 1944 a special Commission had arrived in Auschwitz from Berlin to visit the Czech family camp. During the visit, Eichmann himself had shown the camp to the head of the foreign division of the German Red Cross, Max Niehaus. The Commission had lingered for a while in block 31, where a 'school' had been set up in the wooden stable. The head of the school was a former Berlin gymnastics teacher and Zionist, Freddy Hirsch, who had fled to Prague from Germany in 1938. Pleased with what he saw, Eichmann praised the unique development of a centre of spiritual life in circumstances not entirely conducive to such things. Indeed, during the camp's six month existence, more than a thousand men, women and children had died, and the stench from the crematorium was seldom out of their nostrils.

---

[1] Note by the Secretary of State for Foreign Affairs, 10 March 1944, Cabinet papers, 95/15.

[2] Memorandum by the Secretary of State for Foreign Affairs, 13 March 1944, Cabinet papers, 95/15.

[3] War Cabinet Committee on the Reception and Accommodation of Refugees, 14 March 1944, Cabinet papers, 95/15. For the actual Declaration, as made in the House of Commons, see pages 185–6.

The German Red Cross delegates departed. On March 3 the inmates of the family camp were told to write postcards, saying that they were alive and well, and working. They were also made to date the postcards March 25, 26 or 27, and had to ask their relatives abroad to send them food parcels.

Four days later they were told that they were to be resettled at a nearby labour camp called Heydebreck. But no such 'resettlement' was planned. They were to be sent to the gas chambers only a few hundred yards away from their 'haven'.

On March 6 a Slovak Jewess, Katherina Singer, who worked as a secretary to the Senior SS wardress in the women's camp at Birkenau, overheard by chance an SS remark about 'special treatment' for the family camp inmates. She at once passed on this news to two young Jewish prisoners who were at that very moment, as maintenance men, repairing cauldrons in the kitchen of the women's camp. These two, under the pretext of 'urgent repairs', managed to pass the news that same day to Freddy Hirsch, while urging Hirsch to act. But Hirsch was convinced that there was nothing whatsoever to be done to save the family camp, and that night he took poison. It was not strong enough, however, to kill him, and on the following day, March 7, still in a state of unconsciousness he was taken by truck, together with five thousand other survivors of the family camp, to the gas chamber.[1]

Themselves deceived, these victims of a wider deception were driven into the undressing room of the gas chamber. Realizing suddenly that they really were about to be gassed, they tried to resist, attacking the guards with their bare hands. But the SS were quick to answer back, first with rifle butts and then, when the resistance spread, with flame throwers. Filip Müller, one of the few survivors of the 'special detachments' who were forced to be on duty in the undressing room, later recalled how these family camp victims, 'heads smashed and bleeding from their wounds', were driven across the threshold of the gas chamber. As the gas pellets were released, they began to sing the Czech national anthem, Kde domov muj, 'where is my home', and the Hebrew song Hatikvah: 'hope'.[2]

Of this whole Jewish group of more than five thousand, only forty-five were spared, among them eleven pairs of twins, who had been kept alive so that medical experiments could be performed on them.

On March 15 the truth about Auschwitz was 'revealed' yet again. But once again the revelation passed entirely unnoticed in the west, either among the Allied or Jewish leadership. The source was the Polish underground, and the details were published in Istanbul in a cyclostyled newspaper issued by the Polish Consulate General in Istanbul.

According to this newspaper, some 850,000 Jews had been gassed at Auschwitz between the summer of 1942 and the autumn of 1943, among them 60,000 from Greece, 60,000 from France, Belgium and Holland, and 50,000 from

---

[1] For an account of the destruction of the family camp written in Prague in 1946 by the two maintenance men themselves, see O. Kraus and E. Kulka, The Death Factory, Oxford 1966, pages 172–4. and Erich Kulka, Utek z tabora smrti, Prague 1966, chapter 'Operation Heydebreck' and pages 69–71.

[2] Quoted in Erich Kulka 'Five Escapes from Auschwitz', in Yuri Suhl (editor), They Fought Back: The Story of Jewish Resistance in Nazi Europe, London 1968, page 224.

Slovakia, Bohemia and Moravia. In addition, the newspaper noted, some 15,000 Jews from the Polish cities of Bedzin and Sosnowiec had also been gassed in Auschwitz during the summer of 1943.[1]

These figures were far larger than any that had yet been published in the west for people gassed at Auschwitz. They also made clear the precise location of the 'unknown destination'. But this report of March 15 seems to have been completely ignored by both the Allied and Jewish representatives in Istanbul: no copy of it appears to have been sent either to London, Washington or Jerusalem, and the facts which were at last so fully reported remained as secret as if they had never seen the light of day.

---

[1] *Polska pod Okupacja Niemiecka*, volume 5, number 5, 15 March 1944, issued by the Bureau of the Polish Consul-General in Istanbul, A. N. Kurcyusz.

Chapter 20

The German occupation of Hungary

In March 1944, as the Auschwitz deceptions continued to keep the camp's true purpose secret, both the killing at Auschwitz itself, and the spread of Nazi terror, were intensified. On March 10, only three days after the family camp had been destroyed, the second sealed train in five days reached Auschwitz from western Europe. It came from Paris, and after 110 men and eighty women had been taken off to the barracks and tattooed, the remaining 1,390 deportees were marched to the gas chamber.

In London, the Polish Government-in-Exile had continued to publicize whatever news it received of the wider killings. One such report was issued to the Press on March 13, describing the massacre in the city of Lvov of Russian peasants, Italian officers, Jews and Poles, as Soviet forces approached the city.[1] 'In all,' the report noted, 'over 10,000 victims of various nationalities have been massacred.' The report was detailed:

For the last few weeks Lvov has been covered with clouds of smoke and a suffocating smell of burning blowing in from the eastern outskirts of the city. Day after day heavy lorries have driven out of the town in an easterly direction. First go 3 lorries full of people, then one of tar and then a petrol tanker. Every little while another 5 have passed along the road eastwards; on some of the worst days 90 were counted. . . .

On the outskirts of Lvov there is a sandy height which used to be a favourite haunt of the Lvov people in summer. At its foot some temporary barracks have been erected, not for the victims, but for the executioners. The executions take place in the open. Usually the victims are mown down by machine-gun fire, then the bodies are heaped together and petrol and tar are poured over them and set alight. At first the Germans tried to carry out this mass slaughtering in secret, but now they no longer make any attempt at concealment.[2]

On March 14 A. L. Easterman, the Political Secretary of the European Division of the World Jewish Congress, drew the Foreign Office's attention to this Polish report. There were, he wrote, 'still a considerable number of Jews' in the Lvov area, and these Jews 'are most certainly primarily the victims of German murder'. It was both necessary and 'urgent', in the view of the World Jewish Congress, of Dr Nahum Goldmann, Sydney Silverman and himself, both to issue 'a fresh and emphatic warning to the Germans', and also to speed up 'by all possible means', the work of rescuing Jews from Nazi-occupied territory.[3]

A Foreign Office official, Donald Hall, noted eight days later: 'I have had a talk with Mr Easterman who is for the the moment satisfied that we are con-

---

[1] In transliteration from Russian, Lvov; in Polish Lwow; in German Lemberg.
[2] 'Massacres Precede German Evacuation of Lwow', 13 March 1944. Polish Ministry of Information No. 37. Copy in Foreign Office papers, 371/42790.
[3] Foreign Office papers, 371/42790, W 4298.

sidering all this very thoroughly'.[1] The Foreign Office view, in general, was opposed to any further Allied declarations as far as Germany was concerned. But action on this level was not entirely ruled out. A Foreign Office draft of March 17, of a note to be sent from Eden to Churchill about the earlier address from a group known as the 'Representation of Polish Jews', read:

This question was discussed by the Cabinet Committee on Refugees on March 14th, and their conclusion was that it would be useless to make further declarations in regard to Germany, but that appeals or warnings to the satellite countries might very well be worth while.

The position is complicated by the determination of the United States Government to go ahead independently, unless we agree promptly with a warning addressed to Germany as well, and if we cannot shake them in this we shall have to find some way of associating ourselves with the American declaration, however strong our view that this kind of repetition merely debases the currency.[2]

Easterman did not accept this reasoning. It was the view of the World Jewish Congress, he wrote to Donald Hall on March 21, 'that even if there were only a very limited possibility of an effective result, the extremely critical situation of the Jews threatened by the Germans, justifies such a measure being taken'.[3]

One of the satellite countries to which warnings might have been sent was Hungary, where more than three-quarters of a million Jews were still alive. These 750,000 lived not only in pre-war Hungary, with its population of over 444,000 Jews, but in the four areas annexed by Hungary both before and after the start of the war.[4]

The means of helping these Jews had been discussed in Palestine for nearly two years. One idea was to send a small group of Palestinian Jews into Nazi-occupied or dominated Europe where, from behind enemy lines, they could make contact with the local Jewish resistance, and help to organize escape routes and self-defence.

An early advocate of this idea was a non-Jewish journalist, Eric Gedye, who before the war, as the *Daily Telegraph* correspondent in central Europe, had witnessed the German occupation of both Vienna and Prague. Gedye, who was working for British intelligence in the Middle East, favoured sending a British submarine to the Adriatic coast of Yugoslavia, and putting ashore a group of Jews, who would work their way across the partisan-controlled areas of Yugoslavia to Austria, the country in which he had many contacts.

At the end of 1943 this idea had been revived in connection with Hungary, Rumania, Slovakia and Yugoslavia. Instead of landing by submarine, the Jews were to be parachuted by the Royal Air Force into partisan territory in Yugoslavia. They would then go on foot into Hungary, Rumania and Slovakia, to make contact with Jewish resistance groups, and to help train them, and organize escape routes back through Yugoslavia and then into Italy. The parachutists themselves were trained in Palestine by the British, and on

[1] Foreign Office papers, 371/42790, W 4298.
[2] Foreign Office papers, 371/42790, W 4299.
[3] Foreign Office papers, 371/42790, W 4298.
[4] The areas annexed by Hungary were Southern Slovakia (with 78,000 Jews), Ruthenia (with 72,000 Jews), the Yugoslav region of Backsa (with 20,000 Jews), and the northern and eastern regions of Transylvania (with 149,000 Jews).

March 14 the first group of four emissaries, having been taken from Palestine to southern Italy, were parachuted into German-occupied Europe. One of them, the Yugoslav-born Reuven Dafni, was to remain in Yugoslavia in order to act as their base liaison with Tito's partisans, and to smuggle all Jews sent back across the border to safety in southern Italy. Three of the parachutists were to cross into Hungary. Of these three, one was a woman, the twenty-two-year-old Hannah Szenes, who had emigrated to Palestine from Hungary in September 1939.

Unfortunately, the area in which the four parachutists were dropped was itself under attack by the Germans, who had managed to push the partisans away from the very border area with Hungary which the three had planned to cross. The Yugoslav partisans suggested that the Jews cross at a more distant point, involving a march of some two weeks, and the possibility of clashes with German troops.

For four days the Jewish parachutists worked out the details of the new plan with the local partisans. Then, on March 19, a Yugoslav partisan officer interrupted their deliberations. 'The Germans,' he said, 'have invaded Hungary.' Hannah Szenes burst into tears. 'We are too late,' she sobbed, 'we are too late.'

Although Hannah Szenes and her fellow emissaries knew that they would eventually reach the Hungarian border, cross it and enter Hungary, they also knew that their earlier plan, to merge with false papers among Jews who could travel freely and meet unmolested, could no longer be carried out. 'What will happen to all of them,' Hannah Szenes cried. 'They're in German hands now, and we're sitting here, just sitting.'[1]

For the 750,000 Jews of Hungary, the arrival of the German army was indeed a disaster, even at this late stage of the war, with British and American bombers flying deeper and deeper over the Reich, and with the Red Army poised to cross the Carpathians. For despite this, the full apparatus of Gestapo rule could be imposed on Hungary overnight. Now there would be no way that three young emissaries could organize large-scale escape or resistance: each border Jews might try to cross would be sealed even more securely than the Hungarians had hitherto sealed it, and every community would be isolated, pillaged, sealed off from its neighbours, and doubtless, in due course, deported.

On 15 March 1944, the day on which the Palestinian Jewish parachutists had landed in Yugoslavia, Hitler had summoned the Hungarian regent, Admiral Horthy, to a conference in Germany. The choice, said Hitler, was between a German military occupation, and a German-approved Government.

Horthy chose the latter. On his return to Budapest on March 19, he discovered that a special sleeping car had been attached to his train. In it was the new German Minister to Hungary, Dr Edmund Veesenmayer, an honorary officer in the SS, with the equivalent rank of a Colonel in the army.

On reaching Budapest, Horthy told the Hungarian Crown Council that one of Hitler's complaints was 'that Hungary has not yet introduced the steps necessary to settle the Jewish question'. Horthy added, as the official minutes recorded: 'We are accused, therefore, of the crime of not having carried out Hitler's wishes, and I am charged with not having permitted the Jews to be

[1] Recollections of Reuven Dafni, in conversation with the author, 23 March 1980.

massacred.'[1]

On March 22 a new Government took office in Hungary, its members chosen only with Veesenmayer's approval, as was the new Prime Minister, Dome Sztojay. For three days, German officials had already been taking up their posts in the different Hungarian Ministries, in the army, and in the main areas of Hungarian industry. A special SS unit had also reached Budapest on March 19, headed by one of the most senior SS ranks, equivalent to Lieutenant-General, SS Obergruppenführer Dr Otto Winkelmann. This unit had been formed and briefed at Mauthausen by Eichmann himself.

The Jewish Agency was concerned to suggest measures to alleviate dangers threatening the Jews of Hungary. On March 22 Bernard Joseph telegraphed from Jerusalem to Shertok in London: 'Suggest you seek Allied statement warning new Hungarian Government consequences persecution Jews'. Joseph added that the three Allies, Britain, the United States, and the Soviet Union, 'should request Tito facilitate Jewish refugees escape into Yugoslavia'.[2]

The World Jewish Congress was likewise searching for measures to help Hungarian Jewry, and on March 23, in a telegram from Geneva, Gerhart Riegner suggested a 'world wide appeal of leading Anglo-Saxon personalities, non-Jewish and Jewish', including the leaders of the Protestant and Catholic Churches, and 'outstanding Americans of Hungarian origin', aimed at warning the Hungarian people 'not to admit application of policy of extermination of Jews by German butchers or Hungarian Quislings'. Such warnings should be broadcast 'every night in Hungarian language during the next weeks'.[3]

On March 24 President Roosevelt gave a Press Conference in which he described the 'wholesale, systematic murder of the Jews of Europe' as one of the 'blackest crimes' of all history, a crime, he noted, which 'goes on unabated every hour'. Roosevelt added:

As a result of the events of the last few days, hundreds of thousands of Jews, who while living under persecution have at least found a haven from death in Hungary and the Balkans, are now threatened with annihilation as Hitler's forces descend more heavily on these lands.

That these innocent people, who have already survived a decade of Hitler's fury, should perish on the very eve of triumph over the barbarism which their persecution symbolises, would be a major tragedy.[4]

It was therefore 'fitting', Roosevelt added, that the United States should once again 'proclaim our determination that none who participate in these acts of savagery shall go unpunished'. All who knowingly took part in 'the deportation of Jews to their death in Poland', Roosevelt declared, would be 'equally guilty with the executioner himself'.

Still unknown in the west, the trains of deportees continued to reach Auschwitz at regular intervals. On March 25, the day after Roosevelt's Press Conference, a total of 599 Jews reached the camp from Holland. After 304 men and fifty-six women had been marched off to the barracks, the remaining

---

[1] Minutes of the Crown Council meeting, 19 March 1944, quoted in Eugene Levai (edited by Lawrence P. Davies), *The Black Book of the Martyrdom of Hungarian Jewry*, Zurich 1948, page 78.

[2] Central Zionist Archives. S 25/1678.

[3] Telegram to Stephen Wise, archives of the World Jewish Congress, General Secretariat.

[4] Transcript in Franklin D. Roosevelt Library, 'FDR Press Conference 1933–1945', No. 944, folios 112–5.

239 deportees, including all the children and old people, were taken to the gas chamber.

That same day, a telegram from the Palestine Office in Geneva to the Jewish Agency in Jerusalem, could report only that the Jews of Holland were still being deported 'to Poland or Theresienstadt'. Only those with Palestine certificates were being sent elsewhere, to a camp at Bergen-Belsen. There, the telegram noted, it was presumed that their situation was 'better than those deported Poland'.[1]

Two other transports were to reach Auschwitz in the last week of March: some seven hundred Jews evacuated from the eastern Polish town of Boryslaw on March 28, as the Red Army approached, and 1,025 Jews from France on March 30. Of the French deportees, 520 were gassed immediately on arrival.

The Jewish Agency leaders never gave up their hope that they could prevail upon the Allies, and particularly upon the British, to look with sympathy at their appeals. Pondering the news from Hungary, Weizmann decided to stress the second of Shertok's requests when he wrote direct to Churchill's Private Secretary, John Martin, on March 29. Weizmann's letter read:

Well over a million Jews in Hungary, Roumania, Slovakia and Bulgaria are now caught in a death-trap. Probably only a few will be able to save themselves by escaping—some by sea to Turkey, others by crossing into Yugoslavia. In the latter case, their salvation depends on Tito's attitude—not only on the extension to the fugitives of the protection of his forces, but on active help on their part to make escape possible. Marshal Tito's army already contains considerable numbers of Jews, and it is assumed that every group of Jewish refugees crossing into the part of Yugoslavia under his control will yield a proportion of fighting men.

May I ask you to put these considerations before the Prime Minister, and transmit to him our plea that he should send a personal message to Marshal Tito asking him to do his level best to save our people by facilitating their escape so far as this may prove practicable?[2]

John Martin at once passed Weizmann's request to the Foreign Office, where Eden gave it his immediate attention. 'Dr Weizmann's request,' Martin informed Churchill on March 31, 'quite harmonises' with Eden's policy, and 'he would welcome anything that can be done to help.'[3]

On the previous day, March 30, Eden had been asked in the House of Commons, by Sydney Silverman, if, as a result of the German occupation of Hungary, he had any statement to make 'with reference to the urgent and immediate peril which now threatens Jews and other victims of Nazi persecution in these countries'. Eden replied by making a formal Declaration which met all the points for which the Jewish Agency had asked. This Declaration was even stronger than Roosevelt's had been six days before, and read:

Evidence continues to reach His Majesty's Government and Allied Governments, that the Nazi policy of extermination has not been halted. The persecution of the Jews has in particular been of unexampled horror and intensity. On this His Majesty's Government, in common with their Allies, now that the hour of Germany's defeat grows ever nearer and more certain can only repeat their detestation of Germany's crimes and their determination that all those guilty of them shall be brought to justice.

[1] Central Zionist Archives, S 26/1281.
[2] Premier papers, 4/51/10, folio 1424.
[3] Premier papers, 4/51/10, folio 1421.

186 The German occupation of Hungary 1944

But apart from direct guilt there is still indirect participation in crime. Satellite Governments who expel citizens to destinations named by Berlin must know that such actions are tantamount to assisting in inhuman persecution or slaughter. This will not be forgotten when the inevitable defeat of the arch-enemy of Europe comes about.

Happily there are individuals and even official authorities among the satellites who have resisted the evil German example and have shown toleration and mercy. These things are known to the Allies, and in the hope of encouraging such good deeds and increasing their number His Majesty's Government are concerned to make it clear that those who have followed the right path will also not be forgotten in the day of final reckoning.

The time of respite is short, but there is still opportunity for the merciful to multiply their acts of humanity, for the guilty to try to make amends for their deeds of shame by releasing their victims and making, so far as is possible, restitution to them.

His Majesty's Government are confident that they are expressing the sentiments of all the Allied Governments in calling upon the countries allied with or subject to Germany to join in preventing further persecution and co-operate in protecting and saving the innocent.

His Majesty's Government, for their part, are firmly resolved to continue, in co-operation with all Governments and private authorities concerned to rescue and maintain so far as lies in their power all those menaced by the Nazi terror.[1]

The Eden Declaration of 30 March 1944 was, for the Jewish Agency, both positive and helpful. Also helpful was the outcome of a meeting that same day between the Colonial Secretary, Oliver Stanley, and Moshe Shertok, who was accompanied by Professor Namier and Joseph Linton. In telegraphing the result of this meeting to the Jewish Agency in Jerusalem, Shertok explained that he had asked the British Government to interpret as liberally as possible the new policy whereby any Jew reaching Istanbul from Nazi-occupied Europe was to be admitted to Palestine. 'Eventually,' Shertok wrote, 'Stanley agreed liberal interpretation', based on individual applications which the Jewish Agency should itself recommend.

Stanley also agreed to 'keep matters elastic, reviewing policy in light actual escape from Nazi lands', and to make an official British approach to the Turkish Government 'for liberal transit'.[2]

The result of the Shertok-Stanley meeting was quickly seen, for on April 8 Chaim Barlas telegraphed from Istanbul to Jerusalem with the news that the steamship *Maritza*, carrying 244 Jewish refugees from Rumania, had arrived that same day in Istanbul, and that the passengers would be leaving the city in two days' time for Palestine.[3]

It was not only the escape of Jews from Europe that had been discussed at the Shertok-Stanley meeting. A second priority for the Jewish Agency in its dealings with the Colonial Office had been the state of the deportees in Mauritius. In December 1940 the British Government had deported 1,600 'illegal' refugees to this island in the Indian Ocean. Originally from Germany, Czechoslovakia and central Europe, these Jews had been intercepted in the Mediterranean, escorted into Haifa Bay by the Royal Navy, and then deported. The fact that they were not to be allowed back to Palestine, and the unpleasant conditions of their detention, had been a cause of friction between the Jewish Agency and the British authorities for more than three years. Shertok therefore used the opportunity of the meeting to argue that there

[1] Hansard, 30 March 1944.
[2] Telegram of 3 April 1944. Central Zionist Archives, S 25/1678.
[3] Central Zionist Archives, S 25/1678.

was no justification for leaving the deportees to 'languish [or] deteriorate [in] exile'. On this issue the meeting was less successful. The deportees were to remain in Mauritius. But Stanley did agree to consider the 'possibility' of post-war admission of the deportees to Palestine, and also promised to consider the admission of individual deportees to 'Palestinian units'.

There was a third topic raised at the Stanley-Shertok meeting of March 30, which was recorded fully in the Colonial Office account of the discussion. It concerned Jewish terrorism in Palestine. It was exactly a week since five British deaths in Tel Aviv, Haifa and Jerusalem at the hands of the Stern Gang.

Oliver Stanley told the Jewish Agency representatives 'that he had a personal message' from Churchill, to whom he had given a report on the recent killings. 'The Prime Minister,' Stanley said, 'who had always been a sincere friend of the Jews, had been horrified at these outrages, which in his view could do nothing but harm to the Jewish cause.'

Stanley went on to tell the Jewish Agency leaders that he had explained to Churchill that the killings 'were the work of an irresponsible minority which had been condemned by all responsible Jewish authorities'. Nevertheless, Stanley noted, Rabbi J. L. Fishman, a member of the Jewish Agency Executive, had, according to a Jewish Telegraphic Agency report of March 28, while condemning 'the acts of terror', gone on to say that the British Administration in Palestine had 'brought about such despair among those who resort to violence that they do not know what they are doing'.

Stanley pointed out that Rabbi Fishman's remarks 'did not conform' to the statements made by other responsible Jewish leaders who had condemned the killings. In reply, Shertok was emphatic, telling Stanley that these 'outrages' should be regarded 'as the acts of people who were really insane', while Professor Namier commented: 'these people were criminal lunatics'.[1]

The Eden Declaration and the Shertok-Stanley meeting were, for the Jewish Agency, satisfactory. But the continuance of good working relations was again threatened, in the first week of April, by an upsurge of Jewish terrorism in Palestine itself. The Jewish Agency took immediate action. On April 6 Eliahu Golomb, speaking at a Press conference in Tel Aviv on behalf of the Jewish National Council of Palestine stated that if the 'mad career of the terrorists continued', despite Palestinian Jewry's efforts to stop them by moral force, then physical force would be needed: 'We would be obliged,' he said, 'to punish the culprits because they are a vital danger to ourselves.' The Stern Gang, he said, consisted only of 'about 200 to 300 misguided youths who rejected any Jewish or Zionist discipline', and whose first target was the Jews and then the British.

On the following day, April 7, the Haifa correspondent of the *Palestine Post* reported the view of the senior Police Officer in Haifa, that the death of two Jewish terrorists recently shot by the police was the result of 'the co-operation of the public, which had given valuable information to the police'. Copies of this report from Haifa, as well as the Press report of Golomb's speech, were shown to Churchill by Lord Melchett, in an attempt to counter the arguments of those who portrayed Palestinian Jewry as a whole as secret

[1] 'Record of an Interview. . . .', Colonial Office papers, 733/462.

supporters of terrorism.[1]

In the three weeks following the German occupation of Hungary, Dr Weizmann himself had limited the use of his name and influence to a single request made to Churchill, for a British initiative to ask Tito to help receive any Jews who managed to escape from Hungary into Yugoslavia. In the second week of April Churchill agreed that a special message on this subject should be sent to Tito, while preferring it to come from Eden rather than from himself. 'A Foreign Office message can be sent,' Churchill minuted on April 9. 'But I do not want to weaken my contacts with Tito by too much use of them.' He added: 'Let me see what you would send and how you would send it.'[2]

The telegram, as sent to Cairo, to the British Chargé d'Affaires to the Yugoslav Government, declared that 'in view of great public interest in refugees' any action which Tito could take 'to rescue and maintain all fugitives from German persecution would be welcome. Refugees fit for military service could presumably join the Partisan Forces'. Those who could not be accepted for military service would need, if sent on to Italy or the Mediterranean area, to be found 'adequate facilities for their reception and maintenance'.[3]

It was extremely difficult for the Jewish Agency to know what else could be done to help save Hungarian Jewry. On March 30 Richard Lichtheim had written from Geneva to inform Jerusalem of an approach which had been made to the Papal Nuncio in Switzerland. The Catholic Church, it was hoped, 'might exercise some influence on the Hungarian politicians now responsible for the Government'. But even here, Lichtheim noted, 'nobody knows to what extent they can act independently from their German masters'.

Such messages as had earlier been sent by the Jews of Hungary to the Swiss listening-posts had now ended. It was therefore impossible to know what the leaders of Hungarian Jewry felt should be done, or tried. No contact could be made with Budapest, Lichtheim pointed out, as 'we have to be careful not to endanger our friends'.[4] Hungarian Jews living in Switzerland, however, having set up a special Relief Committee, pressed on April 4, after consultation with the Jewish Agency and World Jewish Congress representatives in Geneva, for a Soviet declaration similar to those just made by Roosevelt and by Eden, and for pamphlets to be dropped over Hungary by Allied aircraft warning the Hungarians against anti-Jewish measures and encouraging 'all elements willing to assist the Jews'. At the same time the Committee asked the Allied Governments to 'declare their readiness' to save as many Hungarian Jewish children as possible by granting them visas, and at the same time 'to approach the neutral States – Sweden, Switzerland and Turkey – with a view to encourage them to give temporary shelter to these children, provided means and ways can be found by official or unofficial ways to enable the exit of these children from Hungary.'[5]

[1] Premier papers, 4/52/5, folio 981.
[2] Premier papers, 4/51/10, folio 1413.
[3] Foreign Office draft, W 4878/15/48. Copy in Premier papers, 4/51/10, folio 1417. On 21 June 1944 a secret Foreign Office note stated: 'Marshal Tito has consented to facilitate the escape of Jewish refugees through his lines from Hungary, with the idea that they should reach southern Italy, via Dalmatia': paragraph II, 'Summary of Recent Activities of His Majesty's Government on behalf of refugees, Cabinet papers, 95/15.
[4] Central Zionist Archives, L 22/135.
[5] 'Memorandum Concerning the Jews of Hungary', Geneva, 4 April 1944, archives of the World Jewish Congress, General Secretariat.

In the first week of April the Jewish Agency received one small budget of good news, the arrival in Istanbul of a second ship from Rumania, the *Milca*. On board this small steamer were a further 250 Rumanian Jewish refugees, who were at once allowed to proceed by train across Asia Minor, through Syria, to Palestine, their Palestine visas having been issued by the British Passport Control Officer in Istanbul, A. W. Whittall.

On April 4 Dr Kahany passed on this good news to the British Legation in Berne, the staff of which had been active in persuading the Swiss Government to intercede with the Rumanians on all matters of transit. 'But in the meantime, unfortunately!' he added, 'the remnants of European Jews in Hungary have to face the disaster of Nazi invasion, with all its consequences for them'.[1]

[1] Central Zionist Archives, L 22/56.

Chapter 21

Escape from Auschwitz, April 1944

Following the Allied occupation of southern Italy, the existing 'enemy' airbase at Foggia had been taken over in December 1943 as the main operational centre for British and American heavy bombers flying into central Europe. The distance these bombers could fly and bomb was dictated by the range of their fighter escort, which up to December 1943 had been limited to just over four hundred miles, but which, with the introduction of the Mustang fighter, was extended to an average of up to 850 miles. With such a range, the Allied bombers could now seek out targets throughout Hungary, Slovakia, Rumania, southern Poland, and Upper Silesia. Auschwitz itself came within their range, although it had still not been identified as the destination of the continuing deportations from western Europe.

The Allied bombing targets during the spring of 1944 remained those set out in Operation Pointblank a year earlier: the factories on which Germany's war effort depended, and above all, the oil storage depots and synthetic oil production plants. The Normandy landings, a closely guarded secret, were to take place in the first week of June. Meanwhile, every attempt was being made to seek out Germany's most important oil targets.

On April 4 a United States aerial reconnaissance plane flew, at 26,000 feet, over the I.G. Farben synthetic oil and rubber manufacturing plant at Monowitz. This plant was a known factor in the German war effort, and one of the potential Allied bombing targets in Upper Silesia. The technique of aerial photography then in use involved the pilot turning on his camera shortly before reaching the site to be photographed, and turning it off when he judged that he had flown past his objective.

Monowitz lay four kilometres east of Auschwitz. The pilot turned on the camera when he was approaching his target, and turned it off some six kilometres later. The result: twenty exposures, on three of which Auschwitz itself appeared for the first time.

The intelligence personnel who developed and studied the photographs of April 4 at the Royal Air Force station at Medmenham, in the Thames Valley west of London, were looking for specific industrial installations. These were quickly identified, including 'a power station, carbide plant, synthetic rubber plant and synthetic oil (Bergius) plant'. Each of these plants was then analysed in detail.[1] The oil production method was seen to be similar to that already in use at Blechhammer-South, one of the existing high priority bombing targets.

[1] The analysis made at the time is in 'Interpretation Report D.377A' of 18 April 1944, 'Locality Oswiecim (Auschwitz): Synthetic Rubber and Synthetic Oil Plant', United States Strategic Bombing Survey, Record Group 243.

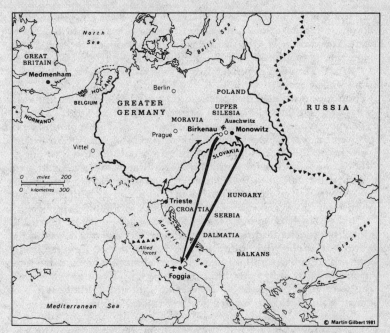

5. The first Allied air reconnaissance over Auschwitz on 4 April 1944, showing also the route of the deportation train from Trieste which reached Auschwitz that same day.

Both the synthetic oil and rubber plants at Monowitz were clearly in 'partial production' already, and while work was still in progress to complete both plants, they were already producing the oil and rubber on which the German war machine depended: and they would soon be capable of doing so on a scale similar to the largest of the plants elsewhere.

The Monowitz interpretation report of April 4 was sent to both American and Royal Air Force intelligence. With so much relevant and important detail visible in the factory zone, the interpreters found no need to comment on the row upon row of huts at Auschwitz I; huts which resembled hundreds of other barracks, army camps, prisoner-of-war camps and labour camps in the Silesian region. Nor did these first photographs include the far more extensive hutted area of Auschwitz-Birkenau, where some 52,000 Jews were being held captive, in addition to the 15,000 in barracks at Monowitz. It was not for another seven weeks, until May 31, that Birkenau itself was photographed, although even then no intelligence assessment was made of it.[1]

At Birkenau itself, the process of gassing continued without respite. On April 4, the day on which this first photograph was taken, a train reached the camp from Trieste. Of its 132 deportees, twenty-nine were sent to the barracks, registered and tattooed, while the remaining 103 were gassed.

On the same day, it was learnt in Geneva that those Polish Jews who had

[1] See page 216.

received South American passports a year earlier, had been sent to Vittel instead of Treblinka, and had awaited German permission to proceed to safety. They were now, Dr Kahany reported to the British Legation in Berne, 'in imminent danger of deportation from Vittel to the extermination camps in Poland'.[1] The camp chosen for them was, in fact, Auschwitz, but this was unknown in Geneva.

From Auschwitz itself, the postcard deception continued. In the first week of April a young Czech Jew, Alfred Kantor, had sent his postcard to a relative in Prague. On it he had been allowed to write only his name, his date of birth, 7 November 1923, and his address, 'Birkenau bei Neuberun, Oberschlesien', together with the name and address of the person to whom he was writing.

Kantor had addressed his postcard to Prague. But the camp administration had sent it first, unfranked, to Berlin, where its six pfennig stamp, with Hitler's head, was franked on April 6. As well as the date stamp, the Berlin Post Office added its public service slogan of the hour: 'Speak *briefly* on the telephone!!'[2]

On these family camp cards, the sender's address, Neu Berun, referred to a small town more than five miles northwest of Birkenau. It was chosen deliberately by the Nazis so that no one receiving a card from the family camp would link it with the standard letter-heading, 'Konzentrationslager Auschwitz o/s' used by other Birkenau prisons on the rare occasions when they were given permission to write. Thus Birkenau's identity was kept separate from Auschwitz, and appeared to be quite a different location.[3]

On April 7 two trains reached Auschwitz from western Europe. The first, from Holland, contained 240 Jews, of whom sixty-two men and thirty-eight women were tattooed and sent to the barracks, and the remaining 140, including twenty-two children, were gassed. Later that same day a second train arrived from Belgium, and 206 men and a hundred women were tattooed and sent to the barracks, while the rest, 319 in all, including fifty-four children, were sent straight to the gas chamber.

The destruction of the family camp on March 7 had made a profound impression on a young Slovak Jew, Walter Rosenberg, who subsequently changed his name to Rudolf Vrba. Several of Vrba's close friends had perished in the family camp, and he felt an urgent need to inform the outside world both of what had already happened at Auschwitz, and of the preparations which those in the camp knew to be taking place to kill a substantially increased number of victims, most probably from Hungary. 'I was attracted,' Vrba later wrote, 'by the possibility to damage the plans of the Nazis by divulging them to the Hungarian Jewish population while they are still in freedom, and can take to the streets.'[4]

Vrba had been in Auschwitz since June 1942, and for nearly two years he had found ample opportunity to observe the killing process at work. On three

[1] Central Zionist Archives, L 22/56.
[2] *The Book of Alfred Kantor*, New York 1971, facing plate 51.
[3] I am grateful to Erich Kulka for pointing out to me this particular refinement of deception, after he had read my account of the Kantor postcard. Letter to the author, 17 September 1980.
[4] Rudolf Vrba, letter to the author, 30 July 1980.

Top
1. 'Illegal' Jewish refugees on their way by boat to Palestine.

Above
2. 'Illegal' Jewish refugees approach the shore of Palestine.

Opposite top left
3. Richard Lichtheim, Jewish Agency representative in Geneva during the second world war.

Opposite top right
4. Gerhart Riegner, representative of the World Jewish Congress, Geneva.

Opposite bottom left
5. Chaim Pozner, of the Palestine Office, Geneva.

Opposite bottom right
6. Front cover of an El Salvador passport, prepared in Switzerland by the Consul-General of El Salvador, for dispatch into German-occupied Poland, as soon as photographs of those it was intended to save had reached Switzerland.

Above right
7. Naked Jews in German-occupied Russia, apparently about to be shot. This picture was the first photograph of the Nazi killing-squads' victims to be smuggled out of Nazi Europe, and brought to Switzerland, early 1942.

Centre right
8. Germans 'disposing' of dead Jews: a further picture reaching Geneva.

Below right
9. A corpse being 'disposed' of: the third picture to reach Geneva. Those receiving these three pictures were not entirely certain as to whether they showed Jews being killed, or Soviet prisoners-of-war.

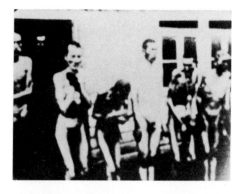

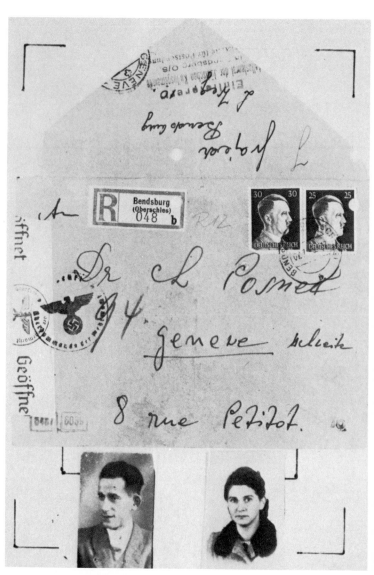

10. A letter posted from Bedzin (Bendsburg) in Upper Silesia, backstamped by the Jewish community council there, and sent to the co-director of the Palestine Office in Geneva, enclosing two photographs to be affixed to a Latin American passport, and then sent back to Bedzin. The envelope had been opened by the German censor, and bears his tape down the side, as well as his swastika marking, and the Geneva postmark on the back.

11. A card from a Polish Jew being held in a labour camp at Liebenau, in Germany, to the co-director of the Palestine Office in Geneva, seeking a Palestine certificate for his four year old daughter, whose photograph he had stuck on the other side of the card. The card has been stamped both by the camp administrator, and by the German censor.

12. The poet Yitzhak Katznelson, and his son. A photograph taken at the Polish mountain resort of Zakopane shortly before the outbreak of war.

Hitler Murdered Three Million Jews In Europe

Hitler has murdered or cestroyed by planned starvation, pogroms, forced labour, and deportations, more than 3,000,000 of Europe's Jews, according to a statement of the Institute of Jewish Affairs, published in the United States.

Russia and other countries have given asylum to 2,000,000 exiles, says the report, leaving only 3,300,000 of Europe's pre-war Jewish population of 8,300,000 unaccounted for.—B.U.P.

Above

13. The front page of the Sunday newspaper, the *People*, 17 October 1943.

Left

14. The news item appearing at the bottom of the page shown above.

15. The first three photographs to be smuggled out of Transnistria, to Switzerland. They are reproduced here the same size which they reached Switzerland, (see pages 197–8).

16. Money issued in the Theresienstadt ghetto. This note was printed on 1 January 1943, and is signed by Jakob Edelstein, the ghetto 'Elder'.

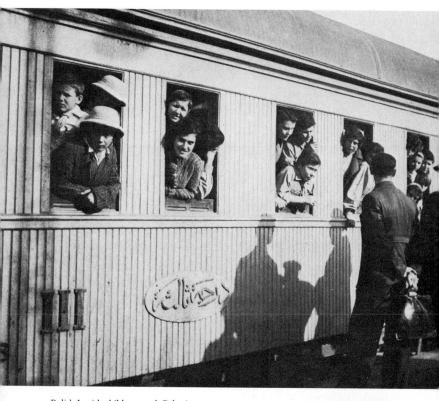

17. Polish Jewish children reach Palestine on 17 February 1943, after their journey across Russia, Persia and the Indian Ocean.

18. One of these 'Teheran' children photographed on 17 February 1943. The woollen shawl is her only memento of her mother, murdered by the Nazis.

Top
19. Crematorium II at Birkenau, shortly before it was put into operation in the winter of 1942.

Above
20. Crematorium IV at Birkenau, shortly before it was ready to be put into operation in the spring of 1943.

Above
21. Rudolf Vrba, who escaped from Auschwitz-Birkenau in April 1944.

Right
22. The Gestapo telegram announcing the escape of Vrba and Wetzler from Auschwitz (see page 196).

Below
23. The watchtowers, electrified wire and barracks of Birkenau, seen from just outside the northern perimeter. It was in the area from which this photograph was taken, known as 'Mexico', that the new barracks were being built for Hungarian Jews, and in which Vrba and Wetzler hid in a pile of timber.

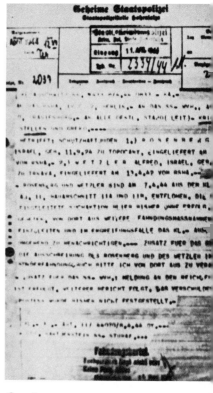

Opposite
24. The railway line and main gate at Birkenau; a photograph taken in 1980.

Opposite top

25. Pilots and crew of Operation Frantic, summer 1944. Back row, far left, is Carl Foreman, who was responsible for making the film of the Operation that summer.

Opposite bottom

26. The single-track railway line from Hungary to Auschwitz, just inside Poland; across the river is Lubotin (see map on page 247).

Below:

27. An aerial photograph taken on 26 June 1944, showing Auschwitz I (Main Camp), Auschwitz II (Birkenau), and Auschwitz III (Buna), as well as the I.G. Farben synthetic oil plant at Monowitz (see page 249).

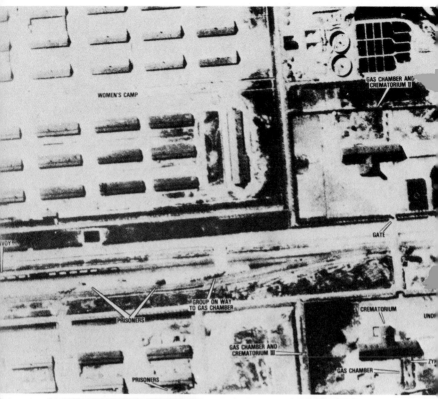

WOMEN'S CAMP

GAS CHAMBER AND
CREMATORIUM II

GATE

VOY

GROUP ON WAY
TO GAS CHAMBER

CREMATORIUM

UND

PRISONERS

GAS CHAMBER AND
CREMATORIUM III

ZY

PRISONERS

GAS CHAMBER

Above
28. Detail from an aerial photograph taken on 25 August 1944, of the railway sidings, or 'ramp' at Birkenau. The photograph also shows Crematorium II, with its entrance gate open, Crematorium III, and the underground undressing rooms, and the largely underground gas chambers, of both crematoria.

Left
29. Hungarian Jewish children on arrival at Birkenau.

Opposite top
30. SS men 'select' Hungarian Jews on the ramp at Birkenau. To the left, able-bodied men who are to be sent to the barracks; to the right, old people, women and children, who will be marched in a few moments from the ramp to the nearby gas chamber.

Opposite bottom
31. The group of old people seen sitting by the cattle truck in the foreground of the above picture.

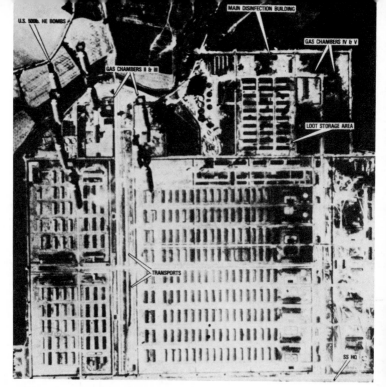

Main disinfection building

U.S. 500lb. HE bombs

Gas chambers IV & V

Gas chambers II & III

Loot storage area

TRANSPORTS

SS HQ

32. An aerial photograph of Birkenau taken on 13 September 1944 showing eight high explosive bombs falling by mistake on the camp (see page 315).

Above

33. A part of the women's camp at Birkenau, and the railway sidings; a photograph taken in 1980.

Right

34. The gate and ruins of Crematorium III, with the railway siding in the foreground, and the birch wood behind; a photograph taken in 1980.

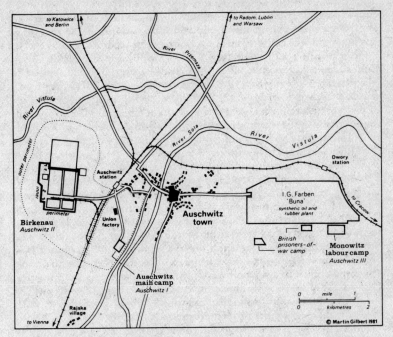

6. Birkenau concentration camp, Auschwitz main camp, Auschwitz town and the I.G.
Farben synthetic oil and rubber plant at Monowitz, with its satellite labour camps.

previous occasions he had made plans to escape, in December 1942, May 1943
and January 1944, but had been unable to carry them out. Now, together with
a fellow Slovak, Alfred Wetzler, he contacted the secret International Resistance Group inside the camp, and put his plan of escape to David Szmulewski,
one of the representatives of the resistance leaders. 'I have been told,' Vrba
later wrote, 'that due to my inexperience, personal volatility (impulsiveness)
and other factors the leadership dismissed my intentions as unreliable.'[1]

The resistance leaders understood, however, Vrba's intense personal feelings
about the destruction of the family camp, and gave him their assurance that,
even if they could not help him escape, no obstacle would be put in his way.
On March 31 his resistance contact, Szmulewski, saw him again, to tell him of
the resistance leaders' decision. 'Szmulewski himself,' Vrba later recalled 'was
very sorry because of the unfavourable "higher decision" but expressed the
hope that in the case of "no success" I would be able to avoid interrogation
and thus avoid a catastrophe for those who had had contact with me before.'

The two escapees were determined to alert the outside world to the reality
of Auschwitz, and to the fate that seemed to be in store for the Jews of Hungary.
Wetzler, who was twenty-six, had been an actual witness of the destruction of
the Theresienstadt family camp. Vrba was nineteen and a half. Both had been

[1] Rudolf Vrba, letter to the author, 11 July 1980.

born in Slovakia. Both had been brought to Auschwitz nearly two years before. What these two men had seen and learned during those two years was to provide the basis for the first comprehensive report to reach the west.

From August 1942 to June 1943 Vrba had worked in a special 'Clearing Commando', known colloquially as 'Canada', then situated in Auschwitz Main Camp. On the arrival of each train at the railway sidings, the Commando's task was to drag out the dead bodies, and then take all the luggage of the deportees for sorting, and to prepare it for dispatch to Germany. Thus for ten months Vrba was present at the arrival of almost every train, and committed to memory their place of origin and the number of deportees in each.

In June 1943 Vrba was transferred from 'Canada' to become one of the registrars in the Quarantine Camp at Birkenau, and as a registrar he had the opportunity of speaking to those new arrivals who had been selected from the incoming trains for slave labour, instead of for gassing. Here again, he both knew and memorized the details of the incoming transports, including the sequence of tattoo numbers allocated to each group as it arrived. In addition, many of the trucks taking people from the railway sidings to Crematorium IV drove past within only a few yards of Vrba's 'office'. As Vrba himself later wrote: '. . . it was part of my duty to make a summarized report of the whole registration office, which report was daily conveyed to the so-called Political Department of the concentration camp Auschwitz. Having this duty enabled me again and again to obtain first hand information about each transport which arrived in the area of the Auschwitz concentration camp.'[1]

From his 'office', Vrba also witnessed the construction of a new railway siding inside Birkenau itself. Work on this siding, or 'ramp', had begun on 15 January 1944. 'The purpose of this ramp,' Vrba later recalled, 'was no secret in Birkenau, the SS were talking about "Hungarian Salami" and "a million units". . . . My lavatory was 30 yards from the new ramp, my office about 100 yards.'

Vrba had also been able to make contact with the Czech family camp, as his work as registrar enabled him to move during the daytime between several sections of Birkenau. He could make full use of this ability, he later recalled, 'by taking a bundle of papers' with him, moving to a section of Birkenau adjacent to the family camp. Then he could contrive to 'get lost' among the prisoners in that section, and without even having to shout, he could speak across the barbed wire between the sections, to other prisoners. There were even times when he had been able to pass written messages across to the family camp, and to receive messages in reply.

Two days before the actual gassing of the family camp, the SS had imposed an internal camp curfew. But a number of those marked out to die had at the same time been transferred to the very section in which Vrba was then a registrar. 'Thus, for the last two days of their lives,' he later recalled, 'I had unlimited contact with them.'[2]

Like Vrba, Alfred Wetzler had also been a registrar, but in different parts of

---

[1] 'Deposition by Doctor Vrba . . . for submission at the trial of Adolf Eichmann', Israel Embassy, London, 16 July 1961, Vrba papers.
[2] Rudolf Vrba, letter to the author, 30 July 1980.

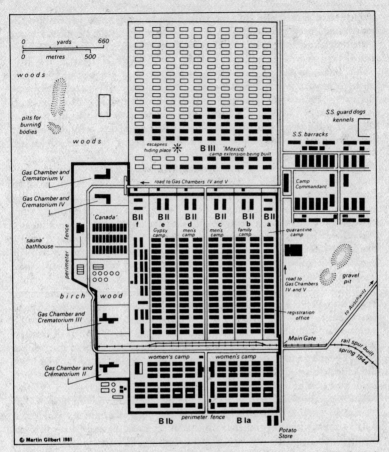

7. The huts, lay-out, gas chambers and crematoria of Birkenau, with its electrically charged perimeter fence, and rail spur built in spring 1944.

Birkenau, including the mortuary. He too had established contacts which enabled him to collect information about every aspect of the killing process. The facts which he and Vrba were able to assemble and to memorize, included the number of Jews 'put to death by gas at Birkenau' from April 1942 to April 1944, listed by their country of origin, and the dimensions of the camp.

While planning their escape, Vrba and Wetzler had even been able to make contact with several of the Jews forced by the SS to drag the corpses from the gas chambers to the crematorium. These Jewish slave labourers were formed into a special unit, or *Sonderkommando*. At regular intervals, they too would be gassed, and then replaced by a new group. But those whom Vrba and Wetzler contacted were able to give them details about the size and workings of the gas chambers themselves. These facts also the two men committed to memory.

Two hours before the evening roll-call of April 7 Vrba and Wetzler were hidden by their colleagues in a specially prepared hide-out which a number of inmates had prepared during work on an extension of the camp which was then under construction beyond the camp's inner perimeter. This area, known as 'Mexico', was being prepared to house the expected Hungarian Jews.

The hide-out was a gap in a woodpile, made up of wooden boards. These boards were being stored as part of the building material for the extension of the camp. Before the inmates returned to their barracks within the inner perimeter, they sprinkled the surrounding area with petrol soaks and tobacco, to prevent the two hundred guard dogs of Birkenau, kept there for just such occasions, from sniffing out the would-be escapees. This latter advice had come from the experience of Soviet prisoners-of-war.

At evening roll-call, after the 'Mexico' workers had returned to their barracks, the sirens sounded. Two prisoners were missing. The guards and dogs began their search. For three days and nights there was a high security alarm, with continuous roll-calls and searches.[1] Throughout those three days a tight cordon of SS guards was kept around both the inner and outer perimeters.

But the hide-away remained undiscovered, and by the evening of April 10, the camp authorities assumed that the two men had already got away. The cordon of SS guards which had surrounded the outer perimeter of the camp was withdrawn.

On April 9 the head of the SS units responsible for guarding the camp, Waffen SS Major Hartenstein had already telegraphed news of the escape to Gestapo headquarters in Berlin. Copies of his telegram were sent to the SS administrative headquarters at Sachsenhausen, to all commanders of Gestapo and SD units in the east, to all Criminal Police units, and to all frontier police posts. The telegram gave the names of the two men, identified them as Jews, and added: 'Immediate search unsuccessful. Request from you further search and in case of capture full report to concentration camp Auschwitz'.[2]

The telegram went on to state that Himmler himself had been informed of the escape, and that the fault 'of any guard' had not so far been determined.

The search within the outer perimeter of the camp having been called off at 10 p.m. on April 10, Vrba and Wetzler slipped past the outer line of watch-towers, and with incredible courage set off southwards toward Slovakia.

After their escape, Vrba and Wetzler had worked their way southwards from Birkenau, 'without documents, without a compass, without a map, and without a weapon'.[3] Carefully avoiding the German 'new settlers' who lived, as at Kozy, in former Polish homes, who were often armed, and had the authority to shoot 'unidentifyable loiterers' at sight, they headed steadily towards the mountains, shunning all roads and paths, and marching only at night. One evening they were fired on by a German police patrol, but managed to escape into the forest. Later they met a Polish partisan, who guided

---

[1] The horror of roll-calls at Auschwitz has been described by many survivors – such as Filip Müller, *Auschwitz Inferno*, London 1979, pages 1–6. On 28 October 1940, for example, 84 Poles died during a single morning's roll-call in Auschwitz Main Camp (report sent by the Polish underground on 31 October 1942, received in London on 28 May 1943, Polish Institute and Sikorski Museum archive, PRM 76/1/13).

[2] Text of the telegram in Erich Kulka, 'Five Escapes from Auschwitz', in Yuri Suhl (editor), *They Fought Back: The Story of Jewish Resistance in Nazi Europe*, London 1968, page 232.

[3] Rudolf Vrba, letter to the author, 29 November 1980.

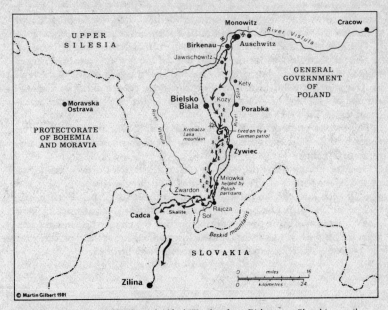

8. Escape route of Rudolf Vrba and Alfred Wetzler, from Birkenau to Slovakia, April 1944, showing the main deportation railway from Slovakia, Austria and Hungary to Auschwitz (through Zilina), and their own route southwards (indicated by arrows).

them towards the frontier, and then, on the morning of Friday April 21, they crossed into Slovakia, finding refuge with a farmer on the Slovak side, in the small village of Skalite.

On April 6, the day before Vrba and Wetzler began their escape, Reuven Zaslani of the Jewish Agency had already warned British intelligence in Cairo of a German radio broadcast in which the Germans 'propose eliminating a million Jews in Hungary'.[1]

On the following day, as Vrba and Wetzler crouched in their woodpile, and were hiding within half a mile of Crematorium IV, the Geneva Zionists were once again telling the Allied representatives in Switzerland what they knew of the fate of European Jewry. This time they told their story to the United States Minister in Berne, Leland Harrison, and his first Counsellor of Legation, J. Klahr Huddle.

Once more Gerhart Riegner and Richard Lichtheim, who headed the delegation, reported for more than an hour on the news which had reached them from Nazi Europe. Several thousand Dutch Jews, they said, had been saved from deportation as a result of receiving Palestine certificates. But the Polish Jews interned in Vittel were less fortunate: recently the Government of Paraguay 'had refused to recognise' those documents and passports which had

[1] Report of an interview, Foreign Office papers, 921/152, 6(5) 44/14, Top Secret. Zaslani's purpose, the interviewer recorded, was to advance further the Jewish Agency's scheme 'for infiltrating Jews into Hungary and Rumania to stimulate resistance among the Jews there'.

been issued by the Paraguayan consul in Berne, while several other South American consuls who had issued similar documents 'had been dismissed'.

The Zionists and the American diplomats then had what was described as 'a general discussion' about the 'tragic fate' of the Jews of Europe. Riegner handed Harrison two photographs. One showed 'the dead bodies of the Jews in Transnistria', Rumanian Jews who had been deported eastward in the autumn of 1941, and the other showed what Riegner called 'one of the death-chambers in Treblinka'.

This second photograph, Riegner told Harrison, 'was corroborating evidence to the report lately issued by Polish circles and describing the death-camp of Treblinka'.[1]

Once again, there was no mention of Auschwitz. Not even its name appeared in the report of this long meeting. Yet the gas chambers there had already been in operation for nearly two years. And as Vrba, Wetzler, and their terrible information began the journey southward, the SS were making plans to build two more gas chambers, to repair the crematoria, and to begin what they hoped would be the rapid, uninterrupted, and secret destruction of the 750,000 Hungarian Jews whose fate they now controlled.

---

[1] 'Note re visit to American Legation Berne on Friday 7 April 1944', Geneva, 11 April 1944, copy in Central Zionist Archives, L 22/92.

Chapter 22

Zionism at bay: rescue at risk

The Jewish Agency's alarm at the German occupation of Hungary did not prevent it from pursuing its other concerns throughout April. On April 10 the head of the Political Department of the Agency, Moshe Shertok who was then in London, received a telegram from Jerusalem, instructing him 'urgently' to obtain a 'minimum' of six thousand Palestine certificates for all Jewish refugees then in Italy, Spain, Aden, Tangiers, Casablanca and Turkey; refugees who were now beyond the range of Nazi terror, and whose lives were in no danger.

As for the Jews still under Nazi control, Shertok was told, the possibility of saving them was 'greatly reduced' and as evidence of this the telegram added: 'Since events Hungary not a single Jew escaped'.[1] Nor had any letters yet been smuggled out of German-occupied Hungary. But news was nevertheless beginning to filter through, and on April 14 the Political Intelligence Centre, Middle East, in a dispatch from Cairo, sent the War Office in London notes pieced together by Balkan Political Intelligence. In Hungary, according to these notes, the new Government 'has published a comprehensive decree for dealing with Jews. This has been accompanied by a strenuous anti-semitic propaganda drive. 'Nevertheless,' the note continued, 'it remains to be seen whether a serious effort will be made to liquidate so large a class.'[2]

Two possible methods of rescue of at least some Hungarian Jews seemed to be the South American and exchange list schemes. For nearly a year, since May 1943, several hundred Polish Jews spared deportation to Treblinka, had waited at Vittel in France with their South American passports. To make their departure from Europe doubly sure, many of them had also been included since December 1943 on a list of 'veteran Zionists and special cases' for the next Palestinian-German exchange. On April 17, however, Richard Lichtheim and Gerhart Riegner telegraphed from Geneva to warn the Jewish leaders in New York that as no German candidates for exchange had presented themselves in areas under Allied control, 'Germany is now becoming impatient, and certificate holders who so far have been kept in special camps are in danger of deportation'.

Lichtheim and Riegner stressed the need for the War Refugee Board to draw up 'as quick as possible' a full list of all Germans eligible for exchange in North and South America, and in the British Empire, and to transmit this list, through the Swiss Government, to the German authorities. They added that this plan of action was of 'special importance' in view of what they described

---

[1] Central Zionist Archives, S 25/1682.
[2] Balkan Political Intelligence Notes, Hungary, War Office papers, 201/1619.

as the 'desperate situation Jews Hungary, who also could profit from Palestine certificates or other authorised documents or visas'. Their telegram ended: 'This view is shared by Papal Nuncio Berne, and all diplomatic representatives we have lately approached.'[1]

That same day, April 17, Lichtheim wrote to the Counsellor of the American Legation in Berne, J. Klahr Huddle, to point out that Spain, the Protecting Power for several Latin American States, had not yet been informed which of those States was willing to honour their Swiss-issued passports, and had therefore 'refused to confirm that the papers are valid'.[2]

For the majority of the Vittel deportees, this initiative came as their own situation worsened. On April 18 a total of 173 of them, including the poet Yitzhak Katznelson and his son, were sent from Vittel to the Drancy internment camp on the outskirts of Paris. Four days later, Huddle informed Lichtheim that Paraguay now 'recognized the documents issued by its consuls as valid'. But it was still not known, the Legation reported, whether the Spanish Foreign Office in Madrid had instructed its Ambassador in Berlin 'to act on behalf of the persons affected'.

In his letter of April 22 Huddle passed on, 'from a reliable source', the attitude of the various Latin American States. Bolivia, Chile, Paraguay and Uruguay were willing to issue passports for Polish Jews. Cuba would only do so 'if Great Britain and the United States interpose no objection'. Costa Rica and Nicaragua would do so 'to a number up to eight families', but unless these families were farmers or industrialists, they would have to leave when the war was over. Haiti and Peru, Huddle added, 'could take no action', while Panama, Guatemala and Salvador 'have taken negative action'.[3]

That same day, having sent this letter, the American Legation in Berne learned that the War Refugee Board and the State Department had informed the Spanish Government of 'the preoccupation' of the United States in the matter of the Vittel and other passport holders. The State Department had added, in its message to Madrid, that the German Government should be told by Spain, as the Protecting Power, that it should accord the Jewish internees involved 'the same treatment which it wishes extended to German civilians in the Western Hemisphere'.[4]

On April 28 the Polish Embassy in Washington sent an urgent message to the State Department. Polish Jews formerly in Vittel, the message read, were now detained in Drancy, which, 'according to our information, is a transit concentration camp'. The message continued:

. . . reliable information having been received that their lives are actually in danger and that every hour counts, the Polish Ambassador urges the necessity of immediate action which might probably require the kind offices of the Spanish and Swiss Government as protecting Powers, in view of obtaining that the passports issued by the Latin American Republics should be respected and that in some cases their validity be prolonged.[5]

[1] Central Zionist Archives, L 22/92, telegram to Stephen Wise.
[2] Central Zionist Archives, L 22/92.
[3] Central Zionist Archives, L 22/92.
[4] Central Zionist Archives, L 22/92, Huddle to Lichtheim of 24 April 1944.
[5] 'Memorandum', Secret, Urgent, United States National Archives, 840/48 Refugees/605.

This inter-Allied activity came too late. On April 29 all 173 of the Vittel deportees in Drancy, including Katznelson and his son, were deported to Auschwitz, where they were gassed.

At the very moment when the Jews of Hungary were being closed into ghettoes, the rescue of Jews from Rumania was gaining momentum. On April 24 a small boat, the *Bella Citta*, reached Istanbul from a Rumanian port, Constanta. On board were 130 Jewish children, accompanied by twenty adults. Of the children, 120 were orphans evacuated from Transnistria on the eve of the arrival of the Red Army. On reaching Istanbul, all of them received permits to enter Palestine. On the following day Chaim Barlas, of the Jewish Agency, wrote to the United States Ambassador in Ankara, Laurence A. Steinhardt:

I met this group today, and I may say they are the most unfortunate children who survived misery and massacre in Transnistria during the last 3 years.

They are now miraculously saved, and will leave on Friday by train to Palestine.[1]

Throughout April, while the SS prepared to deport the Jews of Hungary, other Jews were being brought to Auschwitz as before. On April 9 the first of three trains reached Auschwitz from the Majdanek concentration camp, which was evacuated as the Red Army drove steadily westwards. For eight days these 'evacuees' had been shunted towards Auschwitz in a sealed train, without water, or medical help. During the journey, twenty of them cut their way out of the train at a wayside station, and tried to escape. All were shot. A further ninety-nine were found dead on arrival at Auschwitz. The survivors were tattooed, and sent to the barracks.

On the following day, April 10, a train reached Auschwitz from Italy, and on April 11 from Athens. Of 1,500 deportees in this second train, 1,067 were gassed. On April 29 a further train arrived from Paris, including the Vittel deportees with their once precious, now valueless Latin American passports. On April 30, from a train from Italy, only thirteen men were sent to the barracks, while all the women, children and old people were gassed.

Equally unknown to the Allies, the Jews of Hungary were being prepared for deportation to Auschwitz. The first stage of the Nazi plan, the sealing of the Jews into ghettoes, had already begun on April 16, in Ruthenia. Nine days later, the question of rescue took an unexpected, dramatic turn: on April 25, Joel Brand, a leading Hungarian Zionist, was taken to SS headquarters in Budapest. As Brand recalled two months later, Eichmann 'snapped' at him, as soon as he was seated:

You know who I am. I solved the Jewish question in Slovakia. I have stretched out my feelers to see if your international Jewry is still capable of doing anything. I will make a deal with you. We are in the fifth year of the war. We need—[2] and we are not immodest. I am prepared to sell you all the Jews. I am also prepared to have them all annihilated. It is as you wish. It is as you wish. Anyway, what do you want? I presume for you the most important are the men and women who can produce children.

---

[1] Central Zionist Archives, L 15/117 I.
[2] Left blank in the original text of the interrogation.

Brand then recalled the following conversation:

Brand: I am not the man to decide that old men and women should be left behind, and
            only people capable of producing children should be saved.
Eichmann: Quite. Well, I want goods for blood.
Brand: I did not understand at first and thought Eichmann meant money.
Eichmann: No. Goods for blood. Money comes second.
Brand: What goods?
Eichmann: Go to your international authorities, they will know. For example—lorries.
            I could imagine one lorry for a hundred Jews, but that is only a suggested figure.
            Where will you go?
Brand: I must think. . . .[1]

This meeting between Brand and Eichmann, unknown at the time either
to the Jewish Agency or to the Allies, was to lead within a few weeks to both
the Agency and the Allies becoming directly involved in the fate of Hungarian
Jewry, and in an SS act of deception on a massive scale: for Eichmann wanted
Brand to make contact with the Jewish Agency representatives in Istanbul,
and with the Allies, and to offer a commercial barter, the Jews of Hungary,
alive, in exchange for goods and money: 'Goods for blood', as Eichmann had
expressed it.

With the truth about Auschwitz still unknown in the west, such an offer
contained a tantalizing appeal. But at the very moment when it was being
made, evidence was reaching the Jewish leadership in Slovakia which contained full and horrific details of the gassings at Auschwitz. The source of this
news was the two Auschwitz escapees, Rudolf Vrba and Alfred Wetzler, whose
message had begun its westward journey with their escape from Auschwitz
on April 10 and their meeting with the Slovak farmer at Skalite on April 21.

As Vrba later recalled: 'We met accidently on the march within one kilo-
metre of the German-Slovak border. He was working in his fields. He saw
that we had crossed the border "on our stomachs", and invited us for lunch.'

The farmer's name was Canecky. During lunch he explained to Vrba and
Wetzler that 'in almost all the neighbouring villages' there were Jewish
doctors who had been exempt from deportation in the summer of 1942 because of the 'dire lack' of doctors in Slovakia. The exemption had covered the
doctor's wife and children, but not his parents, brothers or sisters.

The farmer then told the escapees that in the town of Cadca there was one
such Jewish doctor, a Dr Pollak. Vrba realized that this was the same man
whom he himself had met at the time of his own deportation in June 1942, and
who, as a doctor, had been deleted at the last moment from the deportation list.

To walk over the mountains to Cadca would have taken the two men at
least three days. But if they could wait in Skalite until Monday morning, they
could take a train. This they did, dressed as local peasants, and pretending to
transport the farmer's pigs for sale in Cadca's Monday market. As the local
train was controlled by local Slovak gendarmes, and not by Germans, the risk
for someone speaking Slovak, and dressed as a peasant, was relatively small.
So it was that the two men reached Cadca without incident. There, as Vrba
later recalled:

[1] Interrogation report, File No. SIME/P 7769, page 18, in Foreign Office papers, 371/42811. The in-
terrogating officer was Lieutenant W. B. Savigny.

I walked into Dr Pollak's surgery pretending to be a patient. There was a female nurse present in his office, so I pretended I came to complain about a 'gentleman's disease' and I said I wanted the woman nurse to go out. Once alone with Dr Pollak I explained to him briefly who I was and from where I knew him and from where I now came.

When Dr Pollak learned from me that all his 'resettled' relatives were dead, he became somewhat shaky, and asked me what he could do for me. I asked him to immediately contact the Jewish Council in Bratislava. Before I left his office he, Dr Pollak, suggested that he put bandages on my feet so that the nurse would not suspect something unusual, because I was a long time in his office (about fifteen minutes).

He gave me the address of some of his friends, and we, i.e. Wetzler and myself, slept in Cadca. We travelled to Zilina next morning by train, dressed as peasants. On the morning of Tuesday, April 25, at about 10 a.m. we met the first representative of the Jewish Council, Mr Erwin Steiner, in a park in Zilina. We (Wetzler and I) were drinking slivovitz in the park and waiting for Steiner. Without hair, in peasant shirts and drinking slivovitz in public we attracted no attention, as this was a common habit of newly recruited (already shorn) soldiers in Slovakia. Thus we met the Jewish Council, with my feet still in bandages provided by Dr Pollak.[1]

On hearing the two escapees' story, Steiner at once contacted the Jewish community in Bratislava, the Slovak capital. The man to whom he spoke, by telephone, in Bratislava was Oskar Krasnansky, a chemical engineer, and a leading Slovak Zionist. Although Jews were not normally allowed to travel by train, Krasnansky managed to obtain permission from the Police, and made his way to Zilina.

At Steiner's house Krasnansky found the two escapees: 'They were in poor health, and undernourished', he later recalled. 'They had eaten almost no food for three weeks'.

Krasnansky was impressed by the escapees' 'wonderful memory', and for two days he cross-examined them on the 'reality' of Auschwitz. Then, after providing them with false Aryan papers, he sent them for safety to the town of Lipovsky Mikulas.[2]

Using Council documents brought specially from Bratislava, Krasnansky checked the escapees' account of the arrival of trains from Slovakia to Auschwitz with the Council's own statistics of the departure of these trains from Slovakia to their previously 'unknown destination'. Then Krasnansky wrote a covering note to their report, stating that it contained 'only what one or other, or both, experienced, witnessed, or had knowledge of directly'. Krasnansky added:

The statements coincide with the reports, undoubtedly only fragmentary, but reliable, that have been received up until now, and the information supplied on individual transports corresponds exactly with the official listings.

Hence the statements are to be considered as completely authentic.[3]

The question was now discussed in Bratislava: what was to be done with this Vrba-Wetzler report? According to Krasnansky, he himself wrote it out in

[1] Rudolf Vrba, letter to the author, 30 July 1980.

[2] Oskar Krasnansky, conversation with the author, Tel Aviv, 22 December 1980.

[3] Quoted in Erich Kulka, 'Five Escapes from Auschwitz', Yuri Suhl (editor), *They Fought Back: The Story of Jewish Resistance in Nazi Europe*, London 1968, page 233. Krasnansky's note was first published by the War Refugee Board in Washington on 26 November 1944. as part of the official publication of the Vrba-Wetzler report (see pages 328–9 of this volume).

German, and gave it to a typist, Gisi Farkas, who made several copies. 'One copy', he later recalled, 'we sent to Istanbul. But it never arrived there. The man to whom we gave it, who was making the journey, had been sent from Istanbul as a "reliable courier". But possibly he was a paid spy. As far as we later learned, he gave it to the Gestapo in Budapest'.

Krasnansky handed a second copy of the report to the Slovak Orthodox rabbi, Dov Weissmandel, who had contacts with the Orthodox community in Switzerland, and who offered to try to smuggle it there, for transmission to the west.[1]

A third copy was given to Monsignor Giuseppe Burzio, the Papal Chargé d'Affaires in Bratislava, who went it on to the Vatican on May 22, after himself questioning the two escapees. But the Vatican's own records suggest that Burzio's report only reached there five months later.[2]

The most urgent need, Vrba and Wetzler believed, was to transmit the report to Hungary, and to alert Hungarian Jewry to their own potential fate. Krasnansky himself translated the Vrba–Wetzler report into Hungarian, and prepared to give it to Rudolf Kastner, the head of the Hungarian Jewish rescue committee, on his next visit to Bratislava.

Kastner, who made the short train journey from Budapest fairly frequently, was expected in Bratislava before the end of April. But on April 25, the very day on which Krasnansky was cross-examining Vrba and Wetzler in Zilina, Kastner and the Hungarian Jewish leadership in Budapest were receiving Eichmann's offer to negotiate 'goods for blood': to avoid the death camps altogether in return for a substantial payment.

On that fatal day, April 25, two events had coincided: the truth about Auschwitz had reached those who had the ability to make it known to the potential victims, and the offer had been made to negotiate 'goods for blood'. Those Hungarian Jewish leaders who wished to follow up the negotiations were unwilling to risk the negotiations by publicizing the facts about the annihilation process at Auschwitz. Yet that process was known to them from April 28, three days after Eichmann's first meeting with Brand, when Kastner travelled to Bratislava, where he was given a copy of the Vrba–Wetzler report, and took it back to Budapest.[3] But by then Kastner and his colleagues in the Zionist leadership in Hungary were already committed to their negotiations with Eichmann, and to the dispatch of their colleague, Joel Brand, to Istanbul. They therefore gave no publicity whatsoever to the facts about Auschwitz which were now in their possession.

To this day, Vrba remains convinced that had the facts which he and Wetzler brought to Bratislava been immediately publicized and circulated throughout Hungary, many of the 450,000 Jews who were later to be deported, but who were as yet still in Hungary, would have been stirred to resist, evade or otherwise obstruct their deportation. Had the deportees had

---

[1] Oskar Krasnansky, conversation with the author, Tel Aviv, 22 December 1980.

[2] Report No. 2144 (A.E.S. 7679/44), sent from Bratislava 22 May 1944, annotated in the Vatican, 22 and 26 October 1944. Burzio's covering note of 22 May 1944 is reprinted in full in *Actes et Documents du Saint Siège Relatifs à la Seconde Guerre Mondiale*, volume 10, 'Le Saint Siège et les Victimes de la Guerre', January 1944–July 1945, Vatican 1980.

[3] Statement by Oskar Krasnansky and Dr Neumann, Yad Vashem archives.

'knowledge of hot ovens', Vrba later wrote, 'instead of parcels of cold food, they would have been less ready to board the trains and the whole action of deportation would have been slowed down'.

Not urgent warnings to their fellow Jews to resist deportation, but secret negotiations with the SS aimed at averting deportation altogether, had become the avenue of hope chosen by the Hungarian Zionist leaders. Their people thus became the innocent victims of one of the countless Nazi deceptions of the war; 'a clever ruse', as Vrba himself later reflected, 'to neutralize the potential resistance of a million people', and he added: 'Passive *and* active resistance by a million people would create panic and havoc in Hungary. Panic in Hungary would have been better than panic which came to the victims in front of burning pits in Birkenau. Eichmann knew it; that is why he smoked cigars with the Kastners, "negotiated", exempted the "real great rabbis", and meanwhile, without panic among the deportees, planned to "resettle" hundreds of thousands in orderly fashion. . . .'[1]

During the first two weeks of May the deportations to Auschwitz continued from Paris, from Yugoslavia, from Berlin, and from the industrial labour camp at Blechhammer. On May 14 a train arrived bringing sick and old Jews, and Jewish children, from Plaszow, a slave labour camp in the suburbs of Cracow. All were gassed.

For the Jewish Agency, the dispatch of Palestine certificates continued, their sole known means of rescue. During May the first certificates began to reach Belgium, sent from the Palestine Office in Geneva through the International Red Cross, and these gave protection, it was later discovered 'to some 600 recipients'.[2]

Among the many enquiries that had been made was one on behalf of Yitzhak Gruenbaum, Polish-born chairman of the Rescue Committee of the Jewish Agency, whose son Eliezer had been living in Warsaw on the outbreak of war. Early that spring Gruenbaum himself had telegraphed to Gerhart Riegner in Geneva: 'Find my son'. Riegner's first reaction, as he later recalled, was amazement that Gruenbaum should even imagine that it was any longer possible to find anybody in Poland. 'If anybody knew what the fate of Polish Jewry had been,' Riegner thought, 'it is Gruenbaum. He was the personification of the fight for Jewish rights in Poland before the war. It was a completely crazy idea to find an individual there, to find the son of a father in Poland, after two and a half years of killing. . . .'

But Riegner did not shrug off the request. Instead, he later recalled, 'I had a crazy idea of my own. I sent ten Red Cross packages to ten different camps, each in the name of Yitzhak Gruenbaum's son. And from one camp, confirmation came. . . .'[3]

This was indeed so; on March 1 a postcard from Eliezer Gruenbaum reached the World Congress in Geneva, confirming receipt of the parcel. From Geneva, Richard Lichtheim at once wrote to Jerusalem to inform Eliezer's father that his son was alive, and that the postcard had come from a

[1] Rudolf Vrba, letter to the author, 30 July 1980.
[2] Rescue Committee of the Jewish Agency for Palestine, *Bulletin*, Jerusalem, January 1945, page 7.
[3] Gerhart Riegner, conversation with the author, 1 October 1980.

camp in Upper Silesia. The name of the camp was Jawischowitz. It was, Lichtheim added, 'practically the same place as Birkenau'.[1]

Jawischowitz was in fact one of several industrial regions in the Auschwitz area to which Jewish slave labour from Auschwitz and Birkenau were sent. It was in no way 'practically the same place'. But the name 'Birkenau' like that of 'Auschwitz' still masked its true function from those who used it.

According to Eliezer Gruenbaum's postcard, which had been sent from Jawischowitz on April 29, he had received 'three food parcels' through the World Jewish Congress relief organization, Relico, and it was Relico's Geneva office which had received his postcard, which had taken only six days to make its journey from Upper Silesia to Switzerland.

The name 'Birkenau' again appeared in a Jewish Agency message on May 3, although once again, as in Lichtheim's letter of May 1, it was not linked or associated in any way with the name 'Auschwitz', of which it was so integral a part.

The second mention of Birkenau was in a telegram from Yitzak Gruenbaum's representative in Istanbul, Eliezer Leder, who reported to Jerusalem that the British Consulate in Istanbul had confirmed the Palestine certificates recently issued for Hungary and Rumania, and that he, Leder, now wished to know whether it was 'advisable sending same Birkenau'.[2]

This telegram is a clear pointer of just how little was known of the Auschwitz-Birkenau camp. But ignorance and hope were a powerful combination; and hope that at least some Jews could be rescued was given further encouragement on May 5, when the British Consul in Geneva, H. B. Livingston, informed the Jewish Agency representatives there that the Germans had agreed to a third exchange, 'covering 279 Jews for 111 Germans', and that this exchange could take place 'about mid-May'.[3]

Here was a possibility of saving a further 279 Jews from Nazi Europe; Jews from Poland who, if they could be found, could now be brought out. Both the relatives of Palestinian Jews, and 'veteran Zionists' were eligible. The problem was to find them. In the previous exchange, a majority of those on the list had never been found. They had, in fact, already been deported, and gassed. Now the search began again.

---

[1] Central Zionist Archives, L 22/135. Eliezer Gruenbaum survived the war, and emigrated to Palestine, but was later killed during the first Arab-Israeli war of 1948.

[2] Central Zionist Archives, S 26/1190.

[3] Central Zionist Archives, L 22/56.

Chapter 23

The deportations from Hungary, May 1944

The first news that the Jews of Hungary had been rounded up and forced into ghettoes reached the west while the seizures were still taking place. On May 5 Chaim Barlas telegraphed from Istanbul to the Jewish Agency in Jerusalem: 'Latest information from Hungary indicates new wave persecutions introducing ghettoes etc.' Barlas advised the Jewish Agency to telegraph to Stephen Wise in New York 're warning'.[1] This telegram reached Jerusalem on May 6.

On May 8 Yitzhak Gruenbaum, of the Jewish Agency in Jerusalem, telegraphed to Stephen Wise in New York:

Received information that situation Jews Hungary desperate. Authorities there decided apply same restrictions against Jews like Poland. Restrictions and atrocities just beginning, but will grow very fast. Anxious deportation will begin soon. Imperative take all steps our power prevent or at least slow up action.

Such was the full text of Gruenbaum's telegram. It gave no indication of what he envisaged by the phrase 'all steps our power'.[2]

That same day, May 8, the Commander of the Allied air forces in Italy, Lieutenant-General Ira C. Eaker, having received an enquiry about a possible air attack on the German synthetic oil plant at Blechhammer, replied that not only were strikes on Blechhammer 'feasible', but that the German synthetic rubber factory at Auschwitz, as well as the synthetic oil and coking plant at Odertal 'might also be attacked simultaneously'. Eaker added that to carry out the operation 'with the greatest possibly economy', it should not be attempted 'until our fighter position is stronger, in about another 2 weeks'.[3]

This exchange of correspondence concerned the forthcoming Allied air offensive against German oil targets, in conjunction with the still top secret plans for 'Overlord', the Allied landings in Normandy, planned for June 6. The first of these Allied air attacks on German oil production took place on May 12, when four sites in the Sudetenland were bombed, resulting, as Speer informed Hitler on June 30, in an immediate reduction of daily tonnage from 5,845 tons to 4,821 tons, a drop of more than twenty per cent.[4]

Both the Normandy Landings, and the Oil Campaign, were closely guarded secrets. There was no way in which the Jewish leaders could take them into

[1] Central Zionist Archives, S 25/1682, telegram No. 2308.

[2] Central Zionist Archives, S 25/1682, unnumbered.

[3] Eaker to Spaatz, Spaatz papers, Box 143, F, Operational Planning: Attacks against Oil Targets. I am grateful to Professor David S. Wyman for sending me the full text of this document, which was published in part in his article 'Why Auschwitz Was Never Bombed', in *Commentary*, volume 65, number 5, New York, May 1978, page 42.

[4] Quoted in Sir Charles Webster and Noble Frankland, *The Strategic Air Offensive Against Germany 1939–1945*, volume 4, Annexes and Appendices, pages 326–9.

account in their search for assistance. In the second week of May their efforts continued along the same lines as in April. On May 8 the Chief Rabbi of Great Britain, Rabbi Hertz, appealed direct to Churchill with a new suggestion, based on the fact 'that the Nazi rulers separate Jews from the general population of territories under their control, and doom them to torture and mass extermination'. Hertz asked Churchill for an announcement that all Jews in enemy territories 'are British protected persons', to whom the British Government offered 'the facilities arranged by its Protecting Powers, including the provision of travel-documents, facilities for exchange and place of refuge'. This idea, Hertz added, was 'conceived as quite aside from any steps that H.M. Government may undertake in connection with Palestine'.[1]

On May 16 the Foreign Office informed Churchill's private office of the reasons for rejecting Rabbi Hertz's appeal. 'The Allied Governments,' Pierson Dixon wrote to John Martin, with particular reference to the Polish and Czech Governments in exile, 'might be expected to criticize, if not actively resent, a declaration that certain of their nationals were British protected persons.'

Dixon's letter went on to express feelings which were certainly not calculated to encourage any deeper examination of the proposals, or of some alternative means of rescue. Indeed, had they not remained sealed in the secrecy of the Prime Minister's files, such feelings may well have caused the Jewish Agency representatives, and the Chief Rabbi, to despair of any sympathetic consideration being given to what they considered to be the particularly terrible plight of the Jews of Europe. As Dixon wrote:

Such a declaration would, we are convinced, in any case make no practical difference to the fate of the Jews as far as the Germans were concerned, and it would involve us in most far-reaching and undesirable responsibilities towards the surviving Jews which could only be fulfilled after the danger to them had passed, by when they might well desire to retain their new status.

Dixon's letter went on to warn that in any exchange scheme such a 'protected persons' status would still be 'of no help to European Jewry' as it would be 'readily appreciated that we could not give priority to foreign Jews, including presumably large numbers who are "enemy nationals", over British subjects. . . .' His letter continued:

. . . we have always taken the line although the Germans have attacked the Jews with especial ferocity, they have also attacked and murdered many hundreds of thousands of non-Jews (in Poland the proportions are said to be about equal).[2]

To offer Jews exclusive facilities and priorities of escape as British-Protected persons would not be appreciated by the U.S.S.R. It might stimulate anti-Semitism in enemy-occupied countries where non-Jewish nationals who are in danger from the enemy would resent being treated differently from Jewish nationals. It would in fact, by stereotyping the 'Jew' as a separate category, perpetuate the very Nazi doctrine which we are determined to stamp out.

In addition to these arguments, Dixon also sent Martin the Foreign Office's view of what Chief Rabbi Hertz should be told. It too was blunt. To declare

[1] Premier papers, 4/51/8, folio 443.
[2] Some 3 million Polish Jews were murdered by the Nazis between 1939 and 1945 (out of a total Polish Jewish population of just under 3½ million). A further 3 million Polish non-Jewish were also killed during those same years (out of a total non-Jewish population of more than 25 million).

the Jews under Nazi rule to be British-protected persons would, the Chief Rabbi was to be told, 'bring many disadvantages to the Jews themselves'; the British Government 'associated with other Governments, are determined to aid as far as possible *all* the victims of German tyranny, and this they can do, are doing and will do irrespective of making the futile gesture of declaring one category of persons to be British-protected'.[1]

At Auschwitz, the killing process continued with the gassing of fourteen Jews brought from the nearby ghetto of Sosnowiec on May 16. On the same day, the family camp deception was revived, when 2,503 Jews from Theresienstadt were brought to Auschwitz and sent, as their now murdered predecessors had been, to the stables in the Birkenau section of the camp. Once more, men, women and children were kept together. Once more, they were encouraged to send postcards to say how well they were. Once more, they were allowed to receive food parcels from the Red Cross, and to acknowledge them. And within three days, a further two trainloads of Theresienstadt deportees had brought the total number in this deliberate Nazi deception to more than seven thousand.

Although the Hungarian Jewish leadership had decided that negotiations with the Gestapo would be more effective than publicizing the Vrba-Wetzler report, Rabbi Weissmandel, to whom Krasnansky had given a copy at the end of April, held other views. He had first taken his copy of the report from Bratislava to Nitra, to show to his father-in-law, Rabbi Unger, the head of the Orthodox Jewish community. In Nitra the report was translated into Yiddish, and a copy sent westward by courier.

But by May 15 no answer had come. It was clear that the report had either been lost, intercepted or delayed. And on May 15 the SS began the deportation of Jews from Hungary to Auschwitz. Weissmandel realized that the facts of the Vrba-Wetzler report – the 'truth' about Auschwitz – and the new deportations, were linked. He therefore composed a telegram in simple code, and this telegram, sent on May 16 from the Orthodox community in Bratislava to the Swiss Orthodox leaders, for transmission to the United States, urged the Allies to bombard the railways lines between Kosice and Presov to save those Jews who had 'not yet' been deported.

Weissmandel knew that the Kosice-Presov route was one of those along which the first trains had just passed from eastern Hungary to Poland. But Auschwitz itself was not mentioned, either in this telegram, or in a second telegram sent from Slovakia seven days later; only 'Poland'. Nor did either telegram reach the War Refugee Board in Washington until June 18.[2]

Although the Nazis had begun the deportation to Auschwitz, by rail, of the Jews of eastern Hungary, Translyvania, southern Slovakia and Ruthenia, the fact that the deportations were taking place was not known in the west. But on May 18, news that it nad been planned was brought to Jerusalem by a few Hungarian Jews who had managed to escape overland through Istanbul at the

---

[1] Premier papers, 4/51/8, folio 437–9.
[2] For the texts of these telegrams, and the American Government's reaction to them, see pages 236–7.

beginning of May. It was Eliahu Dobkin, the Head of the Immigration Department of the Jewish Agency, who was among those who cross-questioned the refugees, and who telegraphed on the following day, May 19, to Nahum Goldmann and Stephen Wise in New York:

Refugees who reached Palestine yesterday relate terrible facts regarding Jews in Hungary. There is clear evidence that mass extermination is prepared there according methods in Poland. Over 300,000 Jews from Sziget[1] and Carpatho-Russia are already interned in camps and ghettoes. . . .

Dobkin's telegram then listed twenty-three camps and ghettoes by name, and added: 'preparations have been made for the deportation of large numbers'.[2]

The first train to reach Auschwitz from Hungary arrived at the camp on May 17. Made up of more than forty sealed wagons, with a hundred Jews forced into each, this single train, like each of those that followed it, brought more than four thousand Jews to the specially prepared railway line inside Birkenau itself, only a few yards from two of the gas chambers.

Only seventeen men were sent to the barracks from this first massive transport. The rest of the four thousand deportees were gassed.

A second train arrived from Hungary on May 18. Again, it brought more than four thousand Jews. This time, it was twenty women who were taken to the barracks, while the remaining four thousand were gassed. On May 19 the third four thousand arrived; only seven men were tattooed, and spared. On May 20, from the fourth train in four days, thirty-four men and fifty-eight women were sent to the barracks. In those four days, more than 16,000 Jews had been murdered.

On May 20 there was a deportation from another direction, from Paris to Auschwitz. The train contained 565 men, 632 women and 191 children and youths under the age of nineteen. Only 108 adults survived the war.

It was also on May 20 that the Jewish Agency representatives in Geneva passed back the news to Jerusalem: 'There are no actual exchange possibilities for certificate holders Birkenau.'[3]

On May 21 the railway sidings, gas chambers and crematoria at Birkenau were more active than they had ever been before. For on that one day three trains arrived from Hungary, two from Holland, and one from Belgium. The second Dutch train did not contain Jews, but Gipsies, all of whom were sent to the barracks. From the three Hungarian trains, only eleven men and six women were sent to the barracks, and more than 12,000 gassed. This was the largest number to be gassed in a single day in the history of Auschwitz up to that moment. But it was a number that was now to be repeated day after day.

---

[1] Sziget is more correctly, in Hungarian, Máramárossziget; in Rumanian, Sighet. In 1941 there were 10,144 Jews in Sighet, 39 per cent of the town's population, and the highest proportion of Jews in any Hungarian town. Almost all were deported to Auschwitz; less than 2,000 survived. Among the survivors was the author Elie Wiesel.

[2] United States National Archives, 840.48, Refugees 6/37.

[3] Central Zionist Archives, L 22/135.

On May 23 three trains reached Auschwitz: from Italy, France and Hungary. Most of the Italian deportees, 410 of those from France, and four thousand of those from Hungary were gassed. Only five women of these four thousand were spared, for the time being, and sent to the barracks. On the following day, from yet another train from Paris, 188 men were sent to the barracks, and 1,102 men, women and children were gassed. They had been travelling eastwards for four days in their sealed train.

Chapter 24

A Gestapo offer: 'Unmanageable numbers'

On May 24 the news of the Hungarian deportations, now in progress for nine days, was still not known in the west. But on that day the American Consul-General in Jerusalem, L. C. Pinkerton, telephoned the Jewish Agency building in Jerusalem with a message for Shertok. The message had come from Istanbul, and read:

Wednesday, await at Lydda special mission in connection with Hungary. Wednesday night prepare for urgent Executive meeting. Be ready for sudden trip to Istanbul.[1]

This telegram launched the Brand mission: the arrival in Istanbul of Joel Brand himself, and his companion Andor Gross. That same night the British Ambassador in Ankara, Sir Hughe Knatchbull-Hugessen, telegraphing both to London and Jerusalem, reported that Brand 'is said to represent Jewish community in Hungary and to have brought for Jewish Agency a proposal formally addressed to him by Gestapo for exchanging remaining Jews in Axis occupied territory against either commodities or foreign currency'. The Ambassador added: 'Jewish Agency representatives in Istanbul apparently regard the proposal as serious, as they have sent a certain Pomerantz to Palestine to report to Zionist executive'.[2]

The first British reaction to the news of the Brand mission was a succinct one: 'the US authorities', Ian Henderson minuted 'would look more favourably on these blockade-running schemes than we would'.[3]

On the morning of May 26, in Jerusalem, Ben Gurion and Shertok explained the Brand proposals to the British High Commissioner in Palestine, Sir Harold MacMichael. If the Nazis' offer were rejected, he was told, 'they will proceed with their programme of wholesale liquidation'.

Immediately after this meeting, MacMichael telegraphed a full report of it to London. One paragraph concerned the apparent fate, as Brand reported it, of some 300,000 Hungarian Jews, 'already herded in concentration camps as a preliminary to deportation'. Other Jews, he said, were in the 'process' of being rounded up. Plans had been made 'for daily deportation to Polish slaughter-houses of 12,000 Jews as from the 22nd May', but this deportation, so Ben Gurion and Shertok told MacMichael, 'is presumed to have been deferred, pending negotiations'.

---

[1] Central Zionist Archives, S 25/1678.
[2] Foreign Office papers, 371/42758, W 8465, telegram No. 794, Secret. Pomerantz was a young Polish-born Jew who had been active in Istanbul as one of the Jewish Agency representatives concerned with illegal immigration, and the transfer of messages to and from occupied Europe (see also the biographical sketch on page 351).
[3] Foreign Office papers, 371/42758, W 8465, note of 27 May 1944.

9. Joel Brand's journey by road from Budapest to Vienna, then on by air from Vienna to Istanbul, and finally by train to Aleppo and Cairo.

Ben Gurion and Shertok urged the British Government to take the Brand offer seriously. 'In the light of the above and past experience,' MacMichael noted, 'Agency fears that the fate of Hungarian, Czechoslovakian and Rumanian Jews is sealed unless they can be saved in time.'

MacMichael included in his telegram of May 26 a verbatim statement from the Jewish Agency leaders. It read:

They firmly hope that the magnitude and seemingly fantastic character of the proposition will not deter high Allied authorities from undertaking a concerted and determined effort to save the greatest possible number. They fully realise the overwhelming difficulties, but believe that they might not prove insurmountable if the task is faced with the boldness demanded by unprecedented catastrophe.

The deportations to Auschwitz had in fact begun on May 15. But still, by May 26, neither the Jewish Agency, nor the Allies knew of this fact; indeed, the Brand mission itself seemed an indication that the deportations had not yet begun. Hence the hope of Ben Gurion and Shertok that the Allies would make 'a concerted and determined effort to save the greatest possible number'.

In his telegram of May 26, the High Commissioner went on to report that, according to Brand, as 'an alternative to complete annihilation', the Nazis were 'ready to evacuate 1,000,000 Jews' from Hungary, Czechoslovakia, Rumania and Poland, and, in return for ten thousand motor lorries, and certain quantities of 'coffee, tea, cocoa and soap', to send these Jews to Spain and Portugal, 'though not, as they specifically stated, to Palestine'. The Nazis were also prepared, Brand reported, 'to exchange Jews against German prisoners-of-war'.[1]

The Jewish Agency saw the Brand mission as a chance to save at least some of the hundreds of thousands of Hungarian Jews known to be doomed to death. But for the British policymakers this area of Zionist hopes had another aspect. As R. M. A. Hankey minuted on May 27:

It seems likely that this fantastic offer is just a political warfare stunt by the Germans. They must know that it would be almost impossible to move a million Jews from Eastern Europe across France to Spain and Portugal without preventing our bombing of French railways, interfering with the Second Front, embarrassing our relations with Spain and Portugal, using shipping in the Mediterranean and Atlantic, upsetting the supply position in Spain and Portugal and (if the refugees went to the Middle East) very probably precipitating troubles in Palestine and the Middle East which would immobilise British divisions otherwise available for offensive operations.

Even if we did accept, there would be no means of sending the lorries to Germany without interfering again with shipping and military operations.

Finally, if once we were to agree to be blackmailed in this way we should not have an appeal for a mere million Jews, there would be Poles, Frenchmen, Dutchmen, etc., etc.

In the circumstances it is recommended that the Colonial Office should reply that we are not prepared to discuss an offer of this sort through such channels, that everything possible is being done already to prevent the extermination of the Jews and other peoples under German domination; and that the German emissaries may be informed that any Germans executing Jews in consequence of these or other threats will have to answer with their lives under the arrangements for the trial of war criminals when the war reaches a close.

Hankey added 'We should not inform Dr Weizmann or Dr Goldmann (though W.O. say they know through secret channels).' Hankey's first instinct was to advise rejection of the scheme even before telling the Americans. But his colleague, Randall, commented that the United States Government, 'with Mr Morgenthau very actively engaged in winning Jewish approval, will probably feel embarrassed at being asked to share the odium of rejecting the scheme – at least in its present fantastic scale – but it is, I think, essential that we should put it to Washington, with all the objections we see, and ask for American views.' Randall added: 'The Jewish Agency man in Istanbul is apt to find mares nests, but in the present instance the Germans may really have put up all these suggestions, primarily to embarrass us.'

Reading these two comments, Eden noted: 'I agree with Depts view, but I should like Cabinet confirmation.' Meanwhile Colonel Montgomery, the brother of the Field Marshal, suggested, from his vantage point in Military Intelligence, 'that the whole story of this fantastic offer may have been invented by the Jewish Agency'.[2] Brand meanwhile, instead of being allowed to travel to Jerusalem, was still in Istanbul, awaiting British travel documents.

On May 27 one of the special committees set up by the British War Cabinet, the Technical Sub-Committee on Axis Oil Reports, met to discuss the most

---

[1] Palestine telegram No. 683, Top Secret, copies in Foreign Office papers, 371/42758, W 8626 and Cabinet papers, 95/15.

[2] Foreign Office papers, 371/42758, W 8626, folios 50–3.

recent developments in German oil production. Among its reports, which were circulated to both British and American air intelligence, was one on the synthetic oil plant at Monowitz, which had been photographed on April 4. The item, headed 'Auschwitz', read:

The hydrogenation section at the new plant at Auschwitz is only just coming into use. When the construction now in progress has been completed the output of this plant may be at the rate of 180,000 tons per annum. The planned capacity of the plant is probably to the order of half a million tons per annum.[1]

In their report, the War Cabinet expert advisers stressed the extent to which the German dependence upon oil production was 'vital' to Germany's ability to continue the war. And yet, they pointed out, Germany's position as far as oil production was concerned was 'now more vulnerable than at any previous time', while the destruction 'of from two to four' of the specialized plants manufacturing synthetic oil, would 'slow down the German war machine'.[2]

On May 27 a further escape took place from Auschwitz itself. The escapees were a young Polish Jew, Czeslaw Mordowicz, and a Slovak Jew, Arnost Rosin. Rosin had been the leader of the block in which Alfred Wetzler had been a clerk. After Wetzler's escape, as another Auschwitz prisoner later wrote:

Rosin was called in for questioning and tortured. He was accused of complicity in Wetzler's escape and as punishment was given hard labour in the gravel pit. There he made the acquaintance of another Jewish prisoner, Mordowicz, who had been punished by being transferred to the same detail.

During their work the prisoners discovered in the wall of the gravel pit a short, narrow passageway—a bunker—that had been filled in with broken stones after the escape of other prisoners. From time to time during their work, when they were not being watched, they took turns in getting the bunker ready and waited for a suitable opportunity.[3]

Mordowicz himself had, like Vrba before him, long hoped to escape. Later he recalled how, in preparing the bunker, he was helped by two Polish officers, non-Jews, and how he had insisted that if the bunker were still to remain undiscovered after the escape, it should be used to enable them also to escape.

Mordowicz and Rosin had no intention of going south to Slovakia. Their plan was clear: to strike east from the gravel pit, cross the Sola, work their way east to Cracow and then north to Warsaw, travel on to one of the Baltic ports, possibly Gdynia, and then cross the Baltic to neutral Sweden. Their opportunity came on May 27, when, having hidden in the bunker, and remained undetected during the searches and alarms, they were able to slip out of the gravel pit, and past the outer perimeter.

[1] United States Strategic Bombing Survey, Record Group 243. The records of the Technical Sub-Committee are in Cabinet papers, 77/19–28.

[2] 'The Oil Position in Axis Europe, First Six Months of 1944', War Cabinet Technical Sub-Committee on Axis Oil, Cabinet papers, 77/24, A.D.(44)41 (Final) of 27 May 1944. The Chairman of the Sub-Committe was Sir Harold Hartley, who in the First World War had been controller of Chemical Warfare at the Ministry of Munitions. Another member was S. P. Vinter, of the Prime Minister's Statistical Branch.

[3] Erich Kulka, 'Five Escapes from Auschwitz', in Yuri Suhl (editor), They Fought Back: The Story of the Jewish Resistance in Nazi Europe, London 1968, pages 235–8.

But after two days, and when they were half way to Cracow, they learnt from a Polish peasant woman that all able-bodied males in the region which they intended to cross were being taken for forced labour east of Cracow, to prepare urgently needed anti-tank defences. They therefore decided now to strike southwards, as Vrba and Wetzler had done, to the Slovak border. Fortunately for Mordowicz, who was a Pole, his escape partner Rosin was a Slovak, so that the language problem would not create the same dangers as it would have done for two Polish speakers.[1]

On May 31, as Mordowicz and Rosin moved southwards towards Slovakia, the Brand proposals were about to be discussed in London by a War Cabinet Committee. That same day, at Auschwitz, the SS recorded that a total of 40 kilogrammes of gold had been taken from the teeth of the corpses of Hungarian Jews, who had been gassed in the fifteen days between May 17 and the end of the month. This included those gassed on May 31 itself, from two trains, out of which a thousand men and a thousand women had been sent to the barracks, and more than six thousand gassed.

Also on May 31, the second United States aerial reconnaissance mission flew over Auschwitz. Once again, its photographic objective was the Monowitz industrial plant. But two of its frames showed all of Birkenau, one showed part of Auschwitz Main Camp and part of Birkenau, and three showed part of Auschwitz Main Camp, all photographed from a height of 27,000 feet.[2]

Even before his telegrams of May 16 and May 23, urging the bombing of the railways to Poland, Rabbi Weissmandel had sent a Yiddish version of the Vrba-Wetzler report to Switzerland. But this copy had not yet arrived; nor, in fact, had the telegrams. On May 31 Weissmandel wrote again from Bratislava to his Orthodox colleagues in the west. 'Though we wrote some weeks ago', he declared, 'we have not to date received any indication that the letter was received and are concerned about this'. His second letter, which itself was not to reach the west for more than a month, contained an anguished appeal for action to halt the deportations, which had already been in progress for two weeks.

In his letter of May 31, Weissmandel also set out in detail the Eichmann proposals. 'If the Jews are unwilling to accept or fulfill these terms', he wrote, 'then everyone will be deported'. If the terms were met, 'they will permit a great exodus from this country towards the neutral sea through Germany-France-Spain'. According to the Germans, Weissmandel added, 'those already deported are living in Germany and are being kept as hostages until the Jews meet their terms'. But this particular assertion, he was convinced, was 'an outright lie'. He himself believed that the deportees were sent to Auschwitz-Birkenau, where they 'are all gassed there and cremated, except for a very tiny portion'.

If the offer of negotiations was nevertheless real, Weissmandel wrote, then they must be concluded 'without delay or negligence', and the Jews

---

[1] Czeslaw (now Peter) Mordowicz, conversation with the author, Ramat Gan, Israel, 22 December 1980.
[2] Records of the Defense Intelligence Agency (RG 373), Aerial photographs of Auschwitz and Birkenau, Mission 60 PRS/462, Can D 1508 Exposures 3055-7, Can D 1509 Exposures 4056-8 and Can D 1510 Exposures 5018-20.

'must immediately give substance, not merely with words, but in real terms; more money perhaps, and fewer supplies'. But if the negotiations were, in fact, 'a plot, a maneouvre, a gesture of camouflage' aimed at winning Jewish confidence and undermining 'our already meagre and paltry power to resist', then it was essential to demand 'in the strongest terms' the bombing of the railway lines from Hungary to Poland.[1]

This letter, with its combination of scepticism and hope, was not to reach the west for more than a month. Even as it was being written, the Brand proposals were being discussed at the War Cabinet's Committee on refugees, nominally presided over by Anthony Eden.[2]

It was Randall who opened the discussion, in Eden's temporary absence, telling the meeting 'that the Foreign Office thought there were substantial reasons for having nothing to do with the proposals as they stood'.

In putting this view to the United States Government, however, 'it should be borne in mind', he said, 'that the scheme might secure sympathy beyond its merits in Washington, where the President's War Refugee Board, backed by Mr Morgenthau, had, partly for electoral reasons, committed itself to the "rescue" of Jews'.

The Colonial Office supported the Foreign Office's rejection of the Brand proposals. It should be 'made clear at the outset', Oliver Stanley told the Committee 'that since the evacuation of a million refugees from occupied territories and their maintenance in neutral or allied countries could not be undertaken without a major alteration of the course of military operations, the scheme in its present form could not be considered'.

During the discussion that followed, several 'additional points' were made. These related to what was variously described as the 'danger' and 'dangerous complication' involved if the Brand proposals were in fact carried out. As the official minutes of the meeting recorded:

There seemed to be some danger that an indication that we might negotiate through a Protecting Power with the German Government might be followed up, and lead to an offer to unload an even greater number of Jews on to our hands.

One of the additional points concerned the 'equally strong objections' to a 'large evacuation' of Jews through Turkey, since this, as the minutes noted, 'would involve our being pressed to receive unmanageable numbers into Palestine, and thereby introduce the dangerous complication that the immigration quota would be exceeded at a particularly critical time'.

A further problem which the Committee envisaged, in the event of the Brand proposals succeeding, concerned the United Kingdom itself. Here again the minutes were explicit, noting that: 'since no large number of Jews could be maintained in Spain for long, we should be strongly pressed to accommodate them in this country. Our own capacity to accommodate them

[1] The full text of Weissmandel's letter of 31 May 1944 is in Lucy S. Dawidowicz (editor), *A Holocaust Reader*, New York 1976, pages 321–7.
[2] But Eden was unable to attend the meeting until its discussions were over. The other member of the Committee, who did attend the meeting, was the Colonial Secretary, Oliver Stanley. Also present were G. H. Hall, Parliamentary Under-Secretary at the Foreign Office; Lord Selborne, Minister of Economic Warfare; two Home Office representatives; a representative of the Offices of the War Cabinet, and A. W. G. Randall.

was limited in the extreme'.[1]

The Committee on the Reception and Accommodation of Refugees 'were satisfied', as they reported on Brand's proposal to the War Cabinet on the following day, 'that His Majesty's Government could not possibly accept it'. The War Cabinet of June 1 endorsed this conclusion. 'It was clear,' its minutes recorded, 'that the proposal was simply designed to embarrass the Allied Governments in the prosecution of the war.' But the War Cabinet of June 1, at which Churchill himself was present, also agreed that the British Government should 'make it clear that they would do what they could to provide for any small numbers of Jews whom the German Government might be prepared to release and who might be transferred without interference with military preparations'.[2]

The Foreign Office now proceeded to inform the American State Department of the Brand scheme, elaborating on the War Cabinet's decision. 'Assuming that suggestion was put forward by Gestapo in form conveyed to us,' read the draft of June 2 to Washington, 'then it seems to be a sheer case of blackmail or political warfare.' The implied suggestion 'that we should accept responsibility for maintenance of additional million persons is equivalent to asking the Allies to suspend essential military operations.' The draft continued:

We could not bargain over any scheme with the Gestapo and agree to trade lives against military and economic concessions calculated to stave off Germany's defeat. Demand that we should in effect raise the blockade is totally inadmissible, to give Germany 10,000 lorries would bring important access of military strength to the enemy, and German stipulation of Spain and Portugal as sole exodus seems clearly designed to embarrass Allied military operations.

The Foreign Office draft message to Washington also reflected, and again elaborated on, the positive ending to the War Cabinet's conclusion of the previous day, stating that:

. . . we realise importance of not opposing a mere negative to any genuine proposals involving the rescue of any Jewish and other victims which merit serious consideration by the Allied Governments. Whole record of United States Government and HMG over refugees is a proof of their active sympathy with victims of Nazi terror. Accordingly if the German Government were willing to release Jews in position of extreme distress or danger HMG and the United States Government would be willing to examine possibilities of moving to and accommodating in Spain and Portugal such persons as could be handled without prejudice to vital military operations.[3]

This draft was approved by Eden, and dispatched to Washington on June 3. Meanwhile, the Foreign Office had given Weizmann details of the Brand proposals. 'You may like to know,' Randall telegraphed to Lord Halifax on June 2, 'that Weizmann, on being informed, merely observed that the Gestapo's suggestions looked like one more German attempt to embarrass the British and American Governments'. He had added, however, that 'he would like to reflect on the affair and receive news of any developments'.[4]

[1] War Cabinet Committee on the Reception and Accommodation of Refugees, 2nd meeting of 1944, 31 May 1944, Secret, Cabinet papers, 95/15.
[2] War Cabinet No. 71 of 1944, Conclusion No. 3, Copy in Premier papers, 4/51/10, folio 1396.
[3] Foreign Office papers, 371/42758, W 8507, telegram No. 4936.
[4] Foreign Office papers, 371/42758, W 8507, telegram No. 4938.

As another Foreign Office note, by J. G. Tahourdin, recorded, 'Dr Weizmann's comment was to the effect that this clearly was yet another attempt on the part of the Germans to cause difficulties for us', that is, for the Allies.

According to this note, Weizmann had 'no suggestion to make' of his own. But he 'wondered', as the note put it: 'whether it would not be possible for the Prime Minister and the President to issue a joint warning to the Germans, which he thought might go some way to halt the slaughter of the Jews.'[1]

There was a direct link between the Foreign Office attitude towards the rescue of a million Jews, and its view of the 'danger' of 'unmanageable numbers' of Jews reaching Palestine. On June 1 Eden had sent Churchill a ten-point Top Secret draft Cabinet paper, entitled 'Palestine', in which he warned of the danger 'of losing to America the pre-eminent place we have always held, and which in our own strategic interests, including oil, we ought to continue to hold, in the Arab world'. Eden's proposal was a 'Palestinian State' whose sovereignty would lie with the United Nations, but which would be ruled by a British Governor taking his instructions from London. This would not be a temporary Mandate, but a permanent settlement. It would therefore end the Arab fear of a permanent political settlement based upon a Jewish majority. Up to 400,000 new Jewish immigrants would be permitted, but should come 'within 100,000 of the Arab', and never closer: never, that is, a Jewish majority. Eden added:

It would further help to reconcile Arab opinion if it were possible to point to Jewish immigration being directed to other parts of the world as well as Palestine. If no suitable location for a Jewish settlement can be found in Africa it might be possible to persuade the Americans to allot a separate quota for Jewish immigrants. . . .

Eden was particularly worried that if any form of Partition scheme went ahead, the Arabs would revolt against the Jewish State that resulted, however small that State, and that this Arab revolt, 'protracted, costly, maybe disastrous', would not be led 'by the present Arab rulers and political leaders' but by 'leaders as yet unknown: the potential Titos of the Arab world'.[2]

At the end of his telegram to Shertok on May 29, Yitzhak Gruenbaum, the Chairman of the Rescue Committee of the Jewish Agency, had advised the 'adoption extraordinary measures repeatedly suggested, view interfering deportation'. But he did not say what these measures might be. On June 2, however, the day after the War Cabinet in London had rejected the Brand proposals, Gruenbaum telegraphed, through Pinkerton in Jerusalem, to the War Refugee Board in Washington, asking the United States Air Force to bomb the deportation railways.

Gruenbaum's telegram was in three sections. The first concerned the need to find a ship to help rescue Jews from Rumania, the matter being 'very urgent' as German forces were likely at any moment to occupy the port of Constanta as they retreated before the Red Army. The third section of the telegram

---

[1] Foreign Office papers, 371/42758, W 8507, minute of 2 June 1944.
[2] 'Palestine', Top Secret, Colonial Office papers, 733/461, Part One.

urged financial aid from the War Refugee Board, to help the International Red Cross and 'assist in relief and protection' of the Jews of Hungary. It was the second section that referred to 'a definite German decision to proceed as rapidly as possible' with the systematic deportation of Hungarian Jews to Poland', and went on to state that trains were to be sent to Poland every day. Indeed, Gruenbaum noted, '8,000 from Carpatho Russia[1] have already been taken'. Gruenbaum's telegram continued:

Suggest deportation would be much impeded if railways between Hungary and Poland could be bombed. Also suggest renewal of warning against Hungarian participation and persecution and inclusion of Bulgaria in warning as German influence in that country is rapidly increasing with accompanying massacres.[2]

In fact, by June 2, the date of Gruenbaum's telegram, not 8,000 Jews, but more than 250,000 had been deported from Hungary to Auschwitz, where most of them had been gassed. Gruenbaum's information referred to the first deportations of May 15, when 8,000 Jews from Ruthenia had been deported to Auschwitz, reaching the camp on May 17 and 18. Nor did Gruenbaum mention Auschwitz by name, but only 'Poland', as the destination of the deportees.

Also unknown to Gruenbaum, June 2 was the first day of a new Allied operation, Operation Frantic, through which the bombing of these very same railways could have been effected. Operation Frantic was a shuttle bombing system, whereby the United States forces flying either from Britain or Italy could use the Soviet airbase at Poltava in order to extend their range, and to overfly areas previously outside the limit of their targets.

Operation Frantic had two aims, neither of which by itself automatically barred out its use for the purpose Gruenbaum had suggested. Its first aim was to be 'a veritable model of air warfare in order to impress the Russians with admiration and confidence'. Its second aim was 'to distract the Germans on the eve of the Normandy landings', to be launched in four days' time.[3]

Frantic remained operational for more than four months. The first Frantic, on June 2, dropped a thousand bombs on the railway marshalling yards at Debrecen. This action impaired the railway system considerably. 'All tracks in the main marshalling yards were cut,' the air intelligence reported, 'and a large quantity of rolling stock was damaged. The bombs blasted or fired the central railway station and the chief buildings of an engineering establishment.' But the fate of the Jews of Debrecen was not affected: all that happened was that their electricity and gas supplies were cut. Although Debrecen was a railway junction, linking several of the deportation routes, the object of the raid was to harm German communications in such a way as to help the Soviet forces then in the Carpathians.

The United States bombers waited at Poltava for the return mission. A week

---

[1] Carpatho Russia, also known as Subcarpathian Ruthenia: part of the Austro-Hungarian Empire in 1914; incorporated in Czechoslovakia in 1919; annexed by Hungary in 1939; a part of the Soviet Union since 1945.

[2] War Refugee Board, Box 34, Measures Directed Towards Halting Persecution, F: Hungary, volume 2.

[3] For the origins, aims and targets of Operation Frantic, see Wesley Frank Craven and James Lea Cate (editors), *The Army Air Forces in World War II*, volume 3, Chicago 1951.

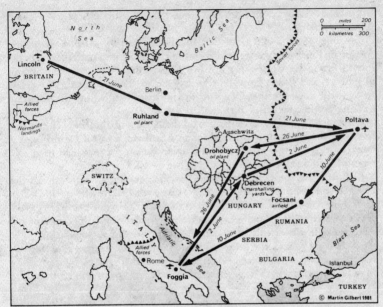

10. Flight paths and targets of 'Operation Frantic' during June 1944, showing also the principal deportation railways from Hungary to Auschwitz between 15 May and 8 July 1944.

of bad weather made flying impossible. Then, returning to their bases in Italy on June 10, the target set, and hit, was the airport at Focsani in Rumania.

The question of the effectiveness of bombing railways was the subject of a memorandum sent from the Ministry of Economic Warfare on June 2. The memorandum had nothing to do with the deportation of Jews to Auschwitz, but it did set out the arguments for and against the bombing of railways. It was in northwestern Europe, according to the memorandum, that such bombing was least effective, 'because the railways form a dense network; with a few hours' or days' work the enemy should be able to open an alternative route which avoids a blockage'. But in southeastern Europe a greater effect had been achieved by dislocating rail traffic. The dislocations as a result of raids on Hungary, Rumania, Serbia and Bulgaria, the memorandum stated, 'are of longer duration than in N.W. Europe because there are few alternative routes and little in the way of repair facilities'.[1]

For the Jewish Agency, at this moment, the Brand proposals were becoming the principal and overriding hope of rescue for Hungarian, and indeed Czechoslovak and Polish, Jewry. As such, the need to follow up these proposals began to dominate the Agency's discussions during June. But neither the British rejection of the proposals, nor the reasons for that rejection, were known. In the shadow of Brand, all other schemes and priorities, including

[1] 'Attacks on Railways in 1944', Foreign Office papers, 898/318.

Gruenbaum's railway line bombing request, held a subsidiary place in Jewish Agency thinking.

On June 5 Brand and Gross left Istanbul by rail for Aleppo. Reaching Aleppo on June 6, they were held in custody by the British until the end of the month, first in Aleppo and then in Cairo, Gross being interrogated from June 6 to June 22, and Brand from June 16 to June 30. This meant further delay, further false hopes, further focussing on the Brand proposals to the exclusion of other possible measures of rescue.

On June 6 the Allied forces landed on the Normandy beaches. The second front, so long awaited, so essential for an Allied victory over Germany, was now in being. Here was the military action which the Jews had been told repeatedly could alone bring any real rescue or relief.

At Auschwitz, the secret arrivals and gassings continued, from France, from Hungary, and from Italy. Of the 496 Jews who reached Auschwitz on D-Day itself, June 6, a total of 99 were taken to the barracks, while 297 were gassed.

On that same day, June 6, a second report on the aerial photographs of Auschwitz III was circulated to British and American air intelligence. The report was six pages long, followed by a detailed plan. The main source was still the aerial reconnaissance of April 4, supplemented, not by the pictures of May 31, but with what was described as 'a consideration of information from available ground sources'.

Once again, no reference was made to the huts or other buildings of Auschwitz I or Birkenau, although five of the photographs of May 31 showed all or part of Auschwitz I, and three showed Birkenau. The aim of the assessment of June 6 was to examine every possible aspect of the synthetic rubber and oil plant, and this was done in remarkable detail: the Monowitz railway system, the location and extent of the factory, and the individual installations. The exact size, purpose and capacity of almost every building was precisely stated, and the buildings themselves were located by numbers on a clear and detailed map. Thus: 'Steam emission from the 123 feet diameter cooling tower (79 on map) serving the compressor houses indicates that gas is being passed through the plant', and again: 'Rundown tanks for the main distillation plant (95) and for the second plant (94) are built in the form of horizontal cylinders. About 35 of them can be seen, and more are already buried. Each measures 38 feet in length by 8 feet in diameter, and could accommodate 1,900 cubic feet; there is therefore visible random capacity for rather more than 1,600 tons of oil. . . .'[1]

The notes to the plan make it clear that the nature of the labour force at Monowitz was known to those who made the intelligence assessment. Thus area 106 is described as 'Concentration Camp', 122 as 'Labour Camp', and 123 again as 'Concentration Camp'. But the intelligence assessment makes no reference to these three areas. In fact, area 123 was the Monowitz camp for Jewish labourers brought from Birkenau, and was accurately located and drawn from one of the aerial photographs taken two months earlier.[2]

[1] Interpretation Report No. D.389. 'Location: Oswiecim (Auschwitz)', United States Strategic Bombing Survey, Record Group 243.

[2] 'Oswiecim: I.G.F. Synthetic Rubber and Synthetic Oil Plant. A.C.I.U. Plant No. D.410. Neg. No. 38618R. Based on Cover of 4.4.44.' United States Strategic Bombing Survey, Record Group 243.

The meaning of what the report of June 6 described as 'ground sources' was revealed two days later to the War Cabinet's Technical Sub-Committee on Axis Oil Reports. The new source was a Belgian student who had been deported from Belgium to Monowitz in May 1942 'to serve as an interpreter'. After escaping in May 1943, he had managed to reach Britain, where he had been interrogated in January 1944 by the British Air Ministry. When completed, the student's report had made clear, 'the plant will be very large, possibly larger than one of the Blechhammer plants.'[1]

It was the facts which the Belgian student had been able to give about the existence, the purpose and the capacity of the synthetic oil plant which led to the increased importance of Monowitz as a target, moving it from the larger list of 'unknown status' plants, to the shorter list of 'known' plants.[2]

Thus two different Auschwitz camps were becoming known to the Allies almost simultaneously: Birkenau with its gas chambers, and Monowitz with its oil. But the knowledge of the oil came first, by nearly two weeks, and it was this oil knowledge that stimulated the rapid, urgent action of air reconnaissance and attack, judged indispensable for the Allied war effort.

On the day after the D-Day landings, unknown either to the Allies or to the Jewish Agency, the Nazis completed the first phase of their Hungarian deportation plan; for on that day the last train reached Auschwitz from Ruthenia and Transylvania, bringing the number of Jews who had been deported to a total of 289,357, and most of them being killed, in only 23 days. Yet the hope still persisted in Jewish circles in Jerusalem and London that the continuing negotiations with Brand were delaying any such deportations.

Also on June 7 Weizmann went to see Anthony Eden to discuss the Brand mission. According to a note by Randall two days later, Weizmann told Eden that he 'had never heard of' Brand, 'but that he might well be a trustworthy person'. In these circumstances, the Foreign Office agreed to allow Shertok to interview Brand in Aleppo, having for two days refused to allow the meeting to take place.

During his meeting with Eden, Weizmann raised the question of 'an official direct approach' by Britain to the Hungarian Government. This approach had also been suggested by Steinhardt, the United States Ambassador to Turkey, to whom the Jewish Agency had also passed on details of the Brand proposals. The very fact of American support roused the scepticism of the Foreign Office. Randall minuted on June 7: 'It has to be remembered that the US Ambassador in Angora has declared his intention of winning the Jewish vote in New York State for the Democrats. . . .'

Another suggestion, put forward originally by Weizmann in a discussion with G. H. Hall at the Foreign Office on June 2, and repeated to Eden at their meeting on June 7, as a means of preventing the deportation of Jews from Hungary, was that Churchill and Roosevelt 'issue a joint warning to the Germans, which he thought might go some way to halt the slaughter of the Jews'. During the discussion Weizmann also proposed that Stalin might join this declaration.

[1] 'Report E.O.C. 74–1, prepared by the Western Axis Sub-Committee of the Enemy Oil Committee in Washington', copy in Cabinet papers, 77/24, A.O. (44)44.
[2] War Cabinet Technical Sub-Committee on Axis Oil Reports, copy in Cabinet papers, 77/24, A.O. (44)44.

Weizmann also suggested an official and direct approach to the Hungarian Government, to warn them not to take any part in the persecutions. But the Foreign Office were opposed to Weizmann's idea. As Frank Roberts minuted on June 8: 'I would rather deprecate this as being on the whole useless'.[1]

One long-nurtured attempt at rescue came to grief at the beginning of June 1944, when on June 7 the young parachutist Hannah Szenes was finally able to cross from Yugoslavia to Hungary. For she was arrested almost at once, and after prolonged tortures, executed by firing squad in a prison courtyard in Budapest. By the end of the year, seven of her thirty-two fellow parachutists had been caught and shot.

On June 2 the American Consul-General in Jerusalem, Pinkerton, had sent to Washington a request from a member of the Jewish Agency Executive, Yitzhak Gruenbaum, for warnings against the deportations to be broadcast to Hungary. 'Gruenbaum may be informed,' Cordell Hull replied to Pinkerton on June 22, 'that warnings regarding treatment of Jews are constantly being shortwaved and otherwise transmitted to Hungary', and also that 'efforts to safeguard' the position of the Jews in Hungary had been made through the International Red Cross, 'and various foreign channels'.[2]

During the second week of June it seemed that the fate of the Jews of Hungary might depend as much upon local considerations inside Hungary itself as upon Gestapo policy. Weizmann had already drawn the Foreign Office's attention to Hungarian dislike of the anti-semitic measures, and on June 9 the Political Intelligence Centre, Middle East, reported to the War Office: 'There is evidence that public opinion has been offended by the violently sadistic attitude towards the Jews which the Government has shown'.[3]

The idea of rescuing Hungarian Jewry through the Brand proposals continued, however, to be seen in the Foreign Office as creating new problems for Britain's Middle East policy. There was always the possibility, R. M. A. Hankey minuted on June 14, 'of letting the Germans flood the M.E. with Jews in order to embarrass us', and he added: 'There is fortunately not much sign of it yet, but it will be very hard to cope with, both politically and from a refugee point of view, if the imbroglio does end that way. A bull point for German political warfare.'[4]

---

[1] The discussion between Weizmann and Eden on 7 June 1944, and the Foreign Office comments on it, are in Foreign Office papers, 371/42758, W 9102.

[2] United States National Archives, 840.48, Refugees, 6193, Secret.

[3] Balkan Political Intelligence Notes, Issue No. 84, War Office papers, 201/1619. The deportation of 12,000 Hungarian Jews to the east in August 1941, and the killing of several thousand Jews in Hungarian-occupied Yugoslavia between January and March 1942 (both during the Bardossy premiership), had been followed in 1943 by the trial of those responsible for the Yugoslav killings, and by the Hungarian Government's refusal to deport Hungarian Jews to German-occupied Poland (both during the Kallay premiership). Hitler himself had protested twice to the Hungarian Government, first in April 1943 and then in March 1944, about its 'irresolute and ineffective' handling of the Jewish question. Even after Kallay's replacement by Sztojay in March 1944, and the German occupation of Hungary, the anti-semitic measures still aroused widespread criticism. Thus on 14 May 1944 the German economy officer in Hungary reported to Berlin that the closing of 18,000 Jewish shops (out of a total of 30,000 shops in the capital) had caused 'considerable disturbance'. And on 15 May 1944, Angelo Rotta, the Papal Nuncio in Budapest, had urged the Hungarian Government 'not to continue this war against the Jews beyond the limits prescribed by the laws of nature and the commandments of God', an appeal echoed during the next three weeks by several leading Hungarian churchmen.

[4] Foreign Office papers, 371/42758, W 9317.

The United States attitude to the Brand proposals was at first somewhat different. On June 10 the State Department telegraphed to their Ambassador to Turkey, Steinhardt, that 'every effort should be made to convince the Germans that this Government is sufficiently concerned with this problem that it is willing to consider genuine proposals for rescue and relief of the Jews and other victims'. For this reason, the United States Government had decided to send Ira Hirschmann as 'a special representative of the War Refugee Board' to Turkey, to see Brand, in order to convince Brand that the United States Government 'has not closed the door'.

The actual Brand proposals could not however be accepted, Steinhardt was told, 'except in consultation with both British and Soviet Governments'. In forwarding the text of this telegram to London, Lord Halifax added that State Department officials 'consider the German proposals to be unacceptable'; that sending Hirschmann to Turkey was 'merely an expedient for gaining time'; and that the 'sole purpose of the manoeuvre is to induce the Germans to hold their hand'.[1]

Thus once more the belief was reiterated that the deportation of the Jews of Hungary would be postponed for as long as the Brand mission was thought to be under serious consideration by the Allies. In fact, on June 11, the day on which Halifax's telegram reached London, and while Hirschmann was only at the start of his journey, a total of 50,000 Hungarian Jews were being deported from Szekesfehervar and Siofok, to Auschwitz; a deportation which took only four days to complete. Also on June 11, the first Frantic shuttle mission, delayed for seven days at Poltava by bad weather, returned to Italy. Its path was a southerly one; its target, Foscani airport in Rumania. The flight from Foscani to Foggia took it within bombing distance of the Szekesfehervar to Budapest railway, but the fact that for four consecutive days the railway line was being used for the deportation of 50,000 people was quite unknown either to the Allies or to the Jewish Agency.

On June 12 Anthony Eden told the War Cabinet that the Foreign Office regarded as 'unacceptable' the suggestion by Chief Rabbi Hertz that the British Government 'should declare all Jews in enemy territory to be British protected persons'. It was agreed that 'a negative reply' should be sent to the Chief Rabbi. A note in the War Cabinet's conclusions recorded that Churchill himself 'has been anxious, however, that the War Cabinet should be aware of the position before a negative reply was sent to the Chief Rabbi'.[2]

The actual reply to the Chief Rabbi was drafted by Randall, for Eden's signature. While assuring Hertz that 'the most careful and sympathetic consideration' had been given by the Cabinet Ministers concerned to discover measures 'within the essential limitations of our war-effort, to help those suffering and persecuted people', the letter also stated:

It would be manifestly impossible to give indiscriminately priority for exchange to Jews of non-British nationality, who would probably include a large number of German, Austrian and stateless persons, over British subjects. Moreover, to offer Jews, and Jews only, priority of escape as British-protected persons would be to overlook the fact that German brutality has

[1] Viscount Halifax No. 3134, Foreign Office papers, 371/42758, W 9317.
[2] War Cabinet 75 of 1944, Conclusion 4, copy in Premier 4/51/8, folio 433.

been directed very extensively, above all in Poland, against non-Jews. We should not wish to cause resentment among our Allies in whose countries large numbers of non-Jewish nationals are in grave danger.

Eden did tell Hertz that an alternative scheme was 'to work patiently at every practicable means of rescuing Jews who are in danger'.[1] But the only scheme currently being considered was the Brand mission, and this was laden with difficulties. On June 12, the day on which Shertok was to meet Brand in Aleppo, the British Ambassador in Ankara, Sir Hughe Knatchbull-Hugessen, informed the Foreign Office that he had discussed the proposals with his American colleague, Steinhardt:

His own view was that scheme was not merely ordinary but [*undecypherable*] black-mail which had no practical foundation. The quid pro quo was much too cheap in that offer to exchange a million Jews for 200 tons of various commodities was ridiculous. If scheme had contemplated exchange of one ton of some commodity against each Jew he would have regarded it as more serious blackmail.

Ambassador seemed to think it was being run by some local people, probably Gestapo agents, feathering their own nests. In any case, it was completely half baked for it was absurd to think of sending a million Jews to Spain and Portugal without ascertaining whether these Governments were prepared to receive them. Mr Steinhardt also doubted whether in last resort it would be practical to send lorries and goods into Central Europe or to transport Jews out.

'On the whole,' Knatchbull-Hugessen concluded, 'it was clear that the United States Ambassador had no intention of taking scheme seriously.'[2]

Throughout June 11, the first day of the Szekesfehervar deportations, Shertok was in Aleppo, questioning Brand for six hours. Brand was emphatic that even if deportations were taking place, those deported were not being killed, but kept alive to form part of the 'goods for blood' exchange.

One of the reasons, Brand reported, for the Germans not allowing Hungarian Jews to leave Nazi Europe through the Balkans was that the Germans 'did not want to offend the Arabs' nor to help the emergence of 'too strong a Jewish state in Palestine'. But the exodus of a million Jews would serve the German purpose in another way, for, as Brand reported, the Germans 'consider the Jews as a spiritual disease and as such wished to distribute them over a wide area as a demoralising factor against the Allies'. In this way the large 'shipment of Jews' proposed by Eichmann, called Eichner in the transcript, was to be regarded 'in the form of a sabotage mission against the Allies'. Another reason for the exchanges, Brand told Shertok, was that the Germans, both as individuals and as a people, 'wished to give themselves a good mark with the Allies and Jewry in general and try to expiate their sin of the extermination of six million Jews by the release of the remaining two million'.

Not only was this the first mention of 'six million' dead; but it also held out, on that June 12 in Aleppo, the prospect of the rescue, not only of one, but of two million, Jews. Brand then detailed what the cost would be: two million cakes of soap; 10,000 kilos of tea; 40,000 kilos of coffee; 10,000 kilos of cocoa, and 10,000 railway wagons 'to ship Jews across Europe'.

[1] Foreign Office papers, 371/42758, W 9616.
[2] Telegram No. 876, Secret, Foreign Office papers, 371/42758, W 9350.

Shertok's first two questions to Brand showed the sense of urgency, and also of hope, in the mind of the Jewish Agency:

Shertok: Was the saving of children specifically mentioned?
Brand: Yes, Eichner agreed that children and old people should go first, but those of working age would have to stay on for some time as the Germans needed them.
  When this question was discussed Eichner to a certain extent went back on his word and said that, of course, there was not enough money in the whole of the world to pay for the evacuation of all the Jews from Europe.
Shertok: Were the Nazis in any way opposed to the saving of children?
Brand: No.

Shertok's third question concerned the deportations, and Brand's answer explains why the hope still persisted that, even if actual deportations were taking place, the Jews themselves would still not die, provided the Brand mission were to succeed. As the transcript records:

Shertok: Did you call for the suspension of deportations pending the outcome of negotiations?
Brand: Yes, but Eichner said the deportations must go on. I said that he might show goodwill by ceasing the deportations, and Eichner said that there would be no killing until the answer was received, but I must hurry as the Germans cannot keep women and children for an unlimited period as it costs money. When Kummey was asked the same question he tried to put my mind at rest and told me not to worry, stating that as soon as they got first news of the success of my mission then the deportations would cease. When the question was raised with Klages and Schroeder the first reaction was a flat denial that deportations were taking place, but later they also tried to soothe me, stating that the treatment would not be too harsh.[1]

Later on in the discussion, Brand told Shertok that if the proposals were turned down, 'there are sure to be great executions', even if he himself returned to Hungary. Were he not to return, 'all Jews will be slaughtered including my mother, wife, children and particularly people closely associated with me'.

Brand went on to tell Shertok about the forcing of Jews into ghettoes in April and May; of five thousand Jews who escaped the round-ups by reaching the Rumanian border; of another escape route into Poland; of 'lorry-loads of Jews' freed by 'local peasants' in the Carpathians; of large numbers of escapees able to bribe the Rumanian police; and of the 'very strict' frontier police on the Yugoslav border, which almost precluded escape southwards.

Two overriding questions remained: were Jews already being deported from Hungary or not? If not, could they be saved by accepting the proposals Brand had brought. While in Istanbul he had received a telegram which read: 'Deportation not interrupted. Large camps have been arranged in Germany for old people and little children'. By itself, this message could mean that no killing was taking place in the camps. But it could also mean that *no* deportations were taking place, as the telegram was signed with a surname, and Brand's agreed code before leaving was that any message signed by a surname 'was to mean the exact opposite of what it said'. Brand told Shertok he was 'unable to make sense' of the message. He had telegraphed 'several times' to Hungary 'making it plain that he could not understand it, and received no answer'.[2]

[1] Kummey: Hermann Krumey, Eichmann's deputy. Otto Klages was the Gestapo commander in Budapest. Schroeder was head of the Gestapo secret police (SD) in Budapest.
[2] The 12-page transcript of the Brand-Shertok interview of 11 June 1944 is in Foreign Office papers, 371/42759, W 10406, Top Secret, Assistant Defence Security Office, Northern Syria, dated 12 June 1944.

In Hungary itself, the illusion of a possible emigration deal was maintained by the Gestapo, who agreed, on June 13, to begin negotiations with the Jewish Agency and Zionist leaders about the release of a token group of a thousand or so Jews as an earnest of Nazi good faith, and for $1,000 a head. That same day, in Ankara, the American Ambassador, Steinhardt, hitherto sceptical, 'expressed agreement' as the British Ambassador reported 'with view of Refugee Board that door should be kept open for serious proposals'.[1]

It was not only from Hungary that the deportations to Auschwitz continued. On June 14 the 1,800 Jews of Corfu were taken by sea to mainland Greece, and then, on June 20, in cattle trucks by rail to Auschwitz, crossing Yugoslavia, Hungary and Slovakia during their terrible eight-hundred mile journey. Sixteen days after leaving Corfu they reached Auschwitz, where as many as 1,500 of them were immediately sent to the gas chambers.

Yet Auschwitz still retained its secret, and when Richard Lichtheim wrote from Geneva to Jerusalem on June 16, about the fate of the Vittel deportees, he was able to report only 'that they had been sent elsewhere', but that 'the name of the place was not revealed'.[2] It was in fact Auschwitz.

On June 15 the Foreign Office discussed a telegram from Washington, giving the views of Nahum Goldmann and Stephen Wise on the Brand proposals. Goldmann believed the scheme to be 'a genuine offer put up by Gestapo leaders (certainly Eichmann and possibly Himmler) with a view to obtaining foreign exchange for their own use when they should have to flee from a defeated and occupied Germany'. The demand for ten thousand trucks was, he believed, one that Eichmann and Himmler must know 'could not possibly be accepted', but that they had probably made it as 'a bargaining counter and would be prepared to consider conversion into cash'. Goldmann added:

Although the offer was manifestly unacceptable in its present form it might well be possible to persuade the Germans in return for large sums of blood money, to keep the Jews alive in concentration camps in Hungary, possibly under International Red Cross or Swiss supervision.

Stephen Wise was more sceptical of the offer, which he felt was 'primarily for purposes of psychological warfare blackmail'. But both he and Goldmann were, as Lord Halifax reported, 'most emphatic on the need to keep the discussion open on the prospect offered of saving at least some Jews' lives', and also on the 'desirability for putting up counter proposals at the earliest opportunity'.[3] The Foreign Office doubted whether such negotiations would achieve anything. 'The Germans are quite capable of taking the money,' A. E. Walker minuted on June 15, 'and of not keeping their bargain.'

Shertok had returned to Jerusalem from Aleppo on June 13. On the following morning he reported to the Jewish Agency Executive, and on June 15, together with Ben Gurion, he went to Government House to report on his meeting with Brand to Sir Harold MacMichael. Shertok told MacMichael that he was convinced that the Nazi proposition was a serious one, sponsored by 'really responsible and highly placed German authorities'. He believed that

[1] Telegram No. 907, Foreign Office papers, 371/42758, W 9449.
[2] Central Zionist Archives, L 22/135.
[3] Viscount Halifax, No. 3188, Secret, Foreign Office papers, 371/42758, W 9523, telegram and comments.

the Nazis hoped that 'by obtaining some credit in our eyes for not now slaughtering 2,000,000 Jews they would get away with the fact that they had slaughtered 6,000,000 Jews already', as well as an attempt to 'save their own skins'. Shertok also reported that Eichmann had told Brand that the 'child-bearing category' of Jew was the 'most difficult to spare at present, since they were wanted for work. Therefore, Jews might have to be content with old people and children in the first instance'.

Shertok went on to say that he was 'convinced' that the German policy 'was in fact to defer the killings, adding', as MacMichael noted, 'that many Germans and their wives seemed genuinely full of compassion, though he conceded this might be spurious'.

Although, at this meeting of June 15, Ben Gurion interrupted Shertok at one point to say 'that it was quite likely that the whole business was a trick', Shertok went on to emphasize 'the urgent and vital need to probe the whole matter and explore every avenue'. It was, he felt, 'essential' for there to be a meeting 'with accredited German representatives', possibly by the Red Cross, the United Nations High Commission for Refugees, or the American War Refugee Board.

As the discussion drew to its close, Ben Gurion asked that 'if there was anything which could humanly be done in such a way as not to be of any advantage to the enemy or prejudice the war effort, he pleaded that it should be done'.

Commenting on Shertok's desire to open more direct negotiations with the Germans, R. M. A. Hankey noted, on June 20:

He, poor fellow, is, after all, solely concerned to extricate as many Jews as he can from the clutches of the Nazis (and incidentally, to pile them into Palestine regardless of the local situation) and possibly does not care very much what the effect is on the war effort.

Hankey added: 'Ben Gurion, who is in many ways more extreme than Mr Shertok, sees the problem more clearly', and he concluded:

It is to be observed that we ourselves from the first have considered this scheme to be 'a fantastic piece of blackmail with political warfare motives' and our opinion is shared by the British and United States Ambassadors in Angora, by the High Commissioner in Palestine, by Lord Moyne and the Commander-in-Chief in the Middle East. It appears to be sympathised with by Mr Ben Gurion and, I rather gather, also by Dr Weizmann.

In these circumstances, I am sure that we should do well not to make too much of the scheme, in our desire to play hide and seek with the Americans over rejecting it. We may eventually find ourselves committed to taking it more seriously than we really wish to do.

'Most of this is fantastic,' another official minuted, 'and I do not like our taking any responsibility for passing on fantasies from one Zionist to another.'[1]

For the British Government, a further and possibly decisive argument against following up the Brand proposals came on June 22, when Randall noted: 'the Soviets are against negotiations of any kind'. This led to a comment by Ian Henderson:

Mr Shertok is undoubtedly playing a game in this business in what he conceives to be the best interests of the Jewish Agency, viz: by aiming at placing the Agency in a position where they

---

[1] Palestine telegram No. 761, Top Secret, Foreign Office papers, 371/42758, W 9647, telegram and comments.

can say that they were primarily responsible for bringing to fruition a gigantic scheme for Jewish rescue.

He would be quite indifferent to any chance of dissension between ourselves and the Russians.

At his meeting with MacMichael on June 15, Shertok had asked for permission to return to London. This was agreed to on June 17 by the Foreign Office. It was also decided on June 17 that Brand should be kept in Cairo 'until Shertok's return', and that he should 'not be allowed to return to Hungary' until the Foreign Office's conversations with Shertok were completed.[1]

On his way to London, Shertok travelled through Cairo. On June 17 Lord Moyne telegraphed to the Foreign Office: 'suggest I try to convince Shertok that complete impracticability of the scheme shows that it is a propaganda plant'. That same day, Ian Henderson noted within the Foreign Office that the point raised by Moyne, as to whether 15,000 trucks were for the German war effort, or to transport Jews westwards, 'tends to confirm the impression that we already have that this whole proposal for Jewish evacuation is a move in political warfare'.[2]

Despite these doubts, the element of possibility still held back a total British refusal. Although it was 'impossible to accept this particular scheme', the Foreign Office telegraphed to Lord Moyne on June 20, 'we also feel importance of not opposing a mere negative to any genuine proposals involving rescue of Jewish victims'.[3]

---

[1] Foreign Office papers, 371/42758, W 9644, telegram No. 1465 and comments.

[2] Foreign Office papers, 371/42758, W 9643.

[3] Foreign Office papers, 371/42758, W 9644.

Chapter 25

The truth about Auschwitz reaches the west, June 1944

During the second week of June 1944 news was finally received in Geneva which was to transform Allied knowledge of Nazi brutality. The source of this news was the information sent from Slovakia, consisting of two separate reports: the detailed account by Vrba and Wetzler of the gassing procedure, and the news brought later by Mordowicz and Rosin, that the deportation of Hungarian Jews was acutally in progress, and that they too were being gassed.

Mordowicz and Rosin had reached the Slovak border on June 6, and had made contact, as Vrba and Wetzler had done, with the Slovak Jewish leadership. The two new escapees told their story, not only the facts once more of the nature of life and death at Auschwitz-Birkenau, as Vrba and Wetzler had told, but also their own eye-witness account of the arrival and destruction of tens of thousands of Hungarian Jews in the week before their escape. As Vrba later commented: 'Wetzler and I saw the preparation for the slaughter. Mordowicz and Rosin saw the slaughter itself'.[1]

On reaching Slovakia, Mordowicz and Rosin had been taken to the small hill town of Lipovsky Mikulas, where, as Mordowicz later recalled, they were brought to a room next to one in which Vrba and Wetzler were already waiting, whereupon the Slovak Jewish leaders, led by Oskar Krasnansky, cross-examined both pairs of escapees, checking one against the other every detail of their descriptions of 'normal life' at Auschwitz: 'how we were dressed, what we ate, the reality of the Auschwitz life. That was the most difficult for them to believe, the reality. We gave them the names of young Slovak Jews who worked in the *Sonderkommando*. Some were known to them. . . .'[2]

Mordowicz and Rosin then made their special report, covering the events at Birkenau between April 7, the day on which Vrba and Wetzler had escaped, and May 27, the day of their own escape. At the beginning of April, they reported, some 1,700 Greek Jews had arrived, of whom 200 had been 'admitted to the camp', and the rest 'immediately gassed'. Between April 10 and April 15 some 5,000 Polish Jews and non-Jews had arrived, including two or three thousand women from Majdanek, of whom 300 were Jewish girls. The new arrivals were given tattoo numbers 'running from approximately 176,000 to 181,000'; then, three days after their arrival in Birkenau, the 300 Jewish girls 'were all gassed and burned'.

At the end of April 3,200 more Greek Jews had reached Birkenau, of whom all but 200 were 'exterminated'. At the beginning of May 'smaller transports'

[1] Rudolf Vrba, 'Footnote to Auschwitz Report', in *Jewish Currents*, March 1966.
[2] Czeslaw (Peter) Mordowicz, conversation with the author, Ramat Gan, Israel, 22 December 1980.

of Dutch, French, Belgian and Greek Jews had arrived, most of whom 'were put to work in the Buna plant' at Monowitz. Then the 'mass transports' from Hungary had begun: 'the spur railroad track which ran into the camp to the crematoria was completed in great haste', Mordowicz and Rosin reported, 'the crews working night and day, so that the transports could be brought directly to the crematoria. Only about 10 per cent of these transports were admitted to the camp; the balance were immediately gassed and burned. Never had so many Jews been gassed since the establishment of Birkenau'.

Even the capacity of the crematoria had not been enough for these new arrivals, Mordowicz and Rosin told their questioners. As a result, 'great pits 30 metres long and 15 metres wide were once more dug in the "Birken-wald" (as in the time before the crematoria) where corpses were burned day and night'.[1]

Shattered by this new information, Krasnansky returned to Bratislava, where he and his colleagues prepared a combined Vrba-Wetzler and Mordowicz-Rosin report, for transmission to the west.[2] 'I put the two reports together, and prepared to send them off again', Krasnansky later recalled.[3] And only seven days later, by means of yet another courier, but this time a reliable one, a copy of the combined report reached neutral Switzerland. Its recipient was Dr Jaromir Kopecky, the Geneva representative of the Czechoslovak Government-in-Exile: it reached Geneva on June 13. Kopecky at once showed the report to Gerhart Riegner. As Riegner read, he came to the section about the Czech family camp which had been in quarantine for six months. 'I had never heard of this before,' Riegner later recalled. 'Then they had been killed, and then there had been another quarantine camp. Six months, I thought to myself, what does it mean? In only seven days time the second quarantine expires.'

Riegner stopped reading. 'Have you seen this paragraph,' he cried out to Kopecky, 'these people are going to be killed in seven days. We must act. We must telegraph to London at once. The BBC can alert the world.'[4]

The Vrba-Wetzler report told of the second family camp reaching Birkenau from Theresienstadt on 20 December 1943. The six-month period would expire on 20 June 1943. Kopecky realized that he must act at once, not merely to make the details of the Vrba-Wetzler report known to the Allies, but even more urgently, to alert the world to the imminent destruction of the family camp, in the hope of averting its destruction. He therefore telephoned a member of the British Legation in Berne, Elizabeth Wiskemann, who was known

---

[1] 'German Extermination Camps – Auschwitz and Birkenau': texts of the Vrba-Wetzler and Mordowicz-Rosin reports, as published on 26 November 1944 by the Executive Office of the President, War Refugee Board, Washington D.C.

[2] Rudolf Vrba has written, of the fate of Mordowicz: 'After his escape from Auschwitz, Mordowicz was apprehended by the Gestapo in Bratislava in September 1944 a second time, but his identity was not discovered. He was arrested while protecting a Jewish family. He was handed over to the Waffen-SS who brought him back to Birkenau. There, he was recognized by prisoners during the tattooing procedure and these prisoners tattooed immediately a new number upon his arm and a fish over the old number. The prisoners in the main registrars office immediately arranged that this "new" prisoner should be put into a transport destined for slave labour in coal mines elsewhere, and thus Mordowicz escaped death'. (letter to the author, 30 July 1980).

[3] Oskar Krasnansky, conversation with the author, Tel Aviv, 22 December 1980.

[4] Recollection of Gerhart Riegner, in conversation with the author, Geneva, 1 October 1980.

to be an expert on Czechoslovakia, and told her about the apparent imminent destruction of the second Czech family camp.

That same day, in sending Miss Wiskemann a summary of the facts, Kopecky wrote:

Here are the details of the urgent message about the group of Jews in danger in Birkenau.

Please do what you can so that the details are sent back as quickly as possible and are broadcast at once over the BBC etc.

But it will be necessary to avoid mentioning the source. One could say simply over the radio: 'We have received this from a reliable source. . . .'

Kopecky added that the request to broadcast the details was made in agreement with the representatives of the Jewish organizations. The report itself, as drafted in telegram style by Riegner on the basis of the Vrba-Wetzler report, and as sent to Miss Wiskemann, read:

According report made by two Slovakian Jews who escaped from Birkenau to Bratislava and whose reliability is assured by Jewish leaders there 3,000 Czechoslovakian Jews who were brought from Terezin[1] to Birkenau on December 20, 1943 will be gassed after six months quarantine on about June 20, 1944.

Appealing most urgently that this news may be broadcasted immediately through BBC and American Radio in order to prevent at last moment this new massacre.

Report which contains horrible detailed description of massacres in gas chambers Auschwitz Birkenau of hundreds of thousands Jews all nationalities occupied Europe states that already first group of about 4,000 Czechoslovakian Jews who arrived from Terezin in Birkenau beginning September 1943 were after 6 months quarantine gassed on March 7, 1944.

Report reveals that treatment both Czechoslovakian transports called SB Transports— Sonderbehandlungstransporte — was strikingly different from usual transports.

Families were not separated, even children, school was allowed and prescription 6 months quarantine absolutely unusual.

View fact that first group was entirely exterminated danger of imminent extermination second group most serious.

Please issue without delay most impressive warning to German butchers who directing slaughters Upper Silesia.

Do not mention Bratislava as source.

Further reports following.

Please inform immediately also the Czechoslovakian Government.

Miss Wiskemann acted at once, passing on both Kopecky's covering letter and Riegner's telegraphic summary to Alan Dulles, head of United States Intelligence in Switzerland, and informing him: 'I have just wired this – could you also?' But Dulles sent it on to the American Minister in Berne, Roswell McClelland, with a covering note that it 'seems more in your line', and McClelland, who received it on June 16, passed it back to Washington.[2]

At last the reality of Auschwitz–Birkenau was clear to the outside world. The 'unknown destination in the east' finally had a name. The camp which had hitherto been believed to be one of the many labour camps in Upper Silesia was revealed to be the largest single killing centre in Europe. The place where it had earlier been reported that several thousand Jews and several thousand

---

[1] The Czech form of Theresienstadt.
[2] War Refugee Board, 'Box 61, General Correspondence of R. McClelland, F: Miscellaneous Documents and Reports re. Extermination Camps for Jews in Poland.'

Poles had been murdered was shown to be the site of the murder, during the previous two years, of a million and a half Jews, brought there not only from Poland, but from all over Europe, and still being brought, at the incredible rate of 12,000 a day, from Hungary.

All those in Geneva who received the Vrba–Wetzler report of the gassings were shocked and bewildered. On June 18 brief details were broadcast over the BBC, as Kopecky had asked, and on the following day Richard Lichtheim set down his own full summary in a letter to the Jewish Agency Executive in Jerusalem. In his letter Lichtheim made it clear that as a result of the new report, 'We now know exactly what has happened and where it has happened'. Not only had 'very large numbers' of European Jews been killed 'systematically' in what Lichtheim referred to as 'the well-known death-camps in Poland (Treblinka etc.)', but also in 'similar establishments situated near or in the labour-camp of Birkenau in Upper Silesia'. Lichtheim added:

There *is* a labour camp in Birkenau just as in many other places of Upper-Silesia, and there *are* still many thousands of Jews working there and in neighbouring places (Jawischowitz etc.).

But apart from the labour-camps proper there is a forest of birch trees near Birkenau (Brezinky) where the first large-scale killings took place in a rather 'primitive' manner, while later on they were carried out in the labour camp of B itself with all the scientific apparatus needed for this purpose, i.e. in specially constructed buildings with gas-chambers and crematoriums.

Lichtheim went on to point out that, according to the new report, not only had 'many hundreds of thousands' of Polish Jews been sent to Birkenau, but also 'similar' numbers of other Jews who had either been deported first to Poland, or 'directly sent to Birkenau in the well-known cattle-trucks from Germany, France, Belgium, Holland, Greece, etc.', and that all of these deportees had been 'killed in these establishments'.

The bodies of all those killed, Lichtheim reported, had been 'burnt in specially constructed stoves'. Also burnt in these stoves were those 'who died by starvation or ill-treatment in the labour camps nearby'. Lichtheim then informed Jerusalem that: 'The total number of Jews killed in or near Birkenau is estimated at over one and a half million'.

Could the Vrba–Wetzler report be believed? In his letter of June 19 Lichtheim told his Jewish Agency superiors in Jerusalem, there were 'many details' in these reports which 'are confirmed by a second report received from another source'. This other source was a further report, the text of which had also reached Switzerland in June, and which had been written by a former Polish officer, a non-Jew, known only as 'the Polish Major'. He had been sent to Auschwitz with sixty other Poles on 24 March 1942, from the notorious Montelupich prison in Cracow, and had himself later escaped. His report of his experiences in Auschwitz was extremely detailed, nineteen pages in all, of which three pages dealt entirely with the Jews. He, too, gave one and a half million as the number of Jews gassed at Birkenau since the spring of 1942.

In his letter of June 19, Lichtheim also repeated the details given in the Vrba–Wetzler report of the fate of the four thousand[1] Jews who had been trans-

[1] In fact, 5,007.

ferred to Auschwitz from Theresienstadt in September 1943, kept in the family camp for six months, and then gassed, with the sole exception of eleven pairs of twins who 'were left alive and were sent to a hospital in Auschwitz for biological experiments'.[1] Reflecting on this terrible episode, Lichtheim wrote:

We knew that not all Jews who were sent to Theresienstadt remained there and that for many of them Theresienstadt only served as a transit camp.

But until the autumn of 1943 we have never heard that Jews who had been for some time in Theresienstadt were to be transferred to Upper-Silesia. Therefore we were much puzzled when we learned that several thousand Jews—men, women and children—were suddenly brought to Birkenau from Theresienstadt.

But at that time we believed that it was done to exploit more Jewish labour in the industrial centres of Upper-Silesia.

Henceforth, there could be no more illusions. Auschwitz–Birkenau was no longer thought to be part of an 'industrial' centre, but was clearly a death camp.

Turning then to the passage in the Vrba–Wetzler report which had so alarmed Gerhart Riegner, Lichtheim warned that a second group of Jews had reached Birkenau on 20 December 1943, from Theresienstadt.[2] They, like the first, had been designated for *Sonderbehandlung*: Special Treatment. 'Now we know what that means,' Lichtheim added. They too had been told they were being kept in the family camp for a six-month 'quarantine'. That six months, he wrote, would expire on June 20. And he went on, basing his comments once again on the Vrba–Wetzler report:

. . . it should be noted that the members of the first group which was killed on March 7th had to write on March 1st to their relatives abroad stating that they were in good health and these letters had to be dated March 23rd or 24th or 25th. Therefore it will prove nothing if letters will arrive from the second group dated later than June 20th. . . .

The second family camp was not in fact 'liquidated' until the second week of July. But precisely on June 20, among those who were killed at Birkenau, was Jacob Edelstein, the former 'Elder' of the Theresienstadt ghetto, who had tried for nearly two years to make life in the ghetto bearable for his fellow Jews. Edelstein had been shot, not gassed. And before being shot, he had been forced to watch while his wife and young son were shot in front of him.[3]

Lichtheim could not know this detail. But he was convinced that the Vrba–Wetzler report was true. And he went on to warn the Zionist leaders in Jerusalem that, 'Apart from the danger which is now hanging over the Jews in Theresienstadt, there are large scale deportations from Hungary'.

What was to be the fate of these Hungarian Jews? Lichtheim's letter of June 19 informed Jerusalem that 'additional reports just received' said that 12,000 Jews 'are now deported from Hungary every day'. These were the reports of the second two escapees, Mordowicz and Rosin, whose account of the daily arrival of Hungarian Jews at Auschwitz had been smuggled into Switzerland

---

[1] In fact, some 45 other family camp inmates were not gassed in March 1944.

[2] In fact, 2,504 on 4 December 1943 (of whom 262 survived the war), and 2,503 on December 18 (of whom 470 survived).

[3] On July 21, a month *after* these executions, Gerhart Riegner telegraphed from Geneva to the Czecho-slovak Government-in-Exile in London: 'Edelstein has been working in the East for some months. His wife Mirjam and son Arieh wrote on the 25.3.1944 from Birkenau, pleading for help and exchange certificates'. (Archives of the World Jewish Congress, General Secretariat).

in June together with the Vrba–Wetzler report. Of these 12,000 deportees a day, Lichtheim wrote: 'They also are sent to Birkenau'.

It had at last become clear what Birkenau was, and what being 'sent' to Birkenau meant. 'It is estimated,' Lichtheim wrote, 'that of a total of 1,800,000 Jews or more so far sent to Upper Silesia, 90 per cent of the men and 95 per cent of the women have been killed immediately, without even being registered for work.'

Only five per cent of the women and ten per cent of the men, 'especially the younger and stronger men', had been, as Lichtheim reported it, 'distributed among the numerous labour camps in Upper-Silesia'.

In his letter of June 19, Lichtheim explained that the administration of the camp at Birkenau was subordinated 'to the camp of Auschwitz (Oswiecim) which is 4 km from Birkenau'. At Auschwitz, he added, many non-Jewish political prisoners had 'perished' as a result of ill-treatment. That was why 'Oswiecim has for long been known as a "death-camp".' But non-Jews reaching Auschwitz, he noted 'have not been slaughtered wholesale on arrival like 90 per cent of the Jews arriving at Birkenau'.

The secret of Auschwitz (Oswiecim) and Birkenau was over: 'we now know in full detail,' Lichtheim wrote, 'how, where and when the Jews of Europe have been killed, apart from the hundreds of thousands who met their deaths in the ghettoes and death-camps of Poland.'[1]

The Warsaw ghetto, the Lodz ghetto, Chelmno, Belzec, Sobibor, Treblinka, Majdanek: all had preceded Auschwitz–Birkenau by as much as two years, and even more, in the correspondence and consciousness of the west. Now, with the truth having reached Geneva, it was to be no more than a week until Auschwitz–Birkenau took its true place at the head of the list of the mass murder sites of Europe.

The Vrba–Wetzler report, although based entirely upon the power of two men's memories, was remarkably accurate in its details. But even before these details had reached Britain, the United States or Palestine, an urgent appeal to bomb the railway lines to Auschwitz had been put before the War Refugee Board in Washington.

The source of the appeal was the two short, coded telegrams sent from Slovakia to Switzerland on May 16 and May 24. Both telegrams had been sent from the Orthodox community in Bratislava to Isaac Sternbuch, the representative in Switzerland of the Union of Orthodox Rabbis. Sternbuch had sent them on to New York, to Jacob Rosenheim, President of the Agudas Israel World Organization.[2] From New York, Rosenheim had sent them to the War Refugee Board, on June 18.

The first of the two telegrams, that of May 16, asked for 'prompt disturbance of all transports, military and deportation', by the Royal Air Force and other 'air raids', and recommended 'bombarding' the railway between Kosice[3] and Presov. The aim of such a bombardment would be 'to save also

---

[1] Central Zionist Archives, L 22/135.

[2] Also known as the 'Union of Universally Organized Orthodox Jewry'.

[3] Kosice, a Slovakian town annexed by Hungary in 1939. Known in Hungarian as Kassa and in German as Kaschau. Between 1918 and 1939, and since 1945, a part of Czechoslovakia.

Jews not yet deported'. The message ended: 'We expect Royal Air Force act very carefully'.

Rosenheim sent the War Refugee Board the text of the telegram, the decoded version quoted above, and a short commentary. In the commentary he noted that the Kosice and Presov railway was 'the single near route from Hungary to Poland', and that all the more eastern routes could not be used for 'traffic to Poland', as there was already fighting in those areas. He added:

> Kaschau is the transit-place and main-junction for all military transports and Presov is the town through which the deportations are continued after passing Kaschau. Therefore the bombarding of these two towns is wanted.
> If these two places and this route be made impassable the deportations would have to be made the long roundabout-way via Austria, which latter route—according to the advice in the wire—seems to be impossible for the Germans.

The second telegram to be sent to Washington on June 18 was that of May 23. It too urged the British and Americans to 'give instructions for mass air raids' of Kosice, Presov and Munkacs in order to 'disturb the railway-lines'. Since May 15, the telegram added, the situation was in dreadful and desperate state on account of not bombing', as 15,000 people were being deported daily. The telegram ended with the terse appeal: 'Must delay not one day. Help at last'.

According to the commentary sent by Rosenheim to Washington, this second telegram made, as its three main demands and points:

> 1 to bomb most urgently without a further delay the railwaylines of Kaschau and Presov, because 15,000 people are forwarded every day over this short and not disturbed route from Hungary to Poland,
> 2 that furthermore the town Munkacs should be bombed,
> 3 the bombing has to be made at once, because day after day less people could be saved and it would be very soon too late for the rescue.[1]

Nearly four weeks had passed between the dispatch of this second telegram from Slovakia and its arrival in Washington. Nor did either telegram refer to Auschwitz or Birkenau: only to 'Poland'. Nevertheless, in forwarding it to Washington, Rosenheim asked Pehle to use his 'decisive influence' to have the plan realized, and asked for the decision to be taken 'after thorough consideration, *without any loss of time*', adding that 'every day counts, as you will see, for the destruction of thousands'.

In a letter that same day to Morgenthau, Rosenheim stated that 'up to now, about 30,000 Jews are said to have been doomed to destruction' by deportation from Hungary 'to the gas chambers of Poland'. And he added that the 'slackening of the process of annihilation' would be achieved 'by paralyzing the railroad traffic from Hungary to Poland, especially by an aerial bombardment of the most important railway junctions of Kaschau and Presov'.[2]

---

[1] The text of the two original telegrams of May 16 and May 23, together with the decodes and commentaries, are in the War Refugee Board archives Box 62, 'General Correspondence of R. McClelland, F: Union of Orthodox Rabbis: Representative in Switzerland (I. Sternbuch), January–June 1944.'

[2] Rosenheim's two letters of 18 June 1944 are in the War Refugee Board archives, Box 35, 'Measures Directed Towards Halting Persecution, F: Hungary No. 5.'

On June 24 Pehle went to see the Assistant Secretary of War, John J. McCloy about the bombing proposal. In a memorandum written later that day, Pehle noted how he had told McCloy 'that I wanted to mention the matter to him for whatever exploration might be appropriate by the War Department'. But Pehle added 'that I had several doubts about the matter'.

Pehle then listed his doubts:

(1) whether it would be appropriate to use military planes and personnel for this purpose; (2) whether it would be difficult to put the railroad line out of commission for a long enough period to do any good; and (3) even assuming that these railroad lines were put out of commission for some period of time, whether it would help the Jews in Hungary.

Having expressed these doubts, Pehle had gone on, as he himself noted, to make it 'very clear to Mr McCloy' that he was not, 'at this point at least, requesting the War Department to take any action on this proposal, other than to appropriately explore it'.

McCloy promised Pehle that he would 'check into the matter'.[1] And two days later the Operations Division of the War Department General Staff recommended that McCloy should reply that the suggested air operation was 'impracticable', for the reason 'that it could be executed only by diversion of considerable air support essential to the success of our forces now engaged in decisive operations'. The Operations Division added that 'the most effective relief to victims of enemy persecution is the early defeat of the Axis, an undertaking to which we must devote every resource at our disposal'.[2]

The principal 'decisive operations' mentioned in this letter remained the Allied attempt to destroy all of Germany's war-making powers based upon the manufacture of synthetic oil. The continuing German success in holding up the Allied advance in Normandy added urgency to the oil campaign.

On June 21, five days before Jacob Rosenheim's request had been considered by the Operations Division in Washington, the second Frantic mission took place, with the United States bombers flying from their English base at Lincoln across Germany, bombing the synthetic oil plant at Ruhland, south of Berlin, and flying on to Poltava. But on arrival at Poltava the Frantic project itself came to grief, when German planes attacked Poltava airport. Not only did the Germans succeed in destroying forty-three B.17s and damaging twenty-six; they also destroyed fifteen of the Mustang fighter escort, and ignited 450,000 gallons of aircraft fuel which had been brought into Russia so laboriously throughout the spring. One American and twenty-five Russians were killed, and the Frantic shuttle was forced to delay the return operation until June 26, and to abandon any flights for the whole of July, until their Poltava fuel store had been replenished by fuel brought by truck along the long road route through Persia and the Caucasus.[3]

---

[1] 'Memorandum for the Files', War Refugee Board, Box 35, 'Measures Directed Towards Halting Persecution, F: Hungary, No. 5.'

[2] Letter of Major General Thomas T. Hardy, Assistant Chief of Staff, National Archives Record Service, RG 165, Records of the War Department General and Special Staff, OPD 383–7, Section II, Case 21.

[3] Wesley Frank Craven and James Lea Cate (editors), *The Army Air Forces in World War II*, volume 3, Chicago 1951. The sound track of a United States film of Operation Frantic, made during the autumn of 1944, states that among the supplies taken to Poltava were fuel oil, 3,000 miles, via Persia; radio equipment and operators, via Egypt and Palestine; and food and other supplies essential for the mission, 2,000 miles from Liverpool to Murmansk, then a further 2,000 miles by rail from Murmansk to Poltava. (I am grateful to Carl Foreman for the text of this sound track).

The destruction of German oil supplies had become the Allies' overriding priority by the second half of June. At the same time, the Jewish Agency's priority remained the rescue of Hungarian Jewry by negotiation with the Gestapo.

At the very moment when the location and purpose of Auschwitz became completely known, the Nazis, determined to complete the destruction of Hungarian Jewry, continued with the massive deception which they themselves had mounted through the Brand mission. It was a deception which had already succeeded for six weeks, reflected in the anguished response of the Jewish leaders in Jerusalem and London, caught in the trap of a false hope which they could not abandon.

Chapter 26

The Gestapo offer: 'Keep the pot boiling'

The Jewish Agency's desire to continue to press the Allies to open negotiations with the Gestapo for the rescue of Hungarian Jewry had been jolted into feverish activity by a telegram sent to Istanbul on June 17 from the Zionist leaders in Budapest. This telegram demanded Brand's immediate return to Hungary. 'If *not*,' it declared, 'all will be in vain.'[1]

Moshe Shertok, who was on his way from Jerusalem to Cairo, received the Budapest telegram on June 19. He at once telegraphed to Weizmann in London, and to Nahum Goldmann in New York, urging both of them to use their influence to persuade the British and American Governments to allow Brand to return to Hungary at once. In his telegram to Weizmann, Shertok set out the hopes which the Jewish Agency Executive had of still being able to use the Brand mission to effect the rescue of a substantial part of Hungarian Jewry. Brand had come, Shertok explained, as an emissary of the 'remnant' of European Jewry, and in an attempt to rescue that remnant he had accepted his mission from the enemy on the 'clear understanding' that he return with a reply.

Although Brand realized that he might be killed immediately by the Nazis if he returned to Hungary without a 'definite answer', he was still 'desperately anxious', as Shertok phrased it, to return with a report of his discussions so far, in the hope that when the Gestapo knew at least that its proposals were being considered 'in high quarters', it would help to gain time, and would 'prevent precipitation of calamity'.

Shertok's telegram to Weizmann continued:

We consider his return is imperative if the slightest chance rescue is to be preserved. We regard this as the first indispensable step towards giving effect to the line agreed by Mr Eden of gaining time and not closing door.

For the same reason, we consider it equally essential that some immediate indication be given to the other side of readiness negotiate regarding rescue of Jews, urging, same time, discontinuation of deportation and slaughter pending meeting.[2]

In his telegram to Nahum Goldmann, Shertok noted that the Jewish Agency Executive's conclusion, after hearing of his talk with Brand, had been that although the 'exchange proposition may be mere eyewash and possibility ulterior motives must be assumed, it is not improbable that even preliminary negotiations might result in salvation substantial number'.

Shertok then set out the Agency's proposal: to explore the possibility of a

---

[1] Central Zionist Archives, S 25/1678.

[2] Foreign Office papers, 371/42759, W 9885, telegram No. 779 from Sir Harold MacMichael to the Secretary of State for the Colonies, enclosing telegram for Weizmann from Shertok.

meeting with 'German representatives' in Lisbon or Madrid, the aim of which would be to 'discuss rescue Jews, urging same time discontinuation deportations and slaughter pending meeting'. The negotiating body appearing 'on behalf' of the Allies, Shertok added, might be the Inter-Governmental Refugee Committee, or the War Refugee Board, or the Red Cross, 'or any other suitable agency'.[1]

On June 19 two of the leading Zionists in Budapest, Moshe Krausz and Rudolf Kastner, managed to telephone a message to Geneva, which was passed on to Jerusalem, urging what they called 'vigorous action' by the Allied Governments. Their demand was twofold; a warning to the Germans that 'reprisals' would be taken if Hungarian Jewry were massacred, and an immediate decision by the Allies 'to grant foreign citizenship to Hungarian Jews'.[2]

A message from several of the Hungarian deportees themselves reached Jerusalem on June 23. It had been sent from Poland a month earlier, on May 21, and had reached Istanbul on June 19: a total journey time of thirty-three days. The message read, as deciphered in Jerusalem:

Am not far from Cousin *Peecham* (Coal Mines). Last week met over there *rezach* (murder) and *kewer* (tomb). Tell *Hafganah* (demonstration) to write Redcross. . . . *Pachad* (fear) with us.[3]

On June 21 the Foreign Office received Shertok's appeal to Weizmann about Brand's immediate return to Hungary. The British Government's reply, Ian Henderson noted, could only be 'that we will not let him go until we have seen Mr Shertok. . . .' Shertok, he added, 'must be interviewed in London, and it is in London and Washington that the chief decisions must be taken.' Henderson also noted that: 'The Soviet Govt have rejected any idea of negotiation.'[4]

This was indeed so. A telegram from the British Ambassador in Moscow, Sir Archibald Clark Kerr, sent and received on June 20, had repeated a message from Andrei Vyshinsky stating categorically that the Soviet Government 'does not consider it expedient or permissable to carry on any negotiations whatsoever with the Government of Hitlerite Germany on questions touched on in your letter'.[5] Commenting on this message two days later, Randall noted: 'This strengthens us for the forthcoming talks with Mr Shertok, who will almost certainly press for contact with the Germans'.

Foreign Office opinion had become decisively sceptical not only of the Brand proposals, but even of the motives of the Jewish Agency. In the Refugee Department, Randall minuted on June 22:

I think the message to Dr Weizmann should be sent on, but I feel we are (as we realised at the beginning we should be if, for political reasons, we refrained from turning the whole scheme down) on a slippery slope and we need expect little help I am afraid from the Jewish Agency to arrest our rapid progress to the bottom. We shall therefore have to apply the brake ourselves. . . .

The Eastern Department was equally emphatic: '. . . we must realize,'

[1] Central Zionist Archives, S 25/1682.
[2] Central Zionist Archives, Z 4/14870.
[3] Central Zionist Archives, S 25/1678.
[4] Foreign Office papers, 371/42759, W 9885.
[5] Moscow telegram No. 1653, Foreign Office papers, 371/42759, W 9875.

wrote Baxter, 'that Mr Shertok's interests in the matter are opposed to those of H.M. Govt., for *his* main object is to fill Palestine with Jews.'

For the Central Department, Frank Roberts stressed the need 'to avoid sliding further down the slope and above all conveying the impression that we are prepared to negotiate with Himmler on this or any other point'.[1]

Later in the evening of June 22, the Foreign Office received a telegram, sent two days earlier from Sir Hughe Knatchbull-Hugessen in Ankara, reporting the views of Ira Hirschmann, the War Refugee Board representative in Turkey. Hirschmann, it appeared, was entirely unconvinced that the Brand proposals were realistic, but 'feels strongly that in order to gain time he ought to be sent back to Hungary with some kind of proposals to keep the pot boiling'.

In a Top Secret and personal telegram sent that same day, the British Ambassador added:

Mr Hirschmann is a go-getter, somewhat tenacious of his own ideas, and impatient of official methods. He is looking at the whole Jewish refugee question mainly from the point of view of the coming Presidential election in the United States and is I think inclined to resent the fact that it is not being dealt with by the United States alone as a purely American concern.[2]

The Foreign Office decision made on June 23 was to detain Brand in Cairo, but not to dismiss the Brand negotiations altogether. As Randall minuted: 'It is a delicate piece of prising we have to do, as between the US Govt. and the Zionists, but for the sake of our relations with the former, I think we must try to carry out the balancing feat, at least until we get the venue of the discussions moved to London.' Randall added '. . . in view of the alleged life and death interests involved, I am of the opinion that the final decision should go higher.'[3]

On June 21, while Shertok was still in Jerusalem, Lord Moyne had refused to allow him to send 'through secret channels' a message to Barlas, in Istanbul. Moyne's reason was that the message gave 'an indication of the British Government's policy as conceived by Shertok which may not in fact prove accurate'. There was also the danger, as Moyne saw it, that the details contained in the message 'would almost certainly reach Budapest within a short time'.[4]

Supported by Shertok, as Randall noted on June 23, Brand himself had pleaded to be sent back, 'with a message that we are continuing this fantastic scheme'. If he were not sent back, he said, 'the direst consequences will ensue for him and the Jews in Europe'[5] But both MacMichael and Moyne were opposed to Brand's return, 'until', as Moyne had telegraphed on June 20, 'the situation is clearer'.

On June 22 Ira Hirschmann, of the War Refugee Board, was allowed to interrogate Brand in Cairo. Brand told Hirschmann that in addition to coffee, chocolate, tea and soap, Eichmann had also asked for money, 'dollars, Swiss

[1] Randall, Baxter and Roberts minutes, Foreign Office papers, 371/42759, W 9885.
[2] Telegram No. 953, Personal and Top Secret, Foreign Office papers, 371/42759, W 10023.
[3] Foreign Office papers, 371/42759, W 9885.
[4] Lord Moyne No. 1494, Top Secret, Foreign Office papers, 371/42759, W 9943.
[5] Foreign Office papers, 371/42759, W 9944.

francs, and some South American money'. The Jewish leaders in Hungary, Brand added, had hoped to be able to offer Eichmann a million dollars. The interrogation continued:[1]

H. What is your opinion of the chances of this working?
B. My opinion is that they would keep their word.
H. Why?
B. First of all because they need things—
H. How do you know?
B. When I left Hungary, I know that they were needing all kinds of things.
H. Things or money.
B. At first I thought, I know they need things. I know from years of work that everyone of them can be bought. I know this from years of work—I am not saying that I have bought Eichmann or Wislizeni.[2] In my work very many of them have been bought and I do believe that criminals of such a low sort as these men are always receptive to offers of money. . . .[3]

When Hirschmann asked Brand what he would like to see done, Brand replied:

The best thing I think would be that one, two or three officers from Hungary should come to a neutral country, say Spain or Turkey or Switzerland, and English and American people, and myself too, and we should try to come to some sort of bargain. That is my recommendation.

Brand believed, he told Hirschmann, that if he went back with such a recommendation 'I could stop persecutions – the worst persecutions – that are going on, at once'. Hirschmann then pressed Brand to tell him about the persecutions themselves. As the notes of their meeting recorded:

H. Are these persecutions still going on?
B. I am sorry to say that they were going on.
H. What number of people have been deported?
B. Until the week I went away, the week I went away they started deporting about 12,000 every day.
H. Where?
B. Kaschau, Klausenberg,[4] Munkacs, Hust.
H. Were they in camps?
B. They were concentrated in places in such terrible conditions that have never been known before.
H. What kind of transportation—trucks?
B. No, railway lorries, 60 and 80 men in a lorry, the lorry sealed down.
H. Did any die on the way?
B. I am certain of it.
H. Where were they taken to?
B. Auschwitz and Birkenau.

To the listeners in Cairo on June 22, these words 'Auschwitz' and 'Birkenau' meant nothing. The first summaries of the report prepared by the two Auschwitz escapees had not yet reached Jerusalem or London. But they were to do so within only a few days.

---

[1] Foreign Office papers, 371/42807, WR 34.
[2] Dieter Wisliceny: active in deporting Jews from Slovakia (1942), Greece (1943) and Hungary (1944). Executed, 1948.
[3] 'Eichmann's cleverest trick in these difficult negotiations', Hannah Arendt has written, 'was to see to it that he and his men acted as though they were corrupt'. Hannah Arendt, *Eichmann in Jerusalem*, Penguin books, London 1977, page 196.
[4] Klausenberg: in Rumanian, Cluj; in Hungarian, Kolozsvar.

On the same day that Hirschmann was conducting this interrogation, Lord Halifax was sending a dispatch from Washington to London, assessing the motives of the War Refugee Board, and warning of the 'danger' of what he called their 'irresponsible interference'. Of the reactions of Hirschmann's boss, Pehle, the Director of the War Refugee Board, Halifax noted that they were 'I fear influenced in large measure by his passion for publicity and by his desire to appear before Jewish World as twentieth century Daniel'. As for Hirschmann's own activities, Halifax added, these were 'dangerously emotional'. His telegram ended:

... it seems to me at this end that there is no great difference between ourselves and the United States Government in our reactions to this proposal and that provided mere emotional chagrin among Zionists and War Refugee Board can be kept under control there is no reason why we should not reach an agreed policy.[1]

In one area, British and American attitudes seemed to be linking up, for on June 24 Knatchbull-Hugessen reported from Ankara that his American colleague, Steinhardt, 'is also becoming exasperated by individual activities of representatives of various Jewish organisations, and is vividly conscious of the bearing of the Jewish refugee question on the Presidential election. . . .'[2]

Whatever its motives, the War Refugee Board maintained its view, as Halifax reported to London, that the Brand proposals 'might conceivably lead to other and perhaps less unacceptable suggestions', and that 'some lives might be saved, if only for the period during which we were able to spin out the negotiations'.[3]

The Jewish Agency Executive's frustration was growing, as the Brand mission remained unresolved. There was bitterness also, in Jerusalem, when the Chief Secretary told Shertok on June 20 that a thousand Yemeni Jews in the no-man's-land between Aden and Yemen could not be given certificates to Palestine, except on the basis of individual applications and needs. 'Stressed utter impracticability procedure individual cases regarding Yemenites', Shertok telegraphed to Linton on June 22, and he added that he had pointed out to the Chief Secretary that for the future of the Jewish people it was, as he phrased it, 'immaterial whether Jew killed by Nazis Europe or dies in Southern Arabia victim starvation epidemic'.[4]

It was not until 23 June 1944 that the Allies first learned that a total of more than 435,000 Hungarian Jews had been deported to Auschwitz in the previous five weeks. For on that day the Co-Director of the Palestine Office in Geneva, Dr Chaim Pozner, was handed a letter which had been sent to him from Budapest, by the Director of the Palestine Office there, Moshe Krausz. The information in this letter made an impact which no earlier information had done, for it was now known in Geneva exactly what 'Auschwitz' meant.

The Krausz letter had been sent from Budapest on June 19, and smuggled into Switzerland by courier. It contained two enclosures. The first was yet

[1] Viscount Halifax, telegram No. 3361, War Cabinet Distribution, Foreign Office papers, 371/42759, W 10024.
[2] Sir H. Knatchbull-Hugessen, telegram No. 973, Top Secret, Foreign Office papers, 371/42759, W 10248.
[3] Viscount Halifax, telegram No. 3433, Foreign Office papers, 371/42759, W 10324.
[4] Telegram No. 214. Central Zionist Archives, S 25/1682.

another copy of the Vrba-Wetzler report describing the annihilation process in Auschwitz. The second enclosure set out the details hitherto unknown in the west, of the deportation to Auschwitz of at least 435,000 Hungarian Jews between 15 May and 19 June. According to this second enclosure, a further 350,000 Jews were assembled in and near Budapest, awaiting deportation.

In his covering letter of June 19, Krausz wrote that the whole Jewish community in Hungary was 'condemned to death', and he added: 'There are no exceptions, there is no escape, there is no possibility of concealment, and we have to face our fate. We have not even the possibility of escaping to a neighbouring country'.

The urgent need revealed in the Krausz letter was to save the surviving 350,000 Hungarian Jews from deportation to Auschwitz.

In his letter to Pozner, Krausz made certain requests 'in case', as he wrote, 'the Christian world should endeavour to take steps in our favour'. According to Krausz 'it would be possible to save a few thousand persons by issuing Palestinian passports, i.e. granting Palestinian citizenship to the certificate holders'. In this event, Krausz added, the Swiss Legation in Budapest would have to be authorized to issue such passports, 'after the necessary passport forms have been put at their disposal'. But this would have to be done 'immediately, otherwise it is too late'.

As well as Palestinian passports, Krausz added, the passports 'of neutral states' might also be issued. His letter ended: 'I beg you to intervene wherever possible and to appeal to every person of sentiment. We are sure that the Americans and English will help us. Please help us.'[1]

Pozner, and the Jewish representatives in Switzerland to whom he showed Krausz's letter, acted at once, informing the British and American authorities in Switzerland of the news that had reached them. Also on June 23, Dr Pozner sent a telegram to Istanbul, for onward dispatch to Jerusalem, urging 'necessary speedy action', as well as a 'reply about Haftzazis proposals in this matter'.[2] Once more, a proper name hid a Hebrew word, haftzaza: bombing. This was the proposal to bomb the railway lines leading to Auschwitz, and to try to bomb the crematoria themselves, a proposal which had first been sent from Slovakia by Rabbi Weissmandel on May 16, and was at that very moment being turned down by the War Department in Washington.

That same day, the Czechoslovak representative in Geneva, Dr Jaromir Kopecky, together with Dr Riegner of the World Jewish Congress, and Riegner's Czech colleague Dr Ullmann, went together to the International Red Cross and, as Riegner later reported to his superiors in New York, 'appealed most seriously for immediate action Red Cross, view stopping by all possible means deportation and extermination'.[3]

Action was now swift: on the following day, June 24, Riegner gave a

[1] Yad Vashem archive, Pazner papers, 12/88.

[2] Central Zionist Archives, L 15/80.

[3] Three days later, on 26 June 1944, Riegner had again gone to see the International Red Cross in Geneva, 'urging again', as he later reported to New York, 'immediate despatch of eminent Red Cross representative to Budapest', and on 4 July 1944 the Swiss Jewish jurist Professor Guggenheim urged the President of the International Red Cross, Max Hüber, to send a 'personal handwritten appeal' to the Regent of Hungary, Admiral Horthy, to halt the deportations. (Riegner to Nahum Goldmann, telegram of 5 July 1944, Archives of the World Jewish Congress, General Secretariat).

summary of the Vrba-Wetzler report to Roswell McClelland, the American Minister in Berne. Riegner stressed, in a covering note, that these were 'reliable reports', and he also included a reference to the Polish Major, together with details from the Major's report. Riegner added that, in agreement with Dr Kopecky, the Representative of the Czechoslovak Government, six proposals were submitted to Washington:

1) The Allied Governments should issue a warning to the Germans and the Hungarians that they will use reprisals against the Germans living in the Allied countries.
2) The camps of Auschwitz and Birkenau and especially the buildings containing the gas-chambers and crematoriums, recognisable by their high chimneys, as well as the sentries around the railings and the watch-towers and the industrial installations should be bombed from the air.
3) The following main railway-lines which are used for the daily transports should also be bombed:
   a) Kosice (Kaschau)–Kysak–Presov–Novy-Sandz[1]
   b) Nove Mesto pod Saterom–Medzilaborce
   c) Munkacs–Lawoczne
   d) the railway-junction Cop
   e) Galanta–Leopoldov–Trnava–Nove Mesto–Puchov–Trenzin–Zilina–Cadca
   f) Legenye–Satoraljaujhely
4) Without mentioning in any way where this report comes from the foregoing report should be given widest publicity by radio and newspapers, so that the Germans may know that the outside world is fully informed about their atrocities.
5) The public warnings of the Allied Nations over the radio and at other occasions should be constantly repeated.
6) The Holy See should be asked to issue a strong condemnation of these crimes.[2]

McClelland acted immediately on receiving Riegner's letter, telegraphing details of the Vrba-Wetzler report to Washington that same day. In his telegram, after listing the principal railway deportation routes which were being used, number one being, as on Riegner's list, the Kosice-Presov line, he continued: 'It is urged by all sources of this information in Slovakia and Hungary that vital sections of these lines, especially bridges along *one* be bombed as the only possible means of slowing down or stopping future deportations'.

McClelland's telegram continued with the suggestion that in order to 'check' such continued deportations 'we recommend British and Soviet broadcasts and especially leaflets' with which the Vatican 'should be prevailed upon associate itself'. The telegram ended:

There is little doubt that many of these Hungarian Jews are being sent to the extermination camps of Auschwitz (Oswiecim) and Birke Nau (Rajska) in eastern upper Silesia where according to recent reports, since early summer 1942 at least 1,500,000 Jews have been killed. There is evidence that already in January 1944 preparations were being made to receive and exterminate Hungarian Jews in these camps. Soon a detailed report on these camps will be cabled.

On reaching the War Refugee Board, McClelland's telegram made a particular impact on Benjamin Akzin, one of the Board's officials. In an inter-

---

[1] In Polish, Nowy Sacz; in German, Neu Sandez.
[2] Archives of the World Jewish Congress, General Secretariat.

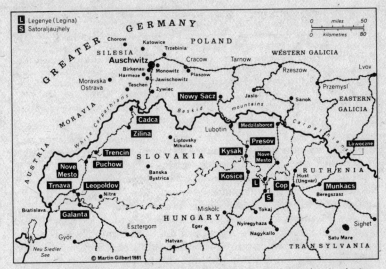

12. The principal railway lines along which Hungarian Jews were deported to Auschwitz between 15 May and 8 July 1944, showing also (in white lettering) the towns mentioned in the appeal sent from Bratislava that these lines should be bombed.

office communication on June 29, Akzin argued that the destruction of the 'physical installations' at Auschwitz and Birkenau 'might appreciably slow down the systematic slaughter at least temporarily'.

Akzin's letter was a sustained attempt to argue in favour of the bombing of the gas chambers and crematoria. The 'methodical German mind', he believed, would require some time to rebuild the installations, 'or to evolve elsewhere equally efficient procedures of mass slaughter and of disposing of the bodies'. During this time, some lives at least might be saved. But the saving of lives might also be 'quite considerable', since, as he wrote, 'with German manpower and material resources gravely depleted, German authorities might not be in a position to devote themselves to the task of equipping new large-scale extermination centres'.

Akzin also argued in favour of the bombing 'as a matter of principle', as it would constitute, he wrote, 'the most tangible—and perhaps the only tangible—evidence of the indignation aroused by the existence of these charnel-houses'.

One other factor was raised by Akzin in favour of bombing Auschwitz and Birkenau; that during the bombing there would also be many deaths 'among the most ruthless and despicable of the Nazis'.

In bombing Auschwitz, Azkin added, there would be no 'deflecting' of United States aerial strength from any important zone of military objectives, as Auschwitz itself was in just such a zone, the 'mining and manufacturing centres' of Katowice and Chorzow, 'which play an important part in the industrial armament of Germany'. Akzin ended:

Presumably, a large number of Jews in these camps may be killed in the course of such bombings (though some of them may escape in the confusion). But such Jews are doomed to death anyhow. The destruction of the camps would not change their fate, but it would serve as visible retribution on their murderers and it might save the lives of future victims.

It will be noted that the inevitable fate of Jews herded in ghettoes near the industrial and railroad installations in Hungary has not caused the United Nations to stop bombing these installations. It is submitted, therefore, that refraining from bombing the extermination centers would be sheer misplaced sentimentality, far more cruel than a decision to destroy these centers.[1]

Nothing came of Akzin's appeal. 'It wasn't my job to write this sort of memorandum', he later recalled. 'Sometimes, when I got excited, I put it on paper. But I was the only European fellow there – I had been born in Riga. All the others were typical Americans who knew little about Europe'.[2]

On the day that Benjamin Akzin made his plea for the bombing of Auschwitz and Birkenau, his superiors on the War Refugee Board sent a copy of McClelland's telegram to the Assistant Secretary of War, John J. McCloy. McCloy's executive assistant, Colonel Harrison A. Gerhardt, had already been involved in the rejection of the Rosenheim railway bombing request only three days before. He at once noted for McCloy, on this second bombing suggestion: 'I know you told me to "kill" this but since those instructions, we have received the attached letter from Mr Pehle. I suggest that the attached reply be sent.' The attached reply, duly signed and sent by McCloy on July 4, turned down the request, using similar reasons to those of the Operations Division in turning down the Rosenheim proposal.[3]

Meanwhile, on the same day that McClelland had sent his telegram to Washington, a further summary of the Vrba–Wetzler report had been sent, this time to London, by Walter Garrett, the representative in Switzerland of the British news service, Exchange Telegraph. Garrett's telegram of June 24 gave news both of the forcing into ghettoes and of the deportation of Jews from Hungary. It also pointed out that on May 15 'deportation began unknown destination but later revealed Auschwitz'. Garrett also reported receipt of what the telegraphic language summarized as:

Dramatic account one darkest chapters modern history revealing how 1,715,000 Jews put death annihilation camp Auschwitz, Birkenau and Harmansee[4] bracket upper Silesia unbracket where also awful destiny HungJews today fulfilling itself.

In his telegram of June 24, Garrett informed his London office that the reports on which he was basing his account came from 'two Jews who escaped Birkenau correctness whereof confirmed'. Garrett then listed in his telegram the figures of the Vrba–Wetzler report, omitting by mistake the figure of 50,000 Lithuanian Jews, hence the total figure in his telegram of 1,715,000.

Garrett's telegraphic summary of the Vrba–Wetzler report ended: 'Absolute

---

[1] War Refugee Board, Box 35, Measures Directed Towards Halting Persecution, F. Hungary No. 5.

[2] Benjamin Akzin, conversation with the author, Jerusalem, 23 December 1980.

[3] Gerhardt's note is quoted in David S. Wyman, 'Why Auschwitz was never Bombed', in *Commentary*, volume 65, number 5, New York, May 1978, page 39.

[4] In Polish, Harmeze: a village two kilometres southwest of Birkenau; it was within the Auschwitz camp administrative region, and served as a farm labour-camp annex.

exactness above report unquestionable and diplomat Catholic functionaries well known Vatican desire widest diffusion worldwide'.[1]

From Hungary, the deportations continued without respite, and on June 25, the day after McClelland's telegram had reached Washington and Garrett's had reached London, more than 15,000 Hungarian Jews were deported to Auschwitz.

On June 26, while these deportations were still in progress, the second Frantic shuttle, now recovered from the German attack on Poltava airport, flew back to Italy. On its return it bombed the synthetic oil plant at Drohobycz. In all, 71 Flying Fortresses and 51 Mustangs took part in this return flight.[2] Their flight path took them across several of the main deportation railways.

Also on June 26, the third aerial reconnaissance to fly over Auschwitz and Birkenau recorded, from an altitude of 30,000 feet, the layout of both camps. As on the two previous occasions, the object of the photographs was to locate and portray the I.G. Farben factory at Monowitz. But as before, further photographs had been taken to ensure that Monowitz really was within view of the camera, with the result that one of the frames showed the whole of Auschwitz and the whole of Birkenau.[3]

One of the photographs showed the whole of Monowitz, Auschwitz I and Birkenau within a single frame. Twenty showed Monowitz alone. But it was not Auschwitz I or Birkenau, but Monowitz, at which the camera had been aimed, it was Monowitz alone which, if the detail in the photographs could be exact enough, would become a target for Allied bombers.

The first analysis of the Monowitz photograph was made two days later. 'Although the gas plants are active,' it was noted, 'there is no evidence of production of synthetic oil.' One of the generators of the water gas plant did, however, have 'a smoking chimney', and five gas-holders were full. In the synthetic rubber section, 'considerable progress had been made. A second kiln had been completed and a third was 'well advanced'. Elsewhere, progress in construction had been 'considerable', and it seemed probable that the synthetic rubber section 'is now working at about half its planned capacity'.[4]

The photographs of June 26 were analysed in even greater detail three days later. 'The works sidings,' it was noted, 'are served by the Oswiecim-Dziedzice railway. There are generally good rail and road connections with the surrounding area and with the other refineries and synthetic oil plants in this vicinity.' Construction work at the synthetic oil plant had been 'proceeding rapidly', since the first reconnaissance of April 4: 'one of the three sets of hydrogenations stalls appeared completed; the other two pairs appear almost complete.' As for 'personnel', these were 'seen scattered throughout area', as were large numbers of trucks, 'seen in many parts of the plant—some in motion'. Mechanical excavators 'are seen at work in many sections of the plant' while

[1] Quoted in full in Jenó Lévai, Zsidósors Európában, Budapest 1948, pages 68–72. Garrett's telegram was 837 words long, and was sent to London in four separate sections.

[2] Wesley Frank Craven and James Lea Cate (editors), The Army Air Forces in World War II, volume 3, Chicago 1951.

[3] Exposure 5022, Can C1172, Mission 60/PR522 60 SQ, Scale 1:60,000, United States Strategic Bombing Survey, Record Group 373.

[4] Interpretation Report No. D326R, Prints 4043 to 4048, United States Strategic Bombing Survey, Record Group 243.

visible throughout the plant area were 'piles of construction materials and equipment awaiting erection'.

The aerial photographs of June 26 showed, nevertheless, that completion of 'all the installations' would take a 'considerable time', but that once they were completed, Monowitz would have a capacity to produce 20,000 tons of synthetic rubber a year from its 'Buna' installation, and an eventual 375,000 tons of synthetic oil. But the immediate synthetic oil production, using the single completed hydrogenation stall was estimated at only 62,500 tons a year, while if the two stalls under construction were also in use, as they 'appear almost complete', this figure would be increased to 180,000 tons. The intelligence report noted that the foundations had been laid for four more stalls, hence the eventual high productive capacity.[1] And hence also the urgency for bombing.

One of the June 26 photographs of Monowitz was attached to this second report, and a total of sixty-two items marked on it, including the completed, partially completed, and planned stalls in the synthetic oil plant, and the whole process of synthetic rubber production in the Buna Plant. Also identified was a Light Metal plant for the reduction of aluminium, then under construction, and the 'Concentration Camp' which had also been identified on the photographs and plan of April 4.

No reference was made in either of the two intelligence reports to the photograph which also showed Auschwitz I and Birkenau. This section of the photograph was clearly of no relevance to those whose task was to pinpoint the industrial production of oil and rubber. Looking at the photograph today, one can identify in it several of the features mentioned in the Vrba–Wetzler report, including the small wood, the four gas chambers, the four crematoria, and the special railway spur running from the main line into Birkenau. There is even a train on the siding inside Birkenau.

That same day, June 26, Richard Lichtheim, writing to Jerusalem from Geneva, stressed that all the provinces of northern and eastern Hungary were already *judenrein*, and that 'even from Budapest we have received letters saying that our friends there no longer have any hope to be spared. In fact they are saying good-bye to us'. From the Hungarian provinces, Lichtheim added, '10,000 to 12,000 are daily deported to the death camps'. His letter ended, 'the only method which would be effective (and which has also been suggested) has so far never been used: reprisals'.[2]

The idea of reprisals against Germans in Allied hands had long been considered by the Allies to be a two-edged weapon, especially with so many Allied prisoners-of-war, including pilots and air crew, in German hands. More than 40,000 British troops had been taken prisoner at Dunkirk alone.[3]

[1] Mediterranean Allied Photo Reconnaissance Wing, Report No. H.1.11(P) of 1 July 1944, 'Activity at the I.G. Farbenindustrie Synthetic Oil and Synthetic Rubber Works at Oswiecim (Poland)'. United States Strategic Bombing Survey, Record Group 373.

[2] Central Zionist Archives, L 22/135.

[3] A British Intelligence estimate of 5 September 1944 gave a figure of 160,000 for the total number of British and Commonwealth prisoners-of-war in Allied hands (over 100,000 of them east of the Elbe), and over 30,000 Americans (three-quarters of them east of the Elbe), M. R. D. Foot and J. M. Langley, *M.I.9*, London 1979, page 288.

On June 26 the Jewish Agency representatives in Portugal sent a telegram through the American Embassy in Lisbon to the two leaders of American Jewry, Stephen Wise and Nahum Goldmann, transmitting the Budapest message of June 19 'that 400,000 Jews already sent Poland', and passing on the request of two of the Jewish leaders in Budapest, Krausz and Kastner, for 'vigorous action' by the United Nations 'to save rest'.

The second paragraph of this Lisbon telegram, forwarded by the War Refugee Board in Washington to the Zionist leaders in New York, raised a completely separate problem, the possibility of Jewish children to leave Rumania, provided shipping was available. These Rumanian children were in no immediate danger of deportation. Nevertheless, the chance of bringing them to Palestine would ensure their safety. 'We are informed by Istanbul,' the Lisbon emissaries reported, 'sea transport available for 7,600,' and they added: 'Vast sums necessary immediately', including a War Refugee Board 'subsidy'.[1]

The Jewish organizations in Switzerland were anxious to get the information about Auschwitz and the Hungarian deportations to Churchill himself. 'I shall be grateful if you will kindly cable the attached urgent message to London,' Lichtheim wrote to Douglas MacKillop at the British Legation in Berne on June 26. And he added: 'More and more reports are coming in about the awful fate of the Hungarian Jews and the mass murders committed by the Germans in the death-camps of Poland and Upper Silesia.'[2]

MacKillop acted immediately, and shortly before eight o'clock in the evening of June 26, the British Minister in Berne, Clifford Norton, telegraphed to the Foreign Office the text of a message from Lichtheim for the Jewish Agency. The telegram, marked urgent, reached London at four o'clock in the morning of June 27. Its first part summarized the Krausz letter of June 19, and read:

Received fresh reports from Hungary stating that nearly one half total of 800,000 Jews in Hungary have already been deported at a rate of 10,000 to 12,000 per diem. Most of these transports are sent to the death camp of Birkenau near Oswiecim in Upper Silesia where in the course of last year over 1,500,000 Jews from all over Europe have been killed.

We have detailed reports about the numbers and methods employed. The four crematoriums in Birkenau have a capacity for gassing and burning 60,000[3] per diem.

In Budapest and surroundings there are still between 300,000 and 400,000 Jews left including those incorporated in labour service but no Jews are left in eastern and northern provinces and according to a letter from our manager of Palestine office Budapest, the remaining Jews in and around Budapest have no hope to be spared.

[1] Lisbon telegram No. 1981, United States National Archives, 840.48, Refugees 6–2644. The Jewish Agency representatives in Lisbon were Eliahu Dobkin and Fritz Lichtenstein. Their telegram was sent by the American Legation in Lisbon to the State Department in Washington, where it was received at 6.30 that same evening.

[2] Central Zionist Archives, L 22/56.

[3] This figure was a telegraphic error. The correct figure, as given in the original message, was 12,000 a day. In the fifty consecutive days between 18 May and 7 July 1944, more than 400,000 Hungarian Jews had been murdered in the four gas chambers at Birkenau, making a minimum daily average over the whole period of between 8,000 and 9,000.

12. The route by which the Vrba-Wetzler and Mordowicz-Rosin reports about Auschwitz went from the camp at Birkenau to London.

The second part of the Lichtheim telegram set out the measures which the Jewish organizations in Geneva felt were urgent. The first was that the facts themselves, 'which are confirmed by various letters and reports from reliable sources', should be given the 'widest publicity' and that the Hungarian Government 'should again be warned that they will be held responsible because they are aiding the Germans with their own police to arrest and deport and thus murder the Jews'. There then followed four further suggestions: the first, 'reprisals against Germans in Allied hands'; the second, 'bombing of railway lines leading from Hungary to Birkenau'; the third, 'precision bombing of death camp installations'; and the fourth, the bombing of 'all Government buildings' in Budapest. The Lichtheim telegram ended: 'Please consider these or other proposals, also inform Jerusalem and New York about situation'.[1]

Although Lichtheim's telegram reached the Foreign Office on the morning of June 27, it was not sent on to the Jewish Agency until July 1. But it was copied by the Foreign Office on June 27 for immediate distribution to the War Cabinet. It was at this moment that the Hungarian deportations became known to Churchill. He at once minuted to Eden: 'What can be done? What can be said?'[2]

On the very morning that Lichtheim's telegram had reached the Foreign Office, an indication of the fate of the Jews of Hungary was published in the *Manchester Guardian*, albeit on an inside page. The headline read:

FATE OF JEWS IN HUNGARY
MASSACRE BEGINS

The newspaper report began: 'Information that the Germans are systematically

[1] Norton telegram, No. 2949, Urgent, War Cabinet Distribution, copy in Premier papers, 4/51/10.
[2] Premier papers, 4/51/10.

exterminating Hungarian Jews has lately become substantial', and it went on to say that it had been reported 'from Poland' that 'thousands of Jews have arrived at the concentration camp of Oswiecim'.

According to the *Manchester Guardian*, another source had just arrived 'tonight', that is, June 25, which had given the approximate figure of 100,000 Hungarian Jews 'who had already perished in the death camps established by the Germans in Poland'. Although these reports were 'not confirmed in London', the newspaper added, 'it is known that for some time past Germany has threatened to exterminate Hungarian Jewry'.

The source of the report of June 25 must have been Garrett's telegram sent from Switzerland on the previous day. Another source quoted by the *Manchester Guardian* on June 27, in a separate column, was the Polish National Council's Jewish representative, Dr E. Scherer, who had received a message from Poland 'yesterday' saying 'that in the Oswiecim concentration camp the Germans are now gassing and slaughtering the remnants of Polish Jews'. Yet another message, the *Manchester Guardian* stated, said that 'one hundred thousand Hungarian Jews had been brought to Oswiecim and slaughtered there in the course of May'.

Knowing nothing on June 27 of the message from Switzerland with its news of the Hungarian deportations, and its appeal for bombing, the Jewish Agency's priority still lay in pursuing the Brand proposals. Shertok had flown to Cairo to speak to Hirschmann on June 21. He had seen Lord Moyne on June 23, and had then returned by air to Jerusalem. On June 24 he flew back again to Cairo, and on the following morning, had been given a place on the flight to England, reaching London that same evening.

The Foreign Office and the War Office, however, were both still very much against the Brand proposals. On June 26 a letter from A. J. Kellar, of Military Intelligence, to Randall, reported the view of Special Intelligence Middle East, that the Jewish Agency 'is endeavouring to push us into an early response to German proposal when we are still uncertain of motive behind it'.[1] In a second letter to Randall that same day, Kellar sent on two further points from Brigadier Maunsell of Special Intelligence Middle East, who had spoken to Ira Hirschmann, and reported that Hirschmann 'is evidently taking a much more objective and reserved attitude to the case than the Jewish Agency representatives in Palestine and Turkey have done. . . .' In addition, Maunsell warned: 'The greatest objection to Brand's return is the risk that he might convey a secret and unauthorised message from the Jewish Agency representatives in the Middle East or Turkey.'

Brigadier Maunsell advised Military Intelligence not to allow any more Jewish representatives to see Brand; he had already, he said, with Lord Moyne's consent, refused to allow Shertok to have a second meeting with Brand. As for Brand's companion Gross, he was 'a multiple agent working for the Intelligence organisations of six different countries'.[2]

Also on June 26, Randall himself suggested that in view of Shertok's

[1] Foreign Office, 371/42759, W 10266, folios 148–9.
[2] Foreign Office, 371/42759, W 10266, folios 150–1.

arrival 'and the growing pressure from the Jewish Agency', the Cabinet Refugee Committee should be informed 'of the latest stages of the Gestapo offer about the Jews', and a note drafted by him that same day was prepared for circulation under Eden's signature.[1]

The Foreign Office note of June 26 stated that the answer to Shertok's desire to open negotiations should be twofold; one that 'to start talking about material recompense (so many Jews released for so many tons of soap etc.) would open an unending series of blackmail, and must be firmly refused'; and two, that it would be impossible for the British or American Governments to have anything to do with the Gestapo or 'even the German Government' on the basis proposed by Brand 'above all in the face of the firm refusal of the Soviet Government, whose military interest, as being nearest to Hungary where most of the remaining compact Jewish communities are placed, is most important'.[2]

On June 27 Shertok went to the Foreign Office, accompanied by Joseph Linton. The Foreign Office representatives were Randall, Walker and Henderson. Shertok agreed at the outset that any publicity regarding the Brand proposals 'was to be deplored', but he went on to urge that, on the assumption that the proposals were 'serious', Brand should be allowed to return at once to Budapest 'with a message for the Gestapo that HMG and the United States Government were considering these proposals and that the German Government would hear from them shortly'.

Shertok agreed with the Foreign Office representatives that the 'correct channel of approach' from the British to the German Government 'could only be through the Protecting Power'. He added that he was anxious that British and American Government representatives should meet representatives of the German Government both 'for the purpose of dangling a carrot in front of the Germans' and also in the hope 'that from such a meeting some practical proposals might arise'.

The Foreign Office representatives pointed out that no such meeting could take place without the concurrence of the Soviet Government, 'and that this was almost certainly impossible to obtain'. Shertok replied 'that the Agency fully recognised this', but suggested that the War Refugee Board might make 'direct contact with the Germans'. It was also suggested that the Spanish or International Red Cross 'might be a suitable intermediary'.

Shertok agreed with his questioners that 'any approach made by HMG and the United States Government through the Protecting Power should be concerned with counter-proposals', and that 'in the first instance' various schemes should be carried out; the record of the meeting referred to two such schemes, 'transport of 20,000 Jewish children to Switzerland, and of 5,000 Jewish children and their escorts from the Balkans'.

When Anthony Eden saw this report he noted, against Shertok's wish for British and American Government representatives to meet representatives of the German Government: 'This is out of the question'.[3]

---

[1] Foreign Office papers, 371/42759, W 10386.
[2] 'Note by the Secretary of State for Foreign Affairs', 26 June 1944, Cabinet papers, 95/15.
[3] 'Record of Interview with Mr Shertok, Jewish Agency for Palestine', Foreign Office papers, 371/42759, W 10260, folio 146.

On June 28, at Weizmann's suggestion, Shertok asked to see Eden himself. Eden was reluctant to agree to a meeting, minuting that same day to his Private Secretary: 'What do you say? Must I? Which of my colleagues looks after this? Minister of State or Mr Hall? At least the one of them responsible should be there to see these two Jews. Weizmann doesn't usually take much time'.[1]

It was George Hall who agreed to see Shertok and Weizmann, without Eden having to be present, on June 30. At that meeting, Shertok again asked that Brand be allowed to leave Cairo, and return to Budapest. His return should only be delayed, Shertok argued, 'if there were a chance of his being thus enabled to take a definite answer'.

Shertok then stressed that 'as time was desperately short' two immediate steps should be taken: a message should be sent by the Allied Governments, through the Protecting Power to the German Government to say 'that the Allies are prepared to meet the Germans to discuss rescue of the Jews in general'; while at the same time the War Refugee Board 'should meet representatives of the Gestapo'.

Shertok favoured using the War Refugee Board in order to avoid any official approach through the Protecting Power meeting with 'a formal refusal'. Any reply to the Brand proposals, he added, should include a statement that the Allies expected that the deportations 'would stop in the meanwhile'.

The meeting ended with Shertok making two further suggestions; 'that there might be a wireless warning to the railwaymen of Hungary not to carry Jews to death camps', and that 'death camps should be bombed', a suggestion, he said, which had originated with Krausz.[2]

Shertok's first point, the wireless warning, was taken up at once and was put into immediate effect. Five days later, on July 5, the Political Warfare Executive arranged for a senior Trade Unionist, Mr Marchbanks, of the International Transport Workers Federation, to broadcast an appeal, which was repeated on the following day, warning Hungarian railway workers not to carry Jews to the death camps, and on July 11 a further similar appeal was arranged at the specific request of the Foreign Office.[3]

The second point passed on by Shertok, that the death camps should be bombed, was also taken up. Although the distance from British bases was too great for a precision night bombing attack by the Royal Air Force, it was however within the range of a daylight raid by the United States Air Force. But it would need to be given a very high priority indeed, with Germany's oil resources still a grave danger to the Allied advance both from east and west. For this reason the Americans were at that very moment turning down the earlier Jewish request to bomb the railways. 'The War Department,' McCloy wrote to Pehle on July 4, 'is of the opinion that the suggested air operation is impracticable,' and he went on to explain:

---

[1] Foreign Office papers, 371/42807, WR 49, folio 70.
[2] 'Record of an Interview granted by Mr Hall to Dr Weizmann and Mr Shertok', Foreign Office papers, 371/42807, WR 49, folio 73.
[3] Foreign Office papers, 371/42807, WR 49, folios 70–1.

It could be executed only by the diversion of considerable air support essential to the success of our forces now engaged in decisive operations and would in any case be of such very doubtful efficacy that it would not amount to a practical project.[1]

One opponent of the proposal to bomb the camps themselves was Leon Kubowitzki, the head of the Rescue Department of the World Jewish Congress. At the same time that the War Department were turning down the railway bombing request, Kubowitzki was warning the War Refugee Board that the destruction of the death installations 'can not be done from the air, as the first victims would be the Jews who are gathered in these camps'.

Kubowitzki had a second objection. Such a bombing, he wrote, 'would be a welcome pretext for the Germans to assert that their Jewish victims have been massacred not by their killers, but by the Allied bombing'.

The plan which Kubowitzki favoured, and which he had already mentioned to the War Refugee Board at a meeting on June 28, was for an American approach to the Soviet Government 'with the request that it should dispatch groups of paratroopers to seize the buildings, to annihilate the squads of murderers, and to free the unfortunate inmates'. At the same time, Kubowitzki wrote, the Americans should ask the Polish Government 'to instruct the Polish underground to attack these and similar camps to destroy the instruments of death'.[2]

Kubowitzki's appeal for a paratroop action was not even put by the War Refugee Board to the War Department. As Pehle himself explained to Morgenthau two months later:

At this stage of the war, it did not seem proper to suggest to the War Department the diversion of military equipment or military personnel to non-military purposes. Furthermore, aerial and paratroop raids of this kind must entail casualties on the part of the raiders and we did not feel justified in asking the War Department to undertake a measure which involved the sacrifice of American troops.

Pehle also commented on Kubowitzki's request that the Polish Government-in-Exile should 'direct its underground forces to destroy the death camps and free the prisoners there', a request, he said, first made on June 27 by Dr Schwarzbart, of the Polish National Council, to the Polish Prime Minister. This request had not been acted on, Pehle noted, and he added:

In view of the apparently deep-rooted anti-Semitism on the part of a large segment of the Polish Government and underground movement, it seemed most unlikely that the Poles would, in good faith, undertake to attack the death centers effectively unless strong political pressure involving political support were asserted.

As a matter of fact, it is very doubtful whether the Poles had the necessary forces to carry out any such operation.[3]

Another, earlier request by the Jewish Agency, was also being followed up at the end of June; Weizmann's appeal for a link with Tito and the rescue of

[1] Quoted in David S. Wyman, 'Why Auschwitz was Never Bombed', in *Commentary*, volume 65, number 5, New York, May 1978, page 39.

[2] Letter of 1 July 1944, War Refugee Board, Box 35, Measures Directed Towards Halting Persecutions, F: Hungary No. 5.

[3] Letter of 6 September 1944, War Refugee Board, Box 33, Measures Directed Towards Halting Persecutions, F: Hungary No. 1.

Hungarian Jews through Yugoslavia. Churchill had given this project his support, and on June 28, when the Jewish Agency asked for permission for Reuven Zaslani to go to Bari and make contact with Tito's representative there, Velebit, Lord Moyne telegraphed to the British Minister resident in Algiers: 'I am not able to assess prospects of project but would hesitate without good reason to put difficulties in the way of any scheme which may assist the escape of Jews from Axis occupied Europe'.[1]

In London, the result of Shertok's two interviews at the Foreign Office had been to confirm official reluctance to take up the Jewish Agency's request for negotiations between the Allies and the Germans. When Eden himself read the record of Shertok's interview with George Hall, he underlined Shertok's principal request, that the Allies should send a message to the German Government to say that 'the *Allies are prepared to meet* the Germans' to discuss the rescue of Jews, and minuted in the margin: 'We are NOT'.[2]

Meanwhile, on June 29 the *Manchester Guardian* had published a message from the World Jewish Congress, to the effect that news had reached them on June 17 'that in the period from May 15 to May 27 the Germans transported from Hungary 62 railway trucks laden with Jewish children aged between two and nine years, and that six railway trucks laden with Jewish adults passed daily through the station of Plaszow, near Cracow, bound for an unknown destination'.

In this particular report, no mention was made of Auschwitz or Birkenau. The report added that the Polish Government in London now had a message, dated June 14, confirming that 100,000 Hungarian Jews had been 'slaughtered by mass gassing in the lethal chambers of the notorious German death camps in Polish Galicia',[3] and that 750,000 Jews in Hungary were 'in the most imminent peril'.

Eden had already opposed any negotiations with the Germans for the 'rescue' of Jews. His opposition was unknown however to the Jewish Agency leaders, for whom two telegrams arriving from Jerusalem on June 30 only made their request for negotiations seem more urgent. The first, sent from Gruenbaum on June 27, relayed the Lichtheim telegram, and then set out the measures which the Jewish Agency Executive felt were essential. The first suggestion was one made by the Geneva Zionists, that 'we demand larger number certificates and quicker settlement formalities, also issue special protection documents based on immigration certificates'.

The Agency Executive, Gruenbaum continued, was convinced that 'nothing but unprecedented drastic measures can halt wholesale slaughter Hungarian Jewry'. The Executive had five points which it wished to be taken up at once.

The first four points concerned specific measures for saving individuals by means of documents: an approach to the British Foreign Office for 'some official document' which the Swiss Government could give to all Jews in

---

[1] Foreign Office papers, 371/42810, WR 331, Cairo telegram No. 369.
[2] Foreign Office papers, 371/42807, WR 49, folio 73.
[3] Before 1914 Auschwitz had been a frontier town at the western extremity of the Austro-Hungarian province of Galicia. Between 1919 and 1939 it was within the borders of southwestern Poland, and in October 1939 it was annexed to the German province of Upper Silesia, in the sub-district of East Upper Silesia.

Budapest who were 'included in our approved lists'; the speeding up of the transmission of these lists before the individuals were deported, making use of the direct contact between British and Swiss diplomats in Turkey, and the link between the Swiss diplomats in Turkey and the Swiss Legation in Budapest; the issuing of 'large numbers of permits' for Hungarian Jews to proceed to the large refugee camps in North Africa which the American Government had announced that it was setting up; and a personal approach by Weizmann himself to the 'leading figures' in Switzerland, with a view to what was called 'more effective collaboration' as far as the rescue of Jews was concerned between the International Red Cross and other Swiss relief agencies.

The fifth point in Gruenbaum's telegram was to 'reiterate' his previous suggestions for the prevention of the deportation of Hungarian Jews to the 'death camps Poland'. 'In my view,' Gruenbaum ended, 'our effort gravely imperilled if deportations continue. Material may disappear.'[1]

The second telegram to reach Shertok on June 30 was also from Gruenbaum, and had been sent from Jerusalem on the previous day. It referred directly to Brand's mission, reporting that information had been received from Istanbul stating 'expressly' that the continued detention of Brand and Gross was the 'direct cause speeded and intensified deportation'. Gruenbaum repeated Krausz's earlier demand that the 'responsibility' for the deportations should be 'placed [on the] shoulders [of] those [who] decided detention'. His telegram ended with a desperate plea on behalf of the Executive for one final effort to follow up the Brand initiative:

Please impress competent authorities we asked their help fully trusting that if cannot assist will at least not make things worse. This done by detention two men.

Therefore please one, immediate return two men; two, immediate agreement to meet Lisbon; three, meanwhile adoption extraordinary measures repeatedly suggested view interfering deportation.

The one measure referred to in Gruenbaum's telegram was again one which Krausz had pressed for earlier: 'retaliatory measures against Germans detained allied countries'. Such measures, Gruenbaum wrote, were regarded 'as only effective way stopping murder'.[2]

At Auschwitz, one train had arrived from Hungary on June 28, and two on June 29. Two further trains arrived on June 30, but not from Hungary. The first brought two thousand Jews from Athens and Corfu, of whom 1,423 were gassed on arrival. The second brought a thousand Jews from the internment camp at Fossoli, in German-occupied northern Italy. Of these, 582 were gassed, making a death toll on June 30 of just over two thousand.

Beginning in July 1944, Jews were not only being brought to Auschwitz almost every day, but were also being sent away from Auschwitz to labour camps in central and western Germany. So effective had the Allied bombing of Germany become that Jewish labour was now judged essential if the munitions factories of the Reich were to be kept in operation. Thus, on July 1, two

[1] Foreign Office papers, 371/42807, WR 49, folio 75.
[2] Foreign Office papers, 371/42807, WR 49, folio 74.

thousand Jewish women were taken from the women's camp at Birkenau, and sent by train to two factory camps controlled by Büchenwald concentration camp, one at Gelsenkirchen and the other at Essen. As it crossed central Germany, the train was caught up in an Allied bombing raid, and 266 of the women were killed.

At Birkenau, between July 2 and July 11, the second family camp of Jews from Theresienstadt was destroyed. More than three thousand women and children were gassed, but at the same time two thousand women were sent to labour camps at Stutthof and Hamburg, while a thousand of the younger men and teenage boys were sent to the badly damaged German synthetic oil plant at Schwarzheide, astride the Berlin–Dresden autobahn.

While not giving up its primacy as a killing centre, Auschwitz now also began to serve as a labour reserve for the rest of the Reich.

On the evening of July 1 Eden approved a telegram to Lord Halifax describing the discussions with Shertok. The telegram, which had been drafted by Randall, informed the Ambassador that the Brand proposals were being 'kept in play in the hope of staving off disaster and seeing whether something acceptable might not emerge'.

Adopting a more positive tone than hitherto, the telegram stated that it was possible that the Government might decide to send Brand back to Hungary with a message 'that he had found Allied circles concerned with the fate of the Jews and that he understood allies were conveying their views through the Protecting Power, and the German Government might shortly expect to hear something'.

If this were to be decided upon, Halifax was told, 'then we suggest that British and United States Ministers in Berne would be instructed to address the Swiss Government. . . .'

There then followed the text of the suggested instruction, based on the British acceptance of the transfer of 'a stated number of Jews in conditions of distress to the responsibility of other countries', beginning with a German 'earnest of good faith', the grant of permits, long ago asked for, to enable five thousand Jewish children from southeastern Europe to go to Palestine, and the departure of 1,500 Jewish children 'who would be given temporary hospitality in Switzerland'. Two further suggestions to enable the Germans to show 'an earnest of good faith' were also set out in the proposed instructions to the Swiss Government, for communication to the German Government:

(c) the transport of Jewish refugees to the various homes offered them has been hindered by the absence of German safe-conducts for the various ships proposed to be employed. The German Government is requested to withdraw its objection to the safe-conducts, in particular in the case of the s.s. 'Tari', which would be used solely for the transport of civilian refugees.

(d) for some considerable time past lists of Jews who would be given immediate entry into Palestine have been communicated to the German Government. It is suggested that as many of the persons as can be identified should now be given permits to leave, and on learning that this has been done transport arrangements will be taken in hand by the United Kingdom and United States Governments.[1]

[1] Foreign Office to Washington, telegram No. 5958, 1 July 1944, War Cabinet Distribution, Cabinet papers, 95/15.

In a second telegram that same evening, Halifax was asked to discuss this suggestion with the 'appropriate' United States authorities, 'and ask whether they would join in the proposed approach to the Swiss Government. . . .'[1]

Both these telegrams were printed for distribution to the War Cabinet. On reading them, Churchill minuted to Eden, on July 2: 'Surely we cannot negotiate with the Germans on this matter, certainly not without the Cabinet being consulted. This is not the time to have negotiations with the enemy'.[2] To this, Eden replied four days later that the telegrams also made clear 'that in our view there can be *no* direct contact between the Allies and the Germans'. But, Eden continued, 'as we could not entirely disregard Jewish interest in the matter, we thought it as well to explain our view of all the possible courses of action very fully to the U.S. Govt.'[3]

The deportations from Hungary to Auschwitz continued throughout the first week of July, as did deportations from Holland and France, news of which reached the Jewish Agency in London on July 3, in the form of a further telegram from Lichtheim in Geneva. According to information which had reached Geneva, the number of Jews 'transferred to Westerbork to Belsen and Theresienstadt not known: Full lists names both camps, and other particulars, especially names certificate holders, not obtainable'. Lichtheim's telegram continued:

Red Cross or neutral envoys cannot visit these camps. Have many names Theresienstadt where number inmates during last two years about 40,000, while deportations were constantly going on, probably to make room for newcomers. Only certain privileged categories can write.

Lichtheim also passed on the bad news that while 283 of the four to five hundred Jews with foreign passports who had been interned in Vittel were still there, a total of 163 'are said to have been deported two months ago to an unknown destination'. The destination had, in fact, been Auschwitz.

Despite the pressure of the Allied forces in Normandy even Drancy was still being used to deport Jews from Paris to the east. As Lichtheim telegraphed: 'Drancy now only transit camp for deportees. Deportations starting whenever number inmates reaches 1,000 to 1,500.'[4] This was indeed true; unknown in the west, on June 30 a total of 1,153 Jews had been deported from Paris to Auschwitz by train, travelling through eastern France, the Rhineland, Saxony and Silesia to their destination, at the very moment when the Allied armies were battling in the Normandy salient, less than 150 miles to the west. On reaching Auschwitz, on July 4, more than two hundred women and nearly four hundred men were sent to the barracks. But more than four hundred women, children and old people were gassed.

The news from Hungary, by contrast, seemed to open up a small area of hope, for on the morning of July 4 the Foreign Office received a telegram for Shertok, from the Zionists in Switzerland, to the effect that a 'portion of

[1] Foreign Office to Washington, telegram No. 5959, 1 July 1944, War Cabinet Distribution, Cabinet papers, 95/15.
[2] Prime Minister's Personal Minute, M 782/4, Foreign Office papers, 371/42759, W 10025, folio 68.
[3] Reply drafted by Valentine Lawford, Foreign Office papers, 371/42759, W 10025, folio 69.
[4] Central Zionist Archives, S 25/1678.

Hungarian Jews expelled to Poland are held Germany probably as emigration candidates'.

This news referred to the 1,658 Jews released by the Gestapo from camps in Budapest, and sent by train to Bergen-Belsen, as the first part of the deal, if deal indeed it were to be, intended to cover the 350,000 Jews still alive in Hungary after the May 15 to June 30 deportations.

This telegram, which had reached London through the Jewish Agency representative in Portugal, reported that 'possibility exists for 1,000 refugees to enter Spain', and that the Spanish Government was also prepared to admit five additional groups of three hundred children each. In addition, $800,000 had been made available in New York for the 'transportation of Balkan refugees through Istanbul'.[1]

Another long-advocated Zionist concern was pressed by Weizmann during the first week of July 1944. It was a request that had first been made, and made even then with urgency, in the first month of war, nearly five years before, for the creation of a specifically Jewish military formation, to fight, as a Jewish unit, alongside the other Allied armies, British, American, Free French, Czech and Polish.

The current request, as put forward by Weizmann, was for the setting up of a Jewish Brigade Group. This was discussed at the War Cabinet on July 4, when Churchill spoke in favour of granting Weizmann's request, telling the War Cabinet: 'In view of the sufferings the Jewish people are at present enduring, there is a strong case for sympathetic consideration of projects in relation to them'.

In reply, the Commander-in-Chief Middle East strongly opposed the setting up of any specifically Jewish force. This demand, he said, was 'purely political, as a first step towards creating a Jewish Army', and he went on to warn that a Jewish Brigade Group might be brought back to Palestine, a move which would 'inevitably lead to large scale disturbances'. In any case, he added, there was 'no equipment' available for so large a force.

The War Cabinet concluded that the idea of setting up a Jewish force would be 'carefully examined'. But Churchill was sceptical. 'When the War Office say they will carefully examine a thing', he wrote to the Cabinet Secretary on July 10, 'they mean they will do it in'.[2]

---

[1] Sir R. Campbell, telegram No. 1163, Foreign Office papers, 371/42807, WR 55.
[2] War Cabinet Conclusions and Churchill's comment, in Premier papers, 4/51/9.

Chapter 27

'Do all in your power'

On July 4 a summary of the Vrba–Wetzler report finally reached the Foreign Office. The route of this particular summary was through the Czechoslovak representative in Geneva, Jaromir Kopecky, to the Acting Czechoslovak Minister for Foreign Affairs, Hubert Ripka, then in exile in London. The information in the report of the two Jewish escapees had been 'further considerably supplemented', the Czechoslovak Government noted, 'by reports which a Polish major who escaped from Oswiecim furnished to the underground organisation in Slovakia'.[1]

In sending the Foreign Office an eight-page summary of the report, Ripka suggested that the Allied Governments issue 'an emphatic protest and solemn warning to the German Government in respect of these barbarous crimes'. President Beneš himself, Ripka had reported, was ready 'to associate himself with any protest which might be organised'.

The summary of these two reports, as received at the Foreign Office on July 4, read, in full:

OSWIECZIM[2] and BIRKENAU

The concentration camp at Oswieczim was originally intended for political prisoners, and about 15,000 Germans, Czechoslovaks, Poles and Russians were there in 'protective detention'. Besides this, professional criminals were sent there and asocial elements, homosexuals, Bible students, and later Jews from the occupied countries. Over the entrance is the inscription in German 'Arbeit macht frei'.

The Birkenau labour camp, which lies 4 km. from Oswieczim, and the agricultural work of the Harmense camp, are both under the control of the governor of the Oswiecim camp. Inside Oswieczim camp are work-shops of the German armaments concerns Siemens and Krupp. The huts in the camp are in three rows covering an area of 500 × 300 metres. They are surrounded by a double fence 3 metres high charged with high tension electricity. At every 500 metres is a watch-tower 5 metres high with machine-guns and searchlights. This is the 'kleine Postenkette'. Another line of watch-towers runs in a circle of 2 kilometres and the work-shops are between the two rows of watch-towers.

Birkenau camp is formed of three blocks covering an area of 1,600 × 850 metres and is also surrounded by two rings of watch-towers. The outer ring is connected with the outer ring of watch-towers of Oswieczim camp and they are only separated by the railway-lines. Birkenau camp is called after the small forest of Birkenwald (in Polish Brzezinky) nearby. The local population used to call this place 'Rajsko'.

Working conditions at Birkenau and Oswieczim are unimaginable. Work is carried on either in the camp or in the neighbourhood. Roads are built. Reinforced concrete buildings are put up. Gravel is quarried. Houses in the neighbourhood are knocked down. New buildings are put up in the camps and in the work-shops. Work is also done in the neighbouring coal mines or in the factory for synthetic rubber. Some persons also work in the administration of the camps.

---

[1] British Embassy to the Czechoslovak Government, letter No. 91, in Foreign Office papers, 371/42809, WR 218, folio 34.

[2] Misspelt throughout this report. The correct Polish spelling of Auschwitz is Oswiecim.

Any person who does not carry out his work to the satisfaction of the overseer is flogged or beaten to death. The food is 300 grammes of bread per head every evening, or 1 litre per head of turnip soup and a little coffee. That is for the Jews. Non-Jews receive rather more. Anyone who cannot work and has a temperature of at least 38.6 degrees is sent to the 'Krankenbau', the hut for the sick.

The German doctor divides sick persons into two groups: curable and seriously ill. The seriously ill are disposed of by a phenol injection in the region of the heart. Among non-Jews this is done only to those who are really seriously ill, while among the Jews 80 to 90 per cent of all those ill receive it. 15,000 to 20,000 persons have already been got rid of in this way by injections.

Particularly inhuman scenes took place when the sick were killed wholesale during the process of delousing when a typhus epidemic broke out. Near the 'Krankenbau' is the 'hygiene institute' where sterilisation and artificial insemination of the women are carried out and blood tests are made for blood transfusion. For these experiments chiefly Jews are used.

Since March, 1942 enormous transports of Jews have come to Oswieczim and Birkenau. A very small number of them have been sent to the labour camp, while an average of 90 per cent of those who have come have been taken straight from the train and killed. These executions took place at the beginning in the forest of Birkenwald by gas suffocation in a special building constructed for the purpose. After the suffocation by gas the dead bodies were burnt.

At the end of February, 1943, four new crematoria were built, two large and two small, in the camp of Birkenau itself. The crematorium contains a large hall, a gas chamber and a furnace. People are assembled in the hall which holds 2,000 and gives the impression of a swimming-bath. They have to undress and are given a piece of soap and a towel as if they were going to the baths. Then they are crowded into the gas chamber which is hermetically sealed.

Several SS men in gas-masks then pour into the gas chamber through three openings in the ceiling a preparation of the poison gas megacyklon, which is made in Hamburg. At the end of three minutes all the persons are dead. The dead bodies are then taken away in carts to the furnace to be burnt. The furnace has nine chambers, each of them with four openings. Each opening will take three bodies at once. They are completely burnt after $1\frac{1}{2}$ hours. Thus each crematorium can burn 1,500 bodies daily. The crematoria can be recognised from the outside by their lofty chimneys.

On principle only Jews are put to death by gas, this only done to Aryans in exceptional cases. Aryans are shot with pistols on a special execution ground which lies between blocks 10 and 11 of Oswieczim camp. The first executions took place there in the summer of 1941 and reached their peak a year later when they were carried out by hundreds. Later when this aroused attention a large number of non-Jews who were condemned to death, were taken straight from the train to the execution ground and not entered on the lists of the camp.

According to careful calculations during the period from April, 1942, to April, 1944, from $1\frac{1}{2}$ to $1\frac{3}{4}$ million Jews were put to death by gas or in some other way, half of these being Polish Jews, other Jews from Holland, Greece, France, Belgium, Germany, Yugoslavia, Czechoslovakia, Italy, Norway, Lithuania, Austria and Jews of various other nationalities who were brought to Oswieczim from other camps in Poland.

About 90 per cent of the members of the transports arriving in Birkenau and Oswieczim were taken straight from the train to be put to death and about 10 per cent became inmates of the camp. Each of the new inmates was registered and received a number. In April, 1944, 180,000 persons in all had been registered as inmates of the camp, counting Jews and non-Jews together. Of the whole number who had arrived before there were only 34,000 in the camp at the beginning of April this year, 18,000 of them being non-Jews. (In both sources we have quoted this number includes the membership of both camps together.) The remainder had been killed by hard work, illness, especially epidemics of typhus and malaria, ill treatment, and finally 'selection'. Twice a week the camp doctor indicated persons destined for selection. Those selected were all gassed.

In a single block of Birkenau camp the average number of deaths a week was as much as 2,000, 1,200 of these being natural deaths and 800 'selection'. A special book entitled 'S.B. Sonderbehandelte' is kept dealing with the 'selected'. Notice of the deaths of the others is sent to the supreme commander of the camp at Oranienburg.

At the beginning of 1943 the 'political section (camp Gestapo) at Oswieczim received

500,000 forms for release. The governor had them all made out in the names of persons who had already been gassed and lodged them in the archives of the camp. Among the persons responsible for the savagery in both camps we must mention:

Hoess, governor of the camps, Untersturmfuehrer Schwarzhuber, director of the camp, the Tyrolese chief of the political department (Lagerfuehrer), Oberscharfuehrer Palitsch, Scharfuehrer Stiwett, SS-Scharfuehrer Wykleff, SS Mann Kler, the garrison doctor Wirt, the camp doctor Entrest.

In addition, professional criminals who have killed Jews in the camp:

Reich Germans Alexander Newmann, Albert Haemmerle, Rudi Ostringer, Rudi Berekert, Arno Boem, Zimmer and the political prisoners Alfred Kien and Alois Stahler.

Such, the Czechoslovak government informed the Foreign Office on July 4, was the contents of the two documents which it had just received. In addition, it explained, those who had managed to secure 'the transmission of the documents to a neutral country' had added both extra information, and a series of suggestions for action.

The added information was that 12,000 Jews were being deported daily from Ruthenia, Translyvania and the Kosice district 'where there used to be 320,000 Jews' and that those deported were being sent to Auschwitz, '5,000 going by train via Slovakia daily and 7,000 via Carpathian Ruthenia'.

There then followed the four suggestions for action which had been added to the Vrba-Wetzler report while it was on its way to Switzerland: that the Allied Governments should jointly address to the Hungarians and Germans 'a threat of reprisals directed at the Germans in the hands of these Governments'; that the crematoria at Auschwitz and Birkenau, 'which are recognizable by their high chimneys and watchtowers' should be bombed, together with the main railway lines connecting Slovakia and Ruthenia with Poland; that public warnings to the Germans and Hungarians 'should be repeated'; and that the Vatican 'should be requested to pronounce a severe public condemnation'.[1]

In a covering note to the Foreign Office, Hubert Ripka commented: 'Even if it should happen that the report is incorrect in a few concrete details for instance, if it exaggerates the number of victims in some cases,[2] it is indisputable that these terrible cruelties are being carried out wholesale, systematically, and on a deliberately organised plan'. To try to counter this, the Czech government would welcome 'a joint manifestation' by all the Allied Governments 'condemning these incredible savageries perpetrated by Nazi Germany upon the Jews', believing that it was necessary for the Allied Governments to 'utter an emphatic protest and a solemn warning to Hitler's government which is undoubtedly responsible through its organs for this organized perpetration of barbarous crime'.[3]

---

[1] 'Report on Conditions in the Concentration Camps of Oswiecim and Birkenau', Note No. 4951/duv/44 of the Czechoslovak Government, Foreign Office papers, 371/42809, WR 218, folio 44. The copy of this report as sent to the State Department is in United States National Archives, 840.48, Refugees 7/544, received by the War Refugee Board on 14 July 1944.

[2] The principal features of the Vrba-Wetzler report, the arrival of deportation trains at Auschwitz between March 1942 and April 1944, the gassing of the majority of the deportees on arrival, and the numbers gassed, are fully borne out by the facts and figures in Danuta Czech, 'Kalendarium der Ereignisse im Konzentrationslager Auschwitz-Birkenau', published in *Hefte von Auschwitz*: volume 3, Auschwitz 1960, volume 4, Auschwitz 1961, volume 6, Auschwitz 1962, and volumes 7 and 8, Auschwitz 1964.

[3] Foreign Office papers, 371/42809, WR 218, folio 35.

In summarizing the Ripka letter and enclosure for the purpose of its own internal discussions, the Foreign Office made no reference to the four suggestions for action added to the Vrba-Wetzler report itself. Instead, it focused on Ripka's personal proposal for an Allied protest, replying to the Czechs three weeks later that 'we share to the full their indignation at the treatment of Jews in these camps', and that Britain was taking, and 'will take' all practicable measures of rescue 'consistent with the successful prosecution of the war' while at the same time considering the question of 'a formal declaration by Allied Governments'.[1]

No mention was made in this reply of the request for reprisals, or for the bombing of the crematoria or main railway lines.

On July 5, the day after the summary of the Vrba-Wetzler report and the Polish Major's report had reached the Foreign Office, Anthony Eden was asked in the House of Commons by Sydney Silverman whether he had any information about the 'mass deportation of Jews now proceeding from Hungary to Poland for the purpose of massacre', and whether there were any steps 'which the United Nations can take to prevent in the moment of victory the total annihilation of European Jewry by Hitlerite Germany'.

In his reply, Eden stated that 'the German and Hungarian authorities have already begun these barbarous deportations', and that in the course of them 'many persons have been killed'. His answer continued:

. . . there are unfortunately no signs that the repeated declarations made by His Majesty's Government in association with the other United Nations of their intention to punish the instigators and perpetrators of these frightful crimes have moved the German Government and their Hungarian accomplices either to allow the departure of even a small proportion of their victims or to abate the fury of their persecution.

'The principal hope,' Eden added, 'of terminating this tragic state of affairs must remain the speedy victory of the Allied nations.'

Silverman went on to make a specific request of the British Government, asking Eden if 'any further appeal' could be made by the Allies 'not to the butcher gang now running German affairs, but to the Hungarian Government who, in the past, have not resorted to this sort of activity except under German pressure'. Might not such an appeal 'still be made?'

Eden had in fact told the War Cabinet two days before that he was against warnings 'to which we could not give effect', as this 'tended to reduce their value'.[2] But in his remarks to the House of Commons he limited himself to recalling Roosevelt's initiative of March 24 and his own declaration of March 30. 'I do not think we can add anything to that,' Eden said, 'although we shall, of course, use the BBC to bring home to the Hungarian Government the feelings of this House and the nation on the matter.'[3] Indeed, it was on that very same day, July 5, at Shertok's request, that the BBC broadcast the appeal from the International Transport Workers Federation to the Hungarian railway workers, urging them not to help in the transport of Jews to the death camps.

[1] Foreign Office papers, 371/42809, WR 218, draft by I. L. Henderson, folio 45.
[2] War Cabinet 85 of 1944, copy in Premier papers, 4/51/10, folio 1388.
[3] Hansard, 5 July 1944.

The deportations from central Hungary continued. But on the evening of July 4, Admiral Horthy told the German Minister, Veesenmayer, that he was being bombarded every day with telegrams, including messages, from the Vatican, the King of Sweden, and the President of the International Red Cross, urging him to stop the deportations.[1] On the following evening, July 5, the Hungarian Prime Minister, Sztojay, told Veesenmayer that his Government was being 'deluged' with telegrams; that the Papal Nuncio was calling on him 'several times' a day; and that the Turkish, Swiss and Spanish Governments had also urged an end to the deportations.

The Hungarian Prime Minister then read out to the German diplomat three telegrams, intercepted he said – but perhaps in reality they had been leaked, for these were the messages sent from Berne on June 26 by the British and United States Ministers – giving details of the Vrba-Wetzler report, including the information that a million and a half Jews had been killed at Auschwitz even before the start of the Hungarian deportations.

According to the Hungarian Prime Minister, there was another detail in the three telegrams which had upset the Hungarian Government: the proposal that the Allies should not only bomb the railway lines to Auschwitz, but that they should begin 'target bombing of all collaborating Hungarian and German agencies' in Budapest itself. According to Sztojay, this request for an Allied air attack on Budapest had actually included 'exact and correct street and house numbers in Budapest' of Hungarian and German institutions involved in the deportations, together with the names of seventy Hungarian and German individuals who were stated to be most directly involved in sending Jews from Hungary to Auschwitz.

Sztojay gave Veesenmayer the impression that the three Berne telegrams had frightened the Hungarian Government even more than the Papal and Swedish protests. One of the telegrams, he said, had asked for 'world-wide propaganda with detailed descriptions of the state of affairs'.[2] The Hungarian Government felt isolated and vulnerable. No German effort could protect Budapest from Allied air attack, or lessen the threat of guilt implied by the list of names. Clearly, the Allies might be in a position quite soon to exact the retribution which would be demanded, a fact which had been underlined by an unusually heavy American bomber attack on the marshalling yards of Budapest on July 2.

Despite the world-wide protests, on July 6 a total of 1,180 Jews were deported from the southern Hungarian city of Pecs to Auschwitz. But on that same day less than twenty-four hours after Sztojay's talk with Veesenmayer, the German Minister was summoned again to the Hungarian Prime Minister, and told that Horthy himself had ordered the deportations to be stopped.[3]

[1] Report of Veesenmayer to Ribbentrop, 6 July 1944, Nuremberg Trial Documents, NG 5684.
[2] Report of Veesenmayer to Berlin, 6 July 1944, Nuremberg Trial Documents, NG 5523.
[3] Report of Veesenmayer to Berlin, 6 July 1944, Nuremberg Trials Documents, NG 5523.

Chapter 28

'Get anything out of the Air Force you can'

On 6 July 1944 the Jewish Agency's two most senior representatives in London, Chaim Weizmann and Moshe Shertok, went to the Foreign Office to see Anthony Eden. The Agency's principal objective throughout this meeting was to accelerate the return of Brand to Budapest, and by this means to hold out at least some possibility of offering the Germans a deal for the rescue of the remaining Jews of Hungary. Nothing was known of Horthy's order to halt the deportations. Indeed, for another twelve days both the Allies and the Jewish Agency believed that the deportations were still in full force.

During their discussion Weizmann told Eden that originally he had thought 'that time might still be gained' for Hungarian Jewry. Now, however, he said, 'the catastrophe was right on them'. What he and the Jewish Agency hoped was that Brand would be allowed 'to go back' to Budapest. In addition, Weizmann told Eden, 'an offer had been made from the other side to one of their friends in Istanbul, Mr Bader, to go to Budapest, guaranteeing his safe return'. Weizmann suggested that 'it would be a good thing' if this second emissary, Menahem Bader, were to go to Budapest with Brand.

It was Moshe Shertok who stressed what he called the 'significant fact' of the Bader proposal. This showed, he said, 'that the matter was still alive, and that the Germans seemed prepared to strike a bargain'. Even if Brand was not allowed to return to Budapest, Bader 'should be allowed to proceed'. It might be a trap. But, on the other hand, 'all it might boil down to might be a question of money'. The Jewish Agency believed, Shertok told Eden, 'that if that was so, the ransom should be paid'.

Eden rejected, however, all idea of 'anything that looked like negotiating with the enemy'. It was, he said, 'too dangerous'. As for Brand, however, Eden now revealed that the British Government 'would be prepared to let him go back'. The problem was that 'Soviet consent was essential', and that was clearly not forthcoming.

Shertok replied that unless Brand could report to the Germans 'that there would be a meeting', there was 'little point in his returning', and he added: 'The Germans—at any rate that particular group—seemed anxious to meet, and the whole question was whether that desire of theirs could not be used as a lever for saving Jews'.

Eden confirmed that 'it was intended to put through the Protecting Power' certain proposals, such as the admission of 20,000 Jewish children into Switzerland, and 'a similar proposal' regarding Sweden, as well as the emigration of people on 'approved lists' to Palestine.

According to the Jewish Agency's own note of the interview, Weizmann then 'ran briefly through the other items' of an Aide-Memoire which he had brought with him, those items 'not connected with Joel Brand's mission'. Eden 'promised consideration', and was, as the note recorded, 'particularly impressed by the proposal that Marshal Stalin should be approached with a view to his issuing a warning to the Hungarians'.[1]

The Aide-Memoire from which Weizmann read, and which he left with Eden, comprised six paragraphs. The first was based on the reports that had been received from Geneva and Istanbul, and particularly the Krausz letter of June 19, and spoke of the deportation already of 400,000 'to the death-camps', of Birkenau itself, 'where there are four crematoriums with a capacity for gassing and burning 60,000 a day, and where, in the course of the last year, over 1,500,000 Jews from all over Europe are reported to have been killed'. The first paragraph ended: 'In and around Budapest there are still over 300,000 Jews awaiting their doom. According to the Istanbul message their deportation was to have started this week'.

The second paragraph of the Aide-Memoire stated that what is called 'the stage of temporising in the hope of prolonging the victims' lives' appeared to be over, and that 'some definite steps must immediately be taken' if what was described as 'the admittedly remote chance of saving Hungarian Jewry was 'not to be missed'.

The Jewish Agency realized, as the second paragraph expressed it, that its 'proposals for action' were 'unorthodox, and perhaps unprecedented'. They were, nevertheless, considered 'warranted by the present tragedy, which is also without parallel or precedent'.

There then followed the Jewish Agency's proposals, beginning with the one which had dominated the actual discussion with Eden and which had been at the centre of the Jewish Agency's request since Shertok's interview with Brand in Aleppo on June 12, more than three weeks before, that 'an intimation should be given to Germany that some appropriate body is ready to meet for discussing the rescue of Jews'. This proposal was elaborated in the Aide-Memoire as follows:

... a representative of the American War Refugee Board, if necessary seconded by a British official, should be ready to meet at Istanbul a member of the Nazi group in Budapest, to explore possibilities of rescue.

Joel Brand, and if only possible, his former escort, should be allowed to return to Hungary; Brand being authorized to inform the other side of the course that will have been decided upon.

The Jewish Agency could not abandon, perhaps it had no right to abandon, hope that a deal with the Gestapo was possible. That any Gestapo offer to release Jews 'must have ulterior motives—avowed or hidden' was, the Aide-Memoire stressed, fully appreciated. 'It was not however improbable,' it continued, 'that in the false hope of achieving these ends, they would be prepared to let out a certain number of Jews—large or small.' Hence the belief of the Agency that if it was in the last resort only a question of money, 'the ransom should be paid'.

The Jewish Agency's Aide-Memoire ended with a sixth paragraph,

[1] 'Note of Interview with the Right Hon. Anthony Eden, Foreign Office, Thursday, July 6th, 1944, at 3.15 p.m.', Secret, Central Zionist Archives, Z 4/14870.

setting out, 'apart from the question of Joel Brand's mission', five 'urgent suggestions'.

The first suggestion was that the Allies should publish a declaration 'expressing their readiness to admit Jewish fugitives to all their territories, and stating that they have in this the support of neutrals – Switzerland, Sweden, Spain and possibly Turkey – who were preparing to give 'temporary shelter' to Jewish refugees escaping 'massacres'.

The second suggestion was that the Swiss Government 'in particular' should be asked to instruct its representatives in Hungary that it was willing to allow Jewish refugees into Switzerland and would at the same time 'issue such documents to the largest possible number of people as might in the interim afford them some protection'.

The third Jewish Agency suggestion was that a 'stern warning to Hungarian officials, railwaymen, and the population in general, be published and broadcast, to the effect that anyone convicted of having taken part in the rounding-up, deportation and extermination of Jews will be considered to be a war criminal and treated accordingly'.

It was the fourth proposal in the Jewish Agency Aide-Memoire which had impressed Eden. This was that Stalin should be approached 'to issue a similar warning to Hungary on part of the Soviet Union'.

The fifth and final Jewish Agency request was a brief but positive one: 'that the railway line leading from Budapest to Birkenau, and the death-camps at Birkenau and other places, should be bombed'.[1]

Towards the end of their discussion, referring to this last point, Eden told Weizmann and Shertok that 'as regards bombing', he had 'already got in touch with the Air Ministry about the bombing of the death camps. He would now add the suggestion about bombing the railway'.

The meeting was about to end. As one last point, Weizmann told Eden of what he believed to be 'the one conclusion to be drawn from the whole tragedy; to create a state of things which would soon make its recurrence impossible'. Here was the nub of the Zionist case: the need for a Jewish self-governing authority in its own land. 'He hoped,' Weizmann said, 'that an opportunity would soon present itself of discussing this aspect of the problem with Mr Eden.'[2]

The Weizmann-Shertok-Eden interview was over. In sending an account of it to Churchill that same day, Eden reported Weizmann's appeal 'that we should do something to mitigate the appalling slaughter of Jews in Hungary'. Eden added that according to the Jewish Agency's 'information', 60,000 Jews a day were being 'gassed and burnt at the death camp of Birkenau', and he commented: 'This may well be an exaggeration'. It was indeed an exaggeration, the result of a telegraphic error: for Mordowicz-Rosin and Krausz had both accurately reported a daily death toll of 12,000.

Nevertheless, Eden raised with Churchill three of the suggestions which Weizmann had made following their discussion of the Brand mission, informing Churchill that Weizmann 'recognized that there was little His

[1] 'Aide-Memoire', Central Zionist Archives, Z 4/14870.
[2] 'Note of Interview . . .', Central Zionist Archives, Z 4/14870.

Majesty's Government could do', but suggesting that something might be done 'to stop the operation of this death camp' by bombing the railway lines to it, and to 'similar camps', and also by bombing the camps themselves 'so as to destroy the plant used for gassing and cremation'.

Eden told Churchill that the idea of bombing the railway lines had 'already been considered',[1] but that he had told Weizmann 'that I would now re-examine it and the further suggestions of bombing the camps themselves'. Eden told Churchill: 'I am in favour of acting on both suggestions'.

Weizmann had suggested that 'a greater impression might be made upon the obduracy of the Hungarians' if Stalin were to issue a warning to them 'couched in the strongest terms', and Eden added:

I told Dr Weizmann that I would consider this suggestion. I am in favour of it. You will remember that the Soviet Government joined His Majesty's Government and the United States Government in 1942 in a declaration condemning similar atrocities and pledging themselves to exact retribution. The most appropriate form of approach would, I think, be a message from yourself to Marshal Stalin. Would you be willing to do this?

Eden also told Churchill of Weizmann's suggestion that Menahem Bader should be allowed to visit Hungary, and of his own dislike of anything 'which might be interpreted as negotiation with the enemy'. Moreover, Eden told Churchill, 'there would be no hope of inducing Marshal Stalin to make the proposed declaration if he suspected that we were in contact with the enemy behind his back'.[2]

As soon as Churchill read Eden's minute, he replied with support both for the bombing proposals, and for the appeal to Stalin, but rejecting any follow-up of the Brand mission. His minute to Eden, dated July 7, read:

Is there any reason to raise these matters at the Cabinet? You and I are in entire agreement. Get anything out of the Air Force you can, and invoke me if necessary. Certainly appeal to Stalin. On no account have the slightest negotiations, direct or indirect, with the Huns. By all means bring it up if you wish to, but I do not think it is necessary.[3]

Effectively, from this Churchill minute of June 7, the Brand mission, on which the Jewish Agency had, throughout almost the whole period of the actual deportations, put its principal hopes, was in eclipse, though not yet formally discarded. But there still remained the proposed Allied declaration on 'temporary shelter', the issuing of 'protection' documents by the Swiss, the stern warnings to the Hungarians, the 'similar' Soviet warnings, and the bombing proposals, in that order, of the Jewish Agency's Aide-Memoire.

The priority of documents and certificates over bombing can easily be understood. It was by means of Palestine certificates and foreign passports that, over the past four years, several thousand Jews had been rescued from Nazi-occupied Europe, by a process, as those who worked in the Palestine

---

[1] Both in his discussion, and in his report of it to Churchill, Eden referred to a previous British consideration of the bombing request. But, so far, neither my own researches in the archives of the Prime Minister, the Foreign Office or the Air Ministry, nor the researches of others, have found any other reference to what was meant by this, or what, if anything, had been already done.

[2] Foreign Secretary's Minute, P.M. 44/501, Premier papers, 4/51/10, folios 1365–7.

[3] Prime Minister's Personal Minute, M 800/4, Premier papers, 4/51/10.

Offices in Geneva or Bucharest have confirmed, at once slow, frustrating, and rewarding. Thus on July 6, the very day of the Aide-Memoire, Chaim Barlas was able to telegraph from Istanbul to Jerusalem: 'exchange transport 283 refugees from Holland arrived, including 222 from concentration camp Bergen-Belsen, and 61 from Vittel. Leaving tonight by train for Palestine'.[1]

These were, of course, 'legal' immigrants as far as the British were concerned, some because they were Palestinian subjects who had been caught in Europe at the outbreak of war, others because they were in possession of valid certificates. All of them were being exchanged for a group of German civilians who had been living in Palestine at the outbreak of war.[2]

One of those who was exchanged, Rosine de Jong, subsequently recalled several episodes of the train journey from Belsen to Istanbul, dominated by the meeting in Vienna with Hungarian Jews going in the opposite direction. She also recalled how even the Red Cross men did not want to talk to the Jews for fear of becoming contaminated with disease, and walked around with gloved hands. Then there was the arrival in Turkey with the festive meal offered by the Turks, after which everyone became ill: their first shower, the white bread, offered them in Syria in a British army camp, the train entering Palestine with everyone glued to the windows and, at the end, the train blowing its whistle all along its way in Palestine, with hundreds of people standing near the rails, throwing flowers.[3]

The 283 'exchangees', the first to be allowed out of Nazi Europe since November 1942, reached Haifa four days after leaving Istanbul. Joshua Behar, the Secretary of the Immigration Department of the Jewish Agency, who met the group when they reached Haifa, noted in his report of their arrival: 'The whole group made a very pathetic impression. All the people lack weight and strength. Signs of great suffering in the past are visible on their faces. No less than 80 people were found ill and 40 were in need of hospital treatment. All suffer from undernourishment. The impression is terrible'.[4]

Ironically, Allied air power had almost prevented this train of refugees from leaving Europe, for at the Bulgarian border the railway line had been attacked 'by an Allied bomber formation'.[5]

Churchill's minute of July 7 had given Eden the authority to follow up two of the Jewish Agency's requests, the bombing of Auschwitz, and the Stalin declaration. Eden at once took action on both. To the Secretary of State for Air, Sir Archibald Sinclair, he wrote on July 7, his letter marked 'Secret' and 'Immediate', of his meeting with Weizmann on the previous day. Weizmann had brought him, he said, 'further information' about the 'appal-

---

[1] Central Zionist Archives, S 25/1678.

[2] Among the Jews who had been released from Belsen and Vittel was Dr Max Plaut, the last President of the Hamburg Jewish Community; Gertrud Van Tijn, a veteran Zionist from Holland who had been active in helping German refugees in Holland between 1933 and 1940; Rabbi Lazar Duenner, a former Rabbi in Cologne and then Chief Rabbi of Amsterdam; Jacob von Belitz, a Dutch Socialist leader; Ignatz Bergenthal, a German banker and economist; and Professor Albert Levkovitz, a teacher at the Breslau Rabbinical Seminary.

[3] Recollections communicated by Rosine de Jong's nephew, Yaacov Yannay, letter to the author, 23 June 1980.

[4] 'A Note in Connection with the Group of Immigrants Who Arrived Under the Exchange Scheme', Central Zionist Archives, Z 4/15136.

[5] Jewish Telegraphic Agency report, printed in its Daily News Bulletin, 12 July 1944.

ling persecution' of Jews in Hungary, 'the main point of which was that, according to these reports 400,000 Hungarian Jews had already been deported to what he called "death camps" at Birkenau in Upper Silesia. . . .' Eden's letter continued:

Dr Weizmann admitted that there seemed to be little enough that we could do to stop these horrors, but he suggested, *and both the Prime Minister and I are in agreement with his suggestion,* that something might be done to stop the operation of the death camps by

(1) bombing the railways lines leading to Birkenau (and to any other similar camps if we get to hear of them); and

(2) bombing the camps themselves with the object of destroying the plant used for gassing and burning.

I should add that I told Weizmann that, as you may know, we had already considered suggestion (1) above that I would re-examine it and also the further suggestion of bombing the camps themselves.

'Could you let me know,' Eden asked Sinclair, 'how the Air Ministry view the feasibility of these proposals?' and he added: 'I very much hope that it will be possible to do something. I have the authority of the Prime Minister to say that he agrees.'[1]

Eden's letter had been drafted for him by A. E. Walker. Before signing the draft, Eden deleted the phrase in italics. Also deleted were the words 'some time soon' in the sentence, 'Could you let me know *some time soon* how the Air Ministry view the feasibility of these proposals?'[2]

Also on July 7, Eden prepared a draft of a personal message to be sent from Churchill to Stalin. The draft was based entirely upon the points which the Jewish Agency had wished the British Government to make. The draft began by recalling the inter-Allied Declaration of 17 December 1942, which had drawn attention 'to the bestial measures of extermination' being applied by the Germans to the Jews under their control, and 'solemnly affirming that those responsible for these crimes should not escape retribution'. The draft continued, as if in Churchill's words:

In spite of an unbroken series of military reverses during the past two years and the certainty of final defeat the Germans are in no way desisting from their barbarous treatment of the Jews. Indeed the contrary would appear to be the case. All our information goes to show that since the Germans occupied Hungary measures of gassing and burning have been applied with ever-increasing ferocity by the Germans and that the Hungarians are collaborating as willing accomplices in these outrages. As a result appeals are frequently made to H.M. Government to issue some further declaration condemning these crimes.

It has occurred to me that, given the victorious advance of the Soviet armies, a declaration by your Government couched in terms of unambiguous frankness and proclaiming that the Soviet Armies and retribution for these crimes would enter Hungary together, might have the effect of at least reducing the scale of these horrible outrages against the Jewish population.[3]

The instruction to the Air Ministry to report on the feasibility of bombing both the railways to Auschwitz, and the camp itself, and the draft message to Stalin, were both dated July 7. They had thus both been put in hand within twenty-four hours of Weizmann's request, and on the same day that Churchill

---

[1] Air Ministry papers, 19/218.
[2] Draft in Foreign Office papers, 371/42809, WR 276/10/9, Folio 141.
[3] Draft in Premier papers, 4/51/10, folio 1359.

had given them his explicit approval. More than that, Churchill had been so aware of the urgency as to tell Eden to by-pass the Cabinet. Nor, in the context of the wider war, was this a period free from anxiety for Britain, or for Churchill. On July 6, the day of the Weizmann-Shertok interview with Eden, Churchill himself had announced in the House of Commons a total of 2,752 British civilian dead in flying bomb raids since mid-June, a period of only three weeks.[1] Throughout July 6, 7 and 8, the overriding priority had been to release the Allied army from the Normandy beachhead. One month and three days after the Normandy landings, both Caen and St Lô, at the perimeter of the landings, were still in German hands. It was to be another week and a half before St Lô was captured and the Allied forces were capable of making any substantial advance into France.

[1] Hansard, 6 July 1944.

Chapter 29

'The biggest outcry possible'

Not only bombing, but also documents, continued to trouble the Jewish Agency leaders. On July 7 Moshe Shertok went to the Colonial Office to urge, as 'the most helpful way of protecting some at any rate' of the surviving Hungarian Jews, some 'fictitious device' whereby they might be regarded, for the purpose of rescue, 'as Palestinian citizens', without, Shertok hastened to add, becoming Palestinian citizens 'for permanency'.

To offer this fictitious citizenship, Shertok added, 'would of course be completely unorthodox', but the position of these Hungarian Jews 'was a tragedy without parallel'. To encourage the British to agree to the device, the Jewish Agency would give a written undertaking 'that no claim to full Palestinian citizenship would be made' on the strength of any such document. It was possible, Shertok said, that the Hungarian Government 'would refuse to accept' the Palestinian citizenship, 'but it might be tried'.

The Colonial Office did not reject Shertok's proposal out of hand. Sir George Gater, the Permanent Under-Secretary of State, 'recognized', as the minutes recorded, 'the desperate situation', and understood that what the Jewish Agency wanted 'was some kind of document which would appear to be a document of Palestinian citizenship but which could really be a fake, and could be acknowledged as such once the present emergency was passed'. Gater did not 'rule out' this proposal in advance, and undertook to give it 'sympathetic consideration'. Shertok stressed that 'speed was essential'.[1]

Within three weeks, however, the British Government had turned down the proposal, as well as a further proposal emanating from non-Jewish circles, that the protective device of British citizenship should be tried. Speaking in the House of Commons on July 28, a Conservative MP, Squadron Leader Fleming, asked the Foreign Secretary if he would 'consider the advisability' of granting British nationality 'to the remaining Jews in Nazi-occupied territory' on similar terms to the offer of common nationality which had been made to the French people in 1940, 'in order to maintain their morale and to help them in their struggle for freedom from destruction'. But the Parliamentary Under-Secretary of State, George Hall, replied that the British Government was 'convinced' that to give 'what in fact would be merely verbal British protection would bring no advantages to Jewish individuals in German-occupied territories'. Hall added: 'Although the Germans have specially attacked Jews, they have also attacked and murdered many thousands of non-Jews (in Poland the proportions are said to be about equal)'.[2]

---

[1] 'Record of Discussions with members of the Jewish Agency at the Colonial Office on the 7th July, 1944', Colonial Office papers, 733/462.

[2] Hansard, 28 July 1944. This line of reasoning was not new (see page 208).

Eden's two directives, on the Auschwitz bombing and the Soviet declaration, had both been issued on July 7. On the following day, the last mass deportation from Hungary took place.

Auschwitz itself was still receiving transports from elsewhere. But these other deportations were not yet known to the Jewish Agency, and it was to be another six weeks before they were put forward as a reason for bombing the railways or the camp. Meanwhile, on July 8, the fourth Allied photographic reconnaissance of Monowitz took place. Sixteen of the photographs showed, as was intended, the I.G. Farben complex, but only its eastern part.[1] One photograph alone again included part of Auschwitz I, just as the cameras were about to be switched off.[2] But once again, there was no intelligence commentary for anything but Monowitz.

The ending of the Hungarian deportations after July 8 was still not known in the west. Indeed, on that same day, a member of the State Department, Fletcher Warren, in conversation with a member of the British Embassy in Washington about the Swiss 'protection' documents and the Brand mission, remarked that despite a first payment to the Nazis by Hungarian Jewry, the deportations had continued, 'and these were still going on'. Warren added: 'It had been the hope of all concerned that by keeping the door open and by not turning down these proposals out of hand we were holding position and to that extent benefiting Jews in question. Information received however did not support this hope'.[3]

Some of that information was circulated by the War Refugee Board on July 8. It consisted of a report from the American Minister in Sweden, Herschel V. Johnson, that according to 'evidence reaching the Swedish Foreign Office', the Hungarian deportees 'are now being killed *en masse*, many of them by means of a gas chamber across the Hungarian frontier in Poland'. Johnson reported that according to the Swedish Foreign Ministry spokesman:

. . . people of all ages, children, women and men, are transported to this isolated spot in box cars packed like sardines and that upon arrival many are already dead.

Those who have survived the trip are stripped naked, given a small square object which resembles a piece of soap and told that at the bath house they must bathe themselves. The 'bath house' does in fact look like a big bathing establishment, being a large building built by the Germans. Into a large room with a total capacity of two thousand packed together closely the victims are pushed. No regard is given to sex or age and all are completely naked.

When the atmosphere of the hall has been heated by this mass of bodies a fine powder is let down over the whole area by opening a contraption in the ceiling. When the heated atmosphere comes in contact with this powder a poisonous gas is formed which kills all occupants of the room.

Trucks then take out the bodies, and burning follows.[4]

This report was not made public. But it was made available by the War Refugee Board to all United States Government departments, as part of the Board's weekly confidential summary of events in Europe, and in due course

---

[1] Mission 325–72. Can B8803. Scale 1:59,000. Strategic Bombing Survey, Record Group 243.
[2] As above, Exposure 5015. There are right and left oblique views of the same area in Exposures 1016 and 2016.
[3] Viscount Halifax, telegram No. 3682. Copy in Premier papers, 4/51/10.
[4] War Refugee Board, Confidential Weekly Report for 3 to 8 July 1944.

a copy even reached Churchill's desk, sent to him, not by the War Refugee Board, the State Department, or Roosevelt, but by his own son, Randolph, who had been shown it by chance more than a month and a half later.[1]

Churchill himself continued to watch over the process of the initiatives which he had supported, minuting on July 8, to Eden, about the draft message to Stalin:

Are you aiming at a tripartite declaration by Britain, the United States and Russia, or are you aiming at a British declaration to be supported by a Russian declaration; or are you aiming at a Russian declaration to be supported by a British declaration? This is not clear to me from your paper.

I will support any of these solutions, but I think they ought to go through you to Molotov rather than from me direct.

'I am entirely in accord,' Churchill added, 'with making the biggest outcry possible.'[2]

In answer to Churchill's question, Pierson Dixon wrote to John Martin on July 8: 'Mr Eden feels that H.M. Government have made so many declarations condemning German atrocities against the Jews that there would be little use in making another one on this occasion, and that a Russian declaration by itself would be more likely to have effect'.[3]

Churchill continued to press his advisers for action on the various Jewish Agency requests with which he had been involved. On July 10, only a week after the War Cabinet's decision to examine 'carefully' the idea of setting up a Jewish Brigade Group, Churchill pressed the Cabinet Secretary for an early decision. 'I certainly understood,' he wrote, 'and hold very strongly the view that a brigade group should be made. . . . The matter must therefore be set down for an early meeting of the War Cabinet this week, and the Secretary of State for War should be warned of my objection.'[4]

Another area in which Churchill intervened during the second week of July was the dispute which had arisen over the thirty-two Hungarian Jews who had bought their freedom and been flown from Hungary to Lisbon. On July 8 a telegram from Sir Ronald Campbell, the British Ambassador in Lisbon, had warned of the State Department's fear that the arrival of these Hungarian Jews 'is a German move to plant suspicion in Soviet minds', suspicions concerning a separate peace between Germany and the western Allies.[5] But Churchill dismissed the State Department's apprehension out of hand, writing to Eden on July 10:

Surely this only means that these poor devils have, at the cost of 90 per cent of their worldly possessions handed over in useful condition, procured an opportunity to escape from the butcheries to which their fellow-countrymen are doomed.

As to para 3 of Campbell's telegram the only suspicion planted in my mind is that some of these German murderers have lined their pockets well with a view to their future. I presume

[1] This report was given personally by Randolph Churchill to his father on 26 August 1944. No copy had been sent earlier to the Prime Minister or to his Office.

[2] Prime Minister's Personal Minute, M 806/4, Premier papers, 4/51/10, folio 1357.

[3] Premier papers, 4/51/10, folio 1341.

[4] Prime Minister's Personal Minute, C 45/4.

[5] Sir R. Campbell, telegram No. 3685, copy in Premier papers, 4/51/10, folio 1329.

you will discount any far-fetched Russian suspicions by telling them all about it, and even possibly mentioning the kind of interpretation I put upon this action. It is a naked piece of blackmail on threats of murder.[1]

Even the Brand proposals had not entirely disappeared from the area of British policy discussion following Churchill's minute of July 7. Three days later Churchill's secretariat set out for him, at his own request, a note on the Foreign Office view of 'what reply should be made to the German proposals', and of the use of Brand to take back a message to Hungary to the effect 'that the Allies were conveying their views through the Protecting Power'. Commenting on this, Churchill's secretariat pointed out that while it was indeed true that the Brand proposals, if taken up, would amount 'to indirect negotiation with the enemy', it was nevertheless 'quite usual to negotiate with the enemy through the Protecting Power', as had been done in arranging exchanges of prisoners of war. 'It has even been done in other instances,' Churchill was told, 'with the object of getting Jews out of German hands.'

Churchill's Secretariat added, however, that the Foreign Office view was somewhat different: not only did the Foreign Office 'not feel strongly' about the approach through the Protecting Power, but it had 'mainly been keeping the ball in play because of the dangers of a point-blank refusal, and the continual clamour of Jews in London'.

'You may feel,' the note ended, 'that in any case it is illogical to negotiate with the Germans and at the same time to threaten them with dire consequences if they use their only pawn in the game.'[2]

On July 11 Churchill finally made up his mind to reject the Jewish Agency's idea of using Brand to begin negotiations with the Germans through the Protecting Power. His minute to Eden read in full:

There is no doubt that this is probably the greatest and most horrible crime ever committed in the whole history of the world, and it has been done by scientific machinery by nominally civilized men in the name of a great State and one of the leading races of Europe. It is quite clear that all concerned in this crime who may fall into our hands, including the people who only obeyed orders by carrying out the butcheries, should be put to death after their association with the murders has been proved.

I cannot therefore feel that this is the kind of ordinary case which is put through the Protecting Power as, for instance, the lack of feeding or sanitary conditions in some particular prisoners' camp. There should therefore in my opinion be no negotiations of any kind on this subject. Declarations should be made in public, so that everyone connected with it will be hunted down and put to death.

The project which has been put forward through a very doubtful channel seems itself also to be of the most nondescript character. I would not take it seriously.[3]

The Jewish Agency, however, still had hopes that the Brand mission could be revived, and Jewish lives saved as a result of indirect negotiations between the Allies and the Germans. In an effort to set the mission in motion again, the Jewish Agency Executive decided to approach President Roosevelt direct. It was their first effort to do so. The telegram, sent on July 11, through the United States Consul-General in Jerusalem, spoke of a proposal 'received by

[1] Prime Minister's Personal Minute, M 818/4, Top Secret, Premier papers, 4/51/10, folio 1331.
[2] Premier papers, 4/51/10, folios 1346–8.
[3] Prime Minister's Personal Minute, M 844/4, Foreign Office papers, 371/42809, WR 274.

this Agency emanating from apparently influential enemy sources at Budapest indicating Nazi readiness release one million Hungarian Rumanian Jews on certain conditions known to State Department, and proposing negotiations to that end'.

The Jewish Agency telegram informed Roosevelt of Brand's detention in Cairo, and went on to plead that whereas 'war exigencies' were clearly the 'prime consideration', Roosevelt should nevertheless 'not allow this unique and possibly last chance of saving remnant European Jewry' to be lost.

Even if 'some doubts' could be entertained about the Brand proposal 'in its present form', the Jewish Agency went on, 'we would urgently and respectfully submit that door should not be closed and that suitable arrangements be made [to] discuss proposal with representatives of enemy group from which it emanated'.

The Jewish Agency then asked Roosevelt to give his support to the proposals which it had already submitted to the British Government: 'firstly, immediate intimation to other side, through appropriate channels, of readiness to nominate representative to discuss rescue and transfer largest possible number Jews', combined with a further intimation to the 'other side' that the 'preliminary condition' to any discussion was the 'immediate discontinuation' of the deportations.[1]

In a second telegram from Jerusalem on July 11, the Jewish Agency asked Roosevelt to follow up the Brand proposals by allowing representatives of the War Refugee Board to meet 'members of Budapest group' in Istanbul, to enable Brand to 'return immediately' to Budapest, and to 'carry with him decision readiness to negotiate'.

If waiting for such an Allied decision would delay Brand's return, he should still be sent back 'immediately', the Jewish Agency suggested, 'and be instructed to report to the other side that he had delivered his message, that it was under consideration in the highest quarters, and that early action would follow'.[2]

The Jewish Agency Executive's telegrams to Roosevelt made no mention of bombing, or of any other measure than the return of Brand to Budapest with a positive offer. In London, however, the Jewish Agency had prepared a 'Note on the Proposal For Bombing the Death Camps'. The Note gave details of the working of the gas chambers at Auschwitz, and added that all the information available pointed 'to the fact that deportees are put to death immediately on arrival'. Enclosed with the Note was a Jewish Telegraphic Agency report, emanating from Czechoslovak underground sources, and already given by the Czechoslovak Government-in-Exile to the British Government a week before, which contained an appeal to the Allies to bomb the Auschwitz crematoria, 'easily recognisable by their chimney and watchtowers', and the railway lines from Slovakia and Ruthenia into Poland, 'especially the bridge at Cop'.[3] But all the details of deportation in the report referred to the period of late May, and June, when the eastern Hungarian deportations were actually in progress. The aim of the appeal was to save

---

[1] Jerusalem telegram No. 97, United States National Archives, 840.48, Refugees/7-1144.
[2] Central Zionist Archives, S 25/1682.
[3] Central Zionist Archives, Z 4/14870.

Jews who had in fact already been murdered. It had reached the Jewish Telegraphic Agency at least a month too late.

In its Note of July 11, the Jewish Agency gave as its opinion that the bombing of the death camps was 'hardly likely to achieve the salvation of the victims to any appreciable extent'. Indeed, it added, the physical effects of the bombing could only be 'the destruction of plant and personnel, and possibly the hastening of the end of those already doomed'.

The dislocation of 'the German machinery for systematic wholesale murder' might however, the Note continued, cause delay in the execution of the remaining 300,000 Jews still in Hungary, and this 'in itself is valuable as far as it goes, but it may not go very far, as other means of extermination can be quickly improvised'.

According to the Jewish Agency's Note, the 'main purpose' of the bombing of Auschwitz 'should be its many-sided and far-reaching moral effect'.

The Note went on to explain what this moral effect would be:

It would mean, in the first instance, that the Allies waged direct war on the extermination of the victims of Nazi oppression—today Jews, tomorrow Poles, Czechs, or whatever race may become the victim of mass murder during the German retreat and collapse.

Secondly, it would give the lie to the oft-repeated assertions of Nazi spokesmen that the Allies are not really so displeased with the work of the Nazis in ridding Europe of Jews.

Thirdly, it would go far toward dissipating the incredulity which still persists in Allied quarters with regard to the reports of mass extermination perpetrated by the Nazis.

Fourthly, it would give weight to the threats of reprisals against the murderers by showing that the Allies are taking the extermination of Jews so seriously as to warrant the allocation of aircraft resources to this particular operation, and thus have a deterrent effect.

Lastly, it would convince the German circles still hopeful of Allied mercy of the genuineness of Allied condemnation of the murder of the Jews, and possibly result in some internal pressure against a continuation of the massacres. The first report that the R.A.F. or the American Air Force had bombed the death camps in Upper Silesia is bound to have a demonstrative value in all these directions.

The Jewish Agency's Note of July 11 ended by drawing 'special attention' to the fact mentioned in the Czech report, 'that the Oswiecim camp contains workshops of the German armament concerns Siemens and Krupp'.[1]

On July 11 the BBC broadcast a formidable warning to all those involved in the deportation of Jews to the death camps. The speaker was Professor Lindley Fraser, the leading BBC news commentator in its broadcasts to Germany. During the last month, he said, 'the persecution of the Jews, that most loathsome outcrop of national socialist ideology, has entered upon a new phase. This time the scene is Hungary'. And he went on to tell of reports that 'no less than 400,000 Jews, men and women, old people and young children were deported to a concentration camp in Poland', where they were subjected 'to treatment by one of those technical innovations of which Hitler is so proud—the gas chamber'.

Lindley Fraser went on to say that there were still 350,000 Jews left in Hungary, but the 'present German and Hungarian rulers of Hungary have now decided that they too are to be deported to Poland for death by gassing'. This policy, he added, had aroused 'the disgust and execration of the world'. His broadcast ended:

[1] Central Zionist Archives, Z 4/14870.

What the National Socialists are today proposing to do in Hungary is of course only the continuation of what they have already done, on an even larger scale, in Poland itself. We know the kind of people these men are who order and carry out such a policy. But let them be warned. Everybody who takes part in these murders will be called to account and made to suffer the full penalty for his crimes.

And let him also ask himself whether the last stage of a war which is already lost is a good time in which to brand himself as a war criminal and a murderer.

I issue this warning to *all* concerned—whether soldier or civilian, initiator or executant, German or Hungarian. Let them take heed. Those who carry out the National Socialist policy of exterminating the Jews will have no place in the world of the future.[1]

In Jerusalem, it was the Brand mission which still held its priority in the policy of the Jewish Agency. On July 13 Ben Gurion himself telegraphed to Shertok that the Berlin Foreign Office had 'sent urgent instructions' for Brand's substitute, Menahem Bader, to be found, and flown to Berlin on the weekly flight, leaving on July 8. As he had not been found, he was now expected on the July 15 flight. Bader himself had commented that the Germans still did not seem to be aware that he was both a Jew and an enemy subject, holding as he did a Palestinian passport.

In his telegram of July 13, Ben Gurion asked Shertok: 'Please communicate immediately Bader latest decision'.[2] His telegram crossed with one from London, also sent on July 13, in which Shertok reported: 'Joel affair still subject inter-allied consultations'.[3] That same day a War Refugee Board memorandum noted that although most of the various 'large scale and fantastic' proposals for saving the Jews of Hungary were 'of dubious reliability', nevertheless the policy of the Board was 'to avoid the outright rejection of any one of these, in the hope that some valid and acceptable proposal might be received'.[4]

But also on July 13, in London, the War Cabinet's refugee Committee heard from the Foreign Office representative, A. W. G. Randall, that a report had just been received which showed that 'the approach by Brand and Gross' had been intended, not to rescue Jews, but 'as cover for a separate peace intrigue'. The object of the Gestapo had been to put forward 'vague hints of peace proposals' which might 'embarrass' Britain with the Soviet Union.

Commenting on this information, Eden said it confirmed the refugee Committee's earlier suspicion that the Brand proposals were 'a mere trap'.

The question then arose as to the attitude of the United States. According to Sir Herbert Emerson, even the Chairman of the War Refugee Board, John W. Pehle, 'had shown himself alive to the danger that the Germans might play the card of offering an unmanageable number of refugees to the United Nations'. Emerson added, however, that the American Government was under 'great pressure from the Jews' of America, so much so that he had heard it said that an 'unfavorable response' to the Brand proposals 'might even cost the Administration the vote of New York State'.

[1] 'Sonderbericht, Room 407, Hungarian Jews', BBC Written Archives Centre.
[2] Central Zionist Archives, S 25/1682. For Bader's own account, see Menahem Bader, *Sad Missions*, Tel Aviv 1979.
[3] Central Zionist Archives, S 25/1678.
[4] 'Summary of Steps Taken by War Refugee Board with Respect to the Jews of Hungary', War Refugee Board, Box 33, Measures Directed Towards Halting Persecutions in Hungary, No. 1.

In conclusion, the refugee Committee agreed that either the Germans 'or the Jews themselves' might at any moment make the as yet secret story into a public one, 'to our disadvantage'. It was however agreed that the British Government should 'lay aside entirely the idea of any kind of negotiations, whether direct or indirect. . . .'[1]

The British were continually being made aware of Russian suspicions. Only two days after this decision, the British Ambassador in Moscow, Sir Archibald Clark Kerr, wrote to Eden, in a personal letter, that the former Soviet Ambassador to London, Ivan Maisky, had complained about the pace of the Normandy advance, implying that the western Allies were 'short of punch'. Maisky's 'other fear', the Ambassador reported, 'was that we would be gentle with the Germans when the time came. This feeling is fairly widespread and will need watching'.[2]

The Jewish Agency persevered in an attempt to by-pass the Brand and Bader stalemate, despite the British Government's clear unwillingness to authorize even the most indirect of negotiations between Britain and the Nazis. On July 14 Shertok telegraphed to Ben Gurion: 'Foreign Office has vetoed Bader's going', but went on to suggest that Dr G. G. Kullmann, a Swiss citizen, and Sir Herbert Emerson's 'deputy' in the Inter-Governmental Committee on Refugees, 'should be asked to go to Budapest provided facilities from other side forthcoming, with view to exploring possibilities'.[3]

In a letter to the Foreign Office on July 14, Shertok stressed that in the view of the Jewish Agency, the latest message received from Istanbul 'goes to my mind a long way to show that the matter is still alive, and that the Germans have something to propose and are ready to discuss things'. This feeling, Shertok went on, 'adds considerable weight to our suggestion about Mr Kullmann's mission to Budapest'.[4]

The Foreign Office dismissed the Jewish Agency's hopes. 'Of course,' noted Ian Henderson, 'the Germans (or at least high Gestapo circles) wish to keep the matter alive as a means of pretending to negotiate peace, or in fact to put out peace feelers, and to divide us from the Russians.'[5]

Although no further deportations took place from Hungary after July 8, several trains which had earlier set off from Hungary continued on their way. Two reached Auschwitz on July 8, one on July 9, three on July 10 and the last two on July 11. From most of these trains, only two or three individuals were sent to the barracks, and the remaining four or five thousand were gassed: a total death toll of more than 30,000 in only four days.

The Jewish Agency's Aide-Memoire of July 6 had asked the Allies to declare their readiness 'to admit Jewish fugitives to all their territories', and to declare that they had 'the support of neutrals' in this. On July 15 Sir Hughe Knatchbull-Hugessen, in a telegram from Ankara, informed the Foreign Office that, 'in

---

[1] War Cabinet Committee on the Reception and Accommodation of Refugees, 13 July 1944, Cabinet papers, 95/15.
[2] Foreign Office papers, 800/302, folio 106.
[3] Foreign Office papers, 371/42809, WR 238, folio 70.
[4] Foreign Office papers, 371/42809, WR 238, folio 67.
[5] Foreign Office papers, 371/42809, WR 238, folio 66.

virtue of authority in your telegram No. 842 I have just informed the President of the Council in writing that all Jewish refugees reaching Turkey will forthwith be given entry visas to Palestine'. There was, however, in the Ambassador's view, the danger, as he reported it, that the Turks would think 'that we regarded mass influx as in prospect. This would frighten them and would be liable to set the clock back rather than to advance matters'. For this reason, he would mention only 'incidentally' the British Government's previous intimation 'of readiness to help with food or money if necessary. . . .', reserving any 'more formal assurance until such time, if ever, as a mass influx seems to be imminent'.[1]

When A. L. Easterman, of the World Jewish Congress, wrote to George Hall at the Foreign Office on July 15 to suggest a warning by Churchill, Roosevelt and Stalin, 'calling on the peoples of the occupied countries to protect the Jews', Ian Henderson persuaded Hall to give a negative answer. 'In view of the apparent change in the Jewish policy of the Hungarian Govt,' Henderson wrote, 'it would be hardly politic in the interests of the Jews themselves to pursue this idea at the moment,' and he added: 'The Soviets have always been reluctant to get mixed up in Jewish affairs. . . .'[2]

On July 18 the synthetic oil and rubber plant at Monowitz was designated a target for the first time, following the careful scrutiny of the four earlier photographic missions. It was to be just over a month before the first bombing raid, but the lines were now laid down for just what should be attacked. First, the target was located two miles east 'of the centre of Oswiecim', adjacent to a sparsely built-up area to the north, 'while hutted workers camps' were to the west and south.

The synthetic oil and rubber plants were both 'still under construction', but production of both oil and rubber was already 'in progress'. The oil was produced by the 'Bergius' process, using hard coal obtained in the vicinity. The buildings were dispersed 'in the usual manner of synthetic oil plants'. The obstruction to low flying within the target area consisted of chimneys and cooling towers, 'the highest being the chimney on the Boiler House (7 on map) which is approximately 400 feet high. A power line runs N. from the Transformer Station (16 on map) with pylons 90 feet high. . . .'

The target details included a section on the 'vital parts' to be hit. This noted that whereas the hydrogenation stalls were 'largely invulnerable to attack' owing to their heavy construction to suit the high internal operating pressures, and were furthermore usually protected 'by heavy concrete boxes', the operations of the whole factory depended on its gas generating plant. Once this plant was destroyed, all synthetic oil production would cease. In addition, of all the items at Monowitz, the gas generating plant 'would take the longest to repair'. It therefore constituted a 'Primary Vital Part', and was indicated as such on the accompanying map, which listed twenty-four such targets, building by building. Each target was part of the oil or rubber production process. The slave labour camp at Monowitz, although on the photograph, was not identified in the key nor, of course, was it an industrial target.

[1] Sir H. Knatchbull-Hugessen, telegram No. 1095, Foreign Office papers, 371/42809, WR 265, folio 93.
[2] Foreign Office papers, 371/42809, WR 291, folios 161 and 163.

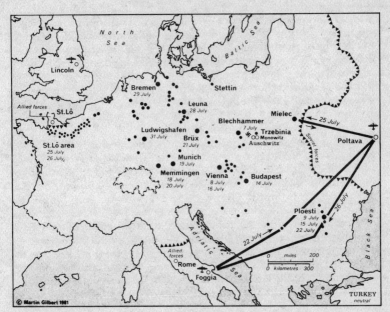

13. Allied bomber targets (black circles) during July 1944 against German oil storage, refining and production targets, together with the 'Operation Frantic' missions of 22, 25 and 26 July 1944.

The instructions of July 18 also told that on the basis of the photographs of April 4, 'no camouflage or smoke screens are observed', and went on to place the I.G. Farben plant among Germany's twelve major synthetic oil refineries, each capable of producing between 200,000 and 650,000 tons annually.[1]

The Allied bombing raids on German oil targets had continued throughout July. So effective were they that the production of synthetic oil fell from a maximum 1,043 tons a day on July 1 to a minimum 120 tons on July 21. By July 25, despite considerable efforts at repairs, and accelerated production, only 417 tons were produced that day. The effectiveness of these bombing raids was such that in a letter to Hitler on July 28, Albert Speer urged the total abandonment of all German passenger and courier air services in order to save fuel.[2]

But this Allied success had only been achieved by what the Chief of the Air Staff described, in a letter to Churchill on July 31, as 'comparatively heavy losses' incurred during the lightest nights, when the moon and lack of cloud cover exposed the bombers to anti-aircraft fire. These losses, he added, although not 'necessarily typical', were 'another pointer to the increasing efficiency of the enemy's night defences and the increasingly severe opposition

---

[1] Target Information Sheet, GS.5612, of 18 July 1944. 'Target No. 2(f)38. Place Oswiecim or Auschwitz, Category: Chemicals and Explosives. Sub-Category: Rubber and Plastics'. Strategic Bombing Survey, Record Group 243.

[2] Published in Sir Charles Webster and Noble Frankland, *The Strategic Air Offensive Against Germany 1939–1945*, volume 4. Annexes and Appendices, pages 326–9.

Bomber Command have to face over Germany'. The Chief of Staff's report went on: 'It is clear that the enemy is surmounting the difficulties presented by our radio counter-measures and that great flexibility of tactics and improved defences by our heavy bombers and by accompanying the night fighters will be needed if losses are to be kept down'.

It was nevertheless hoped, the Chief of the Air Staff added, 'to extend the scope of our daylight operations and to attack suitable targets in Germany as experience is gained'.[1]

On July 14 Churchill himself took a further personal initiative on behalf of another group of Hungarian Jewish refugees. They had arrived in Greece, after having paid substantial sums of money, not only to the Germans to be allowed to leave Hungary, but also to Greek communists, to be allowed to travel southwards through Greece to the Aegean coast. Lord Moyne had been perturbed by the idea of the communist involvement, and also at the apparent support of the United States for the transaction. But Churchill took another view, writing to Eden on July 14 that while it was 'quite possible that rich Jews will pay large sums of money to escape being murdered by the Huns', and while it was undoubtedly 'tiresome' that this money should get into the hands of the Greek communists, 'why on earth we should go and argue with the United States about it I cannot imagine'. Churchill added:

We should take a great responsibility if we prevented the escape of Jews, even if they should be rich Jews. I know it is the modern view that all rich people should be put to death whenever found, but it is a pity that we should take up that attitude at the present time. After all, they have no doubt paid for their liberation so high that in future they will only be poor Jews, and therefore have the ordinary rights of human beings.[2]

In London, the Foreign Office continued to exert its influence on behalf of the Jewish Agency. When told by the Agency that 1,500 Hungarian Jews, the first token exchange group, might have problems at the Spanish border, a telegram was sent on July 15 to Sir Samuel Hoare, the British Ambassador in Madrid, asking him to ask the Spanish authorities 'to facilitate entry of such refugees'. The telegram continued:

Presumably those not eligible for admission into Palestine might obtain permission to enter Canada (as has happened to many others who have succeeded in escaping to the Iberian Peninsula) or could be sent to Fedhala where accommodation has been reserved for this kind of influx of refugees over the Pyrenees.[3]

On that same day, Randall, who had approved of the Madrid telegram, informed Shertok that, with reference to Weizmann's 'latest' appeal, 'his suggestions regarding bombing are receiving attention with the appropriate authorities'.[4] This was indeed so, but the outcome was not hopeful. Also on July 15, the Secretary of State for Air, Sir Archibald Sinclair, wrote to Eden:

[1] Premier papers, 3/14/4.
[2] Prime Minister's Personal Minute, M 862/4.
[3] Telegram No. 861, Foreign Office papers, 371/42807, WR 55.
[4] Central Zionist Archives, Z 4/14870.

You wrote to me on the 7th July to ask if anything could be done by bombing to stop the murder of Jews in Hungary.

I entirely agree that it is our duty to consider every possible plan that might help, and I have, therefore examined:

    (a) interrupting the railways

    (b) destroying the plant

    (c) other interference with the camps.

I am advised that (a) is out of our power. It is only by an enormous concentration of bomber forces that we have been able to interrupt communications in Normandy; the distance of Silesia from our bases entirely rules out our doing anything of the kind.

Bombing the plant is out of the bounds of possibility for Bomber Command, because the distance is too great for the attack to be carried out at night. It might be carried out by the Americans by daylight but it would be a costly and hazardous operation. It might be ineffective and, even if the plant was destroyed, I am not clear that it would really help the victims.

There is just one possibility, and that is bombing the camps, and possibly dropping weapons at the same time, in the hope that some of the victims may be able to escape. We did something of the kind in France, when we made a breach in the walls of a prison camp and we think that 150 men who had been condemned to death managed to escape.[1] The difficulties of doing this in Silesia are, of course enormously greater and even if the camp was successfully raided, the chances of escape would be small indeed.

Sinclair's letter ended:

Nevertheless, I am proposing to have the proposition put to the Americans, with all the facts, to see if they are prepared to try it. I am very doubtful indeed whether, when they have examined it, the Americans will think it possible, and I do not wish to raise any hopes. For this reason, and because it would not be fair to suggest that we favoured and the Americans were unwilling to help I feel that you would not wish to mention the possibility to Weizmann at this stage. I will let you know the result when the Americans have considered it.

Eden was not pleased with Sinclair's reply. 'A characteristically unhelpful letter', he noted on July 16, and added: 'I think that we should pass the buck to the ardent Zionists, in due course, i.e. tell Weizmann that we have approached Sir A. Sinclair & suggest he may like to see him'.

Against Sinclair's comment that 'even if the plant was destroyed, I am not clear that it would really help the victims', Eden noted: 'He wasn't asked his opinion of this; he was asked to act'.[2]

Neither Eden, nor any of his Foreign Office officials, took up Sinclair's suggestion that weapons might be dropped to help Jews escape from Birkenau. But within two weeks of Sinclair's letter, special efforts such as those which the bombing of Auschwitz would have required were to be organized by the Air Ministry itself, to send volunteer and regular aircrews to drop help by air to the Warsaw uprising.

Sinclair's proposal to have the bombing proposals 'put to the Americans' effectively ensured that these proposals were now at the mercy of the United States War Department, which, unknown to Sinclair or the Air Ministry, had already rejected them eleven days earlier. The Brand proposals were likewise being brought to an end. On July 16 Eden explained to Churchill the reasons for the Cabinet Committee's decision of three days before:

---

[1] This was 'Operation Jericho', carried out by the Royal Air Force in March 1944 against Amiens prison.

[2] Foreign Office papers, 371/42809, WR 277, folios 147–8.

We had before us a report from British secret sources, only just received, which confirmed our original feeling (which we suppressed out of regard for Dr Weizmann's appeal and the views of the United States Government) that it would be of the greatest danger to send Brand back to the Germans or even to make any approach to them which could be interpreted as a response to the preposterous proposals from the Gestapo.

The new evidence suggested that these proposals were intended by the Gestapo to cover an attempt to initiate peace-talks with ourselves or the Americans, no doubt not seriously but with the object of prejudicing our relations with the Soviet Government.

Having given the actual reasons, Eden went on to refer to that aspect of the Brand affair which had caused the British Foreign Office to take it, perhaps, more seriously than they would have liked. As Eden phrased it:

We were very conscious of the differences of opinion we shall probably encounter in Washington, where electoral necessities and the War Refugee Board backed by Mr Morgenthau dictate a willingness to play with any scheme, however objectionable, (e.g. licences for foreign currency to be expended for Jews in enemy territory, and overbidding the guides in our escape between France and Spain), which can be represented as rescuing European Jews.

Our considered opinion, however, is that we should totally ignore the combined Brand-Gestapo approach.

Churchill minuted on Eden's letter: 'I entirely agree'.[1]

The new information arose from the interrogation of Andor Gross, who made it clear that he had been sent to Istanbul with Brand, not merely to act as a bodyguard or check on his activities, but specifically to try to institute discussions for a separate peace between the Gestapo on the one hand, and the British and Americans on the other; a peace which would leave Russia isolated, and alone at war with Germany. According to Gross, he had been entrusted by Otto Klages, SD Commander in Budapest and Eichmann's nominal chief, to try to 'arrange a meeting in any neutral country between 2–3 high SD officers, and 2–3 high British and American officers for the purpose of opening negotiations on the subject of separate peace between the SD and the Allies, excluding Russia'. Gross had replied that he could bring about such a meeting 'much more easily than Brand would be able to buy lorries. . . .'[2]

Two days later, on July 18, the Hungarian Jewish story took a dramatic turn. For on that day the Foreign Office telegraphed to the British Ministers in both Berne and Stockholm: 'Jewish circles here state that a halt has been called to the deportation of Jews from Hungary'.

The telegram went on to suggest that the reason for this halt, which appeared to be true, was possibly 'due to difficulties of transport'. But 'Jewish circles suggest that Hungarians and possibly Germans have been impressed by protests, and might at this junction be impressed by similar further action'.[3]

News of the reported halt to the deportations became public on July 19, when the Associated Press correspondent in Berne reported a promise made by Admiral Horthy that no more Jews would be deported from Hungary. The

[1] Foreign Secretary's Minute, P.M.44/530, Premier papers, 4/51/10, folios 1335–7.
[2] SIME report No. 3, SIME/P.7755, Top Secret, Foreign Office papers, 371/42811, page 37.
[3] Telegrams No. 581 (to Stockholm) and No. 2355 (to Berne), Foreign Office papers, 371/42809, WR 215.

Jewish Agency's London daily news summary headlined the story:

DEPORTING OF JEWS TO STOP—HORTHY

The Associated Press correspondent also reported that according to reports circulating in Berne, Horthy had authorized the Red Cross 'to direct the evacuation of Jewish children to countries willing to receive them', and had also authorized 'the evacuation to Palestine of any Jews possessing visas'.[1]

The reaction inside the Foreign Office to the news of the Horthy offer was as much concerned with Britain's Palestine policy as with the possibility of saving lives. 'This raises big issues,' Randall noted on July 19, 'i.e. we may have a flood of applications to enter Palestine etc. We shall have to be careful.'[2]

To the Jewish Agency, as well as to the British Government, it had become clear that the fate of the Jews of Hungary now no longer depended upon negotiations with the Gestapo, or the bombing of camps or railway lines, but on the goodwill of the Hungarian Government. This goodwill appeared, at first sight, to be a positive factor. On July 20 the Foreign Office sent the Jewish Agency a copy of a telegram just received from the British Ambassador in Ankara, dated July 19. The telegram read:

I understand from Jewish Agency representatives that Apostolic delegate at Istanbul has appealed to the Hungarian Government through the Catholic Church in Hungary on behalf of 5,000 Jews whose admission into Palestine has been approved. The Hungarian Government are stated to have replied that they will respect the persons of these 5,000 Jews provided that they hold Swiss certificates. . . .[3]

The Apostolic Delegate in Istanbul whose appeal had just reached Budapest was Roncalli, the same Catholic diplomat who had earlier interceded with the King of Bulgaria to save the Jews of Bulgaria from deportation to the death camps.[4]

From Lisbon, on July 20, came further news which more than confirmed the new era, marking, as Ian Henderson noted, a 'radical & favourable change in Hungarian policy towards the Jews'. The Lisbon information was that the Hungarian Government had already 'received and approved' three proposals: an offer from the Swedish Government to permit 'the emigration to Sweden or Palestine of Jews who have relations living in Sweden or who have business connections there'; an offer from the Swiss Government, 'on behalf of the British Government', to renew the previously suspended permission to emigrate for Jews possessing valid visas for Palestine; and an offer by the War Refugee Board to admit Red Cross assistance 'for Jews in camps or ghettos' in Hungary, and for the 'dispatch of Jewish children under 10 years of age to Palestine'. The report ended:

While these measures are being carried out, the deportation from Hungary of Jews for purposes of labour abroad—for which only part of them have been employed, while the rest, similarly to gentile Hungarians, are doing labour service within the country—is suspended.[5]

[1] Daily Press Survey, volume 5, No. 460.
[2] Foreign Office papers, 371/42809, WR 285, folio 150.
[3] Ankara telegram No. 1108, Foreign Office papers, 371/42810.
[4] Fourteen years later he was to become Pope, as John XXIII.
[5] Foreign Office papers, 371/42811, WR 443.

The Jewish Agency now sought new priorities and new areas of pressure on the western Allies. Following Horthy's change of policy, the imperative need became that for certificates, documents, and avenues of refuge. On July 20 Shertok went again to the Foreign Office, where he discussed the Hungarian offer with Randall. The Jewish Agency priority was now clear, to press for as many Hungarian Jews as possible to be brought to Palestine. There was no reason, Shertok told Randall, 'why Palestine should not receive up to 400,000 Jews'. Palestine, he said, was 'the obvious and best destination for potential emigrants'.[1]

The Jewish Agency's new request roused old fears in the Foreign Office mind, setting the policy, and the clash of priorities, on a familiar course, not of Jewish rescue versus the Allied war effort, but of Zionist ambitions versus Britain's Palestine policy.

Unknown to the western world, other deportations to Auschwitz continued; the 1,200 Jews of Rhodes were being taken, first by ship across the Aegean on July 24, and then by train through the Balkans, and indeed through Hungary, reaching Auschwitz on August 17, where most of them were immediately killed.

The Jewish Agency's principal requests after July 20 were for visas and transport facilities, principally to Palestine. As Randall noted, in a sentence intended for Lord Halifax, but deleted at the last moment: 'Please ascertain US Govts views on this. But leave them in no doubt that, while willing to help to utmost extent compatible with military and economic situation in Palestine, we cannot, in view of other commitments contemplate an illimitable flow now being directed on Palestine from Hungary.'[2]

[1] Foreign Office papers, 371/42810, folio 216.
[2] Foreign Office papers, 371/42810, folio 217.

Chapter 30

Fears of a flood

The Foreign Office continued to react with suspicion and hostility to the prospect of tens, or even hundreds of thousands of Hungarian Jews seeking asylum in Palestine. 'Representatives of the Jewish Agency,' Lord Halifax was informed on July 21, 'appear to be about to exert heavy pressure in favour of greatly increased Jewish immigration to Palestine as a corollary to the offer of the Hungarian Government.' This identical telegram was sent to the British High Commissioners in Canada, Australia, New Zealand and South Africa. 'Question of alternative destinations,' the telegrams noted, 'must therefore be examined without delay.'

The Foreign Office did make several suggestions for such alternative havens: that the American Government 'might agree to accept more Jewish refugees' into the United States; that Britain and America might jointly approach the Latin American Republics 'to accept more Jewish refugees'; and that a similar joint approach might be made to the Portuguese Government 'in the hope of finding an asylum for Jews in Angola'.

In addition, in order to show that 'no avenue of escape is being closed to the Jews', the Foreign Office suggested that the Dominion Governments, Canada, Australia, New Zealand and South Africa, 'may wish to consider whether there is any action which they can usefully take. . . .'[1]

In Madrid, the British Embassy was active in the last week of July in persuading the Spanish Government to allow the 1,500 Hungarian Jews who had been transferred to Belsen to enter Spain. 'United States Embassy are also sending in a note in support of move,' Sir Samuel Hoare telegraphed to the Foreign Office on July 24, 'making a similar request based on humanitarian interests.'[2]

Other areas of rescue were also opening up in the last week of July, through the War Refugee Board representative in Ankara, Ira Hirschmann. On July 24 the Jewish Agency Executive telegraphed from Jerusalem to the Zionist Federation in Johannesburg: 'Hirschmann persuaded Allies support our demand transport facilities Turkey. This gave valuable help rescue activities which may result our shipment thousands from Rumania, possibly Bulgaria, near future'.[3]

The Jewish Agency representatives in Geneva, through whom first the news of the Hungarian deportations, and then the bombing requests had been made, were themselves caught up in the new mood and new situation. 'Red Cross now discussing best organisational form of assistance,' Lichtheim tele-

[1] Foreign Office papers, 371/42810.
[2] Sir S. Hoare, telegram No. 1,118, Foreign Office papers, 371/42811, WR 418.
[3] Central Zionist Archives, S 24/1682.

graphed to London on July 24. 'Representative War Refugee Board here actively cooperating, has offered financial help.'

Lichtheim's telegram continued with several even more positive details. Switzerland, he said, was prepared to accept 'certain number of children', and Sweden had declared 'willingness admit all Hungarian Jews, for whose maintenance Swedish people will guarantee, such guarantees being given in large numbers'.[1]

It was on July 26 that the first complete version of the Vrba-Wetzler report finally reached London. This version was sent together with the nine-page description by Krausz of the ghettoization of Hungarian Jews three months before. The Vrba-Wetzler section consisted of a twenty-five page typescript, together with a five-page summary. These documents had been sent from the British Legation in Stockholm on July 19. 'We send these in the original German,' the Legation wrote in a covering letter, 'to save time since we fear that their translation will take several days.'[2]

On reaching the Foreign Office in London on July 26, this full text of the Vrba-Wetzler report was sent first to the Refugee Department. 'Even if one allows for customary Jewish exaggeration,' Ian Henderson minuted on August 26, 'these stories are frightful.'

No one inside the Foreign Office had suggested publication of the July 4 summary of the Vrba-Wetzler report, handed to them by the Czechoslovak Government-in-Exile. Nor did anyone suggest publication now, on receipt of this second, much fuller text through Stockholm. But Ian Henderson thought that the details would, as he wrote, be 'of interest to anyone dealing with "War Criminals",' and the document was therefore sent on to the Central Department. There, however, its circulation came to an end, after David Allen minuted on August 15: 'I am afraid this looks as though it would not help greatly towards identifying individuals responsible'.[3]

That same week the Vrba-Wetzler report was filed away. In Washington also it made no impact, until resurrected three and a half months later, together with the Polish Major's report, and circulated to the Press. But by then the gassings at Auschwitz had ended, and the killing machinery was being dismantled for dispatch to other camps inside Germany itself.

On July 27 there was further hopeful news from Hungary, for on that day Eliezar Kaplan of the Jewish Agency, who had been in Turkey, telegraphed to Shertok in London that not only did the Hungarians now 'agree recognize validity all immigration certificates' issued to Hungarians to go to Palestine, but that the Hungarian Government 'want their departure begin immediate'. Kaplan added: 'understand they undertake discontinue expulsions whilst actions under these schemes continued'.[4]

Also at the end of July Eden wrote to a Labour Member of Parliament,

---

[1] Telegram received in London on 27 July 1944, and forwarded that same day by the Foreign Office to the Jewish Agency, Foreign Office papers, 371/42811, WR 452.

[2] Foreign Office papers, 371/42811, WR 402. The file was headed, inside the Foreign Office, 'Situation of the Jews in Hungary', although only nine of its thirty-nine pages referred to Hungary, while thirty pages were about Auschwitz.

[3] Henderson and Allen notes, Foreign Office, 371/42811, WR 402.

[4] Central Zionist Archives, S 25/1682.

Emanuel Shinwell, himself a Jew, that any Hungarian Jews who had been granted Palestine certificates would be admitted to Palestine 'without further question' once the Hungarian Government allowed them to leave. The numbers involved, Eden added, were 'considerable'.[1]

In London, Churchill continued to press the War Office to agree to the formation of a Jewish Brigade Group, writing in a Top Secret minute to the Secretary of State for War on July 26: 'I like the idea of the Jews trying to get at the murderers of their fellow-countrymen in Central Europe, and I think it would give a great deal of satisfaction to the United States'.

The War Office opposed a special flag for the Jewish Brigade Group. But Churchill was not convinced. 'I cannot conceive,' he wrote in his minute of July 26, 'why this martyred race, scattered about the world, and suffering as no other race has done at this juncture, should be denied the satisfaction of having a flag.'[2]

Two and a half months were to pass until, on September 19, the War Office announced the formation of a Jewish Brigade Group 'to take part in active operations'. Thus five years had gone by; five years of war, during which the Jews had been denied their reiterated appeal to participate, as a specifically Jewish force, in the Allied fight against Nazism.

Jewish refugees from Rumania were now reaching Istanbul in increasing numbers. But these developments were not so welcome in London. On July 28 Christopher Eastwood of the Colonial Office, wrote to Ian Henderson at the Foreign Office, to express his department's 'concern' at the 'increasing influx of refugees into Palestine from the Balkans', and to suggest setting up a refugee camp 'as far from Palestine as possible'. Unless this were done, Eastwood warned, 'pressure to admit them into Palestine, despite the White Paper, may become very great'. There was only 'limited room', and he added: 'We are afraid that we may be on the verge of a flood of refugees'.

Henderson noted on Eastwood's letter: 'Refugee Dept. are acutely aware of the desirability of finding for Jewish refugees, especially the large number that may now emerge from Hungary, destinations alternative to Palestine'.

One possible camp site suggested by Henderson was Sicily, 'which has the merit', he wrote to Eastwood, 'of having been proposed by President Roosevelt as a possible haven for Jewish refugees from Yugoslavia'. Henderson added: 'We share your dislike of Syria, as being too near Palestine.'[3]

Not all the Colonial Office decisions were negative. On July 28 Eastwood himself informed Henderson that the Colonial Secretary had agreed that the Swiss Government should be authorized 'to go ahead' with the issue of certificates for Hungarian Jews which would entitle the holder to enter Palestine 'as an immigrant . . . at any time at which he (she) may reach that country'. After two years' residence, the certificate holder would then be entitled to obtain Palestinian citizenship.[4]

In a further British gesture of help, the Ministry of Economic Warfare

[1] Foreign Office papers, 371/42811, WR 437.
[2] Prime Minister's Personal Minute, M.901/4, Premier papers, 4/51/9.
[3] Foreign Office papers, 371/42811, WR 453.
[4] Foreign Office papers, 371/42811, WR 454.

agreed on June 28 to allow extra food supplies to be taken through the Baltic blockade to Sweden for all Hungarian Jewish children who were received in Sweden, the Hungarian authorities having already assured the International Red Cross that 'all Jewish children under ten years of age who are in possession of visas to the reception countries could leave Hungary'.[1]

A sense of relief now pervaded the telegrams and messages about Hungarian Jewry. 'Situation Budapest more quiet', Lichtheim telegraphed to Bernard Joseph on July 28 from Geneva,[2] and on that same day Clifford Norton telegraphed to the Foreign Office from Berne: 'Swiss Government inform me that according to a telegram being sent to Swiss Legation Budapest, measures taken against Jews in Hungary have been suspended until emigration organised by Swiss Legation has been carried out'.[3]

On August 1 a report by the International Red Cross delegation in Budapest seemed further to dispel the fears that the Jews of Budapest were in danger. According to the report, a copy of which was telegraphed to the Foreign Office that same night from Berne, the Jews in Budapest had 'sufficient food and clothing', were allowed to shop between 10 a.m. and 5 p.m., could be visited in their homes and internment camps by Red·Cross representatives and could receive food in the camps. Sick Jews, according to the report, 'are being properly cared for in hospitals'.

The Red Cross report went on to announce that 40,000 Jewish men, women and children, together with a thousand orphans, would be sent from Hungary to Palestine, via Rumania. The first train would leave Budapest with two thousand people 'in about ten days', accompanied by a Red Cross delegate as far as Constanta. They would be travelling on a collective Swiss passport, and the Rumanian Government had already given the Red Cross an assurance 'that everything will be done to facilitate transport across Rumania'.[4]

No further news had reached the Allies from Auschwitz itself in the last two weeks of July. But even with the halt to the Hungarian deportations, the gassing there had continued. During two weeks, trains had arrived from several Silesian and Polish labour camps, from Berlin, from Paris, from Trieste, and from the concentration camp at Majdanek, the evacuation of which was in progress as Soviet troops drew near.

The sending of Jews away from Auschwitz, to concentration camps in Germany itself, also continued throughout the second half of July, with prisoners being sent from the barracks at Birkenau to camps at Hamburg, Buchenwald, Ravensbrück and Dachau, and then from these camps being sent on to hundreds of factories where Jewish slave labour was quickly becoming an integral part of the the German effort to repair bomb damage and to maintain industrial production.

Further details of the nature of Nazi atrocities had continued to reach the Allies after the arrival of the Vrba-Wetzler report. One account of the murder

[1] Foreign Office papers, 371/42811, WR 481.

[2] Central Zionist Archives, S 25/1678.

[3] Mr Norton, telegram No. 3521, Foreign Office papers, 371/42811, WR 479.

[4] Mr Norton, telegram No. 3587, Foreign Office papers, 371/42814, War Cabinet Distribution, copy in Cabinet papers, 95/15.

of Jews in Lithuania had been published in a Stockholm evening newspaper on 13 April 1944, but only forwarded to Washington ten weeks later, on June 29, by the American Minister in Sweden, Herschel V. Johnson. This account, by a Lithuanian non-Jew, also gave details of the enormous efforts which the Germans had been making since December 1943 to obliterate all traces of the mass murders near Vilna and Kovno by digging up the corpses with steam shovels, and burning the remains in 'enormous iron furnaces'.[1]

On July 24 the United States Embassy in Lisbon had forwarded to Washington a detailed account of Nazi treatment of Jews in both Holland and Poland. The source of this account, which reached the War Refugee Board on August 2, was four American citizens who had recently been repatriated. The report had been compiled by a member of the Embassy, Robert C. Dexter, who noted that the stories of one of the four women, Mrs Ida Johnson, 'are particularly valuable, as she is obviously not Jewish'.

The non-Jewish woman told Dexter that in Holland she had seen one old man 'apparently 60 years of age, who was knocked down then deliberately kicked to death'. She had also seen another man 'hit in the face with a brick until his face was badly crushed'.

One of the Jewish women, Miss Fanny Flinders, had been imprisoned in Berlin, at the prison on the Alexanderplatz. 'If the guards happened to feel like it,' she told Dexter, 'they would take out the prisoners to special cells which were covered with broken glass, and either make the prisoners dance on the broken glass or roll around on it. If they survived this ordeal, they would then come back to the ordinary cell, streaming with blood.' While in Poland, Miss Flinders added, she had seen 'the bodies of young girls' thrown into the streets after having been raped and tortured by the Gestapo. 'They were treated so badly,' she added, that 'they were streaming with blood and many of them were viciously mutilated.'

Both Mrs Johnson and Miss Flanders were 'obviously telling the truth', Dexter reported, 'although it is difficult to understand how any individuals could be as cruel as they reported the Gestapo and German guards to have been'.[2]

Also on August 2, news reached the Church of Scotland that one of their missionaries, Jane Haining, the matron of the girls' home in the Budapest Mission of the Church of Scotland, had been deported from Budapest to Auschwitz. Later they were to learn that this dedicated missionary, who had been more than ten years in Budapest, had been accused of working among Jews, and of weeping when she had to sew the yellow star on the dresses of her girls before they went from the home to school. Miss Haining had died in Auschwitz on July 17. A month later the Church of Scotland received a second communication through the Swiss Government: Miss Haining's death certificate forwarded by the German Legation in Budapest. The certificate read:

Miss Haining who was arrested on account of justified suspicion of espionage against Germany, died in hospital, July 17, of cachexia following intestinal catarrh.[3]

[1] Stockholm telegram No. 3610, United States National Archives, 840.48, Refugees/6-2444.
[2] Lisbon dispatch No. 764, United States National Archives, 840.48, Refugees/7-2444.
[3] Quoted in David McDougall, *Jane Haining of Budapest*, Edinburgh 1949, page 19.

Cachexia is a wasting of the body, leading to a general collapse of the system, and can be caused by starvation, cancer, or tuberculosis.

During August a delegate of the International Red Cross visited the Commandant at Auschwitz. After a conversation with the Commandant, conducted in the presence of some 'polite but taciturn' German officers, the delegate inferred that Red Cross parcels which had been addressed to people in the camp were handed over intact. During the journey by road from Teschen to Auschwitz, the delegate had seen a number of prisoners working under SS supervision at the roadside, and noticed that the prisoners' faces had 'pale grey skin colouring'. But he was not able to talk to them, nor visit the camp itself. Nor did he feel in any position to raise or investigate the query which had been put to him by the chief representative of the British prisoners-of-war whom he had visited at Teschen, concerning rumours of the existence of a 'modern bathroom complete with shower, in which prisoners were gassed'.[1]

On a small but persistent scale, the rescue of Jews from Rumania had continued. Any Rumanian Jews who reached Istanbul now automatically received a collective British visa for Palestine. On August 3 three motor boats had left the Rumanian port of Constanta for Istanbul: the *Morina*, with 308 refugees, which reached Istanbul on August 6, the *Bulbul*, with a further 390 refugees, which anchored in the Bosphorus on August 6, and the *Mefkure*, with 320 refugees on board. Each ship was to receive its collective visas from the British Passport Control Office in Istanbul, and the refugees to go on by train to Palestine.

On August 5 the *Mefkure*, was attacked and machine-gunned by a German submarine shortly after reaching the Turkish coast. Amid scenes of horror she was then sunk. 'Only five survivors', Barlas telegraphed to London as soon as the scale of the tragedy was known.[2]

One of the five passengers who had been saved, the twenty-two-year-old Ladislav Fülop, had been a well-known amateur swimmer in Hungary. Fülop had been able to save his eighteen-year-old wife, Veronika, then eight months pregnant, and herself a backstroke champion.

Among those drowned in the *Mefkure* were many couples with young children. Most were from Bucharest and Czernowitz, but some were refugees who had already fled from Poland to Rumania in 1939 and 1940. Of those who were drowned, thirty-seven were children between the ages of seven and twelve. Eleven were under the age of seven. Veronika Fülop saw both her mother and brother killed by machine gun fire, while the ship was being attacked.

The five survivors of the *Mefkure* were taken on board the *Bulbul*, and added to its collective passport. Also added was the Fülop baby, born between the sinking and the departure of the train from Istanbul to Palestine.[3]

Other boats followed despite the sinking of the *Mefkure*. On August 8 the

---

[1] Danuta Czech, 'Kalendarium der Ereignisse im Konzentrationslager Auschwitz-Birkenau', published in *Hefte von Auschwitz*, volume 8, Auschwitz 1964.

[2] Central Zionist Archives, L 15/117 II.

[3] 'Report on the Sinking of the M/V "Mefkure",' Central Zionist Archives, L 15/117 II. There is also an account of the sinking, as recalled by Fülop himself, in Ehud Avriel, *Open the Gates!: A Personal Story of Illegal Immigration to Israel*, London 1975, pages 171–3.

Kazbek reached Istanbul with 752 Jewish refugees on board, most of them teenage children who had been brought back to Rumania from the death camps of Transnistria, and almost all of whom had seen their parents and relatives murdered, or die of starvation and disease.[1]

One of those who reached Palestine on board the *Kazbek* was Jona Schärf, a fifteen-year-old schoolgirl. Born in Czernowitz, she had been deported in 1941, when she was twelve years old, with both her parents, her eighteen-year-old sister and her grandmother to one of the Transnistrian concentration camps, Verhovka. Within ten days of reaching the camp, both her parents and her grandmother had died, and for more than two years Jona had been a daily witness of savage brutality, hunger, disease and death.

On her arrival in Palestine, Jona was shocked and angered to discover that no one wanted to believe her stories of the horrors of the concentration camp, not even her brother and other relatives who had been living in Palestine since before the war. 'They didn't believe a word I was telling them,' she later recalled. 'My own brother didn't believe me,' and she added:

They didn't believe that people were killed in concentrations camps: their own relations. They didn't believe that people were made to dig their own graves, and were then shot to death.

I suppose it was really too horrible to believe. But a certain amount of indifference also came in. They lived very well in Palestine.

One lady said to me: 'People don't like to hear such stories and people don't like to see such sad faces. People want hopeful stories, Jona, not stories that will disturb their well-ordered lives.'

It would have helped a lot if people had believed us. They said I had made it up. But I couldn't have made it up if I had wanted to—this is what people couldn't understand.

When I told my brother about our parents he said: 'Are you sure?', and looked at me in a funny way.[2]

In late July and early August 1944, with the rapid advance of the Soviet army and the liberation of Lublin, the Jewish Agency was confronted by new problems, and sought new help from the Allies. On August 1 the Jewish Agency Executive telegraphed to Shertok, who was still in London, asking him to approach the Soviet Ambassador 'for permission send relief to Jews in liberated Poland', and also to ask the Russians, the British and the Americans if a representative of the Agency might himself proceed to the liberated areas.[3]

The other pressure from Jerusalem concerned the certificates which the Colonial Office now agreed could be issued by the Swiss Government for Hungarian Jews to proceed to Palestine. The existence of this new procedure seemed to open up a far wider hope, similar to the hope stirred by the arrival of Brand in Istanbul two and a half months before, even though the total number that could be saved was now susbstantially less. If the certificate scheme could be extended to countries other than Hungary, the Agency telegraphed to Shertok on August 3, it could mean 'saving remnant our people western Europe, and extend much needed protection (Zionist) veterans Balkan countries. . . .'[4]

[1] Central Zionist Archives, L 15/117 II.
[2] Conversation with the author, 24 March 1980.
[3] Central Zionist Archives, S 25/1682.
[4] Central Zionist Archives, S 25/1682.

Speaking in the Canadian Parliament on August 4, a Liberal member, Arthur Roebuck, declared his support for a generous Allied response to the Horthy offer. 'We must either be rescuers or accomplices', he said, and went on to assert that large numbers of these refugees, 'could be accommodated in Palestine today if the British empire governments and the United States would insist that the door be opened'.[1]

On the same day that Roebuck was making his appeal in Canada, the War Cabinet's Committee on refugees met in London to discuss the Horthy offer. Although it came to no conclusion, its minutes reveal the dilemma with which three government departments, the Foreign Office, the Colonial Office, and the Home Office believed themselves to be faced: refusing to offer a haven in Palestine to Hungarian Jews might lead to 'arousing hostile opinion here and in the USA'; but accepting them might mean 'risking civil war in Palestine owing to an inroad of Jews from Hungary into the Levant'.

One of these present, the Colonial Secretary, Oliver Stanley, 'objected strongly to the arrangements proposed by the International Red Cross whereby 41,000 Jews would shortly leave Hungary for Turkey via Roumania'. The general feeling of the meeting, the minutes recorded, was against joining with the United States Government in 'signing a blank cheque which we could not honour'.

The senior Home Office representative present, Sir Frank Newsam, agreed with the Foreign Office view 'that we should accept the "Horthy offer" as a gesture, informing the Americans at the same time that they must not face us with the impossible in the question of providing accommodation'. Newsam also pointed out 'that the offer might be inspired by Hitler who would wish to create fundamental difficulties for the Allies in the Near East by allowing an exodus of Jews'.

It was finally decided that the 'above mentioned dilemma' should be referred to the War Cabinet.

Oliver Stanley, in further remarks to his Committee colleagues, also observed 'that the sudden influx of large numbers of Jewish refugees into Palestine would immediately bring about a most critical situation'. Stanley added:

It was not clear that the figure of 40,000 might not turn out to be much larger and he recalled that the Brand proposals recently considered by the Committee had spoken of 800,000 to a million Jews. He felt most strongly that it was imperative that urgent action should be taken to stop this movement pending decisions of our general line of action and to prevent matters from slipping still further.

At the same time, it should be made clear to the International Red Cross that they had no right to attempt to send refugees to territories for which His Majesty's Government had responsibility without permission.

Towards the end of the discussion Osbert Peake, the Parliamentary Under-Secretary at the Home Office, 'observed that there was now negligible accommodation' in Britain itself, while Oliver Stanley told the Committee that 'repeated investigations' by the Colonial Office had shown that there were

[1] Dominion of Canada, Official Report of *Debates: House of Commons*, volume 6, 1944, page 5952.

'no other possible places' for Jews to find refuge in the British Empire, or in other territories over which Britain had control'.[1]

On his return from a visit to the Normandy battlefield, Churchill found that there was still hostility towards the twenty-two Hungarian refugees who had arrived in Lisbon by air in mid-July. Once more, the State Department feared a Russian accusation of separate peace negotiations. Churchill urged Eden to ignore this fear, writing on August 6:

> This seems to be a rather doubtful business. These unhappy families, mainly women and children, have purchased their lives with probably nine-tenths of their wealth. I should not like England to seem to be wanting to hunt them down. By all means tell the Russians anything that is necessary, but please do not let us prevent them from escaping.
>
> I cannot see how any suspicion of peace negotiations could be fixed on this miserable affair.[2]

In an unsent version of this same minute, Churchill had written: 'I do not think we ought to go to war with this crowd. They have purchased their lives with nine-tenths of their possessions. Who is suspicious of peace negotiations now? At any rate, I do not wish to join in the hunt'.[3]

On August 8, the Foreign Office circulated a memorandum to the War Cabinet on the Horthy offer. The memorandum was signed by Eden, who had not been present at the Cabinet Committee discussion four days before, and stressed how 'difficult' it would be to find 'accommodation' for the refugees, in view of the Colonial Office's concerns about Palestine. It appeared for various reasons that the existing camps in French North Africa, Tripolitania, Egypt, southern Italy, Sicily and Cyprus, were full. 'Transit' camps in Syria and Palestine were opposed by the Colonial Office. But the view of the Foreign Office, Eden's memorandum added, 'is that immediate problems presented by the flow of Jewish refugees into the Levant may become so acute that as a practical measure the establishment of a transit camp in Syria should be immediately considered', in advance of 'the provision of permanent destinations'. These latter, Eden felt, might best be secured by consultation with the Dominion Governments.[4]

The War Cabinet discussed the Horthy offer at its evening meeting on August 9, when it was pointed out that this offer was 'quite distinct' from the Brand proposals. George Hall stated that in the Foreign Office view 'we must make it clear to the Americans that in practice we were not in a position to accept an indefinite commitment'. Oliver Stanley said that no more than 11,000 Jews could be taken into Palestine 'without any conflict' with the 1939 White Paper. Switzerland, however, had offered 'to take 50,000 Jewish children'. This, said Stanley, was 'a very generous offer which would go far to relieve the situation'.

The members of the War Cabinet then expressed general agreement that

---

[1] War Cabinet Committee on the Reception and Accommodation of Refugees, 4th meeting of 1944, Cabinet papers, 95/15.

[2] Prime Minister's Personal Minute, M.928/4. Premier papers, 4/51/10, folio 1322.

[3] Churchill to Eden, signed but cancelled, Premier papers, 4/51/10, folio 1323.

[4] 'Hungarian Offer to Allow Jews to Leave Hungary', War Cabinet paper 434 of 1944, Foreign Office papers, 371/42814, WR 682.

'the extent' to which Britain had made provision for refugees since the outbreak of the war 'was not realized by the United States Government' and that
if the Horthy offer were to result in 'a considerable exodus' of Jews from
Hungary, the British Government would have to press the Americans
'strongly' to undertake what was described in the War Cabinet as 'their fair
share of the burden'.

The War Cabinet agreed to inform the United States of the gist of this
decision, stressing, as Lord Halifax was informed, that the British Government
could only participate 'to the extent of their resources', and reiterating that
the Americans must 'take their fair share of the burden'. But three days later,
Lord Halifax replied that the War Refugee Board could not accept this
formula, as it appeared to commit the United States Government to 'unlimited liability'.

Jewish terrorism was also discussed at the War Cabinet of August 9,
following an attempt on the life of Sir Harold MacMichael. It should be
'made clear to the responsible Jewish leaders', Churchill told his colleagues,
'that we looked upon them to take all practicable steps in their power to
stamp out the gangs responsible for such outrages'. It was also agreed to
resume 'at an early date' discussion of what were called 'the general issues
affecting our Palestine policy'.[1]

---

[1] War Cabinet 104 of 1944, Cabinet papers, 65/43.

Chapter 31

Bombing Auschwitz:
'Cost . . . to no purpose'

At the beginning of August a new Allied priority arose, with the Warsaw uprising, and the attempt by the Poles to throw off the German yoke before Soviet forces reached Warsaw. Britain and the United States were determined to give whatever aid they could to the insurgents. Stalin, however, afraid that a non-Communist government would emerge, opposed this aid, and refused to allow the Allies to use any of the airfields in eastern Poland which he now controlled to drop arms and supplies on Warsaw.

The western Allies decided, however, to send aid to Warsaw from Foggia in southern Italy. Because of the danger involved in flying so far beyond their usual range, mainly volunteer crews were used in these missions. Dozens of airmen volunteered. On some of these missions, more than one in six of the aeroplanes failed to return. The first flight from southern Italy to Warsaw took place on August 4, followed by two more on August 8 and August 9. Then, for six consecutive days from August 12 to August 17, two full Royal Air Force squadrons, and one South African squadron, were detailed to carry out these flights, losing seventeen aircraft out of a total of ninety-three taking part. As a result of these high losses, only volunteer Polish crews flew to Warsaw in the following month.

On August 12 Churchill appealed direct to Stalin to send the machine guns and ammunition for which the Poles had implored. 'Can you not give them some further help,' Churchill asked, 'as the distance from Italy is so very great?'[1]

On August 13 the second of the Royal Air Force missions flew from Italy to Warsaw. Three of the twenty-eight aircraft were lost, while much of the aid fell, not in areas held by the Poles, but in areas under German control. On August 20, following the withdrawal of regular Royal Air Force flights, Churchill and Roosevelt telegraphed jointly to Stalin, whose forces had halted just to the east of Warsaw, seeking Soviet help, and telling him:

We are thinking of world opinion if the anti-Nazis in Warsaw are in effect abandoned. We believe that all three of us should do the utmost to save as many of the patriots there as possible.

We hope that you will drop immediate supplies and munitions to the patriot Poles in Warsaw, or will you agree to help our planes in doing it very quickly. We hope you will approve.

'The time element,' Churchill and Roosevelt added, 'is of extreme importance.'[2]

At the War Cabinet of August 16, both the Warsaw uprising and the

[1] Winston S. Churchill, *The Second World War*, volume 6, London 1954, page 117.
[2] Winston S. Churchill, *The Second World War*, volume 6, London 1954, pages 119–20.

Horthy offer had been discussed. In Churchill's absence at the Italian front, Clement Attlee presided over the meeting, which Eden opened with a detailed account of the help being sent to Warsaw. Eden then spoke again of the Horthy offer, telling his colleagues that the American Government had agreed to take 'any balance for which we could not provide'.

The actual demands made, Eden stressed, 'would not exceed the accommodation we could provide'. In addition, Britain would not accept responsibility for ' "all Jews" permitted to leave Hungary', but only for a maximum of sixty to seventy thousand in the 'specific categories' of the Horthy offer. Even so, he explained, in view of the reported 'difficulties of transportation', the number of refugees for which provision would have to be made 'might be much smaller'.[1]

Six days later, on August 17, the British and United States Governments issued a joint declaration that, 'despite the heavy difficulties and responsibilities involved', they had both decided to accept the Hungarian Government's offer 'for the release of Jews', and would 'make arrangements for the care of such Jews leaving Hungary who reach their frontiers from Hungary'.

In accepting the Horthy offer, the joint declaration emphasized, Britain and the United States 'do not in any way condone the action of the Hungarian Government in forcing the emigration of Jews as an alternative to persecution and death'.[2]

Commenting on the Allied acceptance of the Horthy offer, Ian Henderson noted, in a Foreign Office minute on August 25, that the British Government would 'undoubtedly be subjected to severe pressure in the US and elsewhere to allow such people to enter Palestine'. Such a proposal, he added, 'could not be entertained for one moment'. As long as the war lasted, he wrote, it was 'essential' not to exceed the White Paper limit on Jewish immigration. If this limit were not maintained, he warned, there would be 'a risk of serious consequences in the Near East gravely prejudicial to the conduct of the war'.

Henderson stressed that an alternative destination to Palestine must be found, at least until the end of the war, and he added that the Colonial Secretary, Oliver Stanley, 'urges (and I agree) that such an alternative destination shd not (repeat not) be near Palestine'.[3]

Where their destination could be was not clear. Enquiries were made in New Zealand and South Africa. But seven weeks later the Dominions Office noted that:

The New Zealand Government have decided that for the time being they are unable to help in view of a commitment which they have undertaken to receive some 840 Polish refugee children. The Union Government have indicated that they consider themselves already to have their hands full with war refugees and evacuees to the number of 14,488 and in view of this and the commitment which they have undertaken in accommodating Italian prisoners of war, they do not feel that they can afford any assistance in receiving Hungarian Jews.[4]

Despite the news on July 19 of the ending of the Hungarian deportations, and its own pessimistic assessment of the possibilities of bombing Auschwitz,

[1] War Cabinet 107 of 1944, items 1 and 2, copy in Premier papers, 4/52/5.
[2] Foreign Office papers, 371/42814, WR 705, folio 138.
[3] Foreign Office papers, 371/42814, WR 708, folio 156.
[4] Foreign Office papers, 371/42818, WR 1246, letter of 12 October 1944 to Australia House.

the Air Ministry had continued to approach the Americans in an effort to seek a means of carrying out the Churchill-Eden request, and on July 26 the Air Minister's Assistant Private Secretary had reported that the Vice-Chief of the Air Staff was to raise the matter with United States General Spaatz 'when he is next in the Air Ministry'.[1]

A week later, on August 2, Spaatz was reported by the Deputy Chief of the Air Staff, N. H. Bottomley, to have been 'most sympathetic'. But it was 'necessary', Bottomley informed the Acting Chief of the Air Staff, 'to know more about the precise location, extent and nature of the camps and installations at Birkenau'. It was 'particularly necessary', he noted, to have 'photographic cover'. Bottomley added:

Will you please have this produced as early as possible, so that the operational possibilities of taking some effective action from the air can be studied by the operational Commands and the Deputy Supreme Commander. I need not emphasize the need for absolute secrecy in this investigation.[2]

This request for photographic intelligence was passed on to the Foreign Office. But despite a telephone call from the Foreign Office on August 5, the Air Ministry heard no more.

Meanwhile, the Soviet-American Frantic shuttle was ready to be resumed, after nearly six weeks when it had been unable to operate because of the German air-raid on the Poltava base. The first renewed Frantic set out on August 6, when seventy-six bombers and sixty-four fighters of the United States Air Force, flying from England, struck on the way out at the Focke-Wulf aircraft factory in Gydnia, and in a special raid, on August 7, at the oil refineries at Trzebinia and Blechhammer. The intelligence survey of the Trzebinia raid reported 'good results and some losses'.[3]

The Trzebinia refineries, bombed on August 7, were only thirteen miles northeast of Auschwitz. On August 8 a further cluster of Allied aircraft, this time Polish, again passed within only a few miles of Auschwitz while flying from Foggia, in southern Italy, to drop supplies on Warsaw. These were manned by volunteer crews, accepting the risk of flying beyond their normal range.

Twenty-two such flights to Warsaw and back were made in the following six weeks, by Royal Air Force units until August 17, and then by volunteer Polish units. Of a total of 181 aircraft sent, 31 of them failed to return.[4]

For the Jews inside Birkenau, the continual passage of Allied aircraft far overhead, searching for their more distant targets, was galling. As Hugo Gryn, a fifteen-year-old Jewish boy from eastern Hungary, later recalled: 'one of the most painful aspects of being in the camp was the sensation of being totally abandoned'.[5]

The deportation of Jews to Auschwitz had continued throughout the first three weeks of August: from France, from Belgium, from northern Italy,

[1] Air Ministry papers, AIR 19/218, M 8694.

[2] Air Ministry papers, AIR 19/218, S of S 475, 15/28.

[3] Wesley Frank Craven and James Lea Cate (editors), *The Army Air Force in World War II*, volume 3, Chicago 1951.

[4] Hilary St. George Saunders, *Royal Air Force 1939–1945*, volume 3, London 1954, pages 239–41.

[5] Hugo Gryn, conversation with the author, 21 October 1980.

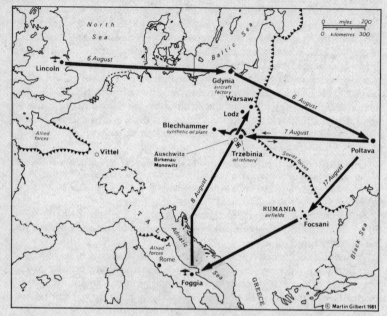

14. 'Operation Frantic' raids of 6, 7 and 17 August, and Allied airborne aid to Warsaw on 8 August 1944.

from Berlin, from Slovakia, and from the labour camps of Silesia.

On August 7 the Jews of Lodz, the largest of all the remaining ghettoes, were marked out for destruction. More than 60,000 Jews were still in Lodz, working for the Germans as slave labour in hundreds of textile and other factories in the city.

The first train to reach Auschwitz from the Lodz ghetto arrived on August 15. Two more followed on August 16, one on August 21, one on August 22, and three on August 24, bringing more than half of those deported to their deaths.

Nothing was known to the Allies of these Lodz deportations, nor of the train which reached Auschwitz on August 16 from the island of Rhodes. In July 1944, with an Allied invasion of Rhodes imminent, the Jews of the island had been taken by ship to the Greek mainland, and then deported by train northwards. On reaching Auschwitz, 346 men and 254 women were sent to the barracks, while the remaining 1,202 deportees, including all the children and old people, were gassed. Of the six hundred who were 'spared', most died six months later of starvation and ill-treatment at Mauthausen and Ebensee: only 150 survived the war.

On August 9 there had been a fifth United States aerial photographic reconnaissance above Auschwitz. But although both Auschwitz Main Camp, Birkenau, and Monowitz were photographed, much of the film was too badly overexposed to be of use, and some was out of focus.

On August 12 there was a sixth aerial reconnaissance over Auschwitz.

Once again, although all of Auschwitz Main Camp, Birkenau and Monowitz were photographed, the quality of the images was poor.[1]

Despite the halting of the Hungarian deportations, enough was known of the continuing deportations to Auschwitz from elsewhere, including Paris, to stimulate a further Jewish request for the bombing of the camps. This came on August 8, when the World Jewish Congress appealed to the War Refugee Board in Washington, on behalf of Ernest Frischer, a member of the Czechoslovak Government-in-Exile in London, to bomb the gas chambers, crematoria, and railways leading into Auschwitz. Frischer wrote:

I believe that destruction of gas chambers and crematoria in Oswieczim by bombing would have a certain effect now. Germans are now exhuming and burning corpses in an effort to conceal their crimes.

This could be prevented by destruction of crematoria and then Germans might possibly stop further mass exterminations especially since so little time is left to them.

Bombing of railway communications in this same area would also be of importance and of military interest.[2]

Five days later on August 14, this appeal was rejected by John McCloy, the Assistant Secretary of War. The operation proposed, he wrote yet again, 'could only be executed by the diversion of considerable air support essential to the success of our forces now engaged in decisive operations elsewhere and would in any case be of such doubtful efficacy that it would not warrant the use of our resources'. These were the same phrases which McCloy and his assistant, Gerhardt had used a month before. McCloy added, in a new line of argument: 'There has been considerable opinion to the effect that such an effort, even if practicable, might provoke even more vindictive action by the Germans'.[3]

Meanwhile, confused by Horthy's order to halt the Hungarian deportations to Auschwitz, the Foreign Office discussed whether Auschwitz was still a priority as far as the bombing proposal was concerned. On August 10 Eden's Assistant Private Secretary, Guy Millard, minuted to Roger Allen: '. . . Birkenau is in Upper Silesia, formerly Poland, and is presumably being used by the Germans for incinerating German & Polish Jews as well as Hungarian?' and he went on to ask: 'Have we any information to suggest that it is still being used? If it is, presumably the Jews will still want us to bomb it'.

Allen doubted whether bombing Auschwitz was still a priority. 'I know of no information,' he replied, 'other than that in WR 276/10/9, suggesting that Jews are being gassed and burnt at Birkenau. It may well be so but I cannot recall having seen any recent confirmation. . . .'[4]

In London, the Air Ministry's annoyance at the Foreign Office delays in providing photographic intelligence on Auschwitz led to a protest from Air

[1] Records of the Defense Intelligence Agency (RG 373), Aerial Photographs of Auschwitz and Birkenau, Mission USEC/R–79 (9 August 1944), Exposures 1018–25, and Mission USEC/R–82 (12 August 1944), Exposures 3017–9.

[2] War Refugee Board, Box 35, 'Measures Directed Towards Halting Persecutions, F: Hungary, No. 5.'

[3] Quoted in David S. Wyman, 'Why Auschwitz was Never Bombed', in *Commentary*, volume 65, number 5, New York, May 1978, page 40. For the earlier version, see pages 255–6.

[4] Millard and Allen minutes, Foreign Office papers, 371/42809, WR 731. For Allen's WR 276 reference, see pages 271–2.

Commodore Grant to William Cavendish-Bentinck. Grant's letter began: 'I am perturbed at having heard nothing more from the Foreign Office about the problem of Birkenau since Allen telephoned me on the 5th of this month,' and he added:

You will appreciate that as the Secretary of State for Air has instructed the Air Staff to take action on Mr Eden's request it is a matter of the greatest urgency for me to obtain photographic cover of the camps and installations in the Birkenau area. The information at present in our possession is insufficient for a reconnaissance aircraft to have a reasonable chance of obtaining the cover required and only the Foreign Office can obtain the information which I need.[1]

Grant went on to say that in view of the 'urgency of the problem', which Eden himself had raised, he would 'be grateful if I can have a reply, whether it be positive or negative, to my request with the utmost expedition'. Grant then explained to Cavendish-Bentinck that:

In his conversation Allen hinted that the Foreign Office were tending to reconsider the importance that they had placed upon the liberation of the captives at Birkenau. This however does not help me. If in fact further information about the Germans' intentions in that particular camp has caused the Secretary of State for Foreign Affairs to revise his opinion it will be necessary for him to inform the Secretary of State for Air who will, no doubt, then modify or rescind the instructions which he has issued to the Air Staff.

Only if and until such official action were taken, Grant noted, could the priority cover of Birkenau, 'which is now of the very highest', be lowered, and his letter ended: 'I therefore shall be most grateful for all the help you can give me either to let me have the information which I require to get the job done or else to clear the position in the event of the Foreign Office having modified its views as to the importance of the task'.[2]

Reading this exchange on August 15 Sinclair himself noted that Grant had done 'all and more than all that could reasonably be expected of him', and he added: 'The ball is in the F.O. court'.[3]

The Foreign Office now turned to the Jewish Agency, suggesting that in view of the reported end to the Hungarian deportations, the Agency might like to withdraw its request for bombing. But Joseph Linton, replying on August 16, would not allow the request to be dropped, writing to Ian Henderson:

The reasons which were advanced for the bombing of the death-camps are still valid. There are still many Jews in the hands of the Germans who can be sent to these camps to their doom. There is another reason why the destructions of the camps is urgent: in the situation in which

[1] The necessary photographic cover had in fact existed since 31 May 1944 (see page 216), with further aerial photographs of Birkenau having been taken on June 26 (see page 249). The photographs had hitherto been submitted to intelligence scrutiny only for their Monowitz cover. But within a few days of being taken, they were readily available for further intelligence scrutiny if required, at Medmenham, fifty miles west of London. No search was made for them, however, and hence no use of them, for their Birkenau cover, at any stage during the Jewish Agency's enquiries of August, September and October 1944. Indeed, the first analysis of the Birkenau photographs, pinpointing on them the gas chambers, crematoria, railway sidings, trains in the sidings, huts etc, was not made until February 1979, with the publication in Washington of Dino A. Brugioni and Robert G. Poirer, *The Holocaust Revisited: A Retrospective Analysis of the Auschwitz-Birkenau Extermination Complex.*
[2] Foreign Office papers, 371/42814, WR 749, folio 190.
[3] Air Ministry papers, 19/218/M.8565/S.2294.

the Germans find themselves today, it will be more difficult for them to construct new camps, and this might be the means of saving Jewish lives.[1]

Linton was not to be deterred from what he saw as an urgent task. On August 18 Shertok telegraphed from London to the Jewish Agency in Jerusalem: 'Informed carrying out Gruenbaum's idea fraught technical difficulties. They wonder whether we wish it pursued view changed situation. Replied affirmatively'.[2] When, on telephoning the Foreign Office on August 18, Linton learned that it was a lack of topographical information which was causing the delay, he at once obtained plans and descriptions of both Auschwitz and Treblinka from the Polish Government-in-Exile in London, and forwarded them to the Foreign Office.[3]

But inside the Foreign Office the attitude towards the bombing was already emphatic. As Ian Henderson minuted that same day, August 18:

Mr Grant of the Air Ministry says that this idea would cost British lives and aircraft to no purpose. I think it is fantastic, and should be dropped. But if the Air Ministry have strong objections they should say so and we can return a negative reply to the Jewish Agency.[4]

Henderson's attitude was challenged by Roger Allen, who minuted three days later, on August 21:

We cannot now shift the responsibility to the Air Ministry, by asking them to say that for technical reasons they are opposed to the whole venture. If the political situation has changed and we no longer wish on political grounds to proceed with this project, it is up to us to tell the Air Ministry so in a form that will have the effect of revoking the Secretary of State's previous communication to Sir A. Sinclair. From the Air Ministry point of view this matter is urgent, since the reconnaissance has been given the highest priority and they can do nothing about it until either (a) we put them in touch with the source of the topographical information or (b) we tell them that the whole scheme is now dead.[5]

Linton's letter, and the ground plans of both Auschwitz and Treblinka, reached the Foreign Office on August 22. 'These plans may be of interest to the Air Ministry', A. Walker minuted three days later. 'On the other hand I take it that we do not intend to pursue the camps bombing scheme (see minute for the S. of S.)'.[6] The minute to which Walker referred had been drafted for Eden by Ian Henderson earlier that same day, August 25. It described in general terms the halting of the Hungarian deportations, and the

[1] Foreign Office papers, 371/42814, WR 749, folio 191.

[2] Central Zionist Archives, S 25/1678.

[3] Foreign Office papers, 371/42806, WR 823, folios 31–34 (Auschwitz plan and key), folios 35–39 (Treblinka plan and key). The sketch map of Auschwitz showed 28 specifically numbered features of Auschwitz Main Camp (including towers, sentries with machine guns, ammunition dump, crematorium, stores of belongings taken away from prisoners, SS barrack room and dwelling houses for officers); and at Auschwitz-Birkenau 'SS barracks, square, kennels, concentration camp for women, gas chambers in a wood west of Brzezinki/Birkenau', and 'crematorium in a wood, probably west of the barracks'. There were some mistakes in the Birkenau section of the sketch, but the general layout and relationship of the buildings was correct, and the hutted area of the women's camp was particularly detailed and accurate.

[4] Foreign Office papers, 371/42814, WR 749, folio 188.

[5] Foreign Office papers, 371/42814, WR 749, folio 188.

[6] Foreign Office papers, 371/42806, WR 823, folio 27.

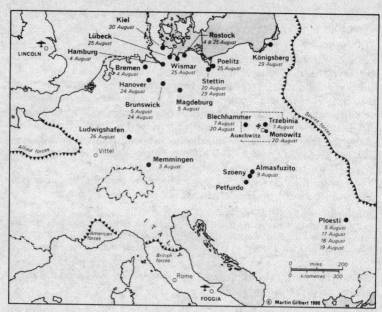

15. Allied bomber targets (black circles) during August 1944, against German oil production, refining and storage targets.

technical difficulties involved in the bombing. Six days later, on September 1, Richard Law, the Minister of State at the Foreign Office wrote direct to Weizmann, referring back to Weizmann's request of July 6 for the bombing of the camps, or of the railway lines to them. 'I am sorry to have to tell you,' Law wrote, 'that in view of the very great technical difficulties involved, we have no option but to refrain from pursuing the proposal in present circumstances.'[1]

This letter was originally to have been signed by Eden himself. In it were two passages which were cut out of the letter as sent. After referring to the 'very great technical difficulties involved', the original draft had gone on to say: 'not to mention the diversion which would be necessary of material of vital importance at this critical stage of the war'. A second passage in the original draft had referred to the British reasons, technical and material, being 'reinforced by our information that the deportations have virtually ceased'. This passage was also deleted before the letter was sent.[2]

The Jewish Agency knew, as they had informed the Foreign Office, that the deportations were continuing, even if news of them took weeks, and sometimes months to emerge. Thus on August 17, Linton telegraphed from London to the Jewish Agency in Jerusalem, that among the Vittel detainees sent to Drancy, and then to an 'unknown destination', were Katznelson the

[1] Foreign Office papers, 371/42814, WR 749, folio 200.
[2] Foreign Office papers, 371/42814, WR 749, folio 199.

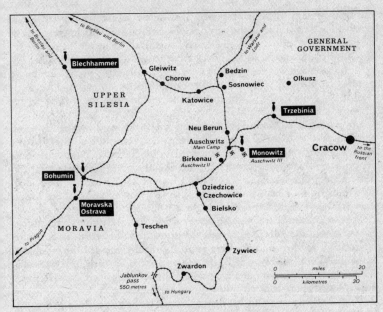

16. Allied bomber targets against oil production, refining and storage targets in the Auschwitz region during August and September 1944.

poet and his wife.[1] The destination, Linton added, was 'probably Oswiecim'.[2]

The first bombing raid on the synthetic oil and rubber plant at Monowitz took place on August 20. The raid was flown by the 15th United States Air Force, from their base at Foggia, in southern Italy. During the raid, which began at 10.32 in the evening, and lasted for twenty-eight minutes, 127 Flying Fortresses dropped a total of 1,336 five hundred pound high explosive bombs, from an altitude of between 26,000 and 29,000 feet.

Only one of the bombers was shot down. Against the nineteen German fighters that rose to intercept them, the Americans had been able to send an escort of a hundred Mustangs.

The intelligence reports on the Monowitz raid of August 20 were completed three days later, following a scrutiny of aerial photographs taken immediately after the raid. The 'main weight of the attack' it appeared, had fallen on the central and eastern part of the works, 'where there is very considerable damage to installations and buildings'. Owing to the dispersed nature of the various plants, however, 'many hits have been scored on the open ground between buildings and damage is therefore not so spectacular as it might otherwise be'. It seemed 'probable' that the blast from these hits

---

[1] In fact, Katznelson's wife and two of their three children had been deported from Warsaw to Treblinka, and murdered there, nearly two years earlier. Katznelson and one of his sons had been deported from Drancy to Auschwitz on 29 April 1944, and killed there: Linton's information was correct.

[2] Central Zionist Archives, S 25/1678.

on open ground 'must have caused a considerable amount of damage to installations' not visible on the photographs. Several buildings in the synthetic oil plant were seen to have been 'severely damaged', and there was 'probably also some blast damage' to one of the three active hydrogenation stalls.

Heavy damage was recorded by the aerial photographs in the aluminium production plant, as well as 'considerable damage to stores, buildings, contractors sheds and offices, and to huts and buildings in the various labour camps adjoining the works'.[1]

Among those at Monowitz who were sheltering in one of these labour camp 'huts' was Arie Hassenberg, a twenty-one year old Jew from Bedzin. He was among thirty thousand Jewish slave labourers in Monowitz's own concentration camp, Auschwitz III, that August 20. Thirty-six years later he recalled: 'The bombing was really a happy day for us,' and he added: 'We thought, they know all about us, they are making preparations to free us, we might escape, some of us might get out, some of us might survive.'

There was another feeling, also, in the minds of those pitiful slaves, forced to work until they dropped from exhaustion, surrounded by barbed wire, guarded by SS dogs and machine guns. 'We really enjoyed the bombing,' Hassenberg recalled. 'We wanted once to see a killed German. Then we could sleep better, after the humiliation never to be able to answer back. To see a killed German: that was why we enjoyed the bombing.'[2]

The Monowitz target lay less than five miles to the east of the gas chambers of Birkenau, and the aerial photographs taken during the raid include three which covered both Auschwitz I and Birkenau.[3] Two days later, on August 22, a further 261 Flying Fortresses attacked the oil refineries at Blechhammer and Bohumin,[4] flying within forty miles of Auschwitz on their return journey.

'We saw many times the silver trails in the sky', one of the prisoners at Birkenau, Erich Kulka, later recalled, and he added:

All the SS men would go into the bunkers but we came out of our huts, and prayed that a bomb will fall, or soldiers and weapons will be parachuted, but in vain.

Whenever there was a raid the SS ran away. We were always left alone, completely left alone. Perhaps we could have run away. But being totally powerless and feeling helplessly forgotten, we had nowhere to go.[5]

Also on August 22, a train reached Auschwitz from the Austrian concentration camp at Mauthausen. After ninety-three men had been sent to the barracks, the remaining 326 were gassed. That same day, from a train from Slovakia, only three men were 'selected' to live. Two days later, on August 24, as the Allied air-raids throughout Upper Silesia continued, another train reached Auschwitz from the Lodz ghetto, so many of whose inhabitants had

[1] Mediterranean Allied Photo Reconnaissance Wing, Interpretation Report No. D.B.189 of 23 August 1944, GS–5612: Poland, Oswiecim (11.15 hours) Synthetic Oil and Rubber Works. United States Strategic Bombing Survey, Record Group 243.
[2] In conversation with the author, 24 July 1980.
[3] Mission USEC/R86. Can B, 10658. Exposures 5018, 5019 and 5020. Scale 1:52,000. Altitude, 26,000 feet.
[4] Wesley Frank Craven and James Lea Cate (editors), The Army Air Force in World War II, volume 3, Chicago 1951.
[5] Erich Kulka, conversation with the author, Jerusalem, 4 February 1980.

now been gassed. One of those in this particular deportation was a twenty-five-year-old girl from Lodz, Sarah Cender, who later recalled how:

Upon arrival we were separated from the males and brought in front of a building where heaps of clothing were lying on the ground. We were ordered to undress quickly and naked we were pushed into a pitch dark chamber (what we naively and hopefully thought to be a bath facility—although no soap or towel were given to us).

The doors closed behind us. Anxious seconds and minutes passed. Nothing seemed to happen for a while. Only cries and laments and hysterical screams were heard from every corner of the chamber. Some of the women started to cough incoherently, believing being choked by gas. The situation became unbearable. . . .

Suddenly a tremendous rumble shook the place. In the few minutes we could not understand what has happened, but soon enough we recognized the familiar sound of over-flying bombers. The shattering noises and rumblings continued throughout the night. Exhausted, neither dead nor alive, holding on to each other, cramped and entrapped we waited in darkness for the inevitable to come.

A long time passed by. It seemed like eternity. We lost track of time. We sank into delirium.

And then all of a sudden noises and harsh voices were heard. The doors opened. We were ordered to come out. Broken down in body and spirit, completely naked we were gathered in the nearby field and again we waited and waited. . . .

Several hours later a group of young Nazis arrived, looked us over, selected the younger looking women and ordered the rest to be taken away. . . .[1]

All those taken away were gassed. Those who remained were then sent to the bath house, and then to the barracks. There, with their heads shaven and their forearms tattooed, they joined nearly 40,000 other women labourers, awaiting dispatch to the slave labour camps of the Auschwitz region, and of Greater Germany.

That day, August 24, there were, including the women, a total of some 135,000 Jews at Auschwitz, of whom 30,000 were working at Monowitz.

On the following day, August 25, American aeroplanes again flew over Auschwitz. Once more their task was to photograph the Monowitz industrial plant. Once more, the camera also took pictures of Auschwitz Main Camp, of Birkenau, of the railway sidings, the gas chambers and the crematoria. The approximate location of these areas, and in particular the location of the gas chambers, the crematoria and the birch wood, had already been indicated, together with the huts in women's camp at Birkenau and the huts in Auschwitz Main Camp, in the sketch-map sent by Linton to the Foreign Office on August 18, and acknowledged by the Foreign Office four days later. One of the photographs of August 25 actually showed Jews on the way from a train to a gas chamber and crematorium, the gate of which is seen open to receive them.

Two gas chambers and crematoria are visible in the photograph of August 25. The outline of the underground gas chambers is seen, as are the vents in the gas chamber ceiling. Part of the deliberate Nazi deception can also be made out: the special landscaped garden built inside the entrance which was designed to lull those who were being led to their deaths into some sense of normality.

In the photograph of August 25, Crematorium II and its chimney stand out particularly boldly in the sunlight. There is also a large pit behind Crematorium II: probably one of the pits which was being used for the open burning

[1] Letter of 17 January 1980 from Sarah Altusky (née Cender) to Lilli Kopecky, Kopecky papers.

of bodies when the capacity of the crematorium itself was exceeded. In another part of the same photograph, recently arrived deportees can be seen queueing outside the registration building.

No attempt was made to link the details on Linton's sketch-map with any of the aerial photographs of Birkenau, which dated back to May 31. Meanwhile, plans for the bombing of the Auschwitz area continued to be made. On August 25 a second intelligence report on the Monowitz raid of five days before revealed 'considerable activity' of pedestrians, motor vehicles and light railway engines 'over the whole area of the plant', as progress was made in clearing the bomb damage, 'and particularly with roof repairs'. Two of the buildings which had been slightly damaged, a gas holder and a water gas plant, were both being repaired, and the water gas plant 'now appears to be operative'. It looked as if an attempt was also being made to start an anti-aircraft smoke screen, 'from smoke pots scattered about the factory area'.[1]

The sole purpose of the photographic reconnaissance over Auschwitz on August 25 was to look yet again at the damage done during the raid of August 20, and to see what further repairs were being made. Once more, both Auschwitz I and Birkenau appear in part in five of the photographs.[2] But the intelligence assessment made no reference to these exposures, nor did it have any reason to do so. Over Monowitz it noted, 'some slight clearances and repairs were seen', but as to the six 'primary objectives', at the first, the boiler house and generator hall, 'no damage seen'; at the second, the water gas plant, 'no damage seen'; at the third, the H_2S removal plant, 'no damage seen'; at the CO_2 and CO removal plant 'small installation partly wrecked'; at the gas conversion plant, and at the injector houses, 'no damage seen'.

This was a disappointing result. 'The damage received,' the report concluded, 'is not sufficient to interfere seriously with synthetic fuel production, and should not greatly delay completion of this part of the plant.'[3]

A photograph attached to this report showed one of the aerial shots taken over Monowitz on August 25. In it, hundreds of bomb craters are clearly visible. The photograph was accompanied by a plan on which all damaged and destroyed buildings were marked. Also identified were 151 different buildings, including a group of buildings at the southeastern edge of Monowitz listed as 'Concentration Camp'. This was, in fact, the slave labour camp at Auschwitz III, with 30,000 Jews who had been brought from Birkenau. But this was not known to the interpreters. More than seventy huts and other buildings were visible, but not specifically identified, inside this particular complex, recognized as a camp, but not commented on further in any way.[4]

[1] Mediterranean Allied Photo Reconnaissance Wing, Interpretation Report No. D.B.191 of 25 August 1944. G.S.5612: 'Poland, Oswiecim, (10.35 Hours) Synthetic Oil and Rubber Works.' United States Strategic Bombing Survey, Record Group 243.

[2] Exposures 3182 to 3185, Mission 60 PR/694, 60 SQ, Can F5367, Scale 1:10,000, Altitude 30,000 feet. United States Strategic Bombing Survey, Record Group 143.

[3] Mediterranean Allied Photo Reconnaissance Wing, Interpretation Report No. D.P.95 of 30 August 1944. 'G.S.5612, Poland, Locality: Oswiecim (Auschwitz).' United States Strategic Bombing Survey, Record Group 243.

[4] The photograph was Exposure 4176. Mission 60 PR/694. 60 Squadron. 25 August 1944. Altitude 30,000 feet. The plan was 'Oswiecim: I.G.F. Synthetic Rubber and Synthetic 0.7 Plant. D. Section. Map RW. Copied from A.C.I.U. Plan No. D/410.' United States Strategic Bombing Survey, Record Group 243.

The Allied bombing of synthetic fuel plants in the Auschwitz-Birkenau area continued. On August 27 a further 350 heavy bombers struck at Blech-hammer, and on August 29 a total of 218 heavy bombers struck Moravska Ostrava and Bohumin,[1] both within forty-five miles of Auschwitz I and Birkenau.

Although Allied bombers on their various missions continued to fly over Birkenau, the pilots, navigators and bombing officers were totally unaware of what lay below them.

But for some of those below, even this overflying was memorable. One group of Jews who may have owed their lives to the chance of Allied bombers flying overhead, were those who had been brought to Auschwitz a few weeks before from the slave labour camp at Starachowice. These Jews had tried to escape from their labour camp as the Red Army approached, but most had been shot down by the guards. The rest had been sent to Auschwitz in sealed goods wagons, in which many had died. On reaching Auschwitz, they had been taken to a part of the Gipsy camp, only a few days before the Gipsies themselves were taken away by force to the gas chambers. 'I still remember well their cries at midnight,' one young man, Shalom Lindenbaum, later recalled, 'as they were forced to move—men, women and children—while our barracks were locked.'

A week later, shortly before sunset, Lindenbaum and his fellow evacuees from Starachowice were suddenly ordered to a roll-call, in the direction of the camp gate. As he later wrote, they were:

. . . . afraid that now it was our turn, because normally before dusk there were no transports to other camps. On the nearby road, which led to the 'sauna' (bath house) and gas chambers a new transport, which had arrived from ghetto Lodz, as we later learned, mostly women and children, passed by. There was no doubt where they were taken. This even strengthened our bad feeling. I remember how I ran ahead to my father in order to be together in what seemed to be our last hour.

At that time Allied bombers appeared in the sky. It will be difficult to describe our joy. We prayed and hoped to be bombed by them, and so to escape the helpless death in the gas chambers. To be bombed meant a chance that also the Germans will be killed. Therefore we were deeply disappointed and sad when they passed over, not bombing.

Fortunately we were taken back to the barracks, after a search on our bodies. But we didn't speak about our unexpected return, survival, only about the bombers, about the Allies' reluctance to bomb the gas chambers.

'We didn't pray for our life,' Lindenbaum added, 'we had no hope for that—but for revenge, for human dignity, for punishment to the murderers.'[2]

---

[1] Wesley Frank Craven and James Lea Cate (editors), *The Army Air Force in World War II*, volume 3, Chicago 1951.
[2] Letter to the author, 13 June 1980.

Chapter 32

'These wailing Jews'

Despite the War Department's rejections of the various appeals to bomb the railways leading to Auschwitz, or the gas chambers and crematoria in the camp itself, one officer of the War Refugee Board continued to press his superiors for action. This was Benjamin Akzin, who on September 2 wrote direct to Pehle to point out that the War Department rejection 'quite likely stems from the habitual reluctance of the military to act upon civilian suggestions'.

Akzin reminded Pehle that the War Refugee Board had been created precisely in order to 'overcome the inertia', and even in some cases the 'insufficient interest' of the various Government departments 'in regard to the saving of Jewish victims of Nazi Germany', and he went on to urge Pehle to go direct to Roosevelt. 'I am certain,' Akzin added, 'that the President, once acquainted with the facts, would realize the values involved and, cutting through the inertia-motivated objections of the War Department, would order the immediate bombing of the objectives suggested.'

No such approach was made to Roosevelt. Nor was any action taken on a further appeal forwarded by Akzin, from Isaac Sternbuch in Switzerland, on behalf of the Rabbi of Nitra, in Slovakia, pleading for the bombing of railroad junctions between Budapest and Silesia, on the grounds that, since August 28, the 'deportations of Jews from Budapest' had begun, and that 12,000 Jews had already been deported 'to Oswiecim, in Upper Silesia'.[1]

Day by day the Jewish Agency in London had likewise sought new means of rescue and relief: greater Red Cross activity, including visits to camps inside Germany, more certificates for Palestine, the dispatch of Agency emissaries and aid to the newly liberated countries, and approaches to the Soviet Union. The list was long, the requests frequent, and the agony apparent in every appeal.

The very act of appealing seemed sometimes to offend. When on September 7, A. G. Brotman, Secretary of the British Board of Deputies, asked the Foreign Office to approach the Soviet Union on behalf of Jews in those areas of Rumania which were being liberated by the Red Army, one official, A. R. Dew, noted: 'In my opinion a disproportionate amount of the time of the Office is wasted on dealing with these wailing Jews'. He was, however, rebuked. The Jews, wrote one of his colleagues, Lady Cheetham, 'have been given cause to wail by their sufferings under the Nazi regime'.[2]

The Board of Deputies' request was turned down by Eden on September 9.

[1] War Refugee Board, Box 34, 'Measures Directed Towards Halting Persecutions, F: Hungary, No. 5.
[2] Foreign Office papers, 371/42817, WR 993, Dew minute, 1 September 1944, Cheetham minute, 7 September 1944.

'In view of the delicacy of such a suggestion,' Eden wrote to the War Cabinet's refugee Committee, 'and of the absence of any concrete plan it is proposed to suggest that the Jewish societies should approach the Russians direct.' And Eden added: 'they have contacts with the Soviet Embassy and otherwise.'

Eden also informed the refugee Committee of the International Red Cross plan of August 1, to allow 40,000 Jews to leave Hungary via Rumania, in groups of two thousand. A Red Cross report made it clear that the plan had broken down, as the German occupying authorities had 'refused to grant exit visas', and as the Hungarian-Rumanian frontier 'is now closed'. The Red Cross had suggested a joint British, United States and German safe-conduct for the first two thousand to go down the Danube, by river steamer to the Bulgarian border. But in London the Admiralty and Air Ministry had stressed 'that a safe conduct is not feasible in view of the fact that the Danube has been systematically blocked by mines for some time past'. Even so, the Swiss had been asked by the British 'urgently to explore whether there is any other method of egress for this party of 2,100 Jews, e.g. in the direction of Switzerland itself'.

Eden's note to his Committee colleagues had gone on to discuss 'possible destinations' for 'such persons as may be allowed to leave Hungary'. The Portuguese Government was willing to take them 'in groups of 300 or so, suggesting that they have a large number in mind'. The figure of five thousand children was mentioned. Others might be allowed into Tangier; the Spanish Government having agreed to the granting of 'a certain number of visas for this purpose'. The Brazilian Government was 'prepared to take 500 children'. And the United States were prepared both to offer five thousand visas for the United States itself, and also to 'intervene' with the Eire Government on behalf of further refugees.[1]

These efforts were frustrated by the German Government. On September 22 the War Refugee Board representative in Switzerland, Roswell McClelland, informed Washington that although two thousand Hungarian Jews now held both Palestinian certificates and a collective passport issued by the Swiss Legation at Budapest 'in late July', the Germans had argued that since 'the departure of these people for Palestine would disturb "German relations with Arabs" they could not permit these people to go'. The German Foreign Office might, however, view the emigration more favourably 'if these Jews were going to American or British territory'. McClelland told Washington:

It might be possible, in order to ease the problem of settlement of such a group in the postwar, if this could be done without German suspicion being aroused, to select Hungarian Jews who desired to return to their country when the war is over. The idea of getting Jews out of Europe permanently is an obsession in certain Nazi circles and they will not tolerate the departure of those they feel may come back again.

An additional alternative of a more positive nature would be to make a concrete offer to admit a group of 1,000 or more Hungarian Jewish children into the United States, for instance, those whose parents have been deported. . . .[2]

---

[1] 'Note by the Secretary of State for Foreign Affairs', written 9 September 1944, circulated 29 September 1944, War Cabinet Committee on the Reception and Accommodation of Refugees, Cabinet papers, 95/15, J.R.(44)23.
[2] Berne telegram No. 6276, United States National Archives, 840.48, Refugees/9–2244.

On September 30 the War Refugee Board informed McClelland that the American Legation in Berne already had 'broad authority' to grant visas 'for entry into the United States', including four thousand American visas for children in Hungary which had been authorized on August 21. In addition, Ireland and 'various Latin American Republics' had now given assurances 'that they will receive at least 2,000 children'. Mexico was also now willing to take in refugees 'for the duration of the war'. Spain had authorized two thousand visas for children, and Sweden had agreed to admit both children and 'numerous adults'.[1] It was therefore up to the Germans to respond: if they were sincere, there were already places waiting for thousands of children, once they were allowed to reach the Spanish, Swiss or Swedish borders.

The Germans, however, made no response, even with the armies of the western Allies on the outskirts of Paris, and the Red Army on the banks of the Vistula.

In the first week of September more Jews reached Auschwitz, from Slovakia, Lodz, Sosnowiec, Holland and Saarbrücken. Of the 1,019 brought from Holland on September 5, a total of 549, including seventy-nine children, were among those 'selected' for the gas chamber. On September 7 four trains reached Auschwitz, from Lodz, Vienna, Trieste and Berlin, and on September 8 there were three trains in all, two from Lodz and one from France. The numbers involved were becoming smaller. Fifty-six men from the transport from Trieste were gassed, thirty-nine from the train from Berlin. Three days later, a hundred Jewish women were sent out of Auschwitz, westwards to Flossenbürg, where they were dispersed among the factories of the region. On September 12 three hundred Jewish children reached Auschwitz from Kovno. All but sixty-five were gassed.

These deportations and killings were unknown in the west. But throughout the early part of September, news of yet more deportations from Hungary had begun to reach the Jewish Agency in Jerusalem, following the overthrow of Admiral Horthy, and the return of the Gestapo to Budapest. As the American Consul-General, L. C. Pinkerton, telegraphed to Cordell Hull in Washington on September 1, for transmission to the Zionist leaders:

Have just received new of renewed deportations from Hungary twelve thousand daily. Those nearer Hungary demand renewed and strengthened sharp warnings to government officials and population of Hungary, also frequent air dropped leaflets and broadcasting. Strong approach to Pope and maximum activization of Red Cross most important.[2]

Reading of the new threat to Hungarian Jewry, Yitzhak Gruenbaum made one further effort to persuade the Allies to look again at the request to bomb Auschwitz. On September 13 he telegraphed from Jerusalem, to Shertok in London, that the newly installed Hungarian Government had ordered the deportations to begin again.[3] 'Daily transports,' he wrote, 'ten, twelve thousand Jews being prepared Oswiecim via Zilina, Pruska.' Others, some

---

[1] Telegram No. 3378, United States National Archives, 840.48, Refugees/9–2244.
[2] Jerusalem telegram No. 124, United States National Archives, 840.48, Refugees/9–2244.
[3] Sztojay had been replaced as Prime Minister of Hungary by General Lakatos on August 25.

15,000 according to a 'reliable report', had been deported, not to Auschwitz, but to Germany.

Gruenbaum proposed three immediate measures: a proclamation by the United Nations that Hungarian acquiescence in these renewed deportations 'will gravely impair Hungary's position'; that the railway line leading to Auschwitz through Zilina and Pruska 'be bombed, destroyed'; and that 'Oswiecim itself be bombed'.[1]

Enclosed with Gruenbaum's telegram was a list of five separate railway routes from Hungary to Auschwitz. Two of these, however, were already largely in Soviet hands.

On the day that Gruenbaum sent his telegram, the American Air Force attacked synthetic oil plants at both Oderthal and Monowitz. At Monowitz they met intense and accurate anti-aircraft fire, but hit their target,[2] which lay within five miles of the still active gas chambers.

They also, by mistake, dropped a number of bombs on Auschwitz I, accidentally hitting and destroying the SS barracks there, and killing fifteen SS men. A further twenty-eight SS men were badly injured. The clothing workshop was also hit and destroyed, and forty camp inmates working there, including twenty-three Jews, were killed. During the raid, a further sixty-five inmates were severely injured.

During this same bombing attack of September 13, a cluster of bombs was dropped in error on Birkenau. One of the bombs damaged the railway embankment leading into the camp, and the sidings leading to the crematoria. A second bomb hit a bomb shelter located between the crematoria sidings, killing thirty civilian workers.

Five miles away, the I.G. Farben plant at Monowitz, the object of the raid, was slightly damaged, and some three hundred slave labourers injured. On the following day, those who had been injured were given flowers, milk, and a double portion of margarine in the camp hospital.

For the Jews themselves, trapped as slave labourers at Monowitz, the impact of the raid had been considerable. Among those who witnessed it was Shalom Lindenbaum, who had been sent from Birkenau to Monowitz only a few days before. As the American bombers appeared in the sky, he later wrote:

We ceased to work, and the German soldiers and civilians ran to the shelters. Most of us didn't. So probably, we expressed our superiority feeling, and a kind of revenge. We had nothing to lose, only expected to enjoy the destruction of the big factory which we were building for the I.G. Farben Industrie. It was naturally so.

This happy feeling didn't change also after the Americans indeed, began to bomb, and obviously we had casualties too—wounded and dead. How beautiful was it to see squadron after squadron burst from the sky, drop bombs, destroy the buildings, and kill also members of the Herrenvolk.

Those bombardments elevated our morale and, paradoxically, awakened probably some hopes of surviving, of escaping from this hell. In our wild imagination we also saw a co-ordination between the Allies and the indeed small underground movement in the camp, with which I was in touch. We imagined a co-ordinated destruction and escape; destruction

---

[1] 'Copy of cable from Jewish Agency, Jerusalem, dated 13th Sept, 1944', Foreign Office papers, 371/42818, folio 31. The list of the railway routes is folio 32.

[2] Wesley Frank Craven and James Lea Cate (editors), The Army Air Force in World War II, volume 3, Chicago 1951.

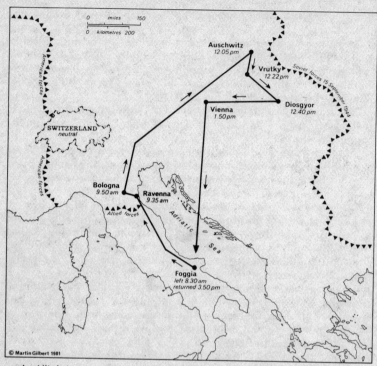

17. An Allied air reconnaissance sortie over Auschwitz, 16 September 1944, showing the time at which the aircraft flew over each of its objectives.

from above by the bombers, and from our hands, while escaping, even if we have to be living bombs—to be killed. Unfortunately this never occurred.[1]

The Monowitz raid of September 13 had lasted for only thirteen minutes, from 11.17 a.m. to 11.30 a.m. Ninety-six heavy bombers took part, dropping just over a thousand 500-pound bombs from 24,000 feet.

Like the raid of August 20, this one was also part of the continuing Allied efforts to destroy Germany's synthetic oil production. According to the interpretation of aerial photographs taken during the raid, 'only slight damage' was done, mostly to the 'small stores, buildings and labour barracks'. Two buildings in the 'concentration camp' were seen also to have been hit. Normal motor transport movement was seen. So too were the repairs to 'previous damage' in the raid of August 20, 'and new construction continuing'.[2]

[1] Letter to the author, 13 June 1980. Lindenbaum added in his letter: 'Maybe that such recollection will appear as superficial, as a retroactive imaginative reconstruction. To prove it, I called up four of my friends from Monowitz who live in my neighbourhood, and asked for their recollections. All of them had the same. It doesn't mean that there were no other reactions, probably were, but as I—and also they—could remember, we thought little about our life, rather enjoyed the bombings, mixed with natural human fear'.

[2] Photographic Interpretation Report No. G361. 'I.G.F. Synthetic Oil and Rubber Plant, Oswiecim, Poland (15.15 hours).' Based on Exposures 4053, 4054 and 4055. United States Strategic Bombing Survey, Record Group 243.

As part of the air attack on September 13, yet another photographic mission had flown over both Auschwitz and Birkenau, as well as over Monowitz. Its camera even recorded, twice, the falling bombs.[1] Also visible in the Birkenau photographs of September 13 are the gas chambers and Crematoria IV and V: the latter being hidden from the inmates of the camp by the birchwood.

Inside Birkenau, September 13 had seen both arrivals and departures. The arrivals were non-Jews: 929 Polish men and boys, and 900 Polish women and children who had been seized by the Gestapo in Warsaw at the beginning of the uprising. That same day 524 Jews were sent away from Auschwitz, to the concentration camp at Flossenbürg, to work in nearby factories.

The dual policy continued throughout September, Jews arriving from Lodz on the 15th and 18th being gassed, and Jews being sent out on the 17th to Mauthausen and on the 18th to Flossenbürg. The selection inside Auschwitz also continued. On September 19, the Jewish New Year, SS doctors visited each of the barracks in order to make a special selection of the 'sick'. They chose a hundred men, and the last sixty-five children who had been brought from the Kovno ghetto. All were gassed.

On September 16 two pilots from 680 Squadron, Flight Lieutenant Tasker and Flight Sergeant Murphy, left Foggia to photograph eight of the recently attacked oil plants and stores. Their sortie took them over Ravenna, Bologna, Auschwitz, Vrutky, Diosgyor and Vienna. Passing over Monowitz at five minutes after midday, the photographs which they took covered only the western third of the plant, the section least affected by the attack three days before. But they did show that the cooling tower serving the main distillation had been destroyed, and a purified gas-holder burned out.[2]

Two days later, on September 18, a second reconnaissance sortie by Major Allam and Lieutenant Roth of 683 Squadron was more successful in photographing the areas hit during the September 13 air-raid on Monowitz, but noted that owing to the dispersed nature of the buildings, 'fresh damage is not as heavy as it might otherwise be'. In addition to the damage noted by the camera two days before, the new photographs, when analysed, showed slight blast damage to the water gas plant, but found no other primary or even secondary objectives to have been 'visibly affected'. There was however some clear 'fresh' damage to stores, workshops, and 'in the labour camps to the south and south-west of the plant'. The camera also photographed clearance of bomb damage, and roof repairs, 'in progress around several points of earlier damage'.[3]

Further photographs were taken over Monowitz on September 18 by 60 Squadron. Air Intelligence confirmed the findings of Allam and Roth, but noted that there were 'no signs' of operative activity in any part of the plant, apart from a wisp of smoke or steam issuing from the southern end of the blower-house for the water gas plant', and the presence of gas in five gasholders.

[1] The bombs over Birkenau are seen in Exposure 3VI. Mission 464 BG: 4 M97. Can B8413, Scale 1:23,000. Altitude, 23,000 feet. The bombs over Auschwitz are seen in Exposure 4V2. In all, Birkenau appears in two of the photographs, Auschwitz in six. United States Strategic Bombing Survey, Record Group 243.

[2] Mediterranean Allied Photo Reconnaissance Wing, Interpretation Report No. D.B.214 of 16 September 1944, Prints 4044 and 4045. United States Strategic Bombing Survey, Record Group 243.

[3] Mediterranean Allied Photo Reconnaissance Wing. Interpretation report No. D.B.217 of 18 September 1944. Prints No. 3019–3024, 4019–4025 and 4022. United States Strategic Bombing Survey. Record Group 243.

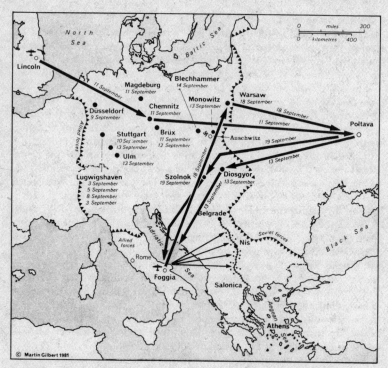

18. 'Operation Frantic' raids of 11, 13, 18 and 19 September 1944, including Allied air aid to Warsaw on 18 September, and Allied bombing targets connected with German oil production, refining and storage during September 1944.

The only other activity recorded was 'the usual movement' of trucks, personnel, 'cranes and hopper wagons and presence of rail cars'. The fresh damage, the intelligence analysts concluded, 'is not likely greatly to delay the work of completion of the synthetic oil plant'.[1]

Gruenbaum's appeal that the bombing of Auschwitz should again be considered reached London on September 20. It was at once sent on by Linton to Paul Mason at the Foreign Office. In his covering letter, Linton wrote:

You will note that three proposals are made. As regards the second, I am attaching a note of the four railway routes from Budapest to Poland.

About the third proposal, we were informed some time ago that there were technical difficulties in the way of bombing the Camp at Oswieczim. Since then however, we understand that the fuel depots in that area have been bombed on two occasions.

If the position has changed, it might perhaps be possible to reconsider the question of bombing the Camp.

'We should be very grateful,' Linton added, 'for anything you may be able to do in the matter.'[2]

---

[1] Mediterranean Allied Photo Reconnaissance Wing. Interpretation report No. D.P.110 of 21 September 1944. Prints No. 4020–4023. United States Strategic Bombing Survey, Record Group 243.

[2] Foreign Office papers, 371/42818, WR 1174, folio 30.

Linton's request for a second consideration of bombing was not pursued any further by the Foreign Office. Ironically, when he sent it to the Foreign Office on September 20, the officials there were still commenting on the earlier request, and on their own decision not to pass on to the Air Ministry the plans of Auschwitz which Linton had sent them, at their own instigation, a month before, on August 18.

On September 6 the Deputy Chief of the Air Staff, N. H. Bottomley, had written to Lieutenant General Spaatz:

The Foreign Office have now stated that Jews are no longer being deported from Hungary and that in view of this fact and because of the serious technical difficulties of carrying out bombing they do not propose to pursue the matter further.

This being so we are taking no further action at the Air Ministry and I suggest that you do not consider the project any further.[1]

No mention was made by Bottomley of the Air Ministry's request for intelligence, nor of the Jewish Agency's prompt provision of just such material. 'We are therefore technically guilty,' Paul Mason minuted on September 18, 'of allowing the Air.Min. to get away with it without having given them (tho' we had it) the info they asked for as a prerequisite.' Mason nevertheless agreed not to pursue the matter further. In all the circumstances, he minuted, 'I think perhaps (tho' I feel a little uneasy about it) we had better let this go by'.

Pondering Mason's reflection about British guilt, Eden's Assistant Private Secretary, Guy Millard, wrote on September 20: 'Surely this information was taken into consideration when the decision was taken not to pursue the matter'. 'That's the whole point,' Mason replied on September 21, 'It looks as if it wasn't.'

That same day, in a further minute, to William Cavendish-Bentinck, Paul Mason wrote: 'I cannot see that the topographical information made available to us by the Jewish Agency was ever communicated to the Air Ministry', and he added: 'I don't know whether, had the Air Ministry been sent this information (which doesn't look all that good) they would have modified their objections. But I am not quite happy about it'.

The point remained an 'actual one', Mason noted, since 'the Jewish Agency has just weighed in with a new suggestion, based upon fresh information about German extermination plans, that the camps should be bombed'. Mason's own view, like that of Lady Cheetham, was that 'if anyone is to do the job, it should be the Red Air Force which is much nearer'.

Roger Allen felt less uneasy than Mason. 'Even with the information,' he noted on September 22, 'the Air Ministry were reluctant to risk valuable lives & aircraft in a possibly futile reconnaissance.'[2] They would only have done so,

---

[1] Air Ministry papers, 19/218, 12/22.

[2] British airborne aid to the Warsaw uprising had also been affected by the argument of unnecessary risk, but to a much lesser extent. At the time of the first three flights across Poland, on August 4, 8 and 9, the Deputy Commander-in-Chief of the Mediterranean Allied Air Force, Sir John Slessor, had opposed further flights on the grounds of risk. But under pressure, he agreed to further Royal Air Force and South African Air Force flights on six consecutive days, August 12 to August 17. On these six days, 17 out of 93 aircraft were lost, after which Slessor insisted that all future flights were carried out by Polish volunteers. As for the risk of *reconnaissance* flights, as raised by Roger Allen, such flights were by September a regular feature of the follow-up of bombing raids for intelligence purposes, and none of the intelligence flights actually sent over Auschwitz, to photograph Monowitz (on September 16, September 18 – twice – and October 6), came to grief (see also map on page 316).

he added, 'if the Foreign Office had been strongly in favour of the attempt'. In fact, he noted, 'as is quite clear' from its minutes 'the Foreign Office were cooling off'. Allen continued:

In these circumstances, although I doubt if we have been quite fair to the Air Ministry in representing our failure to do what the Jewish Agency wanted as due to the technical reasons alone, I do not think that the fact that we did not pass on the topographical information will have greatly affected the Air Ministry's attitude. . . .

I suggest that this be allowed to go by, unless the question is raised again, in which case the topographical details will have to be sent to the Air Ministry.[1]

In fact, the question had been raised again, by Linton, in his letter of September 20. But the plans were not sent on to the Air Ministry.

Linton's letter and Gruenbaum's renewed appeal were received by the Foreign Office on September 22. They prompted two comments. The first, by Lady Cheetham on September 25, noted that according to the Swiss and Swedish Governments, the Hungarians had denied that Jews had been deported 'for any reason except to work in Germany in conditions similar to those accepted by Hungarian nationals'. In addition, the Hungarian Government had told the Swiss 'that they are ready to release Jews', but that the Germans would not grant exit permits for transit across Germany to either Switzerland or Sweden. Nor owing to the military situation, was it possible for Jews to escape across the border from Hungary to Rumania.

There was no proof, Lady Cheetham noted, that Hungarian policy had been 'reversed again', and she added: 'As to bombing the railway lines to Oswiecim, possibly the Soviets might consider doing this'.

Commenting on Lady Cheetham's minute, Paul Mason wrote:

The first question is, is there any authentic reason to suppose that the Hungarian Government have reversed the policy which existed early in August and are now preparing (doubtless under strongest German pressure) to send further people to the extermination camps in Silesia? I certainly would not accept what the Jewish Agency say without confirmation.

Mason suggested sending a 'short telegram' to the Swiss and Swedish Governments, to ask if either Government had reason to believe 'that a policy of deporting Jews to extermination camps is imminent or is actually taking place'. On the basis of their replies, he felt, 'would depend consideration of the further alternatives suggested by Mr Linton', none of which, he added, 'at first sight, to my mind, are really in any way practicable'.[2]

In the United States, one further bombing request had been sent by the War Refugee Board to the War Department. Its source was a telegram from James Mann, Assistant Executive Director of the Board, who, while on a visit to England, had been told by the Polish Government-in-Exile that 'in all Polish concentration camps the Germans are increasing their extermination activities'. According to a telegram from Mann to Pehle:

The War Refugee Board is urged by them again to explore with the Army the possibility of bombing the extermination chambers and German barracks at largest Polish concentration

---

[1] Minutes in Foreign Office papers, 371/42806, WR 823.
[2] Foreign Office papers, 371/42818, WR 1174, folio 29.

camps which, they say, are subject to precision bombing since they are sufficiently detached from the concentration camps.

Mann added that the Poles 'have promised to furnish me with recent maps which I will forward to Washington by air-mail, although I assume the Army authorities have maps of such camps'.[1]

On October 3, Pehle sent a copy of this appeal to John McCloy at the War Department. Two days later Harrison Gerhardt recommended to McCloy that 'no action be taken on this since the matter has been fully presented several times previously'. It was the War Department's position, he added, that any such bombing should be within the 'operational responsibility' of the Russian forces.[2]

Still in the United States, one further request for bombing the camps had been pressed on the War Department, this time by Nahum Goldmann. who raised it personally with McCloy. Goldmann later recalled, in a letter to the author: 'McCloy indicated to me that, although the Americans were reluctant about my proposal, they might agree to it, though any decision as to the targets of bombardments in Europe was in the hands of the British. I was therefore advised to approach the British representative on the Allied High Command, General Dill. . . .'

With some difficulty Goldmann managed to obtain an interview with General Dill. Their talk, he recalled, was 'one of the most unforgettable and depressing of my long career', and he added:

General Dill took from the start a completely negative attitude. His argument was that bombing the camps would result in the death of thousands of prisoners.

I replied to him that they were destined to being gassed anyhow and explained that the idea to bomb the death camps had been suggested to us by the Jewish underground in Poland, with whom we were in a certain contact through the Polish government in exile in London, which regularly conveyed messages from the Jewish Nazi victims to us—mainly Rabbi Stephen Wise and myself—via the American State Department.

General Dill thereupon revealed his real motivation, by declaring that the British had to save bombs for military targets and that the only salvation for the Jews would be for the Allies to win the war.

I answered that the few dozen bombs needed to strike the death camps would not influence the outcome of the war and pointed out that the Royal Air Force was regularly bombing the I.G. Farben factories, a few miles distant from Auschwitz.

At the end of our talk, which lasted over an hour, I accused General Dill and his colleagues of lack of human understanding for the terrible tragedy of the extermination camps. He regarded it as discourteous for me to be so outspoken in my criticism.[3]

Unknown to Goldmann, there had been a further aerial reconnaissance over Auschwitz on October 16. Once again, its sole purpose had been to examine the progress of repairs at the I.G. Farben plant at Monowitz, now that just over a month had passed since the second of the two bombing attacks. The sortie, by Captain Barry and Lieutenant Jefferys, revealed 'a great deal of repair and constructional activity' in both the synthetic oil and synthetic rubber plants since the last report in mid-September. Although assessment was 'hampered by hazy prints', it was still 'obvious' that repairs had progressed

---

[1] War Refugee Board, Box 35, Measures Directed Towards Halting Persecution, F: Hungary, No. 5.

[2] National Archives and Records Service, RG 107, 400.38 Jews.

[3] Letter to the author, 27 February 1980.

'at almost all points'. There then followed an analysis of the repair of thirteen separate groups of buildings.[1]

As Monowitz continued production, it remained a primary target. Indeed, in October 1944, it accounted for Germany's third highest production of synthetic oil, after Blechhammer North and Odertal.[2]

The Jewish Agency's alarm about Hungarian Jews being again deported to Auschwitz had not been misplaced, although the reported numbers of the renewed deportations, 'twelve thousand daily', were far in excess of the numbers now involved. Trains with Hungarian Jews had indeed reached Auschwitz on September 4, 5, 15 and 18, but with only several hundred Jews in each. A fifth train had reached Auschwitz from Budapest on September 20. Eight men were sent to the barracks but the remaining fifty-two were gassed. Later that same day a second train arrived from Hungary: 31 men and 22 women were sent to the barracks. The remaining 146 were gassed.

The one special Allied air effort that continued throughout September remained the sending of help to the Poles still fighting against the Germans in Warsaw. On September 18 the American Air Force Eighth Bomber Group had flown the last of the Frantic missions. They had left from England, dropped their supplies over Warsaw, and flown on to Poltava. A total of 107 Flying Fortresses took part, dropping 1,284 containers of arms and supplies. Nearly a thousand fell into German hands. Less than a hundred reached the Polish Home Army.[3] Two days later, on September 20, the last Polish volunteer flight from Foggia to Warsaw took place, also to drop supplies. Of twenty aircraft that took part, five were shot down. Since the beginning of August, 200 pilots had been killed on these Warsaw raids.

From a map in Churchill's papers, the flight paths to Warsaw can be seen passing just to the west of Cracow, virtually over Auschwitz itself.[4] But it was the agony of Warsaw, not the agony of the Jews, that had come to dominate the telegraphic exchanges of the Allied leaders.

---

[1] Interpretation Report No. D.B.241, 60 Squadron. Sortie 60/792 of 16 October 1944. 'Poland Oswiecim Syn. Oil and Rubber Plant (13.49 hours).' Prints 3011–15. United States Strategic Bombing Survey, Record Group 243.

[2] German synthetic oil production in October 1944, in tons: Blechhammer North, 3,400 tons, Odertal 2,600 tons. Monowitz 2,000 tons. Lower in the scale were Trzebinia, 1,500 tons, Kolin, 1,500 tons, Schwechat, 800 tons and Pardubice, 200 tons. Mediterranean and South Air Forces Weekly Intelligence Survey No. 9, dated 5 March 1945. United States Strategic Bombing Survey, Record Group 243.

[3] Wesley Frank Craven and James Lea Cate (editors), The Army Air Force in World War II, volume 3, Chicago 1951.

[4] Premier papers, 3/352/11. On 2 October 1944 Stalin vetoed the use of Poltava for any further British or United States flights in support of the Warsaw uprising.

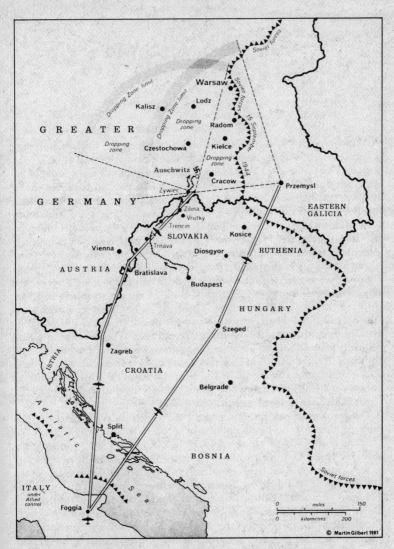

19. Allied airborne aid to Warsaw between early August and late September 1944, showing the two main flight paths and the principal dropping zones, as well as the front line positions of the Red Army on 15 September, and the renewed deportations by rail from Budapest to Auschwitz on 4, 5, 15, 18 and 20 September 1944.

Chapter 33

The end of Auschwitz

At Auschwitz itself, the process of destruction continued. On September 30 a thousand prisoners in Auschwitz Main Camp were 'selected' as unfit, and gassed. That same day, 2,499 Jewish men and women were brought to Birkenau from Theresienstadt. No more than five hundred were sent to the barracks: the rest were gassed. A further 1,500 Jews arrived from Theresienstadt on October 2, and all but three hundred were gassed. A similar number arrived on October 3: some six hundred were sent to the barracks, and nine hundred were gassed. On October 6, from another train which reached Auschwitz from Theresienstadt, 271 women and a hundred men were sent to the barracks, and the rest, 1,230 men, women and children, were gassed.

Unknown to the Allies, on October 7 one of the groups of Jewish prisoners who were being forced to pull the bodies out of the gas chambers, and take them to the crematoria, revolted. Throwing a Gestapo overseer into the flames, these *Sonderkommando*, as they were called, then killed four other SS men, blew up the crematorium itself, Crematorium IV, and ran off towards the camp fence. About six hundred *Sonderkommando* managed to break out of the camp. But the alarm had been raised, and all were hunted down and shot. Two days later four women, who had been arrested in the women's camps in Auschwitz I and Birkenau, were charged with smuggling explosives to the *Sonderkommando*, tortured, and then hanged.

The revolt destroyed one of the four Birkenau crematoria. The remaining three continued to operate without a break. On October 9, only two days after the revolt, and on the day on which the four girls were hanged, two thousand Jews who had arrived from Trieste and Theresienstadt were gassed, as well as two thousand Jewesses specially 'selected' from Birkenau.

Rumours of an impending increase in the pace of gassing had reached the Foreign Office and the State Department from the Polish Government-in-Exile, which circulated an appeal by the Council for the Rescue of the Jewish Population in Poland. The appeal warned that the Germans were preparing the mass murder of 'all persons imprisoned' at both Auschwitz and Birkenau, and asked all the Allied Governments 'to do everything possible' to deflect the Germans from their apparent intention, which included the 'annihilation' of the 'remnants of the Jewish population in Poland'.[1]

On October 8 the Deputy Under-Secretary of State at the Foreign Office, Sir Orme Sargent, telegraphed to Eden, who was on his way with Churchill to Moscow, about growing pressure for an Allied statement. This pressure

---

[1] Ambassador Winant to Secretary of State, telegram No. A–1225, United States National Archives, 840.48, Refugees/10/944.

came not only from the Poles, he explained, but from 'other minor Allies', including the Czechoslovak Government. The Foreign Office view, Sargent added, was that a statement should indeed be issued, 'in view of increasing Polish pressure and of interest taken by Jewish and humanitarian organizations'. Unfortunately, Sargent explained, Churchill himself had opposed any such declaration, and had expressed his opposition in a terse minute before he had left for Moscow: 'Surely publicity given about this might ban a chance of saving the multitudes concerned'.[1] Such, apparently, was Churchill's view.

In fact, the Churchill minute had been wrongly copied by a secretary. What Churchill had actually written was: 'Surely publicity given about this might *have* a chance of saving the multitudes concerned'.[2] As soon as this error was noticed, the British Government consulted both the United States and Soviet Government as to how to respond. The Americans replied that they wished to issue a solemn warning that 'if these plans are carried out, those guilty of such murderous acts will be brought to justice and will pay the penalty for their heinous crimes'. The Soviet Government made no reply. The British therefore agreed with the United States to join in issuing the warning, which was broadcast from Washington at 12 noon on October 10, and from London, over the BBC, at 6 p.m. and 9 p.m. that same evening. 'We should welcome publicity,' the Foreign Office had stated.[3]

Neither the broadcast itself, nor the Declaration, made any mention of the Jews. The Declaration referred to German plans for 'mass execution of the people in the concentration camps Oswiecim and Brzezinky'. At these camps, it stated, 'thousands of people from many European countries are imprisoned'. The Declaration continued with a warning 'that if this plan, or any similar plan elsewhere, is carried out', the British Government 'will hold responsible all those who are in any way involved, from the highest to the lowest. In full co-operation and agreement with the Allies, they will spare no effort to bring the guilty to justice'.[4]

To the surprise of the Allies, their warning of October 10 brought an instant response from Berlin. 'These reports are false from beginning to end,' the German Telegraph Service announced on October 11. Commenting on this announcement, an official in the Central Department of the Foreign Office, Frank Roberts, noted: 'A satisfactory reaction. Our declaration may for once have been worth while'.[5]

But the Allied warning, issued so promptly and phrased so clearly, led to no relaxation of the slaughter. On the day of the warning eight hundred Gipsy boys and girls had been gassed, and two days later, on October 12, three thousand Jewish women were 'selected' from the barracks at Birkenau and gassed in Crematorium II. A further three thousand women were taken from the barracks and gassed on October 13, as were 1,360 men, women and children who had arrived from Theresienstadt on the previous day. Every

[1] Premier papers, 3/352/4, folios 78 and 80.

[2] Premier papers, 3/352/4, folio 70.

[3] Foreign Office papers, 371/39454, C 13943.

[4] Home News Bulletin, 6 p.m., 10 October 1944, page 11, BBC Written Archives Centre. The final text of the Declaration is in Foreign Office papers, 371/39454, C 13943.

[5] Foreign Office papers, 371/39454, C 13914.

day saw further gassings. Even those working for I.G. Farben at Monowitz were not spared. On October 17 a total of two thousand were selected as 'unfit for further work', and gassed, as were 155 women, bringing the death toll for that single week to eight hundred Gipsies and 17,392 Jews. Not for four months had such a rate of killing been achieved. The Anglo-American warning had been in vain. Nor did the following seven days see any end to the killing: on October 18, three thousand Jews brought from Slovakia, three hundred Jews brought from Budapest and thirteen Polish non-Jews were gassed. That same day the Polish Government-in-Exile announced that the Germans had begun 'the mass murder of Poles in gas chambers' at Auschwitz, and that 12,400 civilians 'driven from Warsaw' after the uprising were among those 'in danger'.[1] The announcement made no mention of Jews.

On the following night, in a broadcast to Germany, in German, Professor Lindley Fraser read out the names of seven Germans 'from among the personnel in the camps', including 'the political chief' of Auschwitz. Fraser described Auschwitz as 'perhaps the most horrible in reputation of all the concentration camps set up by the Nazis'. His broadcast ended:

Let all the other people concerned be warned. These atrocities are capital crimes which will be punished. Let all those concerned in them whether as initiators or as executives or in any other way, reflect whether they are wise to behave like this at the end of an already lost war.

And let the German people remember that the men who are now calling on it to commit national suicide on their behalf are the men who are directly responsible for a series of crimes which have left an indelible stain on the honour of their country.[2]

The gassings at Auschwitz continued, particularly of Jews from Theresienstadt. So intense was the killing that by the end of October more than 33,000 Jews had been murdered in thirty-one days. But when, on October 12, A. G. Brotman, on behalf of the Board of Deputies of British Jews, asked Paul Mason to consider bombing the camp in conjunction with the Soviet Air Force, Mason, 'invited his attention to the risk of Germany claiming that *we* had done our best, by bombing the camp, to exterminate the inmates ourselves'.[3]

On September 29 a telegram had reached Istanbul, from Krausz in Budapest, to say that 'only 200,000' of Hungary's 800,000 Jews were still alive.[4] On October 6 the Jewish Agency learned that the Swedish representative in Budapest, Raoul Wallenberg, had arranged to issue five thousand 'protective passports', with a further four thousand which would be ready in the next few days, and that as Germany had now definitely refused transit facilities for passport holders, these Jews were being put into special houses in Budapest 'under Swedish protection'.[5] Despite this, nearly 100,000 Jews were assembled in Budapest at the end of the month, and forced to march westwards, towards

[1] *Daily Telegraph,* 19 October 1944, under the headline 'Mass Murder of Poles'.

[2] 'More Polish Atrocities', copy of broadcast transcript in Foreign Office papers, 371/39454, C 14402.

[3] Foreign Office papers, 371/39454, C 14201.

[4] The telegram had been sent from Budapest to Istanbul on September 4. It was forwarded from Istanbul to London on September 29, arriving on October 7. Copy in Foreign Office papers, 371/42818, WR 1301.

[5] Central Zionist Archives, S 25/1678.

the Austrian border. Tens of thousands perished during this march: the victims of hunger, exposure, individual brutality and mass shooting.

On October 29 a total of 547 Rumanian Jews reached Istanbul on board the *Selahedine*. All were sent straight on to Palestine on a collective passport.

At Auschwitz on November 1 a total of seventy-three women were taken from the barracks and gassed. But a far larger number, 1,717 women and 634 men, were sent from Auschwitz by train to Ravensbrück and Bergen-Belsen, to fill the growing reservoir of slave labourers needed in central and western Germany, as the Allied armies advanced eastward from France towards the Rhine. On November 2, four women were gassed, and 795 sent westward. But the process could still work in reverse, and on November 3, of a total of 509 Jews reaching Auschwitz from the Slovak labour camp at Sered, 481 were gassed on arrival.

The mass killings at Auschwitz were almost over. As Soviet forces stood poised in the Carpathians for its next westward offensive, more and more of the inmates of Auschwitz were sent by train to concentration camps in Germany to join the slave labour reserve, while fewer and fewer trains reached Auschwitz itself.

It was only now, after the gas chambers at Auschwitz had almost ceased their work, that the full text of the Vrba-Wetzler report, the Mordowicz-Rosin report, and the Polish Major's report actually reached the desk of the Director of the War Refugee Board, John W. Pehle.

Upset by what he had read, Pehle wrote on November 8 to McCloy at the War Department. These eye-witness descriptions, he wrote, 'have just been received' from Roswell McClelland in Switzerland. No report hitherto received by the Board, Pehle added, 'has quite caught the gruesome brutality of what is taking place in these camps of horror. . . .'

At last, Pehle himself was in favour of bombing the camps. As he explained to McCloy:

The Germans have been forced to devote considerable technological ingenuity and administrative know-how in order to carry out murder on a mass production basis, as the attached reports will testify. If the elaborate murder installations at Birkenau were destroyed, it seems clear that the Germans could not reconstruct them for some time.

Until now, despite pressure from many sources, I have been hesitant to urge the destruction of these camps by direct, military action. But I am convinced that the point has now been reached where such action is justifiable if it is deemed feasible by competent military authorities.

I strongly recommend that the War Department give serious consideration to the possibility of destroying the execution chambers and crematories in Birkenau through direct bombing action.

Pehle's letter to McCloy continued with further reasons why the bombing should now be carried out:

It may be observed that there would be other advantages of a military nature to such an attack. The Krupp and Siemens factories, where among other things cases for handgrenades are made, and a Buna plant, all within Auschwitz, would be destroyed. The destruction of the German barracks and guard-houses and the killing of German soldiers in the area would also be accomplished.

The morale of underground groups might be considerably strengthened by such a dramatic exhibition of Allied air support and a number of the people confined in Auschwitz and Birkenau might be liberated in the confusion resulting from the bombing.

That the effecting of a prison break by such methods is not without precedent is indicated by the description in the enclosed copy of a recent New York Times article of the liberation from Amiens prison of 100 French patriots by the R.A.F.[1]

Pehle ended his letter by pleading 'the urgency of the situation' as his reason for making this appeal, and asked for McCloy's reply 'as soon as possible'.[2]

Once again, but now far too late, the bombing request was sent through the War Department on yet another futile journey to the Operations division, where once again it was turned down with the same arguments that had been used so decisively in June, July and August, that it would divert air power from vital industrial targets.

The War Refugee Board learned of these arguments in a letter from McCloy, sent from the War Department on November 18. The letter added that Auschwitz could only be hit by American heavy bombers, based in Britain, which 'would necessitate a hazardous round trip flight unescorted of approximately 2,000 miles over enemy territory'. No reference was made to the Foggia airbase or to the fact that the round trip, which was far less than two thousand miles,[3] had already been carried out many times by United States planes bombing industrial targets throughout the Auschwitz region, and that for each raid a fighter escort had not only been provided, but had proved effective. Indeed, it was the range of the fighter escort, not of the bombers, that had made possible these bombing raids, including the raids over Monowitz and Trzebinia, the targets nearest to Auschwitz.

McCloy also told Pehle:

At the present critical stage of the war in Europe, our strategic air forces are engaged in the destruction of industrial target systems vital to the dwindling war potential of the enemy, from which they should not be diverted. The positive solution to this problem is the earliest possible victory over Germany, to which end we should exert our entire means.[4]

On receiving this bombing negative, the War Refugee Board decided to take one final step, the publication in full of the three reports, and these were issued to the Press on November 25. The three reports were prefaced by a page of explanation, including the War Refugee Board's comment that: 'So revolting and diabolical are the German atrocities that the minds of civilized people find it difficult to believe that they have actually taken place'. Nevertheless, the Board continued, 'the Governments of the United States and other countries have evidence which clearly substantiates the facts' and 'recently' according to this introduction, the Board had received 'from a representative close to the scene, two eye-witness accounts of evidence which occurred in notorious extermination camps established by the Germans'. The introduction ended:

[1] This was 'Operation Jericho', carried out in March 1944, and already cited, four months before, by the British Secretary of State for Air, as a possible model (see page 285 of this volume).

[2] War Refugee Board, Box 6, German Extermination Camps.

[3] The distance from the American airbase at Foggia to Auschwitz and back, including diversions to avoid the area immediately above the Soviet-German front line, was just under 1,300 miles.

[4] National Archives and Records Service, RG 107, ASW 400.38, Countries-Germany.

The Board has every reason to believe that these reports present a true picture of the frightful happenings in these camps. It is making the reports public in the firm conviction that they should be read and understood by all Americans.

The Vrba-Wetzler report was headed 'No. 1, The Extermination Camps of Auschwitz (Oswiecim) and Birkenau in Upper Silesia', and filled thirty-three pages. The Mordowicz-Rosin report followed, as a seven-page addition to the Vrba-Wetzler report. The Polish Major's report was headed 'No. 2. Transport (The Polish Major's Report)', and filled nineteen pages.[1]

All three reports were given substantial publicity in the *New York Times* of November 26, which published as one of its front page headlines:

U.S. BOARD BARES ATROCITY DETAILS
TOLD BY WITNESSES AT POLISH CAMPS

The story that followed described 'the first detailed report' made by a United States Government agency offering 'eye witness proof of mass murder by the Germans', atrocities which, the newspaper declared, 'transcend the horrors of Lublin'. While at Lublin, the newspaper summary continued, 1,500,000 people were said to have been killed in three years, at Birkenau from April 1942 to April 1944 '1$\frac{1}{2}$ million to 1,765,000 persons were murdered in the torture chambers'.[2] There had been 'many thousands of other deaths,' the report continued, by 'phenol injection, brutal beatings, starvation, shootings etc.'[3]

The inside page continued for five and a half columns giving details from both the Vrba-Wetzler report and the Polish Major's report, as published by the War Refugee Board, and on the following day, at a special meeting of the World Jewish Congress in Atlantic City at which Nahum Goldmann, Stephen Wise and Chaim Weizmann each spoke, there was a renewed appeal for the removal of the existing restrictions on Jewish immigration into Palestine as well as an appeal for the removal of restrictions on Jewish land purchase which had been a part of the 1939 White Paper.[4]

In Budapest, both Swedish and British documents had continued to protect several thousand Hungarian Jews from pogroms and death marches. On November 3 Paul Mason noted that 4,500 Jews were holders of Swedish 'protective passports', and eight thousand of 'certificates for admission into Palestine'. These certificates, however, 'do not, of course entitle their holders to anything more than visas for temporary admission into Palestine', and he went on to point out that the Colonial Office had only agreed to issue these certificates 'in the belief that they would never have to be honoured'. He had even heard a Colonial Office opinion 'the other day' which suggested 'they

---

[1] Executive Office of the President, War Refugee Board, 'German Extermination Camps—Auschwitz and Birkenau'. At the Nuremberg Trial this 59-page document was submitted as document 022-L.
[2] Other than at Auschwitz, more than two million Jews had been killed in the death camps of German-occupied Poland between January 1942 and January 1944. The approximate number of killings in these camps has been estimated after the war at 840,000 (Treblinka), 600,000 (Belzec), 360,000 (Chelmno), 250,000 (Sobibor) and 125,000 (Majdanek). The Lublin area had long been associated in western minds with privation and killing, from the earlier days of the Lublinland 'reservation' (see page 13). Majdanek is 2 miles from Lublin, Sobibor 60 miles, Belzec 80 miles, Treblinka 110 miles and Chelmno 220 miles.
[3] *New York Times*, 26 November 1944.
[4] *New York Times*, 27 November 1944.

regarded these certificates as "bogus" and would not honour them on presentation'.

Mason expressed his 'alarm' at this attitude. If it became known, he commented, 'we could never hope to get any other Jews holding such certificates out of German clutches', and his colleague G. Hall Patch noted: 'If genuine certificates have been issued it is inconceivable, to my mind, that there should be any suggestion that they would be dishonoured on presentation. Action of this sort is more in keeping with the traditions of a disreputable Balkan or South American Government, than with those of HMG.'[1]

Since July, Jewish rescue efforts, particularly of Jews in Hungary, had been coordinated on a daily basis with the International Red Cross, the Swedish Government, the Swiss, the Americans and the British. But at the beginning of November cooperation with the British, essential in all matters concerning certificates for Palestine, was suddenly thrown into turmoil by the assassination of Lord Moyne by two members of the Stern Gang. On November 8 David Ben Gurion and Moshe Shertok telegraphed to the Egyptian Prime Minister, Ahmed Maher Pasha: 'Entire organised Jewish community Palestine and Jewish public throughout world were shocked and horrified by assassination in Cairo in broad daylight of Lord Moyne British Minister resident in Middle East.' The telegram continued: 'We execrate murderers as traitors to their peoples cause and express sympathy with Egyptian Government in grave embarrassment caused to them by this assassination'.[2] This condemnation of Lord Moyne's murder by the leaders of the Jewish Agency Executive was endorsed that same day by Chaim Weizmann, who was then in London. 'Count every effort will be made stamp out this dreadful evil,' he telegraphed to his colleagues in Jerusalem, and on the following day Lord Moyne's son replied by telegram to Shertok's condolences: 'Deeply touched by your message of sympathy and especially by the personal tribute which you pay to my father. . . .'[3]

Despite Lord Moyne's assassination, the British Government made no change in its open door policy at Istanbul. The eighty-eight Jewish children who had reached Istanbul on November 8 and 9 from Bulgaria were given immediate visas, and were able to leave by train for Palestine on November 10.[4]

On November 11 the Allied Combined Intelligence Unit prepared a Top Secret report on the principal sites of German synthetic oil production. At Auschwitz-Monowitz, it was clear, 'progress has been made with construction' of the Buna plant. Two of the lime kilns 'are now complete and the third is nearing completion'. As a result of the bombing attacks on August 20 and September 13, it now appeared, there had been 'a cessation of production for two or three months', and the production recently restored was at only two-thirds its earlier capacity. The probable annual production of synthetic oil was estimated at between 24,000 and 33,000 tons.[5]

[1] 'Jews in Hungary', Foreign Office papers, 371/42828, WR 1814.
[2] Central Zionist Archives, S 25/1682.
[3] Central Zionist Archives, S 25/1678.
[4] Central Zionist Archives, L 15/106 II.
[5] Interpretation Report No. D.907R of 11 November 1944, 'German Buna Plants'. United States Strategic Bombing Survey, Record Group 243.

As a result of this report, a further attack on Monowitz was planned for November 29. Meanwhile, unknown to the Allies, on November 26 Heinrich Himmler ordered the crematoria at Auschwitz to be destroyed. That same day, as Crematorium II was being dismantled, its motor was crated up for dispatch to Mauthausen, and its gas conduits for dispatch to Gross Rosen. Also on November 26, a total of thirty prisoners in the *Sonderkommando*, their horrific 'tour of duty' done, were gassed in Crematorium V.

The dismantling of Crematorium II continued, and is clearly visible in the United States aerial reconnaissance photographs taken four days later, on November 29. For the first time since the earliest of the aerial photographs of April 4, no train was to be seen at the Birkenau railhead. The destroyed Crematorium IV, blown up during the *Sonderkommando* revolt on October 7, can also be identified.[1]

In the intelligence report that followed the reconnaissance, no mention is made of the crematoria area at Birkenau. But for the first time there is a direct reference to the number and nature of the trains in the Auschwitz-Birkenau 'marshalling yard'. Although the photographs themselves were of 'dark quality', they revealed, in the 'North Yard', approximately 220 to 240 'mixed wagons', five locomotives 'in steam', and two other locomotives, while in the 'South Yard' the Allied analysts noted 160 mixed wagons, one locomotive 'in steam', and twenty-three box cars on the railway sidings 'in industrial plant West of South Yards', as well as two locomotives 'in steam in an unidentified area' to the southwest.[2]

It is clear from this analysis that nothing was known by those who made it of the purpose or role of Birkenau and its sidings. In the same report, the scrutiny of Monowitz was as detailed, and as specific as always. Smoke and steam issuing from several smoke stacks and installations indicated 'the plant to be active'. Five small work trains, two small locomotives, and several lorries were seen 'moving in the plant area'. In addition the report noted that 'numerous personnel can also be seen moving about', that further repairs had been carried out to damaged installations, and that 'new construction' had continued. Some thirty railway wagons were to be seen on the Monowitz sidings, and approximately a hundred wagons 'on the railway sidings east of the plant area'.[3]

From this it was clear that Monowitz was still operational, and on December 18 the Allied bombers attacked again, some bombs hitting the plant, and others the labour camp, the latter to such an extent that the first intelligence analysis revealed that five huts had 'suffered partial destruction from direct hits'. But there was also wastage, a cluster of twelve bombs having fallen in the 'open area'.[4] A second intelligence report five days after the raid was to

[1] Records of the Defense Intelligence Agency (RG 373), Aerial Photographs of Auschwitz and Birkenau, Mission 15 S 6/887 5PG, Can D 1610, Exposures 4058–61.

[2] Photographic Interpretation Report No. G.430 of 29 November 1944. 'Poland, Marshalling Yard: Oswiecim/Brzezinka (and Industry)'. Photo 3068–70, 4059 and 4060. United States Strategic Bombing Survey, Record Group 243.

[3] Photographic Interpretation Report No. G.430 of 29 November 1944. 'Poland. Oswiecim Synthetic Oil and Rubber Plant (13.15 Hours)'. Photos 4036–67. United States Strategic Bombing Survey, Record Group 243.

[4] Photographic Interpretation Report No. G.453 of 21 December 1944. 'Poland, Oswiecim Synthetic Oil and Rubber Works', Photos 4027–30. United States Strategic Bombing Survey, Record Group 243.

reveal 'particularly heavy damage' to the injector house, compressor house and north workshop, but at the same time reported substantial 'repairs and construction' in the distillation plant, cooling plant, lime kiln and railway shed. In addition, in the 'concentration camp', that is to say, Monowitz's own slave labour camp, 'three heavily damaged buildings have been repaired'.[1]

On December 4 another ship from Rumania, the *Toros*, brought 908 Jewish refugees to Istanbul. Of these, 380 were Jewish orphans from Transnistria, 420 were Hungarian refugees, and a hundred were Jews from Rumania. All were given a collective visa by the British Passport Control Office in Istanbul, and left by train for Palestine three days later.[2]

At Auschwitz, the destruction of the evidence continued. On December 5 a group of fifty Jewish women was formed into a special 'commando' and given orders to dig out all the corpses which had been tossed into mass graves around Crematorium IV, and to burn the bodies in open pits.

In photographs taken by a further United States photographic reconnaissance on December 21, the sole aim of which was to show the extent of the damage at Monowitz during the bombing raid three days before, many of the electrified fences and guard towers of Birkenau can now be seen to have been dismantled. At Crematorium II the undressing room roof adjacent to the gas chamber had been removed, and the roof and chimney of the Crematorium itself were in the process of being dismantled. The fences around the Crematorium can also be seen to have been removed. Around Crematorium III the fences are also gone, and the whole building surrounded by debris. But none of this was looked for, noticed, or in any way suspected by those whose only purpose in studying the photographs was to learn more about Monowitz and its synthetic oil production.

Auschwitz main camp remained, as did the women's camp in Birkenau, and conditions continued harsh, intensified by severe cold and frequent snow falls. During December 2,093 women died in Auschwitz, leaving 18,751 on the camp roll-call on December 27.

Allied bombers had continued to attack the nearby industrial zones, and in a further American raid on Monowitz on December 26, a cluster of bombs had fallen by mistake on the SS sick bay in Birkenau. One of those who witnessed this attack was Erich Kulka. Thirty-five years later he recalled how:

I and a colleague working in the maintenance squad had been called to the SS sick bay in Birkenau because the central heating pipes had been damaged by frost over Christmas. We were ordered to repair it, and hurried across to the SS rooms. In the room we found oranges, figs and chocolates, things I had not seen for five years. Being left alone for a few moments to do the repairs, we took the food and hid it under our jackets, then we began the repairs.

Suddenly we heard the sirens. The SS took us into the heating cellar. As we hid in the cellar we heard the sound of bombs falling. There were about five bombs. One of the bombs crashed near this heating building. We were covered with rubble and ashes.

When the smoke cleared and we came out of the cellar we found one SS man dead by the

---

[1] Photographic Interpretation Report No. G.286 of 23 December 1944. 'Poland, Oswiecim Synthetic Oil and Rubber Plant (12.09 Hours)'. Prints 4065-71. United States Strategic Bombing Survey, Record Group 243.

[2] Central Zionist Archives, L 15/106 II.

doors, another by the windows. About five SS men were killed during the raid. We were exactly one mile from the annihilation plant area.

After the raid we were escorted back to our camp. Entering our barrack, dirty and bleeding, we took our the figs and oranges—as a Christmas gift to our friends.

'We saw it,' Kulka added, 'as an adventure.'[1]

The raid of December 26 was judged a success, the photographic intelligence experts reporting that in the synthetic oil plant 'a good concentration of hits has been scored throughout the plant'. Many of the installations had received direct hits. Many more had 'probably' been damaged by blast. Nevertheless, although the roof of the coke intake had been 'heavily damaged by blast', the operation in that sector of the plant 'has apparently been resumed'. In the synthetic rubber plant, several important buildings had been hit, but the gantry crane had apparently not been damaged at all, 'although many hits were scored in the area'.[2]

Some parts of the synthetic oil and production processes, although much damaged, were still working after the raid of December 26, and the slave labour camp at Monowitz, as well as the dozens of other factories in the Auschwitz region, continued to employ thousands of Jewish men and women from Auschwitz. On December 30 there were 2,036 women registered in the Monowitz group of factories, and 1,088 at the Union factory nearby. Of the male inmates at Auschwitz 35,000 were working at Monowitz, and another 31,000 in other factories in the region.

As the Jewish refugees from Rumania now grew in number, with the collapse of German influence there, and as the Rumanian ports were opened to civilian traffic, the problem of British policy in Palestine re-emerged. On December 22 the Jewish Agency protested to both London and New York that 608 refugees on board the *Stara Zagora* had been sent back to Bulgaria by the Turkish Government, after the British had refused to give them Palestine visas.[3] The British authorities argued that the December quota of 1,500 had already been exceeded.[4] Other refugees from Rumania were being held at the Bulgarian border, with very little food and no medicine, and had been refused permission by the Turks to proceed to Istanbul.

But the crisis was shortlived, and on December 30 instructions reached the British Embassy in Ankara to make immediate arrangements to allow the refugees on the *Stara Zagora* to proceed to Palestine.[5] On 5 January 1945 they returned to Istanbul, and two days later they were on the train to Palestine. Most, it emerged, were refugees who had been born in Poland and Hungary.

The Red Army was now approaching Auschwitz. It had already reached Lublin, and had published for the world to see photographs of corpses and skele-

[1] Conversation with Erich Kulka, Jerusalem, 4 February 1980.

[2] Photographic Interpretation Report No. D.B.245 of 4 January 1945. Sortie 328/635 (Lt. Smith). 'Poland, Oswiecim O/R and Synthetic Rubber Plant (11.10 hours).' Prints 4002–08. United States Strategic Bombing Survey, Record Group 243. Among the aircraft taking part in this reconnaissance was one from 60 Squadron, South African Air Force (Lieutenant Rodseth and Flying Officer Starbuck).

[3] Goldin telegram, No. 6154, Central Zionist Archives, L 15/116.

[4] Foreign Office papers, 371/42824.

[5] Barlas telegram, No. 5032, Central Zionist Archives, L 15/116.

tons lying pell-mell in the courtyard of Majdanek. This evidence of Nazi atrocities was difficult for many people to take in. 'The British and American people,' wrote Captain D. MacLaren, of the Psychological Warfare Division, on 3 January 1945, 'are still not as a whole willing to believe that German atrocities abroad and the Gestapo reign of terror at home, has been anything like what it is.' A special publication should be prepared, he believed, with photographs, 'setting forth the record of the Gestapo'.

Captain MacLaren's boss in the Political Intelligence Department, Ritchie Calder, approved this plan, but was sceptical of its effect. There was, he wrote, 'a saturation point in human psychology, and people who would be likely in peacetime to respond to cruelty to a child or to an animal will, after years of being told of brutalities, become anaesthetised even to a Lublin'.

Ritchie Calder also argued that the Germans 'do not believe or do not want to believe' what their enemies told them about their atrocities, and that there was 'a danger that they may become convinced that we are building up these excesses only to justify our subsequent excesses'. Nevertheless, he added, 'the charge sheet has to be made out. . . .'[1]

On what facts, however, was that 'charge sheet' to be based? One document which reached the British Foreign Office on January 9 was a seven-page memorandum compiled by the Inter-Governmental Committee on Refugees, entitled 'Jewish Refugee Problem'. The purpose of the memorandum was to estimate the number of Jews who, after the war, would seek refugee status and new homes. Part of the problem of estimating the numbers of refugees revolved around the estimate of the number of deaths. Ian Henderson commented on January 11: 'One notable tendency in Jewish reports on this problem is to exaggerate the numbers of deportations and deaths and thereby to underestimate considerably the number of survivors presenting a problem'.[2]

At the end of the first week of January, as the Red Army drew nearer to Auschwitz, the Gestapo began to organize the evacuation of more than 65,000 Jewish prisoners.[3] The first to leave were a thousand women, sent from Birkenau to Bergen-Belsen on January 6.

On January 14 the United States Air Force flew its twelfth photographic reconnaissance flight over Monowitz. Once more, all of Auschwitz and all of Birkenau were included. Studying the photographs today, the continuing dismantling of the gas chambers and crematoria is evident. So also is the substantial bomb damage at Monowitz, where forty-four damaged buildings, and more than 940 bomb craters can be seen. And yet the factory was still working, and the paths in the snow leading to the barracks of Auschwitz III are clearly visible.[4]

Similar repair activity, as well as the apparent successful working of the

---

[1] Foreign Office papers, 898/422.

[2] Foreign Office papers, 371/51134, WR 89/14/48, folio 59.

[3] On 7 January 1945 the number of Jewish prisoners at Auschwitz was: at Auschwitz Main Camp, 10,000 men and 6,000 women; at Birkenau, 10,000 women and 4,000 men; and at Monowitz, 35,000 men and women.

[4] Photographic Interpretation Report No. G.494 of 14 January 1945. 'Poland: Oswiecim Synthetic Oil and Rubber Plant (12.30 Hours).' Photos 3018–20 and 4020. United States Strategic Bombing Survey, Record Group 243.

boiler house of the synthetic oil plant, was seen in the eight photographs brought back on January 15 by Squadron Leader Friend and Flying Officer Wheeler. There had also been 'movement and probably turnover' of rolling stock near the coal and gas intakes, while in the synthetic rubber plant, roof repairs and new construction 'continues'.[1]

Despite the four bombing raids on Monowitz, some synthetic oil was still being produced. But the total production in the first two weeks of January was only 500 tons, compared with 1,200 tons for December, and 2,000 tons each for November and October.[2] From the aerial reconnaissance of January 15, it was clear that a substantial number of the factory buildings were either without their roofs, or were damaged in some other way.

On the day of this last aerial reconnaissance, the sound of distant artillery fire could already be heard by those in Auschwitz, and three days later, on January 18, the SS ordered the camp to be evacuated. Only those who were too sick to walk were left behind: nearly 2,000 at Auschwitz, just over 6,000 at Birkenau, of whom 4,400 were women, and 850 at Monowitz.

As the first thousand Jews set off on foot from Monowitz on January 18, the 850 who could not march were left in the care of eighteen doctors.

Throughout January 18 and 19 enormous columns, some with as many as 2,500 prisoners, set off on foot, in the freezing weather, westwards towards the cities of Silesia. Anyone who fell, and could not rise again, was shot. The slightest protest was met with savage brutality from the armed guards. The death marches had begun. In one column of eight hundred men, only two hundred survived the eighteen days of marching and savagery. In another column of 2,500, a total of seventy-one were shot during the first day's march.

As the marchers continued westwards on January 19, Allied bombers struck once more at the Monowitz industrial plant.[3] As a result of the bombardment, the 850 sick who had been left behind were without water or light. In the week to come, two hundred of them died.

Not only from Auschwitz, but from all the slave labour camps of Upper Silesia, the Jews were being marched away. At the same time, United States bombers continued to strike at the whole region. On January 20 they hit the hydrogenation plant at Blechhammer,[4] where nearly four thousand Jews worked as slave labourers: all of them former inmates of Auschwitz.

During the bombing of Blechhammer the SS abandoned the watch-towers, and forty-two Jews were able to escape through a hole made in the wall by one of the bombs. One of the escapees was shot, but the rest managed to reach the shelter of a nearby wood, from where they were able to reach an outlying unit of the advancing Soviet forces.

At Birkenau on January 20, the SS blew up the already largely dismantled

[1] Photographic Interpretation Report No. D.B.300 of 15 January 1945. 'Poland: Oswiecim Synthetic Oil and Rubber Plant (13.50 Hours).' Prints 3002–06, and 4003–05. United States Strategic Bombing Survey, Record Group 243.

[2] Mediterranean and Southern Air Forces Weekly Intelligence Summary No. 9 of 5 March 1945. United States Strategic Bombing Survey, Record Group 243.

[3] Wesley Frank Craven and James Lea Cate (editors), The Army Air Force in World War II, volume 3, Chicago 1951.

[4] Wesley Frank Craven and James Lea Cate (editors), The Army Air Force in World War II, volume 3, Chicago 1951.

Crematorium II and Crematorium III. That same day they shot two hundred of the 4,200 sick women. Meanwhile the death marches continued into Upper Silesia, with hundreds being shot each day, as well as all who were too weak even to stand up when morning came. Reaching the larger cities, the marchers were then put in trains, and sent to the concentration camps at Gross Rosen, Ravensbrück, Sachsenhausen, Nordhausen, Buchenwald and Bergen-Belsen. Often they were forced to travel in open goods wagons. Each night the temperature fell far below zero. Of four thousand men sent by train from Gleiwitz to Nordhausen on January 22, six hundred died on the journey. That same day, sixty men and women who were among the Jews who had been left at Birkenau set off on foot, in search of safety. An hour later a Gestapo unit went after them, and opened fire. Ten managed to work their way back to Birkenau. The rest were killed.

The Jewish Agency continued to try to set up a further civilian exchange. As a result of a smuggled document, it was learned that there were some six thousand 'Palestinians' at Bergen-Belsen: Jews with certificates entitling them to enter Palestine. But where could Germans be found for whom they could be exchanged? On January 22 a count was made. The largest number of potential exchangees were the furthest away, six hundred German civilians interned in New Guinea. In the Near East there were a further 237, and in the Belgian Congo, seventy-five.[1]

On January 25 the Gestapo shot 350 Jews in the sick bay at Auschwitz: 150 men and 200 women. On the following day Gas Chamber and Crematorium V were blown up.

[1] Central Zionist Archives, L 22/56.

Chapter 34

'The worst of all the camps'

At 3 p.m. on January 27, Soviet troops reached Auschwitz. They found 648 corpses, and 7,600 survivors: 1,200 survivors in Auschwitz Main Camp, 5,800 at Birkenau, including four thousand women, and 650 survivors at Monowitz.[1] Since the first gas chamber had begun operations more than two and a half years earlier, a minimum of two million Jews had been killed there, as had as many as two million Soviet prisoners-of-war, Polish political prisoners, Gypsies, and non-Jews from all over Europe.

Although Auschwitz had been reached by Soviet troops, the facts about the camp did not immediately become known. More than two weeks later, on February 15, the Foreign Office telegraphed to the British Ambassador in Moscow: 'Press reports suggest that the Soviet forces have recently liberated the so-called "extermination" camp at Oswiecim in Upper Silesia: possibly the similar camp at Birkenau has been overrun'.[2] As the British Government had made a declaration in October 'about the appalling conditions there', the Ambassador was told, 'people here are naturally beginning to ask whether we have any information about what may have actually been discovered'.[3]

Four days later, on February 19, the British Ambassador passed on the request for 'any information' about Auschwitz to the Soviet Foreign Minister, Vyshinski.[4] But five weeks later, despite a reminder from the Ambassador, no such information was forthcoming. 'I should like to try again,' Paul Mason noted on April 25, when the Soviet message reached him, and he suggested that 'Perhaps the Buchenwald and Belsen disclosures may stimulate the Russians?'[5]

Two days later a brief telegram arrived from the Embassy in Moscow. Vyshinski 'now writes', the Embassy reported, 'that it has been found from investigations from the Oswiecim group of concentration camps that more than 4,000,000 citizens of various European countries were destroyed by the Germans'. And Vyshinsky added: 'No British were found among the survivors.[6]

Reading this telegram in London on April 30, Paul Mason commented: 'It is an odd telegram: read literally, it might mean that 4 million were killed at the Oswiecim group (i.e. ? Os and Birkenau) but that is not what is meant,

---

[1] Danuta Czech, 'Kalendarium der Ereignisse im Konzentrationslager Auschwitz-Birkenau', published in *Hefte von Auschwitz*, volume 8, Auschwitz 1964.

[2] Auschwitz and Birkenau were of course sections of a single camp, and just over a mile apart: since May 1942 the gassing of all Jewish deportees had taken place at the four gas chambers in the Birkenau section.

[3] Telegram No. 703, Foreign Office papers, 371/51185, WR 514.

[4] British Embassy, Moscow, 220/5/45, Foreign Office papers, 371/51185, WR 514.

[5] Foreign Office papers, 371/51185, WR. 874. British troops had entered Belsen on 15 April 1945.

[6] Foreign Office papers, 371/51185, WR 874.

I think. I think it means the records there allow this deduction to be drawn in respect of all Europe; otherwise, the figure is certainly much exaggerated'.[1]

Beginning at the end of February 1945, a number of reports about Auschwitz were made public. The first, by a Polish officer, Lieutenant Witlinski, was published on February 23 in the *Polpress Bulletin* in a dispatch from Lublin. 'Those who survived,' he wrote, 'don't look like human beings, they are mere shadows,' and he told of the medical experiments, of the gassing, and of the fact that the number of victims at Auschwitz 'was so great that it was impossible to burn all bodies in stoves. The Germans were obliged to burn them in bonfires'.[2]

On 7 May 1945 the Soviet News Agency Tass issued a Special Bulletin giving a full report of the gassing and cremation process at Auschwitz, as described by a Soviet enquiry commission which had interviewed more than two thousand survivors.[3] In the British Foreign Office, Ian Henderson noted, after he had read this report: 'It is generally agreed that Oswiecim was the worst of all the camps'.[4]

---

[1] Foreign Office papers, 371/51185, WR 1208. More than fifty British-born Jews had been killed at Auschwitz, most of them young men and women who had emigrated between the wars to France, Belgium or Holland. In addition to Miss Jane Haining, the Foreign Office also listed, as actual British subjects believed to have been in Auschwitz, Mrs Alice Nathan, born in Trieste in 1867 or 1868, Mrs Helen Bulford, Mrs L. Franz and her children, and Mr Samuel Richter (Foreign Office papers, 371/51185, WR 1417, note of 27 June 1945.)

[2] *Polpress Bulletin*, No. 16.

[3] *Soviet Monitor*, No. 5999, 'Special Bulletin: The Oswiecim Murder-Camp'.

[4] Foreign Office papers, 371/51185, WR 1417.

Epilogue

Most of Europe's Jews had already been murdered several months before the facts of the concentration camp killings were fully known, and more than a year and a half before Auschwitz itself was identified as a main killing centre.

Throughout 1942, the problem confronting both the Allies, and the Jews in Allied lands, had been lack of information. This arose from the deliberate Nazi policy of deception, whereby the destination of the deportees, and their fate, was cloaked and concealed. But as the details of the killings in eastern Europe began to filter through to the west early in the summer of 1942, it was clear that the scale of the massacres was substantial and horrific; so much so that by the end of the year they were described in the widely publicized Allied Declaration of 17 December 1942 as 'bestial crimes'.

During this time, it was difficult for the Allies to do anything other than to issue warnings and declarations. It was the German army which dominated Europe, from the Atlantic to the Black Sea. At the same time, one problem for both Jews and non-Jews outside Nazi-dominated Europe was to take in the enormity of what was happening. For some of those who read the reports, there was also an unwillingness to take them in.

As the details of the killings began to reach the west in an increasing flow, several responsible Government officials went so far as to ascribe the stories to what one official called 'customary Jewish exaggeration'. In these same official circles there was also continuing reluctance to adopt an open door policy on behalf of those few Jewish refugees who did manage to escape, even though such a policy had been called for in several major debates in the British Parliament.

Many of the policymakers who opposed the appeals on behalf of refugees were particularly 'afraid' as they expressed it, of the 'danger' of 'flooding' Palestine, and indeed Britain, with Jews. They argued that even the arrival of a few thousand Jewish refugees in Britain itself would provoke an outburst of anti-semitism. These same policymakers were also wary of what they regarded as a parallel 'danger' of falling for what one of them referred to as Jewish 'sob-stuff': in that particular instance a series of reports brought to the west in November 1942 by Jews who had been exchanged for German citizens in Allied hands, and who had given an account of Nazi atrocities which they themselves had seen.

The name and location of the four death camps, Chelmno, Treblinka, Sobibor and Belzec, had become known in the west by the summer of 1942. But from the first week of May 1942 until the third week of June 1944, the gas chambers at Auschwitz-Birkenau had kept their secret, both as the principal mass murder site of the Jews of Europe, and also as the destination of so many hundreds of deportation trains from France, Holland, Belgium, Italy, Greece and elsewhere.

The fact that these deportations were taking place from western and southern Europe was well known to the Allies. But for two years their actual destination had remained unknown, repeatedly reported as an 'unknown destination', at first believed to be located 'somewhere in the east', and as time went on, 'somewhere in Poland'. Where in Poland was not known. Nor was it entirely clear during those two years whether the deportees were being murdered, or being used principally as a vast reserve of slave labour.

The actual name of Auschwitz, as a concentration camp, had been known in the west throughout the first two years of its operation, and even earlier. But it was known and publicized solely as a camp where terrible things happened to Polish non-Jews: above all, to 'Aryan' Poles seized for resistance activity inside Poland itself.

Between May 1942 and June 1944, almost none of the messages reaching the west had referred to Auschwitz as the destination of Jewish deportees, or as a killing centre. Nor had the name of Auschwitz made any impression on those who were building up what they believed to be an increasingly comprehensive picture of the fate of the Jews. The names Chelmno, Treblinka, Sobibor and Belzec, as well as Majdanek and Mauthausen, were all mentioned in Allied declarations and reports, or in Jewish appeals: Auschwitz-Birkenau was not mentioned. It formed no part of the re-iterated and well-known list of killing centres. In the vast majority of reports reaching the west about the murder of Jews, the name Auschwitz-Birkenau had no place, even after Chelmno, Treblinka, Sobibor and Belzec had ceased operation, and indeed, by the middle of 1943, had completed their task.

As this book has shown, a few references to the killing of Jews at Auschwitz did reach the west. None, however, for different reasons, made any impact: not the report of the woman from Sosnowiec on 25 November 1942 (see page 92), nor the report dictated in London on 18 April 1943 (see page 130), nor the brief reference in *The Times* on 26 May 1943 (see page 145), nor the further, longer reference in *The Times* on 1 June 1943 (see page 145), nor the letter smuggled out of the Polish town of Bedzin on 17 July 1943 (see page 151), nor the report smuggled out of Bratislava on 1 September 1943 (see page 154) nor the cyclostyled newspaper report printed in Istanbul by the Polish Consulate General on 15 March 1944 (see pages 179–80).

Looking back with the advantage of hindsight, even with the hindsight possible in June 1944, these 'lost' references to Auschwitz-Birkenau do add up to a definite and detailed picture, which, had it been taken in, might well have served as a basis for general knowledge and for requests for publicity, warnings or action. In the event, there could be no Allied response as far as Auschwitz was concerned for the first two years of its operation; two years during which more than a million and a half Jews had been murdered.

When the truth about Auschwitz did become known, as a result of the messages brought by the four escapees, the request for bombing was only one of many requests made by the Jewish organizations in the west, mainly because, from mid-May to mid-July 1944, these organizations, and particularly the Jewish Agency, were themselves the victims of a deliberate

Nazi deception, that negotiations with the Gestapo were possible, and could indeed be the principal means of saving more than a million Jewish lives. This delusion, carefully fostered by the Gestapo, lasted until the second week of July, when the Jewish Agency made the bombing request its priority.

The test of the Allied response came in the summer of 1944, when the British and American policymakers were asked to bomb Auschwitz. At the time of this request the American Government possessed a great deal of information about Auschwitz, including both its location and its function, together with the technical ability to bomb both the railway lines leading to the camp and the gas chambers in the camp itself. The British policymakers had, in addition, Churchill's personal authority to examine a bombing scheme with a view to positive action. Yet even then, a few individuals scotched the Prime Minister's directive because, as one of them expressed it at the time, to send British pilots to carry it out would have then risked 'valuable' lives. At that very moment however Allied lives were being risked, and risked willingly by volunteer crews, to drop supplies on Warsaw during the Polish uprising: and during these missions, these very same pilots had actually flown across the Auschwitz region on their way to Warsaw.

The American War Department likewise rejected all appeals to try to destroy the gas chambers at Auschwitz, although American bombers regularly overflew the camp throughout August and September 1944, had already photographed it from the air on a number of occasions, and had even dropped bombs on it by mistake. The War Refugee Board itself, set up in Washington in January 1944 specifically to examine methods of rescue, passed on several bombing requests to the War Department, but did not give them its official support for more than three months, by which time it was too late.

In part, the story of the negative Allied response to many of the Jewish appeals for help was one of lack of comprehension and imagination, in the face of the 'unbelievable'. Many Jews likewise found the scale of the slaughter difficult to grasp. But one man who did understand the enormity of the crimes was Churchill, who wrote to Anthony Eden in July 1944: 'There is no doubt that this is probably the greatest and most horrible single crime ever committed in the whole history of the world'. In the making of Allied policy, however, Churchill was not always the final arbiter, and in many cases, not least among them the bombing of Auschwitz, other voices and other considerations prevailed.

But above all, the story told in these pages is one of many failures, and of two successes. The failures, shared by all the Allies, were those of imagination, of response, of Intelligence, of piecing together and evaluating what was known, of co-ordination, of initiative, and even at times of sympathy. The successes lay elsewhere, with the Nazis; in the killings themselves, and in a series of bizarre deceptions which enabled those killings to be carried out on a gigantic scale, for more than three years, almost without interruption.

Biographical Notes

on some of the principal characters in
this book, prepared by the author

BENJAMIN AKZIN, born in Riga in 1904. Educated at Russian and German schools. Studied at Vienna University (1922) and Paris (1926); Assistant, Harvard University, 1934–36; studied in London, 1936–38. Active in Zionist work, as a Revisionist. Joined US Government service in Washington as a specialist in international law, 1941, with the Library of Congress Legislative Reference Service. Seconded to the War Refugee Board, 1944. Political Secretary of the American Zionist Emergency Council, New York, 1947–48. Emigrated to Israel, 1949. Subsequently Professor of Political Science and Constitutional Law, Hebrew University of Jerusalem.

CHAIM BARLAS, born in Brest Litovsk, 1898. Director of the Palestine Office, Warsaw, 1919–25. Emigrated to Palestine, 1925. Director of the Immigration Department of the Jewish Agency, based in Jerusalem, 1929–39; based in Istanbul, 1940–45. Jewish Agency Representative in Geneva, 1939–40; in Turkey, 1940–45. World Jewish Congress Representative in Turkey, 1941–45. Director-General, Ministry of Immigration, Israel, 1948–49. Resident in Jerusalem (1981).

DAVID BEN GURION, born in Plonsk (Russian Poland), 1886. Emigrated to Palestine, 1906. Served in the Jewish Legion of the British Army, 1918. General Secretary, Jewish Labour Union in Palestine (Histadrut), 1921–35. Chairman of the Jewish Agency Executive, 1935–48. Prime Minister of Israel, 1948–53 and 1955–63. He died in 1974.

NORMAN BOTTOMLEY, born 1891. Served in the Royal Flying Corps, 1915–18. Senior Air Staff Officer, Headquarters, Bomber Command, 1938–40. Commanded a bomber group, 1940–41. Deputy Chief of the Air Staff, 1941 and 1943–45. Knighted, 1944. Commanded Bomber Command, 1945–47. Director of Administration of the BBC, 1948–56. Died in 1970.

JOEL BRAND, born in Hungary in 1906. Educated in Erfurt, Germany, where his father had founded a firm for the setting up of telephone installations. Joined the Labour Zionist youth movement, 1919; the Communist Youth Movement, 1921. Graduated from the Erfurt Technical School, 1923. Travelled in America, 1924–26, working in various motor car factories and building firms. Returned to Germany to become co-director of his father's firm (his father having died). Returned from Communism to Zionism, 1931. After Hitler's rise to power, imprisoned in Erfurt for a year, 1933–34. Started a small knitting factory in Budapest, 1935. Elected to the Central Committee for the Hungarian Zionist Organisation, 1939. Member of the Committee of the Palestine Office in Hungary, 1940. Member of the Zionist Assistance and Rescue Committee, founded in January 1943, and in charge of the underground rescue of Jews from Poland. Mission to Istanbul, May 1944. Held by the British first in Aleppo, then in Cairo, May–October 1944. Released in Jerusalem, 7 October 1944. A witness at the Eichmann trial, Jerusalem, 1961. He died in Frankfurt in 1964, while giving testimony against Eichmann's aides, including Hermann Krumey.

BORIS OF BULGARIA, born 1896. Became King after the abdication of his father, 'Foxy' Ferdinand, in October 1918. Survived an assassination attempt, 1925. Maintained Bulgaria's neutrality, 1939–41. Under pressure from Hitler, he aligned Bulgaria with the Axis in the spring of 1941, and allowed his Government to declare war on the western Allies, but not on the Soviet Union, December 1941. Opposed the increasing Nazi demands on Bulgaria, 1942–43. He died after an interview with Hitler on 28 August 1943, either murdered, or of a heart attack.

WILLIAM CAVENDISH-BENTINCK, born 1897. Entered the British Diplomatic Service, 1919, as 3rd Secretary, Warsaw. Attended the Conference at Lausanne (1922–24) and Locarno (1925). Chairman of the Joint Intelligence Committee of the Chiefs of Staff, 1939–45. Ambassador to Poland, 1945–47.

SARAH CENDER, born in 1919 in Lodz, where she attended High School. Lived in Zdunska Wola, 1940–42. Deported with her parents from Zdunska Wola to the Lodz Ghetto, 1942. Deported to Auschwitz, 1944. After the war she emigrated to the United States, where she married Hirsh Altusky, editor of the Warsaw Ghetto Resistance Organisation publications.

WILLIAM CLUSE, born in 1875. An orphan from the age of five. Apprenticed to a printer at the age of 15. Served in the Royal Army Medical Corps, 1914–18. A Labour Member of Parliament, 1923–31 and 1935–50. Parliamentary Private Secretary to the Minister of Transport, 1940–41, and to the Minister of Aircraft Production, 1942–45. He died in 1955.

ARTHUR COLEGATE, Company director; President of the Industrial Property Committee of the International Chamber of Commerce, 1925–29. A Conservative Member of Parliament, 1941–45 and 1950–55. Vice-President of the Midland Union of Conservative Associations. Knighted, 1955. He died in 1956.

LORD CRANBORNE, born 1893. Conservative MP, 1929–41. Secretary of State at the Dominions Office, 1940–42 and 1943–45. Secretary of State for the Colonies, 22 February 1942 to 21 November 1942. Succeeded his father as 5th Marquess of Salisbury, 1947. Leader of the House of Lords, 1951–57. Secretary of State for Commonwealth Relations, 1952. He died in 1972.

NORMAN H. DAVIS, born in Tennessee in 1878. Entered banking as a young man. After becoming a millionaire at the age of 35, he withdrew from active business to enter public service. Entered the US Treasury as financial adviser on foreign loans, 1917. A US delegate to the World Disarmament Conference, Geneva, 1931. A personal friend of President Roosevelt, and Roosevelt's Ambassador-at-Large, 1933–38, he was also an adviser to the White House on European affairs. Appointed by Roosevelt as Chairman of the American Red Cross, 1938. President of the Council on Foreign Relations, November 1943. He died in July 1944.

ARMINIUS DEW, born in 1906. Entered the British diplomatic service, 1928. Served in Moscow, 1938–39 and in Belgrade, 1940–41. Transferred to the Foreign Office, 1941. Killed in an air crash (with several other Foreign Office officials) on the way to the Yalta Conference, 1945.

ELIAHU DOBKIN, born in Bobruisk, Russia, in 1898. Educated at Kharkov University. Emigrated to Palestine, 1932. Director of the Immigration Department of the Jewish Agency, Jerusalem, 1939–45. Subsequently Chairman of the Central Committee of the United Israel Appeal. He died in 1976.

BLANCHE DUGDALE, born in 1880. A niece of Lord Balfour, and friend of Chaim Weizmann. Worked in the Naval Intelligence Department of the Admiralty,

1915–19. Head of the Intelligence Department of the League of Nations Union, London, 1920–28. A member of the Zionists' inner circle and policy-making group in London, 1930–45. She died on 16 May 1948, two days after the establishment of the State of Israel.

IRA C. EAKER, born 1898. An outstanding United States' pilot, on 17 August 1942 he led the first US bombing raid over western Europe. A leading advocate of daylight bombing. Commander of the 8th Air Force, 1943. Commander-in-Chief of the Allied Forces in Italy, January 1944; of the Allied Air Forces for the invasion of southern France, August 1944.

ALEXANDER EASTERMAN, born in Scotland in 1890. A journalist. Foreign Editor of the *Daily Express*, 1926–33. Chief Foreign Correspondent of the *Daily Herald*, 1934–40; War Correspondent in Paris, 1940. Political Secretary of the World Jewish Congress, British Section, 1941–45. Chairman of the Palestine Committee of the Board of Deputies of British Jews, 1943–49. A representative of the World Jewish Congress at the Nuremberg trials, 1945–46, at the San Francisco conference which inaugurated the United Nations, 1946. Living in Britain, 1981.

ADOLF EICHMANN, born in Germany in 1906. His parents moved to Linz, in Austria, when he was eight years old. At school in Linz. A travelling salesman for the Socony Vacuum Company, 1928–33. Joined the Nazi Party, 1932. Served as a corporal in Dachau concentration camp, 1934. Worked in the Jewish Section of the Secret Service (S.D.), visiting Palestine on an intelligence mission. Sent to Vienna to promote Jewish emigration, March 1938, and forced thousands of Jews to leave Austria. Established a 'Centre for Jewish Emigration' in Prague, March 1939. Promoted Captain. Director of the German Centre of Jewish Emigration, Berlin, 1939–41. Head of the Gestapo's Section IVB4, March 1941, dealing with Jewish affairs, expulsion, deportation and (from January 1942) extermination. Lieutenant-Colonel, 1941–45. Chief of the *Sonderkommando*, Hungary, March–July 1944. Escaped from an American Prisoner-of-War camp, 1945. Kidnapped by Israeli agents, Argentina, May 1960. Tried in Jerusalem, 1961, and executed, May 1962.

HERBERT EMERSON, born 1881. Entered the Indian Civil Service, 1905. Knighted, 1933. Governor of the Punjab, 1933–38. High Commissioner for Refugees, League of Nations, 1939–46 and Director of the Intergovernmental Committee on Refugees, 1939–47. Died 1962.

HAROLD FARQUAR, born in 1894. Entered the British Diplomatic Service in 1922, as a 3rd Secretary, Warsaw. Subsequently served in Madrid, Budapest, Rome, Mexico and Helsinki. Consul-General, Barcelona, 1941–45. Minister Plenipotentiary, Addis Ababa, 1946. Ambassador in Stockholm, 1948–51. Knighted, 1950. Died, 1953.

WILHELM FILDERMANN, born in Bucharest in 1882. A member of the Central Committee of the Union of Rumanian Jews since 1913. A member of the Committee of Jewish Delegations at the Paris Peace Conference in 1919. A non-Zionist delegate to the Zurich Congress of the Jewish Agency in 1929. President of the Jewish community of Bucharest in 1931. He survived the war, emigrated to Paris in 1948, and died in 1963.

JUDAH FISHMAN, born in Bessarabia, 1875. Rabbi of Ungeni, Bessarabia, 1905–13. Emigrated to Palestine, 1913. Helped to establish the Chief Rabbinate of Palestine, 1918. Representative of the Mizrachi movement on the Zionist Executive from 1935. Opposed the suppression of Jewish terrorists by the Haganah, 1944–45. Acting Chairman of the Jewish Agency, June 1946, when he was imprisoned by the British. Minister of Religion and Minister in charge of War Casualties in the Israel Provisional Government, 1948. He died in 1962.

ERNEST FRISCHER, from Moravska Ostrava. A leading Jewish public figure in interwar Czechoslovakia. Member of the Jewish National Council from 1925. In 1935, Jewish Party candidate for the Czech Senate; Chairman of the Jewish Party, 1935–39. Member of the Czechoslovak Government-in-Exile, and of the Czechoslovak State Council (in London), 1940–45, representing the interests of Czech Jewry. The first President of the Jewish Community in Prague after the war, he rebuilt the community. Died in Czechoslovakia.

HARRISON A. GERHARDT, born 1909. A graduate of West Point, he served at the Military Academy, 1939–43, and as Executive Assistant to the Secretary of War, 1943–45. Colonel, 1944. Staff Officer to the Secretary of War at the Cairo (1943) and Potsdam (1945) Conferences. US Secretary, Allied Control Council, Berlin, 1945–48. Special Assistant to the US High Commissioner, Germany (John J. McCloy), 1949–51. Served with the NATO Ministerial Council, 1952–54. Brigadier-General, 1957. Chief of Staff, I Corps, Korea, 1958–59. Commanding General, Southern European Task Force, 1962–64.

NAHUM GOLDMANN, born in the Lithuanian region of Russia, 1895. His parents emigrated to Germany when he was five. Visited Palestine, 1913. Member of the Jewish Section of the German Foreign Ministry, 1914–18. Chairman of the Political Committee of the 17th Zionist Congress, 1931. Left Germany, 1933. Representative of the Jewish Agency at the League of Nations, 1935. Co-founder (with Stephen Wise) of the World Jewish Congress, 1936. Moved to New York, 1939, and established the Zionist Emergency Council. Co-Chairman of the Executive of the Zionist Organization, 1948–56; President, 1956–1968. President of the World Jewish Congress from 1949. President of the Claims Conference, 1951, and of its successor, the Memorial Foundation for Jewish Culture, 1965. Left the United States to become a citizen of Israel, 1962. Took Swiss citizenship, 1968.

ANDOR GROSS, or Grosz, known as 'Bandi', alias Andre Gyorgy, alias Andreas Grainer. Born in Beregszasz (then part of the Austro–Hungarian Empire), 1905. Attended a Jewish School in Budapest, 1915–19; the Commercial High School, 1919–23. Joined a transport firm, 1923. Bought a café, 1926, but went bankrupt, 1929. Began smuggling and black market activities, 1931. Engaged in gold smuggling between Hungary and Switzerland, 1938. Known in Budapest as the 'smuggler king'. Sentenced to 1 years in prison for smuggling offences, 1941. The Germans helped him to avoid serving this sentence, in return for espionage. In May 1942 he was sent by the Germans on an espionage mission to Switzerland, the first of many journeys to neutral countries. Imprisoned in Turkey for espionage, 1946–53.

YIZHAK GRUENBAUM, born in Warsaw, 1879. Journalist and orator. A delegate at the 7th Zionist Congress, 1905. Member of the Polish Parliament, 1919–32. Co-founder of the Minorities' Block, 1922. Emigrated to Palestine, 1933. Member of the Jewish Agency Executive, and Head of the Labour Department, 1935–48. Head of the Rescue Committee of the Jewish Agency, 1939–45. Minister of the Interior in the Provisional Government, Israel, 1948. A strong advocate of the secularization of the State. Treasurer of the Jewish Agency, 1949–50. He died in 1970.

JANE HAINING, born in 1897. Worked as a typist, 1917–22. Began work for the Jewish Mission Committee of the Church of Scotland, 1922. Matron of the Girls' Home in the Budapest Mission of the Church of Scotland, 1932–44, bringing Christianity to Jewish children. Deported to Auschwitz, May 1944, and died there two months later.

GEORGE HALL, born in Wales, 1881. Began work in a colliery at the age of 12. Labour Member of Parliament, 1922–46. Civil Lord of the Admiralty, 1929–31. Parliamentary Under-Secretary of State, Colonial Office, 1940–42; for Foreign Affairs, 1943–45. Secretary of State for the Colonies, 1945–46. First Lord of the Admiralty, 1946–51. Created Viscount, 1946. Died 1965.

R. M. A. HANKEY, born in 1905. Entered the British diplomatic service, 1927. Served in the Foreign Office, 1939–45. Subsequently British Ambassador at Stockholm (1954–60) and Chairman of the Foreign Office Economic Policy Committee (1960–65). Succeeded his father as 2nd Baron Hankey, 1963.

LELAND HARRISON, born in New York, 1883. Educated at Harvard and Harvard Law School. Entered the American diplomatic service, 1907. Diplomatic Secretary of the American Commission to Negotiate Peace, Paris 1919. Minister to Sweden, 1927–29; to Uruguay, 1929–30; to Rumania, 1935–37; to Switzerland, 1937–46. Died 1951.

ARIE HASSENBERG, born in Bedzin, southwestern Poland, 1923. A High School student, 1933–39. Worked in an electrical shop, 1941–42; a shoemaking shop, 1943. Deported to Auschwitz, 1943. Sent to the I.G. Farben works at Buna-Monowitz, March 1944. During the evacuation of Buna he escaped from the train, 22 January 1945, and was liberated by the Red Army near Gleiwitz five days later. Active in organizing 'illegal' immigration from Poland to Palestine, August 1945. Reached Palestine himself, 'illegally', October 1946. Deported by the British to Cyprus, and interned. Returned to Palestine, April 1947. Served in the Haganah, November 1947 to April 1948; in the Israel Defence Forces, May 1948–September 1949. Graduated in Law from the Hebrew University of Jerusalem, 1950. Practiced as a lawyer in Tel Aviv since 1957. In 1979 he began historical research into the wartime role of the Red Cross in connection with the concentration camps.

IAN HENDERSON, born 1906. Entered the British Consular Service, 1924. Consul at Innsbruck, 1933. Served as an Observer in the Sudeten–German districts of Czechoslovakia, during their transfer to Germany under the Munich Agreement, 1938. Employed in the Foreign Office, 1942–45. Commercial Counsellor, Prague, 1946. Ambassador to Paraguay, 1952–53; to Panama, 1956. Knighted, 1958. Retired, 1960.

JOSEPH HERTZ, born in Slovakia in 1872. Taken to the United States at the age of 12. Rabbi in Syracuse, New York, 1894–96. Rabbi of Johannesburg, South Africa, 1896–1911. Returned to New York, 1911–13. Chief Rabbi of the United Hebrew Congregations of the British Commonwealth from 1913 until his death in 1946.

CARDINAL ARTHUR HINSLEY, born in 1870. Catholic Archbishop of Westminster from 1935 until his death in March 1943. Created Cardinal in 1937.

IRA HIRSCHMANN, born in Baltimore, Maryland, 1906. A banker and businessman. Contributor to Nazism: An Assault on Civilisation, 1934. Special Assistant, National War Labor Board, 1942–44. Special Representative of the War Refugee Board in Turkey, 1944. Special Inspector-General, United Nations Relief and Rehabilitation Agency (UNRRA), 1946. Author of Lifeline to a Promised Land, 1949.

AXEL HOJER, born in Sweden in 1890. City Medical Officer, Malmo, 1930–35. Director-General of Medicinalstyrelsen, Stockholm, 1935–52. Principal of Trivandrum Medical School, India, 1952–54. World Health Organization assignments in Assam, India, 1956–57 and Ghana, 1958–60. He died in 1974.

MIKLOS HORTHY, born in 1868. An Admiral in the Austro–Hungarian Navy. Regent of Hungary, 1919–44. Forced to abdicate by the Germans, October 1944, and interned by the Germans. Held by the Americans, 1945–48. The Americans refused to extradite him to Hungary, and he was released in 1948. Subsequently in exile in Estoril, Portugal, where he died in 1957.

BERNARD JOSEPH, born in Montreal, 1899. President of the Young Judaea Zionist movement in Canada, 1917. Joined the Jewish Legion and served in Palestine, 1918. Settled in Jerusalem, 1921. A lawyer; Legal Adviser to the Jewish Agency's Political Department. Member of the Jewish Agency Executive, 1945–46. Military Governor of Jerusalem, 1948. Entered the Israeli Cabinet as Minister of Supply and Rationing, 1948; subsequently Minister of Trade and Industry, Justice, Development, Health and again Justice (1961–66). He died in 1980.

MENAHEM KAHANY, born in Cracow, then a part of the Austro-Hungarian Empire, in 1898. On active service on the Italian front, 1916–18, (one of his brothers was killed in action on the Rumanian front). Wanted to be a physician, but unable to study medicine at Cracow University owing to the Polish restrictions on the percentage of Jewish students. Doctor of Law, Cracow, 1922. In Palestine, 1922–24. In Paris, as a newspaper correspondent of a Cracow daily paper, 1924–26. Political Secretary of the Jewish Agency at the League of Nations, Geneva, 1926–46, and Jewish Agency representative with the Permanent Mandates Commission, Geneva, 1926–39. A member of the Committee of Foreign Correspondents in Switzerland, 1940–44. Since 1948, Special Adviser to the Israeli Delegation at the United Nations, Geneva. Resident in Switzerland, 1981.

JAN KARSKI, born in Lodz (then a part of Russian Poland) in 1914. Studied law at Lvov University. Served in the Polish Army, 1935–36. Entered the Polish Foreign Ministry, 1938. Lieutenant, Mounted Artillery, 1939. Captured by the Russians, but disguised himself as a private, and repatriated (all officers being kept in captivity). Served as a courier between Warsaw and the Polish National Council, first in France, then in Britain. Lived underground in Warsaw, 1941–42. Reached London in November 1942, then travelled to the United States. In 1944 he published *Story of a Secret State*. Resident in the United States since 1945: Professor in the Department of Government at Georgetown University.

RUDOLF KASTNER, born in Cluj, Transylvania (then part of the Austro-Hungarian Empire), 1906. Also known as Reszo Kasztner. Worked for the Hungarian language Zionist daily newspaper in Cluj, 1925–40. Secretary of the National Jewish Party's Parliamentary group, 1925–40. Head of the Budapest Jewish Rescue Committee, and deputy Chairman of the Hungarian Zionist Organization, 1943–45. His wartime negotiations with the SS in Hungary led to a trial in Israel, where accusations against him as a collaborator were upheld by the District Court. On 3 March 1957, following the Court's decision, Kastner was assassinated by a young man who had been influenced by the accusations. On 17 January 1958 the District Court's decision was reversed by the Supreme Court.

HUGHE KNATCHBULL-HUGESSEN, born 1886. British diplomat. Knighted 1936. Ambassador to China, 1936–37; to Turkey, 1939–44; to Belgium, 1944–47. Died 1971.

ARTHUR KOESTLER, born in Budapest in 1905. Educated at Vienna University. Worked as a journalist in the Middle East, Paris and Berlin, from 1926. *News Chronicle* reporter in the Spanish Civil War, 1936–37. Imprisoned by Franco. Served in the French Foreign Legion, 1939–40; in the British Pioneer Corps, 1941–42. Among his earlier publications were *Spanish Testament* (1938), *Darkness at Noon* (1940), *Scum of the Earth* (1941), *Arrival and Departure* (1943), and *Promise and Fulfilment* (1949). Living in London, 1981.

JAROMIR KOPECKY, a Czechoslovak diplomat. Between the wars he served as both Permanent Czechoslovak Delegate in Geneva representing the Czechoslovak Red Cross, and as Permanent Czechoslovak representative at the League of Nations. He continued to hold both these posts during the war. Returned to Czechoslovakia, 1945, where he worked, after 1948, as a historian.

OSKAR KRASNANSKY, born in Nitra, Slovakia (then part of the Austro-Hungarian Empire), 1902. Educated at Vienna in the Commercial High School and College of Foreign Trade. Slovak Representative of the Cement Trust in the 1930s. Active in Zionist circles in Bratislava. One of the Slovak representatives at the Zionist Congress, Geneva, 1939. Active in organizing 'illegal' immigration from Slovakia to Palestine, 1939–40. A member of the Rescue Committee of the Jewish community in Bratislava, 1942–44. Emigrated to Israel, 1949. An Attaché of Israel in Cologne in the 1950s. Living in Tel Aviv, 1981.

MIKLOS KRAUSZ, born in 1908 in a small village in eastern Hungary. Known also as Moshe. Joined the Zionist Organization in Hungary, 1929. Secretary-General of the Palestine Office of the Jewish Agency, Budapest, 1932; head of the Palestine Office, Budapest, 1937–44. A delegate to the 22nd Zionist Congress, in Switzerland, 1946. Emigrated to Israel, 1948, becoming head of the Rehabilitation Department at the Ministry of Social Welfare. Living in Jerusalem, 1981.

LEON KUBOWITZKI, born in Lithuania in 1896. Emigrated to Belgium, where he became a prominent lawyer. One of the leaders of Belgian Jewry between the wars, and active in the anti-Nazi boycott movement, 1933. In the United States from 1940, he became Head of the Department of European Jewish Affairs, of the World Jewish Congress, 1943–44. Secretary General of the World Jewish Congress, 1945–48. Emigrated to Israel, 1948. Took the surname Kubovy. Israel's Minister to Poland and Czechoslovakia, 1949–53; to Argentina, Chile and Paraguay, 1957–58. Chairman of the Yad Vashem Remembrance Authority, Jerusalem, from 1959 until his death in 1966.

ERICH KULKA, born in Moravia in 1911. A technical expert in the wood-working industry. Arrested by the Gestapo, 1939. In Dachau, 1940; Neuengamme, 1941. Deported to Auschwitz, October 1942. During the evacuation from Auschwitz, he escaped with his 12-year-old son, and was hidden by partisans in the mountains on the Slovak-Moravian border. Free-lance writer since 1946, first in Czechoslovakia, in Israel from 1968. His many publications include *Five Escape from Auschwitz* (1975). Living in Jerusalem, 1981.

LEO LAUTERBACH, born in Drohobycz, in the Galician province of Austria-Hungary, 1886. Educated at the Universities of Vienna and Lvov. Chairman of the Zionist Students' Association of Galicia, 1912–13. On active service in the Austro-Hungarian army, 1915–18. Joined the staff of the World Zionist Organization, London 1919; director of its Organization Department, 1921; Executive Secretary, in London 1935–36, in Jerusalem, 1936–48. He died in Jerusalem in 1968.

RICHARD LAW, born 1901. Son of the British Prime Minister, Andrew Bonar Law. Conservative MP, 1931–50. Parliamentary Under-Secretary of State at the Foreign Office, 1941–43; Minister of State, 1943–45. Minister of Education, 1945. Created Baron Coleraine, 1954. Died, 1980.

RICHARD LICHTHEIM, born in Berlin, 1885. Educated in Berlin and Freiburg. Joined the Zionist students society, 1905. First visit to Palestine, 1910. Journalist and editor of the principal Zionist newspaper in Berlin, 1911–13. A leading Zionist emissary to Constantinople, 1914–17, he urged the Turks to refrain from extreme measures against the Jews in Palestine. Member of the Zionist Executive, London, and head of its Organization Department, 1921–23. An opponent of Weizmann's policies, in 1925 he joined Jabotinsky's Revisionist Party, but left it in 1933 in protest against what he called 'its separatist and fascist tendencies'. Manager of an Insurance Company in Berlin, 1923–33. Emigrated to Jerusalem, 1934. Jewish Agency Representative in Geneva, 1939–45. He died in Jerusalem in 1963.

SHALOM LINDENBAUM, born in 1926 in Przytk, the Polish village in which a notorious anti-Jewish pogrom took place in 1936. Deported in 1940 into central Poland, then to a forced labour camp in which, on one occasion, 120 of the 600 prisoners were executed in front of the others. Evacuated to Auschwitz, July 1944. Subsequently transferred to Monowitz. Evacuated from Monowitz, 18 January 1945, on 'death march' to Buchenwald on which over 80 per cent were shot, or died of cold, hunger and sickness. Escaped from the death march, 22 January 1945. Sheltered by two Polish women near Gleiwitz. Liberated by the Red Army, 27 January 1945. Joined the IZL (Irgun), 1946. Emigrated to Palestine, August 1946; detained in Cyprus until April 1947. Served in the Israel Defence Forces, 1948–50. Worked in Haifa as an unskilled dock worker, a school janitor, and then as secretary in the school. Worked in a bank. Took his B.A. in Hebrew Literature and History, 1956. Lecturer, Bar-Ilan University, Israel, since 1959.

JOSEPH LINTON, born in Ozorkow, near Lodz (Russian Poland) in 1900. Emigrated to England shortly before the First World War. Began Zionist work in London in 1919. Known as Ivor. Financial and Administrative Secretary of the Jewish Agency in London, 1930–40; Political Secretary, 1940–48. Israel Consul-General and Counsellor of Embassy, London, 1949–50. Minister of Israel in Australia and New Zealand, 1950–52; in Japan, 1952–57; in Thailand, 1954–57. Ambassador to Switzerland, 1958–61. Resident in London since 1961.

H. B. LIVINGSTON, born 1895. Entered the British Consular Service, 1919. Consul at Leipzig, 1933–36; at Dresden, 1936–38 and at Geneva, 1938–45. Consul-General, Los Angeles, 1945. Served with the Control Commission for Germany, 1946. Consul-General, Baden-Baden, 1946–50; Marseilles, 1950–51. He died in 1968.

BRECKENRIDGE LONG, born in St Louis, Missouri, 1881. A lawyer. Entered the Foreign Service, 1917. Unsuccessful Democratic Candidate for the US Senate, 1928. Ambassador to Italy, 1933–36. Assistant Secretary of State, 1940–44. He died in 1958.

ROSWELL MCCLELLAND, born in Palo Alto, California, 1914. Studied at Duke University, Munich, and Perugia, 1936–37. Delegate in Switzerland of the American Friends Service Committee, 1940–44. War Refugee Board Representative in Switzerland, 1944–45. Special Assistant to the American Minister, Legation of the United States of America, Berne, 1945–49. Desk Officer, State Department, 1949–53. Served in Spain (1953–56), Senegal (1960–64) and Rhodesia (1964–65). American Minister to Greece, 1967–70; Ambassador to Niger, 1970.

JOHN J. MCCLOY, born in Philadelphia 1895. On active service 1917–18 (Distinguished Service Medal). Practiced law in New York, 1921–40. Assistant Secretary of War, April 1941 to November 1945. President of the World Bank, 1947–49. US Military Governor and High Commissioner for Germany, 1949–52. (Under his 'Clemency Act' of January 1951 many convicted Nazis had their sentences substantially reduced.) Banker and businessman. Co-ordinator of US Disarmament Activities, 1961–63. Chairman of the President's General Advisory Committee on Arms Control and Disarmament, 1961–74.

DOUGLAS MACKILLOP, born 1891. Educated at Manchester and Lyons universities. Entered the British Diplomatic Service, 1919. Chargé d'Affaires, Moscow, 1936–37; Counsellor of Embassy, Peking, 1937; Riga, 1938–40; Berne, September 1940–November 1945. Subsequently head of the Refugee Department and Claims Departments of the Foreign Office, 1945–49. Consul-General, Munich, 1949–51. He died in 1959.

HAROLD MACMICHAEL, born in 1882. Joined the Sudan Political Service, 1905. Served in the Sudan, 1905–33. Knighted 1932. Governor and Commander-in-Chief, Tanganyika Territory, 1933–37. High Commissioner and Commander-in-Chief for Palestine, 1938–44. Special Government Representative, Malaya, 1945. Constitutional Commissioner, Malta, 1946. Died, 1969.

LUIGI MAGLIONE, born near Naples, 1877. Entered the Secretariat of State at the Vatican, 1908. Papal Nuncio in Switzerland, 1920; then in France. Created Cardinal, 1935. Papal Secretary of State from 1939 until his death on 22 August 1944.

JOHN MARTIN, born 1904. Entered the Dominions Office, 1927. Secretary of the Palestine Royal Commission, 1936. Private Secretary to Winston Churchill, 1940–41; Principal Private Secretary, 1941–45. Deputy Under-Secretary of State, Colonial Office, 1956–65. British High Commissioner in Malta, 1965–67. Knighted, 1952.

KINGSLEY MARTIN, born in 1897. Assistant Lecturer at the London School of Economics, 1923–27. Editor of the *New Statesman and Nation* from 1930 to 1960. Died in 1969.

PAUL MASON, born 1904. Entered the British Diplomatic Service, 1928. Served in Lisbon, 1941–43. Head of the Refugee Section of the Foreign Office, 1944. Minister to Sofia, 1949–51. Assistant Under-Secretary of State, 1951–54. Ambassador to the Hague, 1954–60. Permanent UK Representative to NATO, 1960–63. Head of the Permanent UK Delegation on Disarmament and Nuclear Tests, Geneva, 1963. Knighted, 1954.

GUY MILLARD, born 1917. Entered the British Foreign Office, 1939. Assistant Private Secretary to Anthony Eden, 1941–45. Private Secretary to Eden (then Prime Minister), 1955–56. Ambassador to Sweden, 1971–74 and to Italy, 1974–76. Knighted, 1972.

CZESLAW MORDOWICZ, born in Mlawa, Poland in 1921. Deported to Auschwitz in 1943; escaped, May 1944. After the war, he worked in an electrical equipment enterprise in Bratislava. Emigrated to Israel, 1966. Resident in Israel, 1981.

HENRY MORGENTHAU, born in New York City in 1891. A farmer and agriculturalist. Joined Roosevelt's administration as head of the Federal Farm Board and Farm Credit Administration, 1933–34. Secretary of the Treasury, 1934–45. Proposed the partition of Germany, and its conversion into an essentially agrarian area (the Morgenthau Plan), 1945. General Chairman of the United Jewish Appeal, 1950–53; and of the Israel Bond Drive, 1951–54. He died in 1967.

HERBERT MORRISON, born 1888. Mayor of Hackney, 1920–21. Labour Member of Parliament, 1923–24, 1929–31 and 1935–59. Minister of Transport, 1929–31. Home Secretary and Minister of Home Security, 1940–45. Member of the War Cabinet, 1942–45. Deputy Prime Minister, 1945–51. Secretary of State for Foreign Affairs, 1951. Created a Life Peer, 1959. Died 1965.

LORD MOYNE, born 1880. Conservative MP (as Walter Guinness), 1907–31. On active service, 1914–18. Created Baron Moyne, 1932. Secretary of State for the

Colonies, 8 February 1941 to 22 February 1942 (when he was succeeded by Lord Cranborne). Deputy Minister of State, Middle East, 1942–44. Resident Minister in the Middle East from 28 January 1944 until his assassination in Cairo by Jewish terrorists (from the Stern Gang) on 6 November 1944.

LEWIS NAMIER, born in Galicia in 1888, of Jewish parents who had converted to Roman Catholicism. Educated at the universities of Lvov, Lausanne, the London School of Economics and Balliol College, Oxford. Naturalized as a British subject, 1913. Worked in the Propaganda Department, London, 1917–18; the Political Intelligence Department of the Foreign Office, 1918–20. Political Secretary of the Jewish Agency in London, 1929–31. Professor of Modern History at Manchester, 1931–53. A leading adviser to the Jewish Agency Executive in London, 1936–39. Seconded to the Jewish Agency for war work, 1939–45. Baptised into the Russian Orthodox Church (on his marriage), 1947. Knighted 1952. He died in 1960.

CLIFFORD NORTON, born 1891. On active service at Gallipoli and in Palestine, 1914–18. Political Officer, Damascus, Haifa, Deraa, 1919–20. Entered the British Diplomatic Service, 1921. Counsellor, Warsaw, 1937–39. Minister, Berne, 1942–46. Ambassador, Athens, 1946–51. Knighted, 1946.

FRANCIS D'ARCY OSBORNE, born 1884, a direct descendent of the 5th Duke of Leeds (Secretary of State for Foreign Affairs, 1783–91). Minister Plenipotentiary, Washington, 1931–35; the Holy See, 1936–47. 12th Duke of Leeds, 1963; died 1964.

EUGENIO PACELLI (a Pope), born in Rome, 1876. Entered the Secretariat of State, Vatican, 1901. Papal Nuncio to Germany, 1925–35. Instrumental in negotiating the Concordat between the Holy See and the Third Reich, 20 July 1933. Pope, as Pius XII, from 1939 until his death in 1958.

OSBERT PEAKE, born 1897. On active service in the Coldstream Guards, 1916–18. Barrister, 1923. Conservative Member of Parliament, 1929–55. Parliamentary Under-Secretary of State at the Home Office, 1939–44. Financial Secretary to the Treasury, 1944–45. Minister of Pensions and National Insurance, 1953–55. Created Viscount Ingleby, 1955. Died 1966.

JOHN W. PEHLE, born 1909. Specialist in monetary problems at the US Treasury, 1934–40. Director of Foreign Funds Control, Washington, 1940–44. Assistant to the Secretary of the Treasury, 1940–44. Executive Director of the War Refugee Board, February 1944 to January 1945, after which he returned to the Treasury.

VENYA POMERANTZ, born in eastern Poland in 1918. A Zionist-Socialist, he emigrated to Palestine at the age of fifteen. Worked at Kibbutz Ramat Rahel, just south of Jerusalem, 1933–42. Sent to Istanbul by the organizers of illegal immigration in 1942. Active in organizing illegal immigration in Istanbul, Paris and Sofia, 1942–48. Subsequently, as Zvi Hadari, Professor of Engineering Sciences in the Department of Nuclear Engineering, Ben Gurion University of the Negev, Israel.

CHAIM POZNER, born in 1899 in Russian Poland. Active in Zionist educational circles from 1918. Educated at Königsberg and Basel. Chairman of the Palestine Office, Danzig, 1934–38. Co-Chairman of the Palestine Office, Geneva, 1940–45. European representative of the Finance Department of the Jewish Agency, 1945–48; of the Finance Ministry of Israel, 1948–53. Settled in Israel, 1953 (taking the surname Pazner). Worked in the Finance Ministry, 1953–57. Economic Counsellor at the Israel Embassies in the Argentine and Uruguay, 1957–60. Minister for Economic Affairs, Israel Embassy, Sweden, 1960–62. Director, Revenue and Services Department, Foreign Exchange Division, Ministry of Finance, Israel, 1963–67. From 1967, Vice-Chairman of Yad Vashem, the Holocaust memorial and archive, Jerusalem.

EDWARD RACZYNSKI, born in Poland in 1891. Educated at Cracow and Leipzig Universities, and at the London School of Economics. Entered the Polish Ministry for Foreign Affairs, 1919. Ambassador to London, 1934–45; acting Minister for Foreign Affairs (in London), 1941–42; Minister of State for Foreign Affairs in General Sikorski's Cabinet, 1942–43. Chairman of the Polish Research Centre in London. Polish President-in-Exile since 1979.

A. W. G. RANDALL, born 1892. Entered the British Foreign Office, 1919. Served in the Refugee Section, 1939–42; Head of the Refugee Department, 1942–44. Ambassador to Denmark, 1947–52. Knighted, 1949. Died, 1977.

ELEANOR RATHBONE, born 1872. The first woman member of Liverpool City Council, 1909–34. Independent MP for the Combined English Universities, 1929–46. Secretary of the Parliamentary Committee for Refugees. Died, 1946.

GERHART RIEGNER, born in Berlin, 1911. A student of law, he completed his studies in Germany, became assistant to a judge, and intended to work to become a Professor of Jurispridence. Suspended from public office by the law of 1 April 1933. Emigrated to France, May 1933. Took up legal studies in Paris, but hampered by a French law which forbad legal practice for ten years after naturalization. Fellow of the Graduate Institute of International Studies, Geneva, 1934. Joined the newly created World Jewish Congress (an organization set up in 1936 to combat persecution of the Jews); Legal Secretary, 1936; Director of the Geneva Office, 1939–45; Member of the Executive, 1948; Secretary-General, 1964. Negotiated (with A. L. Eastermann) in North Africa for the rights and status of North African Jewry (1950s). Active in the sphere of Jewish relations with the Christian Churches, including the Vatican and the World Council of Churches (1960s). Resident in Geneva, 1981.

HUBERT RIPKA, born in 1895. Lecturer in International Politics at Prague University, and editor of a Prague daily newspaper, 1934–39. Escaped to France, March 1939. Escaped to England, June 1940. Deputy Secretary of State (and acting Minister) for Foreign Affairs of the Czechoslovak Government (in London), 1940–45. Minister of Foreign Trade, Prague, 1945–48. Resigned, 1948. In exile in England from 1948 until his death in 1958.

FRANK ROBERTS, born in 1907. Entered the British Foreign Office, 1930. Served in Paris and Cairo. Returned to the Foreign Office, 1937–45. Later Ambassador to Belgrade (1954–57), to Moscow (1960–62) and to Bonn (1963–68). Knighted, 1953.

ANGELO RONCALLI, born in Bergamo, Italy, 1881. Apostolic Delegate to Bulgaria, 1931–34; to Turkey and Greece, 1934–44. Gave help to individual Jews and Jewish groups in Slovakia, Yugoslavia, Hungary, Italy and France. Appointed Papal Nuncio in Paris after the liberation of the city in August 1944. Cardinal, and Patriarch of Venice, 1953. Became Pope, as John XXIII, in 1958. In 1959 he ordered the use of the term 'perfidi' with reference to the Jews to be deleted from the Good Friday prayer. He died in 1963.

JACOB ROSENHEIM, born in Frankfurt in 1876. One of the founders, at the Katowice conference of 1912, of the Agudas Israel organization of Orthodox Jews. Editor of the Agudas Israel weekly journal, *Der Israelit*, 1905–35. Emigrated to London, 1935; to New York, 1941; to Israel 1950. Died in Jerusalem in 1965, a few days before his 95th birthday.

ARNOST ROSIN, born in Slovakia in 1914. Deported to Auschwitz in April 1942; escaped, May 1944. Worked as an administrative official in television in Bratislava, 1945–68. An official of the Jewish Community in Düsseldorf since 1968, and its emissary in Jerusalem, 1978–80.

JONA SCHARF, born in Czernowitz, 1929. Deported with her family to Transnistria, 1941. Reached Palestine on the *Kazbek,* 1944. Completed her schooling, and then worked as a secretary in Israel. Married; now, as Jona Malleyron, she lives in Tel Aviv.

IGNACY SCHWARZBART, born in the Galician province of Austria-Hungary in 1888. Chief editor of a Polish-language Zionist daily newspaper, 1921–24. Chairman of the Zionist Federation of West Galicia and Silesia. A member of the Zionist General Council from 1933, of the Polish Parliament, 1938–39, and of the Polish National Council in London, 1940–45. Lived in the United States from 1946, and served as director of the administrative department of the World Jewish Congress. Author of a book on Jewish life in Cracow between the wars, published in 1958. He died in 1961.

MOSHE SHERTOK, born in Kherson, Russia, in 1894. Settled in Palestine in 1906. Served in the Turkish Army, 1915–17. A student at the London School of Economics, 1921–24. Head of the Political Department of the Jewish Agency, 1933–48. Changed his name to Sharett in 1948; first Foreign Minister of the State of Israel, 1948–56. Prime Minister, 1955–56. Chairman of the Jewish Agency Executive from 1960 until his death in 1965.

WLADYSLAW SIKORSKI, born 1881. Educated at Lvov. Lieutenant-Colonel of the Polish Legions, 1914–18. Active in the defence of Lvov and Przemysl against the Ukrainians, 1918. Commander of the 5th and 3rd Army Corps against the Bolsheviks, 1920. Prime Minister of Poland, 1922–23. Minister of Military Affairs, 1923–25. Prime Minister of the Polish Government-in-Exile (the London Poles), and Commander-in-Chief of the Polish Army, from October 1939 until his death in an air crash on 4 July 1943.

ARCHIBALD SINCLAIR, born 1890. Succeeded his father as 4th Baronet, 1912. On active service, 1915–18. Private Secretary to Churchill, 1918–22. A Liberal MP, 1922–45. Leader of the Parliamentary Liberal Party, 1935–45. Secretary of State of Air, 1940–45. Created Viscount Thurso, 1952. Died, 1970.

KATERINA SINGEROVA, born in Slovakia. Known as Katja. One of the first Jewesses to be brought to Auschwitz in the spring of 1942; her tattoo number was 2098. Erich Kulka writes: 'She was a young, beautiful, strong girl, mastered good German, and was taken as runner to the women's camp wardress. Later she became secretary and in this capacity she helped many women prisoners and was in contact with the conspiracy movement also in the men's camp' *(letter to the author, 6 November 1980).* Surviving the war, she lived in Prague from 1948, married, and became the Director of the Czechoslovak National Fund for Creative Artists.

THOMAS SNOW, born in 1890. Educated at Winchester and New College Oxford. Entered the British diplomatic service, 1923. Served in Cuba, 1935–37 and Finland, 1937–40. Head of the Refugee Department of the Foreign Office, 1940–41. Served in Colombia, 1941–44; Ambassador, 1944–45. Counsellor, Switzerland, 1946–49. Retired 1950. Resident in Switzerland.

CARL SPAATZ, born in Pennsylvania, 1891. Served in Mexico (1917) and on the western front (1918). Commander-in-Chief, United States Strategic Air Forces in Europe, January 1944–May 1945; in Japan, 1945–46. Chief of Staff, Air Force, 1947–48.

OLIVER STANLEY, born 1896, a son of the 17th Earl of Derby. Conservative Member of Parliament, 1924–50. Secretary of State for War, 1940; for the Colonies, 22 November 1942 (in succession to Lord Cranborne), until 23 May 1945; for the Dominions, May–July 1945. He died in 1950.

LAURENCE A. STEINHARDT, born in New York, 1892. On active service, 1917–18. A lawyer with the War Department, 1918–19. In private law practice, 1920–33. An early supporter of President Roosevelt's Presidential campaign, 1932. Subsequently American Minister to Sweden, 1933, and to Peru, 1937, then Ambassador to the Soviet Union, 1939–41; to Turkey, 1942–45; to Czechoslovakia, 1945–48 and to Canada, 1948–50. He died in 1950.

DOME SZTOJAY, born in 1883. Hungarian Minister to Germany, 1935–44. Prime Minister of Hungary, March–August 1944. Tried, for his part in the deportation of Hungarian Jews, and executed in Budapest, January 1946.

MYRON C. TAYLOR, born 1874. Lawyer and industrialist. Chairman of the Board of US Steel, 1932–38. US Representative, Evian Conference on refugees (and Chairman of the Conference), 1938. President Roosevelt's (and later President Truman's) Personal Representative to Pope Pius XII, 1939–50. Helped to reorganize the Italian Red Cross, 1946. Died, 1959.

FRITZ ULLMAN, born in Karlsbad (then a part of the Austro-Hungarian Empire), 1902. Active in the Zionist Organization of Czechoslovakia, 1929–39. Represented the interests of Czech Jewry in Geneva, 1939–45. Member of the Organization Department of the Jewish Agency, Jerusalem, 1946; seriously wounded in the Arab terrorist attack on the Jewish Agency building, 1947. He died in 1972.

EDMUND VEESENMAYER, born in 1894. An SS officer, he transferred to the German Foreign Office, and was active on the eve of its Nazification in 1938. Appointed 'Plenipotentiary for Ireland' in 1940 when he made plans for using members of the Irish Republican Army (IRA) against England. In September 1941, while in Belgrade, he recommended the deportation of all Serbian Jews. In May 1943 he complained to Ribbentrop about Hungary's failure to deport Jews. German Minister to Hungary, 1944. Sentenced to 25 years' imprisonment at the Nuremberg Trials, 1946. His sentence was later commuted to 10 years by John J. McCloy, US High Commissioner in Germany, and he was in fact released in December 1951.

RUDOLF VRBA, born in Czechoslovakia in 1924. Deported first to Majdanek (where his brother Sam was among 18,000 Jews executed during a single day in November 1943), then to Auschwitz. Escaped, April 1944. Served with the Partisan units of the Czech Army, September 1944–April 1945; discharged 'with honour', 3 May 1945. Studied at the Department of Organic Chemistry, Czech Technical University, Prague, 1945–49; Engineer of Chemistry, 1949; Department of Biochemistry and Fermentation, 1949–51. Attached, as a Pharmacologist, to the Ministry of Health, Prague, 1953–58. Emigrated to Israel, 1958, when he joined the Veterinary Research Institute of the Ministry of Agriculture. Emigrated to Britain, 1960, becoming a Member of the Neuropsychiatric Research Unit of the Medical Research Council. Emigrated to Canada, becoming Associate Professor, Department of Pharmacology, University of British Columbia, 1967–75; Faculty of Medicine, since 1975. Author of more than fifty scientific papers; also, *I Cannot Forgive* (1963) and *Factory of Death* (1964).

DOV WEISSMANDEL, an Orthodox rabbi, born in one of the regions of the Austro-Hungarian Empire which was to become a part of Czechoslovakia after the first world war, and subsequently became, in 1938, the independent State of Slovakia. Deported to Auschwitz, 1944, but managed to hide a saw in a loaf of bread, cut a hole in the floor of the carriage, and jump from the train. After the war he emigrated to the United States, where he set up an Orthodox seminary. He died in 1957.

CHAIM WEIZMANN, born in Russia in 1874. Educated in Germany. A delegate at the 2nd Zionist Congress, 1898. Assistant Lecturer in Chemistry at Geneva University, 1902. Reader in Biochemistry at the University of Manchester, 1906. Naturalized as a British subject, 1910. Director of Admiralty Laboratories, 1916–19. Instrumental in the issuing of the Balfour Declaration of 2 November 1917, in which the British Government supported a 'Jewish National Home' in Palestine. President of the World Zionist Organization, and the Jewish Agency for Palestine, 1921–31 and 1935–41. First President of the State of Israel from 1949 until his death in 1952.

ALFRED WETZLER, born in Nitra, Czechoslovakia, in 1918. At Auschwitz, worked as a clerk. Escaped, May 1944. In 1945 he published, in Kosice, a booklet: 'Auschwitz, the grave of 4 million people', in which he included the full Vrba-Wetzler and Mordowicz-Rosin reports. Joined the Czechoslovak Communist Party. Later arrested and expelled from the Party. Subsequently rehabilitated. Worked as an editor in a small Slovak newspaper in Bratislava. Living in Bratislava (1981).

STEPHEN S. WISE, born in Budapest in 1874. Taken to the United States at the age of 17 months. Ordained a rabbi in New York, 1893. A founder of the New York Federation of Zionist Societies, 1897. Secretary of the Federation of American Zionists, 1898–1904. Co-founder in 1909 of the National Association for the Advancement of Coloured People (NAACP). President of the Zionist Organization of America, 1936–38. Co-founder and head of the World Jewish Congress, 1936. Chairman of the American Emergency Committee for Zionist Affairs, 1940–45. Died 1949.

ELIZABETH WISKEMANN, educated at Newnham College, Cambridge. Worked at Chatham House, travelling widely in Europe from 1930. In July 1936 she was arrested by the Gestapo in Berlin, and expelled from Germany. In 1938 she published Czechs and Germans. Worked in Berne on intelligence work, 1940–44, as Assistant Press Attaché, with particular reference to occupied Czechoslovakia. Correspondent of the Economist in Rome, 1946–47. Professor of International Relations at Edinburgh University, 1958–61. Tutor in Modern European History, University of Sussex, 1961–64. She died in 1971.

REUVEN ZASLANI, born in Jerusalem in 1909. An expert on Arab affairs, and a member of the Political Department of the Jewish Agency since 1936. In charge of co-ordinating with the Allies the war effort of Palestinian Jewry. Subsequently leader of the Israel delegation which in 1949 negotiated the cease-fire with Transjordan. Having changed his name to Shiloah, he set up the political intelligence service of the new State of Israel, and was active in establishing secret contacts with Arab statesmen. From 1953 to 1957 he was Minister at the Israel Embassy in Washington. He died in 1959.

SZMUL ZYGIELBOJM, born in the Lublin province of Russian Poland, 1895. Delegate for Chelm at the first convention of the Polish branch of the General Jewish Workers' Union Party (the Bund). Member of the Bund Central Committee, Warsaw, from 1924. Member of the Warsaw Municipal Council, 1926; the Lodz Municipal Council, 1936. Sent by the Bund, to tell of conditions in German-occupied Poland, first to Belgium, 1940, then to the United States, 1940–42 and to Britain, 1942. Bund representative on the Polish National Council, London, 1942–43. Committed suicide in London on 12 May 1943.

Index

362

Index

Laski, Harold: complains to Churchill, 148
Latvia: fate of Jews of, 81, 84–5
Lauterbach, Leo: in Jerusalem, 35, 48, 67, 82; biographical sketch of, 348
Laval, Pierre: 96, 118
Law, Richard: and the Riegner telegram, 59; and the Karski report, 93–5; and the Bermuda Conference, 132–3; and Jewish refugees, 163; and the bombing of Auschwitz request, 306; biographical sketch of, 348
Leder, Eliezer: in Istanbul, 206
Lehman, Governor: his tennis shoe, 44
Lesitz: telegraphic error for Belzec, 92
Les Milles: internment camp, 67, 68
Libya: and Jewish refugees, 139
Lichtheim, Richard: his messages from Geneva, 28–30, 32–3, 34, 35, 39, 47–8, 53, 61, 64–7, 69–73, 78, 81–7, 88, 90–1, 105, 114, 120–1, 122–3, 129, 143–4, 152, 155, 156, 174, 188; his report of 7 April 1944, 197–8; further reports and warnings from, 199–200, 205–6, 228; and the truth about Auschwitz (June 1944), 234–6, 250, 251, 257, 260; and Hungarian Jewish refugees, 289–90, 292; biographical sketch of, 348–9
Lichtenstein, Fritz: and refugees, 174, 251n.1
Lidice: reprisals at, 50; 'never heard of', 170
Lincoln: air base at, 238
Lindenbaum, Shalom: his recollections, 311, 315–16; biographical sketch of, 349
Linton, Joseph: in London, 29, 73, 88, 98–9, 101, 117, 122, 135, 164, 186, 244, 254; and the bombing of Auschwitz appeal, 304–5, 309, 310, 319–20; reports the fate of a poet, 306–7; biographical sketch of, 349
Lipovsky Mikulas: Auschwitz escapees at, 203, 231
Lipson, Daniel: his awkward question, 173
Lisbon: 173, 251, 276, 287
Lithuania: fate of Jews in, 85, 151, 263, 293
Little, Dr: urges help for Jews, 119
Livingston, H. B.: in Geneva, 57, 59, 206; biographical sketch of, 349
Locker, Berl: and Jewish refugees, 98
Lodz: ghetto in, 16, 32, 40, 43, 71, 90; 'doomed to die', 151, 236; Jews deported to Auschwitz from, 302, 311, 314, 317
Long, Breckenridge: 172; biographical sketch of, 349
Lourie, Arthur: 30, 47, 48, 67, 71, 101
Lowrie, Donald A.: his report, 64
Lublin: fate of Jews in, 41, 43, 47, 51, 52, 54, 86, 151; liberated, 295, 333; total deaths in region of, 329; public 'anaesthetised' to, 334
'Lublinland': proposed Jewish reservation, 13–14; Jewish deportees in, 51, 52, 54, 100
Lucas, Senator: at Bermuda, 132
Luke, S. E. V.: and Jewish refugees, 22
Luxembourg: Jews of, 14
Lvov (Lwow, Lemberg): fate of Jews in, 19, 40, 43, 52, 65, 113; resistance at, 162; report of killings in (March 1944), 181
Lyons: protests in, 68, 69

Macaulay, T. B.: and the effect of distress on the human mind, 138
McClelland, Roswell: 233, 246, 248–9, 313–4, 327; biographical sketch of, 349
Macedo, Carlos de: and deportation of Jews, 17
Macedonia: Jews deported from, 122, 125, 157
Mack, John: 'they have no status in any land', 140
MacLaren, Captain D.: and Nazi atrocities, 334
McCloy, John J.: and the Auschwitz bombing appeals, 238, 248, 255–6, 303, 321, 327–8; biographical sketch of, 349
Mackillop, Douglas: in Geneva, 78, 174, 251; biographical sketch of, 250
MacMichael, Sir Harold: and Jewish refugees, 24, 33–4, 36, 80, 133; and an incident in Palestine (November 1943), 165; and Jewish rescue squads, 171; and the 'goods for blood' proposal, 212–3, 228–9, 230, 242; assassination attempt on, 298; biographical sketch of, 350
Madagascar: and Jewish refugees, 109; a possible Jewish colony, 147
Maglione, Cardinal: 69, 71, 104; biographical sketch of, 350
Maher Pasha, Ahmed: 330
Maisky, Ivan: 97, 101, 281
Majdanek: Jews gassed at, 62, 86, 105, 121; report of gassing at, reaches the west, 149–50; further slaughter at (November 1943), 162; Jews deported to Auschwitz from (April 1944), 201, 231; mentioned, 236; more deportations to Auschwitz from (July 1944), 292; death toll at, 329n.2; photographed at liberation, 333–4
Malines: internment camp, 153
Mallet, Victor: reports on deportations, 16
Manchester Guardian: reports killing of Jews, 43; urges Hitler's threats to be taken seriously, 85; reports truth about Auschwitz, 252–3; a further report in, 257
Mandel, Georges: 96
Mann, James: and a Polish appeal, 320–1
Marchbanks, Mr: and an urgent appeal, 255, 265
Maritza, the: refugees on, 186
Martin, John: 106, 185, 208, 276; biographical sketch of, 350
Martin, Kingsley: and a New Statesman article on Nazi atrocities (9 January 1943), 110–1 and 110n.1; biographical sketch of, 350
Masaryk, Jan: and the Jews, 74
Mason, Paul: and the bombing of Auschwitz, 318–20, 326; and Jewish refugees from Hungary, 329–30; and the liberation of Auschwitz, 337–8; biographical sketch of, 350
Maunsell, Brigadier: his objection, 253
Mauritius: 24, 98, 114, 186–7
Mauthausen: concentration camp, 15, 30, 302; Dutch Jews reported murdered at (December 1942), 105; Hungarian Sonderkommando trained at, 184; a deportation to Auschwitz from (August 1944), 308; a deportation from Auschwitz to (September 1944), 317; crematorium motor sent to (November